MW01130332

SELECTED SHORTER
WRITINGS

SELECTED SHORTER
WRITINGS

J. Gresham Machen

EDITED BY
D.G. HART

P&R
PUBLISHING
P.O. BOX 817 • PHILLIPSBURG • NEW JERSEY 08865-0817

Page design by Lakeside Design Plus
Typesetting by Andrew MacBride

Printed in the United States of America
Library of Congress Cataloging-in-Publication Data

Machen, J. Gresham (John Gresham), 1881–1937.
    [Selections. 2003]
    Selected shorter writings / edited by D.G. Hart.
      p. cm.
    Includes bibliographical references and index.
    ISBN 0-87552-570-9
    1. Presbyterian Church—Doctrines. 2. Reformed Church—Doctrines.
  3. Theology, Doctrinal. 4. Machen, J. Gresham (John Gresham),
1881–1937—Bibliography.   I. Hart, D.G. (Darryl G.). II. Title.

BX9175.3.M262 2004
230'.51—dc22

                                        2003065626

CONTENTS

Introduction: The Forgotten Machen? 1

Part One: Christ and the Witness of Scripture

1. What the Bible Teaches about Jesus   23
2. The Witness of Paul   33
3. The Witness of the Gospels   45
4. The Virgin Birth of Christ   57
5. The Resurrection of Christ   75

Part Two: Christianity and Modern Substitutes

6. What Is Christianity?   91
7. History and Faith   97
8. Does Fundamentalism Obstruct Social Progress?   109
9. What Fundamentalism Stands for Now   116
10. What Is the Gospel?   123

Part Three: The Task of Christian Scholarship

11. Christian Scholarship and Evangelism   135
12. Christian Scholarship and the Defense of the Faith   143
13. Christian Scholarship and the Building Up of the Church   153
14. The Necessity of the Christian School   161
15. Forty Years of New Testament Research   175

Part Four: Theological Education

16. Westminster Theological Seminary: Its Purpose and Plan   187
17. Facing the Facts before God   195
18. Consolations in the Midst of Battle   202

19. Servants of God or Servants of Men 206

20. The Minister and His Greek Testament 210

Part Five: The Nature and Mission of the Church

21. The Parting of the Ways 217

22. The Mission of the Church 228

23. The Christian View of Missions 237

24. The Truth about the Presbyterian Church 243

25. Is There a Future for Calvinism in the Presbyterian Church? 267

26. The New Presbyterian Hymnal 274

Part Six: The Presbyterian Controversy

27. Statement to the Special Commission of 1925 291

28. Statement to the Committee to Investigate Princeton 299

29. The Attack upon Princeton Seminary: A Plea for Fair Play 310

30. Statement to the Presbytery of New Brunswick 332

Part Seven: Church and Society

31. Christianity and Liberty 355

32. The Responsibility of the Church in Our New Age 364

33. The Church in the War 377

34. Voices in the Church 381

35. Statement on the Eighteenth Amendment 395

Part Eight: Christianity and Culture

36. Christianity and Culture 399

37. Relations between Jews and Christians 411

38. The Christian and Human Relationships 421

39. Mountains and Why We Love Them 429

40. The Benefits of Walking 438

Part Nine: Reviews

41. Review of Speer's *Some Living Issues* 443

42. Review of Fosdick's *Modern Use of the Bible* 455

43. Review of McGiffert's *God of the Early Christians* 469

44. Review of Mullins's *Christianity at the Cross Roads*   507
45. Karl Barth and "The Theology of Crisis"   533

Part Ten: Autobiographical
46. Christianity in Conflict   547

For Further Reading   571
Index   577

Introduction

THE FORGOTTEN MACHEN?

A mong the functions that anthologies serve, sometimes they perform inspirational purposes, and on other occasions they help to satisfy intellectual curiosity. In the case of this collection of shorter writings by J. Gresham Machen, the expectation of many readers is likely to be a book that pays tribute to one of the leading conservative Protestants of the twentieth century, thus memorializing a hero of the faith. For readers who regard Machen as an enemy of theological progress and example of ecclesiastical tolerance, such a volume may also prove inspirational by commemorating an enemy of forward thinking. In either case, this collection may only reinforce well-established understandings of the author. To be sure, inspiring affection or resentment is a legitimate service of *Selected Shorter Writings*. But this anthology may also involve more than meets the eye.

With regard to this extra dimension, readers may be interested to know that many of the essays assembled here were originally published in 1951 in a volume edited by Ned B. Stonehouse, entitled *What Is Christianity?* A junior member of the New Testament department of Westminster Seminary when Machen taught there from 1929 to 1937, Stonehouse decided to assemble his mentor's shorter and occasional writings, which was the second in a three-volume labor of love. The first was a collection of Machen's sermons, published in 1949 as *God Transcendent*. *What Is Christianity?* followed two years later. And Stonehouse completed these posthumous anthologies with his own account of Machen's life in *J. Gresham Machen: A Biographical Memoir*, published in

1

1954. As an accomplished New Testament scholar, a churchman who served on various denominational committees of the Orthodox Presbyterian Church, and editor of the *Presbyterian Guardian*, Stonehouse had a fairly full plate of duties. But his regard for his former professor and mentor prompted him to devote at least the better part of seven years to the preservation and commemoration of Machen's life and writings.

Of Stonehouse's three volumes, only the collection of sermons and the biography have remained in print. The anthology of shorter essays and addresses, *What Is Christianity?*, has never been reprinted, however. This volume is an effort to make up for this curiosity in publishing history. It also includes a selection of other essays and book reviews designed to fill out the themes under which the original essays have been reorganized. Before introducing its contents, a word or two of explanation may be in order for the neglect of Machen's shorter writings and occasional addresses.

DEFENDER OF HISTORIC CHRISTIANITY

The highlights of Machen's life are relatively well known and need little rehearsal.[1] The middle son of a successful Baltimore attorney, Machen grew up in the genteel culture of his Southern parents and a society that was fast losing its capacity for gentility, thanks to the factors of modern economic and industrial development. He excelled as a student, doing his undergraduate work at the Johns Hopkins University in classical Greek, and adding to that with a year of graduate study at his alma mater before attending Princeton Seminary from 1902 to 1905. After a year of study in Germany, Machen returned to teach New Testament at Princeton Seminary, first as a lecturer until 1914 when he was ordained as a Presbyterian minister, a status that facilitated his promotion to assistant professor.[2]

Except for a year of service in the Y. M. C. A. during World War I, Machen labored away as a seminary professor in relative obscurity. He showed signs

---

1. For Machen's own understanding of his life and accomplishments, see chapter 46 in this anthology.
2. For biographical treatments of Machen, see Ned B. Stonehouse, *J. Gresham Machen: A Biographical Memoir* (Grand Rapids: Eerdmans, 1954); and D. G. Hart, *Defending the Faith: J. Gresham Machen and the Crisis of Conservative Protestantism in Modern America* (Phillipsburg, N.J.: P&R, 2003).

of academic accomplishment by writing *The Origins of Paul's Religion*, published in 1921, and a grammar for New Testament Greek, published the following year. Machen would continue to keep a hand in New Testament scholarship during the 1920s, writing *The Virgin Birth of Christ* (1930), a book he considered the culmination of his scholarly endeavors.

He gained notoriety not for his academic work, however, but for his involvement in the so-called fundamentalist controversy of the northern Presbyterian Church (PCUSA). His most popular book, *Christianity and Liberalism* (1923), argued that historic Christianity and liberalism differed on the basic doctrines of the faith, so much so that they constituted two distinct religions. As controversial as that thesis was, a number of other circumstances transported Machen into the national spotlight. One was the fact that he was a minister in a socially prominent denomination whose proceedings received coverage in daily newspapers. *Christianity and Liberalism*, along with *What is Faith?*, which came out two years later, at times simply functioned as a resource for inquiring journalists to figure out the logic behind Machen's public statements. These books also gave ammunition to many conservative Protestants in a variety of denominations who knew that something was wrong with contemporary preaching and church life but could not always identity the source. Thus, during the 1920s Machen emerged as the thoughtful fundamentalist. He was learned enough to win a measure of respect from secularists and sufficiently orthodox to gain support from conservative Protestants.

The reception of Machen's arguments among Presbyterian clergy and leaders was not a happy one, however.[3] By making the confessional character of the church so important, he was swimming against a current in American Protestantism that had been running strongly for almost four decades. As a result, from 1925 until the end of his life he became something of a pariah within mainline Presbyterian circles. The reorganization of Princeton Seminary in 1929 was partly an effort to clamp down on dissent at the denomination's oldest theological school. Machen took the leading role in founding Westminster Seminary in 1929 to perpetuate the Old

---

3. See Bradley J. Longfield, *The Presbyterian Controversy: Fundamentalists, Modernists, and Moderates* (New York: Oxford University Press, 1991); and William J. Weston, *Presbyterian Pluralism: Competition in a Protestant House* (Knoxville: University of Tennessee Press, 1997).

Princeton tradition and to give conservative dissent an institutional out-let. He also saw that a new denomination was likely to be necessary if a Presbyterian witness were to persist. The first step in that direction occurred with the founding in 1933 of the Independent Board for Presbyterian Foreign Missions. This agency also functioned as a protest to a 1932 report on American Protestant missions. In the eyes of Machen, *Re-Thinking Missions* revealed how the largest denominations had replaced the salvation of men and women with the advance of Western civilization by affirming Christianity's commonality with other world religions.[4] The Presbyterian hierarchy responded by declaring the new board illegal and demanding Machen's presbytery to bring him to trial. In 1935, without giving Machen the chance to question the denomination's ruling, the Presbytery of New Brunswick declared him guilty on six counts, and the following year he was suspended from the ministry. His suspension, along with those of other conservatives on the Independent Board, led to the creation in 1936 of the Orthodox Presbyterian Church.

Implicit in this brief summary of Machen's professional life is a rendering of the man that makes him a hero to conservatives and a reactionary to those in the mainline. Yet this collection of writings reveals another side to Machen's thought. In fact, one of the reasons why the original collection of his short addresses and essays, *What Is Christianity?*, has never been reprinted may be that both his modern-day sympathizers and revilers think he can be understood simply on the binary categories of conservative and liberal. For all his conservatism, however, Machen approached any number of issues in ways that today's conservatives might think liberal. Meanwhile, for all his antipathy to liberalism, Machen's defense of historic Christianity was not dependent on recent views of biblical authority or novel ideas about creation or Christ's return; instead, it was thoroughly in the mainstream of Augustinian Christianity.[5] One purpose of this book, then, is to reveal a depth and complexity to Machen's views that the cari-

4. See William R. Hutchison, *Errand to the World: American Protestant Thought and Foreign Missions* (Chicago: University of Chicago Press, 1987).
5. The standard study in American fundamentalism is George M. Marsden, *Fundamentalism and American Culture: The Shaping of Twentieth-Century Evangelicalism, 1875–1925* (New York: Oxford University Press, 1980). Part of my aim in *Defending the Faith* was to show how Machen did not fit the mold of funda-

catures of him as gospel defender or liberal loather generally miss. Because of these other sides to his thought, the following essays may also do something more than inspire veneration or contempt. They may actually provide an occasion for a better understanding of the Christian message, the church's ministry, and the believer's social and cultural responsibilities.

MACHEN AND FUNDAMENTALISM

One reason for forgetting Machen is the close association that many American Christians draw between him and the fundamentalist–modernist controversy of the 1920s. Some might think that the debates of that decade are part of a different time in the life of American Protestantism and that developments since then render the concerns of fundamentalists, although appropriate in their day, no longer relevant. For others, who believe that writings from the 1920s and 1930s will simply reveal the severe limitations of creationism or dispensationalism, the thought of collecting a leading fundamentalist's occasional essays and addresses is an invitation to return to theological obscurantism.

On this score the following selections reveal how unusual a fundamentalist Machen was, so much so that it might be better to give him another designation. Especially in the first two parts of this book, Machen's views provide support for his own estimate of himself, as follows:

> I never call myself a "Fundamentalist." There is, indeed, no inherent objection to the term; and if the disjunction is between "Fundamentalism" and "Modernism," then I am willing to call myself a Fundamentalist of the most pronounced type. But after all, what I prefer to call myself is not a "Fundamentalist" but a "Calvinist"—that is, an adherent of the Reformed Faith.[6]

Part of the reason for Machen's disavowal of the term "fundamentalist" was that he himself was not partial to either of the doctrines upon which

---

mentalism. For another effort that explores the limitations of the conservative and liberal categories for understanding American Protestantism, see D. G. Hart, *The Lost Soul of American Protestantism* (Lanham, Md.: Rowman & Littlefield, 2002).

6. Quoted in Stonehouse, *J. Gresham Machen*, 426.

fundamentalists drew most heavily, namely, dispensationalism and creationism.[7] Neither did Machen stress the doctrine of biblical inerrancy, even though he had studied under and worked with Benjamin B. Warfield at Princeton Seminary, whose doctrine of biblical infallibility was as erudite as it is legendary.[8] Machen did affirm inerrancy, but it was a side issue in his estimation.[9] Yet because fundamentalism was and still is so heavily associated with idiosyncratic ideas about human origins and Christ's return, or with a wooden approach to the Bible's authority, Machen's contemporaries in the Presbyterian church, and later evangelical leaders, could dismiss him as something of a theological bumpkin.

What the essays in Parts One and Two reveal, however, is just how vanilla, in a Reformed sense, Machen's theology was. When he articulated the central claims of Christianity, Machen did not try to be flashy or say something unusual. In fact, having memorized the Westminster Shorter Catechism as a boy and having studied with Warfield, Machen's understandings of Christ and the significance of his life, ministry, death, and resurrection were remarkably conventional. Even his approach to the virgin birth, the fruit of almost twenty-five years of research, was not to find the one doctrine by which he could beat all comers. Instead, his articulation and defense of Christ's miraculous birth reflected an awareness of modern debates about this historic affirmation of the church. The apparent blandness of Machen's doctrinal position has at times made him less appealing among his own denomination where the search for a theological linchpin has sometimes generated doctrinal novelty. Yet his conventionality did not permit avoiding the battles that fundamentalists were fighting. Consequently, instead of opposing liberalism because of evolution, vague ideas about Christ's kingdom

7. On the peculiar doctrines of fundamentalism, see Timothy P. Weber, *Living in the Shadow of the Second Coming: American Premillennialism, 1875–1925* (New York: Oxford University Press, 1979); Paul Boyer, *When Time Shall Be No More: Prophecy Belief in Modern American Culture* (Cambridge, Mass.: Harvard University Press, 1992); and Ronald L. Numbers, *The Creationists: The Evolution of Scientific Creationism* (New York: Alfred A. Knopf, 1992).

8. See Mark A. Noll, *The Princeton Theology, 1812–1921: Scripture, Science, and Theological Method from Archibald Alexander to Benjamin Warfield* (1983; Grand Rapids: Baker, 2001).

9. See D. G. Hart, "Fundamentalism, Inerrancy, and the Biblical Scholarship of J. Gresham Machen," *Journal of Presbyterian History* 75 (1997): 13–28.

INTRODUCTION

and return, or the inspiration of the Bible, Machen criticized modernist preachers and theologians for departing from Augustinian notions about human sinfulness and the sufficiency of divine mercy in Christ.

The apparent militancy of his opposition to liberalism qualifies him, according to the estimate of many who have studied the controversy of the 1920s, as a fundamentalist. But that term may actually obscure more than it clarifies if the word "fundamentalist" means simply angry evangelicals. Christians, both Roman Catholic and Protestant, may have had good reasons to be upset if some ministers were teaching and preaching ideas contrary to the church's historic affirmations in the Apostles' Creed, or if other ministers and church leaders could not see the problem with such erroneous teaching and preaching. For Machen, the positive presentation of the gospel (Part One) necessarily involved doctrinal controversy (Parts Two and Nine).

THE TASK OF CHRISTIAN SCHOLARSHIP

Part of what made Machen an odd participant in the fundamentalist controversy was his work as a New Testament scholar. Of course, some of the leading modernists were academics. Union Seminary in New York City and the University of Chicago Divinity School, for instance, were important centers in liberal Protestant networks.[10] But on the conservative side, Machen's scholarly reputation was unusual. Even so, as the address "History and Faith" (Selection 7) shows, Machen's positive statements of Christian truth and his polemical theology stemmed from his own scholarly investigations.

Much has been written of late by evangelical academics about the nature of Christian scholarship.[11] Machen's own example, coupled with his understanding of his responsibilities as seminary professor and minister of the Word, reflects an older Protestant notion about Christian scholarship. John Calvin, for instance, argued for four offices in the government of the church—pastors, elders, deacons, and doctors. The last office was not en-

10. See William R. Hutchison, *The Modernist Impulse in American Protestantism* (Cambridge, Mass.: Harvard University Press, 1976).
11. See, for instance, George M. Marsden, *The Outrageous Idea of Christian Scholarship* (New York: Oxford University Press, 1997); and Mark A. Noll, *The Scandal of the Evangelical Mind* (Grand Rapids: Eerdmans, 1994).

tirely different from that of pastor; it required the same sort of training and allowed a man to preach and administer the sacraments. But it also included a responsibility to educate those training for the ministry.[12] Machen obviously fits this category. In addition, his work as a New Testament scholar was, as Parts Three and Four show, never isolated from the edification of the church. One reason for the direct relevance of Machen's scholarship to officers and laity alike was its subject matter. Had he pursued a Ph.D. in classical Greek literature, as he at one point contemplated, his academic work would have been only indirectly relevant to the ministry of the church and the building of Christ's body. But as a scholar who investigated Scripture, Machen recognized that this book was not merely an object of study; it was a source of faith and life. The religious nature of Scripture did not mean that all study of it involved the resolution of practical spiritual problems. Machen kept up with the scholarly literature in the field and welcomed the insights of scholars who did not appreciate the sacredness of the Bible (e.g., Selection 15). Nevertheless, he was also highly aware of a duty to serve the church with his learning (e.g., Selections 11–13). In this sense, what made Machen's scholarship Christian was not so much his own faith as the object and aim of his studies; he believed he was investigating a book that was explicitly religious, and he used his learning to contribute to the life of the church.[13]

Of course, Machen also served the church by teaching at an agency of the Presbyterian Church in the U.S.A., Princeton Seminary. The oldest Presbyterian seminary in the United States, Princeton was established for the sake of training a learned ministry.[14] This was the same goal that Machen took to Philadelphia in 1929 when he founded Westminster Seminary (e.g., Selection 16). He reflected often on the importance and limitations of the-

12. See E. Harris Harbison, *The Christian Scholar in the Age of the Reformation* (New York: Charles Scribners' Sons, 1956).
13. See Hart, *Lost Soul*, ch. 4; and idem, "Taking Every Thought Captive: The Ministry of the Word and the Limits of Christian Scholarship," in Gary L. W. Johnson and R. Fowler White, eds., *Whatever Happened to the Reformation?* (Phillipsburg, N.J.: P&R, 2001), 185–203.
14. See David C. Calhoun, *Faith and Learning, 1812–1868*, vol. 1 of *Princeton Theological Seminary* (Carlisle, Pa.: Banner of Truth Trust, 1994); and idem, *The Majestic Testimony, 1869–1929*, vol. 2 of *Princeton Theological Seminary* (Carlisle, Pa.: Banner of Truth Trust, 1996).

ological education, as the selections in Part Four demonstrate. Some of these thoughts reflect an awareness of the difficulties seminarians face when finally taking up their work in the pulpit, and some show more systematic reflection on the best course of study for future pastors. In both cases, Machen articulated the Princeton/Westminster ideal of the pastor scholar. This involved a minister who knew the original languages of the Bible, and spent long hours in the study preparing for the all-important work of Word and sacrament. This model has sometimes been criticized for producing men more cerebral than pastoral. But Machen's understanding of the ministry did not divorce study from edification. In his view, the work of pastors in articulating, expositing, and defending the truths contained in Scripture was of eternal significance. To slight the hard work of seminary training, or the ongoing labor of sermon preparation and study, was a dereliction of the minister's duty.

THE PRESBYTERIAN CONTROVERSY

Because Machen was a seminary professor with a keen eye on serving the church, his emergence as a combatant in the Presbyterian controversy of the 1920s and 1930s was natural if not inevitable. Yet he came to this task with a distinct disadvantage. For almost forty years his communion, the PCUSA, had been operating at the denominational level with the outlook that "doctrine divides, ministry unites." This was precisely the motto of liberals in the Presbytery of New York during the 1890s when Charles Briggs came to trial. It also began to seep into other quarters of the church, most noticeably in its ecumenical relations. Presbyterian officials provided important leadership to the formation of the Federal Council of Churches (1908) and to the failed plan in 1920 for an organic union of the largest denominations in the United States. In both cases, Protestant ecumenism was premised upon the notion that cooperation for a common purpose of religious service was more important than the creeds and polities of the different denominations.[15]

The logic behind this form of cooperation was exactly the opposite of

15. See D. G. Hart, "The Tie That Divides: Presbyterian Ecumenism, Fundamentalism, and the History of Twentieth-Century American Protestantism," *Westminster Theological Journal* 60 (1998): 85–107.

Machen's. As the essays in Part Five indicate, he believed the church's primary task was one of proclaiming the forgiveness of sins provided exclusively in Jesus Christ. Thus, doctrine mattered; it was not a peripheral area of church life that could be developed when ministers and laity had free time. In fact, Machen's emergence as a critic of Protestant liberalism stemmed directly from his opposition to church policies that divorced mission from proclamation. He had been commissioned for the first time to the General Assembly of 1920 where he heard plans for the union of Presbyterians with Baptists, Congregationalists, Methodists, and some of the other larger denominations.[16] There he began to connect the dots between Protestant ecumenism and Protestant modernism; the former's purpose of uniting Protestants in a mission of transforming American society depended on the latter's understanding of theology as merely the reflection of religious experience. This faith, Protestant leaders believed, was the same in all denominations no matter the particular differences in doctrine, worship, or church polity. Machen's opposition to liberalism, then, was deeply bound up with a Reformed understanding of the nature and mission of the church.

As the selections in Part Six reveal, Machen's critique of liberal Protestants came with significant costs. He was, after all, a professor at the second oldest Protestant seminary in the United States, and because of his standing his ideas automatically gained a wider hearing. Yet Presbyterian leaders did not care for the exposure that Machen's ideas received, partly because he was critical of trends in the denomination and partly because he did not represent a form of faith that showed that Presbyterians were progressive. As a result, Machen became a wrench in the machinery of the Presbyterian bureaucracy. In 1925 the General Assembly appointed a special committee to study the cause of controversy in the denomination. This investigation was not so much aimed at Machen, but it did find conservatives who made arguments like Machen's to be the source of the church's troubles.[17] (Selection 27 is Machen's testimony before this committee.) This committee's report led to the formation of another study committee, this one aimed more directly at Machen. In 1926 and 1927 another General Assembly committee had the responsibility for investigating Princeton Sem-

16. See Hart, *Defending the Faith*, ch. 3.
17. See Longfield, *Presbyterian Controversy*, chs. 7–8.

inary, the institutional voice of conservative dissent in the Presbyterian church, to explore the nature of conservative criticisms of the denomination. (Selection 28 is part of Machen's testimony before this committee, and Selection 29 is his plea for Presbyterians not to let the committee change Princeton's character.)

This committee recommended the reorganization of Princeton Seminary. Its decision removed the seminary from conservative control and prompted the founding of Westminster Seminary. Still, Presbyterian officials were not finished with Machen. The controversy surrounding the layman's report on foreign missions, *Re-Thinking Missions*, occasioned the last run-in between Machen and denominational bureaucrats. In 1933 Machen formed a rival missions board, and the Presbyterian hierarchy instructed his presbytery to bring him to trial.[18] (Selection 30 is part of his testimony leading up to the trial.) Only after the PCUSA suspended Machen from the ministry in 1936 did he found a new denomination, the Orthodox Presbyterian Church, one that he hoped would not separate doctrine from work but instead see the two as being inextricably connected.[19]

CHRISTIANITY AND CULTURE

If the anthology included only Machen's writings on the gospel, the Bible, seminary education, and the church, many readers might be content. After all, what else did Machen do aside from his work as a biblical scholar, seminary professor, and churchman? Some might find his writings even at this point more particularly Presbyterian than necessary. Still, evangelicals and Reformed should be able to find enough in Machen's shorter writings on Christianity and the church to appreciate, even discounting his persistence about Calvinism.

18. See Hutchison, *Errand to the World*; and Edwin H. Rian, *The Presbyterian Conflict* (Grand Rapids: Eerdmans, 1940).
19. On the OPC, see Charles G. Dennison and Richard C. Gamble, eds., *Pressing toward the Mark: Essays Commemorating Fifty Years of the Orthodox Presbyterian Church* (Philadelphia: Committee for the Historian of the OPC, 1986); and D. G. Hart and John R. Muether, *Fighting the Good Fight: A Brief History of the Orthodox Presbyterian Church* (Philadelphia: Committee on Christian Education and Committee for the Historian of the OPC, 1995).

Parts Seven and Eight reveal a side of Machen that few would expect from a conservative Presbyterian. Indeed, one reason why *What Is Christianity?* was never reprinted may be that his essays on society and culture left conservative evangelical and Reformed Christians scratching their heads.[20] How could a man who defended the virgin birth of Christ oppose prayer and Bible reading in public schools? Or why would someone who took great comfort from the doctrine of the vicarious atonement oppose federal legislation that prohibited the sale and distribution of alcohol? Even more puzzling is how a man who believed in the Lordship of Christ over all spheres of creation could defend the civil liberties of Communists, Roman Catholics, and Mormons to disseminate propaganda for their views. Machen's quirky notions about society and culture, and the Christian's duty in those spheres, go a long way to explaining why the collection of essays that Ned B. Stonehouse assembled fifty years ago were never reprinted. Yet to ignore this part of Machen's thought is to turn him from a three-dimensional figure into a cardboard cutout.

Although most of Machen's work and support was in the Northeast, he was a Southerner with politics to match.[21] As such, he was a lifelong Democrat who defended the prerogatives of local government against national consolidation. He was also a civil libertarian who jealously guarded against the intrusions of government into spheres where it was unneeded. Consequently, Machen's politics never lined up well with the membership of the northern Presbyterian Church (PCUSA), which was overwhelmingly Republican, or with his successors in the Orthodox Presbyterian Church, who—especially after the New Deal (which Machen opposed mightily)—were also more sympathetic to Republican than to Democratic administrations. Perhaps the greatest difference between these two political traditions is the issue of cultural uniformity. Republicans have generally favored economic efficiency, which tends toward political centralization, and

---

20. The one exception here is a collection of essays that reveals Machen's libertarian politics. See J. Gresham Machen, *Education, Christianity and the State*, ed. John W. Robbins (Jefferson, Md.: Trinity Foundation, 1987).
21. Longfield, *Presbyterian Controversy*, especially makes this point. For a good overview of the Southern political tradition, see Eugene D. Genovese, *The Southern Tradition: The Achievement and Limitations of an American Conservatism* (Cambridge, Mass.: Harvard University Press, 1994).

cultural homogeneity as the best way of building a great nation. Democrats, in contrast, have generally opposed centralization and favored cultural diversity as the best way of preserving liberty.[22]

Still, Machen's ideas about the relationship between Christianity and society were not simply the product of political instincts he inherited from his father (a native Virginian) and mother (a native Georgian). (Selection 46 provides some insights into Machen's relationship to his parents as well as his cultural sensibilities more generally.) As Selection 32 demonstrates, Machen's notions about drawing a proper line between religion and public life stemmed directly from his understanding of the gospel and the mission of the church. Thus, trying to separate Machen's political and cultural interests is a feat not easily accomplished. In a nutshell, Machen believed that spiritual liberty was markedly different from civil liberty. To him both were vital, one to the church, the other to the United States of America. But that did not mean that it was unnecessary to distinguish neatly between the spiritual and eternal things of the church and the physical and temporal matters of the state and cultural life. In fact, to neglect this distinction was to run headlong into the clutches of a social gospel that liberal Protestants fashioned into a full-blown social gospel and that fundamentalists developed into a program for Christian America. For Machen, the spiritual nature of the church meant that the ministry of Word and sacrament was designed to achieve spiritual ends (i.e., the kingdom of the Lord Jesus Christ) through spiritual means (Word, sacrament, and discipline).[23]

Machen's ideas about culture and politics veered in a direction different from the Reformed transformation-of-culture model established first by Abraham Kuyper and then reinforced by H. Richard Niebuhr.[24] By distinguishing between the church in its corporate capacity and the church in political and cultural spheres, Machen suggested a less aggressive and triumphalist vi-

---

22. Allen C. Guelzo, *Abraham Lincoln: Redeemer President* (Grand Rapids: Eerdmans, 1999), contrasts these two positions exceptionally well through a contrast between Lincoln and Thomas Jefferson.
23. See D. G. Hart, "The Spirituality of the Church, the Westminster Standards, and Nineteenth-Century American Presbyterianism," in *Recovering Mother Kirk: The Case for Liturgy in the Reformed Tradition* (Grand Rapids: Baker Book House, forthcoming).
24. Abraham Kuyper, *Lectures on Calvinism* (Grand Rapids: Eerdmans, 1931); and H. Richard Niebuhr, *Christ and Culture* (New York: Harper, 1951).

sion of Christian cultural involvement. On the one hand, the church in its official capacity was to refrain from any activity not sanctioned in Scripture, from political declarations to humanitarian assistance. The work of the church, though outwardly ordinary and insignificant, was actually the chief site of the history of redemption. If the church neglected her spiritual task for social or cultural pursuits, she was abandoning the most glorious work imaginable. On the other hand, God called individual Christians in their vocations to be engaged in social and cultural endeavors that they shared with nonbelievers. Rather than calling this common work Christian, it was better to describe it as human. Machen believed it was important to reserve the terminology of redemption for the mission of the church.

Because of these distinctions, some have regarded Machen's understanding of culture as less than Reformed, bordering on fundamentalist.[25] It does appear that the neat distinction that Machen makes between the church and society grants autonomy to a variety of realms of human existence, as if the church, both as individuals and corporately, does not have a word to speak on military spending, gay marriage, or public-school textbooks. Yet it is important to see, as the selections in Parts Seven and Eight show, that Machen was not implying that Christianity is unrelated to any range of activity beyond the ministry or fellowship of the church. Instead, he was raising questions about the much more difficult issue of how Christianity is related to these other areas of human activity. And as these selections also reveal, Christians, even Reformed ones, may actually give different answers to questions about the best form of government, cultural and religious diversity in a single nation, the value of mountain climbing, or the significance of advanced learning.

REMEMBERING MACHEN

What, then, do the essays in this volume add up to? Do they confirm the verdict of Caspar Wistar Hodge, Machen's old friend and longtime colleague at Princeton Seminary, who wrote on the occasion of Machen's death that

25. This is the implication of Albert M. Wolters, *Creation Regained: Biblical Basics for a Reformational Worldview* (Grand Rapids: Eerdmans, 1985); and Brian J. Walsh and Richard J. Middleton, *The Transforming Vision: Shaping a Christian World View* (Downers Grove, Ill.: InterVarsity Press, 1984).

the church had lost "the greatest theologian in the English-speaking world"?[26] Or how about the perspective of H. L. Mencken, the most popular journalist of Machen's day, who thrilled to see Protestantism on the defensive but who also thought Machen had a point? That point, as Mencken explained in his obituary of Machen, was that the Westminster professor was completely unable "to square the disingenuous evasions of Modernism with the fundamentals of Christian doctrine." Consequently, he drew the ire of the Presbyterian leaders who were trying to "convert the Presbyterian Church into a kind of literary and social club, devoted vaguely to good works."[27] Or perhaps the observation that Harvard church historian William R. Hutchison made almost forty years after Machen's death, one that resembled Mencken's more than Hodge's, is the one that unifies the orthodox Presbyterian's thoughts. Hutchison wrote that Machen's main contribution during the fundamentalist controversy was to reassert the old Princeton refrain that the gospel's binding address required a "clean"choice between Christian orthodoxy or no Christianity at all."[28]

Although significance, like beauty, is usually in the eye of the beholder, Hutchison's read on Machen may be the best to account for the complexity of Machen's views. This Presbyterian stalwart did not simply insist that those officers in his communion choose between honoring or dishonoring their Calvinistic heritage. Throughout his writings Machen also argued that it was impossible to have it both ways. Trusting the message of the gospel involved consequences, some blessed and some painful (and sometimes even the sufferings were blessed). Regardless of whether Machen's admirers today will agree with the alternatives that he elaborated, what stands out in these essays is an awareness of the nature of the choices that follow Reformed Christians living in culturally diverse, liberal, democratic, secular societies such as Canada, England, the Netherlands, and especially the United States. Machen's understanding of the claims of the gospel differs in some important respects from that of the likes of John Calvin, John Owen, Jonathan Edwards, and Abraham Kuyper. This may help to explain why parts of Machen have been forgotten; his arguments do not always reassure that

26. Hodge, quoted in "Recent Tributes to Dr. Machen," *Presbyterian Guardian* 3 (13 Feb. 1937): 189.
27. Mencken, "Doctor Fundamentalist," *Baltimore Evening Sun*, 18 Jan. 1937.
28. Hutchison, *Modernist Impulse*, 258.

Calvinists will prevail in the marketplace of ideas, the debates of legislatures, or the collections of art museums. But that sobering conviction may be the best reason for remembering Machen.

SELECT BIBLIOGRAPHY

Books by J. Gresham Machen

For a complete bibliography of Machen's published writings, readers should consult the one compiled by James T. Dennison Jr. and Grace Mullen in *Pressing Toward the Mark* (see below).

The Christian Faith in the Modern World. New York: Macmillan, 1937.
The Christian View of Man. New York: Macmillan, 1936.
Christianity and Liberalism. New York: Macmillan, 1923.
Education, Christianity and the State. Edited by John W. Robbins. Jefferson, Md.: Trinity Foundation, 1987.
God Transcendent. Edited by Ned B. Stonehouse. Grand Rapids: Eerdmans, 1949.
New Testament Greek for Beginners. New York: Macmillan, 1922.
The Origins of Paul's Religion. New York: Macmillan, 1921.
Virgin Birth of Christ. New York: Harper and Bros., 1930.
What Is Christianity? And Other Addresses. Edited by Ned Bernard Stonehouse. Grand Rapids: Eerdmans, 1951.
What Is Faith? New York: Macmillan, 1925.

Books about Machen

Chrishope, Terry A. *Toward a Sure Faith: J. Gresham Machen and the Dilemma of Biblical Criticism, 1881–1915*. Fearn Ross-shire: Christian Focus, 2001.
Coray, Henry W. *J. Gresham Machen*. Grand Rapids: Kregel, 1981.
Hart, D. G. *Defending the Faith: J. Gresham Machen and the Crisis of Conservative Protestantism in Modern America*. Baltimore: Johns Hopkins University Press, 1994.
Marsden, George M. *Understanding Fundamentalism and Evangelicalism*. Grand Rapids: Eerdmans, 1991.
Russell, C. Allyn. *Voices of Fundamentalism: Seven Biographical Studies*. Philadelphia: Westminster Press, 1976.

INTRODUCTION

Stonehouse, Ned B. *J. Gresham Machen: A Biographical Memoir*. Grand Rapids: Eerdmans, 1954.

Woolley, Paul. *The Significance of J. Gresham Machen Today*. Phillipsburg, N.J.: P&R Publishing, 1977.

Books about Princeton Seminary

Calhoun, David C. *Faith and Learning, 1812–1868*, vol. 1 of *Princeton Theological Seminary*. Carlisle, Pa.: Banner of Truth Trust, 1994.

———. *The Majestic Testimony, 1869–1929*, vol. 2 of *Princeton Theological Seminary*. Carlisle, Pa.: Banner of Truth Trust, 1996.

Kerr, Hugh Thomson. *Sons of the Prophets; Leaders in Protestantism from Princeton Seminary*. Princeton: Princeton University Press, 1963.

Loetscher, Lefferts A. *Facing the Enlightenment and Pietism: Archibald Alexander and the founding of Princeton Theological Seminary*. Westport, Conn.: Greenwood Press, 1983.

Noll, Mark A., ed. *The Princeton Theology, 1812–1921: Scripture, Science, and Theological Method from Archibald Alexander to Benjamin Warfield*. 1983; Grand Rapids: Baker Book House, 2001.

Vander Stelt, John C. *Philosophy and Scripture: A Study in Old Princeton and Westminster Theology*. Marlton, N.J.: Mack Publishing, 1978.

Books about Twentieth-Century American Presbyterianism

Coalter, Milton J., John M. Mulder, and Louis B. Weeks, eds. *The Confessional Mosaic: Presbyterians and Twentieth-Century Theology*. Louisville: Westminster/John Knox, 1990.

———. *The Diversity of Discipleship: Presbyterians and Twentieth-Century Christian Witness*. Louisville: Westminster/John Knox, 1991.

———. *The Mainstream Protestant "Decline": The Presbyterian Pattern*. Louisville: Westminster/John Knox, 1990.

———. *The Organizational Revolution: Presbyterians and American Denominationalism*. Louisville: Westminster/John Knox, 1992.

———. *The Pluralistic Vision: Presbyterians and Mainstream Protestant Education and Leadership*. Louisville: Westminster/John Knox, 1992.

———. *The Presbyterian Predicament: Six Perspectives*. Louisville: Westminster/John Knox, 1990.

Coalter, Milton J., John M. Mulder, and Louis B. Weeks. *The Re-Forming Tradition: Presbyterians and Mainstream Protestantism*. Louisville: Westminster/John Knox, 1992.

Dennison, Charles G. and Richard C. Gamble, eds. *Pressing toward the Mark: Essays Commemorating Fifty Years of the Orthodox Presbyterian Church*. Philadelphia: Committee for the Historian of the OPC, 1986.

Hart, D. G. and John R. Muether. *Fighting the Good Fight: A Brief History of the Orthodox Presbyterian Church*. Philadelphia: Committee on Christian Education and Committee for the Historian of the OPC, 1995.

Loetscher, Lefferts A. *The Broadening Church: A Study of Theological Issues in the Presbyterian Church since 1869*. Philadelphia: University of Pennsylvania Press, 1954.

Longfield, Bradley J. *The Presbyterian Controversy: Fundamentalists, Modernists, and Moderates*. New York: Oxford University Press, 1991.

North, Gary. *Crossed Fingers: How Liberals Captured the Presbyterian Church*. Tyler, Tex.: Institute for Christian Economics, 1996.

Rian, Edwin H. *The Presbyterian Controversy*. Grand Rapids: Eerdmans, 1940.

Weston, William J. *Presbyterian Pluralism: Competition in a Protestant House*. Knoxville: University of Tennessee Press, 1997.

Books about American Theology and Culture, 1870–1940

Boyer, Paul. *When Time Shall Be No More: Prophecy Belief in Modern American Culture*. Cambridge, Mass.: Harvard University Press, 1992.

Brereton, Virginia Lieson. *Training God's Army: The American Bible School, 1880–1940*. Bloomington, Ind.: Indiana University Press, 1990.

Carpenter, Joel A. *Revive Us Again: The Renewal of American Fundamentalism*. New York: Oxford University Press, 1997.

Crunden, Robert M. *Ministers of Reform: The Progressives' Achievement in American Civilization, 1889–1920*. New York: Basic Books, 1982.

Gorrell, Donald K. *The Age of Social Responsibility: The Social Gospel in the Progressive Era, 1900–1920*. Macon, Ga.: Mercer University Press, 1988.

Hankins, Barry. *God's Rascal: J. Frank Norris and the Beginnings of Southern Fundamentalism*. Lexington, Ky.: University of Kentucky Press, 1996.

Hart, D. G. *The Lost Soul of American Protestantism*. Lanham, Md.: Rowman & Littlefield, 2002.

———. *The University Gets Religion: Religious Studies and American Higher Education*. Baltimore: Johns Hopkins University Press, 1999.

Himmelstein, Jerome L. *To the Right: The Transformation of American Conservatism*. Berkeley, Calif.: University of California Press, 1990.

Hutchison, William R. *The Modernist Impulse in American Protestantism*. Cambridge, Mass.: Harvard University Press, 1976.

———. *Errand to the World: American Protestant Thought and Foreign Missions*. Chicago: University of Chicago Press, 1987.

Kuklick, Bruce. *Churchmen and Philosophers: From Jonathan Edwards to John Dewey*. New Haven: Yale University Press, 1985.

———. *Puritans in Babylon*. Princeton: Princeton University Press, 1996.

Lears, T. J. Jackson. *No Place of Grace: Antimodernism and the Transformation of American Culture, 1880–1920*. New York: Pantheon, 1981.

Levine, Lawrence. *Defender of the Faith: William Jennings Bryan, 1915–1925*. New York: Oxford University Press, 1965.

Lichtman, Allan J. *Prejudice and Old Politics: The Presidential Election of 1928*. Chapel Hill, N.C.: University of North Carolina Press, 1979.

Marsden, George M. *Fundamentalism and American Culture: The Shaping of Twentieth-Century Evangelicalism*. New York: Oxford University Press, 1980.

Marty, Martin E. *The Noise of the Conflict, 1919–1941*, vol. 1 of *Modern American Religion*. Chicago: University of Chicago Press, 1991.

May, Henry F. *The End of American Innocence: The First Years of Our Time, 1912–1917*. New York: Alfred A. Knopf, 1959.

Noll, Mark A. *Between Faith and Criticism: Evangelicals, Scholarship, and the Bible in America*. San Francisco: Harper & Row, 1986.

Numbers, Ronald L. *The Creationists: The Evolution of Scientific Creationism*. New York: Alfred A. Knopf, 1992.

Ribuffo, Leo P. *The Old Christian Right: The Protestant Far Right from the Great Depression to the Cold War*. Philadelphia: Temple University Press, 1983.

Sandeen, Ernest R. *The Roots of Fundamentalism: British and American Millenarianism, 1800–1930*. Chicago: University of Chicago Press, 1970.

Trollinger, William Vance Jr. *God's Empire: William Bell Riley and Midwestern Fundamentalism*. Madison, Wis.: University of Wisconsin Press, 1990.

Turner, James. *Without God, Without Creed: The Origins of Unbelief in America*. Baltimore: Johns Hopkins University Press, 1985.

Wacker, Grant. *Augustus H. Strong and the Dilemma of Historical Consciousness*. Macon, Ga.: Mercer University Press, 1985.

Weber, Timothy P. *Living in the Shadow of the Second Coming: American Premillennialism, 1875–1925*. New York: Oxford University Press, 1979.

PART ONE

CHRIST AND THE WITNESS OF SCRIPTURE

1

WHAT THE BIBLE
TEACHES ABOUT JESUS

The subject which I have been bold enough to propose for the three addresses which I shall have the privilege of attempting to deliver is this: "Is the Bible Right about Jesus?" And, after all, that is the real test of the authority of the Bible. If the Bible is really right about Jesus, the probability is that it is right about other things as well. But before we discuss that question, it does seem to me to be important to discuss what the Bible teaches about Jesus. If you are going to determine whether the Bible is right in what it says, it does seem to be important that you should first ask yourself what it says. In other words, I am old-fashioned enough—I know it is quite out of date—to think that it is important to examine a thing before you begin to express an estimate or criticism of it. So it does seem to me that we should first ask ourselves what the Bible teaches about Jesus before we ask ourselves whether that which the Bible teaches is true or false.

In the prologue to the third gospel we have words which, literally translated, are approximately as follows: "Forasmuch as many have taken in hand to draw up a narrative concerning those matters which have been fulfilled among us, even as they delivered them unto us, who from the beginning were

"What the Bible Teaches about Jesus" is an address originally delivered on June 10, 1927, in London before the Bible League of Great Britain, and published in *The Evangelical Student* 3 (October 1928) 4–11. Reprinted in *What Is Christianity?* ed. Ned Bernard Stonehouse (Grand Rapids: Eerdmans, 1951).

eyewitnesses and ministers of the word it seemed good to me also, having traced the course of all things accurately from the first, to write to thee in order, most excellent Theophilus, that thou mightest know the certainty concerning the things wherein thou wast instructed" (Luke 1:1–4 ASV).

It is a very wonderful sentence from the point of view of style: the sense is held in abeyance until the very end; it is like a wave gradually forming on the shore until it reaches its climax in those words "the certainty." The man who wrote that sentence was a man gifted from the point of view of style, especially when we observe in the passage that follows, where he was dealing with the delicate details of Palestinian life, that he did not there attempt a classical Greek style, but was possessed of taste enough to catch the wonderful spirit of those Semitic narratives which came to him upon Palestinian ground.

But more interesting than the style of the passage is its content. I do not know that there is any passage in the whole of the Scriptures which needs to be taken to heart more earnestly just now than these words. That Theophilus to whom the third gospel and the book of Acts are dedicated was probably an immature Christian, one at least who needed intellectual guidance, in whose case intellectual difficulties needed attention. It is very interesting to learn how the author of a very large portion of the whole New Testament deals with the intellectual needs of such a man. In the first place, there is no evidence that the author treated the doubts or difficulties that Theophilus may have had as being necessarily sinful. There, I think, he provides a lesson for us when we try to lead people today. But still more important is it to observe that he did not treat those intellectual questionings as though they were a matter of no moment. He did not adopt the modern slogan that "it makes no difference"; that men can be equally close to Jesus no matter what they think of Jesus. But he plainly recognized what is recognized in the whole of the New Testament: that the Christian religion is founded squarely upon a body of facts. In other words, the method of this writer in dealing with intellectual difficulty is, first of all, to get the matter straight.

That is a method which has gone out of fashion at the present time. If there is one thing in the church in America and, if what I read is correct, also in the church elsewhere in the world—if there is one thing that is characteristic of the church of the present day, it is the alarming growth of plain stark ignorance. Suppose you are leading a Bible class that is dealing with the kingdoms of Judah and Israel. It may be well to begin with a little review. Suppose you say: "Now let us get this matter straight. Who was the first king of the united Israel?" There will perhaps be an eloquent silence for a little while, and then there will be various suggestions. Solomon, perhaps, will be a prominent candidate for the position. Finally, a gray-haired gentleman, the oldest member of the congregation, product of a better day in education, may suggest that it was Saul. You will say that that is correct, and that Saul did not exactly make a go of it. And then you will say that the next one was David, and the next Solomon, and then the kingdom was divided. When you get through, they will come up and say: "We never heard anything like it." Try that method in teaching a class. You may make a great hit! It is an entirely new notion to some people just to get the Bible straight.

Now I had it fairly straight when I was very young, not by attendance at any sort of school, not by the operation of elaborate schemes of pedagogy, but by half an hour with my mother on Sunday afternoons at home. I could tell you the kings of Israel and Judah in order. The kings of Israel are easy, because they were all bad. But I could tell you just which ones of the kings of Judah were good and which bad, at a very tender age. But, it may be asked, what is the use of it? What is the use of learning all those mere details? There is a great deal of use of it, I think. For if you get the notion that there was a true progress of history in Old Testament times, then you come to have certain conviction that is entirely absent from the minds of many persons who try to be good Christians at the present day—the conviction that when our Lord Jesus came into this world for our salvation, he came at a definite point of time, and that if we had been living there we could have seen him; that like the author of the fourth gospel we could have touched him with our hands, seen him with our eyes, and heard him with our ears. In other words, you have formed the fundamental conviction that, unlike other religions, the Christian religion is founded squarely upon a body of historical fact. Very well, it is rather important, I think, for us to try to get straight in our minds what the Bible says about Jesus.

But it is quite impossible to understand what the Bible says about Jesus unless you know also some of the things that the Bible says about other matters as well; and so if you will begin to read your Bible, you will find at least two important things in the Old Testament. At the very beginning, of course, you find the doctrine of creation, that doctrine that is so much despised today: "In the beginning God created the heavens and the earth." You have there a clear view of a personal God, the Creator and Ruler of the world.

Unfortunately, that view of a personal God is lost in large sections of the modern church. Men say that the doctrine of creation is a matter of metaphysics without importance for the Christian. We cannot solve the problem, it is said, as to how the world came into being; those things do not belong to the sphere of religion at all. Our God, men say, is a God of love, and we are indifferent to the question whether there is a God of power. Well, of course, there are many objections to such a way of thinking. A God who is only a God of love and has no power to act is not a person; and a God who is not a person but merely an abstraction is not a God who can love us and whom we can love. But of course the Christian heart negates this lack of interest in the question of the Creator and Ruler of the world. As for us, we say still, as we contemplate the "woodlands robed in the blooming garb of spring," or dark mountains capped with dazzling white: "This is God's world; its majesty and its beauty came from him."

One thing that is to be regretted in the religious life of the present day is the decline in natural religion. But as for me, I am bound to say that I will not yield to the pantheists in my sense of the friendliness of nature; and when I toil up upon one of our mountains in America—for there we have to pay for our view; we have not the bare mountains you have in Britain— when I toil up, and the trees, as I ascend, become smaller and smaller until the prospect bursts upon my view, as I am far away from the troubles of the valley below, sometimes I have a feeling of the friendliness of nature, the friendliness of nature as over against the hostility of man, which is somewhat in the spirit of the pantheists of all ages, except that in our case it is a far deeper thing; for as we come thus into contact with nature we can think of that holy and living person who has provided its majesty and its beauty because of his love for us.

And then at the very beginning of the Bible you have also the other great presupposition of what the Bible tells us about Jesus—namely, the awful fact of sin. The consciousness of sin is deepened all through the Old Testament; in the teachings of our Lord, too, and all through the New Testament. It is deepened by a proclamation of the law of God. The law is the schoolmaster to bring us to Christ; and unless by learning the lesson of the law we come to have the consciousness of sin, I fear we shall never come to Jesus as our Savior.

On that point I desire not to be misunderstood. I do not mean for one moment that all Christian experience is alike. I do not mean that everyone, when he comes to Christ, has to go through a prior period of agony of soul until he comes into the joy of acceptance of the gospel. I remember a very interesting meeting that I attended some years ago. It was a meeting of an evangelical type, an experience-meeting; and the persons who were there present were asked to say where they were born the first time, and when and where they were born the second time. One person said that he was born the first time in such and such a city, and that he was born the second time on a railway train at such and such a moment, of such and such an hour, and on such and such a day. It was a very interesting record of the truest Christian experience, and God forbid that we should say aught against it. But then one lady rose to her feet in a very modest way and said something to the effect that she was born the first time in such and such a place, and she could not tell when she was born the second time because she had grown up in a Christian home. I do not remember her exact words, but the notion was that as she had come to the consciousness of sin, she had come also to the consciousness of Jesus as her Savior. That was a true Christian experience too, and we should never disparage it. My friends, do not misunderstand me. I do believe that there is a definite instant when the wonderful event occurs in the life of everyone who becomes a Christian—the wonderful event when he or she is born again—but I do believe also that there are many who cannot tell when that instant was; it is known to God, but not to them. There are many Christians who cannot give the day and hour of their conversion, who do not pass through prior agonies of soul. Certainly such Christian experience is not at all inferior to the experience of those who could give the very day and hour of their conversion. Both kinds of Christian experience, it seems to me, are true forms of Christian experience; and God forbid that we should deprecate either of them. But even in the case of those who grow up in Christian homes and are children of the covenant from tender years, there is logically connected with their acceptance of Christ as Savior the consciousness of the fact that without him they are lost in sin. So those are the two great presuppositions of the Christian message: the awful holiness, the awful transcendence of God, and the terrible separateness of sinful man from the Holy God.

Then, after the preparation for the coming of our Lord under the old dispensation, at last the fullness of the time had come. In what wondrous fashion the Savior, according to the New Testament, came into this world! He who was so great did not despise the virgin womb; he was content to be born as a man and to lie as a babe in a manger and to be subject to earthly parents. How wondrous the story is! How different from anything that could have been expected, yet how full of a divine majesty!

In the New Testament there is the record of the life of our Lord upon this earth. And even in the days when he was on earth, he manifested his glory. The writers of the New Testament are conscious of the fact that even when our Lord was subject, in his human nature for the most part, to the petty limitations of human life, yet the glory of the incarnate Word shone forth. With what a trembling wonder the author of the fourth gospel says that "the Word became flesh . . . and we beheld His glory"!

At that point, of course—in our dependence upon the Bible for the facts with regard to Jesus—we meet the opposition of many modern men. A great many persons are telling us that we should emancipate ourselves from the slavish dependence upon a book, and that our true authority is Christ alone. So they tell us that every race and every generation must interpret Christ for itself. We think in this connection, for example, of that beautiful but harmful little book, *The Christ of the Indian Road,* by E. Stanley Jones, where truth is mixed with error in such a way as to lead many astray. The notion seems to be that every race may interpret Christ for itself.

If that meant simply that every race has its contribution to make to the rich store of our understanding of what God has told us in his Word, then we could no doubt agree. If it meant that the Indian race could understand some aspects of what the Bible says better than other races, in order that when that race had seized some aspects of the truth about Jesus it might share that newly discovered truth with us—if that were what is meant, we might agree. But I fear that something very different is meant or, if not consciously meant, at least logically involved in what is said; I fear that what is involved is that the interpretation of Christ which every race attains is an interpretation that is valid for that race alone—as when it is often said, in accordance with the pragmatist skepticism of the day, that "Western creeds" must not be forced upon the "Eastern mind." When you arrive at that point—when you hold that every race may interpret Christ for itself— you are in great danger of substituting just the imagination of your own heart for contact with the real person, Jesus of Nazareth, whom God has presented to all nations in the whole of his Word, not only in the four gospels, but also, just as truly, in the epistles of Paul.

I do believe, indeed, with all my heart, that there is a direct contact of the risen Christ with the human soul. But I also believe that if that were all, the whole coming of our Lord upon this earth would have been in vain, and that it is for us when we come into contact with Jesus not to despise the plain record of what he said and did.

There is the first aspect, then, of what the Bible tells us about Jesus. The Bible tells us what manner of person Jesus was and is, and the part of the Bible that tells us that is contained particularly in the four gospels. But if that were all that we knew about Jesus, we should be of all men most miserable. If we knew only what sort of person Jesus was and is, we should look with hopeless envy upon those who, when he was on earth, pushed in through the crowd where he sat amid scribes and Pharisees, and had the wonderful experience of looking upon his face. We should be conscious, as we read about that experience, of a wealth of glory from which we should be forever shut out. No, there is something else that we need also to know, how we of the twentieth century can come into contact with him. And surely that is not such a very simple thing. We cannot observe him as we go through our busy streets. We are separated from him by nineteen centuries. How is the wonder to be accomplished that we who live in the twentieth century should have personal contact with one who lived so long ago?

If you will read the religious writers of the present day, you will constantly observe that they assume it as an axiom that we ought to return to the experience of those who came into contact with our Lord in Galilee. I do not believe for one moment that they are right. In book after book, in sermon after sermon, it seems to be assumed that we ought to take the first disciples in Galilee as our models today. "They did not know anything about the Nicene and Chalcedonian doctrine of the person of our Lord," it is said in effect; "and so therefore these things are matters of indifference to us." Such is the argument. But do you not see that if we are to have contact with one who lived in the first century, we must know far more about him than was known by those who came into direct contact with him when he was on earth? We need to know, for one thing, that he has risen from the dead and that he is still alive; and then we need to know how, if he is still alive, we can come into his presence.

There is where the other great division of what the New Testament says about Jesus Christ comes in; and that other great division is found especially in the epistles of Paul. The gospels tell us what manner of person Jesus was and is; and the epistles tell us—what it is equally important for us to know—how we can come into contact with him. Do not misunderstand me. The division is not an absolute one. The epistles tell us not only how we can come into contact with Jesus, but also what sort of person he was and is; the great Christological passages in the epistles enrich greatly and clarify our knowledge of the person of our Lord. And the gospels, on the other hand, tell us not only what sort of person Jesus was, but also, by way of prophecy, how future generations could come into contact with him. But after all, it is not surprising that the full explanation of our Lord's redeeming work should be made known only after the redeeming work was done, and so I have little sympathy with those who regard the words of our Lord when he was on earth as somehow more necessary for our needs than the words of the Holy Spirit that are found, for example, in the epistles of Paul. You could summarize what we need to know about Jesus by saying that we need to have, first, the record of Jesus' life in the gospels to tell us what sort of person Jesus is, and then we need to have the eighth chapter of Romans and the rest of the epistles of Paul to tell us how it is that he can become our Savior today.

What is it that our Lord did, not merely for the men of long ago but for us today? The answer of the whole New Testament, of the whole Bible indeed, is abundantly plain. For us he did more than heal our bodily infirmities. For us he died upon the cross. There is the point of contact between Jesus and our souls. I do not think that what the New Testament says about the cross of Christ is particularly intricate. It is, indeed, profound, but it can be put in simple language. We deserved eternal death; the Lord Jesus, because he loved us, died in our stead upon the cross. It is a mystery, but it is not intricate. What is really intricate and subtle is the manifold modern attempt to get rid of the simple doctrine of the cross of Christ in the interests of human pride. Of course there are objections to the cross of Christ, and men in the pulpits of the present day pour out upon that blessed doctrine the vials of their scorn; but when a man has come under the consciousness of sin, then as he comes into the presence of the cross, he says with tears of gratitude and joy: "He loved me and gave himself for me."

Men have objections in plenty. The Christian doctrine of the cross, as it is found in the Bible, is objected to, in the first place, because it depends upon history. But of course it must depend upon history if it is to be a gospel; for "gospel" means "good news"; and "news" means an account of something that has happened. With regard to the same objection, we might say also that though this way of salvation begins in history, it proceeds to present experience. When we read the blessed record, we can take it to our souls and come into contact now with our risen Lord. Men exalt "experience" at the present day, and set it in opposition to the Word of God, but why do they not attend to that Christian experience which testifies that the Word of God is true?

Then men say, in the second place, that it is absurd that one man should die for another man's sins. Of course it is absurd. Certainly one man cannot die for another man's sins, and the human analogies that have been proposed for the atonement made by Christ usually just show how totally unable the natural man is to understand the doctrine of the cross. When men appeal to the sacrifice of individuals at the present time as though that were in any full sense analogous to the gift of the Lord Jesus on the cross, they show that they have never come into any real contact with the cross of Christ; for when a man comes into contact with the cross, he is impressed, not with the similarity between that act of self-sacrifice and other acts of self-sacrifice, no matter how noble they may be, but he is impressed with the profound difference, and so he says:

> There was no other good enough
>   To pay the price of sin,
> He only could unlock the gate
>   Of heaven, and let us in.

Because one mere man cannot suffer for another man's sins, it does not follow that the Lord Jesus could not suffer for our sins. And that is why we cling, with all our souls, to the Christian doctrine of the deity of our Lord, for if he is not God, then he cannot be our substitute.

But men say: "What a low view it is of the love of God if you represent an angry God as though he were waiting coldly for a sacrifice to be made!" It is really astonishing to me how preachers of the present day, who are able to read, who have some sort of contact with the Christian literature of all the centuries, should so misrepresent the Christian doctrine of the cross. Of course I need not point out to you where the error lies. The very point of the Christian view of the cross is that God does not wait for someone else to pay the price of sin, but in his infinite love has himself paid the price for us—God himself in the person of the Son, who loved us and gave himself for us; God himself in the person of the Father, who so loved the world that he gave his only-begotten Son.

It is a strange thing that when men talk about the love of God, they show by every word that they utter that they have no conception at all of the depths of God's love. If you want to find an instance of true gratitude for the infinite grace of God, do not go to those who think of God's love as something that cost nothing, but go rather to those who in agony of soul have faced the awful fact of the guilt of sin, and then have come to know with a trembling wonder that the miracle of all miracles has been accomplished, and that the eternal Son has died in their stead.

Thus if we put what the Bible says about Jesus together, we can even now have contact with him. I am bound to say that there was a time when I was greatly troubled in my faith by the defection of the modern world from Jesus of Nazareth as he is set forth in Scriptures; but as I observe what is becoming of the world when the contact with Jesus is broken, my faith is no longer so much troubled by the argument from modern authority, and I have come to wonder whether, after wandering in devious ways, we shall not be forced to come again, as little children, to the Lord Jesus Christ as he is set forth in the Holy Scriptures and offered to us in the gospel.

Let us unite in a word of prayer:

Almighty God, our Heavenly Father, we give you thanks for the wonder of your grace in the gift of Christ our Lord and Savior. How can we ever find words which shall not seem vain as we think of his love for us? How can we, without shame, try to give you thanks for that grace of Christ our Savior who died for us, the Just for the unjust? And how can we think, without shame, of the ill way in which we have requited you for your love? But we rejoice in the knowledge that when by your Holy Spirit we have been united to Christ through faith, we are his forever. We pray that thus we may be kept safe by one stronger than we are. And we pray with all our souls for those who have not found Christ as Savior, that they may be led through the mists of error and doubt into the clear shining of the light of faith— that when they have sought other saviors and their souls are still restless, they may, through Christ, find their rest in you. And all that we ask is in the name of Christ Jesus, our Lord and Savior. Amen.

2

THE WITNESS OF PAUL

We are considering the question whether the Bible is right about Jesus. This morning we considered, in a necessarily very brief and summary way, what the Bible says about Jesus, because obviously it is necessary to determine what the Bible says before we can consider the question whether what the Bible says is true. Certainly what the Bible says about Jesus contains many mysteries; but the distinctive features of it at least can be put almost in a word. Jesus of Nazareth, according to the Bible, was no product of this world, but a Savior come voluntarily into this world from without. His entrance into the world was a stupendous miracle. While he was on earth he manifested a wondrous control over the forces of nature. His death was no mere holy martyrdom, but an event of cosmic significance, a sacrifice for the sins of the world. His resurrection was no mere vain aspiration in the hearts of his disciples, but a mighty act of God. That is what the Bible says about Jesus.

That account, in practically all of the larger churches today, is faced by an alternative account. According to that alternative account, Jesus of Nazareth was the fairest of the children of men. He lived a life of wonderful purity and unselfishness. He was conscious of a wonderful closeness to

"The Witness of Paul" is an address originally delivered on June 10, 1927, in London before the Bible League of Great Britain, and published in *The Evangelical Student* 3 (January 1929) 7–15. Reprinted in *What Is Christianity?* ed. Ned Bernard Stonehouse (Grand Rapids: Eerdmans, 1951).

God. He felt that he had a mission to bring others to that closeness of relationship with God that he himself had. In order to express his sense of that mission, he was unfortunately forced to use the categories of thought that prevailed in his day, and so he made the claim to be the Jewish Messiah. At first he won the favor of the crowd, but since he would not be the kind of leader that they desired, he fell under their condemnation. He fell a victim, finally, to the hostility of the leaders of his people and the cowardice of the Roman governor, and died the common death of the criminals of that day upon the cross. After his death, his disciples were utterly discouraged. Even when he had been with them they had been far inferior to him in spiritual discernment and in courage, and now that he was taken from them what little power they might have had seemed to be gone. They fled from him in cowardly flight in the hour of his dire need. But then after his death they began to meditate upon his life with them, and as they mused thus upon their intercourse with him, the impression that his person had made upon them was too strong for them to believe that he had perished. Predisposed psychologically in that way they experienced certain hallucinations—experiences in which the optic nerve is really affected, but affected by a pathological condition in the subject himself, not by something in the external world. They thought they saw him, and perhaps they thought they heard a word or two of his ringing in their ears. These pathological experiences were the means by which the influence of Jesus was continued upon the earth; they were the means by which those weak, discouraged disciples were changed into the spiritual conquerors of the world! It was really, we are told, just the personal influence of Jesus; but the personal influence of Jesus made itself felt, according to this account, in that pathological form.

The really great question in the modern church is this: Which of these two accounts of Jesus is correct? People often obscure this issue, and tell us that we should not pay too much attention to theological controversy. Let us just be good Christians, we are told, and have faith in Jesus, and not bother our heads about the theological issue of the present day! Of course, such a way of thinking ignores the central question at issue. The central question is whether Jesus of Nazareth was such a one as that faith in him for men of the twentieth century is absurd, or whether he was such a one as the Bible presents to us, in whom we can have confidence for this world and for the world to come.

How shall we as historians investigate this all-important question? It is customary in modern discussion of the question to begin with certain interesting documents which have come down to us from the first century of our era. I refer to the epistles of Paul. There we have a fixed starting point in all controversy. All serious historians of the present day, whether they are Christians or not, are agreed that most of the epistles of Paul, to say the least, were actually written by the man whose name they bear. There we have at least a fixed point in controversy.

Now, if you will examine the epistles of Paul, you will discover, even on the basis of those epistles alone, quite apart from the gospels and quite apart even from the book of Acts (though the general outline of the life of Paul in the book of Acts is generally accepted even by skeptical historians of the present day), that the Paul who wrote those letters was actually a contemporary of the Jesus of Nazareth whose life we are studying today. He speaks in one of the universally accepted epistles of having come into contact with the brother of this Jesus (namely, in Galatians 1:19). So Paul was a contemporary of Jesus, a man of the first Christian generation, a man who according to his own testimony had been in direct contact with the brother of Jesus and with Peter, the chief of the intimate friends of Jesus.

The testimony of such a man with regard to the all-important question of the origin of our religion, which is also the question of the truth of our religion, is certainly of the utmost value.

If you will examine the epistles of Paul, you will discover one fact at least—you will discover that Paul was a man who had among his other gifts a remarkable gift of self-revelation. It is perfectly true that we know comparatively little of the details of his life; even if we use all the sources of information which are contained in the New Testament, long years of his life are a complete blank. During a large part of his life we cannot trace his movements; we are left entirely in the dark. Despite that fact, however, we are given in the epistles such intimate contact with the man himself that it is a true word which, I believe, has somewhere been spoken that Paul is probably the best-known man of antiquity.

There are men whom one never comes to know. There are men with whom I have had contact day after day and year after year, and whom yet I have never come to *know*. There are other men into communion with whom I can come by the briefest intercourse. So it is with the apostle Paul. Without a touch of morbid introspection, without vanity, in the most natural and genuine way, he has allowed us a glimpse into his very inmost soul. He has revealed to us the depths of his life; he has revealed that which makes him great in the history of the world, namely (if I may use the fashionable modern term), his wonderful "religious experience."

As it is looked at thus from the outside by modern historians, the religion of Paul is a matter about which there can be some agreement. The religion of Paul, it is discovered, is distinctly a religion of redemption. It is a religion of redemption in that it begins with the most thoroughgoing pessimism with regard to the condition of humanity that could possibly be imagined. You may understand the difference between a religion of redemption and what is not a religion of redemption by comparing the religion of Paul with the religion of the Modernist church. The religion of the Modernist church is a distinctive example of a religion which is *not* a redemptive religion. It begins with optimism as to the present condition of humanity. It begins with what a famous preacher in America has designated as an article which should certainly be put into our creed, namely, "I believe in man." That is not a religion of redemption.

But the religion of Paul—as it is recognized just as clearly, in some instances at least, by modern historians who do not at all accept that religion for themselves as it is by conservative scholars—the religion of Paul is distinctly a religion of redemption. It begins with the most radical pessimism with regard to the present condition of mankind that could possibly be imagined. Such pessimism, of course, fills with disgust and horror the modern historians of whom I have spoken; but they must recognize the fact that whether they themselves like it or not, such was the religion of Paul. Paul believed that the human race is lost in sin, and that a divine event took place outside the walls of Jerusalem when Jesus of Nazareth died apparently as a criminal upon the cross—that there an event took place which put a new face upon the world, an event of cosmic significance that brought about a revolution in those who were affected by it so far as their relation to God is concerned.

Of course, that character of the religion of Paul as a redemptive religion involves necessarily a certain view of the one by whom redemption was wrought. It is inconceivable that a mere man could by his death thus effect something of cosmic significance. So it is not surprising that Paul held a very peculiar view of this Jesus of Nazareth. It is perfectly plain—I mean on the basis of the epistles alone—that Paul separated Jesus from ordinary humanity, and placed him on the side of God. It is indeed disputed, though I think wrongly, by modern historians whether he ever applied to Jesus the Greek word which we translate by the word "God" in our English Bible. According to any commonsense interpretation of Romans 9:5, he certainly did; and the fact is recognized even by some whose general view of the religion of Paul might make another interpretation to them more agreeable. But that is a question of minor importance, because it is perfectly plain, at any rate, that Paul constantly applies to Jesus the Greek term which is translated "Lord"; and that term is the term which is used in the Greek Old Testament that Paul used to translate the word "Jehovah," the most awful and holy name of the God of Israel.

Moreover, it is interesting to observe that just the most recent research has demonstrated, or thinks it has demonstrated, the fact that even in the pagan world of that day, that word "Lord" was distinctly a term of divinity. Hence it is a case where "a little learning is a dangerous thing" when some modern preachers never use the word "Lord" in reference to Jesus, but use only the word "Master." It is perfectly true that the Greek word *kyrios* ("Lord") is used to designate "master" in ordinary human relationship, but it is also perfectly clear that its connotation as it is used in the New Testament is entirely different. Modern men sometimes use the word "Master" predominantly with reference to Jesus with the notion that they need a simple word used in ordinary life. But as a matter of fact, they should not seek an ordinary word if they are to translate the word *kyrios*; but they should seek a highly specialized word—and such a word is the word *kyrios* in the epistles of Paul. Paul's terminology for the Trinity is this: *theos*, "God"; *kyrios*, "Lord"; *pneuma*, "Spirit."[1] But it is just the same Trinity of three persons in one God as that which is designated by "God the Father, God the Son, and God the Holy Ghost."

So the terminology bears out the fact that Paul regards Jesus as clearly on the side of God. But we do not need to depend upon the terminology, because the thing itself is perfectly plain. At the beginning of the epistle to the Galatians, we have these truly stupendous words—to modern skeptical historians they seem to be most extraordinary, however familiar they may have become to us—"Paul, an apostle not from men nor through a man,

1. See Warfield, *The Lord of Glory* (1907), 231.

but through Jesus Christ, and God the Father, who raised Him from the dead." There we have a separation of Jesus Christ from ordinary humanity and the placing of him on the side of God!

It is true that Paul elsewhere speaks of Jesus as a man. He speaks elsewhere of "the man Christ Jesus." But if you will examine those passages, you may discover that Paul speaks of Jesus as a man as though it were something strange, something wonderful that he should be a man; and at any rate, the prevailing way in which he speaks of Jesus involves a clear separation of Jesus from ordinary humanity and a placing of him on the side of God.

But you do not need to appeal to individual passages, because the outstanding fact is that Paul stands everywhere in a religious relationship to Jesus Christ. The religion of Paul does not consist merely in having faith in God like the faith which Jesus had in God, but it consists essentially in having faith in Jesus Christ. Modern skeptical historians again may be our teachers here, for they regard that as the supreme problem in the history of the church. The supreme problem to these historians is the problem how in the world a faith in God like the faith which Jesus had in God and which these historians regard Jesus himself as having inculcated in his disciples can ever have given place, by a stupendous, a momentous change, upon which nineteen centuries of history have been based, to a faith in Jesus himself. And that change took place before the time of Paul. That is a fact which cannot be denied—Jesus was for Paul not primarily an example for faith but an object of faith.

Of course, if you hold, as most of us here present no doubt hold, that Jesus was truly God, then this attitude of Paul is cause for no surprise. But far different is it if you occupy the position of modern historians who regard Jesus as a mere man. In that case, you have Jesus, a mere man; and then you have Paul, one of his contemporaries, according to the epistles (whose genuineness everyone admits), separating this Jesus from ordinary humanity and placing him on the side of God. If that is the way in which we are to look at it, what we have here is an extraordinary instance of deification, the attribution of deity to a mere man on the part not of later generations, but of one of his contemporaries.

I have often quoted (for I think it is significant) the admission of a man who, I suppose, was the typical representative of that view of Jesus which regards Jesus as a mere man, namely, the late H. J. Holtzmann. Holtzmann said that for this extraordinary deification of the man Jesus as it appears in the epistles of Paul, he was able to cite no parallel in the religious history of the race.[2] Oh, you may say, how about the deification of the Roman emperors, either at their death or during their lifetime? But that is totally different in its lack of seriousness—and far more important than all that, it is totally different from this deification of the man Jesus because it is found in a polytheistic environment. If Paul had been a polytheist who could believe in many gods, then perhaps he might have added Jesus to the gods that he already worshiped. But Paul was clearly a monotheist; for if the Pharisaic Judaism of the first century was anything, it was an enthusiastic monotheism. I suppose its insistence upon monotheism was not exceeded even by the Mohammedanism of the present day. Monotheism was the very center and core of their belief—a horror of many gods, and a separation of God from the world. Yet it was this monotheist, sprung from a race of monotheists, who in his epistles everywhere places the man Jesus, who had lived a short time before and had died a shameful death, clearly on the side of God, and pays to him homage that is due to God alone.

If we went no further, we should be led to ask who this Jesus was who could thus be raised to deity by one of his contemporaries. But our surprise as historians reaches its height when we observe this curious fact—that Paul does not argue about this strange view of Jesus. Paul does not seem, in his earlier epistles at least, where he is dealing with Palestinian Judaism, to regard this lofty view of Jesus as a thing about which one word of argument was needed. "Oh," you may say, "Paul, of course, was not in the habit of arguing!" Well, was he not? When it came to matters about which there was a dispute in the churches of his day, we may thank God that Paul was not a man who was averse to argument or controversy, because if Paul had been a man averse to controversy, as many leaders of the Modernist church say that they are, we should have no Christianity today—I mean, when we look at the thing from the human point of view. God might have raised up another instrument, but as a matter of fact it was through the apostle Paul and men like him that our Christianity was preserved.

No, Paul certainly was in the habit of arguing. He argues about the place of the law, for example, and the all-sufficiency of faith and the like; but when it comes to this truly stupendous view which he has of Jesus, he seems

2. Holtzmann, in *Protestantische Monatshefte*, 4 (1900), pp. 465 ff., and in *Christliche Welt*, 24 (1910), col. 153.

to assume that his view is also the view even of his bitter opponents like the Judaizers attacked in the epistle to the Galatians. Nowhere does there appear to have been in the early apostolic age any color of support for disagreement with the view held by Paul of the person of Christ.

One can hardly avoid the conclusion, on the basis of a study of the epistles of Paul, that when Paul does not argue about this matter it is because no argument was needed, because Paul's view was accepted as a matter of course. That involves this stupendous conclusion: that Peter and the very brother of Jesus, men who had walked and talked with Jesus on earth, who had seen him subject to the petty limitations of human life—that these men actually agreed with this stupendous view of Jesus as a supernatural person, an object of worship, as he is presented in the epistles of Paul.

On the basis of the epistles alone, therefore, we should ask ourselves: "Who was this Jesus? What manner of person was he that he could thus be raised to divine dignity, not by later generations, but by his own intimate friends?"

The religion of Paul is a phenomenon of history that requires an explanation, and the modern historians have been willing to accept the challenge. The central problem, I suppose, which has confronted modern historians who have tried to construct the origin of Christianity without building it upon a supernatural Christ is the problem of the origin of this religion of Paul. Four hypotheses with regard to it may be distinguished.

The first is the simple one that Paul's religion was founded upon the real Christ; that Paul came to believe Jesus to be a supernatural person for the simple reason that as a matter of fact Jesus was a supernatural person—in other words, that Paul's religion is founded upon the actual descent of a supernatural person into this world for its redemption, whose death was an event of cosmic significance, and whose resurrection followed as the completion of his redeeming work. That is the supernaturalistic hypothesis, and if that is accepted, the whole problem is solved.

But there are other explanations which have been proposed in recent years, and they are alike in denying the entrance into this world of any creative act of God in distinction from the use by God of the forces of nature. The first of these explanations is the "Liberal" or Ritschlian view, which has been dominant in many quarters in the church for a good many years. There are some indications that among scholars this reconstruction is tottering to its ruin, but still in America, and I believe in this country as well,

CHRIST AND THE WITNESS OF SCRIPTURE

it dominates the popular presentation of Christianity from the modern naturalistic point of view. According to this explanation, Paul was a true disciple of Jesus in his religious experience, but Paul's theology was the mere temporary form in which in his day that religious experience had to be expressed. That is the hypothesis. You must distinguish the kernel from the husk, it is said. Paul was really affected by the lofty moral life of the real human person, Jesus of Nazareth; but he had to express what he owed to Jesus in the (now outworn) categories of his time—the notion of the atoning death of Christ and the like. It is the business of the modern Christian, according to that view, to discard the husk in order to retain the precious kernel. Paul's religion, according to that formula, comes from the real Jesus, and is a permanent possession of the human race, while Paul's theology, being the mere temporary husk to preserve that kernel, was derived from other sources, and may now safely be discarded by the modern church.

That hypothesis has been set forth in dozens or hundreds of brilliant books. But in 1904 it suffered a most extraordinary attack, not from a conservative scholar, but from a radical historian, namely William Wrede of Breslau, who pointed out that the whole separation between Paul's religion and Paul's theology is quite unhistorical, that the religion of Paul is intimately connected with his theology, and that in the epistles of Paul you do not find quotations of the words of Jesus and citations of his example, but what you do find is the reiteration again and again of the cosmic significance of his death and resurrection.

Of course it was easy for the "Liberal" or Ritschlian historians to point out the excesses of Wrede's view. It was perfectly easy for them to show that Wrede was wrong in supposing that Paul knew little or nothing about the details of the words and deeds of Jesus. It was easy to show that Paul tells in his epistles more than Wrede supposed, and that he knew far more than in the epistles he has chosen to tell. The incidental way in which he refers to the institution of the Lord's Supper, for example, seems clearly to show that his information was taken from a fund of further information which was given to the churches in the beginning. "The Lord Jesus, the night in which He was betrayed"—do you not see that it presupposes a whole account of the events connected with the betrayal? We know what is meant because we have read the story in the gospels, but it would be a riddle if we did not know about the betrayal by Judas. And elsewhere, as well as in this passage, it is easy to see that Paul had evidently told the churches far more than in the epistles he has found occasion to repeat. And indeed that is altogether natural, because if these people in the churches were asked to take a man who had lived but a few years before as their Savior, the object of their adoration, questions would have to be asked and answered as to what manner of person this was.

Wrede's opponents in the camp of modern Liberalism were able to point out the defects of his reconstruction, but they utterly failed to refute him at the central point; it is perfectly clear, as Wrede observed, that the very center of Paul's religious life is found just in those things which the Liberal historians had rejected or had minimized as a mere temporary expression of some deeper experience, namely, the significance of the cross of Christ, and so on. Where does the current of Paul's religious life run full and free? Surely it is in the great theological passages of the epistles—the second chapter of Galatians, the fifth chapter of 2 Corinthians, the eighth chapter of Romans. Those are the passages in which you have the very center of Paul's life; and so much, at least, Wrede observed, even though he himself did not believe for himself one word of what Paul teaches in these matters. Never was Wrede really refuted by his opponents in the Liberal camp. According to Wrede, Paul's religion and his theology go together; and if his theology came from somewhere else than the real Jesus, his religion came from somewhere else too. So Wrede ventured on the assertion that Paul was the second founder of Christianity, a more powerful influence in historic Christianity, perhaps, though not a more beneficent influence, than Jesus himself. If you hold that Jesus was a mere man, do you not see the justification for that view? Liberal historians had produced a Jesus who had really little in common with the apostle Paul, and the radical view of Wrede was the nemesis to which they were naturally subjected. So a vast literature on the subject sprang up. But you have a feeling, as you read the works of the Liberal historians, that in refuting Wrede they get nowhere. They refute him in detail, but they do not touch the central point.

What would the solution be? It is perfectly plain. The Liberal theologians were quite right as over against Wrede in holding that Paul knew much more about the details of the life of Jesus than Wrede supposed. There the Liberal historians were right. But Wrede was entirely right as over against them in holding that the Jesus upon whom Paul's religion was based was not the reduced Jesus of modern naturalism, but the stupendous Person who is presented in the epistles themselves. What, then, is the solution? It is perfectly simple, as I have said. It is simply that Paul's religion was based upon the Jesus whose death and resurrection were events of cosmic significance, that that Jesus was the real Jesus, that there was not that amazing break between the man Jesus and the one whom Paul, with abundant opportunity of acquainting himself with his life, presented in his epistles, that the Jesus of the epistles of Paul was the real Jesus who walked this earth.

But then, if you reject this supernaturalistic solution and hold, with Wrede, that Paul's religion was not based upon the real Jesus, whence did it really come? Wrede said that it came from pre-Christian Judaism, that Paul had a lofty idea of the Messiah before he was converted, and that no essential change was wrought by his conversion except that he came to believe that this Messiah had come to this earth. But that view has been generally felt to break down; there are few who hold it today. It must be rejected for many reasons, and particularly for the reason that the loftiest view of the Messiah which you find in the apocalyptic books that are thought to preserve for us the doctrine upon which Paul is supposed to be dependent falls far short of the view which Paul holds of Jesus. There is no doctrine of the deity of the Messiah in those Jewish apocalyptic books, and no trace of the warm religious relationship between the believer and the Messiah. So you would be obliged to come to this extraordinary conclusion: that when the lofty Messiah of pre-Christian Jewish speculation was identified with a mere human being, that identification with a mere human being, instead of drawing down this pre-Christian Jewish notion of the Messiah, lifted it far beyond men's wildest dreams.

The last of the naturalistic hypotheses is that Paul's religion and theology came essentially from the religion of the contemporary pagan world. But that hypothesis is faced with many difficulties with which we have not here time to deal—the difficulty, for instance, of answering the question how contemporary paganism could ever have influenced the life of Paul at the center either before or after his conversion, and the difficulty found in the fact that the supposed parallels on examination really break down. Therefore, I think, we may say that unless Jesus is the kind of person that is presupposed in the epistles of Paul, the attempts which have so far been made to explain in some other way the origin of the religion of Paul have not yet attained success. In the epistles we discover a problem which leads us on beyond our easy complacency in a naturalistic view of the world toward what modern men think of with antipathy as the abyss of supernaturalism; and then we are led to the question whether the stupendous Savior who is presented in the epistles of Paul was not truly one who came to this earth for our redemption, and in whom we may have confidence alike for this world and for the world to come.

Let us unite in a word of prayer:

We thank you for the witness of the apostle Paul, who was your chosen messenger. We rejoice in the glory of these matchless books which have enabled men to live lives of victory over sin and have stayed their souls. And we pray that this great apostle may again be heard, that the darkness may be dispelled, and that men may find here the great charter of Christian liberty, that without merit of their own, but through the blood of Christ, they may be free forevermore. Amen.

3

THE WITNESS OF
THE GOSPELS

Today we have been considering the question: "Is the Bible Right about Jesus?" This afternoon we considered the witness of Paul. We observed that in the epistles of Paul we have a fixed starting point in all the controversy of the present day, since the genuineness of these epistles is not denied by any serious historian—at least the genuineness of the chief of them. In the epistles of Paul, we have Jesus presented clearly as a supernatural person, not primarily as an example for religious faith, but as the object of religious faith. We observed further that that stupendous presentation of the person of Jesus which is found everywhere in the epistles of Paul is so presupposed as a matter beyond debate that the historian can hardly avoid the extraordinary conclusion that that lofty view of Jesus was also the view of those with whom Paul had come into contact, namely, the intimate friends of Jesus who had lived with him when he was upon this earth.

Therefore, as we examine the phenomenon of the religion of Paul, which is a fact of history that no serious historian denies, this question arises in our minds: Who was this Jesus who thus could be raised to divine dignity, and that not by later generations, but by his own contemporaries in the first

"The Witness of the Gospels" is an address originally delivered on June 10, 1927, in London before the Bible League of Great Britain, and published in *The Evangelical Student* 3 (April 1929) 11–20. Reprinted in *What Is Christianity?* ed. Ned Bernard Stonehouse (Grand Rapids: Eerdmans, 1951).

Christian generation—so raised even by those who had seen him subject to all the limitations of human life in their intercourse with him while he was upon this earth? Even if the historian possessed only the epistles of Paul as sources of historical information about Jesus, he would have enough to give him pause. But as a matter of fact we have other sources of information about Jesus, for in the four gospels we find an extended picture of him, an extended account of his life upon earth.

I shall not stop here to consider certain very important questions with regard to the gospels, namely, questions of literary criticism with regard to the date and authorship of these books, except to say just in passing that the evidence for the authorship of one of these books—the gospel according to Luke—is of such a singularly cogent kind that to the astonishment of the learned world it has within recent years convinced some scholars whose view as to the origin of Christianity is just as much out of accord with the traditional view of the authorship of these books as could possibly be imagined. You have the extraordinary phenomenon that scholars like Professor von Harnack, of Berlin, whose view as to the origin of Christianity is of a thoroughly naturalistic kind, as far removed as possible from that which is present in the Lucan writings, have been so much impressed by the argument from literary criticism that they have actually come to the traditional view that the gospel according to Luke was written by Luke the physician and companion of Paul, who was in Palestine in the year A.D. 58, and was there in A.D. 60, and probably during the interval (these dates being pushed back a few years if another chronology is adopted), so that he actually came into direct contact with James, the brother of this Jesus whom we are studying tonight.

I might point out, too, with regard to all of the gospels, that there is a certain self-evidencing quality in their narrative. Personal testimony is a very subtle thing; and when you face a witness on the witness stand, the credence which you will give to his testimony is dependent very often upon the subtle impression that you obtain of the person testifying. That sort of evidence, which often attains a high degree of value, has a larger place in the production of Christian conviction than often is supposed. If you are troubled with doubts about the truth of this extraordinary narrative which you have in the four gospels, I should commend to you the exercise of reading one of the gospels through from beginning to end with something like the rapidity which you apply every morning to the morning newspaper or to any book of the day. At other times study the gospels, but for once just *read* the gospels. I sometimes think that perhaps that is the reason why God has given us one gospel which is so short as the gospel according to Mark—that at one sitting we might easily read the whole book through. In the gospel according to Mark you are not asked to sit quietly at the feet of Jesus and listen in an extended way to his teaching. You are not taken into the intimacy of his circle as is the case in the gospel according to John. But you are asked to look at him with something of the wonder which was in the minds of those first observers in the synagogue at Capernaum. It is a gospel that makes a first impression; and I tell you, when you read it, if you will brush out of your mind everything you have read about it, and will let the total impression of it be made upon your mind, there will come to you an overpowering impression that that witness is telling the truth.

So it is also with the gospel according to John. It has been my business for a great many years to read a great many things that have been said against the trustworthiness of the gospel according to John, and sometimes, as I have read, I have been impressed with the plausibleness of much that is said. But at other times, after filling my mind with what is said about the gospel according to John, I have just conceived the notion of reading, not what is said *about* the book, but the book itself; and when I have done that, the impression has been overpowering. It does seem perfectly plain that the author of this book is claiming to be an eyewitness of the wonderful events that he narrates. There is no writer of the New Testament who lays greater stress upon the plain testimony of the senses than he, and the keyword of the gospel, I think, is found in the words: "And the Word was made flesh, and dwelt among us, and we beheld His glory." You cannot sublimate those words into meaning merely that we human beings have heard about the incarnate Word, but they spring from the wondering gratitude of a man who himself had had the inestimable privilege of touching with his hands and hearing with his ears and seeing with his eyes the incarnate Word of God. When you read the book, you have the overpowering impression that the author is telling the truth; and the hypothesis to which you are logically forced if you hold that the book is not true—the hypothesis that this writer is engaging in a refined bit of deception by subtly making the false impression of being an eyewitness when he was no eyewitness at all—this hypothesis becomes, when you become acquainted with the man by reading his narrative for yourself, a monstrous hypothesis indeed.

Tonight I propose not to examine these questions of literary criticism in detail, but just to take for a moment the total picture of Jesus that is provided in the gospels. And I may say at the start that that picture is a picture of just the kind of person that is presupposed in the epistles of Paul. Yet there does not seem to be the slightest evidence of any dependence of the writers of the gospels upon the epistles. In the epistles of Paul there is presupposed everywhere a Jesus who was a supernatural person and yet lived a life upon this earth, and you have just such a person presented in all the gospels.

There are three things that need to be said about the modern reconstruction of Jesus as distinguished from the Jesus who is presented to us in the gospels. In the first place, that reconstruction involves the elimination of the supernatural from the life of Jesus, because the Jesus of all the gospels is clearly a supernatural person. It used to be held, perhaps, that you have a difference in the gospels in this respect: at one time, perhaps, the divine Christ of John was contrasted with the human Christ of Mark. But modern criticism of the gospels has tended powerfully against any such distinction as that, and it is admitted by the dominant school of criticism today that in the gospel according to Mark as well as in the gospel according to John you have presented to you not a mere teacher but a supernatural person whose death had some sort of redeeming significance, not a teacher of righteousness merely, but a Savior, essentially the sort of supernatural Christ that is presented in the epistles of Paul.

Here is a strange problem: the Jesus of the gospels is a supernatural person; he is plainly a real person who lived upon this earth; and yet from the point of view of modern naturalistic criticism a supernatural person can never be real, because by such criticism the supernatural has been eliminated from the pages of history.

Perhaps it may be well to say a word in passing as to what we mean by the "supernatural," what we mean by a "miracle." It is true, there is nothing more unpopular in the discussion of religious questions at the present day than this humble matter of the definition of terms; many persons are very angry when they are asked to check the flow of their thought by so humble a thing as a definition! Many definitions of the word "miracle" have been proposed, but I confess that the only one of them that seems to me satisfactory is one which I learned many years ago. "A miracle," according to that definition, "is an event in the external world that is wrought by the *immediate* power of God." That does not mean that while other events are not wrought by God, a miracle is wrought by him. But it means that in the case of other events, God uses means—whereas in the case of a miracle, he puts forth his creative power just as truly as in that mighty act of creation which underlies the whole process of the world.

When you adopt that definition of a miracle, you have based all your thinking upon a certain very definite philosophy, and that definite philosophy upon which you have based your thinking is called theism—if you will pardon a technical term for a very simple thing. It is the view of the world which Jesus of Nazareth held, as well as the view of the world which has been held by many philosophers. In a truly theistic view of the world, it is almost as necessary to assert the real existence of an order of nature as it is to assert the real existence of a personal God. People say nowadays that we who hold to a belief in miracles are doing away with the possibility of science—science which seeks to set forth the orderly course of this world. As a matter of fact, we are being much more kind to science than science is kind to itself, because we are asserting that the order of nature has a real objective existence, a thing which, as I understand it, the scientists of the present day, from the scientific point of view, do not find it necessary to assert at all. We assert that there is such a thing as a really existent order of nature, created by God, upheld at every moment by God, not a machine set going by God and let alone, but something that is under God's control and yet a really existent thing. And what is meant from that point of view as a miracle is the entrance of the *creative* power of God at some point in the course of the world. I do not see how if you really believe in creation at all—and I do not see how unless you believe in creation you can hold to a theistic view of the world—you can have any objection of principle to the entrance of creative acts of God within the course of the world.

So much for the definition of "miracle." From that point of view, it is clear that the miracles of the New Testament have a stupendous significance. Someone will say: "What a degrading thing it is that we should suppose that this order of nature had to be broken into. You are requiring us to suppose that there have been unaccountable and meaningless events and our reasonable view of the world is gone!" Not at all, my friends. A miracle from the Christian point of view is not a disorderly thing, but it springs from the source of all the order that there is in the world—namely, the will of God.

Very well, in the New Testament you have Jesus presented as a supernatural person, and you have in the New Testament an account of miracles. At that point many persons enter upon a very peculiar line of thought. Many devout persons nowadays, even persons who believe in the fact of the miracles, will tell you that while miracles used to be an aid to faith, now they are a hindrance to faith; that people used to believe in Jesus because of the miracles, but that now when they already believe in him on other grounds they may then come to a belief in miracles, so that although the miracles may be a hindrance that can be overcome, still they are not an aid to faith, but a hindrance that people used to believe in Jesus *because of* the miracles, but now they believe *in spite of* the miracles. Such a way of thinking involves a very curious confusion. Of course, it is perfectly true from one point of view that miracles are an obstacle to faith—but who ever denied it? The more commonplace a narrative is, the easier it is to believe. If I told you that as I walked the streets of this city I met several of my fellow-beings, my narrative would be very much superior to the narrative of the New Testament in one particular: it would certainly be far easier to believe. But then, it is not likely that anyone would be very much interested in it. So, without miracles, the narrative of the gospels would certainly be far easier to believe; but, do you not see, it would not be worth believing. Without the miracles, the thing that you would be believing would be a totally different thing from that which you are believing now. Without the miracles, you would have in Jesus a teacher and example; but with the miracles you have a Savior from your sins.

So the Jesus presented in the gospels is a supernatural person. But from the point of view of the presuppositions of Modernism, a supernatural person never existed upon this earth. What is the conclusion? It would seem to be that this Jesus never lived at all. There have been here and there a few who have held that view—Kalthoff and Drews in Germany, and W. B. Smith in America. These men have held that there was no real person corresponding to the Jesus of the gospels at all. But that view is not held by really important historians. It is perfectly plain that we have here an account of a real person living at a definite time upon this earth, and that if the whole picture is to be regarded as fictitious, then there is no way in the sphere of history of distinguishing truth from sham.

So this Jesus was a real person; he was a supernatural person; and yet, according to Modernist historians, a supernatural person is never real! What is the solution from the Modernist point of view? The solution proposed is that you have two elements in the gospels—first a picture of the real, the purely human Jesus; and secondly, a defacement of that picture by miraculous ornamentation—and that it is the duty of the modern historian to recover the picture of the true human Jesus; it is his duty to remove the coating of the supernatural which in the gospels has almost completely defaced the portrait, to tear away from Jesus these tawdry trappings of the supernatural, in order that the true presentation of the man Jesus may burst upon the world.

It seemed at first, from the naturalistic point of view, to be a very hopeful task. You might say, of course, that the way to do it would be to claim that while the gospels as we have them are full of the supernatural, if you get back to the original sources it would not be so at all. But the trouble is that in the earliest sources reconstructed, rightly or wrongly, by modern criticism you have similar supernatural elements. So you have to go to work in some other way. All you can do is simply to go through the gospels and just take the supernatural out. So a hundred years ago men went very hopefully to work. They said that the events narrated in the gospels were historical, but not really supernatural; that the first observers put a false supernaturalistic interpretation upon events that were really perfectly natural. When, for example, it is said in the first chapter of Luke that Zacharias went into the temple, certainly it was true that a man of that name went into the temple, and that in the dim religious light he saw the smoke of the incense rising up, and thought in the solemnity of the moment that it was an angel, and that as he had been thinking about certain things he thought that the angel spoke words to him. That is an example of what is called technically the rationalizing method of dealing with the miracle narratives.

The most powerful critic, perhaps, of the rationalizing method was not an orthodox theologian; but it was David Friedrich Strauss. The famous *Life of Christ* of Strauss appeared in 1835. It was directed against two opponents. In the first place, it was directed against the supernaturalistic view of Jesus, which takes these stories of the miracles at their face value and believes that they are sober fact. Strauss directed all the power of his attack against that view of the believing Christian about the miracles in the gospels. And I should like to say that if you want a really powerful criticism of the gospel narratives on the negative side, a really powerful attack against their truthfulness, you cannot do better than go back to the original *Life of Christ* by

Strauss, because you will find that most of those who deal with the matter today are far inferior to Strauss in acumen and in the other qualities that are necessary to the task.

But Strauss also attacked the rationalizing method to which I have just referred. He pointed out how ridiculous it is, when the thing for which the whole narrative exists is the miracle in it, to take away the miracle and think you have anything left. No, said Strauss; the whole reason for which these narratives were formed is found in the miracles that they contain; and if the miracles are not historical, the thing to say is that nothing is historical and that these miracle narratives are just the clothing of some religious idea in historical form.

That is the mythical view of Strauss—that the narratives are to be taken as a whole and are to be regarded as the clothing in historical form of a religious idea. So if you are to get the miracles out of the gospels, you have to go to work much more subtly than was thought necessary by Paulus and the early rationalizers. It is clear that you cannot just take out the miracles and leave the rest, but that if you are going to take out the miracles, you must also take a great deal of the rest of the narrative which exists simply for the sake of the miracles.

Here, then, is the phenomenon that has appeared in the modern criticism of the gospels. You proceed to take the miracles out; in doing so you find to your consternation that great shreds of the rest have to come out also. It is like pulling a pound of flesh out of a living body. Very naturally, therefore, there is a tendency in recent criticism to approach nearer and nearer to the absurd view that it is *all* unhistorical. That is the first difficulty in reconstructing your purely human Jesus—the difficulty of separating the miracles from the rest—because the whole picture is not an agglomeration, but an organism.

Then there is a second difficulty. Suppose you have taken the miracles out of the gospels and have got a purely human Jesus. It cannot be done, but let us suppose it could be done—you have your human Jesus who never worked miracles (except miracles that you could explain away, such as faith healing and the like, which are not miracles at all). It would look as though, from the naturalistic point of view, you were in a hopeful condition. At last you have the real Jesus whom we moderns can accept. But the trouble is that when you have reconstructed your purely human Jesus, you find that he is an entirely unbelievable figure. He is not only a person who never *did* exist, but he is one who never *could* have existed. He has a moral and psychological contradiction at the root of his being. That moral and psychological contradiction arises from the stupendous fact of the Messianic self-consciousness of Jesus. It is a fact that the Jesus of the gospels really did hold that he was the Messiah; and that he held that he was the Messiah not in some lower political sense, as though it meant merely that he was a king of David's line, but in the stupendous sense that he was actually to sit on the throne of God and be the instrument in judging the earth.

Jesus called himself the Son of Man. There is much misinterpretation of the term "Son of Man" on the part of the readers of the gospels, but it seems perfectly plain that the term does not set forth the human nature of Jesus as over against the divine nature at all, but is a reference to the tremendous scene in the seventh chapter of Daniel, in which one like unto a son of man is represented as being present with the Ancient of Days. The term "Son of Man" is perhaps a more lofty, a more stupendous, a more supernatural designation of Jesus in the gospels than the term "Son of God," at least as that term might be understood in the minds of the people.

People sometimes say: "We are not interested in theology and metaphysics and all that; we are not interested in the doctrine that the creeds set forth about the person of our Lord. It is sufficient for us to read the Sermon on the Mount and try to do what Jesus there says and get rid of all theology." Well, the Sermon on the Mount contains a most stupendous theology, and it contains a stupendous theology just in its presentation of the person of Jesus. If there is one passage in the whole of the New Testament which is loved by the Modernist church, it is the passage in which Jesus represents the scene at the last judgment, where it is said: "Not every one that saith unto me, Lord, Lord, shall enter into the kingdom of heaven; but he that doeth the will of my Father which is in heaven." But just in that very passage you have the stupendous notion presented by Jesus himself that *he* is to be the one who will sit on the throne of God at the final judgment and be the judge of human beings who have lived in all the periods of history. Why, it is a perfectly stupendous theology, a perfectly stupendous presentation of the majesty of the person of Jesus. What would you think of a mere man who should look out upon his contemporaries and say that *he* was to be the one who was to determine their eternal destiny at the last judgment? You would say he was unbalanced or insane. Some persons are saying that about Jesus today. They have written long and learned books to show the particular kind of insanity with which Jesus was afflicted. It does not worry me a bit. Indeed, I think it is a hopeful sign of the times that these alienists should be investigating the case of a mere man who thought he was divine. At the time when there were emperors of China, it used to be thought a pretty sure sign of insanity for a man to declare that he was emperor of China; but, you know, if actually the emperor of China had declared that he was *not* the emperor but someone else, that would have been an equally sure sign of insanity. So these alienists are investigating the case of a man who thought he was divine and was *not* divine; but against one who thought he was divine and *was* divine they have, obviously, nothing to say.

In other words, you have here in modern form the old problem of the stupendous claims of Jesus. How could Jesus have made these claims if they were not true? Some have held that Jesus never really made the claims, that he never claimed to be the Messiah at all. But that view has been held by comparatively few modern scholars, because it is faced by such an overpowering weight of contrary evidence. It was the claim to be the Messiah that cost Jesus his life. That claim is thus deeply rooted in the narrative. Usually, therefore, modern scholars pursue a different policy. They say that Jesus did not know how to express his sense of a mission except in the (somewhat unsatisfactory) category of Messiahship. Sometimes they have held that it was at the baptism that he came to think that he was the Messiah. Very interesting popular presentations of some such view have appeared in modern times. When I was a student in Germany, about twenty years ago, everyone was reading Frenssen's *Hilligenlei*, a novel which incidentally brings in a very interesting psychological reconstruction of Jesus. Jesus is represented as thinking about the Savior that was to come, and at last he comes to the conclusion that he is that Savior himself. It is a very dramatic representation of the way in which he came to that conclusion—and it is also totally unconvincing. It does not make one bit of difference whether you put this acceptance of Messiahship at the baptism or, as many modern scholars have done, at some later time; whether you put it late or early, it does—unless the claim was really justified—put a moral stain upon the character of Jesus. And that means putting a moral stain upon the character of a stainless one. Even modern men are forced to admit that as a whole the character of Jesus was totally inconsistent with any lack of mental balance. Thus at the very center of the being of the reconstructed, purely human Jesus, there is a hopeless contradiction. The reduced Jesus of modern naturalism is a monstrosity, whereas the Jesus presented in the gospels, though he is full of mystery, is yet a person whom a man can love, and a person who might, by the wonderful grace of God, really have lived upon this earth.

That, then, is your second difficulty—your reconstructed Jesus is an unbelievable figure. Then there is a third difficulty. It is found when you raise the question how your purely human Jesus ever could have become a divine Jesus in the belief of the church. Certainly that step must at least have been taken at a very early time. It is a very extraordinary thing how people can tell us in the modern church that we have to take a reverse step, that we have to go back from the apostolic church to Christ himself. These modern men admit that in the early apostolic church Jesus was made not merely the example for faith, but the object of faith. But it is said that Jesus did not present himself in that way; he did not present himself as an object of faith; and we have to reverse the step which was taken by the primitive apostolic church and get back to the real Jesus! It does seem to be an extraordinary thing that you have the Christian church appealing to Jesus of Nazareth and yet that the whole thing is found to be a total mistake, that the mistake was made at the very beginning, and that the whole power of the church comes from that mistake! We have to go back, we are told—back from the gospel which sets forth Jesus as Redeemer to the gospel which Jesus himself preached. It is strange how people who say that seem to think they are bringing us nearer to Jesus. Constantly we hear it asked: "Why should we trouble ourselves with all this puzzling theology about the death of Christ and the resurrection? It is a barrier between us and Jesus. Even such of it as is presented by Paul and by the primitive Jerusalem church must be wiped out; we must preach the gospel *of* Jesus instead of the gospel *about* Jesus."

But the gospel *of* Jesus, if that is all you have, does not mean that you have any close touch with him. You can have a gospel of D. L. Moody, but not a gospel about him; a gospel of Paul, but not a gospel about him. "Was Paul crucified for you?" When we say we have a gospel about Jesus, we mean that we have a gospel of which Jesus is not the mere author or proclaimer, but the very substance. Jesus proclaimed not only a gospel, but a gospel which had his own person in the center of it. When you read the gospels a little closer, you will find that everywhere Jesus presented himself as Savior, not merely as a teacher or an example. If he did not present himself as a Savior, then his teaching is the most gloomy teaching that there ever was in this world. You may talk about the thunderings of Sinai. But what are they compared with the terrifying law of the Sermon on the Mount? How much higher, how much more terrible that is than the law that is set forth in the Old Testament! How shall we stand if only such persons as those whom Jesus there describes can come into the kingdom of God? When you read the Sermon on the Mount, you are led straight to the foot of the cross; if such is the law of God, you need Christ not merely as a teacher but as a Savior.

When we come to the Lord Jesus, let us not take him as reconstructed for ourselves in a way after our own choosing, but let us receive the Lord Jesus Christ "as he is offered to us in the gospel." When we so receive him, we have a wonderful confirmation of the documentary evidence. Possibly you may have a certain feeling of dissatisfaction with what I have been saying tonight; possibly you may feel that while we may argue about these intricacies of historical criticism, somehow what we want is immediacy of conviction with regard to Jesus. Well, you may have such immediacy of conviction, because by accepting this gospel message you may come into living communion with Christ. But right there is where modern men go wrong. They say: "We have our communion with the living Christ, and so we do not care whether the Bible is true or not. We care nothing for the element of history in the Bible. The Bible is infallible only in the sphere of the inner life." That is very sad. It looks as though you had climbed up to the heights of Christian experience by means of the Bible, and when you are there you kick your ladder down, thus preventing others from coming up by it. But as a matter of fact, the Bible is not a ladder but a foundation. Here is what Christian experience does: it does not give you Christ whether the Bible is true or not, but it is confirmatory evidence to show you that as a matter of fact the Bible *is* true. What I think we ought to be opposed to is a partial view of the evidences of Christianity. Let us not appeal to experience as over against the Bible; let us take along with the documentary evidence in the gospels the great wealth of evidence that comes to us in other spheres, the evidence provided by the consciousness of sin, of the need of salvation, the need of a Savior. Then we can come to the wonderful message of the gospel. It has then evidencing value enough. Accept it, and come to the feet of Jesus, and hear him say to you, as you contemplate him upon the cross: "Thy faith hath saved thee. Go in peace."

4

THE VIRGIN BIRTH
OF CHRIST

Accordint to the belief of all the historic branches of the Christian church, Jesus of Nazareth was born without human father, being conceived by the Holy Ghost and born of the virgin Mary. In the present lecture we shall consider very briefly the origin of this belief. The belief of the Christian church in the virgin birth of Christ is a fact of history which requires an explanation. And two kinds of explanation are possible. In the first place, the belief may be explained as being based upon fact. It may be held that the church came to believe in the virgin birth because as a matter of fact Jesus was born of a virgin. Or in the second place, it may be held that the belief arose in some other way. The task of the historian is to balance these two kinds of explanation against each other. Is it easier to explain the belief of the church in the virgin birth on the hypothesis that it originated in fact or on the hypothesis that it arose in some other way?

We shall first examine the former hypothesis—that the belief in the virgin birth is based upon fact. Of course, the most obvious thing to say is that this belief appears in the New Testament in the clearest possible terms. And

"The Virgin Birth of Christ," the substance of a popular address delivered at Winona Lake Bible Conference, originally appeared in *The Bible To-Day* 19 (1924) 75–79, 111–15. Reprinted in *What Is Christianity?* ed. Ned Bernard Stonehouse (Grand Rapids: Eerdmans, 1951).

most of our time will be taken up in examining the New Testament evidence. But before we come to examine the New Testament evidence, it may be well to glance at the later Christian literature.

At the close of the second century, when the Christian literature outside of the New Testament becomes abundant, when we have full information about the belief of the church at Alexandria, in Asia Minor, at Rome, and in the West, we find that everywhere the virgin birth was accepted as a matter of course as one of the essential things in the Christian view of Christ. But this same kind of belief appears also at an earlier time; for example, in the old Roman baptismal confession which was the basis of our Apostles' Creed, in Justin Martyr at the middle of the second century, and in Ignatius, bishop of Antioch, at the beginning of the century. There were, it is true, denials of the virgin birth not only by opponents of Christianity but also by some who professed a kind of Christian faith. But all of these denials look far more as though they were due to philosophical prepossession than to any genuine historical tradition. The plain fact is that the virgin birth appears just as firmly fixed at the beginning of the second century as at the end of it; it is quite impossible to detect any gradual establishment of the doctrine as though it had to make its way against opposition. Particularly the testimony of Ignatius and of the Apostles' Creed shows not only that the virgin birth was accepted at a very early time, but that it was accepted as a matter of course and as one of the facts singled out for inclusion even in the briefest summaries of the most important things which the Christian needed to know about Christ. Even this evidence from outside the New Testament would suffice to show that a firm belief in the virgin birth existed in the Christian church well before the close of the first century.

But still more important is the New Testament evidence, and to that evidence we now turn.

The virgin birth is attested in two of the New Testament books, the gospel according to Matthew and the gospel according to Luke. The value which will be attributed to this testimony depends, of course, to a considerable extent upon the view which one holds of each of these two gospels as a whole. Obviously, it will not be possible to discuss these questions here; it would carry us too far afield to discuss the evidence for the early date and high historical value of the two gospels in which the virgin birth appears. But one remark at least may be made in passing: it may at least be observed that the credit of the great double work, Luke–Acts, has been steadily rising in recent years even in circles which were formerly most hostile. The extraordinary strength of the literary evidence has led even men like Professor Harnack of Berlin, Professor C. C. Torrey of Yale, and the distinguished historian Professor Eduard Meyer, despite their rejection of the whole supernatural content of the book, to accept the traditional view that Luke–Acts was actually written by Luke the physician, a companion of Paul. It will not be possible here to review that literary evidence in detail, but surely the evidence must be very strong if it has been able to convince even those whose presuppositions render hypothesis of Lucan authorship so extremely uncomfortable.

But if the third gospel was really written by Luke, its testimony as to events in Palestine must surely be received with the greatest possible respect. According to the information derived from the use of the first-person plural in the book of Acts, Luke had been in contact with James, the Lord's own brother, and with many other members of the primitive Jerusalem church. Moreover, he was in Palestine in A.D. 58 and appears there again two years later, so that presumably he was in the country during the interval. Obviously, such a man had the fullest possible opportunity for acquainting himself not only with events concerning the Gentile version of Paul but also with events in the life of our Lord in Palestine. It is therefore a matter of no small importance that the virgin birth is narrated in the third gospel.

But the virgin birth is not merely narrated in the third gospel; it is narrated in a very peculiar part of that gospel. The first two chapters of the gospel are possessed of very remarkable literary characteristics. The hand of the author of the whole book has indeed been at work in these chapters, as the elaborate researches of Harnack and others have clearly shown; but the author's hand has not been allowed to destroy the underlying literary character of the narrative. And that underlying character is very strongly marked. The truth is that the first two chapters of Luke, with the exception of the typical Greek sentence in Luke 1:1–4, are in spirit and style nothing in the world but a bit of the Old Testament embedded in the midst of the New Testament. Nowhere is there a narrative more transparently Jewish and Palestinian than this. It is another question how the Palestinian character of the narrative is to be explained. Some have supposed that Luke used a written Palestinian source, which had already been translated into

Greek or which he himself translated; others have supposed that without written sources he has simply caught the truly Semitic flavor of the oral information that came to him in Palestine. At any rate, however the Palestinian character of the narrative is to be explained, that Palestinian character itself is perfectly plain; in the first two chapters of Luke we are evidently dealing with a narrative that came from Palestinian soil.

That fact is of great importance for the question of the virgin birth. It shows that the virgin birth was narrated not merely in Gentile Christian documents but also in the country which was the scene of the narrated event. But there is still another reason why the Palestinian character of the narrative is important. We shall observe in the latter part of the lecture that the great majority of these modern scholars who reject the fact of the virgin birth suppose that the *idea* of the virgin birth was derived from pagan sources. But if that hypothesis is accepted, the question arises how a pagan idea came to be attested just by the most transparently Jewish and Palestinian portion of the whole New Testament. The Palestinian Judaism of the first century was passionately opposed to pagan influences, especially that loyal type of Palestinian Judaism which appears with such beautiful clearness in Luke 1 and 2. How could a pagan idea possibly find a place in such a narrative?

The question is really unanswerable; and in order to attempt to answer it, many modern scholars have had recourse to a truly desperate expedient—they have maintained that the virgin birth was not originally contained in the Palestinian narrative found in the first two chapters of Luke but has been later inserted into that narrative by interpolation. This interpolation theory has been held in two forms. According to the more radical form, the virgin birth has been interpolated into the completed gospel. This hypothesis is opposed by the great weight of manuscript attestation, there being not the slightest evidence among the many hundreds of manuscripts containing the gospel of Luke that there ever was a form of that gospel without the verses narrating the virgin birth. A more cautious form of the interpolation theory has therefore sometimes been preferred. According to that more cautious form, although the words attesting the virgin birth formed an original part of the third gospel, they did not form an original part of the Palestinian source which the author of the gospel was using in the first two chapters, but were interpolated by the author himself into the source which elsewhere he was closely following.

What shall be said of this interpolation theory? Very often the best and only refutation of an interpolation theory is the refutation which Dr. Francis L. Patton is once said to have applied to theosophy. A lady is reported to have asked Dr. Patton after one of his lectures to give her the strongest argument against theosophy. "Madam," said Dr. Patton, "the strongest argument against theosophy is that there is no argument in its favor." Similarly, it may be said that the burden of proof is clearly against those who advance an interpolation hypothesis; if no clear evidence can be adduced in its favor, the hypothesis must be rejected and the narrative must be taken as it stands. Even such a consideration would be decisive against the interpolation theory regarding the virgin birth in the infancy narrative of the third gospel. The advocates of the theory have signally failed to prove their point. The virgin birth is not merely narrated with great clearness in Luke 1:34–35, but is implied in several other verses; and no reason at all adequate for supposing that these portions of the narrative have been tampered with has yet been adduced. But as a matter of fact, we are in the present case by no means limited to such a merely negative method of defense. The truth is that in the present case we can do far more than disprove the arguments for the interpolation hypothesis; we can also actually prove positively that that hypothesis is false. A careful examination shows clearly that the virgin birth, far from being an addition to the narrative in the first chapter of Luke, is the thing for which the whole narrative exists. There is a clear parallelism between the account of the birth of John and that of the birth of Jesus. Even the birth of John was wonderful, since his parents were old. But the birth of Jesus was more wonderful still, and clearly it is the intention of the narrator to show that it was more wonderful. Are we to suppose that while narrating the wonderful birth of John the narrator simply mentioned an ordinary, nonmiraculous birth of Jesus? The supposition is quite contrary to the entire manner in which the narrative is constructed. The truth is that if the virgin birth is removed from the first chapter of Luke, the whole point is removed and the narrative becomes quite meaningless. Never was an interpolation hypothesis more clearly false.

But personally I am very glad that the interpolation hypothesis has been proposed, because it indicates the desperate expedients to which those who deny the virgin birth are reduced. The great majority of these who reject the virgin birth of Christ suppose that the idea arose on pagan ground, and admit that other derivations of the idea are inadequate. But in order to hold this view, they are simply forced to hold the interpolation theory regarding the first chapter of Luke; for only so can they explain how a pagan idea came to find a place in so transparently Jewish a narrative. But the interpolation theory being demonstrably false, the whole modern way of explaining the idea of the virgin birth of Christ results in signal failure. The naturalistic historians, in other words, are forced by their theory to hold the interpolation hypothesis; they stake their all upon that hypothesis. But that hypothesis is clearly false; hence the entire construction falls to the ground.

So much then for the account of the virgin birth in Luke. Let us now turn to the gospel according to Matthew. Here the virgin birth is narrated with a plainness which leaves nothing to be desired. Some men used to say that the first two chapters of the gospel are a later addition, but this hypothesis has now been almost universally abandoned.

The value of this testimony depends, of course, upon the view that is held of the gospel as a whole. But it is generally admitted by scholars of the most diverse points of view that the gospel was written especially for Jews, and the Jewish character of the infancy narrative in the first two chapters is particularly plain.

If this lecture were being delivered under the conditions that prevailed some years ago, it might be thought necessary for us to enter at length into the question of Matthew 1:16. Some time ago the textual question regarding this verse was discussed even in the newspapers and created a good deal of excitement. It was maintained by some persons that an ancient manuscript of the gospels which was discovered in the monastery of St. Catherine on Mount Sinai provided a testimony against the virgin birth. The manuscript referred to is the so-called Sinaitic Syriac, a manuscript of an ancient translation of the gospels into the Syriac language. This manuscript is not, as has sometimes been falsely asserted, the most ancient New Testament manuscript, since it is later than the two greatest manuscripts, the Codex Vaticanus and the Codex Sinaiticus, which also have the inestimable advantage of being manuscripts of the original Greek, not of a mere Syriac translation. But the Sinaitic Syriac is a very ancient manuscript, having been produced at about 400 A.D., and despite the fact that the extravagant claims made for it have now for the most part been abandoned, a few words about it may still be in place.

The Sinaitic Syriac has a curious reading at Matthew 1:16. But the importance of this witness must not be exaggerated. In order to accept the

CHRIST AND THE WITNESS OF SCRIPTURE

witness of the Sinaitic Syriac against all other documents, one must suppose (1) that this manuscript has correctly reproduced at the point in question the ancient Syriac translation from which it is descended by a process of transmission, (2) that this ancient Syriac translation (which was probably produced in the latter part of the second century) correctly represents at this point the Greek manuscript from which the translation was made, and (3) that that Greek manuscript correctly represented at this point the autograph of the gospel from which it was descended by a process of transmission. All of this is exceedingly uncertain in view of the overwhelming mass of evidence on the other side. To accept one witness against all the other witnesses is a very precarious kind of textual criticism where the evidence is so exceedingly abundant as it is in the case of the New Testament.

But as a matter of fact, the Sinaitic Syriac does not deny the virgin birth at all. It attests the virgin birth in Matthew 1:18–25 just as clearly as do the other manuscripts, and it implies it even in Matthew 1:16. The reading of the Sinaitic Syriac which has given rise to the discussion is as follows: "Jacob begat Joseph; Joseph, the husband of Mary, of whom was born Jesus, who is called Christ." That would be self-contradictory if the word "begat" meant what it means in English. But as a matter of fact, the scribe of the Sinaitic Syriac, if he thought of what he was doing and was not simply making a careless mistake, clearly used the word "begat" in the sense "had as a legal descendant." It is interesting to note that Professor F. C. Burkitt, the greatest British authority on the Syriac manuscripts, who certainly is far from being prejudiced in favor of the virgin birth, holds that even if the original text were simply "Joseph begat Jesus" (which as a matter of fact appears in no manuscript), it would be absolutely without significance as a testimony against the virgin birth, for it would only mean that Joseph had Jesus as his legal heir. The author of the first gospel is interested in two things, in one of them just as much as in the other. He is interested in showing (1) that Jesus was the heir of David through Joseph and (2) that he was a gift of God to the house of David in a more wonderful way than would have been the case if he had been descended from David by ordinary generation.

Thus, even if the Sinaitic Syriac did represent the original text, it would not deny the virgin birth. But as a matter of fact, it does not represent the original text at all. The original text of Matthew 1:16 is exactly the text that we are familiar with in our Bibles.

Accordingly, we have an unequivocal double witness to the virgin birth of Christ in the gospel according to Matthew and in the gospel according to Luke. These two witnesses are clearly independent. If one thing is clear to modern scholars—and to every commonsense reader—it is that Matthew has not used Luke and Luke has not used Matthew. The very difficulties of fitting the two infancy narratives together is, to the believer in the virgin birth, a blessing in disguise, for it demonstrates at least the complete independence of the two accounts. The unanimity of these two independent witnesses constitutes the very strongest possible testimony to the central fact about which they are perfectly and obviously agreed.

But at this point an objection is often made. The rest of the New Testament, we are told, says nothing about the virgin birth; Paul says nothing about it, and neither does Mark. Hence the testimony in favor of it is often said to be weak; men are often impressed with this argument from silence.

And the argument from silence needs to be used with a great deal of caution. The silence of a writer about any detail is without significance unless it had been shown that if the writer in question had known and accepted that detail, he would have been obliged to mention it.

But that is just exactly what cannot be shown in the case of the silence about the virgin birth. Paul, for example, does not mention the virgin birth, and much has been made of his silence. "What is good enough for Paul," we are told in effect, "is good enough for us; if he got along without the virgin birth, we can get along without it too." It is rather surprising, indeed, to find the Modernists of today advancing that particular argument; it is rather surprising to find them laying down the principle that what is good enough for Paul is good enough for them, and that things which are not found in Paul cannot be essential to Christianity. For the center of their religion is found in the ethical teaching of Jesus, especially in the Golden Rule. But where does Paul say anything about the Golden Rule, and where does he quote at any length the ethical teachings of Jesus? We do not mean at all that the silence about such things in the epistles shows that Paul did not know or care about the words and example of our Lord in the days of his flesh. On the contrary, there are clear intimations that the reason why the apostle does not tell more about what Jesus did and said in Palestine is not that these things were to him unimportant but that they were so important that instruction about them had been given at the very beginning in the churches and so did not need to be repeated in the epistles, which are addressed to special needs. And where Paul does give details about Jesus, the incidental way in which he does so shows clearly that there is a great deal else which he would have told if he had found occasion. The all-important passage in 1 Corinthians 15:3–8 provides a striking example. In that passage Paul gives a list of appearances of the risen Christ. He would not have done so if it had not been for the chance (humanly speaking) of certain misunderstandings that had arisen in Corinth. Yet if he had not done so, it is appalling to think of the inferences which would have been drawn from his silence by modern scholars. And yet, even if the occasion for mentioning the list of appearances had not happened to arise in the epistles, it would still have remained true that that list of appearances was one of the absolutely fundamental elements of teaching which Paul gave to the churches at the very beginning.

That example should make us extremely cautious about drawing inferences from the silence of Paul. In the epistles Paul mentions very few things about the earthly life of Jesus; yet clearly he knew far more than he has found occasion to tell in the epistles. It does not at all follow, therefore, that because he does not mention a thing in the epistles he did not know about it. Hence the fact that he does not mention the virgin birth does not prove that the virgin birth was to him unknown.

Moreover, although Paul does not mention the virgin birth, the entire account which he gives of Jesus as an entirely new beginning in humanity, as the second Adam, is profoundly congruous with the virgin birth and profoundly incongruous with the view that makes Jesus the son, by ordinary generation, of Joseph and Mary. The entire Christology of Paul is a powerful witness to the same event that is narrated in Matthew and Luke; the religion of Paul presupposes a Jesus who was conceived by the Holy Ghost and born of the virgin Mary.

The silence of Mark is of just as little importance as the silence of Paul. The gospel according to Mark was preeminently the missionary gospel; it was not intended to give all the facts about Jesus, but simply those which needed to be given first to those who had not already been won to Christ. Reading the second gospel, you stand in astonishment like those who were in the synagogue at Capernaum in the scene described in the first chapter. You see the wonderful works of Jesus; you stand afar off looking at him; you are not introduced to him with the intimacy of detail which one finds in Matthew and Luke. The fact that Mark does not narrate the virgin birth does not prove that he does not believe in the virgin birth or that it is to him less important than other facts, but shows merely that the narration of the birth of Jesus in any form is quite contrary to the plan of his gospel, which begins with the public ministry. The most important things that need to be said are not always the first things; and Mark is concerned with the first things that would make an impression even upon those who had not already been won to Christ.

The New Testament does indeed imply that the contemporaries of Jesus in Palestine were unaware of the story of the virgin birth, and perhaps it also makes probable that the virgin birth formed no part of the earliest missionary preaching of the apostles in Jerusalem. But all that is just what could be expected even if the virgin birth were a fact. The virgin birth was a holy mystery which was capable of the grossest misunderstanding; certainly it would not be spoken of by a person like Mary, whose meditative character is so delicately and so vividly depicted in the first two chapters of Luke. It would not be spoken of to the hostile multitude, and least of all would it be spoken of to the brothers of Jesus. Also, it would certainly not be mentioned in the earliest public missionary preaching before the crowds in Jerusalem. Only at some time after the resurrection, when the miracle of the virgin birth had at last been vindicated by the resurrection and exaltation of Jesus, would Mary breathe the mystery of Jesus' birth to sympathetic ears. Hence it found its way into the wonderful narrative preserved by Luke and from there into the hearts of Christians of all the ages.

Such is the course of events which would be expected if the virgin birth were a fact. And the attestation of the event in the New Testament is just exactly what is suited to these antecedent probabilities. The attestation in the very nature of the case could not be equal to that of an event like the resurrection, of which there were many eyewitnesses; but it is just what it would naturally be if the event really occurred in the manner in which it is said to have occurred in Matthew and Luke.

But the full force of the New Testament evidence can be appreciated only if the accounts are allowed to speak for themselves. These narratives are wonderfully self-evidencing; they certainly do not read as though they were based on fiction; and they are profoundly congruous with that entire account of Jesus without which the origin of the Christian religion is an insoluble puzzle.

If this testimony is to be rejected, what is to be put in its place? If the belief of the Christian church in the virgin birth was not founded upon fact, how did it actually originate? The consideration of this question constitutes the second main division of our subject. If the virgin birth is not a fact, how did the idea find a place in the New Testament and at the center of the church's belief? If Jesus was really born of Joseph and Mary, how shall we explain the fact that in the New Testament we have this strange false account of his birth?

The first explanation which has been proposed is that the false idea arose in Jewish–Christian ground. We have observed that the New Testament narratives of the virgin birth are strikingly Jewish in character; it is natural then to find the origin of the idea among the Jews. Some scholars therefore have supposed that the virgin birth was attributed to Jesus because devout Jewish Christians desired to find a fulfillment for the prophecy of Isaiah 7:14, "Behold the virgin shall conceive." But this method of explaining the origin of New Testament narratives has come into general disfavor in recent years; and such disfavor is particularly well deserved with regard to Isaiah 7:14. There is not the slightest evidence for supposing that verse was ever interpreted by the pre-Christian Jews as indicating a virgin birth of the Messiah. We do not mean that Isaiah 7:14 is not a true prophecy; on the contrary, we regard it as a very precious prophecy of the virgin birth of the Lord. But it is one thing to understand such a prophecy after the event and quite a different thing to understand the prophecy before the event. In general, adherents of the mythical theory about the New Testament have become much less confident than they formerly were about supposing that the myths arose in order to show fulfillment of Old Testament prophecies. Usually it is admitted to be clearly the other way around; only after certain things came to be believed about Jesus on independent grounds were the Old Testament prophecies interpreted as referring to him.

But the advocates of the Jewish derivation of the idea of the virgin birth also point to the wonderful birth of heroes like Isaac. Isaac, it is said, was born by a kind of miracle after his parents were old; it was therefore only a slight step to suppose that there was an even greater miracle in the case of one who was greater than Isaac, and thus in the case of Jesus the human father was excluded altogether. This explanation ignores the characteristic Jewish attitude toward marriage and the begetting of children. There was among the Jews not the slightest tendency toward asceticism; and far from being only a slight step in advance, the exclusion of the human father makes the birth of Jesus totally different from that of Isaac. The very point of the narrative about Isaac is that Abraham actually was in a physical sense his father; it is just the paternity of Abraham which the narrative stresses. There is nothing in the story of Isaac, therefore, which could have caused the development of the story of the virgin birth among the Jews. It is no wonder then that most modern scholars are inclined to agree with Adalbert Merx in saying that the idea of the virgin birth is "as un-Jewish as possible."

If then the Jewish derivation of the supposed myth of the virgin birth is impossible, recourse is often had to pagan influences. Sometimes, it is true, attention has been called to the philosophic Judaism of Philo of Alexandria, who combined a strange allegorical interpretation of the Old Testament with acceptance of the doctrines of Greek philosophy. But there is not to be found in the works of Philo any real parallel to the virgin birth of Christ, the apparent parallels being due to the fact that in his treatment of Old Testament characters such as Abraham and Isaac Philo has often lost sight of the literal significance of the history and is thinking only of the allegorical interpretation in accordance with which these characters represent only spiritual qualities or the like. Moreover, the whole atmosphere of Philo is as remote as anything could possibly be from the Palestinian atmosphere that appears with such wonderful clearness in the infancy narratives of Matthew and Luke. It is no wonder then, in view of the obvious insufficiency of the Jewish derivation of the idea of the virgin birth, that the majority of modern scholars who have denied the fact have had recourse, for the explanation of the origin of the idea, to purely pagan sources.

But at this point a double protest must be raised. How could a pagan idea find a place in primitive Christianity? Against the entrance of such an idea there was a twofold barrier. In the first place there was the barrier that separated all of primitive Christianity from the pagan world. Christianity at its inception involved a tremendous protest against paganism, and nothing would have been more abhorrent to the early Christians than the introduction into their thought about Jesus of the crassly pagan idea of the begetting of men by the gods, an idea which belonged not merely to paganism but to paganism in its most revolting and immoral aspects. That was the first barrier that needed to be surmounted before a pagan idea could find a place in the infancy narratives of Matthew and Luke. This barrier has been rightly and very ably insisted upon by Professor Harnack, though in the interests not of a defense of the virgin birth but of a derivation of the idea from Jewish sources.

But even if this barrier were surmounted, another question would still remain. Even if the supposed pagan idea could have attained a place in the belief of the early church, how could it ever have entered, not into Gentile Christian documents, but into the most clearly Jewish and Palestinian narratives in the whole New Testament, particularly into the infancy narrative of Luke? This question constitutes an insuperable objection, at the start, to the whole hypothesis of pagan influence, unless the interpolation theory regarding Luke 1 and 2 is correct. The hypothesis of pagan influence is absolutely bound up with the interpolation theory. But that interpolation theory, as we have already observed, is clearly false. The virgin birth is an integral part of the narrative in Luke, to say nothing of its place in Matthew. But in reading the infancy narrative in Luke we are simply breathing the atmosphere of Palestine, and are separated by whole worlds from the life of the Gentiles. Every word breathes the spirit of the Jewish expectation of the Messiah, and of Jewish life and thought. And yet it is supposed that a crassly pagan idea has found a place in such a narrative!

Thus the double barrier remains against the entrance of a pagan idea into the infancy narratives: first, the barrier that separated the whole of primitive Christianity, whether Jewish or Gentile, from pagan ideas; and second, the barrier that separated Palestinian Judaism from the Gentile world. In view of these initial objections, it is only for the sake of the argument that we examine the alleged pagan parallels at all. And as a matter of fact, the parallels upon examination all break down.

The Modernist preachers of the day, in their attack upon the New Testament account of our Lord, sometimes speak of "virgin births" in pagan mythology as though they were the commonest things in the world. But as a matter of fact, in Greek mythology at least, there is no such thing as a virgin birth at all. Certain heroes were regarded as having been born without human father, but that means not that they were born of virgin mothers, but that the Greek gods were conceived of in a thoroughly anthropomorphic way as possessing human passions and as falling into very human sins. The children begotten of certain women by Zeus, in the course of his numerous amours, were certainly not virgin-born. The same notion was transferred to certain historical characters such as Plato and Alexander the Great and the emperor Augustus. Whether seriously or not, these characters by a form of flattery were sometimes said to have been begotten, like the demigods of old, by some god, who took the place of the human father. But such a conception was possible only because of the grossly anthropomorphic way in which the Greek gods were conceived.

But in the infancy narratives in Matthew and Luke, we find ourselves in an entirely different circle of ideas. In these narratives Jesus is represented as conceived by the Holy Ghost. But certainly the divine Spirit is not regarded in any anthropomorphic way. Indeed, as has often been observed, the word for "Spirit" in Hebrew is not of masculine but of feminine gender. And what is more important still is the character of the narrative as a whole. In these chapters the lofty spiritual monotheism of the Old Testament prophets is preserved to the very full; and the conception of our Lord in the womb of the virgin Mary is regarded not in an anthropomorphic way but as a creative act of the same divine Spirit who was active in the first creation in accordance with the majestic narrative of Genesis. It is inconceivable that such a narrative should be the product of invention; but it is still more inconceivable that it should have been derived from the most degraded and immoral parts of Greek mythology.

But one more explanation for the origin of the idea of our Lord's virgin birth has been proposed in recent years. Certain scholars belonging to the most "advanced" school of comparative religion, having detected the impossibility of the hypotheses which we have just considered, have advanced a new hypothesis of their own. They have recognized the fact that the idea of the virgin birth is "as un-Jewish as possible," and so have rejected the derivation of the supposed virgin-birth myth on Jewish ground. On the other hand, they have recognized the integrity of the narrative in Luke 1 and have rejected the interpolation hypothesis which makes the virgin birth a later insertion. A pagan idea—that of the virgin birth—does stand, therefore, they hold, in a Jewish narrative. But, they suppose, this curious fact was possible because even before the time of Christ the Jews had, under the influence of oriental paganism, already come to believe in a virgin birth of the coming Messiah. Thus, in the New Testament the virgin birth appears in a Jewish narrative; but that means, it is supposed, not that the idea was originally Jewish, but only that a pagan idea had become so well naturalized among the pre-Christian Jews that in the first century its pagan origin had been forgotten.

This hypothesis is an interesting testimony to the defects of the alternative theories. But in itself it is improbable in the extreme. What evidence is there that late pre-Christian Judaism had come to expect a virgin birth for the Messiah? There is really no evidence whatever. We do know something of the late pre-Christian Jewish doctrine of the Messiah, and what we know not only contains no mention of a virgin birth but is rather contrary to any such idea. Surely it is quite inadmissible to posit such an idea without any positive evidence and simply in the interests of a theory regarding the Christian doctrine of the virgin birth of Jesus.

Thus, all of the modern theories regarding the origin of the idea of the virgin birth supposing it not to have been founded on fact have been tried and found wanting. And it is interesting to observe how the advocates of one theory are often the best critics of the others. Thus Harnack, in the interests of his Jewish derivation of the idea, does excellent service in showing the impossibility of the entrance of such an idea from pagan sources; advocates of the pagan derivation have well demonstrated the insufficiency of the Jewish derivation; and finally the most recent school of comparative religion has triumphantly and quite correctly insisted upon the falsity of the interpolation theory regarding Luke 1 upon which the ordinary hypothesis of pagan derivation is based. The truth is that if the belief in the virgin birth of Christ is not founded upon fact, no other satisfactory way of explaining the origin of the belief and its inclusion in Matthew and Luke has yet been proposed.

Shall we then simply accept the attestation of the virgin birth, which we have seen is very strong and very early? We should probably not be able to do so, despite all that has been said, if the virgin birth stood absolutely alone, if it were a question simply of a virgin birth of a man of the first century about whom we knew nothing. For the virgin birth is a stupendous miracle, and if it stood alone there would be a tremendous burden of proof against it. But as a matter of fact it does not stand alone, but is supported by a great mass of other facts; it is not a question simply of a virgin birth of some man of the first century about whom we know nothing, but it is a question of the virgin birth of one about whom we know a great deal, namely, Jesus of Nazareth. If the New Testament picture of Jesus is false as a whole, then of course we shall not accept the virgin birth; but if Jesus was really in general what the New Testament represents him as being, then we shall believe with the utmost firmness, on the basis of abundant evidence, that he was conceived by the Holy Ghost and born of the virgin Mary.

But what is the importance of the matter? That question has loomed large in recent discussion, and some have held that although they accept the virgin birth of Christ themselves, they can make common cause in Christian service with those who do not accept it. But this indifferentist position is really almost worse from the Christian point of view than any doctrinaire denial could be. As a matter of fact, the virgin birth is of central importance for Christian faith.

In the first place, it is important because of its bearing upon the question of the authority of the Bible. No one denies that the attestation of the virgin birth forms an integral part of the Bible; it is not a question whether the Bible teaches the virgin birth but whether, teaching the virgin birth as it admittedly does, the Bible is true or false. We must therefore face the question frankly. If the Bible has allowed myth to enter at this point into the representation not of something on the periphery but of Christ himself, then Scripture authority is gone, and some different basis must be sought for Christian doctrine and Christian life. Deny the virgin birth of Christ, and you must relinquish the authority of the Bible; accept the virgin birth, and you may continue to regard the Bible as the very Word of God.

In the second place, the virgin birth is a test as to the view which a man holds in general about Christ. Two opposite views of Jesus of Nazareth are struggling for the ascendancy in the church today. According to one view, he was a teacher who initiated a new type of religious life, who founded Christianity by being the first Christian; according to the other view, he was the eternal Son of God who came voluntarily into this world from outside the world and who founded Christianity by redeeming men from the guilt and power of sin. The conflict between these two views is the conflict between naturalism and supernaturalism; and that is a conflict not between two varieties of Christianity, but between two mutually exclusive religions. But how can we tell which view any individual holds? Conceivably one might ask him whether he believes in the deity of Christ. But unfortunately the word "deity" or the word "god" has been degraded so low in Modernist parlance that when the Modernist says that "Jesus is God," he means something even far more remote from Christian belief than the Unitarian meant when he said that "Jesus is not God." Or it may conceivably be asked whether the individual in question believes in the resurrection. But here again the answer may mean nothing, since the word "resurrection" is often interpreted (quite absurdly, it is true) to mean simply the continued existence of Jesus

CHRIST AND THE WITNESS OF SCRIPTURE

or his continued influence, and not to involve the miracle of the emergence of his body from the tomb. But, over against all such ambiguities, when a man says that he believes Jesus to have had no human father, one can tell pretty clearly where he stands.

The impression is indeed often produced that many men who reject the virgin birth maintain in general the New Testament account of our Lord. But that impression is entirely false. There have been, it is true, a few men in the history of the modern church who have rejected the virgin birth and yet have accepted the supernatural Christ and have believed in his true resurrection from the dead. But these men have been few and far between, and it would probably be impossible to name a single one of any prominence who is living today. Particularly false is the notion that many men who deny the virgin birth yet accept the incarnation, for the men who deny the virgin birth usually mean by "incarnation" almost the exact opposite of what Christians mean by that term. The truth is that the conflict about the virgin birth is only one phase of the great religious conflict of the day. And that conflict is a conflict between the Christian religion and a naturalistic or agnostic Modernism which is anti-Christian to the core.

In the third place, the virgin birth is important in itself—even aside from its importance as being connected with the question of the authority of Scripture and as being a test for the differentiating of naturalism from supernaturalism. The Christian world, in other words, has a clearer and better conception of Christ than it would have had if God had never told us of the virgin birth and had allowed us to think that Jesus was the son, by ordinary generation, of Joseph and Mary. Conceivably indeed we might have been Christians even if God had never told us of the virgin birth. Certainly never to have heard of the virgin birth would have been a much less serious thing than it is to reject it now that we have heard of it. But it is easy to see the errors which might then have arisen, or which would have attained additional momentum, if God had never told us of the virgin birth of our Lord. What the knowledge of the virgin birth does is to fix with inescapable clearness the supernaturalism of the life of Jesus from the very beginning; the virgin birth, for example, intensifies the impossibility of holding that our Lord only grew up gradually into his divinity, or of holding in Gnostic fashion that the Son of God descended upon a man Jesus at the baptism. All such errors are excluded by many things in the New Testament. But they are excluded with special clearness in the precious narrative of the virgin birth. That narrative represents our Lord clearly as no product of sinful humanity but as one who came into the world by a mighty creative act of God. And that representation is at the very center and core of the Christian faith.

No doubt the virgin birth is not the point at which one should begin in trying to convince a man who has not yet come to Christian faith. No doubt one should begin rather with the resurrection, in which the direct testimony is, and must be in the very nature of the case, vastly more abundant. But when a man has once been convinced that Jesus is truly the risen and ascended Lord and when he has once accepted him as Savior, then his faith will be unstable and incomplete unless he goes forward to accept the precious testimony of Matthew and Luke as to our Lord's entrance into the world.

The truth is that the New Testament account of Christ is a wonderfully unitary thing, and an integral part of it is the virgin birth. Believe that Jesus is simply the fairest flower of humanity, and the infancy narrative of the gospels, despite its marvelous beauty, will be to you abhorrent; but accept the dear Lord and Savior presented to you in the Word of God, and you will believe and confess, with a heart full of gratitude and love and joy, that he was "conceived by the Holy Ghost, born of the Virgin Mary."

5

THE RESURRECTION
OF CHRIST

S ome nineteen hundred years ago, in an obscure corner of the
Roman Empire, there lived one who, to a casual observer, might
have seemed to be a remarkable man. Up to the age of about thirty
years, he lived an obscure life in the midst of a humble family. Then he began
a remarkable course of ethical and religious teaching, accompanied by a ministry of healing. At first he was very popular. Great crowds followed him
gladly, and the intellectual men of his people were interested in what he had
to say. But his teaching presented revolutionary features, and he did not satisfy the political expectations of the populace. And so, before long, after
some three years, he fell a victim to the jealousy of the leaders of his people
and the cowardice of the Roman governor. He died the death of the criminals of those days, on the cross. At his death, the disciples whom he had
gathered about him were utterly discouraged. In him had centered all their
loftiest hopes. And now that he was taken from them by a shameful death,
their hopes were shattered. They fled from him in cowardly fear in the hour
of his need, and an observer would have said that never was a movement
more hopelessly dead. These followers of Jesus had evidently been far infe-

"The Resurrection of Christ," the substance of a popular address delivered at Winona
Lake Bible Conference, originally appeared in *The Bible To-Day* 19 (1925) 223–27,
265–68. Reprinted in *What Is Christianity?* ed. Ned Bernard Stonehouse (Grand
Rapids: Eerdmans, 1951).

rior to him in spiritual discernment and in courage. They had not been able, even when he was with them, to understand the lofty teachings of their leader. How, then, could they understand him when he was gone? The movement depended, one might have said, too much on one extraordinary man, and when he was taken away, then surely the movement was dead.

But then the astonishing thing happened. The plain fact, which no one doubts, is that those same weak, discouraged men who had just fled in the hour of their Master's need, and who were altogether hopeless on account of his death, suddenly began in Jerusalem, a very few days or weeks after their Master's death, what is certainly the most remarkable spiritual movement that the world has ever seen. At first, the movement thus begun remained within the limits of the Jewish people. But soon it broke the bands of Judaism, and began to be planted in all the great cities of the Roman world. Within three hundred years, the Empire itself had been conquered by the Christian faith.

But this movement was begun in those few decisive days after the death of Jesus. What was it which caused the striking change in those weak, discouraged disciples, which made them the spiritual conquerors of the world?

Historians of today are perfectly agreed that something must have happened, something decisive, after the death of Jesus, in order to begin this new movement. It was not just an ordinary continuation of the influence of Jesus' teaching. The modern historians are at least agreed that some striking change took place after the death of Jesus and before the beginning of the Christian missionary movement. They are agreed, moreover, to some extent even about the question what the change was; they are agreed in holding that this new Christian movement was begun by the belief of the disciples in the resurrection of Jesus; they are agreed in holding that in the minds and hearts of the disciples there was formed the conviction that Jesus had risen from the dead. Of course, that was not formerly admitted by everyone. It used to be maintained, in the early days of modern skepticism, that the disciples of Jesus only pretended that he had risen from the dead. Such hypotheses have long ago been placed in the limbo of discarded theories. The disciples of Jesus, the intimate friends of Jesus, it is now admitted, in a short time after his death came to believe honestly that he had risen from the dead. The only difference of opinion comes when we ask what in turn produced this belief.

The New Testament answer to this question is perfectly plain. According to the New Testament, the disciples believed in the resurrection of Jesus because Jesus really, after his death, came out of the tomb, appeared to them, and held extended intercourse with them, so that their belief in the resurrection was simply based on fact.

Of course, this explanation is rejected by those modern men who are unwilling to recognize in the origin of Christianity an entrance of the creative power of God, in distinction from the laws which operate in nature. And so another explanation has been proposed. It is that the belief of the disciples in the resurrection was produced by certain hallucinations in which they thought they saw Jesus, their teacher, and heard perhaps words of his ringing in their ears. A hallucination is a phenomenon well known to students of pathology. In a hallucination, the optic nerve is affected, and the patient therefore does actually in one sense "see" someone or something. But this effect is produced not by an external object, but by the pathological condition of the subject himself. That is the view of the "appearances" of the risen Christ which is held today by those who reject the miraculous in connection with the origin of Christianity.

It is also held, it is true, that what was decisive in the resurrection faith of the early disciples was the impression which they had received of Jesus' person. Without that impression, it is supposed, they could never have had those pathological experiences which they called appearances of the risen Christ, so that those pathological experiences were merely the necessary form in which the continued impression of Jesus' person made itself felt in the life of the first disciples. But after all, on this hypothesis, the resurrection faith of the disciples, upon which the Christian church is founded, was really based upon a pathological experience in which these men thought they saw Jesus, and heard perhaps a word or two of his ringing in their ears, when there was nothing in the external world to make them think that they were in his presence.

Formerly, it is true, there were other explanations. It used to be held sometimes that the disciples came to believe in the resurrection because Jesus was not really dead. When he was placed in the cool air of the tomb, he revived and came out, and the disciples thought that he had arisen. A noteworthy scholar of today is said to have revived this theory because he is dissatisfied with the prevailing idea. But the great majority of scholars today believe that this faith of the disciples was caused by hallucinations, which are called "appearances" of the risen Lord.

But let us examine the New Testament account of the resurrection of Jesus, and of the related events. This account is contained particularly in six of the New Testament books. Of course, all the New Testament books presuppose the resurrection, and witness is borne to it in all of them. But there are six of these books, above all others, which provide the details of the resurrection. These are the four gospels, the book of Acts, and the first epistle of Paul to the Corinthians.

According to these six books, if their witness is put together, Jesus died on a Friday. His body was not allowed to remain and decompose on the cross, but was buried that same evening. He was placed in a grave chosen by a leader of the people, a member of the Sanhedrin. His burial was witnessed by certain women. He remained in the grave during the Sabbath. But on the morning of the first day of the week, he arose. Certain women who came to the grave found it empty, and saw angels who told them he had risen from the dead. He appeared to these women. The grave was visited that same morning by Peter and the beloved disciple. In the course of the day Jesus appeared to Peter. In the evening he appeared to two unnamed disciples who were walking to Emmaus, and apparently later on the same evening he appeared to all the apostles save Thomas. Then a week later he appeared again to the apostles, Thomas being present. Then he appeared in Galilee, as we learn from Matthew 28. Paul is probably mentioning this same appearance when he says that "He appeared to above five hundred brethren at once" (1 Corinthians 15:6). It was probably then, also, that he appeared to the seven disciples on the Sea of Galilee (John 21). Then he appeared in Jerusalem, and ascended from the Mount of Olives. Sometime in the course of the appearances there was one to James, his own brother (1 Corinthians 15:7). Later on he appeared to Paul. Such is the New Testament account of the resurrection appearances of our Lord.

There are two features of this account to which great prominence has been given in recent discussions. These are (1) the place and (2) the character of the appearances of Jesus.

According to the New Testament, the place was first Jerusalem, then Galilee, and then Jerusalem again. The appearances took place, not only in Galilee and in Jerusalem, but both in Jerusalem and in Galilee; and the first appearances took place in Jerusalem.

So much for the place of the appearances. As for the character of the appearances, they were, according to the New Testament, of a plain, physical kind. In the New Testament Jesus is represented even as holding table companionship with His disciples after his resurrection, and as engaging in rather extended intercourse with them. There is, it is true, something mysterious about this intercourse; it is not just a continuation of the old Galilean relationship. Jesus' body is independent of conditions of time and space in a way that appeared only rarely in his previous ministry. There was a change. But there is also continuity. The body of Jesus came out of the tomb and appeared to the disciples in such a way that a man could put his finger in the mark of the nails in his hands.

In two particulars, this account is contradicted by modern scholars. In the first place, the character of the appearances is supposed to have been different. The disciples of Jesus, it is supposed, saw him just for a moment in glory, and perhaps heard a word or two ringing in their ears. Of course this was not, according to the modern naturalistic historians, a real seeing and hearing, but a hallucination. But the point is that those who regard these appearances as hallucinations are not able to take the New Testament account and prove from it that these appearances were hallucinations and were not founded upon the real presence of the body of Jesus, but are obliged first to reduce the New Testament account to manageable proportions. The reason is that there are limits to a hallucination. No sane men could think that they had had extended companionship with one who was not really present, or could believe that they had walked with him and talked with him after his death. You cannot enter upon the modern explanation of these happenings as genuine experiences but at the same time mere visions, until you modify the account that is given of the appearances themselves. And if this modified account is true, there must be a great deal in the New Testament account that is legendary. You must admit this if you are going to explain these appearances as hallucinations. So there is a difference concerning the *nature* of the appearances, according to modern reconstruction, as over against the New Testament.

And there is a difference also concerning the *place* of the appearances. According to the customary modern view of naturalistic historians, the first appearances took place in Galilee, and not in Jerusalem. But what is the importance of that difference of opinion? It looks at first sight as though it were a mere matter of detail. But in reality it is profoundly important for the whole modern reconstruction. If you are going to explain these experiences as hallucinations, the necessary psychological conditions must have prevailed in order for the disciples to have had the experiences. Therefore, modern historians are careful to allow time for the profound discouragement of the disciples to be gotten rid of—for the disciples to return to Galilee, to live again in the scenes where they had lived with Jesus, to muse upon him, and to be ready to have these visions of him. Time must be permitted, and the place must be favorable. And then there is another important element.

We come here to one of the most important things of all—the empty tomb. If the first appearances were in Jerusalem, why did not the disciples or the enemies investigate the tomb, and refute this belief by finding the body of Jesus still there? This argument is thought to be refuted by the Galilean hypothesis regarding the first appearances. If the first appearances took place not till weeks afterward and in Galilee, this mystery is thought to be explained. There would be no opportunity to investigate the tomb until it was too late; and so the matter could have been allowed to pass, and the resurrection faith could have been allowed to pass, and the resurrection faith could have arisen. Of course, this explanation is not quite satisfactory, because one cannot see how the disciples would not have been stimulated to investigate the tomb, whenever and wherever the appearances took place. We have not quite explained the empty tomb, even by this Galilean hypothesis. But you can understand the insistence of the modern writers that the first appearances took place in Galilee.

So there is a difference between the modern historian and the New Testament account in the matters of the *manner* and of the *place* of these experiences. Were they of a kind such that they could be explained as hallucinations, or were they such that they could only be regarded as real appearances? Was the first appearance three days after Jesus' death, and near the tomb, or later on in Galilee?

Let us come now to the New Testament account.

The first source that we should consider is the first epistle of Paul to the Corinthians. It is probably the earliest of the sources. But what is still more important—the authorship and date of this particular source of information have been agreed upon even by the opponents of Christianity. So this is not only a source of first-rate historical importance but it is a source of *admitted* importance. We have here a fixed starting point in all controversy.

We must examine, then, this document with some care. It was probably written, roughly speaking, about 55 A.D., about twenty-five years after the

death of Jesus, about as long after the death of Jesus as 1924 is after the Spanish–American War. That is not such a very long period of time. And of
course, there is one vital element in the testimony here which does not prevail in the case of the Spanish War. Most people have forgotten many details of the Spanish–American War because they have not had them
continuously in mind. But it would not be so in the case now under consideration. The resurrection of Jesus was the thing which formed the basis
of all the thought of the early Christians, and so the memory of it when it
was twenty-five years past was very much fresher than the memory of an
event like the Spanish–American War of twenty-five years ago, which has
passed out of our consciousness.

Let us turn, then, to 1 Corinthians 15, and read the first verses. "Moreover, brethren, I declare unto you the gospel which I preached unto you,
which also ye have received, and wherein ye stand; by which also ye are
saved, if ye keep in memory what I preached unto you, unless ye have believed in vain. For I delivered unto you first of all that which I also received."
"First of all," or "among the first things," may mean first in point of time, or
first in point of importance. At any rate, this was a part of Paul's fundamental preaching in Corinth, in about the year 51 or 52. So we get back a
little farther than the time when the epistle was written. But these things
were evidently also first and fundamental in Paul's preaching in other places,
so that you are taken back an indefinite period in the ministry of Paul for
this evidence. But then you are taken back by the next words farther still—
"that which I also received." There is a common agreement as to the source
from which Paul "received" this information; it is pretty generally agreed
that he received it from the Jerusalem church. According to the epistle to
the Galatians, he had been in conference with Peter and James only three
years after his conversion. That was the time for Paul to receive this tradition. Historians are usually willing to admit that this information is nothing less than the account which the primitive church, including Peter and
James, gave of the events which lay at the foundation of the church. So you
have here, even in the admission of modern men, a piece of historical information of priceless value.

"For I delivered unto you first of all that which I also received, how that
Christ died for our sins according to the scriptures; and that he was buried,
and that he rose again the third day according to the scriptures." Why does
Paul mention the burial of Jesus? The impression which the mention of the

burial produces upon every reader who comes to it as for the first time is that Paul means to say that the body of Jesus was laid in the tomb. The burial, in other words, implies the empty tomb. And yet a great many modern historians say that Paul "knows nothing" about the empty tomb! Surely such an assertion is quite false. Paul does not indeed mention the empty tomb in so many words; he does not give a detailed description of it here. But that does not mean that he knew nothing about it. Those to whom he was writing believed in it already, and he is simply reviewing a previous argument in order to draw inferences from it with regard to the resurrection of Christians. To say that Paul knows nothing about the empty tomb ignores the fact that the mention of the burial is quite meaningless unless Paul had in mind the empty tomb. I do not see how anyone can get any other impression. Moreover, is not that what "resurrection" means, after all? Modern historians say that Paul was interested simply in the continued life of Jesus in a new body which had nothing to do with the body which lay in the tomb. That is rather strange in this connection. Paul is arguing, in this passage, not against men who denied the immortality of the soul, but against men who held the Greek view of the immortality of the soul without the body. The view that they were holding would logically make of the resurrection of Jesus just the simple continuance of his personal life. There is no point at all, then, in what Paul says against them unless he is referring to the resurrection from the tomb. Unless he is referring to this, he is playing into the hands of his opponents. But many men nowadays have such a strangely un-historical notion of what "resurrection" meant to the early disciples. They talk as though the resurrection faith meant that those disciples simply believed that Jesus continued to exist after his crucifixion. This is absurd. Those men believed in the continued existence after death of every man. There is not the slightest doubt about that. They were thoroughly imbued with this belief. They were not Sadducees. Even in those first three days after Jesus' crucifixion, they still believed that he was alive. If that is all that resurrection meant, there was nothing in it to cause joy. Conviction of the continued life of Jesus would not make him any different from other men. But what changed sadness into joy and brought about the founding of the church was the substitution, for a belief in the continued existence of Jesus, of a belief in the emergence of his body from the tomb. And Paul's words imply that as clear as day.

"And that he rose again *the third day*." Of all the important things that

Paul says, this is perhaps the most important, from the point of view of modern discussion. There are few words in the New Testament that are more disconcerting to modern naturalistic historians than the words "on the third day." We have just observed what the modern reconstruction is. The disciples went back to Galilee, it is supposed, and there, sometime after the crucifixion, they came to believe that Jesus was alive. But if the first appearance took place on the third day, this explanation is not possible. The modern reconstruction disappears altogether if you believe that the first appearances were on the third day. If Paul's words are to be taken at their face value, the whole elaborate, psychological reconstruction of the conditions in the disciples' minds, leading up to the hallucinations in Galilee, disappears.

Many men, it is true, have an answer ready. "Let us not," they say in effect, "go beyond what Paul actually says! Paul does not say that the first appearance occurred on the third day, but only that Christ rose on that day. He might have risen some time before he first appeared to them; the resurrection might have occurred on the third day and yet the first appearance might have occurred some weeks after, in Galilee."

But why, if nothing in particular happened on the third day, and if the first appearance occurred some weeks after, did the disciples hit upon just the third day as the day of the supposed resurrection? Surely it was very strange for them to suppose that Jesus had really risen a considerable time before he appeared to them and had left them all that time in their despair. So strange a supposition on the part of the disciples surely requires an explanation. Why was it, if nothing happened on the third day, that the disciples ever came to suppose that the resurrection occurred on that day and not on some other day?

One proposed explanation is that the third day was hit upon as the day of the supposed resurrection because Scripture was thought to require it. Paul says, it will be remembered, that Jesus rose the third day *according to the Scriptures*. But where will you find in the Old Testament Scriptures any clear reference to the third day as the day of the resurrection of Christ? No doubt there is the "sign of Jonah," and there is also Hosea 6:2. We are certainly not denying that these passages (at least the former) are true prophecies of the resurrection on the third day. But could they ever have been understood before the fulfillment had come? That is more than doubtful. Indeed, it is not even quite clear whether Paul means the words "according to the Scriptures" to refer to the third day at all, and not merely to the central fact of the resurrection itself. At any rate, the Scripture passages never could have suggested the third day to the disciples unless something had actually happened on that day to indicate that Christ had then risen.

But had not Jesus himself predicted that he would rise on the third day, and might not this prediction have caused the disciples to suppose that he had risen on that day even if the first appearance did not occur till long afterward? This is an obvious way out of the difficulty, but it is effectually closed to the modern naturalistic historian. For it would require us to suppose that Jesus' predictions of his resurrection, recorded in the gospels, are historical. But the naturalistic historians are usually concerned with few things more than with the denial of the authenticity of these predictions. According to the ordinary "Liberal" view, Jesus certainly could not have predicted that he would rise from the dead in the manner recorded in the gospels. So for the "Liberal" historians, this explanation of "the third day" becomes impossible. The explanation would perhaps explain "the third day" in the belief of the disciples, but it would also destroy the whole account of the "Liberal Jesus."

Accordingly, it becomes necessary to seek explanations further afield. Some have appealed to a supposed belief in antiquity to the effect that the soul of a dead person hovered around the body for three days and then departed. This belief, it is said, might have seemed to the disciples to make it necessary to put the supposed resurrection not later than the third day. But how far did this belief prevail in Palestine in the first century? The question is perhaps not capable of satisfactory answer. Moreover, it is highly dangerous from the point of view of the modern naturalistic historians to appeal to this belief, since it would show that some interest was taken in the body of Jesus; and yet that is what these modern historians are most concerned to deny. For if interest was taken in the body, the old question arises again why the tomb was not investigated. And the whole vision hypothesis breaks down.

Since these explanations have proved unsatisfactory, some modern scholars have had recourse to a fourth explanation. There was in ancient times, they say, a pagan belief about a god who died and rose again. On the first day the worshipers of the god were to mourn, but on the third day they were to rejoice, because of the resurrection of the god. So it is thought that the disciples may have been influenced by this pagan belief. But surely this is a desperate expedient. It is only a very few students of the history of religions who would be quite so bold as to believe that in Palestine, in the time of Christ, there was any prevalence of this pagan belief with its dying and rising god. Indeed, the importance and clearness of this belief have been enormously exaggerated in recent works—particularly as regards the rising of the god on the third day.

The truth is that the third day in the primitive account of the resurrection of Christ remains, and that there is no satisfactory means of explaining it away. Indeed, some naturalistic historians are actually coming back to the view that perhaps we cannot explain this third day away, and that perhaps something did happen on the third day to produce the faith of the disciples. But if this conclusion is reached, then the whole psychological reconstruction disappears, and particularly the modern hypothesis about the place of the appearances. Something must have happened to produce the disciples' belief in the resurrection not far off in Galilee but near to the tomb in Jerusalem. But if so, there would be no time for the elaborate psychological process which is supposed to have produced the visions, and there would be ample opportunity for the investigation of the tomb.

It is therefore a fact of enormous importance that it is just Paul, in a passage where he is admittedly reproducing the tradition of the primitive Jerusalem church, who mentions the third day.

Then, after mentioning the third day, Paul gives a detailed account, which is not quite complete, of the resurrection appearances. He leaves out the account of the appearances to the women, because he is merely giving the official list of the appearances to the leaders in the Jerusalem church.

So much for the testimony of Paul. This testimony is sufficient of itself to refute the modern naturalistic reconstruction. But it is time to glance briefly at the testimony in the gospels.

If you take the shortest gospel, the gospel according to Mark, you will find, first, that Mark gives an account of the burial, which is of great importance. Modern historians cannot deny that Jesus was buried, because that is attested by the universally accepted source of information (1 Cor. 15). Mark is here confirmed by the Jerusalem tradition as preserved by Paul. But the account of the burial in Mark is followed by the account of the empty tomb, and the two things are indissolubly connected. If one is historical, it is difficult to reject the other. Modern naturalistic historians are in a divided condition about this matter of the empty tomb. Some admit that the tomb was empty. Others deny that it ever was. Some say what we have just outlined—that the tomb was never investigated at all until it was too late, and that then the account of the empty tomb grew up as a legend in the church. But other historians are clear-sighted enough to see that you cannot get rid of the empty tomb in any such fashion.

But if the tomb was empty, why was it empty? The New Testament says that it was empty because the body of Jesus had been raised out of it. But if this was not the case, then why was the tomb empty? Some say that the enemies of Jesus took the body away. If so, they have done the greatest possible service to the resurrection faith which they so much hated. Others have said that the disciples stole the body away to make the people believe that Jesus was risen. But no one holds that view now. Others have said that Joseph of Arimathea changed the place of burial. That is difficult to understand, because if such were the case, why should Joseph of Arimathea have kept silence when the resurrection faith arose? Other explanations, no doubt, have been proposed. But it cannot be said that these hypotheses have altogether satisfied even those historians who have proposed them. The empty tomb has never been successfully explained away.

We might go on to consider the other accounts. But I think we have pointed out some of the most important parts of the evidence. The resurrection was of a bodily kind, and appears in connection with the empty tomb. It is quite a misrepresentation of the state of affairs when people talk about "interpreting" the New Testament in accordance with the modern view of natural law as operating in connection with the origin of Christianity. What is really being engaged in is not an interpretation of the New Testament but a complete contradiction of the New Testament at its central point. In order to explain the resurrection faith of the disciples as caused by hallucinations, you must first pick and choose in the sources of information, and reconstruct a statement of the case for which you have no historical information. You must first reconstruct this account, different from that which is given in the only sources of information, before you can even begin to explain the appearances as hallucinations. And even then you are really no better off. It is after all quite preposterous to explain the origin of the Christian church as being due to pathological experiences of weak-minded men. So mighty a building was not founded upon so small a pinpoint.

So the witness of the whole New Testament has not been put out of the way. It alone explains the origin of the church, and the change of the disciples from weak men into the spiritual conquerors of the world.

Why is it, then, if the evidence is so strong, that so many modern men refuse to accept the New Testament testimony to the resurrection of Christ? The answer is perfectly plain. The resurrection, if it is a fact, is a stupendous miracle, and against the miraculous or the supernatural there is a tremendous opposition in the modern mind.

But is the opposition well grounded? It would perhaps be well grounded if the direct evidence for the resurrection stood absolutely alone—if it were simply a question whether a man of the first century, otherwise unknown, really rose from the dead. There would in that case be a strong burden of proof against the belief in the resurrection. But as a matter of fact, the question is not whether any ordinary man rose from the dead, but whether *Jesus* rose from the dead. We know something of Jesus from the gospels, and as thus made known he is certainly different from all other men. A man who comes into contact with his tremendous personality will say to himself, "It is impossible that *Jesus* could ever have been holden of death." Thus, when the extraordinary testimony to the resurrection faith which has been outlined above comes to us, we add to this our tremendous impression of Jesus' person, gained from the reading of the gospels, and we accept this strange belief which comes to us and fills us with joy, that the Redeemer really triumphed over death and the grave and sin.

And if he is living, we come to him today. And thus finally we add to the direct historical evidence our own Christian experience. If he is a living Savior, we come to him for salvation today, and we add to the evidence from the New Testament documents an immediacy of conviction which delivers us from fear. The Christian man should indeed never say, as men often say, "Because of my experience of Christ in my soul I am independent of the basic facts of Christianity; I am independent of the question whether Jesus rose from the grave or not." But Christian experience, though it cannot make us Christians whether Jesus rose or not, still can add to the direct historical evidence a confirming witness that, as a matter of fact, Christ did really rise from the dead on the third day, according to the Scriptures. The "witness of the Spirit" is not, as it is often quite falsely represented today, independent of the Bible; on the contrary, it is a witness by the Holy Spirit, who is the author of the Bible, to the fact that the Bible is true.

PART TWO

CHRISTIANITY AND MODERN SUBSTITUTES

6

WHAT IS CHRISTIANITY?

I n the trials and conflicts which prevail at the present time, one blessing has been given us. It is the blessing of a renewed and closer Christian fellowship with those with whom we are really agreed. As I sit in many of the councils and meetings of the church at the present day, I have the strange feeling that the deeper things of the heart are being kept in the background, and that we are living merely on the surface of life. It is refreshing, therefore, to be in the company of those with whom one does not need to guard one's every word, but is conscious of the warmth of Christian fellowship which prevails. You—the Free Church of Scotland—have stood for two things. You have stood for liberty of conscience; and you have stood for the Reformed faith, the system of doctrine which is taught in the Scriptures, which are the Word of God. You are a city set on a hill which cannot be hid. Your example has been an encouragement to those all over the world who are facing the same issue which you, by the grace of God, were enabled to face so nobly.

The question for our discussion, "What is Christianity?" has in recent years actually emerged from the seclusion in which it was formerly kept, and has now attained a place upon the front pages of the newspapers and in the popular magazines. A great many persons, indeed, resent our raising

"What Is Christianity?" was first delivered as an address before the General Assembly of the Free Church of Scotland on May 30, 1927. Reprinted in What Is Christianity? ed. Ned Bernard Stonehouse (Grand Rapids: Eerdmans, 1951).

of this question. "If you raise this question," they say in effect, "you will actually interfere with the efficiency of the church." But, after all, "efficiency" simply means doing things, and the important question is whether the things that are being done are good or bad. It is not enough to know that the church is going somewhere, but it is also necessary to know where it is going. More important than all questions as to methods of preaching is the basic question what it is that is to be preached. If the agencies of the church are propagating the gospel of Christ, then it is important that they should be just as well organized as possible; but if they are propagating some other gospel, then the worse organized they are, the better it seems to me to be. We cannot, therefore, avoid the basic question what it is that the church is in the world to do, or, in other words, what Christianity really is.

But how shall we obtain the answer to this question? It does seem to me to be a matter of simple common sense that we can do so only by taking a look at Christianity as it has actually existed in the world. If I were called upon to give a description of the city of Edinburgh, I should not go out somewhere into the central part of the United States and evolve a description of this city out of my own inner consciousness, but I should travel to the city, look at it the best I could, and then try to give some sort of account of it as it actually is. To say that Christianity *is* this or that is very different from saying that it *ought* to have been this or that, or that the ideal religion, whatever its name, *would* be this or that. Christianity is a historical phenomenon like the State of Pennsylvania or the United States of America or the Kingdom of Prussia or the Roman Empire, and it must be investigated by historical means. It may turn out to be a good thing or it may turn out to be a bad thing—that is another question—but if we are to tell what it is, we must take a look at it as it has actually existed in the world.

No doubt we cannot tell all that it is by any such merely historical method as that; we cannot tell all that it is by looking at it merely from the outside. In order that we should tell all that it is, we must ourselves be Christians; we must know Christianity in our own inner lives. But the Christian religion has never been an esoteric type of mysticism—it has always presented itself in the open air, and there are some things about it which should appear to friend and foe alike.

But how shall we take a look at it? It has existed through some nineteen centuries and in a thousand different forms; how can we possibly obtain a common view of it, so as to include in our definition of it what it is and exclude from our definition what it is not? To what point in the long history of Christianity should we turn in order to discover what it really is? Surely the answer to that question is perfectly plain. If we are going to determine what any great movement is, surely we must turn to the beginnings of the movement. So it is with Christianity. We are not asserting at this point in our argument that the founders of the Christian movement had a right to legislate for all subsequent generations. That is a matter for further investigation. But what we are asserting now is that the founders of the Christian movement, whoever they were, did have an inalienable right to legislate for all those subsequent generations that should choose to bear the name "Christian." Conceivably we may change their program; but if we do change their program, let us use a new name. It is misleading to use the old name to designate a new thing. That is just a matter of common sense. If, therefore, we are going to tell what Christianity at bottom is, we must take a look at the beginnings of Christianity.

Now the beginnings of Christianity constitute a fairly definite historical phenomenon, about which there is a certain measure of agreement even between historians that are themselves Christian and historians that are not. Christianity is a great movement that originated a few days after the death of Jesus of Nazareth. If someone should say that it originated at an earlier time, when Jesus first gathered his disciples about him in Galilee, we should not be inclined to quarrel with him; indeed, we might even say that in a sense Christianity originated still farther back, in Old Testament times, when the promise was first given concerning a salvation to come. But if Christianity existed before the death of Jesus, it existed only in a preliminary form. So at least the matter appears to the secular historian, from his superficial and external point of view. Clearly there was a strange new beginning among the disciples of Jesus soon after Jesus' death, and at that time is to be put the beginning of the great world movement which is commonly called Christianity.

What then was Christianity at that time when it began? We can answer the question with more intelligence, perhaps, if we approach it with the fashionable modern answer to it in our mind and ask whether that answer is right or wrong. Christianity, according to that fashionable modern answer, is a life and not a doctrine; it is a life or an experience that has doctrine merely as its symbolic intellectual expression, so that while the life abides the doctrine must necessarily change from age to age.

That answer, of course, involves the most bottomless skepticism that could possibly be conceived, for if everything that we say about God or about Christ or about the future life has value merely for this generation, and if something contradictory to it may have equal value in some future generation, then the thing that we are saying is not true even here and now. A thing that is useful now may cease to be useful in some future generation, but a thing that is true now remains true beyond the end of time. To say, therefore, that doctrine is the necessarily changing expression of religious experience or religious life is simply to give up the search for truth altogether.

Was Christianity at the beginning really such a bottomless skepticism? Was it really a life as distinguished from a doctrine?

Now we want to be perfectly plain about one thing: we desire to guard ourselves just as carefully as we can from what would be the most serious possible misunderstanding of our position. We are certainly not asserting that Christianity at the beginning was not a life. On the contrary, it certainly *was* a life; the early Christians were living lives quite different from the lives of the people about them, and without that distinctive Christian life there could be no Christianity then, as without that life there can be no Christianity now. Christianity at the beginning certainly was a way of life.

But how was that Christian type of life produced? There we come to the crux of the whole question. If one thing is clear to the historian, it is that that type of life was not produced merely by exhortation or merely by the magic of personal contacts; if one thing is clear to the historian, it is that the earliest Christian missionaries did *not* go around the world saying: "We have been living in contact with a wonderful person, Jesus; contact with him has changed our lives; and we call upon you our hearers, without asking puzzling questions, without settling the meaning of his death, without asking whether he rose from the dead, simply to submit yourselves to the contagion of that wonderful personality." That is perhaps what many modern men might have expected the first Christian missionaries to say, but to the historian it is clear that as a matter of fact they said nothing of the kind.

What they did say is summed up in a few words in the fifteenth chapter of the first epistle to the Corinthians, where, as is admitted even by historians of the most skeptical kind, Paul is giving nothing less than a summary of what he "received" from the very first disciples of Jesus in the primitive

CHRISTIANITY AND MODERN SUBSTITUTES

Jerusalem church. "Christ died for our sins according to the Scriptures; he was buried; he rose again the third day according to the Scriptures"—there we have in brief compass what the first Christian missionaries said.

But what is that utterance that we have just quoted? Is it not an account of facts? "Christ died, he was buried, he rose again"—that is a setting forth of things that happened; it is not an exhortation but a rehearsal of events, a piece of news.

The facts that are rehearsed are not, indeed, bare facts, but facts with the meaning of the facts. "Christ died" is a fact; but to know merely that fact never did any good to anyone; it never did anyone any good to know that a Jew who was called Christ died on a cross in the first century of our era. But it is not in that jejune way that the fact was rehearsed by the primitive Jerusalem church; the primitive message was not merely that Christ died, but that Christ *died for our sins*. That tells not merely that Christ died, but why he died, what he accomplished when he died; it gives not merely the fact but the meaning of the fact.

But when you say "fact with the meaning of the fact," you have said "doctrine." We have already arrived, then, at the answer to our question. Christianity at the beginning, we have discovered, was not a life as distinguished from a doctrine or a life that had doctrine as its changing intellectual expression, but—just the other way around—it was a life founded upon a doctrine.

If that is so, if the Christian religion is founded upon historical facts, then there is something in the Christian message which can never possibly change. There is one good thing about facts—they stay put. If a thing really happened, the passage of years can never possibly make it into a thing that did not happen. If the body of Jesus really emerged from the tomb on the first Easter morning, then no possible advance of science can change that fact one whit. The advance of science may conceivably show that the alleged fact was never a fact at all; it may conceivably show that the earliest Christians were wrong when they said that Christ rose from the dead the third day. But to say that that statement of fact was true in the first century, but that because of the advance of science it is no longer true—that is to say what is plainly absurd. The Christian religion is founded squarely upon a message that sets forth facts. If that message is false, then the religion that is founded on it must of course be abandoned; but if it is true, then the Christian church must still deliver the message faithfully as it did on the morning of the first Easter Day.

For our part, we adopt the latter alternative. But it is a mistake to think of us merely as "conservatives"; it is a mistake to think of us as though we were holding desperately to something that is old merely because it is old and as though we were inhospitable to what is new. As a matter of fact, we are looking not merely to a continuance of conditions that now prevail, but to a burst of new power. The Spirit of God will in God's good time again enable men to see clearly, and when they see clearly they will be convinced that the Christian message is true. We long for the coming of that time.

Meanwhile, let us be faithful—as your church has been gloriously faithful—in our witness-bearing. And let us pray God that he may honor not the messengers but the message, that sinful men may be enabled by the gracious power of the Holy Spirit to embrace Jesus Christ as he is offered to us in the gospel.

7

HISTORY AND FAITH

The student of the New Testament should be primarily a historian. The center and core of all the Bible is history. Everything else that the Bible contains is fitted into a historical framework and leads up to a historical climax. The Bible is primarily a record of events.

That assertion will not pass unchallenged. The modern church is impatient of history. History, we are told, is a dead thing. Let us forget the Amalekites, and fight the enemies that are at our doors. The true essence of the Bible is to be found in eternal ideas; history is merely the form in which those ideas are expressed. It makes no difference whether the history is real or fictitious; in either case, the ideas are the same. It makes no difference whether Abraham was a historical personage or a myth; in either case, his life is an inspiring example of faith. It makes no difference whether Moses was really a mediator between God and Israel; in any case, the record of Sinai embodies the idea of a covenant between God and his people. It makes no difference whether Jesus really lived and died and rose again as he is declared to have done in the gospels; in any case, the gospel picture, be it ideal or be it history, is an encouragement to filial piety. In this way, religion has been made independent, as is thought, of the uncertainties of

"History and Faith" is Machen's inaugural address as assistant professor of New Testament at Princeton Theological Seminary, delivered on May 3, 1915 and was published in the *Princeton Theological Review* 13 (1915) 337–51. Reprinted in *What Is Christianity?* ed. Ned Bernard Stonehouse (Grand Rapids: Eerdmans, 1951).

historical research. The separation of Christianity from history has been a great concern of modern theology. It has been an inspiring attempt. But it has been a failure.

Give up history, and you can retain some things. You can retain a belief in God. But philosophical theism has never been a powerful force in the world. You can retain a lofty ethical ideal. But be perfectly clear about one point—you can never retain a gospel. For "gospel" means "good news," tidings, information about something that has happened. In other words, it means history. A gospel independent of history is simply a contradiction in terms.

We are shut up in this world as in a beleaguered camp. Dismayed by the stern facts of life, we are urged by the modern preacher to have courage. Let us treat God as our Father; let us continue bravely in the battle of life. But alas, the facts are too plain—those facts which are always with us. The fact of suffering! How do you know that God is all love and kindness? Nature is full of horrors. Human suffering may be unpleasant, but it is real, and God must have something to do with it. The fact of death! No matter how satisfying the joys of earth, it cannot be denied at least that they will soon depart, and of what use are joys that last but for a day? A span of life—and then, for all of us, blank, unfathomed mystery! The fact of guilt! What if the condemnation of conscience should be but the foretaste of judgment? What if contact with the infinite should be contact with a dreadful infinity of holiness? What if the inscrutable cause of all things should turn out to be a righteous God? The fact of sin! The thralldom of habit! This strange subjection to a mysterious power of evil that is leading resistlessly into some unknown abyss! To these facts the modern preacher responds—with exhortation. Make the best of the situation, he says, look on the bright side of life. Very eloquent, my friend! But, alas, you cannot change the facts. The modern preacher offers reflection. The Bible offers more. The Bible offers news—not reflection on the old, but tidings of something new; not something that can be deduced or something that can be discovered, but something that has happened; not philosophy, but history; not exhortation, but a gospel.

The Bible contains a record of something that has happened, something that puts a new face upon life. What that something is is told us in Matthew, Mark, Luke, and John. It is the life and death and resurrection of Jesus Christ. The authority of the Bible should be tested here at the central point. Is the Bible right about Jesus?

The Bible account of Jesus contains mysteries, but the essence of it can be put almost in a word. Jesus of Nazareth was not a product of the world, but a Savior come from outside the world. His birth was mystery. His life was a life of perfect purity, of awful righteousness, and of gracious, sovereign power. His death was no mere holy martyrdom, but a sacrifice for the sins of the world. His resurrection was not an aspiration in the hearts of his disciples, but a mighty act of God. He is alive, and present at this hour to help us if we will turn to him. He is more than one of the sons of men; he is in mysterious union with the eternal God.

That is the Bible account of Jesus. It is opposed today by another account. That account appears in many forms, but the essence of it is simple. Jesus of Nazareth, it maintains, was the fairest flower of humanity. He lived a life of remarkable purity and unselfishness. So deep was his filial piety, so profound his consciousness of a mission, that he came to regard himself not merely as a prophet, but as the Messiah. By opposing the hypocrisy of the Jews, or by imprudent obtrusion of his lofty claims, he suffered martyrdom. He died on the cross. After his death, his followers were discouraged. But his cause was not lost. The memory of him was too strong; the disciples simply could not believe that he had perished. Predisposed psychologically in this way, they had visionary experiences; they thought they saw him. These visions were hallucinations. But they were the means by which the personality of Jesus retained its power; they were the foundation of the Christian church.

There, in a word, is the issue. Jesus a product of the world, or a heavenly being come from without? A teacher and example, or a Savior? The issue is sharp—the Bible against the modern preacher. Here is the real test of Bible authority. If the Bible is right here, at the decisive point, probably it is right elsewhere. If it is wrong here, then its authority is gone. The question must be faced. What shall we think about Jesus of Nazareth?

From the middle of the first century, certain interesting documents have been preserved; they are the epistles of Paul. The genuineness of them— the chief of them, at any rate—is not seriously doubted, and they can be dated with approximate accuracy. They form, therefore, a fixed starting point in controversy. These epistles were written by a remarkable man. Paul cannot be brushed lightly aside. He was certainly, to say the least, one of the most influential men that ever lived. His influence was a mighty building; probably it was not erected on the sand.

In his letters, Paul has revealed the very depths of a tremendous religious experience. That experience was founded not upon a profound philosophy or daring speculation, but upon a Palestinian Jew who had lived but a few years before. That Jew was Jesus of Nazareth. Paul had a strange view of Jesus; he separated him sharply from man and placed him clearly on the side of God. "Not by man, but by Jesus Christ," he says at the beginning of Galatians, and he implies the same thing on every page of his letters. Jesus Christ, according to Paul, was man, but he was also more.

That is a very strange fact. Only through familiarity have we ceased to wonder at it. Look at the thing a moment as though for the first time. A Jew lives in Palestine, and is executed like a common criminal. Almost immediately after his death he is raised to divine dignity by one of his contemporaries—not by a negligible enthusiast either, but by one of the most commanding figures in the history of the world. So the thing presents itself to the modern historian. There is a problem here. However the problem may be solved, it can be ignored by no one. The man Jesus deified by Paul— that is a very remarkable fact. The late H. J. Holtzmann, who may be regarded as the typical exponent of modern naturalistic criticism of the New Testament, admitted that for the rapid apotheosis of Jesus as it appears in the epistles of Paul he was able to cite no parallel in the religious history of the race.[1]

The raising of Jesus to superhuman dignity was extraordinarily rapid even if it was due to Paul. But it was most emphatically not due to Paul; it can be traced clearly to the original disciples of Jesus. And that too on the basis of the Pauline epistles alone. The epistles show that with regard to the person of Christ, Paul was in agreement with those who had been apostles before him. Even the Judaizers had no dispute with Paul's conception of Jesus as a heavenly being. About other things there was debate; about this point there is not a trace of conflict. With regard to the supernatural Christ Paul appears everywhere in perfect harmony with all Palestinian Christians. That is a fact of enormous significance. The heavenly Christ of Paul was also the Christ of those who had walked and talked with Jesus of Nazareth. Think of it! Those men had seen Jesus subject to all the petty limitations of human life. Yet suddenly, almost immediately after his shameful death, they be-

1. In *Protestantische Monatshefte*, 4 (1900), pp. 465ff., and in *Christliche Welt*, 24 (1910), col. 153.

came convinced that he had risen from the tomb and that he was a heavenly being. There is a historical problem here—for modern naturalism, we venture to think, an unsolved problem. A man, Jesus, regarded as a heavenly being, not by later generations who could be deceived by the nimbus of distance and mystery, but actually by his intimate friends! A strange hallucination indeed! And founded upon that hallucination the whole of the modern world!

So much for Paul. A good deal can be learned from him alone—enough to give us pause. But that is not all that we know about Jesus; it is only a beginning. The gospels enrich our knowledge; they provide an extended picture.

In their picture of Jesus, the gospels agree with Paul; like Paul, they make of Jesus a supernatural person. Not one of the gospels, but all of them! The day is past when the divine Christ of John could be confronted with a human Christ of Mark. Historical students of all shades of opinion have now come to see that Mark as well as John (though it is believed in a lesser degree) presents an exalted Christology, Mark as well as John represents Jesus clearly as a supernatural person.

A supernatural person, according to modern historians, never existed. That is the fundamental principle of modern naturalism. The world, it is said, must be explained as an absolutely unbroken development, obeying fixed laws. The supernatural Christ of the gospels never existed. How then explain the gospel picture? You might explain it as fiction—the gospel account of Jesus throughout a myth. That explanation is seriously being proposed today. But it is absurd; it will never convince any body of genuine historians. The matter is at any rate not so simple as that. The gospels present a supernatural person, but they also present a real person—a very real, a very concrete, a very inimitable person. That is not denied by modern Liberalism. Indeed, it cannot possibly be denied. If the Jesus who spoke the parables, the Jesus who opposed the Pharisees, the Jesus who ate with publicans and sinners is not a real person, living under real conditions, at a definite point of time, then there is no way of distinguishing history from sham.

On the one hand, then, the Jesus of the gospels is a supernatural person; on the other hand, he is a real person. But according to modern naturalism, a supernatural person never existed. He is a supernatural person; he is a real person—and yet a supernatural person is never real! A problem here! What is the solution? Why, obviously, says the modern historian—obviously, there are two elements in the gospels. In the first place, there is genuine historical tradition. That has preserved the real Jesus. In the second place, there is myth. That has added the supernatural attributes. The duty of the historian is to separate the two—to discover the genuine human traits of the Galilean prophet beneath the gaudy colors which have almost hopelessly defaced his portrait, to disentangle the human Jesus from the tawdry ornamentation which has been hung about him by naïve and unintelligent admirers.

Separate the natural and the supernatural in the gospel account of Jesus—that has been the task of modern Liberalism. How shall the work be done? We must admit at least that the myth-making process began very early; it has affected even the very earliest literary sources that we know. But let us not be discouraged. Whenever the mythical elaboration began, it may now be reversed. Let us simply go through the gospels and separate the wheat from the tares. Let us separate the natural from the supernatural, the human from the divine, the believable from the unbelievable. When we have thus picked out the workable elements, let us combine them into some sort of picture of the historical Jesus. Such is the method. The result is what is called "the Liberal Jesus." It has been a splendid effort. I know scarcely any more brilliant chapter in the history of the human spirit than this "quest of the historical Jesus." The modern world has put its very life and soul into this task. It has been a splendid effort. But it has also been—a failure.

In the first place, there is the initial difficulty of separating the natural from the supernatural in the gospel narrative. The two are inextricably intertwined. Some of the incidents, you say, are evidently historical; they are so full of local color, they could never have been invented. Yes, but unfortunately the miraculous incidents possess exactly the same qualities. You help yourself, then, by admissions. Jesus, you say, was a faith healer of remarkable power; many of the cures related in the gospels are real, though they are not really miraculous. But that does not carry you far. Faith healing is often a totally inadequate explanation of the cures. And those supposed faith cures are not a bit more vividly, more concretely, more inimitably related than the most uncompromising of the miracles. The attempt to separate divine and human in the gospels leads naturally to a radical skepticism. The wheat is rooted up with the tares. If the supernatural is untrue, then the whole must go, for the supernatural is inseparable from the rest. This tendency is not merely logical; it is not merely what might naturally be; it is actual. Liberal scholars are rejecting more and more of the gospels; others are denying that there is any certainly historical element at all. Such skepticism is absurd. Of it you need have no fear; it will always be corrected by common sense. The gospel narrative is too inimitably concrete, too absolutely incapable of invention. If elimination of the supernatural leads logically to elimination of the whole, that is simply a refutation of the whole critical process. The supernatural Jesus is the only Jesus that we know.

In the second place, suppose this first task has been accomplished. It is really impossible, but suppose it has been done. You have reconstructed the historical Jesus—a teacher of righteousness, an inspired prophet, a pure worshiper of God. You clothe him with all the art of modern research; you throw upon him the warm, deceptive calcium light of modern sentimentality. But all to no purpose! The Liberal Jesus remains an impossible figure of the stage. There is a contradiction at the very center of his being. That contradiction arises from his Messianic consciousness. This simple prophet of yours, this humble child of God, thought that he was a heavenly being who was to come on the clouds of heaven and be the instrument in judging the earth. There is a tremendous contradiction here. A few extremists rid themselves easily of the difficulty; they simply deny that Jesus ever thought he was the Messiah. A heroic measure, which is generally rejected! The Messianic consciousness is rooted far too deep in the sources ever to be removed by a critical process. That Jesus thought he was the Messiah is nearly as certain as that he lived at all. There is a tremendous problem there. It would be no problem if Jesus were an ordinary fanatic or unbalanced visionary; he might then have deceived himself as well as others. But as a matter of fact, he was no ordinary fanatic, no megalomaniac. On the contrary, his calmness and unselfishness and strength have produced an indelible impression. It was such a one who thought that he was the Son of Man to come on the clouds of heaven. A contradiction! Do not think I am exaggerating. The difficulty is felt by all. After all has been done, after the miraculous has carefully been eliminated, there is still, as a recent Liberal writer has said, something puzzling, something almost uncanny, about Jesus.[2] He refuses to be forced into the mold of a harmless teacher. A few men draw the logical conclusion. Jesus, they say, was insane. That is consistent. But it is absurd.

Suppose, however, that all these objections have been overcome. Sup-

2. Heitmüller, *Jesus* (1913), 71.

pose the critical sifting of the gospel tradition has been accomplished, suppose the resulting picture of Jesus is comprehensible—even then the work is only half done. How did this human Jesus come to be regarded as a superhuman Jesus by his intimate friends, and how upon the foundation of this strange belief was there reared the edifice of the Christian church?

In the early part of the first century, in one of the petty principalities subject to Rome, there lived an interesting man. Until the age of thirty years he led an obscure life in a Galilean family, then began a course of religious and ethical teaching accompanied by a remarkable ministry of healing. At first his preaching was crowned with a measure of success, but soon the crowds deserted him, and after three or four years he fell victim in Jerusalem to the jealousy of his countrymen and the cowardice of the Roman governor. His few faithful disciples were utterly disheartened; his shameful death was the end of all their high ambitions. After a few days, however, an astonishing thing happened. It is the most astonishing thing in all history. Those same disheartened men suddenly displayed a surprising activity. They began preaching, with remarkable success, in Jerusalem, the very scene of their disgrace. In a few years, the religion that they preached burst the bands of Judaism, and planted itself in the great centers of the Greco-Roman world. At first despised, then persecuted, it overcame all obstacles; in less than three hundred years it became the dominant religion of the Empire, and it has exerted an incalculable influence upon the modern world.

Jesus, himself, the founder, had not succeeded in winning any considerable number of permanent adherents; during his lifetime, the genuine disciples were comparatively few. It is after his death that the origin of Christianity as an influential movement is to be placed. Now it seems exceedingly unnatural that Jesus' disciples could thus accomplish what he had failed to accomplish. They were evidently far inferior to him in spiritual discernment and in courage; they had not displayed the slightest trace of originality; they had been abjectly dependent upon the Master; they had not even succeeded in understanding him. Furthermore, what little understanding, what little courage they may have had was dissipated by his death. "Smite the shepherd, and the sheep shall be scattered." How could such men succeed where their Master had failed? How could they institute the mightiest religious movement in the history of the world?

Of course, you can amuse yourself by suggesting impossible hypotheses. You might suggest, for instance, that after the death of Jesus his disciples sat quietly down and reflected on his teaching. "Do unto others as you would have others do unto you." "Love your enemies." These are pretty good principles; they are of permanent value. Are they not as good now, the disciples might have said, as they were when Jesus was alive? "Our Father which art in heaven." Is not that a good way of addressing God? May not God be our Father even though Jesus is now dead? The disciples might conceivably have come to such conclusions. But certainly nothing could be more unlikely. These men had not even understood the teachings of Jesus when he was alive, not even under the immediate impact of that tremendous personality. How much less would they understand after he had died, and died in a way that indicated hopeless failure! What hope could such men have, at such a time, of influencing the world? Furthermore, the hypothesis has not one jot of evidence in its favor. Christianity never was the continuation of the work of a dead teacher.

It is evident, therefore, that in the short interval between the death of Jesus and the first Christian preaching, something had happened. Something must have happened to explain the transformation of those weak, discouraged men into the spiritual conquerors of the world. Whatever that happening was, it is the greatest event in history. An event is measured by its consequences—and that event has transformed the world.

According to modern naturalism, that event, which caused the founding of the Christian church, was a vision, a hallucination; according to the New Testament, it was the resurrection of Jesus from the dead. The former hypothesis has been held in a variety of forms; it has been buttressed by all the learning and all the ingenuity of modern scholarship. But all to no purpose! The visionary hypothesis may be demanded by a naturalistic philosophy; to the historian it must ever remain unsatisfactory. History is relentlessly plain. The foundation of the church is either inexplicable, or else it is to be explained by the resurrection of Jesus Christ from the dead. But if the resurrection is accepted, then the lofty claims of Jesus are substantiated; Jesus was then no mere man, but God and man, God come in the flesh.

We have examined the Liberal reconstruction of Jesus. It breaks down, we have seen, at least at three points.

It fails, in the first place, in trying to separate divine and human in the gospel picture. Such separation is impossible; divine and human are too closely interwoven—reject the divine, and you must reject the human too. Today the conclusion is being drawn. We must reject it all! Jesus never lived!

Are you disturbed by such radicalism? I for my part not a bit. It is to me rather the most hopeful sign of the times. The Liberal Jesus never existed—that is all it proves. It proves nothing against the divine Savior. Jesus was divine, or else we have no certain proof that he ever lived. I am glad to accept the alternative.

In the second place, the Liberal Jesus, after he has been reconstructed, despite his limitations is a monstrosity. The Messianic consciousness introduces a contradiction into the very center of his being; the Liberal Jesus is not the sort of man who ever could have thought that he was the Messiah. A humble teacher who thought he was the Judge of all the earth! Such a one would have been insane. Today men are drawing the conclusion; Jesus is being investigated seriously by the alienists. But do not be alarmed at their diagnosis. That Jesus they are investigating is not the Jesus of the Bible. They are investigating a man who thought he was Messiah and was not Messiah; against one who thought He was Messiah and was Messiah they have obviously nothing to say. Their diagnosis may be accepted; perhaps the Liberal Jesus, if he ever existed, was insane. But that is not the Jesus whom we love.

In the third place, the Liberal Jesus is insufficient to account for the origin of the Christian church. The mighty edifice of Christendom was not erected upon a pinpoint. Radical thinkers are drawing the conclusion. Christianity, they say, was not founded upon Jesus of Nazareth. It arose in some other way. It was syncretistic religion; Jesus was the name of a heathen god. Or it was a social movement that arose in Rome about the middle of the first century. These constructions need no refutation; they are absurd. Hence comes their value. Because they are absurd, they reduce Liberalism to an absurdity. A mild-mannered rabbi will not account for the origin of the church. Liberalism has left a blank at the beginning of Christian history. History abhors a vacuum. These absurd theories are the necessary consequence; they have simply tried to fill the void.

The modern substitute for the Jesus of the Bible has been tried and found wanting. The Liberal Jesus—what a world of lofty thinking, what a wealth of noble sentiment was put into his construction! But now there are some indications that he is about to fall. He is beginning to give place to a radical skepticism. Such skepticism is absurd; Jesus lived, if any history is true. Jesus lived, but what Jesus? Not the Jesus of modern naturalism! But the Jesus of the Bible! In the wonders of the gospel story, in the character of

Jesus, in his mysterious self-consciousness, in the very origin of the Christian church, we discover a problem, which defies the best efforts of the naturalistic historian, which pushes us relentlessly off the safe ground of the phenomenal world toward the intellectual abyss of supernaturalism, which forces us, despite the resistance of the modern mind, to recognize a very act of God, which substitutes for the silent God of philosophy the God and Father of our Lord Jesus Christ, who, having spoken at sundry times and in divers manners unto the fathers by the prophets, has in these last days spoken unto us by his Son.

The resurrection of Jesus is a fact of history; it is good news; it is an event that has put a new face upon life. But how can the acceptance of a historical fact satisfy the longing of our souls? Must we stake our salvation upon the intricacies of historical research? Is the trained historian the modern priest without whose gracious intervention no one can see God? Surely some more immediate certitude is required.

The objection would be valid if history stood alone. But history does not stand alone; it is confirmed by experience.

A historical conviction of the resurrection of Jesus is not the end of faith but only the beginning; if faith stops there, it will probably never stand the fires of criticism. We are told that Jesus rose from the dead; the message is supported by a singular weight of evidence. But it is not just a message remote from us; it concerns not merely the past. If Jesus rose from the dead, as he is declared to have done in the gospels, then he is still alive, and if he is still alive, then he may still be found. He is present with us today to help us if we will but turn to him. The historical evidence for the resurrection amounted only to probability; probability is the best that history can do. But the probability was at least sufficient for a trial. We accepted the Easter message enough to make trial of it. And making trial of it we found that it is true. Christian experience cannot do without history, but it adds to history that directness, that immediateness, that intimacy of conviction which delivers us from fear. "Now we believe, not because of thy saying: for we have heard him ourselves, and know that this is indeed the Christ, the Saviour of the world."

The Bible, then, is right at the central point; it is right in its account of Jesus; it has validated its principal claim. Here, however, a curious phenomenon comes into view. Some men are strangely ungrateful. Now that we have Jesus, they say, we can be indifferent to the Bible. We have the present Christ; we care nothing about the dead documents of the past. You have Christ? But how, pray, did you get him? There is but one answer; you got him through the Bible. Without the Bible you would never have known so much as whether there were any Christ. Yet now that you have Christ, you give the Bible up; you are ready to abandon it to its enemies; you are not interested in the findings of criticism. Apparently, then, you have used the Bible as a ladder to scale the dizzy height of Christian experience, but now that you are safe on top you kick the ladder down. Very natural! But what of the poor souls who are still battling with the flood beneath? They need the ladder too. But the figure is misleading. The Bible is not a ladder; it is a foundation. It is buttressed, indeed, by experience; if you have the present Christ, then you know that the Bible account is true. But *if* the Bible *were* false, your faith would go. You cannot, therefore, be indifferent to Bible criticism. Let us not deceive ourselves. The Bible is at the foundation of the church. Undermine that foundation, and the church will fall. It will fall, and great will be the fall of it.

Two conceptions of Christianity are struggling for the ascendancy today; the question that we have been discussing is part of a still larger problem. The Bible against the modern preacher! Is Christianity a means to an end, or an end in itself, an improvement of the world, or the creation of a new world? Is sin a necessary stage in the development of humanity, or a yawning chasm in the very structure of the universe? Is the world's good sufficient to overcome the world's evil, or is this world lost in sin? Is communion with God a help toward the betterment of humanity, or itself the one great ultimate goal of human life? Is God identified with the world, or separated from it by the infinite abyss of sin? Modern culture is here in conflict with the Bible. The church is in perplexity. She is trying to compromise. She is saying, "Peace, peace," when there is no peace. And rapidly she is losing her power. The time has come when she must choose. God grant she may choose aright! God grant she may decide for the Bible! The Bible is despised—to the Jews a stumbling block, to the Greeks foolishness—but the Bible is right. God is not a name for the totality of things, but an awful, mysterious, holy person, not a "present God," in the modern sense, not a God who is with us by necessity and has nothing to offer us but what we have already, but a God who from the heaven of his awful holiness has of his own free grace had pity on our bondage, and sent his Son to deliver us from the present evil world and receive us into the glorious freedom of communion with himself.

8

DOES FUNDAMENTALISM OBSTRUCT SOCIAL PROGRESS?

T
he term "Fundamentalism" in the title of our discussion is evidently to be taken in a broad sense, not to designate "Premillennialists" but to include all those who definitely and polemically maintain a belief in supernatural Christianity as over against the Modernism of the present day. In what ways has "Fundamentalism," defined thus broadly to include men like ourselves, been held to be inimical to social progress?

In the first place, it has been held to be inimical to social progress because it maintains unchanged certain root convictions in the sphere of history. It is opposed to social progress, we are told, because it is opposed to all progress. It maintains a traditional view of what Jesus was and what Jesus did in the first century of our era, and therefore, we are told, it is opposed to the advance of science. If we no longer hold to the chemistry or physics of the sixteenth century or the fourth century or the first century, why should we hold to the account which those past ages gave of what Jesus said and did?

This objection ignores the peculiarity of history as over against the experimental sciences. A thing that has happened can never be made by the

"Does Fundamentalism Obstruct Social Progress?" originally appeared in *The Survey Graphic* 5 (July 1924) 391–92, 426–27. Reprinted in *What Is Christianity?* ed. Ned Bernard Stonehouse (Grand Rapids: Eerdmans, 1951).

passage of the years into a thing that has not happened; all history is based upon a thoroughly static view of facts. Progress can never obliterate events.

It is a great mistake to suppose that the evangelical Christian is opposed to the discovery of new facts; on the contrary, he welcomes the discovery of new facts with all his mind and heart. But he is a Christian because he maintains certain facts which have been known for many hundreds of years. In particular he believes that on a certain morning some nineteen hundred years ago, the body of Jesus of Nazareth emerged from the tomb in which it had been laid. That belief involves the most far-reaching consequences in every sphere of thought and of conduct; the Christian risks the whole of his life upon his conviction as to the resurrection of Christ.

If indeed that conviction should prove to be ill grounded, it would certainly have to be given up. The Christian ought to welcome to the full the investigation of the resurrection of Christ by all the methods of scientific history. But the point is that that investigation seems to him only to result in a confirmation of his belief. And if it results in a confirmation of his belief, then to relinquish that belief is not progress but retrogression. The grounding of life upon falsehoods is inimical to progress, but the grounding of it upon facts is a necessary condition of any true advance.

In the second place, Christianity is held to hinder social progress because it maintains a pessimistic view of human nature as at present constituted. This charge is sometimes evaded, and the Christian religion is represented as though it were a kind of sweet reasonableness based upon confidence in human goodness. But the evasion reverses the true character of our religion. Confidence in human resources is paganism—or Modernism—whereas Christianity begins with the consciousness of sin, and grounds its hope only in the regenerating power of the Spirit of God.

It is no wonder that the advocates of the Modernist program regard Christians as opponents of social progress. Men who refuse to go with the current and who rebuke the easy self-confidence of their time have always been regarded as enemies of the human race. But this antipathy is well founded only if the pessimism that is objected to is out of accord with the facts. The physician who comforts the patient by a false diagnosis is pleasing for the moment, but the true friend and helper is the one who designates the disease by its true name. So it may turn out to be with the Bible and with the Christian preacher who brings the Bible message to the modern world. Modern social science has erected an imposing building; it has in many respects improved the mechanical aspect of human life—and Christianity certainly has nothing to say against its achievements. But, unless we mistake the signs of the times, there is among the social architects of the present day a vague sense of uneasiness. There is abroad in the world an ill-defined but nonetheless disconcerting sense of futility. The work on the social edifice still goes on, but rifts are beginning to appear in the walls and underneath there are intimations of dreadful things. Shall the trouble with the foundations continue to be ignored? If it is ignored, the enthusiasm of the architects may for a time be maintained, but all the greater will be the crash when at last it comes. Utilitarianism, in other words, is proving to be a quite inadequate basis for the social edifice, and there are those—despised and abused as the enemies of progress and the race—who insist upon facing the underlying facts of personal life. In these men the hope of society really rests. The edifice erected by social science need not be destroyed if the foundations are strengthened in time. And the strengthening is provided by the Christian faith.

In the third place, historic Christianity is thought to be inimical to social progress because it is individual rather than social. The older evangelism, it is said, seeks to win individuals; it invites men to come forward to the mourners' bench, receive salvation, and so escape from this wicked world. The newer and better evangelism, on the other hand—thus the claim runs—instead of rescuing individuals and leaving the world to its fate, seeks so to improve the physical conditions of life and the relations between man and man as to set up what may be called the "kingdom of God" here upon this earth.

This objection depends partly upon a caricature of the Christian religion. It is not true that the Christian gospel offers individual men a selfish escape from the world and leaves society to its fate. On the contrary, Christianity is social as well as individual. Even the relation of the individual to his God is not individual but social, if God exists; certainly it is not regarded by anyone who experiences it as a selfish thing. But the Christian also sustains relationships to his fellow men, and his religion is far from discouraging those relationships. When a man is rescued inwardly from the world, he is not, according to Christian teaching, allowed to escape from the world into a place of mystic contemplation, but is sent forth again into the world to battle for the right.

Nevertheless, despite one-sidedness, the assertion of modern social workers to the effect that historic Christianity is individual rather than social has in it a large element of truth. It is true that Christianity as over against certain social tendencies of the present day insists upon the rights of the individual soul. We do not deny the fact; on the contrary, we glory in it. Christianity, if it is true Christianity, must place itself squarely in opposition to the soul-killing collectivism which is threatening to dominate our social life; it must provide the individual soul with a secret place of refuge from the tyranny of psychological experts; it must fight the great battle for the liberty of the children of God.

The rapidly progressing loss of liberty is one of the most striking phenomena of recent years. At times it makes itself felt in blatant ways, as in the notorious Lusk laws for the licensing of teachers in the State of New York, or in the Oregon school law now being tested in the United States courts. Liberty still has some bulwarks, but even those bulwarks are threatened. In Nebraska, for example, where the study of languages other than English was forbidden and thus literary education was made a crime, all outer defenses were broken through and the enemy was checked only by that last bulwark of liberty, the United States Supreme Court. But unless the temper of the people changes, that bulwark also will fall. If liberty is to be preserved against the materialistic paternalism of the modern state, there must be something more than courts and legal guarantees; freedom must be written not merely in the constitution but in the people's heart. And it can be written in the heart, we believe, only as a result of the redeeming work of Christ. Other means in the long run will fail. Sometimes, it is true, self-interest will accomplish beneficent results. The Lusk laws, for example, which attacked liberty of speech in the State of New York, were opposed partly by the socialists against whom the laws were originally aimed. But the trouble is that socialism, if it were ever put into effect, would mean a physical, intellectual, and spiritual slavery more appalling than that which prevailed under the worst despotisms that the world so far has ever known. The real defenders of liberty are those who are devoted to it for its own sake, who believe that freedom of speech means not only freedom for those with whom they are agreed but also freedom for those to whom they are opposed. It is such a defense of liberty which is favored by the true followers of Christ.

But at this point an objection may arise. "Fundamentalism," it is said, "is a synonym of intolerance; and the writer of the present article desires to cast out of the ministry of his church those who hold views different from his own." How can such a person pretend to be a lover of liberty?

The objection ignores the distinction between voluntary and involuntary organizations. The state is an involuntary organization, an organization to which a man is forced to belong whether he will or not. For such an organization to prescribe any one type of education for its members is an intolerable interference with liberty. But the church is a purely voluntary organization, and no one is forced to enter its ministry. For such an organization to prescribe terms of admission and to insist that its authorized teachers shall be in agreement with the creed or message for the propagation of which the church exists involves not the slightest interference with liberty, but is a matter of plain common honesty and common sense. Insistence on fundamental agreement within a voluntary organization is therefore not at all inconsistent with insistence upon the widest tolerance in the state. Indeed, the two things are not merely consistent, but are connected logically in the closest possible way. One of the essential elements in civil and religious liberty is the right of voluntary association—the right of individuals to associate themselves closely for the propagation of anything that they may desire, no matter how foolish it may seem to others to be. This right is being maintained by "Fundamentalists," and it is being combated subtly but nonetheless dangerously by some of their opponents. The most serious danger to liberty in America today is found in the widespread tendency toward a centralized state monopoly in education—the tendency which has manifested itself crassly and brutally in the Oregon school law, and which manifests itself more subtly in the proposed development of a federal department of education, which will make another great addition to the vast Washington bureaucracy, the bureaucracy which with its discouragement of spiritual initiative is doing so much to drain the lifeblood of the people. The same tendency manifests itself also in the advocacy of anti-theological and anti-evangelical propaganda under the guise of "character-building" in monopolistic public schools. Under these circumstances, it has come about—paradoxical though it may seem—that one of the chief defenders of American liberty is the Roman Catholic church. Catholics and "Fundamentalists," despite their immense differences, are at least agreed, in America, in their insistence upon the right of voluntary association; and such insistence is the very foundation of civil and religious liberty. To *persuade* Catholic parents to send their children to non-Catholic schools is no doubt in many cases wise; to *force* them to do so, no matter how high the motive of the compulsion, is tyranny. The end, we hold, does not justify the means, and violation of sacred rights will in the long run, through the retributive justice of God, bring ruin.

The last objection to historic Christianity is that it is doctrinal rather than practical. There is so much misery in the world, it is said—so many crowded tenements, so many starving children—that there is no time to engage in theological or historical discussions about the death and resurrection of Christ. This objection, we are constrained to believe, betokens a singular narrowness of mind. It seems to be assumed that the church has to choose between examining the basis of her faith and relieving the physical distress of men. As a matter of fact, she ought to do both. Neglect of either one will certainly bring disaster. And today the danger lies altogether in the neglect not of the physical, but of the intellectual and spiritual task. The truth is that the present age is characterized by an unparalleled intellectual and spiritual decline.

The growth of ignorance—certainly in America and probably elsewhere as well—is appalling; poetry is silent; and even the appreciation of fine and noble things seems almost to be lost. Certainly a generation that follows Mr. H. G. Wells in his contemptuous neglect of all the higher ranges of the human mind, or deserts Milton for Van Loon, can hardly convince any thinking man that it is an infallible judge of what is beautiful or good.

We do not therefore seek to evade this last objection, but we meet it squarely in the face. We are opposed with all our might to the passionate anti-intellectualism of the Modernist church; we refuse to separate religion sharply from science; and we believe that our religion is founded not upon aspirations but upon facts. Of course, if the intellectual defense of our faith causes us to neglect our duty to the poor, we have made ourselves guilty of a great sin. And in that case, may God pity us and set us back into the pathway of duty and love! But relief of physical distress, important as it is, is not all that the church has to do. And even that task, we believe, cannot be accomplished if we neglect the intellectual basis of our faith. False ideas are responsible even for the physical evils in the world; the machinery of the world's business will not perform its task if we neglect the soul of man; the best of engines will not run if it is not producing a spark.

Thus we maintain that far from being inimical to social progress, "Fundamentalism" (in the broad, popular sense of the word) is the only means of checking the spiritual decadence of our age. Some men are satisfied with the thought of the time when the physical conditions of life will so be improved by the advance of science that there shall be no poverty and no disease, and when vain aspirations will so be conquered by reason that death will lose its terrors and men will be able to part from their loved ones without a pang. But would such a rule of reason represent an advance over the present state of mankind? For our part, we think not. The deadening of spiritual aspirations and the abolition of individual liberty may bring about a diminution of pain, but they will also bring about the destruction of all that makes life worthwhile. We do not for one moment discourage the relief of distress and the improvement of the physical condition of the race; indeed, these things have obtained their real impetus from the "Fundamentalism" of the past. But if these things prove to be all, then mankind will have sunk to the level of the beasts.

The process of decadence has been going on apace, and it is high time to seek a way of rescue if mankind is to be saved from the abyss. Such a way of rescue is provided by the Christian religion, with its supernatural origin and supernatural power. It is a great mistake to represent us who are adherents of historic Christianity as though we were clinging desperately to the past merely because it is old, and as though we had no message of hope. On the contrary, our eyes are turned eagerly to the future. We are seeking no mere continuation of spiritual conditions that now exist but an outburst of new power; we are looking for a mighty revival of the Christian religion which like the Reformation of the sixteenth century will bring light and liberty to mankind. When such a revival comes, it will destroy no fine or unselfish or noble thing; it will hasten and not hinder the relief of the physical distress of men and the improvement of conditions in this world. But it will do far more than all that. It will also descend into the depths—those depths into which utilitarianism can never enter—and will again bring mankind into the glorious liberty of communion with the living God.

9

WHAT FUNDAMENTALISM STANDS FOR NOW

The term "Fundamentalism" is distasteful to the present writer and to many persons who hold views similar to his. It seems to suggest that we are adherents of some strange new sect; whereas in point of fact we are conscious simply of maintaining the historic Christian faith and of moving in the great central current of Christian life. That does not mean that we desire to be out of touch with our own time, or that we live in a static world without variety and without zest. On the contrary, there is nothing more varied and more interesting than the effect of the Christian religion upon different races and different ages; there is no more absorbing story than that of the relations between Christianity and its changing environment.

But what we do mean is that despite changes in the environment, there is something in Christianity which from the very beginning has remained the same.

This historic continuity of the Christian religion is based upon its appeal to a body of facts—facts about God, about man, and about the way in which, at a definite point in the world's history, some nineteen hundred years ago, a new relationship was set up between God and man by the work

"What Fundamentalism Stands for Now" originally appeared in the *New York Times*, June 21, 1925, 9:1, col. 1. Reprinted in *What Is Christianity?* ed. Ned Bernard Stonehouse (Grand Rapids: Eerdmans, 1951).

of Jesus Christ. There is one advantage about facts—they "stay put." If a thing really happened, it can never possibly be made by the passage of time or by the advance of science into a thing that has not happened. New facts may be discovered, and certainly we Christians welcome the discovery of new facts with all our heart; but old facts, if they are really facts, will remain facts beyond the end of time.

This sheer factual basis of the Christian religion is denied by a large body of persons in the modern church; indeed, at this point we find what is really perhaps the most fundamental divergence in the religious world at the present day. More fundamental than differences of opinion about this truth or that is the difference of opinion about truth as such. When historic Christianity maintains that the Christian religion is based upon a body of truth, a body of doctrine, which will remain true beyond the end of time, it is opposed by a very widespread pragmatism, which maintains that doctrine is merely the necessarily changing expression of an inner experience.

Doctrine, the pragmatist admits, is indeed necessary, but in the very nature of the case it cannot be permanent; it is the mere attempt to express the Christian life in the forms of thought proper to any one generation, and in another generation a different expression will necessarily be in place. Thus, according to the logic of the pragmatist position, two contradictory doctrines may be equally good; one may serve for one generation or for one class of persons, and another may serve for another generation or another class of persons.

Obviously, this attitude involves the most bottomless skepticism; for to say that doctrines which are contradictory to each other are equally true is just the same as saying that the two doctrines are equally false, and that permanent, objective truth in the sphere of religion can never be attained. To such pragmatist skepticism the believer in historic Christianity is sharply opposed; against the passionate anti-intellectualism of a great section of the modern church he maintains the primacy of the intellect; he holds that God has given to man a faculty of reason which is capable of apprehending truth, even truth about God.

That does not mean that we finite creatures can find out God by our own searching, but it does mean that God has made us capable of receiving the information which he chooses to give. I cannot possibly evolve an account of China out of my own inner consciousness, but I am perfectly capable of understanding the account which comes to me from travelers who have been there themselves. So our reason is certainly insufficient to tell us about God unless he reveals himself, but it is capable (or would be capable if it were not clouded by sin) of receiving revelation when once it is given.

God's revelation of himself to man embraces, indeed, only a small part of his being; the area of what we know is infinitesimal compared with what we do not know. But partial knowledge is not necessarily false knowledge, and our knowledge of God on the basis of his revelation is, we hold, true as far as it goes.

Christianity then on our view is not a life as distinguished from a doctrine, or a life of which doctrine is the symbolic intellectual expression; but— just the other way around—it is a life founded upon a doctrine. We refuse, therefore, to abandon to the student of natural science the entire realm of fact in order to reserve to religion merely a realm of ideals; on the contrary, theology, we hold, is just as much a science as is chemistry. The two sciences, it is true, differ widely in their subject matter, and in particular they differ widely in the qualifications required of the investigator; but they are both concerned with the acquisition and orderly arrangement of truth.

The body of truth upon which the Christian religion is based may be divided into three parts. There is first the doctrine of God (or theology proper), second the doctrine of man, and third the doctrine of the relationship between God and man. These three divisions may now be considered briefly in turn.

The basis of the Christian view of God—by no means all of it, but the basis of it—is simply theism, the belief, namely, that the universe was created and is now upheld by a personal Being upon whom it is dependent but who is not dependent upon it. This view is opposed to all forms of the prevalent pantheism, which either makes "God" merely a collective name for the world process itself, or else regards him as related to the world process as the soul of man is related to his body.

All forms of pantheism differ from theism in denying the transcendence of God, the separateness of God from the world. But the transcendence of God, what the Bible calls the "holiness" of God, is at the very root of the Christian religion. God is indeed, according to the Christian view, immanent in the world, but he is also personally distinct from the world and from the finite creatures that he has made.

The Christian doctrine of man is partly involved in the Christian doctrine of God; theism, with its distinction between God and the world, humbles man as creature under the almighty hand of God, while the current pantheism exalts man because his life is regarded as being a part of all the God there is. But another difference of opinion is more important still; it appears in divergent views of moral evil. According to historic Christianity, all mankind are under the just condemnation of God, and are utterly helpless because of the guilt and power of sin. According to another very widespread type of belief, human resources are sufficient for human needs, and self-development, especially the development of the religious nature, is the Christian ideal. This type of belief is optimistic about human nature as it is at present constituted, while historic Christianity regards all mankind as being in itself hopelessly lost.

Many preachers seek to arouse man's confidence in himself; "I believe in Man" is one of the cardinal articles of their creed. But the preacher of historic Christianity tries first of all to destroy man's confidence in himself and to arouse in his soul the dreadful consciousness of sin.

God enveloped in a terrible righteousness, man an offender against his law and under his just wrath—these are the two great presuppositions of the historic Christian gospel. But on the basis of these terrible presuppositions, the Christian preacher comes with a message of hope. The hope is found not at all in any attenuation of the facts about God and man, not at all in any effort to take lightly the curse of God's law, but simply and solely in an account of what God himself has done.

We deserved eternal death, but the Son of God, who was himself God, came into this world for our redemption, took upon himself the just punishment of our sins, died instead of us on the cross, and finally completed his redeeming work by rising from the tomb in a glorious resurrection. There and there alone is found the Christian gospel, the piece of "good news" upon which all our hope is based.

That gospel, as indeed the term "news" implies, is an account not of something that always was true, but of something that happened; Christianity is based not merely on ethical principles or on eternal truths of religion, but also on historical facts.

The redeeming facts upon which the Christian hope is based were things done by the Lord Jesus Christ, and those facts involve the entrance into the course of this world of the creative power of God; in other words, they involve the supernatural.

Acceptance of the supernatural does not, as is often supposed, destroy the basis of science; it does not introduce an element of arbitrariness which would make impossible any exhibition of regular sequences in nature. On the contrary, a miracle, according to the Christian view, is of an arbitrary or purposeless event, but proceeds from the very source of all the order that there is in the world, namely, from the will of God.

God is the author of nature, and we Christians are willing to trust him not to destroy that orderly system in which it is his will that we should live. Indeed, the believer in the supernatural is in some respects kinder to the scientist than the scientist ventures to be to himself; for in order to maintain the distinctness of the supernatural from the natural, we are obliged to hold that there is a real order of nature—not a mere observed set of sequences but a really existent order. Only that order of nature, though really existent, is not self-existent; it was created by the fiat of God's will, and he has never abandoned his freedom in the presence of his world.

We are not saying that while miracles were accomplished by God ordinary events are not accomplished by him, but only that in the case of ordinary events he uses means or "second causes," while in the case of miracles he puts forth his creative power. A miracle then is an event wrought by the immediate, as distinguished from the mediate, power of God; it is not a work of providence but a work of creation.

The outstanding miracle narrated in the New Testament is the emergence of the body of Jesus from the tomb; upon that miracle the Christian church was founded, and the evidence for it is of a singularly varied and cumulative kind. But that event is not isolated; it is connected with a consistent representation of Jesus in the New Testament as a supernatural person—not the fairest flower of humanity, the finest thing the world has to show, not divine only because divinity courses through all things, not God only because he was the highest development of man, but the eternal Son of God who came voluntarily into the world for our redemption.

Acceptance of this New Testament account of Jesus involves a certain attitude toward him which is widely different from the attitude assumed by many persons in the church today. Jesus to us was not only a teacher and example (though he was all that), but he was, and is, our Savior and Lord; he was not the first Christian, the initiator of a new type of religious life, but he stood in a far more fundamental and far more intimate relationship to Christianity than that, because he was the one who made Christianity possible by his redeeming work.

At no point does our attitude appear in more characteristic fashion than just here: many persons hold up their hands in amazement at our assertion that Jesus was not a Christian; we regard it as the very height of blasphemy to say that he was a Christian. "Christianity" to us is a way of getting rid of sin; and therefore to say that Jesus was a Christian would be to deny his perfect holiness.

"But," it is said, "do you mean to tell us that if a man lives a life like the life of Jesus, he is not a Christian even though he rejects the doctrine of the redeeming work of Christ in his death and resurrection?" The question is often asked, but the answer is very simple. Of course, if a man really lives a life like the life of Jesus, all is well; such a man is indeed not a Christian, but he is something better than a Christian—he is a being who has never lost his high estate of sonship with God.

But our trouble is that our lives, to say nothing of the lives of those who thus so confidently appeal to their own similarity to Jesus, do not seem to be like the life of Jesus; we are sinners, and hence we become Christians; we are sinners, and hence we accept with thankfulness the redeeming love of the Lord Jesus Christ, who had pity on us and made us right with God, through no merit of our own, by his atoning death.

Thus we make Jesus not merely an example for faith, but primarily the object of faith. In doing so, we have the whole New Testament on our side; the Jesus who preached "a religion of Jesus" and not "a religion about Jesus" never really was heard of until modern times; the Jesus of all the gospels presented himself not merely as teacher but also as Lord and as Redeemer.

This redeeming work of Christ which is at the center of the Bible is applied to the individual soul, according to our view, by the Holy Spirit; we find no permanent hope for society in the mere "principles of Jesus" or the like, but we find it in the new birth of individual souls. Important indeed are the social applications of Christianity; but as Francis Shunk Downs has well said, there can be no applied Christianity unless there is a Christianity to apply, and there can be no Christianity to apply unless there are Christian men. And men are made Christian by the Spirit of God.

But the means which the Spirit of God uses in making men Christians is faith; and faith is the response of the human soul to the gospel message. A man becomes convicted of sin; he sees himself as God sees him; he is in despair. And then the Lord Jesus is offered to him in the gospel—in the good news that the guilt of sin has been blotted out by the wonderful sacrifice which God himself provided, in his mysterious love for sinners, on Calvary. The acceptance of that message is faith, faith in the Lord Jesus Christ; through faith a man becomes a child of God and then follows a new life, with a victorious battle against sin.

Such is the way of salvation as it is set forth in the Bible and in historic Christianity. It seems to those who have followed it to be the most blessed thing in all the world; who can measure the peace and joy that have been found at the foot of the cross? But to others the message seems strange and full of offense.

The offense comes—and has come ever since the very first days of the Christian church—from the inveterate insistence and exclusiveness of the Christian message. What causes offense is not that we present this way of salvation, but that we present it as the only way. The world according to our view is lost in sin; the gospel provides the only way of escape, and the blackest guilt into which any Christian can fall is to deceive dying souls into thinking that some other way will answer as well.

If our views are wrong, they should be refuted, but what is ethically indefensible is to ask us to hold those views and then act as though we did not hold them. If those views are true, they must determine our every action, in our capacity both as men and as ministers in the church. God has placed us in the world as witnesses, and we cannot in the interests of ecclesiastical harmony or for any other reason allow our witness to become untrue; we cannot consent to deceive men into thinking that they can be saved in any other way than through the gospel that is set forth in the Word of God.

10

WHAT IS THE GOSPEL?

n requesting me to write an article on the theme "What is the gospel?" the editor evidently desired that I should make some reference to an article by the Rev. John Allan MacLean Jr. on the same theme in the July number of the *Union Seminary Review*. In doing so, I may say at the start that the article interested me very greatly. It is certainly interesting to discover what the people who actually form the membership of the churches think with regard to the basic questions of the Christian faith.

Some of the results of the test which was applied to Mr. MacLean's congregation might indeed, superficially considered, cause discouragement. Although many of the answers to the question "What is the gospel?" were excellent, yet others—as, for example, the answer to the effect that the gospel "is the right way of living"—might at first sight seem (whether or not appearances are here deceptive may appear later) to run counter to the very center and core of Christianity as it is found in the grace of God. And in general the test does serve to reveal anew—what is evident in many other ways—that there exists widely in the church today, even in congregations relatively well informed, as the congregation at Greenwood certainly was, considerable confusion of mind.

One reason for such confusion of mind may perhaps be found in the fact that the congregations have not informed themselves with regard to the re-

"What Is the Gospel?" originally appeared in *Union Seminary Review* (Richmond) 38 (1927) 158–70.

ally great issues of the day. "Another inquiry," says Mr. MacLean, "conducted some months ago, as to the kind of sermons or preaching which the people considered most helpful and necessary revealed that only two persons were seriously interested in such things as 'modernism,' or considered its discussion important." Surely that state of affairs is lamentable. Modernism is the greatest menace which the Christian church has faced for hundreds of years. It is overwhelmingly dominant in contemporary religious literature; it is in almost complete control of many of the largest of the formerly evangelical churches; its influence is sometimes felt most strongly just in those ecclesiastical bodies that are most complacent about their freedom from controversy. Surely every intelligent Christian of the present day ought to be interested in such a theme.

Perhaps, indeed, the congregation to which the question was addressed was not quite so indifferent to the issues as it might seem to have been. The term "Modernism," at least in its wider usage, is comparatively new; and the phenomenon that it designates is essentially the same as what was known a generation or so ago as "skepticism" or "unbelief"—only it is now tenfold more dangerous because it is inside the church instead of outside of it. If Modernism had been designated by one of those more familiar terms, possibly the interest of the congregation might have been more keenly aroused. Moreover, the lay mind is interested in what is individual and concrete rather than in what is general and abstract; it is interested in individual manifestations of Modernism rather than in Modernism as a whole. So if instead of putting the question in general terms Mr. MacLean had asked whether the congregation was interested in such questions as "Did Christ rise from the tomb?"; "Was he born of a virgin?"; "Is the Bible true?"—those great questions to which Modernism gives a negative or equivocal answer— I rather think that considerable interest might have been revealed.

Nevertheless, despite such qualifications, it is undoubtedly true that in many quarters there is a most lamentable ignorance regarding the greatest issue of the day. Such ignorance, with the indifference to which it gives rise, is sometimes very disheartening to those who are contending for the faith. They have been in the trenches in the great Christian war; they have tried to defend the heritage of those who stay behind. But then when they get back home, weary and stained with the mud of trench warfare, they are greeted by the exclamation: "What dirty, disgusting fellows those soldiers are! Thank God, we have no unseemly controversy in our church at least!"

124

Far more serious, however, than this discouragement which indifference brings to those who are contending for the faith is the injury to the souls of the indifferent people themselves. In very many cases, people who decry controversy have already lost, or are in process of losing, their own hold upon the great verities of the faith. They may not be conscious of relinquishing a single doctrine or a single fact that the Bible records. But the trouble is that what is not consciously given up in their minds has been removed from their hearts; they live only on the periphery of the Christian religion, and the really great things are lost from view. By such persons, whether in the pulpit or in the pew, the gospel is not indeed denied. But what is almost a worse thing than that is done—the gospel is not denied, but is simply ignored.

I do not mean that every sermon or every other sermon or every tenth sermon ought to be directly polemic; I do not mean that in the pulpit such terms as "Modernism" ought to be constantly used; I do not mean that doubts and questions ought to be needlessly placed in the minds of persons who are still free from them; I do not mean that all congregations ought to be treated alike. On the contrary, the preacher has great need of common sense and of tact. But what I do mean is that, in general and as a whole, the church ought to be made aware of the great issue of the day. Calamity has resulted in many ecclesiastical bodies because the raising of the issue has been postponed too long. The destructive forces have been allowed, quietly and without protestations of orthodoxy, to obtain control of the ecclesiastical machinery; and now disruption, and the destruction of the historic witness of the churches in question, is immediately imminent. Surely it would have been far better to face the issue while the heart of the churches was still sound. An issue that must ultimately be faced had far better be faced bravely at once.

Moreover, controversy, though it should certainly not be fostered where it is not necessary, is by no means an unmixed evil. It is impossible to tell what a thing is without telling what it is not; and the preaching of ministers who seek always to avoid controversy is usually quite colorless and vague. The New Testament itself is very largely a controversial book; Paul's hymn to Christian love in the thirteenth chapter of 1 Corinthians is part of a controversial passage; and much of the most gracious teaching of our Savior is rendered plain by being set over against what was said by the scribes and Pharisees. And in the whole history of the church, it is in times of conflict that great revivals come.

It is discouraging, therefore, to find, according to the former test of which Mr. MacLean speaks, that so few persons in the congregation were interested in Modernism. And so it is discouraging to find, in the later test, that many of the answers (though by no means all of them) were so faulty or so vague. Here also, indeed, as in that former case, our discouragement ought not to be so great as we might at first be tempted to let it be. It is an exceedingly difficult thing to formulate a definition—far more difficult than is generally supposed. Sometimes when I am asked to state in a few sentences my view of some great theme, I am tempted to say to the inquirer: "My dear sir, if you had asked me to write a book on the subject I might perhaps have been bold enough to try to do so, but when you ask me to construct a brief definition— no, I certainly have not sufficient learning or sufficient wisdom for that." So I think that when the members of the congregation at Greenwood were asked to answer in a few sentences the question, "What is the gospel?" they were asked to do an extraordinarily difficult thing. On the whole, I am not surprised, and not too greatly discouraged, at their not doing better than they did; and many of them certainly did very well.

It is evident, moreover, that the faults of those of the answers that were faulty were (very many of them, at least) reducible to one initial fault; they were due to a confusion in the minds of those to whom the question was sent between the question what the gospel *is* and the question what effects the gospel produces in men's lives. So, for example, when it was said that the gospel "is the right way of living," that might at first sight seem to identify the Christian message with the enunciation of ethical principles, quite in the manner of the Unitarian churches. But appearances may here well be deceptive. The person who wrote that answer may have been thinking of those who profess to believe in the gospel and yet do not exhibit any effects of the gospel in their lives, or, better, he may have been thinking of his own struggle against sin, his own difficulties in drawing out the implications of the gospel in his own life. And so, in indignation at false professions on the part of others or in sorrow at his own failures, he may have said, "The gospel is the right way of living." As a definition of the gospel, that answer was just about as faulty as anything that could possibly be imagined, but as an expression of one thing at least (among other things) that the gospel *involves*, it was a very fine Christian utterance indeed.

But how shall we obtain the true answer to the question that has actually been assigned to us; how shall we determine not what the gospel has produced in our lives but what the gospel *is?* It is possible that etymology may help us. Etymology is indeed a snare to preachers; they sometimes employ it when it is not in place. Many words have become worn down in actual usage; the thought of their origin is lost, and to return to it leads to a perversion of their present meaning. But in the case of the Greek word which is translated "gospel" in the English New Testament, such is not the case. That word has certainly retained to the full the freshness of its original meaning.

What then does the word translated "gospel" mean? The question might seem to be unnecessary (were it not apparently ignored in so many sermons and religious books); everyone knows that "gospel" means "good news." But if "gospel" means "good news," then many common notions about the gospel disappear at once. "Good news" is never in the imperative mood; a "gospel" cannot possibly consist in directions as to a way of life or in a complex of worthy ideals. If a man comes running in and says in a tone of great eagerness, "I have news for you," and you ask him what it is, he does not say: "Here is the piece of news I have for you: Keep the commandments of God; love God and your neighbor." Such exhortations are indeed exceedingly important and valuable, but they are certainly not news. News consists always, not in exhortations or commands, but in information about facts; a "gospel" is always in the indicative mood.

But what particular facts are narrated in the Christian gospel? The answer is found, best of all perhaps, in a passage of the New Testament, which summarizes for us in authentic fashion the gospel which all the apostles preached. In 1 Corinthians 15:3ff., the apostle Paul rehearses something that he had "received"; and it is generally agreed by historians of various shades of opinion, even by those who are opposed to Christianity, that the place from which he had received it was the primitive Jerusalem church. What we have in these precious words—perhaps the most important words historically that were ever penned—is nothing less than an authentic summary of the things that were regarded by the earliest Christian church as lying at the foundation of its life. About these things, about this "gospel" (v. 1), Paul says that he was in perfect agreement with those who had been the most intimate friends of Jesus when he was on earth: "Therefore whether it were I or they, so we preach, and so ye believed" (v. 11).

What then, as thus summarized, was the "gospel" of the primitive Jerusalem church? The answer is put in very simple words: "How that Christ died for our sins according to the scriptures: and that he was buried, and that he rose again the third day according to the scriptures."

These momentous clauses do not contain exhortation; they do not set forth a way of life; they do not formulate a program or hold up an ideal. On the contrary, they contain a rehearsal of historical facts; they recount not something that ought to happen, but something that had actually happened. Here we have the sheer factual basis of Christianity. The Christian gospel consists not in an ideal, not even in eternal truth—that is, not in an account of what always was true—but in the narrating of events.

The events, moreover, were not merely what took place in the recesses of men's souls, but they were events in the external world. Christ died; he was buried; he rose again—those were all of the things that could be witnessed by the bodily eye. They are not, first of all, matters of "interpretation," but matters of fact. If Christ really died, really was buried, really rose again, then the gospel may be true; if he did not do so, then the gospel is false. In the latter case it is a gospel still; it is a piece of good news—only the trouble is that the news is not true.

There are many today who rebel against this grounding of Christianity upon historical facts. "Let us have a religion," they say, "that shall be independent of historical science, that shall be able to continue no matter what historians may tell us about events that took place in Palestine in the first century of our era; let us think rather of what Christ does for us today than of what he did or is alleged to have done nineteen hundred years ago."

About such a religion we may have one opinion or another. But one thing is clear—if such is our religion, we have given up the "gospel." We may have discovered useful and inspiring principles, but we have no "good news."

The Christian religion is very different, for it is based squarely upon events; it depends upon historical facts.

The facts upon which it depends are not indeed "bare facts," but they are facts that have a meaning; and the meaning is made known not by experiences of our souls (though it is gloriously confirmed by those experiences), but, as is the case with the facts themselves, by the apostolic message that the New Testament contains. It is said in the same passage in 1 Corinthians with which we have already been dealing not merely that "Christ died" but that "Christ died *for our sins*." That is not a bare fact, but a fact with the meaning of the fact: the gospel tells us not merely that Christ died, but why he died and what he accomplished for us when he died. And what is here put in bare summary becomes in the New Testament as a whole abundantly plain. We deserved eternal death because of sin. But the Son of God, because he loved us and because the Father loved us too, died in our stead upon the cross; and when he had died, he completed his redeeming work by his glorious resurrection. That is the center and core of the gospel that the apostles proclaimed.

But at this point there is often an objection. "We admit," it is said, "that the gospel of the apostolic church is what it has just been represented as being; we admit that the religion of the apostolic church was not a religion of sunny optimism, not a religion based upon confidence in human nature, but in the fullest sense a religion of redemption. But may we not now return from the apostolic church to Jesus himself; must not *his* religion and that alone be the standard for the Christian church?"

The amazing thing about this objection is not that it is raised, for it represents a very widespread way of thinking among modern men. But the amazing thing about it is that the assumption upon which it is based is treated as though it were something that would be accepted as a matter of course by evangelical Christian men. That assumption is that the words of Jesus, spoken while he was on earth, are the sole norm of the Christian religion and that accordingly our relation to Jesus is a mere continuation of the relationship in which his disciples stood to him in Galilee. As a matter of fact, this assumption simply begs the whole question. The question is just exactly whether Jesus came primarily to say something or to do something. If he came primarily to say something, if he came simply to initiate by his words and by his example a new type of religious life, then conceivably his recorded words and the example of his deeds constitute the sole standard by which we can determine what Christianity is. But if he came primarily to do something—namely, in his death and resurrection—then the full meaning of what was done could not be explained until after the doing of it was finished. In the latter case, the eighth chapter of Romans is every bit as important in the determination of what Christianity is as is the Sermon on the Mount.

For our part, in company with the whole of the historic Christian church, we hold to the latter view; and therefore we are quite unwilling to substitute the words of Jesus when he was on earth for the Bible of which they are part, as constituting the seat of authority in religion and the authoritative account of what Christianity is. To do so, we think, would be dishonoring to the words of Jesus themselves; for in those words, he directed men both to the Old Testament Scriptures and to the revelation which was to be given by the Holy Spirit to the apostles.

Nevertheless, even if we take the words of Jesus alone, they are amply sufficient to show that the gospel is what the apostolic church held it to be. Jesus did not, indeed, when he was on earth, set forth the *full* meaning of the redemption that he had come to perform; that he left to the revelation that was to be given by the Holy Spirit to the apostles whom he chose. But, although only by way of prophecy, yet plainly enough, he did point forward to the redeeming event that formed the subject matter of the gospel. When Jesus said at the beginning of the Galilean ministry, "Repent ye, and believe the gospel" (Mark 1:15), what did he mean by the "gospel"? I think we shall not go far wrong if we answer this question by the former part of the same verse. "The time is fulfilled," said Jesus, "and the kingdom of God is at hand." There we have a summary of the gospel that Jesus proclaimed: "The kingdom of God is at hand."

But that summary points forward very plainly, when it is explained by the rest of the four gospels, to the apostolic message with which we have already dealt. There have indeed been those who hold a contrary view; there have been some who have regarded "the kingdom of God" in the teaching of Jesus as designating merely an inner experience in the souls of men. But such a view involves a widespread rejection of important elements in Jesus' teaching as it is recorded in the gospels. Against that view, we may remark in passing, we have just now the support of the ultra-modern hypothesis of "consistent eschatology." According to that hypothesis, "the kingdom of God" in the teaching of Jesus lay altogether in the future; Jesus expected the end of the present order to come in the same year during which his teaching was being carried on; and his ethics, being quite ill-adapted to a permanent society, were intended merely for the brief interim before the expected catastrophe. That is certainly a very one-sided and very false hypothesis, and of course, like the other hypothesis of which we have just spoken, it involves a widespread skepticism with regard to the gospels as they stand; but at least it does call attention to the equal error of that other hypothesis—that other hypothesis which makes the kingdom only a present and inward experience in men's souls. As a matter of fact, the kingdom of Jesus' teaching was both present and future, and to ignore that second feature is to misunderstand the gospels from beginning to end. No, there can

CHRISTIANITY AND MODERN SUBSTITUTES

be no doubt in the mind of any historian who really faces the facts that when Jesus said that "the kingdom of God is at hand," he was thinking of catastrophic events that were to change the face of the world.

One of those catastrophic events is still in the future today—it is the second coming of our Lord in glory. But undoubtedly Jesus also pointed to an event that was nearer at hand—namely, the redeeming event that consisted in his death and resurrection. "The Son of man," he said, for example, "came not to be ministered unto, but to minister, and to give his life a ransom for many" (Mark 10:45). Jesus pointed forward to that event, and the apostles pointed back. But whether the event was in the future or already in the past, always the "gospel" of which the New Testament speaks does set forth an event. Jesus came not primarily to say something but to do something, and the rehearsal of what he did constitutes the center of the good news upon which Christianity depends.

That good news has, of course, in it elements of which we have not now time to speak; certainly, for example, it contains an element of promise as well as an account of what has already been done. And also it has certain presuppositions, and the presuppositions are absolutely necessary if the gospel is to be received. But the presuppositions are not the gospel itself. "God is a Spirit, infinite, eternal, and unchangeable in his being, wisdom, power, holiness, justice, goodness, and truth"—that is a true summary of a large part of the Bible, and it is absolutely necessary for us to know this if we are to be able to understand the gospel of Christ. But it is not the gospel itself. "All mankind, by their fall, lost communion with God, are under his wrath and curse, and so made liable to all the miseries of this life, to death itself, and to pains of hell forever"—that again is a necessary presupposition of the gospel, and again it is a very important thing for us to know. But certainly it does not itself constitute a gospel. But "Christ died for our sins, he was buried, he rose again"—that, with all that goes with it, with the whole saving work of Christ and of the Holy Spirit so gloriously set forth in the Scriptures and so splendidly summarized in the catechism of our church from which we have just quoted—that and that alone constitutes the gospel.

The redeeming work of Christ which the gospel sets forth is applied to the individual soul by the Holy Spirit, and when it is so applied there is Christian experience. But never in the world ought we to look to Christian experience to determine what the gospel is. That we can learn from the Scriptures alone. Christian experience no doubt is needed to enable a man to understand what the Bible says; a man is ill-qualified to understand the Word of God when his mind is still clouded by sin. But never ought experience to be regarded as providing authoritative information about the actual contents of the gospel. To regard it so is fatal to Christian experience itself.

We do not mean that it is not useful to interrogate one's own soul. Some even of the faulty answers in the test reported by Mr. MacLean, for example, were illuminating. They were fine expressions of what the gospel had accomplished in the lives of Christian men and women. How rich and how varied are the effects of the gospel in human lives; in what manifold ways our Savior holds communion with those who are his! But if we cut those experiences loose from their basis in the Word of God, we shall soon lose the experiences themselves. For the question—what the gospel has accomplished in my life and yours—and for one very valuable kind of confirmation of the truth of the gospel, we may look to experience; but to determine what the gospel is, we must turn to the Scriptures and to the Scriptures alone.

So the creeds of the church are not, as is so often supposed, reactions to Christian experience or intellectual expressions of what experience contains, but (just the other way around) they are summaries of what the Bible tells us about the facts and promises upon which Christian experience is based.

What is needed at the present time is a return to those facts. The church is suffering from a woefully exaggerated subjectivism, from a fatal substitution of experience for the Bible as the set of authority in religion. And the curious thing is that this undue preoccupation with experience, this substitution of experience, whether individual or corporate, for the Word of God as the source of authoritative information, is producing a lamentable impoverishment of experience itself. Yet perhaps it is not such a curious thing after all. As a man cannot lift himself from the mire without a helping hand or without something solid upon which he can lay hold, so it is impossible for experience to provide a gospel. If we thought less of our experience and more of the work of Christ, our experience would be much richer than it is. And our service would be much more helpful to burdened souls. All true Christian experience is founded upon the redeeming facts, and the facts are recorded only in the Word of God. Not into our own souls but to the Bible should we look to obtain an answer to the momentous question, "What is the gospel?"

PART THREE

THE TASK OF CHRISTIAN SCHOLARSHIP

11

CHRISTIAN SCHOLARSHIP
AND EVANGELISM

I t seems to me, as I stand here before you today, that there is one blessing in these days of defection and unbelief which we have come to
value as we never valued it before. That is the blessing of Christian fellowship in the presence of a hostile world, and in the presence of a visible
church which too often has departed from the Word of God. Today, during
the three meetings of this League, in the portion of the meetings which has
been allotted to me, I am to have the privilege of delivering three addresses
on the subject "The Importance of Christian Scholarship."

It is no doubt unfortunate that the person who speaks about this subject
should have so limited an experimental acquaintance with the subject about
which he is endeavoring to speak; but in these days of anti-intellectualism
you may be willing to hear a word in defense of the intellect, even from one
whose qualifications for speaking on that subject are so limited as mine.

There was a time when the raising of the question as to the importance
of Christian scholarship might have seemed to be ridiculous; there was a
time when a man who does so much talking as a minister or a Sunday school

"Christian Scholarship and Evangelism" was an address originally delivered on June
17, 1932, in London before the Bible League of Great Britain, and published as
part of the pamphlet, *The Importance of Christian Scholarship* (London: The Bible
League, 1932). Reprinted in *What Is Christianity?* ed. Ned Bernard Stonehouse
(Grand Rapids: Eerdmans, 1951).

teacher does, and as no doubt every Christian ought to do, in the propagation of the faith to which he adheres, would have regarded it as a matter of course that he ought to know something about the subject of which he undertakes to talk.

But in recent years we have got far beyond all such elementary considerations as that; modern pedagogy has emancipated us, whether we are in the pulpit or in the professor's chair or in the pew, from anything so irksome as earnest labor in the acquisition of knowledge. It never seems to occur to many modern teachers that the primary business of the teacher is to study the subject that he is going to teach. Instead of studying the subject that he is going to teach, he studies "education"; a knowledge of the methodology of teaching takes the place of a knowledge of the particular branch of literature, history, or science to which a man has devoted his life.

This substitution of methodology for content in the preparation of the teacher is based upon a particular view of what education is. It is based upon the view that education consists primarily not in the imparting of information, but in a training of the faculties of the child; that the business of the teacher is not to teach, but to develop in the child a faculty which will enable the child to learn.

This child-centered notion of education seems to involve emancipation from a vast amount of drudgery. It used to be thought necessary to do some hard work at school. When a textbook was given to a class, it was expected that the contents of the textbook should be mastered. But now all that has been changed. Storing up facts in the mind was a long and painful process, and it is indeed comforting to know that we can now do without it. Away with all drudgery and all hard work! Self-expression has taken their place. A great pedagogic discovery has been made—the discovery that it is possible to think with a completely empty mind.

It cannot be said that the results of the discovery are impressive. This child-centered notion of education has resulted, particularly in America, where it has been most ruthlessly applied, in a boundless superficiality of which we Americans certainly have little reason to be proud; but it has probably not been confined to America by any means. I wonder when the reaction will come. I wonder when we shall have that revival of learning which we so much need, and which I verily believe might be, in the providence of God, as was the Renaissance of the fifteenth century, the precursor of a reformation in the church. When that revival of learning comes, we may be sure that it will sweep away the present absurd over-emphasis upon methodology in teaching at the expense of content. We shall never have a true revival of learning until teachers turn their attention away from the mere mental processes of the child, out into the marvelous richness and variety of the universe and of human life. Not teachers who have studied the methodology of teaching but teachers who are on fire with a love of the subjects that they are going to teach are the real torchbearers of intellectual advance.

Certainly the present view of education is, when it is applied to the work of the preacher and of the teacher in the church, skeptical to the core. It is summed up in what is called "religious education." I wonder sometimes at the readiness with which Christian people—I do not mean church members, but real Bible-believing Christians—use that term, for the ordinary implications of the term are quite opposed to the Christian religion. The fundamental notion underlying the ordinary use of the term "religious education" is that the business of the teacher in the church is not to impart knowledge of a fixed body of truth which God has revealed, but to train the religious faculty of the child. The religious faculty of the child, it is supposed, may be trained by the use of the most widely diverse doctrinal content; it may be trained in this generation, perhaps, by the thought of a personal God, but in another generation it may be trained equally well by the thought of an ideal humanity as the only God there is. Thus the search for objective and permanent truth is given up, and instead we have turned our attention to the religious faculties of man. In other words, men have become interested today in religion because they have ceased to believe in God.

As over against such skepticism, the Bible, from Genesis to Revelation, presents a body of truth which God has revealed; and if we hold the biblical view, we shall regard it as our supreme function, as teachers and as preachers and as Christian parents and as simple Christians, to impart a knowledge of that body of truth. The Christian preacher, we shall hold, needs above all to know the thing that he is endeavoring to preach.

But if knowledge is necessary to preaching, it does seem probable that the fuller the knowledge is, the better the preacher will be able to do his work. Underlying preaching, in other words, is Christian scholarship; and it is in defense of Christian scholarship that I have thought it might be fitting to say a few words to you today.

Christian scholarship is necessary to the preacher, and to the man who in whatever way, in public or in private, endeavors to proclaim the gospel to his fellow men, in at least three ways.

In the first place, it is necessary for evangelism. In saying so, I am perfectly well aware of the fact that I am putting myself squarely in conflict with a method of religious work which is widely prevalent at the present time. Knowledge, the advocates of that method seem to think, is quite unnecessary to faith—at the beginning a man may be a Fundamentalist or a Modernist; he may hold a Christian or an anti-Christian view of Christ. Never mind; he is to be received, quite apart from his opinions, on the basis of simple faith. Afterwards, indeed, he will, if he has really been converted, read his Bible and come to a more and more correct view of Christ and of the meaning of Christ's death. If he does not come to a more and more correct view, one may perhaps suspect that his conversion was not a real one after all. But at the beginning all that is thought to be unnecessary. All that a man has to believe in at the beginning is conversion: he is saved on the basis of simple faith; correct opinions about God and Christ come later.

With regard to this method, it may of course be said at once that the "simple faith" thus spoken of is not faith at all; or, rather, it is not faith in Christ. A man cannot trust a person whom he holds to be untrustworthy. Faith always contains an intellectual element. A very little knowledge is often sufficient if a man is to believe, but some knowledge there must be. So if a man is to trust Christ, he must know something about Christ; he may know only a very little, but without some knowledge he could not believe at all.

What these advocates of a "simple faith" which involves no knowledge of Christ really mean by "simple faith" is faith, perhaps; but it is not faith in Christ. It is faith in the practitioners of the method, but it is not faith in Christ. To have faith in Christ, one must have knowledge of Christ, however slight, and it is not a matter of indifference whether the opinions held about Christ are true or false.

But is this modern anti-intellectualistic view of faith in accordance with the New Testament? Does the New Testament offer a man salvation first, on the basis of a psychological process of conversion or surrender—falsely called faith—and then preach the gospel to him afterwards; or does the New Testament preach the gospel to him first, set forth to him first the facts about Christ and the meaning of his death, and then ask him to accept the one thus presented in order that his soul may be saved?

That question can be answered very simply by an examination of the examples of conversion which the New Testament contains.

Three thousand were converted on the day of Pentecost. They were converted by Peter's sermon. What did Peter's sermon contain? Did it contain merely an account of Peter's own experience of salvation; did it consist solely in exhortation to the people to confess their sins? Not at all. What Peter did on the day of Pentecost was to set forth the facts about Jesus Christ— his life, his miracles, his death, his resurrection. It was on the basis of that setting forth of the facts about Christ that the three thousand believed, confessed their sins, and were saved.

Paul and Silas were in prison one night at Philippi. There was a miracle; the prisoners were released. The jailer was impressed and said, "What must I do to be saved?" Paul and Silas said: "Believe on the Lord Jesus Christ, and thou shalt be saved." Did the jailer believe then and there; was he saved without further delay? I think not. We are expressly told that Paul and Silas, after that, "spake unto him the word of the Lord." Then and not till then was he baptized, and I think we are plainly to understand that then and not till then was he saved.

Our Savior sat one day by the well. He talked with a sinful woman, and laid his finger upon the sore spot in her life. "Thou has had five husbands," he said, "and he whom thou now hast is not thy husband." The woman then apparently sought to evade the consideration of the sin in her own life by asking a theological question regarding the right place in which to worship God. What did Jesus do with her theological question? Did he brush it aside after the manner of modern religious workers? Did he say to the woman: "You are evading the real question; do not trouble yourself about theological matters, but let us return to the consideration of the sin in your life." Not at all. He answered that theological question with the utmost fullness, as though the salvation of the woman's soul depended on her obtaining the right answer. In reply to that sinful woman, and to what modern religious workers would have regarded as an evasive question, Jesus engaged in some of the profoundest theological teaching in the whole New Testament. A right view of God, according to Jesus, is not something that comes merely after salvation, but it is something important for salvation.

The apostle Paul in the first epistle to the Thessalonians gives a precious summary to his missionary preaching. He does so by telling what it was to which the Thessalonians turned when they were saved. Was it a mere program of life to which they turned? Was it a "simple faith," in the modern sense which divorces faith from knowledge and supposes that a man can have "simple faith" in a person of whom he knows nothing or about whom he holds opinions that make faith in him absurd? Not at all. In turning to Christ, those Thessalonian Christians turned to a whole system of theology. "Ye turned to God from idols," says Paul, "to serve the living and true God; and to wait for His Son from heaven, whom He raised from the dead, even Jesus, which delivereth us from the wrath to come." "Ye turned to God from idols"—there is theology proper. "And to wait for His Son from heaven"—there is Christology. "Whom He raised from the dead"—there is the supernatural act of God in history. "Even Jesus"—there is the humanity of our Lord. "Which delivereth us from the wrath to come"—there is the Christian doctrine of sin and the Christian doctrine of the cross of Christ.

So it is in the New Testament from beginning to end. The examples might be multiplied indefinitely. The New Testament gives not one bit of comfort to those who separate faith from knowledge, to those who hold the absurd view that a man can trust a person about whom he knows nothing. What many men despise today as "doctrine" the New Testament calls the gospel; and the New Testament treats it as the message upon which salvation depends.

But if that is so, if salvation depends upon the message in which Christ is offered as Savior, it is obviously important that we should get the message straight. That is where Christian scholarship comes in. Christian scholarship is important in order that we may tell the story of Jesus and his love straight and full and plain.

At this point, indeed, an objection may arise. Is not the gospel a very simple thing, it may be asked, and will not its simplicity be obscured by too much scholarly research? The objection springs from a false view of what scholarship is; it springs from the notion that scholarship leads a man to be obscure. Exactly the reverse is the case. Ignorance is obscure; but scholarship brings order out of confusion, places things in their logical relations, and makes the message shine forth clearly.

There are, indeed, evangelists who are not scholars, but scholarship is necessary to evangelism all the same. In the first place, though there are evangelists who are not scholars, the greatest evangelists, like the apostle Paul and like Martin Luther, have been scholars. In the second place, the

140   THE TASK OF CHRISTIAN SCHOLARSHIP

evangelists who are not scholars are dependent upon scholars to help them get their message straight; it is out of a great underlying fund of Christian learning that true evangelism springs.

That is something that the church of our day needs to take to heart. Life, according to the New Testament, is founded upon truth, and the attempt to reverse the order results only in despair and in spiritual death. Let us not deceive ourselves, my friends—Christian experience is necessary to evangelism, but evangelism does not consist merely in the rehearsal of what has happened in the evangelist's own soul. We shall, indeed, be but poor witnesses for Christ if we can tell only what Christ has done for the world or for the church and cannot tell what he has done personally for us. But we shall also be poor witnesses if we recount only the experiences of our own lives. Christian evangelism does not consist merely in a man's going about the world saying: "Look at me, what a wonderful experience I have, how happy I am, what wonderful Christian virtues I exhibit; you can all be as good and as happy as I am if you will just make a complete surrender of your wills in obedience to what I say." That is what many religious workers seem to think that evangelism is. We can preach the gospel, they tell us, by our lives, and do not need to preach it by our words. But they are wrong. Men are not saved by the exhibition of our glorious Christian virtues; they are not saved by the contagion of our experiences. We cannot be the instruments of God in saving them if we preach to them thus only ourselves. No, we must preach to them the Lord Jesus Christ, for it is only through the gospel which sets him forth that they can be saved.

If you want health for your souls, and if you want to be the instruments of bringing health to others, do not turn your gaze forever within, as though you could find Christ there. No, turn your gaze away from your own miserable experiences, away from your own sin, to the Lord Jesus Christ as he is offered to us in the gospel. "As Moses lifted up the serpent in the wilderness, even so must the Son of Man be lifted up." Only when we turn away from ourselves to that uplifted Savior shall we have healing for our deadly hurt.

It is the same old story, my friends—the same old story of the natural man. Men are trying today, as they have always been trying, to save themselves—to save themselves by their own act of surrender, by the excellence of their own faith, by mystic experiences of their own lives. But it is all in vain. Not that way is peace with God to be obtained. It is to be obtained only in the old, old way—by attention to something that was done once for all long ago, and by acceptance of the living Savior who there, once for all, brought redemption for our sin. Oh, that men would turn for salvation from their own experience to the cross of Christ; oh, that they would turn from the phenomena of religion to the living God!

That that may be done, there is but one way. It is not found in a study of the psychology of religion; it is not found in "religious education"; it is not found in an analysis of one's own spiritual status. Oh, no. It is found only in the blessed written Word. There are the words of life. There God speaks. Let us attend to his voice. Let us above all things know the Word. Let us study it with all our minds, let us cherish it with all our hearts. Then let us try, very humbly, to bring it to the unsaved. Let us pray that God may honor not the messengers but the message, that despite our unworthiness he may make his Word upon our unworthy lips to be a message of life.

12

CHRISTIAN SCHOLARSHIP
AND THE
DEFENSE OF THE FAITH

n speaking of Christian scholarship before the Bible League, I am somewhat in the position of bringing coals to New Castle, but perhaps you will take what I am saying as being an expression of hearty agreement with that scholarly work which your League has been carrying on so successfully for many years. This morning we considered the importance of Christian scholarship for evangelism. The gospel message, we observed, is not brought to a man after salvation has already been received, but it is brought to him in order that salvation may be received; and the fuller and plainer the message is, so much the more effective is it for the saving of souls.

But Christian scholarship is also necessary, in the second place, for the defense of the faith, and to this aspect of the subject I invite your attention this afternoon. There are, indeed, those who tell us that no defense of the faith is necessary. "The Bible needs no defense," they say; "let us not be for-

"Christian Scholarship and the Defense of the Faith" is an address originally delivered on June 17, 1932, in London before the Bible League of Great Britain, and published as part of the pamphlet, *The Importance of Christian Scholarship* (London: The Bible League, 1932). Reprinted in *What Is Christianity?* ed. Ned Bernard Stonehouse (Grand Rapids: Eerdmans, 1951).

ever defending Christianity, but instead let us go forth joyously to propagate Christianity." But I have observed one curious fact—when men talk thus about propagating Christianity without defending it, the thing that they are propagating is pretty sure not to be Christianity at all. They are propagating an anti-intellectualistic, nondoctrinal Modernism; and the reason why it requires no defense is simply that it is so completely in accord with the current of the age. It causes no more disturbance than does a chip that floats downward with a stream. In order to be an adherent of it, a man does not need to resist anything at all; he needs only to drift, and automatically his Modernism will be of the most approved and popular kind. One thing need always be remembered in the Christian church—true Christianity, now as always, is radically contrary to the natural man, and it cannot possibly be maintained without a constant struggle. A chip that floats downwards with the current is always at peace, but around every rock the waters foam and rage. Show me a professing Christian of whom all men speak well, and I will show you a man who is probably unfaithful to his Lord.

Certainly a Christianity that avoids argument is not the Christianity of the New Testament. The New Testament is full of argument in defense of the faith. The epistles of Paul are full of argument—no one can doubt that. But even the words of Jesus are full of argument in defense of the truth of what Jesus was saying. "If ye then, being evil, know how to give good gifts unto your children, how much more shall your Father which is in heaven give good things to them that ask him?" Is not that a well-known form of reasoning, which the logicians would put in its proper category? Many of the parables of Jesus are argumentative in character. Even our Lord, who spoke in the plenitude of divine authority, did condescend to reason with men. Everywhere the New Testament meets objections fairly, and presents the gospel as a thoroughly reasonable thing.

Some years ago I was in a company of students who were discussing methods of Christian work. An older man, who had had much experience in working among students, arose and said that according to his experience you never win a man to Christ until you stop arguing with him. When he said that, I was not impressed.

It is perfectly true, of course, that argument alone is quite insufficient to make a man a Christian. You may argue with him from now until the end of the world; you may bring forth the most magnificent arguments—but all will be in vain unless there is one other thing: the mysterious, creative power of the Holy Spirit in the new birth. But because argument is insufficient, it does not follow that it is unnecessary. Sometimes it is used directly by the Holy Spirit to bring a man to Christ. But more frequently it is used indirectly. A man hears an answer to objections raised against the truth of the Christian religion, and at the time when he hears it he is not impressed. But afterwards, perhaps many years afterwards, his heart at last is touched: he is convicted of sin; he desires to be saved. Yet without that half-forgotten argument he could not believe; the gospel would not seem to him to be true, and he would remain in his sin. As it is, however, the thought of what he has heard long ago comes into his mind; Christian apologetics at last has its day; the way is open, and when he will believe he can believe because he has been made to see that believing is not an offense against truth.

Sometimes, when I have tried—very imperfectly, I confess—to present arguments in defense of the resurrection of our Lord or of the truth, at this point or that, of God's Word, someone has come up to me after the lecture and has said to me very kindly: "We liked it, and we are impressed with the considerations that you have adduced in defense of the faith; but the trouble is, we all believed in the Bible already, and the persons that really needed the lecture are not here." When someone tells me that, I am not very greatly disturbed. True, I should have liked to have just as many skeptics as possible at my lecture, but if they are not there I do not necessarily think that my efforts are all in vain. What I am trying to do by my apologetic lecture is not merely—perhaps not even primarily—to convince people who are opposed to the Christian religion. Rather, I am trying to give to Christian people—Christian parents or Sunday school teachers—materials that they can use, not in dealing with avowed skeptics, whose backs are up against Christianity, but in dealing with their own children or with the pupils in their classes, who love them and long to be Christians as they are, but are troubled by the hostile voices on every side.

It is but a narrow view of Christian apologetics that regards the defense of the faith as being useful only in the immediate winning of those who are arguing vigorously on the other side. Rather, it is useful most of all in producing an intellectual atmosphere in which the acceptance of the gospel will seem to be something other than an offense against truth. Charles Spurgeon and D. L. Moody, in the latter years of the nineteenth century, were facing a situation entirely different from that which faces the evangelists of today. They were facing a world in which many people in their youth had been imbued with Christian convictions and in which public opinion, to a very considerable extent, was in favor of the Christian faith. Today, on the other hand, public opinion even in England and America is predominantly opposed to the Christian faith, and the people from their youth are imbued with the notion that Christian convictions are antiquated and absurd. Never was there a stronger call of God than there is today for a vigorous and scholarly defense of the faith.

I believe that the more thoughtful of the evangelists are coming to recognize that fact. There was a time, twenty-five or thirty years ago, when the evangelists regarded the work of Christian apologists as either impious or a waste of time. Here are souls to be saved, they said, and professors in theological seminaries insist on confusing their students' minds with a lot of German names, instead of preaching the simple gospel of Christ. But today a different temper often prevails. Evangelists, if they are real evangelists, real proclaimers of the unpopular message that the Bible contains, are coming more and more to see that they cannot do without those despised theological professors after all. It is useless to proclaim a gospel that people cannot hold to be true; no amount of emotional appeal can do anything against the truth. The question of fact cannot permanently be evaded. Did Christ or did he not rise from the dead; is the Bible trustworthy or is it false? In other words, the twelfth chapter of 1 Corinthians is coming again to its rights. We are coming to understand how many-sided is the work of Christ; the eye is ceasing to "say to the hand, 'I have no need of thee.' " Certainly one thing is clear—if Christian apologetics suffers, injury will come to every member of the body of Christ.

But if we are to have Christian apologetics, if we are to have a defense of the faith, what kind of defense of the faith should it be?

In the first place, it should be directed not only against the opponents outside the church but also against the opponents within. The opponents of Holy Scripture do not become less dangerous, but they become far more dangerous, when they are within ecclesiastical walls.

At that point, I am well aware that widespread objection arises at the present time. Let us above all, men say, have no controversy in the church; let us forget our small theological differences and all repeat together Paul's hymn to Christian love. As I listen to such pleas, my Christian friends, I think I can detect in them rather plainly the voice of Satan. That voice is heard, sometimes, on the lips of good and truly Christian men, as at Caesarea Philippi it was heard on the lips of the greatest of the Twelve. But Satan's voice it is, all the same.

Sometimes it comes to us in rather deceptive ways.

I remember, for example, what was said in my hearing on one occasion by a man who is generally regarded as one of the leaders of the evangelical Christian church. It was said at the climax of a day of devotional services. "If you go heresy-hunting for the sin in your own wicked hearts," said the speaker, as nearly as I can remember his words, "you will have no time for heresy-hunting for the heretics outside."

Thus did temptation come through the mouth of a well-meaning man. The "heretics," to use the term that was used by that speaker, are, with their helpers, the indifferentists, in control of the church within the bounds of which that utterance was made, the Presbyterian Church in the United States of America, as they are in control of nearly all the larger Protestant churches in the world. A man hardly needs to "hunt" them very long if he is to oppose them. All that he needs to do is to be faithful to the Lord Jesus Christ, and his opposition to those men will follow soon enough.

But is it true, as this speaker seemed to imply, that there is a conflict between faithfulness to Christ in the ecclesiastical world and the cultivation of holiness in one's own inner life? My friends, it is not true, but false. A man cannot successfully go heresy-hunting against the sin in his own life if he is willing to deny his Lord in the presence of the enemies outside. The two battles are intimately connected. A man cannot fight successfully in one unless he fights also in the other.

Again, we are told that our theological differences will disappear if we will just get down on our knees together in prayer. Well, I can only say about that kind of prayer, which is indifferent to the question whether the gospel is true or false, that it is not Christian prayer; it is bowing down in the house of Rimmon. God save us from it! Instead, may God lead us to the kind of prayer in which, recognizing the dreadful condition of the visible church, recognizing the unbelief and the sin which dominate it today, we who are opposed to the current of the age both in the world and in the church, facing the facts as they are, lay those facts before God, as Hezekiah laid before him the threatening letter of the Assyrian enemy, and humbly ask him to give the answer.

Again, men say that instead of engaging in controversy in the church, we ought to pray to God for a revival; instead of polemics, we ought to have evangelism. Well, what kind of revival do you think that will be? What sort of evangelism is it that is indifferent to the question what evangel is it that is to be preached? Not a revival in the New Testament sense, not the evangelism that Paul meant when he said, "Woe is unto me, if I preach not the gospel." No, my friends, there can be no true evangelism which makes common cause with the enemies of the cross of Christ. Souls will hardly be saved unless the evangelists can say with Paul: "If we or an angel from heaven preach any other gospel than that which we preached unto you, let him be accursed!" Every true revival is born in controversy, and leads to more controversy. That has been true ever since our Lord said that he came not to bring peace upon the earth but a sword. And do you know what I think will happen when God sends a new reformation upon the church? We cannot tell when that blessed day will come. But when the blessed day does come, I think we can say at least one result that it will bring. We shall hear nothing on that day about the evils of controversy in the church. All that will be swept away as with a mighty flood. A man who is on fire with a message never talks in that wretched, feeble way, but proclaims the truth joyously and fearlessly, in the presence of every high thing that is lifted up against the gospel of Christ.

But men tell us that instead of engaging in controversy about doctrine, we ought to seek the power of the living Holy Spirit. A few years ago we had in America, as I suppose you had here, a celebration of the anniversary of Pentecost. At that time, our Presbyterian church was engaged in a conflict, the gist of which concerned the question of the truth of the Bible. Was the church going to insist, or was it not going to insist, that its ministers should believe that the Bible is true? At that time of decision, and almost, it seemed, as though to evade the issue, many sermons were preached on the subject of the Holy Spirit. Do you think that those sermons, if they really were preached in that way, were approved by him with whom they dealt? I fear not, my friends. A man can hardly receive the power of the Holy Spirit if he seeks to evade the question whether the blessed book that the Spirit has given us is true or false.

Again, men tell us that our preaching should be positive and not negative, that we can preach the truth without attacking error. But if we follow that advice, we shall have to close our Bible and desert its teachings. The New Testament is a polemic book almost from beginning to end. Some years ago I was in a company of teachers of the Bible in the colleges and other educational institutions of America. One of the most eminent theological professors in the country made an address. In it he admitted that there are unfortunate controversies about doctrine in the epistles of Paul; but, said he in effect, the real essence of Paul's teaching is found in the hymn to Christian love in the thirteenth chapter of 1 Corinthians, and we can avoid controversy today if we will only devote the chief attention to that inspiring hymn. In reply, I am bound to say that the example was singularly ill-chosen. That hymn to Christian love is in the midst of a great polemic passage; it would never have been written if Paul had been opposed to controversy with error in the church. It was because his soul was stirred within him by a wrong use of the spiritual gifts that he was able to write that glorious hymn. So it is always in the church. Every really great Christian utterance, it may almost be said, is born in controversy. It is when men have felt compelled to take a stand against error that they have risen to the really great heights in the celebration of truth.

But in defending the faith against the attack upon it that is being made both without and within the church, what method of defense should be used?

In answer to that question, I have time only to say two things. In the first place, the defense, with the polemic that it involves, should be perfectly open and aboveboard. I have just stated that I believe in controversy. But in controversy I do try to observe the Golden Rule; I do try to do unto others as I would have others do unto me. And the kind of controversy that pleases me in an opponent is a controversy that is altogether frank.

Sometimes I go into a company of modern men. A man gets up upon the platform, looks out benignly upon the audience, and says: "I think, brethren, that we are all agreed about this"—and then proceeds to trample ruthlessly upon everything that is dearest to my heart. When he does that, I feel aggrieved. I do not feel aggrieved because he gives free expression to opinions that are different from mine. But I feel aggrieved because he calls me his "brother" and assumes, prior to investigation, that I agree with what he is going to say. A kind of controversy that pleases me better than that is a kind of controversy in which a man gets up upon the platform, looks out upon the audience, and says: "What is this? I see that one of those absurd Fundamentalists has somehow strayed into this company of educated men"— and then proceeds to call me by every opprobrious term that is to be found in one of the most unsavory paragraphs of Roget's *Thesaurus*. When he does that, I do not feel too much distressed. I can even endure the application to me of the term "Fundamentalist," though for the life of me I cannot see why adherents of the Christian religion, which has been in the world for some nineteen hundred years, should suddenly be made an "-ism" and be called by some strange new name. The point is that that speaker at least does me the honor of recognizing that a profound difference separates my view from his. We understand each other perfectly, and it is quite possible that we may be, if not brothers (I object to the degradation of that word), yet at least good friends.

In the second place, the defense of the faith should be of a scholarly kind. Mere denunciation does not constitute an argument; and before a man can refute successfully an argument of an opponent, he must understand the argument that he is endeavoring to refute. Personalities, in such debate, should be kept in the background; and analysis of the motives of one's opponents has little place.

That principle, certainly in America, has been violated constantly by the advocates of the Modernist or indifferentist position in the church. It has been violated by them far more than by the defenders of God's Word. Yet the latter, strangely enough, have received the blame. The representatives of the dominant Modern-indifferentist forces have engaged in the most violent adjectival abuse of their opponents, yet they have been called sweet and beautiful and tolerant. The defenders of the Bible and of the historic position of the church have spoken courteously, though plainly, in opposition, and have been called "bitter" and "extreme." I am reminded of the way in which an intelligent American Indian is reported (I saw it in the American magazine *The Saturday Evening Post* a few months ago) to have characterized the terminology used in histories of the wars between the white men and the men of his race. "When you won," said the Indian, "it was, according to your histories, a 'battle'; when we won, it was a 'massacre.'"

Such, I suppose, is the treatment of the unpopular side in every conflict. Certainly it is the treatment which we receive today. Men have found it to be an effective way of making themselves popular, to abuse the representatives of so unpopular a cause as that which we Bible-believing Christians represent.

Yet I do not think we ought to be dismayed. If in these days of unbelief and defection in the church we are called upon to bear just a little bit of the reproach of Christ, we ought to count ourselves honored, and certainly we ought not mitigate in the slightest measure the plainness either of our defense of the truth or of our warnings against error. Men's favor is worth very little, after all, in comparison with the favor of Christ.

But certainly we should strive to keep ourselves free from that with which we are charged. Because our opponents are guilty, that is no reason why we should make ourselves guilty too.

It is no easy thing to defend the Christian faith against the mighty attack that is being brought against it at the present day. Knowledge of the truth is necessary, and also clear acquaintance with the forces hostile to the truth in modern thought.

At that point, a final objection may arise. Does it not involve a terrible peril to men's souls to ask them—for example, in their preparation for the ministry—to acquaint themselves with things that are being said against the gospel of the Lord Jesus Christ?

Would it not be safer to learn only of the truth, without acquainting ourselves with error? We answer, "Of course it would be *safer*." It would be far safer, no doubt, to live in a fool's paradise and close one's eyes to what is going on in the world today, just as it is safer to remain in secure dugouts rather than to go over the top in some great attack. We save our souls, perhaps, by such tactics, but the Lord's enemies remain in possession of the field. It is a great battle indeed, this intellectual battle of today; deadly perils await every man who engages in that conflict—but it is the Lord's battle, and he is a great Captain in the fight.

There are, indeed, some perils that should be avoided—particularly the peril of acquainting ourselves with what is said against the Christian religion without ever obtaining any really orderly acquaintance with what can be said for it. That is the peril to which a candidate for ministry, for example, subjects himself when he attends only one of the theological colleges where the professors are adherents of the dominant naturalistic view. What does such a course of study mean? It means simply this: that a man does not think the historic Christian faith, which has given him his spiritual nurture, to be worthy of a fair hearing. That is my only argument in advising a man to study, for example, at an institution like Westminster Theological Seminary, which I have the honor to serve. I am not asking him to close his eyes to what can be said against the historic faith. But I am telling him that the logical order is to learn what a thing is before one attends exclusively to what can be said against it; and I am telling him further that the way to learn what a thing is is not to listen first to its opponents, but to grant a full hearing to those who believe in it with all their minds and hearts. After that has been done, after our students, by pursuing the complete course of study, have obtained something like an ordinary acquaintance with the marvelous system of truth that the Bible contains, then the more they listen to what can be said against it, the better defenders of it they will probably be.

Let us therefore pray that God will raise up for us today true defenders of the Christian faith. We are living in the midst of a mighty conflict against the Christian religion. The conflict is carried on with intellectual weapons. Whether we like it or not, there are millions upon millions of our fellow men who reject Christianity for the simple reason that they do not believe Christianity to be true. What is to be done in such a situation?

We can learn, at this point, a lesson from the past history of the church. This is not the first time during the past nineteen hundred years when intellectual objections have been raised against the gospel of Christ. How have those objections been treated? Have they been evaded or have they been faced? The answer is writ large in the history of the church. The objections have been faced. God has raised up in time of need not only evangelists to appeal to the multitude, but also Christian scholars to meet the intellectual attack. So it will be in our day, my friends. The Christian religion flourishes not in the darkness but in the light. Intellectual slothfulness is but a quack remedy for unbelief; the true remedy is consecration of intellectual powers to the service of the Lord Jesus Christ.

Let us not fear for the result. Many times, in the course of the past nineteen hundred years, men have predicted that in a generation or so the old gospel would be forever forgotten. Yet the gospel has burst forth again, and set the world aflame. So it may be in our age, in God's good time and in his way. Sad indeed are the substitutes for the gospel of Christ. The church has been beguiled into Bypath Meadow, and is now groaning in the dungeon of Giant Despair. Happy is the man who can point out to such a church the straight, high road that leads over hill and valley to the City of God.

13

CHRISTIAN SCHOLARSHIP AND THE BUILDING UP OF THE CHURCH

We have been discussing today the uses of Christian scholarship. It is important, we showed this morning, for evangelism; it is important, in the second place, as we showed this afternoon, for the defense of the faith. But it has still another use. It is important, in the third place, for the building up of the church.

At this point, as at the first two points, we have the New Testament on our side. At the beginning of the church's life, as we are told in the book of Acts, the apostolic church continued steadfastly, not only in fellowship and in breaking of bread and prayers, but also in the apostles' teaching. There is no encouragement whatever, in the New Testament, for the notion that when a man has been converted, all has been done for him that needs to be done. Read the epistles of Paul, in particular, from that point of view. Paul was the greatest of evangelists, and he gloried particularly in preaching the gospel just in places where it had never been heard; yet his epistles

"Christian Scholarship and the Building Up of the Church" is an address originally delivered on June 17, 1932, in London before the Bible League of Great Britain, and published as part of the pamphlet, *The Importance of Christian Scholarship* (London: The Bible League, 1932). Reprinted in *What Is Christianity?* ed. Ned Bernard Stonehouse (Grand Rapids: Eerdmans, 1951).

are full of the edification or building up of those who have already been won, and the whole New Testament clearly discourages the exclusive nourishment of Christians with milk instead of with solid food.

In the modern church, this important work of edification has been sadly neglected; it has been neglected even by some of those who believe that the Bible is the Word of God. Too often doctrinal preaching has been pushed from the primary place, in which it rightly belongs, to a secondary place; exhortation has taken the place of systematic instruction; and the people have not been built up. Is it any wonder that a church thus nurtured is carried away with every wind of doctrine and is helpless in the presence of unbelief? A return to solid instruction in the pulpit, at the desk of the Sunday school teacher, and particularly in the home is one of the crying needs of the hour.

I do not mean that a sermon should be a lecture; I do not mean that a preacher should address his congregation as a teacher addresses his class. No doubt some young preachers do err in that way. Impressed with the truth that we are trying to present tonight, they have endeavored to instruct the people in Christian doctrine, but in their efforts to be instructive they have put entirely too many points into one sermon and the congregation has been confused. That error, unquestionably, should be avoided. But it should be avoided not by the abandonment of doctrinal preaching, but by our making doctrinal preaching real *preaching*. The preacher should present to his congregation the doctrine that the Holy Scripture contains, but he should fire the presentation of that doctrine with the devotion of the heart, and he should show how it can be made fruitful for Christian life.

One thing that impresses me about preaching today is the neglect of true edification even by evangelical preachers. What the preacher says is often good, and by it genuine Christian emotion is aroused. But a man could sit under the preaching for a year or ten years, and at the end of the time he would be just about where he was at the beginning. Such a lamentably small part of Scripture truth is used; the congregation is never made acquainted with the wonderful variety of what the Bible contains. I trust that God may raise up for us preachers of a different type; I trust that those preachers may not only build upon the one foundation which is Jesus Christ, but may build upon that foundation not wood, hay, stubble, but gold, silver, precious stones. Do you, if you are preachers or teachers in the church, want to be saved merely so as through fire, or do you want your work to endure in the day of Jesus Christ? There is one work at least which I think we may hold, in all humility, to be sure to stand the test of judgment fire; it is the humble im-partation, Sunday by Sunday, or day by day, of a solid knowledge not of what you say or what any man has said, but of what God has told us in his Word.

Is that work too lowly; is it too restricted to fire the ambition of our souls? No, my friends, a hundred lifetimes would not begin to explore the riches of what the Scriptures contain.

Some years ago, when I was still at Princeton Theological Seminary, be-fore the reorganization of that institution, we received one of the countless questionnaires which in America have become, with one's neighbor's radio, one of the nuisances of modern life. The man who sent out the question-naire was threatening, I believe, to write a book on theological education, and afterwards he carried out his threat. The questionnaire begged the ques-tion as many questionnaires do; it was not, if I remember rightly, in the slightest interested in the question whether a high scholarly standard was maintained in the study of the Bible; it did not seem to be much interested in discovering whether the students were or were not required to know the languages in which the Bible is written; but there were all sorts of questions about courses in hygiene and the like. In short, one prominent purpose of sending us the questionnaire seemed to be that of discovering whether Princeton Theological Seminary was or was not a medical school.

I am no longer connected with Princeton Theological Seminary, since its reorganization in 1929, and so cannot speak for that institution. But I may say that Westminster Theological Seminary, which I now have the honor to serve, is not pretending to be a medical school at all. We are not striving to train experts in hygiene or in first aid; we are not trying to make specialists in sociology or even specialists in religion. But what we are try-ing to do is to make specialists in the Bible, and we think that that is a large enough specialty for any man to give to it his life.

What a world in itself the Bible is, my friends! Happy are those who in the providence of God can make the study of it very specifically the busi-ness of their lives, but happy also is every Christian who has it open before him and seeks by daily study to penetrate somewhat into the wonderful rich-ness of what it contains.

A man does not need to read very long in the Bible before that richness begins to appear. It appears in the very first verse of the Bible, for the very first verse sets forth the being of God: "In the beginning God created the heaven and the earth."

We are told today, indeed, that that is metaphysics, and that it is a matter of indifference to the Christian man.[1] To be a Christian, it is said, a man does not need at all to settle the question how the universe came into being. The doctrine of "fiat creation," we are told, belongs to philosophy, not to religion; and we can be worshipers of goodness even though goodness is not clothed with the vulgar trappings of power.

But to talk thus is to talk nonsense, for the simple reason that goodness divorced from power is a mere abstraction which can never call forth the devotion of a man's heart. Goodness inheres only in persons; goodness implies the power to act. Make God good only and not powerful, and you have done away not only with God, but with goodness as well.

Very different from such a pale abstraction, which identifies God with one aspect of the universe, is the God whom the first verse of Genesis presents. That God is the living God; it is he by whom the worlds were made and by whom they are upheld.

No, my friends, it is altogether wrong to say that the Christian religion can do perfectly well with many different types of philosophy, and that metaphysical questions are a matter of indifference to the Christian man. Nothing could be further from the truth. As a matter of fact, everything else that the Bible contains is based upon the stupendous metaphysic that the first verse of Genesis contains. That was the metaphysic of our Lord Jesus Christ, and without it everything that he said and everything that he did would be in vain. Underlying all his teaching and all his example is the stupendous recognition that God is the Maker and Ruler of the world, and the Bible from beginning to end depends upon that same "philosophy" of a personal God.

That philosophy ought to have been clear from an examination of the universe as it is; the Maker is revealed by the things that he has made. "The Heavens declare the glory of God, and the firmament sheweth His handywork." "The invisible things of Him from the creation of the world are clearly seen, being understood by the things that are made, even His eternal power and Godhead." Natural religion has, therefore, the full sanction of the Bible, and at the foundation of every theological course should be philosophical apologetics, including the proof of the existence of a personal God, Creator, and Ruler of the world.

1. With what follows compare the treatment by the lecturer in *What Is Faith* (1925), 46–66.

I know there are those who tell us today that no such study is necessary; there are those who tell us that we should begin with Jesus, and that all we need to know is that God is like Jesus. They talk to us in that sense about the "Christlike God." But do you not see that if you relinquish the thought of a personal God, Creator, and Ruler of the world, you are dishonoring the teaching of Jesus from beginning to end? Jesus saw in the lilies of the field the weaving of God; and the man who wipes out of his consciousness the whole wonderful revelation of God in nature, and then says that all that he needs to know is that God is like Jesus, is dishonoring at the very root of his teaching and of his example that same Jesus whom he is purporting to honor and serve.

The existence of a personal God should have been clear to us from the world as it is, but that revelation of God in nature has been obscured by sin, and to recover it and confirm it we need the blessed supernatural revelation that the Scriptures contain. How graciously that revelation is given! When we rise from the reading of the Bible, if we have read with understanding and with faith, what a wonderful knowledge we have of the living God!

In his presence, indeed, we can never lose the sense of wonder. Infinitesimal are the things that we know compared with things that we do not know; a dreadful curtain veils the being of God from the eyes of man. Yet that curtain, in the infinite goodness of God, has been pulled gently aside, and we have been granted just a look beyond. Never can we cease to wonder in the presence of God, but enough knowledge has been granted to us that we may adore.

The second great mystery that the Bible presents is the mystery of man. And we are not allowed to wait long for that mystery. It is presented to us, as is the mystery of God, in the early part of the first book of the Bible. Man is there presented in his utter distinctness from the rest of the creation, and then he is presented to us in the awful mystery of his sin.

At that point, it is interesting to observe how the Bible, unlike modern religious literature, always defines its terms; and at the beginning, when the Bible speaks of sin, it makes clear exactly what sin is. According to the Westminster Shorter Catechism, if you will pardon an allusion to that upon which your speaker was brought up, "sin is any want of conformity unto, or transgression of, the law of God." I do not remember, at the moment, what proof-texts the authors of the Westminster Standards used to support that definition. But they need hardly have looked further for such proof-texts than to the early part of Genesis. "Ye shall not eat of the tree," said God; man ate of the tree and died. Sin is there presented with the utmost clearness as the transgression of law. So it is presented in the whole of the Bible. Sin and law belong together. When we say "sin," we have said "law"; when we have said "law," then, man being what he now is, we have said "sin."

At the present time, the existence of law is being denied. Men no longer believe that there is such a thing as a law of God, and naturally they do not believe that there is such a thing as sin. Thoughtful men, who are not Christians, are aware of the problem that this stupendous change in human thinking presents to the modern world. Now that men no longer believe that there is a law of God, now that men no longer believe in obligatory morality, now that the moral law has been abandoned, what is to be put in its place, in order that an ordinarily decent human life may be preserved upon the earth? It cannot be said that the answers proposed for that question are as satisfactory as the way in which the question itself is put. It is impossible to keep back the raging seas of human passion with the flimsy mud embankments of an appeal either to self-interest or to what Walter Lippmann calls "disinterestedness." Those raging seas can only be checked by the solid masonry of the law of God.

Men are wondering today what is wrong with the world. They are conscious of the fact that they are standing over some terrible abyss. Awful ebullitions rise from that abyss. We have lost altogether the sense of the security of our Western civilization. Men are wondering what is wrong.

It is perfectly clear what is wrong. The law of God has been torn up, as though it were a scrap of paper, and the inevitable result is appearing with ever greater clearness. When will the law be rediscovered? When it is rediscovered, that will be a day of terror for mankind, but it will also be a day of joy, for the law will be a schoolmaster unto Christ. Its terrors will drive men back to the little wicket gate, and to the way that leads to that place somewhat ascending where they will see the cross.

Those are the two great presuppositions of everything else that the Bible contains; the two great presuppositions are the majesty of the transcendent God and the guilt and misery of man in his sin. But we are not left to wait long for the third of the great mysteries—the mystery of salvation. That too is presented at the beginning of Genesis, in the promise of a redemption to come.

The rest of the Bible is the unfolding of that promise. And when I think of that unfolding, when I try to take the Bible not in part, but as a whole, when I contemplate not this doctrine or that, but the marvelous *system* of doctrine that the Bible contains, I am amazed that in the presence of such riches men can be content with that other gospel which now dominates the preaching in the church.

When I think again of the wonderful metaphysic in the first verse of Genesis—"In the beginning God created the heaven and the earth"—when I think of the way in which throughout the Old Testament the majesty of that Creator God is presented with wonderful clearness, until the presentation culminates in the matchless fortieth chapter of Isaiah—"It is he that sitteth upon the circle of the earth, and the inhabitants thereof are as grasshoppers, that stretcheth out the heavens as a curtain, and spreadeth them out as a tent to dwell in"—when I think of the way in which in that same chapter the tenderness and the gentleness of that same awful God are presented, in a manner far beyond all human imagining—"He shall feed his flock like a shepherd; he shall gather the lambs with his arm, and carry them in his bosom, and shall gently lead those that are with young"—when I think of the wonderful gallery of portraits in the Old Testament, and compare it with the best efforts of men who have sought to penetrate into the secrets of human life and of the human heart; when I think of the gracious dealings of God with his people in Old Testament times, until the fullness of the time was come, and the Savior was born into the world; when I think of the way in which his coming was accomplished, by a stupendous miracle indeed, but in wonderful quietness and lowliness; when I think of the songs of the heavenly host, and the way in which the infant Savior was greeted in the Temple by those who had waited for the redemption of Jerusalem; when I stand in awe before that strange answer of the youthful Jesus, "Wist ye not that I must be about my Father's business?"; when I try to keep my imagination at rest, as Scripture bids me do, regarding those long, silent years at Nazareth; when I think of the day of his showing to Israel; when I think of the sternness of his teaching, the way in which he pulled the cloak from human sin, the way in which, by revealing through his words and his example the real demands of God, he took from mankind its last hope of any salvation to be obtained through its own goodness; when I think, again, of the wonderful kindness of the Savior; when I read how he forgave where none other would forgive, and helped where all other helpers had failed; when I think, above all, of that blessed thing which he did not only for men of long ago, who saw him with their bodily eyes, but for every one of us if we are united with him through faith, when he died in our stead upon the cross, and said in triumph, at the moment when his redeeming work was done, "It is finished"; when I enter into both the fear and the joy of those who found the tomb empty and saw the vision of angels which also said, "He is not here: for He is risen"; when I think of the way in which he was known to his disciples in the breaking of bread; when I think of Pentecost and the pouring out of his Spirit upon the church; when I attend to the wonderful way in which the Bible tells us how this Savior may be our Savior today, how you and I, sitting in this house tonight, can come into his presence, in even far more intimate fashion than that which was enjoyed by those who pushed their way unto him as he sat amid scribes and Pharisees when he was on earth; when I think of the application of his redeeming work by the Holy Spirit:

> Be of sin the double cure,
> Cleanse me from its guilt and power;

when I think of the glories of the Christian life, opened to us, not on the basis of human striving, but of that mighty act of God; when I read the last book of the Bible, and think of the unfolding of the glorious hope of that time when the once-lowly Jesus, now seated on the throne of all being, shall come again with power—when I think of these things, I am impressed with the fact that the other gospel, which is dominant in the church today preached though it is by brilliant men, and admirable though it might have seemed if we had not compared it with something infinitely greater, is naught but "weak and beggarly elements," and that the humblest man who believes that the Bible is the Word of God is possessed of riches greater by far than all the learning of all the world and all the eloquence of all the preachers who now have the ear of an unfaithful church.

14

THE NECESSITY OF THE CHRISTIAN SCHOOL

The Christian school is to be favored for two reasons. In the first place, it is important for American liberty; in the second place, it is important for the propagation of the Christian religion. These two reasons are not equally important; indeed, the latter includes the former as it includes every other legitimate human interest. But I want to speak of these two reasons in turn.

In the first place, then, the Christian school is important for the maintenance of American liberty.

We are witnessing in our day a worldwide attack upon the fundamental principles of civil and religious freedom. In some countries, such as Italy, the attack has been blatant and unashamed; Mussolini despises democracy and does not mind saying so. A similar despotism now prevails in Germany; and in Russia freedom is being crushed out by what is perhaps the most complete and systematic tyranny that the world has ever seen.

But exactly the same tendency that is manifested in extreme reform in those countries is also being manifested, more slowly but nonetheless surely,

"The Necessity of the Christian School" is an address originally delivered in August 1933 before the Educational Convention of the National Union of Christian Schools in Chicago, and appeared in *Forward in Faith* (Educational Convention Year Book, 1933), 5–30. Reprinted in *What Is Christianity?* ed. Ned Bernard Stonehouse (Grand Rapids: Eerdmans, 1951).

in America. It has been given an enormous impetus first by the war and now by the economic depression; but aside from these external stimuli, it had its roots in a fundamental deterioration of the American people. Gradually the people have come to value principle less and creature comfort more; increasingly they have come to prefer prosperity to freedom; and even in the field of prosperity it cannot be said that the effect is satisfactory.

The result of this decadence in the American people is seen in the rapid growth of a centralized bureaucracy which is the thing against which the Constitution of the United States was most clearly intended to guard.

In the presence of this apparent collapse of free democracy, any descendant of the liberty-loving races of mankind may well stand dismayed, and to those liberty-loving races no doubt most of my hearers tonight belong. I am of the Anglo-Saxon race; many of you belong to a race whose part in the history of human freedom is if anything still more glorious. And as we all contemplate the struggle of our fathers in the winning of that freedom which their descendants seem now to be so willing to give up, we are impressed anew with the fact that it is far easier to destroy than to create. It took many centuries of struggle—much blood and many tears—to establish the fundamental principles of our civil and religious liberty, but one mad generation is sufficient to throw them all away.

It is true, the attack upon liberty is nothing new. Always there have been tyrants in the world; almost always tyranny has begun by being superficially beneficent, and always it has ended by being both superficially and radically cruel.

But while tyranny itself is nothing new, the technique of tyranny has been enormously improved in our day; the tyranny of the scientific expert is the most crushing tyranny of all. That tyranny is being exercised most effectively in the field of education. A monopolistic system of education controlled by the state is far more efficient in crushing our liberty than the cruder weapons of fire and sword. Against this monopoly of education by the state the Christian school brings a salutary protest; it contends for the right of parents to bring up their children in accordance with the dictates of their conscience and not in the manner prescribed by the state.

That right has been attacked in America in recent years in the most blatant possible ways. In Oregon, a law was actually passed some years ago requiring all children to attend the public school—thus taking the children from the control of their parents and placing them under the despotic control of whatever superintendent of education might happen to be in office in the district in which they resided. In Nebraska, a law was passed forbidding the study of languages other than English, even in private schools, until the child was too old to learn them well. That was really a law making literary education a crime. In New York, one of the abominable Lusk Laws placed even private tutors under state supervision and control.

It is true that no one of these measures is in force at the present time. The Lusk Laws were repealed, largely through the efforts of Governor Alfred E. Smith. The Oregon School Law and the Nebraska Language Law were declared unconstitutional by the United States Supreme Court, and Justice McReynolds in the decision in the latter case gave expression to the great principle that in America the child is not the mere creature of the state.

Even such salutary decisions as that are not to be contemplated with unmixed feelings by the lover of American institutions. They are based, I suppose, upon the great "Bill of Rights" provisions of the Constitution of the United States. But the original intent of those provisions was that they should be a check upon Congress, not that they should be a check upon the states. The fundamental rights of man were to be guaranteed, it was assumed, by the constitutions of the individual states, so far as the powers reserved to the states are concerned. It is a sign of appalling deterioration when the federal Supreme Court steps in to do what the state courts ought to do. Nevertheless, we cannot help rejoicing at the result. For the present at least, such an excess of tyranny as was put into effect in Oregon and has been seriously advocated in Michigan and other states is postponed.

Yet the forces inimical to liberty have not been discouraged by these temporary checks. They are at work with great persistency just at the present time, busying themselves particularly in the advocacy of two vicious measures, both of which concern childhood and youth.

One of these is the misnamed "child-labor amendment" to the Constitution of the United States. That amendment masquerades under the cloak of humanitarianism; it is supposed to be intended to prevent sweatshop conditions or the like. As a matter of fact, it is just about as heartless a piece of proposed legislation as could possibly be conceived. Many persons who glibly favor this amendment seem never to have read it for themselves. They have a vague notion that it merely gives power to regulate the gainful employment of children. Not at all. The word "labor" was expressly insisted on in the wording of the amendment as over against the word "employment." The amendment gives power to Congress to enter right into your home and regulate or control or prevent altogether the helpful work of your children without which there can be no normal development of human character and no ordinary possibility of true happiness for mankind.

But, someone will say, Congress will never in the world be so foolish as that; the amendment does give Congress that power, but the power will never be exercised. Now, my friends, I will just say this: when I listen to an argument like that, I sometimes wonder whether the person who advances it can possibly be convinced by it himself. If these stupendous powers are never to be exercised, why should they be granted? The zeal for the granting of them, the refusal of the framers of the amendment to word the amendment in any reasonably guarded way, show plainly that the powers are intended to be exercised; and certainly they will be exercised, whatever the intention of the framers of the amendment may be. I will tell you exactly what will happen if this amendment is adopted by the states. Congress will pass legislation which, in accordance with the plain meaning of the language, will be quite unenforceable. The exact degree of enforcement will be left to Washington bureaus, and the individual family will be left to the arbitrary decision of officials. It would be difficult to imagine anything more hostile to the decency of family life and to all the traditions of our people. If there ever was a measure that looked as though it were made in Russia, it is this falsely so-called child-labor amendment to the Constitution of the United States. In reality, it can hardly be called an amendment to the Constitution. Rather, it is the complete destruction of the Constitution, for if human life in its formative period—up to eighteen years in the life of every youth—is to be given to federal bureaucrats, we do not see what else of very great value can remain. The old principles of individual liberty and local self-government will simply have been wiped out.

This so-called child-labor amendment was originally submitted to the states a number of years ago. It was in process of being rushed right through without any more examination than other amendments received. But then fortunately some patriotic citizens in Massachusetts, especially in the organization called "the Sentinels of the Republic," informed the people of the state what was really involved in this vicious measure. Massachusetts had a strict child-labor law; it might have been expected, therefore, in accordance with the customary specious argument, to need protection against states where the child-labor laws are less strict. Yet in a referendum the amendment was rejected by an overwhelming vote. Other states followed suit, and it looked as though this attack upon American institutions and the decencies of the American home had been repelled.

But we are living now in another period of hysteria, a period even worse than that which was found at the time of the war. So the so-called child-labor amendment has been revived. State after state has adopted it, to a total number, I believe, of fourteen. It looks as though the enemies of American institutions might soon have their will, and as though the childhood and youth of our country might be turned over after all to the tender mercies of Washington bureaus. That disastrous result can only be prevented if there is an earnest effort of those who still think the preservation of the American home to be worthwhile.

Another line of attack upon liberty has appeared in the advocacy of a federal department of education. Repeatedly this vicious proposal has been introduced in Congress. It has been consistently favored by that powerful organization, the National Education Association. Now without being familiar with the internal workings of that association, I venture to doubt whether its unfortunate political activities really represent in any adequate way the rank and file of its members or the rank and file of the public-school teachers of this country. When I appeared at a joint hearing before the Senate Committee on Education and Labor and the House Committee on Education in 1926, Mr. Lowrey of the House Committee asked me how it was that the resolution favoring the federal department of education was passed unanimously by the National Education Association although he had discovered that many members of that association were saying that they were opposed to it. Neither Mr. Lowrey nor I seemed to be able to give any very good explanation of this fact. At any rate, I desire to pay the warmest possible tribute to many thousands of conscientious men and women who are teachers in the public schools of this country. I do not believe that in the entire governmental aspect of education these teachers have any really effective representation.

The commission on the subject which President Hoover appointed, for example, was composed hardly at all of teachers, but almost exclusively of "educators." It had within its membership professors of "education," superintendents of schools and the like; but in the entire roll of its membership there was found, if I remember right, hardly a single eminent in any branch of literary studies or of natural science. The composition of that commission was typical of one of the fundamental vices in education in America at the present time—namely, the absurd overemphasis upon methodology in the sphere of education at the expense of content. When a man fits himself in America to teach history or chemistry, it scarcely seems to occur to him, or rather it scarcely seems to occur to those who prescribe his studies for him, that he ought to study history or chemistry. Instead, he studies merely "education." The study of education seems to be regarded as absolving a teacher from obtaining any knowledge of the subject that he is undertaking to teach. And the pupils are being told, in effect, that the simple storing up in the mind of facts concerning the universe and human life is a drudgery from which they have now been emancipated; they are being told, in other words, that the great discovery has been made in modern times that it is possible to learn how to "think" with a completely empty mind. It cannot be said that the result is impressive. In fact, the untrammeled operation of the effects of this great American pedogogic discovery is placing American schools far behind the schools of the rest of the civilized world.

But that is perhaps something like a digression. Let us return to the "educators" and their general demand either for a federal department of education or for federal aid to the states. Such demands are in the interests of uniformity in the sphere of education. There should be, it is said, a powerful coordinating agency in education, to set up standards and encourage the production of something like a system. But what shall we say of such an aim? I have no hesitation, for my part, in saying that I am dead opposed to it. Uniformity in education, it seems to me, is one of the worst calamities into which any people can fall.

There are, it is true, some spheres in which uniformity is a good thing. It is a good thing, for example, in the making of Ford cars. In the making of a Ford car, uniformity is the great end of the activity. That end is, indeed, not always fully attained. Sometimes a Ford car possesses entirely too much individuality. My observation was, in the heroic days before the invention of self-starters, when a Ford was still a Ford, that sometimes a Ford car would start and sometimes it would not start; and if it would not start, there was no use whatever in giving it any encouraging advice. But although uniformity was not always perfectly attained, the aim, at least, was to attain it; the purpose of the whole activity was that one Ford car should be just as much like every other Ford car as it could possibly be made.

But what is good for a Ford car is not always good for a human being, for the simple reason that a Ford car is a machine while a human being is a person. Our modern pedagogic experts seem to deny the distinction, and that is one place where our quarrel with them comes in. When you are dealing with human beings, standardization is the last thing you ought to seek. Uniformity of education under one central governmental department would be a very great calamity indeed.

We are constantly told, it is true, that there ought to be an equal opportunity for all the children in the United States; therefore, it is said, federal aid ought to be given to backward states. But what shall we say about this business of "equal opportunity"? I will tell you what I say about it: I am entirely opposed to it. One thing is perfectly clear—if all the children in the United States have equal opportunities, no child will have an opportunity that is worth very much. If parents cannot have the great incentive of providing high and special educational advantages for their own children, then we shall have in this country a drab and soul-killing uniformity, and there will be scarcely any opportunity for anyone to get out of the miserable rut.

The thing is really quite clear. Every lover of human freedom ought to oppose with all his might the giving of federal aid to the schools of this country; for federal aid in the long run inevitably means federal control, and federal control means control by a centralized and irresponsible bureaucracy, and control by such a bureaucracy means the death of everything that might make this country great.

Against this soul-killing collectivism in education, the Christian school, like the private school, stands as an emphatic protest. In doing so, it is no real enemy of the public schools. On the contrary, the only way in which a state-controlled school can be kept even relatively healthy is through the absolutely free possibility of competition by private schools and church schools; if it once becomes monopolistic, it is the most effective engine of tyranny and intellectual stagnation that has yet been devised.

That is one reason why I favor the Christian school. I favor it in the interests of American liberty. But the other reason is vastly more important. I favor it, in the second place, because it is necessary to the propagation of the Christian faith.

Thoughtful people, even many who are not Christians, have become impressed with the shortcomings of our secularized schools. We have provided technical education, which may make the youth of our country better able to make use of the advances of natural science; but natural science, with its command over the physical world, is not all that there is in human life. There are also the moral interests of mankind, and without cultivation of these moral interests a technically trained man is only given more power to do harm. By this purely secular, nonmoral, and nonreligious training we produce not a real human being but a horrible Frankenstein, and we are beginning to shrink back from the product of our own hands.

The educational experts, in their conduct of their state-controlled schools, are trying to repair this defect and in doing so are seeking the cooperation of Christian people. I want to show you—and I do not think I shall have much difficulty in showing this particular audience—why such cooperation cannot be given.

In the first place, we find proposed to us today what is called "character-education" or "character-building." Character, we are told, is one thing about which men of all faiths are agreed. Let us, therefore, build character in common, as good citizens, and then welcome from the various religious faiths whatever additional aid they can severally bring. Let us first appeal to the children on a "civilization basis"—to use what I believe is the most recent terminology—and then let the various faiths appeal to whatever additional motives they may be able to adduce.

What surprises me about this program is not that its advocates propose it, for it is only too well in accord with the spirit of the age. But what really surprises me about it is that the advocates of it seem to think that a Christian can support it without ceasing at that point to be Christian.

In the first place, when this program of character-education is examined, it will be found, I think, to base character upon human experience; it will be found to represent maxims of conduct as being based upon the collective experience of the race. But how can they be based upon the collective experience of the race and at the same time, as the Christian must hold, be based upon the law of God? By this experiential morality the reverence for the law of God is being broken down. It cannot be said that the results— even judged by "civilization" standards (if I may borrow the terminology of my opponents for a moment)—are impressive. The raging tides of passion cannot successfully be kept back by the flimsy mud-embankments of an appeal to human experience. It is a feeble morality that can say nothing better for itself than that it works well.

For that reason, character-building, as practiced in our public schools, may well prove to be character-destruction. But suppose it were free from the defect that I have just mentioned. I do not see how it can possibly be free from it if it remains, as it must necessarily remain, secular—but just suppose it were free from it. Just suppose we could have moral instruction in our public schools that should be based not upon human experience but upon something that might be conceived of as a law of God. Could a Christian consistently support even such a program as that?

We answer that question in the negative, but we do not want to answer it in the negative in any hasty way. It is perfectly true that the law of God is over all. There is not one law of God for the Christian and another law of God for the non-Christian. May not, therefore, the law be proclaimed to men of all faiths; and may it not, if it is so proclaimed, serve as a restraint against the most blatant forms of evil through the common grace of God; may it not even become a schoolmaster to bring men to Christ?

The answer is that if the law of God is proclaimed in public schools to people of different faiths, it is bound, in the very nature of the case, to be proclaimed with optimism; and if it is proclaimed with optimism, it is proclaimed in a way radically opposed to the Christian doctrine of sin. By hypothesis it is regarded as all that good citizens imperatively need to know; they may perhaps profitably know other things, but the fundamental notion is that if they know this, they know all that is absolutely essential. But is not a law that is proclaimed to unredeemed persons with such optimism at best only an imperfect, garbled law? Is it not very different from the true and majestic law of God with its awful pronouncements of eternal death upon sinful man?

The answer to these questions is only too plain. A proclamation of morality which regards itself as all that is necessary—which regards itself as being capable at the most of nonessential supplementation by additional motives to be provided by Christianity or other faiths—is very different from that true proclamation of the law of God which may be a schoolmaster to bring men to Christ. It is not merely insufficient, but it is false; and I do not see how a consistent Christian can possibly regard it as providing any part of that nurture and admonition of the Lord which it is the duty of every Christian parent to give to his children.

What other solution, then, has the public school to offer for the problem which we are considering just now? Well, many people tell us that the reading of the Bible can be put into the public schools. Every educated man, we are told, ought to know something about the Bible; and no intelligent, broad-minded person, whether a Christian or not, ought to object to the bare reading of this great religious classic. So in many places we find the Bible being read in public schools. What shall we say about that?

For my part, I have no hesitation in saying that I am strongly opposed to it. I think I am just about as strongly opposed to the reading of the Bible in state-controlled schools as any atheist could be.

For one thing, the reading of the Bible is very difficult to separate from propaganda about the Bible. I remember, for example, a book of selections from the Bible for school reading, which was placed in my hands some time ago. Whether it is used now I do not know, but it is typical of what will inevitably occur if the Bible is read in public schools. Under the guise of being a book of selections for Bible-reading, it really presupposed the current naturalistic view of the Old Testament Scriptures.

But even where such errors are avoided, even where the Bible itself is read, and not in one of the current mistranslations but in the Authorized Version, the Bible still may be so read as to obscure and even contradict its true message. When, for example, the great and glorious promises of the Bible to the redeemed children of God are read as though they belonged of right to man as man, have we not an attack upon the very heart and core of the Bible's teaching? What could be more terrible, for example, from the Christian point of view, than the reading of the Lord's Prayer to non-Christian children, as though they could use it without becoming Christians, as though persons who have never been purchased by the blood of Christ could possibly say to God, "Our Father, which art in Heaven"? The truth is that a garbled Bible may be a falsified Bible, and when any hope is held out to lost humanity from the so-called ethical portions of the Bible apart from its great redemptive core, then the Bible is represented as saying the direct opposite of what it really says.

So I am opposed to the reading of the Bible in public schools. As for any presentation of general principles of what is called "religion," supposed to be exemplified in various positive religions, including Christianity, it is quite unnecessary for me to say in this company that such presentation is opposed to the Christian religion at its very heart. The relation between the Christian way of salvation and other ways is not a relation between the adequate and the inadequate or between the perfect and the imperfect, but it is a relation between the true and the false. The minute a professing Christian admits that he can find neutral ground with non-Christians in the study of "religion" in general, he has given up the battle and has really, if he knows what he is doing, made common cause with that synchronism which is today, as it was in the first century of our era, the deadliest enemy of the Christian faith.

What, then, should the Christian do in communities where there are no Christian schools? What policy should be advocated for the public schools?

I think there is no harm in advocating the release of public-school children at convenient hours during the week for any religious instruction which their parents may provide. Even at this point, indeed, danger lurks at the door. If the state undertakes to exercise any control whatever over the use by the children of this time which is left vacant, even by way of barely requiring them to attend upon some kind of instruction in these hours, and still more clearly if it undertakes to give public-school credits for such religious instruction, then it violates fundamental principles and will inevitably in the long run seek to control the content of the instruction in the interests of the current syncretism. But if—as is, it must be admitted, very difficult—it can be kept free from these evils, then the arrangement of the public-school schedule in such manner that convenient hours shall be left free for such religious instruction as the parents, entirely at their individual discretion, shall provide is, I think, unobjectionable, and it may under certain circumstances be productive of some relative good.

But what miserable makeshifts all such measures, even at the best, are! Underlying them is the notion that religion embraces only one particular part of human life. Let the public schools take care of the rest of life—such seems to be the notion—and one or two hours during the week will be sufficient to fill the gap which they leave. But as a matter of fact, the religion of the Christian man embraces the whole of his life. Without Christ he was dead in trespasses and sins, but he has now been made alive by the Spirit of God; he was formerly alien from the household of God, but has now been made a member of God's covenant people. Can this new relationship to God be regarded as concerning only one part, and apparently a small part, of his life? No, it concerns all his life, and everything that he does he should do now as a child of God.

It is this profound Christian permeation of every human activity, no matter how secular the world may regard it as being, which is brought about by the Christian school and the Christian school alone. I do not want to be guilty of exaggerations at this point. A Christian boy or girl can learn mathematics, for example, from a teacher who is not a Christian; and truth is truth however learned. But while truth is truth however learned, the bearings of truth, the meaning of truth, the purpose of truth, even in the sphere of mathematics, seem entirely different to the Christian from that which they seem to the non-Christian; and that is why a truly Christian education is possible only when Christian conviction underlies not a part, but all of the curriculum of the school. True learning and true piety go hand in hand, and Christianity embraces the whole of life—those are great central convictions that underlie the Christian school.

I believe that the Christian school deserves to have a good report from those who are without; I believe that even those of our fellow citizens who are not Christians may, if they really love human freedom and the noble traditions of our people, be induced to defend the Christian school against the assaults of its adversaries and to cherish it as a true bulwark of the state. But for Christian people, its appeal is far deeper. I can see little consistency in a type of Christian activity which preaches the gospel on the street corners and at the ends of the earth but neglects the children of the covenant by abandoning them to a cold and unbelieving secularism. If, indeed, the Christian school were in any sort of competition with the Christian family, if it were trying to do what the home ought to do, then I could never favor it. But one of its marked characteristics, in sharp distinction from the secular education of today, is that it exalts the family as a blessed divine institution and treats the scholars in its classes as children of the covenant to be brought up above all things in the nurture and admonition of the Lord.

I cannot bring this little address to a close without trying to pay some sort of tribute to you who have so wonderfully maintained the Christian schools. Some of you, no doubt, are serving as teachers on salaries necessarily small. What words can I possibly find to celebrate the heroism and unselfishness of such service? Others of you are maintaining the schools by your gifts, in the midst of many burdens and despite the present poverty and distress. When I think of such true Christian heroism as yours, I count everything that I ever tried to do in my life to be pitifully unworthy. I can only say that I stand reverently in your presence as in the presence of brethren to whom God has given richly of his grace.

You deserve the gratitude of your country. In a time of spiritual and intellectual and political decadence, you have given us in America something

THE TASK OF CHRISTIAN SCHOLARSHIP

that is truly healthy; you are to our country something like a precious salt that may check the ravages of decay. May that salt never lose its savor! May the distinctiveness of your Christian schools never be lost; may it never give place, by a false "Americanization," to a drab uniformity which is the most un-American thing that could possibly be conceived!!

But if you deserve the gratitude of every American patriot, how much more do you deserve the gratitude of Christian men and women! You have set an example for the whole Christian world; you have done a thing which has elsewhere been neglected, and the neglect of which is everywhere bringing disaster. You are like a city set on a hill, and may that city never be hid! May the example of your Christian schools be heeded everywhere in the church! Above all, may our God richly bless you, and of his grace give you a reward with which all the rewards of earth are not for one moment worthy to be compared!

15

FORTY YEARS OF NEW TESTAMENT RESEARCH

The forty years that have elapsed since the founding of the *Union Seminary Review* have been a period of such activity in the field of New Testament research that even the barest cataloguing of what has been done would exceed the limits of the present article. The most that we can possibly attempt here is a brief characterization of certain tendencies that have been at work.

In the field of textual criticism, there has been tireless activity. The really decisive labors, it is true, were performed prior to 1888; for by the researches of Tischendorf, Tregelles, and others the principal documentary materials of textual criticism were made available, and the epoch-making edition of Westcott and Hort, which appeared in 1881, established on a firm foundation the principles of the science and the methods of its application to the New Testament. Nevertheless, there has been work in plenty for more recent scholars to do. No new critical apparatus has, indeed, succeeded in taking the place of Tischendorf's monumental eighth edition—for von Soden's apparatus, despite its undoubted value, suffers from an unsatisfactory method of presentation and is generally felt not really to meet the need, while Casper René Gregory, who might well have accomplished what is required, met an untimely end in the Great War. But if a satisfac-

"Forty Years of New Testament Research" originally appeared in the *Union Seminary Review* 40 (1928) 1–12.

tory critical apparatus is still lacking, the materials for its production are being collected with an ever-increasing fullness. Best known, and perhaps most important, of the manuscripts that have been discovered since 1888 is the famous "Sinaitic Syriac" manuscript of the gospels, discovered by Mrs. Gibson and Mrs. Lewis in 1892; but many other finds, and the collation of manuscripts already known, have greatly enriched the documentary materials which present-day textual critics can use. As for the principles of textual criticism, as distinguished from the materials, the conclusions of Westcott and Hort have by no means been accepted everywhere without question. A somewhat more favorable attitude toward the so-called "Western text" has often taken the place of the almost wholesale rejection which the Western readings received at the hands of the great British editors; and the origin of the so-called "Neutral text" has often been found not in a merely naïve and mechanical process of transmission from the autographs, but in a definite recension. On the whole, however, it may probably be said that so far as the actual reconstruction of the New Testament text is concerned, recent developments are not for the most part revolutionary: the text of von Soden, for example, despite peculiarities here and there, is not so very diverse from that of Westcott and Hort; and in general, the high estimate placed by Westcott and Hort upon the Codex Vaticanus and the Codex Sinaiticus has been vindicated by recent research.

The study of the language of the New Testament has received an important impetus from the discovery of the nonliterary papyri. Formerly the Greek language in the Hellenistic age was known for the most part only from the books of the period, but during the past twenty-five or thirty years there have been turning up in Egypt great quantities of private and official documents of various kinds, which are written in the colloquial, as distinguished from the literary, form of the Koiné. The similarities between the language of the New Testament and that of these nonliterary documents have shown with increasing clearness that the New Testament is not written in a special Jewish–Greek dialect, but in the living world-language of the Hellenistic age as distinguished from the "literary" language of the period, which is marred by artificial imitation of classical models. Enthusiasm for the new materials of study has no doubt led sometimes to exaggerations: the Semitic influence upon the Greek of the New Testament is no doubt greater than Deissmann, for example, is willing to admit; and the fact that the New Testament books are not written in the artificial "literary" Greek of the period does not mean that they are not in a high sense literary in purpose and even in form. The epistles of Paul, for example, were not intended merely to be read once and then thrown away, as is the case with the private letters that have turned up on Egyptian rubbish-heaps, but are, though arising out of special circumstances, epistles written in the plenitude of apostolic authority for the edification of the church of God.

Despite such cautions, however, the new materials for the study of the Koiné are exceedingly interesting, and deserve the careful attention which has been paid to them by philologians of the present time. They have not yet been made fully available for New Testament study in any comprehensive lexical work, and the admirable lexicon which Thayer made in 1885 on the basis of Wilke-Grimm remains to this day the best lexicon of New Testament Greek. But the labors of Milligan and Moulton and others have provided an increasing mass of comparative material for the new lexicon whenever it may be produced. In the grammatical sphere, important work has been done, with use of the new sources of information, by Radermacher in Germany, by J. H. Moulton in Great Britain, and by A. T. Robertson in America.

In the sphere of literary criticism, there has been to some extent a tendency to retain traditional views even among those who reject the supernaturalistic account which the New Testament gives of the origin of the Christian religion. Seven of the Pauline epistles are admitted to be genuine by all except a few uninfluential extremists; and among the disputed epistles not only Colossians, but also 2 Thessalonians and Ephesians are on the whole probably gaining in favor. With regard to the pastoral epistles, the issue is more clearly drawn; the genuineness of those epistles is scarcely accepted by any except those who are in general favorable to early Christian tradition and to the supernatural origin of Christianity. In gospel criticism, the Johannine authorship of the fourth gospel is of course rejected generally by those scholars who represent the dominant naturalistic point of view; and the avidity with which the exceedingly feeble and ambiguous indications of an early death of the son of Zebedee based on the de Boor fragment have been seized upon by present-day writers at the expense of the strong tradition as to the Ephesian residence of the apostle constitutes one of the least glorious chapters in the history of modern scholarship. As for the synoptics, the "two-document theory" still enjoys general favor, with "proto-Luke" hypotheses or the like providing subjects of eager debate. It is generally admitted, however, that the modern solution of the synoptic problem cannot in itself lead to the desired establishment of the facts about a non-miraculous Jesus, since the supposed legendary accretions must at least already have found a place in the two chief sources upon which our gospels of Matthew and Luke are rightly or wrongly supposed to be based. It becomes necessary, therefore, to penetrate behind these sources to the materials upon which they in turn may be supposed to be based. An attempt is being made in this direction by the *Formgeschichte* of Bultmann and Dibelius. The ultimate units of the tradition embodied in our synoptic gospels, says Dibelius, were not extended narratives or extended presentations of Jesus' teaching, but detached anecdotes or the like. Such subliterary bits of tradition or legend follow, it is supposed, certain laws that govern their form; by the establishment of those laws, the materials embodied in our gospels may be classified and what is original or early may be freed of later accretions. The advocates of this method of investigation, if we may take Dibelius as their representative, seem to have little hope of arriving at the facts about the real Jesus; because a bit of tradition is early and conforms to the laws governing the class to which it belongs, we must not, according to these scholars, jump to the conclusion that it is historical. In the earliest period, Dibelius supposes, the disciples had such an immediate expectation of the second coming of Christ and the end of the age that they had no motive for committing to writing what they had seen and heard concerning Jesus. Thus this latest method of investigating the gospel materials is made the instrument of a far-reaching skepticism. Certainly the arbitrariness of the method seems rather apparent, and the thesis that at the beginning the expectation of the Parousia was so intense as to destroy in the disciples a historical interest with respect to Jesus seems to be assumed rather than proved.

As over against such skepticism with regard to the ultimate sources of information is to be put the "return to tradition" which has appeared here and there with respect to the Lucan writings. A. von Harnack, for example, has in a series of important monographs argued in defense of the traditional view as to the authorship of Luke–Acts; the double work, he supposes, was really written by Luke the physician, a companion of Paul. The same opinion is also held by the distinguished historian Eduard Meyer and by a number of other scholars who, like Harnack and Meyer, are as far as possible from accepting the supernaturalistic account of the origin of Christianity which the Lucan writings contain. Certainly the conclusion of these scholars with regard to the question of authorship stands in sharp antinomy with their rejection of the supernatural, and it is no wonder that the majority of those who reject the supernatural content of Luke–Acts still deny that it could have been written by a man who stood so close to the events as did Luke the companion of Paul. But just because the naturalistic presuppositions of Harnack and Eduard Meyer are so contrary to the Lucan authorship of the books, their acceptance of that view of the authorship may help to show how strong is the evidence for it in the sphere of literary criticism.

If we turn now from such questions of New Testament introduction to the central historical problem of the origin of Christianity, we find that that problem has in recent years often been approached through a consideration of the apostle Paul. The genuineness of the major epistles of Paul is recognized by all historians worthy of serious considerations; we have in these epistles, therefore, a fixed starting point in all controversy. There is also a certain measure of agreement regarding the contents of the epistles; the religion of Paul, which the epistles attest, is a definite historical phenomenon about the character of which agreement is attainable even by those whose own views about religion are as diverse as possible. The religion of Paul was plainly a religion of redemption: Jesus of Nazareth, according to Paul, was a heavenly being who came voluntarily to earth for the salvation of men, accomplished deliverance by his death and resurrection, and is the object of religious faith for all those who belong to him. How did this religion of Paul arise, and in particular how arose the view regarding Jesus of Nazareth upon which it was based?

This question has been answered by historians who proceed from a Ritschlian background by means of the familiar distinction between religion and theology; Paul's religion, they have maintained, was derived from Jesus, but his theology was the expression of that religion in the (now obsolete) forms of thought that were proper to that age. Jesus, according to the Ritschlian historians, did not work miracles and did not transcend the limits of humanity. He did not, moreover, present himself as the object of faith, but rather sought to lead men to have faith in God like the faith which he himself had. His disciples caught from him the contagion of his filial piety, and Paul in turn caught the same contagion from them. But Paul was obliged to express his debt to Jesus in a doctrine of redemption and of Jesus' own person which was derived from sources with which Jesus himself had little or nothing to do. Thus, in the depths of his religious experience, ac-

THE TASK OF CHRISTIAN SCHOLARSHIP

cording to the Ritschlian historians, Paul was a true disciple of Jesus, but his theology marks a serious decline from the pure gospel of divine fatherhood which Jesus himself preached.

This solution of the problem was attacked by W. Wrede in an important little book on Paul which appeared in 1904. Religion and theology in Paul, Wrede observed, belong together; it is not in connection with any mere following of Jesus' example or obeying of Jesus' commands but in connection with the doctrine of redemption that Paul's religious life runs full and free. But since, according to Wrede, we cannot possibly suppose that there ever existed upon this earth a supernatural Redeemer such as Paul supposed Jesus to have been, Paul's knowledge of the real, purely human Jesus must have been very slight; and the whole edifice of the historic church, being based so largely upon Paul, cannot be based upon Jesus. Thus, according to the logic of Wrede's view, Paul rather than Jesus was the true founder of the Christian religion as it has always been known through all the history of the Christian church.

But if the religion of Paul was not derived from Jesus, whence was it derived? Here opinions diverged. Wrede himself supposed that Paulinism was derived from the pre-Christian Jewish doctrine of the heavenly Messiah, such as it is attested to us, for example, by the Ethiopic book of Enoch. But the dominant tendency is to have recourse rather to the syncretism of the Greco-Roman world. Thus the essentials of Paulinism, it is supposed, including Paul's view of Jesus, were derived not from pre-Christian Judaism, but from the pagan religion of that day.

Was Wrede right as over against the older "Liberalism"? The true answer is that he was both right and wrong. He was right in holding that Paul's religion was not derived from the purely human Jesus of modern naturalistic reconstruction; but he was wrong in holding that such a purely human Jesus was the Jesus who actually lived in Palestine and died upon the cross. Paul's religion was based upon the historic Jesus—about that the "Liberal" opponents of Wrede's radicalism were right—but the historic Jesus was not the mere teacher of righteousness reconstructed by modern historians, but the divine Redeemer whom the epistles of Paul presuppose.

Such a solution of the problem would seem to lie ready to hand. But it involves, of course, an acceptance of the supernatural, and that stupendous step modern naturalistic historians are not willing to take. Thus the "quest of the historical Jesus" goes busily on.

That quest has thus far resulted in failure. Twenty or thirty years ago, it was indeed thought by many to be over. The "Liberal" historians were engaged in presenting the "results" of modern criticism in the form of more or less elaborate biographies of the great prophet of Nazareth who proclaimed the fatherhood of God. Earnest efforts were made to make of that great prophet a living figure on the pages of history; vigorous attempts were made to exhibit as conceivable the facts of his inner life. At last, it was thought, the unfortunate dogmatic accretions had been removed from the figure of Jesus; now at length we had found in Jesus no cold abstraction, no mythical second person of a metaphysical Trinity, but a true man whom, without theology or metaphysics, we could reverence and love.

But alas for human hopes! The critical principles which had removed the supposed theological accretions from the gospel picture were found to attack much of what had been supposed to stand firm, and the purely human Jesus was found to contain at the very center of his being a psychological anomaly due to his lofty claims. Vain have been the efforts made by adherents of the older Liberalism to check the progress of a skepticism only too clearly involved in the principles with which that older Liberalism went to work. Actual denial of the historicity of Jesus has indeed met little favor; but what sort of person Jesus really was must, we are told, remain hidden from the gaze of modern men. Thus Rudolf Bultmann, for example, despairs of producing anything like a biography of Jesus or of penetrating to the facts of his inner life. A comparison of Bultmann's little book on "Jesus" with the popular presentations of twenty years ago will well serve to indicate the trend of the times. Gone is the enthusiasm with which the Jesus of naturalistic reconstruction was held up to the affection and the emulation of men. In popular preaching in America, indeed, that Jesus still holds sway— that Jesus who was "God" simply because he was true man, that Jesus who can be called not "the Lord" but "the Master," that optimistic proclaimer of the fatherhood of God and the brotherhood of man. But among scholars such a figure is with greater and greater thoroughness being erased from the pages of history. Now that the supernatural Jesus of the New Testament has so widely been given up, modern historians despair of any certainty as to what sort of figure is to be put in his place. It is perhaps hardly too much to say that the last forty years in New Testament research have witnessed the rise and fall of "the Liberal Jesus."

The weariness of approaching bankruptcy seems to have fallen, then, upon the modern investigation of the life of Christ and of the beginnings of Christianity. Twenty-five or thirty years ago, there was an influx of new enthusiasm in the rise of the so-called "history-of-religion" school. The method of comparative religion, which had previously been practiced in the Old Testament field, was applied with a new thoroughness by Gunkel and others to the New Testament. A host of willing workers took up the slogan: the origin of Christianity was not to be found in Judaism alone or in the teaching and personality of Jesus, but in the surrounding pagan world; religious ideas and practices are transmitted not merely through the medium of books, but in a mysterious subliterary realm where diverse peoples and nations become one. Thus primitive Christianity, it was supposed, was truly a syncretistic religion; it showed its true worth not by an aloofness from the surrounding world, but by the assimilation and remodeling of what is received.

The "history-of-religion method," so hostile to the supernaturalistic view of Christianity, was scientific in aim; but underlying it there was perhaps something profounder than a purely scientific impulse. Men sought to understand the human phenomenon of religion in order that from their new vantage ground of scientific detachment they might make that phenomenon a help rather than a hindrance to that self-development of humanity which is the goal of modern effort. If such was the purpose, it seems not to have been attained. The substitution of an abstraction called "religion" for the exclusive devotion to one particular religion called Christianity has brought but cold comfort to the human heart.

Into that cold world of scientific detachment there has come in recent years in Germany the imperious tones of a new message—a new message that addresses itself to the soul of every man. It is the message of Karl Barth and Thurneysen and Gogarten and Brunner and other exponents of the so-called "theology of crisis." Barth's famous commentary on Romans is a commentary of a kind strange to the modern world. Not the message of Romans to men of long ago, but its message to men of today, is the subject of this strange exposition of the apostle's words. Many readers hold up their hands in horror. The long battle for grammatico-historical exegesis, they say, seems to have been fought in vain; we are sinking back into the "pneumatic exegesis" dear to allegorizers of ages long gone by. For such criticism we are not without sympathy. The "Epistle to the Romans" of Karl Barth is certainly a very strange book, and the apostle Paul would probably be amazed if he could know that it purports to be an exposition of what he wrote regarding the way of salvation to the Roman church. But as over against his critics Barth has undoubtedly a certain measure of right on his side. A grammatico-historical exegesis so perverted as to involve aloofness of the exegete from his subject matter has given us at the most but an external and mechanical comprehension of what the Bible says. Only the man who comes to the Bible with the despairing question of his own soul, with the question, "What shall I do to be saved?" can really understand the Word of God. That much insight at least is conveyed by the strange commentary of Karl Barth.

It would indeed be a great mistake to regard the Barthian teaching as a real return to the gospel of the Lord Jesus Christ. There are, indeed, in it profoundly evangelical elements. The awful transcendence of God, as over against the pantheizing teaching of Schleiermacher and of great sections of the modern church, the stupendous gulf between the world and God that is found in sin, the necessity and the all-sufficiency of divine grace, the rejection, as profoundly un-Christian, of the boundless modern "tolerance" and indifference in the religious sphere, the necessity above all of hearkening not to human experience, but to God's Word—these are truly Christian convictions in the teaching of Brunner and Barth. But on the other side is to be put the strange epistemology of the Barthian school, which makes us wonder whether these men are not in danger of falling into a skepticism even more complete than that against which they are protesting in the modern world, and the strange indifference to questions of literary and historical criticism with regard to Jesus Christ, an indifference so great that even Bultmann, with his extreme skepticism in the historical sphere, can apparently be regarded as a real member of the Barthian school.

What can be said at any rate is that the Barthian movement, with the remarkable influence that it is attaining among the youth of Germany, has at least thrown the religious world into a state of flux. That fact is only one indication more of what we have already observed—that after the rejection of the New Testament account of the origin of Christianity, modern naturalistic historians have not yet been able to put anything in its place. The most imposing effort in this direction, perhaps, was the "Liberal Jesus" of twenty-five or so years ago. But confidence in that reconstruction has today been undermined. It looks, therefore, as though modern naturalistic criticism of the New Testament were on the verge of bankruptcy. The Christian religion is certainly an important historical phenomenon. How did it come into being? The New Testament has a definite answer to that question. Christianity, according to the New Testament, is based upon the supernatural person of Jesus Christ. But if that answer is to be rejected, what is to be substituted for it? Modern naturalistic criticism has not been able to agree upon any answer.

Upon that fact some hope for the future may reasonably be based. It is unsatisfactory from the scientific point of view to leave the mighty edifice of the Christian religion hanging in the air, and it is unsatisfactory also to the human heart. It may be that in the scientific impasse to which modern naturalistic criticism has come, there may be those who will call in question the naturalistic presuppositions which have led us into such a state; it may be that the naturalistic historians, despite all their brilliancy, may prove to be on the wrong track and that Theodor Zahn, with the other "conservative" scholars of our time, may prove to be on the right track after all; it may be that even in the face of modern skepticism there may be those who will say, not to the reduced Jesus of naturalistic reconstruction and not to the vague figure of a Christ whom every race and every generation is free to interpret for itself, but to the mighty Savior presented in the whole Word of God: "Lord, to whom shall we go? thou hast the words of eternal life."

PART FOUR

THEOLOGICAL EDUCATION

16

WESTMINSTER THEOLOGICAL SEMINARY: ITS PURPOSE AND PLAN

Westminster Theological Seminary, which opens its doors today, will hardly be attended by those who seek the plaudits of the world or the plaudits of a worldly church. It can offer for the present no magnificent buildings, no long-established standing in the ecclesiastical or academic world. Why, then, does it open its doors; why does it appeal to the support of Christian men?

The answer is plain. Our new institution is devoted to an unpopular cause; it is devoted to the service of one who is despised and rejected by the world and increasingly belittled by the visible church, the majestic Lord and Savior who is presented to us in the Word of God. From him men are turning away one by one. His sayings are too hard, his deeds of power too strange, his atoning death too great an offense to human pride. But to him, despite all, we hold. No Christ of our own imaginings can ever take his place for us, no mystic Christ whom we seek merely in the hidden depths of our

"Westminster Theological Seminary: Its Purpose and Plan" was delivered in Philadelphia as the first convocation address at Westminster Theological Seminary on September 25, 1929, and appeared in *The Presbyterian* 99 (October 10, 1929) 6–9. Reprinted in *What Is Christianity?* ed. Ned Bernard Stonehouse (Grand Rapids: Eerdmans, 1951).

own souls. From all such we turn away ever anew to the blessed written Word and say to the Christ there set forth, the Christ with whom then we have living communion: "Lord, to whom shall we go? Thou hast the words of eternal life."

The Bible, then, which testifies of Christ, is the center and core of that with which Westminster Seminary has to do. Very different is the attitude of most theological institutions today. Most seminaries, with greater or lesser clearness and consistency, regard not the Bible alone, or the Bible in any unique sense, but the general phenomenon of religion as being the subject matter of their course. It is the duty of the theological student, they maintain, to observe various types of religious experience, attested by the Bible considered as a religious classic, but attested also by the religious conditions that prevail today, in order to arrive by a process of comparison at that type of religious experience which is best suited to the needs of the modern man. We believe, on the contrary, that God has been pleased to reveal himself to man and to redeem man once for all from the guilt and power of sin. The record of that revelation and that redemption is contained in the Holy Scriptures, and it is with the Holy Scriptures, and not merely with the human phenomenon of religion, that candidates for the ministry should learn to deal.

There is nothing narrow about such a curriculum; many and varied are the types of intellectual activity that it requires. When you say that God has revealed himself to man, you must in the first place believe that God is and that the God who is is one who can reveal himself, no blind world force, but a living person. There we have one great division of the theological course. "Philosophical apologetics" or "theism," it is called. But has this God, who might reveal himself, actually done so in the way recorded in the Scriptures of the Old and New Testaments? In other words, is Christianity true? That question, we think, should not be evaded; and what is more, it need not be evaded by any Christian man. To be a Christian is, we think, a truly reasonable thing; Christianity flourishes not in obscurantist darkness, where objections are ignored, but in the full light of day.

But if the Bible contains a record of revelation and redemption, what in detail does the Bible say? In order to answer that question, it is not sufficient to be a philosopher; by being a philosopher you may perhaps determine, or think you can determine, what the Bible ought to say. But if you are to tell what the Bible does say, you must be able to read the Bible for yourself. And you cannot read the Bible for yourself unless you know the languages in which it was written. We may sometimes be tempted to wish that the Holy Spirit had given us the Word of God in a language better suited to our particular race, in a language that we could easily understand; but in his mysterious wisdom he gave it to us in Hebrew and in Greek. Hence if we want to know the Scriptures, to the study of Greek and Hebrew we must go. I am not sure that it will be ill for our souls. It is poor consecration indeed that is discouraged by a little earnest work, and sad is it for the church if it has only ministers whose preparation for their special calling is of the customary superficial kind.

We are not conducting a school for lay workers at Westminster Seminary (useful though such a school would be), but a theological seminary; and we believe that a theological seminary is an institution of higher learning whose standards should not be inferior to the highest academic standards that anywhere prevail.

If, then, the students of our seminary can read the Bible not merely in translations, but as it was given by the Holy Spirit to the church, then they are prepared to deal intelligently with the question what the Bible means. There we have the great subject of biblical exegesis or biblical interpretation. I hesitate to use that word "interpretation," for it is a word that has been the custodian of more nonsense, perhaps, than any other word in the English language today. Every generation, it is said, must interpret the Bible and the creeds of the church in its own way. So it is said in effect by many modern leaders of the church: "We accept the Apostles' Creed, but we must interpret the Apostles' Creed in a way that will suit the modern mind. So we repeat the assertion of the creed, 'The third day he rose again from the dead,' but we interpret that to mean, 'The third day he did not rise again from the dead.' "

In the presence of this modern business of interpreting perfectly plain assertions to mean their exact opposite, do you know what I verily believe? I verily believe that the new reformation, for which we long, will be like the Reformation of the sixteenth century in that it will mean a return to plain common honesty and common sense. At the end of the Middle Ages the Bible had become a book with seven seals; it had been covered with the rubbish of the fourfold sense of Scripture and all that. The Reformation brushed that rubbish away. So again today the Bible has been covered with an elaborate business of "interpretation" that is worse in some respects than anything that the Middle Ages could produce. The new reformation will brush all that away. There will be a rediscovery of the great Reformation doctrine of the perspicuity of Scripture; men will make the astonishing discovery that the Bible is a plain book addressed to plain men, and that it means exactly what it says.

In our work in exegesis at Westminster Seminary, at any rate, we shall seek to cultivate common sense. But common sense is not so common as is sometimes supposed, and for the cultivation of it true learning is not out of place. What a world of vagaries, what a sad waste of time, could be avoided if men would come into contact with the truly fine exegetical tradition of the Christian church! Such contact with the devout and learned minds of the past would not discourage freshness or originality. Far from it; it would help to shake us out of a rut and lead us into fields of fruitful thinking.

In true biblical exegesis, the Bible must be taken as God has been pleased to give it to the church. And as God has been pleased to give it to the church, it is not a mere textbook of religion written all at one time and in one way. On the contrary, it is composed of sixty-six books written at widely different times and by the instrumentality of widely different men. Let us not regret that fact. If the Bible were a systematic textbook on religion, it would, indeed, possess some advantages: it would presumably be easier to interpret, for much of our present difficulty of interpretation comes from the fact that the biblical books are rooted in historical conditions long gone by. But if the Bible, under those circumstances, would be easier to interpret, it would speak far less powerfully to the heart of man. As it is, God has been very good. He has given us no cold textbook on religion, but a book that reaches every heart and answers to every need. He has condescended to touch our hearts and arouse our minds by the wonderful variety and beauty of his book.

When we have learned to read that book aright, we can trace the history of the revelation that it sets forth. When we do so, we are engaging in an important part of the theological curriculum. "Biblical theology," it is called. Whether it is set forth in a separate course, or whether it is interwoven, as will probably be done in Westminster Seminary, with the work of the Old and New Testament departments, in either case it is a vital part of that with which we have to deal. "God, who at sundry times and in divers manners spake in time past unto the fathers by the prophets, hath in these last days spoken unto us by his Son"—there is the program of biblical theology; it traces the history of revelation through Old and New Testament times.

But biblical theology is not all the theology that will be taught at Westminster Seminary, for systematic theology will be at the very center of the seminary's course. At that point an error should be avoided: it must not be thought that systematic theology is one whit less biblical than biblical theology is. But it differs from biblical theology in that, standing on the foundation of biblical theology, it seeks to set forth, no longer in the order of the time when it was revealed, but in the order of logical relationships, the grand sum of what God has told us in his Word. There are those who think that systematic theology on the basis of the Bible is impossible; there are those who think that the Bible contains a mere record of human seeking after God and that its teachings are a mass of contradiction which can never be resolved. But to the number of those persons we do not belong. We believe for our part that God has spoken to us in his Word, and that he has given us not merely theology, but a system of theology, a great logically consistent body of truth.

That system of theology, that body of truth, which we find in the Bible is the Reformed faith, the faith commonly called Calvinistic, which is set forth so gloriously in the Confession and catechisms of the Presbyterian church. It is sometimes referred to as a "man-made creed." But we do not regard it as such. We regard it, in accordance with our ordination pledge as ministers in the Presbyterian church, as the creed which God has taught us in his Word. If it is contrary to the Bible, it is false. But we hold that it is not contrary to the Bible, but in accordance with the Bible, and true. We rejoice in the approximations to that body of truth which other systems of theology contain; we rejoice in our Christian fellowship with other evangelical churches; we hope that members of other churches, despite our Calvinism, may be willing to enter into Westminster Seminary as students and to listen to what we may have to say. But we cannot consent to impoverish our message by setting forth less than what we find the Scriptures to contain; and we believe that we shall best serve our fellow Christians, from whatever church they may come, if we set forth not some vague greatest common measure among various creeds, but that great historic faith that has come through Augustine and Calvin to our own Presbyterian church. Glorious is the heritage of the Reformed faith. God grant that it may go forth to new triumphs even in the present time of unbelief!

Systematic theology, on the basis of Holy Scripture, is the very center of what we have to teach; every other theological department is contributory to that. That department gives a man the message that he has to proclaim. But we have already spoken of the heritage of the Reformed faith, and of a glorious tradition that has come down to us in the church. And that brings us to speak of another department of the theological curriculum, the department that deals with the history of the Christian church. Our message is based, indeed, directly upon the Bible; we derive the content of it not from the experience of past ages, but from what God has told us in his Word. But it would be a mistake to ignore what past generations, on the basis of God's Word, have thought and said and done. Into many other fields of theological study the study of church history casts a beneficent light. Church history should make us less enthusiastic about a modernity which is really as old as the hills, and amid the difficulties of the present time it should give us new hope. God has brought his church through many perils, and the darkest hour has often preceded the dawn. So it may be in our day. The gospel may yet break forth, sooner than we expect, to bring light and liberty to mankind. But that will be done, unless the lesson of church history is altogether wrong, by the instrumentality not of theological pacifists who avoid controversy, but of earnest contenders for the faith. God give us men in our time who will stand with Luther and say: "Here I stand; I cannot do otherwise, God help me. Amen."

Thus the minister who goes forth from Westminster Seminary will, we hope, be a man with a message. He will also, we hope, be a man who can so deliver his message as to reach the hearts and minds of men; and to help him do that, the department of homiletics and practical theology has an important place. It cannot, indeed, itself teach a man how to preach; that he must learn, if at all, by the long experience of subsequent years. But at least it can help him to avoid errors and can start him in the right way; it can start him out in that long course in homiletics which is provided by all the rest of life.

Such, very feebly and imperfectly presented, is the program of Westminster Theological Seminary; it is far better set forth in the fine article which Dr. Oswald T. Allis has recently contributed to *The Sunday School Times*. Many things are omitted from this brief summary of ours. Some of them are omitted because of the imperfections of the speaker or from lack of time. But others are omitted of deliberate purpose. There are many things—many useful things, too—with which a theological seminary should not attempt to deal. Let it never be forgotten that a theological seminary is a school for specialists. We are living in an age of specialization. There are specialists on eyes and specialists on noses, and throats, and stomachs, and feet, and skin; there are specialists on teeth—one set of specialists on putting teeth in, and another set of specialists on pulling teeth out—there are specialists on Shakespeare and specialists on electric wires; there are specialists on Plato and specialists on pipes. Amid all these specialties, we at Westminster Seminary have a specialty which we think, in comparison with these others, is not so very small. Our specialty is found in the Word of God. Specialists in the Bible—that is what Westminster Seminary will endeavor to produce. Please do not forget it; please do not call on us for a product that we are not endeavoring to provide. If you want specialists in social science or in hygiene or even in "religion" (in the vague modern sense), then you must go elsewhere for what you want. But if you want men who know the Bible and know it in something more than a layman's sort of way, then call on us. If we can give you such men, we have succeeded; if we cannot give them to you, we have failed. It is a large contract indeed, a contract far too great for human strength. But at least, by God's grace, we shall do our best.

Such is the task of Westminster Theological Seminary. It is a task that needs especially to be undertaken at the present time. Fifty years ago many colleges and universities and theological seminaries were devoted to the truth of God's Word. But one by one they have drifted away, often with all sorts of professions of orthodoxy on the part of those who were responsible for the change. Until May 1929 one great theological seminary, the Seminary at Princeton, resisted bravely the current of the age. But now that seminary has been made to conform to the general drift. Signers of the Auburn Affirmation, a formal document which declares that acceptance of the virgin birth and of four other basic articles of the Christian faith is nonessential even for ministers, actually sit upon the new governing board. And they do so apparently with the acquiescence of the rest. Not one word of protest against the outrage involved in their presence has been uttered, so far as I know, by the other members of the board; and a formal pronouncement, signed by the president of the seminary and the president of the board, actually commends the thirty-three members of the board as men who have the confidence of the church. Surely it is quite clear, in view of that pronouncement, as well as in view of the personnel of the board, that under such a governing body, Princeton Seminary is lost to the evangelical cause.

At first it might seem to be a great calamity, and sad are the hearts of those Christian men and women throughout the world who love the gospel that the old Princeton proclaimed. We cannot fully understand the ways of God in permitting so great a wrong. Yet good may come even out of a thing so evil as that. Perhaps the evangelical people in the Presbyterian church were too contented, too confident in material resources; perhaps God has taken away worldly props in order that we may rely more fully upon him; perhaps the pathway of sacrifice may prove to be the pathway of power.

That pathway of sacrifice is the pathway which students and supporters of Westminster Seminary are called upon to tread. For that we can thank God. Because of the sacrifices involved, no doubt many have been deterred from coming to us; they have feared the opposition of the machinery of the church; some of them may have feared, perhaps, to bear fully the reproach of Christ. We do not judge them. But whatever may be said about the students who have not come to us, one thing can certainly be said about those who have come—they are real men.

No, my friends, though Princeton Seminary is dead, the noble tradition of Princeton Seminary is alive. Westminster Seminary will endeavor by God's grace to continue that tradition unimpaired; it will endeavor, not on a foundation of equivocation and compromise but on an honest foundation of devotion to God's Word, to maintain the same principles that the old Princeton maintained. We believe, first, that the Christian religion, as it is set forth in the Confession of Faith of the Presbyterian church, is true; we believe, second, that the Christian religion welcomes and is capable of scholarly defense; and we believe, third, that the Christian religion should be proclaimed without fear or favor, and in clear opposition to whatever opposes it, whether within or without the church, as the only way of salvation for lost mankind. On that platform, brethren, we stand. Pray that we may be enabled by God's Spirit to stand firm. Pray that the students who go forth from Westminster Seminary may know Christ as their own Savior and may proclaim to others the gospel of his love.

17

FACING THE FACTS
BEFORE GOD

In the nineteenth chapter of 2 Kings, we are told how Hezekiah, king of Judah, received a threatening letter from the Assyrian enemy. The letter contained unpalatable truth. It set forth the way in which the king of Assyria had conquered one nation after another—and could the feeble kingdom of Judah escape?

When Hezekiah received the letter, there were three things that he could do with it.

In the first place, he could obey its behest; he could go out and surrender his kingdom to the Assyrian enemy.

In the second place, he could refuse to read the letter; he could ignore its contents. Like another and worse king, with a far better communication than that, he could take out his king's penknife and cut it up and throw it bit by bit contemptuously into the fire.

As a matter of fact, Hezekiah did neither of these two things. He took the letter with all its unpalatable truth and read it from beginning to end; he did not close his eyes to any of its threatening. But then he took the let-

"Facing the Facts before God" was originally presented in 1931 as an address before the League of Evangelical Students, and appeared in *The Evangelical Student* 6 (October 1931) 6–10. Reprinted in *What Is Christianity?* ed. Ned Bernard Stonehouse (Grand Rapids: Eerdmans, 1951).

ter, with all the threatening that it contained, spread it open in the presence of Almighty God, and asked God to give the answer.

Now we too, believers in the Bible and in the blessed gospel that it contains, have received a threatening letter. It is not a letter signed by any one potentate, like the king of Assyria, but it is a collective letter signed by the men who are dominating the world of today and dominating to an increasing extent the visible church. It is a letter breathing out threatenings of extinction to those who hold to the gospel of Jesus Christ as it is set forth in God's Word.

That letter is signed by the men who are dominating increasingly the political and social life of the world. That was not true fifty years ago, at least not in English-speaking countries. Then, to a considerable extent, in those countries at least, public opinion was in favor of the gospel of Christ. Today, almost all over the world, public opinion is increasingly against the gospel of Christ.

The letter of threatening against the gospel is signed also by the men who are dominating the literary and intellectual life of the world. To see that that is true, one needs only to read the popular magazines that appeal to persons of literary and intellectual taste; or one needs only to read the books of the day or listen to what comes "over the air."

The threatening letter is also signed, alas, by the men who are in control of many of the larger branches of the Protestant church. In the Presbyterian Church in the U.S.A., for example, to which the writer of this article belongs, four out of eight ministerial members of the Permanent Judicial Commission, which is practically the supreme guardian of the doctrine of the church, are actually signers of a formal document commonly called the "Auburn Affirmation" which declares to be nonessential even for the ministry the virgin birth of our Lord and four other great verities of the Christian faith; and very slight indeed is the representation of any clear-cut and outspoken evangelicalism in the boards and agencies of the church. In many other ecclesiastical bodies, the situation, from the Christian point of view, is even worse than it is in ours.

But it is in the colleges and universities and theological seminaries that the threatening letter against the gospel of Christ has been most generally signed. In the faculties of some of our great universities today, you can count almost on the fingers of your two hands the men who believe in the gospel in any definite and outspoken way, and in the student bodies individual believers often seem to themselves to be standing nearly alone.

When we receive this threatening letter, there are three things that we may do with it.

In the first place, we may obey its behest; we may relinquish our belief in the truth of the Bible; we may simply drift with the current of the times. Very many students in colleges and universities and theological seminaries have made that choice. They came from Christian homes; they are the subject of the prayers of godly parents. But the threatenings and persuasions of the unbelieving world have apparently been too strong for them. They have been unwilling to adopt the unpopular course. And so they have made shipwreck of their faith.

In the second place, we may refuse to read the threatening letter; we may close our eyes to the unpalatable truth that the letter contains. We may say, as so many are saying today, that the Protestant churches of our own country and of the other countries of the world are "fundamentally sound"; we may cry "Peace, peace; when there is no peace"; we may dig our heads like ostriches in the sand; we may refuse to attend to the real situation in the church and in the world.

I pray God that we may never adopt this method of dealing with the letter of threatening, for if there is one thing that is preventing true prayer today, it is this foolish optimism with regard to the state of the times, this refusal of Christian people to face the true seriousness of the situation in which we stand.

But there is a third choice that we may make when we receive the threatening letter against the gospel of Christ. We may take the letter and read it from beginning to end, not closing our eyes to the threatening that it contains, and then lay the letter, with all its threatenings, open in the presence of Almighty God.

It is to that third choice that the League of Evangelical Students, by its constitution, is irrevocably committed. The prologue to the constitution reads as follows:

> Inasmuch as mutually exclusive conceptions of the nature of the Christian religion exist in the world today and particularly in theological seminaries and other institutions of higher learning; and since it is the duty of those who share and cherish the evangelical faith to witness to it and to strive for its

defense and propagation; and in view of the value for this end of common counsel, united effort and Christian fellowship:

We, the undersigned representatives of Students' Associations in Theological Seminaries and Schools for the Training of Christian Workers, do hereby form a league organized upon the following principles. . . .

There we have a clear facing of the situation as it actually is and a brave willingness, despite that situation, to stand for the defense and propagation of the gospel of Christ.

Certain objections are sometimes raised against this method of dealing with the letter of threatening that has come to us today from a hostile world.

In the first place, we are sometimes told, it will discourage the faith of timorous souls if we tell them thus plainly that the world of today is hostile to the gospel of Christ; it will offend Christ's little ones, men say, if we bid them open their eyes to the real strength of unbelief in the modern world.

But our Lord, at least, never used this method of raising false hopes in those whom he called to be his disciples. He told those who would follow him to count the cost before they took that step, not to be like a man who starts to build a tower before he has funds to complete it or like a man who puts his hand to the plow and then draws back. He never made it easy, in that sense, to be a disciple of him (though in another and higher sense his yoke was easy and his burden light); and any faith in the Lord Jesus Christ which is based upon the vain hope that a man can be a disciple of Christ and still have the favor of the world is a faith that is based on shifting sand. No, it is a poor religion which makes a man willing only to walk in golden slippers in the sunshine; and such a religion is bound to fail in the time of need.

In the second place, however, men say that if we face the real condition of the times, we shall be guilty of stirring up controversy in the church.

No doubt the fact may be admitted. If we face the real situation in the church and in the world, and decide, despite that situation, to stand firmly for the gospel of Christ, we shall be very likely indeed to find ourselves engaged in controversy. But if we are going to avoid controversy, we might as well close our Bibles, for the New Testament is a controversial book practically from beginning to end. The New Testament writers and our Lord himself presented truth in sharp contrast with error, and indeed that is the only way in which truth can be presented in any clear and ringing way.

198

I do not know all the things that will happen when the great revival sweeps over the church, the great revival for which we long. Certainly I do not know *when* that revival will come; its coming stands in the Spirit's power. But about one thing that will happen when that blessing comes I think we can be fairly sure. When a great and true revival comes in the church, the present miserable, feeble talk about avoidance of controversy on the part of the servants of Jesus Christ will all be swept away as with a mighty flood. A man who is really on fire with his message never talks in that feeble and compromising way but proclaims the gospel plainly and boldly in the presence of every high thing that is lifted up against the gospel of Christ.

If we do adopt this method of dealing with the present situation in the church and in the world, if we spread the threatening letter of the adversaries unreservedly before God, there are certain things that God tells us for our comfort. When Hezekiah adopted that method in his day, God sent him Isaiah the son of Amoz, greatest of the prophets, with a message of cheer. But he has his ways of speaking also to us.

In the first place, he tells us for our comfort that this is not the first time of discouragement in the history of the church. Often the gospel has seemed to superficial observers to be forever forgotten, yet it has burst forth with new power and set the world aflame. Sometimes the darkest hour has just preceded the dawn. So it may be in our time.

In the second place, he tells us that even in this time of unbelief there are far more than seven thousand that have not bowed the knee to the gods of the hour. In these days of doubt and defection and hostility, there are those who love the gospel of Jesus Christ. And how sweet and precious is our fellowship with them in the presence of a hostile world!

It is to be God's instrument in giving that comfort that the League of Evangelical Students exists. It is founded to say to students on many a campus who are tempted to think that they are standing alone in holding to the gospel of Christ: "No, brethren, you are not alone; we too hold humbly to the truth of God's Word, and we hold to it not through a mere shallow emotionalism but because to hold to it is a thoroughly reasonable thing, of which a real student need not for one moment be ashamed."

In the third place, God tells us not to be too much impressed by the unbelieving age in which we are living now. Do you think that this is a happy or a blessed age? Oh, no, my friends. Amid all the pomp and glitter and noise and tumult of the age, there are hungry hearts. The law of God has been forgotten, and stark slavery is stalking through the earth—the decay of free institutions in the state and a deeper slavery still in the depths of the soul. High poetry is silent; and machinery, it almost seems, rules all. God has taken the fire of genius from the world. But something far more than genius is being lost—the blessing of a humble and virtuous life. There was a time, twenty-five years ago, when we might have thought that Christian living could be maintained after Christian doctrine was given up. But if we ever made that mistake, we must abandon it today. Where is the sweetness of the Christian home; where is the unswerving integrity of men and women whose lives were founded upon the Word of God? Increasingly these things are being lost. Even men of the world are coming to see with increasing clearness that mankind is standing over an abyss.

I tell you, my friends, it is not altogether an argument *against* the gospel that this age has given it up; it is rather an argument *for* the gospel. If *this* is the condition of the world without Christ, then we may well turn back, while yet there is time, to that from which we have turned away.

That does not mean that we should despise the achievements of the age; it does not mean that we should adopt the "Touch not, taste not, handle not" attitude toward the good things or the wonders of God's world which Paul condemned in his day; it does not mean that we should consecrate to God an impoverished man narrowed in interests, narrowed in outlook upon the marvelous universe that God has made. What it does mean is that we should pray God to make these modern achievements not the instruments of human slavery, as increasingly they are threatening to become, but the instruments of that true liberty which consists in the service of God.

But the deepest comfort which God gives us is not found even in considerations such as these: it is not found in reflections upon God's dealings during the past history of the church; it is not found in our fellowship with those who love the gospel that we love; it is not found in observation of the defects of this unbelieving age. Valuable are all these considerations, and great is the assurance that they give to our souls. But there is one consideration that is more valuable, and one assurance that is greater still. It is found in the overwhelming glory of the gospel itself.

When we attend to that glory, all the pomp and glitter of an unbelieving age seems like the blackness of night. How wonderful is the divine revelation in God's Word! How simple, yet how majestic its presentation of the being of God; how dark its picture of the guilt of man; how bright against

THEOLOGICAL EDUCATION

that background its promise of divine grace! And at the center of all in this incomparable book there stands the figure of one in whose presence all wisdom seems to be but folly and all goodness seems to be but filthy rags. If we have his favor, little shall we care henceforth for the favor of the world, and little shall we fear the opposition of an unbelieving age.

That favor is ours, brethren, without merit, without boasting, if we trust in him. And in that favor we find the real source of our courage in these difficult days. Our deepest comfort is found not in the signs of the times but in the great and precious promises of God.

18

CONSOLATIONS IN THE MIDST OF BATTLE

As you go forth into the gospel ministry, we cannot tell you that you will have an easy time. There are two reasons why we cannot tell you that. In the first place, it would not be true; and in the second place, you would not believe us even if we endeavored to deceive. The world today is opposed to the faith that you profess, and the visible church, too often, has made common cause with the world.

Our Lord himself, when he was on earth, never made it easy to be a disciple of him. He called upon men to count the cost before they would be called by his name. He warned them not to be like the man who starts to build a tower and is unable to complete it, nor like the man who puts his hand to the plough and turns back.

So we at Westminster Seminary, humble followers of Christ, never desire to bring men to this place under the false pretense that if they come to us they will be popular with the world. We are not seeking mere numbers in our student body. Rather are we seeking men like you, the members of this second graduating class, who are ready to bear the reproach of Christ and who are not afraid of earnest labor in the study of God's Word.

As you go forth to face the opposition of the world, and also, alas, the

---

"Consolations in the Midst of Battle" is a commencement address given in 1931 to the graduating class of Westminster Theological Seminary, and appeared in *What Is Christianity?* ed. Ned Bernard Stonehouse (Grand Rapids: Eerdmans, 1951).

opposition of a worldly church, there are certain things that we can tell you for your comfort and strength.

In the first place, we can tell you that one possession, at least, you will always have. It is not a possession that would be valued highly by the world. But we think that it will truly be valued by you. It is the affection and prayers of the little company of men, unpopular with the world, whom you have called your teachers. We are comrades with you in trial and in testimony, and comrades also in the exuberant joy of the gospel of Christ. Our affection will go with you to the ends of the earth. And with us, brethren, there stand today far more than seven thousand who have not bowed the knee to Baal. God has not left himself without a witness even in this unbelieving age.

In the second place, we can tell you that this is not the first time of discouragement in the history of the Christian church. Again and again the gospel has seemed to be forever forgotten; yet always it has burst forth with new power and the world has been set aflame. So it may be in our day. God's Spirit is all-powerful, and he can still bring men to the Savior of their souls.

But what I desire particularly to tell you is not to be too greatly impressed by the pomp and power of this unbelieving age. With all the noise and boasting of the age in which we are living, there are some things that the age has lost.

About one week ago I stood on the one hundred and second story of the great Empire State Building in the city of New York. From there I looked down upon a scene like nothing else upon this earth. I watched the elevated trains, which from that distance seemed to be like slow caterpillars crawling along the rails; I listened to the ceaseless roar of the city ascending from a vast area to that great height. And I looked down upon that strange city which has been created on Manhattan Island within the last five or ten years—gigantic, bizarre, magnificently ugly. It seemed like some weird, tortured imagination of things in another world. I came down from that building very greatly impressed.

But as I reflected upon what I had seen, there came into my mind the memory of other buildings that I had contemplated in the course of my life. I thought of an English cathedral rising from the infinite greenness of some quiet cathedral close and above the ancient trees. I thought of the west façade of some continental cathedral, produced at a time when Gothic architecture was not what it is today, imitative and cold and dead, but a living expression of the human soul; when every carving in every obscure corner, never perhaps to be seen by human eye, was an act of worship of Almighty God.

As I revived these memories, certain thoughts came into my mind. The modern builders, I thought, can uplift the body; they uplifted my body in express elevators twelve hundred and forty feet in record time. But whereas the modern builders, in an age of unbelief, can uplift the body, the ancient builders, in an age of faith, could uplift the soul. As one stands before the tower of a medieval cathedral—with one century laying the foundation there below, another century contributing its quota in the middle distance, and another century bringing the vast conception to its climax in a spire that seems to point upward to the skies—one is uplifted to a height far greater than the twelve hundred and forty feet of the Empire State Building; one is uplifted not by some rebellious tower of Babel seeking to reach unto heaven by human pride, but rather on the wings of faith, up and up until one seems to stand in the very presence of the infinite God.

I am no medievalist, my friends; and I do not want you to be medievalists. I rejoice with all my heart in the marvelous widening of our knowledge of this mysterious universe that has come in modern times; I rejoice in the wonderful technical achievements of our day. I trust that you, my brethren, will never fall into the "Touch not, taste not, handle not" attitude which Paul condemned in his time; I hope you will never fall into that ancient heresy of forgetting that this is God's world and that neither its good things nor its wonders should be despised by those upon whom, through God's bounty, they have been bestowed. I trust that you will consecrate to God not an impoverished man, narrowed in interests, narrowed in mind and heart, but a man with all God-given powers developed to the full.

Moreover, I cherish in my soul a vague yet glorious hope—the hope of a time when these material achievements, instead of making man the victim of his own machines, may be used in the expression of some wondrous thought. There may come a time when God will send to the world the fire of genius, which he has taken from it in our time, and when he will send something far greater than genius—a humble heart finding in his worship the highest use of all knowledge and of all power. There may come a time when men will wonder at their former obsession with these material things, when they will see that these modern inventions in the material realm are in themselves as valueless as the ugly little bits of metal type in a printer's composing room, and that their true value will be found only when they become the means of expressing some glorious poem.

Meanwhile, however, we are living in a drab and empty age. The law of God has been forgotten or despised, and dreary slavery is the result. Do you think that this is a happy or a blessed age? Oh, no, my friends. Amid all the noise and shouting and power and machinery, there are hungry hearts—hearts thirsting for the living water, hearts hungry for the bread that is bread indeed.

That hunger you alone can still. You can do so not by any riches of your own, but as humble ministers of the Lord Jesus Christ. How wonderfully rich you are, my brethren, rich with riches greater by far than all the wealth and power of this world, rich with the inexhaustible riches of God's Word! Oh, may you use those riches! May this graduation day be only the beginning of your study of the Word; may you learn ever to bring forth out of that treasure things new and old! May you be no adherents of some strange new sect; may you maintain your contact with the grand and noble scholarly tradition of the Christian church; may your sermons be born in earnest study and in the agony of your souls! When you come forth into your pulpits, be they great or obscure, may you come forth out of a place of labor and meditation and prayer!

Perhaps it may be objected that that would be a new kind of preaching. Yes, but this is a new seminary, and a new seminary may hope to bring forth some things that are new—new at least to this age. Who can say, my brethren? Perhaps you may be the humble instruments, by the use of whatever talents God has given you, of lifting preaching out of the rut into which too often it has fallen, and of making it again, by God's grace, a thing of power.

Remember this, at least—the things in which the world is now interested are the things that are seen; but the things that are seen are temporal, and the things that are not seen are eternal. You, as ministers of Christ, are called to deal with the unseen things. You are stewards of the mysteries of God. You alone can lead men, by the proclamation of God's word, out of the crash and jazz and noise and rattle and smoke of this weary age into the green pastures and beside the still waters; you alone, as ministers of reconciliation, can give what the world with all its boasting and pride can never give—the infinite sweetness of the communion of the redeemed soul with the living God.

19

SERVANTS OF GOD OR
SERVANTS OF MEN

Y ou will notice that I have written what I shall say to you upon
these few sheets of paper that I hold in my hand. That does not
mean that what I shall say does not come from the heart. It does
not mean that when in deep affection I bid you Godspeed in my own name
and in the name of my colleagues in the faculty I desire to place any cold
medium of a written page between my heart and yours. But it means that I
am conscious of standing here in a very great crisis in the history of the Presbyterian Church in the U.S.A. On such an occasion it is incumbent upon
a man to weigh his words, and to keep precise record of what he says. I am
speaking, indeed, without consultation of my colleagues. I alone am responsible for what I shall say. But I am aware of the momentous issues involved, and I have sent a copy of this little address, insignificant though it
is in itself, to the stated clerk of the General Assembly of the Presbyterian
Church in the U.S.A., and to the stated clerks of the presbyteries of New
Brunswick and Philadelphia.

You are seeking entrance into the Christian ministry. At such a time it

"Servants of God or Servants of Men" is a commencement address given in 1934
to the graduating class of Westminster Theological Seminary, and appeared in *Christianity Today* 5 (May 1934) 9–10. Reprinted in *What Is Christianity?* ed. Ned Bernard
Stonehouse (Grand Rapids: Eerdmans, 1951).

is proper for you to count the cost; it is proper for you to ask just what being a Christian minister means. There is just one thing that I want to say to you in answer to that question. The thing that I want to say to you is that you cannot be a Christian minister if you proclaim the word of man; you can be a Christian minister only if you proclaim, without fear or favor, the Word of God.

In the twenty-second chapter of 2 Kings, we read how a messenger who was sent to call the prophet Micaiah the son of Imlah coached him as to what he should say. "Behold now," he said, "the words of the prophets declare good unto the king with one mouth; let thy word, I pray thee, be like the word of one of them, and speak that which is good." But Micaiah said: "As the Lord liveth, what the Lord saith unto me, that will I speak."

You, my brethren, must be like Micaiah the son of Imlah; you too must say: "As the Lord liveth, what the Lord saith unto me, that will I speak." The Lord does not, indeed, speak to you in the manner in which He spoke to Micaiah. He does not speak to you by direct supernatural revelation. You are not prophets. But he speaks to you through the supernatural book. It is only when you proclaim the words of that book that you are a true minister of Jesus Christ. Only then can you say: "Thus saith the Lord."

The congregations for which you labor may, as the world looks upon them, be but insignificant groups of humble people. But never forget that those insignificant and humble groups are the church of the living God, and that you as their ministers must proclaim to them the awful and holy and blessed Word.

If you obtain your message from any other authority than the Word of God, if you obtain it from the pronouncements of presbyteries or General Assemblies, then you may wear the garb of ministers, but you are not ministers in the sight of God. You are disloyal to the Lord Jesus Christ: you have betrayed a precious trust.

The temptation to you to be disloyal is coming to you in insistent fashion just at the present moment. It is coming to you through the words of cultured and well-meaning gentlemen, and it is coming to you through the unwarranted acts of ecclesiastical councils and courts. In the Presbytery of Baltimore, at a recent meeting, it came through the stated clerk of the General Assembly. The following passage from a letter of the stated clerk of the General Assembly to the stated clerk of that presbytery was read in open session:

If and when any students from Westminster Seminary come before your Presbytery, they should be informed that the Presbytery will neither license nor ordain them until they have given a written pledge that they will support the official agencies of the Church as a part of their pledge of loyalty to the government and discipline of the Church.

The Presbytery of New Brunswick, acting earlier on the same principle and in violation of the Constitution of the Presbyterian Church in the U.S.A., has placed in its manual a provision that no one shall be received into the presbytery without being subjected to an examination as to his willingness to support the regularly appointed boards and agencies.

I feel compelled to say to you, my brethren, with the utmost plainness, that if you sign the pledge demanded of you in that letter of Dr. Mudge and practically implied in that action of the Presbytery of New Brunswick, if you obtain your licensure of ordination in that way, then, quite irrespective of the question whether the boards and agencies are or are not faithful at this moment or at any particular moment, you have become servants of men and are not in the high biblical sense servants of the Lord Jesus Christ. If you promise to adapt your message to shifting majorities in church councils or to the mandates of church officials, if you promise to commend one kind of missions this year and an opposite kind next year, as the General Assembly, newly elected every year, may direct, if you thus take the Bible from your pulpits and place the minutes of the General Assembly in its place, if you thus abandon the Reformation and do despite all the blood and tears that it cost, if you thus abandon the high liberty guaranteed you by the Constitution of the Presbyterian Church in the U.S.A., and if (as, alas, you do if you abandon that liberty) you abandon your allegiance to the Lord Jesus Christ by putting fallible men into the place of authority that belongs only to him, then the ministry has become, as far as you are concerned, merely a profession, and rather a contemptible profession too. You may, by taking such a step, obtain high ecclesiastical preferment, but never can you be ministers of the New Covenant, never can you be ambassadors of God.

If, on the other hand, you choose, as indeed you have already shown very nobly that you have chosen, to obey God rather than men, then you may look to the future with unconquerable joy. If any one door is closed to you by the usurped authority of human councils or officials, be assured that some other and greater door will be opened to you in God's own way. But above all, remember that that Captain is worthy whose service you are thus preferring to the favor of men. He is worthy because of his infinite power and glory. But he is also worthy of something else. There are other things besides the effulgence of his royal majesty which mark him as our Lord:

> Hath He marks to lead me to Him,
>   If He be my Guide?
> "In His feet and hands are wound-prints,
>   And His side."
>
> Is there diadem, as Monarch,
>   That His brow adorns?
> "Yea, a crown, in very surety,
>   But of thorns."
>
> If I find Him, if I follow,
>   What His guerdon here?
> "Many a sorrow, many a labor,
>   Many a tear."
>
> If I still hold closely to Him,
>   What hath He at last?
> "Sorrow vanquished, labor ended,
>   Jordan passed."
>
> If I ask Him to receive me,
>   Will He say me nay?
> "Not till earth and not till heaven
>   Pass away."
>
> Finding, following, keeping, struggling,
>   Is He sure to bless?
> "Saints, apostles, prophets, martyrs,
>   Answer, 'Yes.'"

"Ye were bought with a price," my brethren; "be not ye the servants of men."

20

THE MINISTER AND HIS GREEK TESTAMENT

The widening breach between the minister and his Greek Testament may be traced to two principal causes. The modern minister objects to his Greek New Testament or is indifferent to it, first, because he is becoming less interested in his Greek, and second, because he is becoming less interested in his New Testament.

The former objection is merely one manifestation of the well-known tendency in modern education to reject the "humanities" in favor of studies that are more obviously useful, a tendency which is fully as pronounced in the universities as it is in the theological seminaries. In many colleges, the study of Greek is almost abandoned; there is little wonder, therefore, that the graduates are not prepared to use their Greek Testament. Plato and Homer are being neglected as much as Paul. A refutation of the arguments by which this tendency is justified would exceed the limits of the present article. This much, however, may be said—the refutation must recognize the opposing principles that are involved. The advocate of the study of Greek and Latin should never attempt to plead his cause merely before the bar of "efficiency." Something, no doubt, might be said even there; it might possibly be contended that an acquaintance with Greek and Latin is really necessary to acquaintance with the mother tongue, which is obviously so

"The Minister and His Greek New Testament" originally published in *The Presbyterian* 88 (February 7, 1918) 8–9.

important for getting on in the world. But why not go straight to the root of the matter? The real trouble with the modern exaltation of "practical" studies at the expense of the humanities is that it is based upon a vicious conception of the whole purpose of education. The modern conception of the purpose of education is that education is merely intended to enable a man to live, but not to give him those things that make life worth living.

In the second place, the modern minister is neglecting his Greek New Testament because he is becoming less interested in his New Testament in general—less interested in his Bible. The Bible used to be regarded as providing the very sum and substance of preaching; a preacher was true to his calling only as he succeeded in reproducing and applying the message of the Word of God. Very different is the modern attitude. The Bible is not discarded, to be sure, but it is treated only as one of the sources, even though it is still the chief source, of the preacher's inspiration. Moreover, a host of other duties other than preaching and other than interpretation of the Word of God are required of the modern pastor. He must organize clubs and social activities of a dozen different kinds; he must assume a prominent part in movements for civic reform. In short, the minister has ceased to be a specialist. The change appears, for example, in the attitude of theological students, even of a devout and reverent type. One outstanding difficulty in theological education today is that the students persist in regarding themselves not as specialists, but as laymen. Critical questions about the Bible they regard as the property of men who are training themselves for the theological professorships or the like, while the ordinary minister, in their judgment, may content himself with the most superficial layman's acquaintance with the problems involved. The minister is thus no longer a specialist in the Bible, but has become merely a sort of general manager of the affairs of a congregation.

The bearing of this modern attitude toward the study of the Bible upon the study of the Greek Testament is sufficiently obvious. If the time allotted to strictly biblical studies must be diminished, obviously the most laborious part of those studies, the part least productive of immediate results, will be the first to go. And that part, for students insufficiently prepared, is the study of Greek and Hebrew. If, on the other hand, the minister is a specialist—if the one thing that he owes his congregation above all others is a thorough acquaintance, scientific as well as experimental, with the Bible— then the importance of Greek requires no elaborate argument. In the first place, almost all the most important books about the New Testament presuppose a knowledge of Greek: the student who is without at least a smattering of Greek is obliged to use for the most part works that are written, figuratively speaking, in words of one syllable. In the second place, such a student cannot deal with all the problems at first hand, but in a thousand important questions is at the mercy of the judgment of others. In the third place, our student without Greek cannot acquaint himself with the form as well as the content of the New Testament books. The New Testament, as well as all other literature, loses something in translation. But why argue the question? Every scientific student of the New Testament without exception knows that Greek is really necessary to his work; the real question is only as to whether our ministry should be manned by scientific students.

That question is merely one phase of the most important question that is now facing the church—the question of Christianity and culture. The modern world is dominated by a type of thought that is either contradictory to Christianity or else out of vital connection with Christianity. This type of thought applied directly to the Bible has resulted in the naturalistic view of the biblical history—the view that rejects the supernatural not merely in the Old Testament narratives, but also in the gospel account of the life of Jesus. According to such a view the Bible is valuable because it teaches certain ideas about God and his relations to the world, because it teaches by symbols and example, as well as by formal presentation, certain great principles that have always been true. According to the supernaturalistic view, on the other hand, the Bible contains not merely a presentation of something that was always true, but also a record of something that happened—namely, the redemptive work of Jesus Christ. If this latter view is correct, then the Bible is absolutely unique; it is not merely one of the sources of the preacher's inspiration, but the very sum and substance of what he has to say. But if so, then whatever else the preacher need not know, he must know the Bible; he must know it at first hand, and be able to interpret and defend it. Especially while doubt remains in the world as to the great central question, who more properly than the ministers should engage in the work of resolving such doubt—by intellectual instruction even more than by argument? The work cannot be turned over to a few professors whose work is of interest only to themselves, but must be undertaken energetically by spiritually minded men throughout the church. But obviously, this work can be undertaken to best advantage only by those who have an important prerequisite for the study in a knowledge of the original languages upon which a large part of the discussion is based.

If, however, it is important for the minister to use his Greek Testament, what is to be done about it? Suppose early opportunities were neglected, or what was once required has been lost in the busy rush of ministerial life. Here we may come forward boldly with a message of hope. The Greek of the New Testament is by no means a difficult language; a very fair knowledge of it may be acquired by any minister of average intelligence. And to that end two homely directions may be given. In the first place, the Greek should be read aloud. A language cannot easily be learned by the eye alone. The sound as well as the sense of familiar passages should be impressed upon the mind, until sound and sense are connected without the medium of translation. Let this result not be hastened; it will come of itself if the simple direction is followed. In the second place, the Greek Testament should be read every day without fail, Sabbaths included. Ten minutes a day is of vastly more value than seventy minutes once a week. If the student keeps a "morning watch," the Greek Testament ought to be given a place in it; at any rate, the Greek Testament the Greek should be read devotionally. The Greek Testament is a sacred book, and should be treated as such. If it is treated so, the reading of it will soon become a source of joy and power.

PART FIVE

THE NATURE AND MISSION OF THE CHURCH

21

THE PARTING OF THE WAYS

The Presbyterian Church in the United States of America has apparently come to the parting of the ways. It may stand for Christ, or it may stand against him; but it can hardly halt between the two opinions.

If it stands for Christ, it will do the work which he has put it into the world to do. And that work is the work of witness-bearing. "Ye shall be my witnesses," said the risen Christ, according to the book of Acts; and these words are really a correct summary of New Testament Christianity from beginning to end. New Testament Christianity is not a life as distinguished from a doctrine, or a life which has doctrine as its flower and fruit, but— just the other way around—it is a life founded upon a doctrine. It is a life produced not merely by exhortation, not merely by personal contacts, but primarily by an account of something that happened, by a piece of good news, or a gospel. The apostles set forth the great event after it had occurred—they said "that Christ died for our sins according to the Scriptures, that he was buried, and that he rose again the third day according to the Scriptures." The Savior himself in the days of his flesh proclaimed the same great event by way of prophecy: "Repent ye," he said, "for the kingdom of heaven is at hand," and "The Son of man came not to be ministered unto,

"The Parting of the Ways" originally published (with slight modifications) in *The Presbyterian* 94 (April 17, 1924) 7–9, and (April 24, 1924) 6–7.

but to minister, and to give his life a ransom for many." But whether the event was in the past or in the future, both the apostles and Jesus proclaimed an event; Jesus gave to his disciples a message in which he was to be offered as the Savior of the world.

But if so, it is important above all else to get the message straight. When a witness takes his seat on the witness stand, it does not make much difference what the cut of his coat is or whether his sentences are nicely turned. The important thing is that he tell the truth, the whole truth, and nothing but the truth. So it is with that witness stand which is called the pulpit. It does not make so much difference about the manner in which the message is delivered; there can even be charity for imperfections in the spirit and motives of the messenger; but what is important above all things is that the content of the message should be true.

The content of the Christian message is being contradicted, not only in what is said but even more clearly in what is not said, by the regular preacher in the First Presbyterian Church of New York. Doctrine, says Dr. Fosdick, is the expression of Christian experience, and doctrinal controversies may be ended if we will only translate doctrine back into the life from which it came.

If such assertions are to be approved, if we decide to adopt the pragmatist view that doctrine is merely the necessarily changing expression of Christian experience, we ought at least to understand what that view involves. And what it involves is most abundantly plain—it involves the most abysmal skepticism. If a man holds, for example, that belief in the existence of a personal God, Creator and Ruler of the world, is merely the intellectual form in which the ineffable experience of religion clothes itself in this generation, and that in another generation God may with equal validity be regarded in some other way—such a man does not really hold to that belief in a personal God even now. Or if one holds that the beliefs in the virgin birth and in the bodily resurrection of Christ merely expressed the veneration which the early disciples felt toward Jesus, then one has simply accepted the mythical theory of the New Testament which has been held by opponents of Christianity ever since the days of Strauss—the theory that the miracle narratives are religious ideas, inner experiences, clothed in historical form. Or if the Modernist holds that the divinity of Christ is merely a formula to express what he owes to Jesus, then his assertion of belief in the divinity of Christ is not the most Christian, but the least Christian thing that he says; it simply means that, having given up belief in God as the Creator who brought forth the world by the fiat of his will, he uses the word "divinity" or the word "God" to express his veneration for a holy man; the Modernist preacher says that Jesus is God not because he thinks high of Jesus, but because he thinks desperately low of God.

At this point we find the most fundamental divergence between Modernism and the Christian faith; the Modernist assertion that doctrine springs from life, and may be translated back into the life from which it came, really involves the relinquishment of all objective truth in the sphere of religion. If a thing is merely useful, it may cease to be useful in another generation; but if it is true, it remains true to the end of time. In holding that doctrine is merely the necessarily changing expression of a unitary experience, Modernism has not merely denied some Christian doctrines and retained others but it has denied all doctrines. What used to be regarded as the knowledge of God becomes to the Modernist like the game which the child plays on the nursery floor. The child says, "Let's pretend," and by pretending releases certain pleasurable emotions. But it is all a game, and when years of discretion come, childish things are put away. Similar is the Modernist or pragmatist view of Christian doctrine as the mere expression in human forms of thought of an experience regarded as really ineffable. It makes little difference how much or how little of Christian doctrine the Modernist affirms, since whatever he affirms, he affirms as a mere expression of an inner experience, and does not affirm any of it as fact. Modernism, so far as it is religious at all, is mysticism, whereas Christianity is the worship of one whom (in part only, yet truly) one knows; Modernism is passionately anti-intellectual, whereas Christianity possesses a reasonable faith; Modernism regards itself as independent of science, whereas Christianity must seek to justify its place, despite all the intellectual labor which that involves, in the realm of facts.

Every Christian, then, is primarily a witness; he is in possession of a message which claims to be true. But the Christian witness-bearing is not merely individual; it is also collective. There is a witness-bearing of the individual, but there is also a corporate witness-bearing of the church.

The corporate witness-bearing of the Presbyterian church is carried on especially through the pulpit. Under Presbyterian law, no man can permanently occupy a pulpit of the church without the church's endorsement; the preacher therefore speaks not only for himself, but for the church. That does not mean that the church seeks to impose any beliefs upon any man simply on the ground that they are beliefs of the church; it does not mean that there is the slightest interference with the right of private judgment. But it means that if a man is to speak *in a Presbyterian pulpit,* and obtain the endorsement which is involved in that position, he must be in agreement with the message for the propagation of which the church, in accordance with its constitution, plainly exists.

But many persons seem to regard the duty of witness-bearing as a merely personal or individual thing. "We ourselves," they say, in effect, "will give men the correct, scriptural answer to the question, 'What shall I do to be saved?' But we refuse to object to the answer which other men are giving in the church; we are believers in supernatural Christianity ourselves, but we refuse to involve ourselves in heresy trials or ecclesiastical exclusion of any kind." Men who talk in this way really represent the greatest danger which the church is facing at the present crisis, for in seeming to witness for Christ they are really witnessing against his cause more effectively, in some ways, than those who actually blaspheme his name. It is really quite impossible to place one's life in distinct compartments, and to be Christian in one capacity and anti-Christian in another; it is really quite impossible to be Christian in the prayer meeting or the pulpit and anti-Christian at presbytery or at the General Assembly. It is really quite impossible to be a member of a body and evade the responsibilities involved in membership. Thus, to take a concrete example, it is not merely the preacher in the First Presbyterian Church of New York who is informing the persons who throng that church that our own obedience to the commands of Christ is sufficient, that life produces doctrine and not doctrine life, that a man can first become good by following the example of Jesus and then ask afterwards about the meaning of his death. It is not merely this one preacher who is saying these things so diametrically opposed to the gospel of Christ, but it is the whole Presbyterian church. The constitution of the church plainly regards the preacher as a representative of the whole body, as a man who sets forth the system of doctrine taught in the Word of God, and it plainly gives the courts of the church power to remove any preacher who is preaching what is contrary to that. But with power always goes responsibility. The whole church is saying to many a little one, especially now that the issue has once been raised: "This that you hear in the First Presbyterian Church of New York is the way of salvation; heed the exhortation, and you will be saved."

And the responsibility of the whole church is also the responsibility of every individual member; the government of our church is democratic, and democracy involves responsibility for the individual. Every individual member of the church—to say nothing of ministers who are members of church courts—has a vital responsibility for what is done in the pulpits and still more plainly in the agencies and boards. Individuals must witness for Christ, but the church must also witness in its corporate capacity, and no individual is walking uprightly according to the truth of the gospel if he acquiesces in a corporate witness that is false.

The corporate witness of the Presbyterian church is being undermined in many ways. But two attacks perhaps stand out with special prominence. One is the Report of the Presbytery of New York in the matter of Dr. Fosdick; the other is the Modernist "Affirmation" of the one hundred and fifty ministers.

What is most regrettable about the Report of Presbytery is the extremely low view which it takes of the function of the preacher. This low view appears most clearly perhaps in the following sentences:

> This committee therefore agrees with the Session of the First Church that the sermon, "Shall the Fundamentalists Win?" while seeking a laudable end, was captioned by an objectionable and challenging title that tended to contention and strife. We further agree with the Session that the sermon was open to misunderstanding, and, like the Session, we regret its wide circulation, and deplore the serious distress and disturbances to which it has given rise in many minds. We go further to say that while we are sure that the preaching and teaching in the First Church has never spoken any denial of the church's doctrine of the Virgin Birth of our Lord, it is our judgment that the manner in which the subject was dealt with in the sermon mentioned, is open to painful misconstruction and just objection.

In these sentences, Dr. Fosdick is rebuked for the form of the sermon, and it is intimated below that he will be more discreet in the future. "This Committee," says the Report, "has no reason to doubt that Dr. Fosdick . . . will willingly accept counsel and direction from this Presbytery of which he is a corresponding member." The proposal seems to us to be a thoroughly degrading one—degrading both to those who make it and to the one to whom it is made. Far from being the worst sermon that has been preached in the First Presbyterian Church of New York, the sermon "Shall the Fundamentalists Win?" was to our mind in some respects the best, for it came perhaps nearer than any other to putting the real views of the preacher in words that the plain man could understand. For our part, we believe that a frankness even more complete than that partial lapse into plain-speaking ought to be matter of course. Above all else, a preacher should seek a pulpit where with head erect he can speak his full mind.

But the committee almost seems to favor a policy of concealment. The sermon, it says in effect, would better not have been so widely circulated. Such is exactly the policy which has been pursued by the anti-Christian party in the church for many years. The faith has been undermined week by week, but publicity that might lead to ecclesiastical action has for the most part been avoided. We reject with all our souls any such conception of the preacher's function; the preacher, we believe, ought to say nothing in the pulpit which he could not make known to all the world, and unless he himself repudiates what he has said, he ought not to fear its publication.

Almost equally deplorable is the evident acquiescence of the report in the session's contention that in the sermon "Shall the Fundamentalists Win?" the preacher merely "presented two extreme views on several points of Christian doctrine and did not clearly define his own position with regard to them." This contention is refuted, or rather deprived of all significance, by Dr. Fosdick's letter, in which he speaks of "the unmistakable fact" that "he is committed to the side called 'liberal' "; and to anyone who is familiar with the thoroughgoing naturalism of Dr. Fosdick's whole position, the contention is nothing short of absurd. Either Dr. Fosdick accepts the virgin birth and the other miracles of the New Testament (in that case, he will give joyful testimony to these things) or else he disbelieves them—as of course he does disbelieve them (in that case, it is highly objectionable to suggest, as the committee does, that he should be asked to conceal his disbelief in the pulpit).

Most deplorable of all, perhaps, is the assertion of Dr. Fosdick and of the committee that he believes in the "deity" of Christ. Here we have at its worst that double use of language which so offends the common sense of many men, both within and without the church. Dr. Fosdick does indeed attribute a real meaning to the word "deity," and in that meaning the word is dear to his heart; but he ought to know that the word will be taken in a totally different sense by the rank and file of the church. The word "deity" will be taken in one way by those who hold the transcendent or theistic view of God as the Creator of the world; it is taken in a totally different way by Dr. Fosdick, who regards "fiat creation" as a thing that does not matter to religion (see "The Deepening of Faith," in *The Church Tower* for January, 1924, page 11), and loosely applies the word "deity" to Jesus as a mark of honor for a supreme human being and as an expression of gratitude for a change wrought in the speaker's life by a good example. Thus Dr. Fosdick and with him the Modernist members of the presbytery (though no doubt with good intentions and without realizing what is being done) are offending against the fundamental principle of accuracy in language. In accordance with that fundamental principle, language is accurate not when the meaning attributed to the words by the speaker is in accordance with the facts, but when the impression produced in the minds of the particular persons addressed is in accordance with the facts. Thus the letter of Dr. Fosdick, which is printed in the presbytery's report, would be accurate if it were addressed to a company of men familiar with the pragmatist meaning of the terms employed; but intended as it is to be read by the church at large, it is misleading in the extreme. Every one of the terms employed is used in a sense quite different from its Christian meaning; yet Christian men will suppose that something evangelical and Christian is being said. And from that misunderstanding ecclesiastical advantage for the writer and his supporters is being obtained.

The passionate hostility of Dr. Fosdick to the fundamental things of the Christian religion appears with special clearness in the sermon entitled "The More Abundant Life," preached in the Baptist Temple, Philadelphia, on Thursday evening, February 7, 1924, and published in *The Temple Review*, Vol. 32, No. 12, March 21, 1924. There is indeed in that sermon the customary misleading use of Christian terminology, the customary misleading quotation of the gospel of John (as though Dr. Fosdick held the gospel of John to be true!). But the anti-evangelical animus of the whole discourse is abundantly plain. That animus is directed, first of all, against the Bible, Jesus being represented as rejecting the authority of those Old Testament Scriptures (page 5), which in reality he used as devout "Bible Christians" use the Scriptures today. Secondly, the animus is directed against the Protestant theology which is based upon the Bible. Dr. Fosdick speaks with contempt of "the miserable wranglings" among the denominations "over theological questions that never made any real difference to the richness and fullness of any Spiritual life," and of Lutheranism, the Reformed church, the Episcopal church, . . . "all confusing the souls of men with their various theological policies." Yet it is this same preacher about whom we have the grave assurance of the committee of presbytery that he will respect the obligations due to his position in a creedal church—a creedal church definitely committed by the ordination pledge to the propagation of one of the most clear-cut of those theological systems upon which the preacher pours forth the vials of his scorn!

But the animus of the sermon is directed not only against the Bible, not only against the system of theology which, according to the committee, the preacher is obligated to respect, but also against the entire truth content of the Christian religion.

> Consider in the beginning [says Dr. Fosdick] the way in which people have these experiences for themselves and their fellows, and because they are invariably so simple, they carry those experiences up into their own lives and try to unify, and co-ordinate and rationalize them and make doctrine out of their experiences. When they have contracted a formula, they love it, because the experience for which it stands is precious. Their affections and their loyalty gather around that formula, and the Church walks down the centuries with its shining formula waving like a banner at its head. But then the day unquestionably came when the Church moved out into a new age, with new ways of thinking that never had been on the earth before. And then men began to have trouble with the formula. They don't understand it, and so they don't believe it. Once they fought for it; now they begin to fight about it, and a veritable theological uproar starts, and it is all about the formula. What is the way out of it? It is not hard to see. Translate the formula back into the experience out of which it came. That's the test. Trace any theological question you are troubled about, back into the experience of thought out of which it originally came, for all doctrine comes from life. It endeavors to explain life, and if there is any truth in it, you can take it back to life and test it there.

If that principle, that all doctrine comes from life, is accepted, then of course the agnosticism of Dr. Fosdick becomes inevitable. But the question is whether the principle is true or false. According to the constitution of our church—especially according to the ordination pledge—the principle is false. Doctrine, according to that pledge, is not an explanation of human experience but it is a system revealed in the Holy Scriptures by God. It is not the product of experience, but a setting forth of those facts upon which Christian experience is based.

The constitution of our church is not peculiar at this point, but merely sets forth what is at the very basis of the Christian religion. By Dr. Fosdick that basis is denied, and in its place there is put an agnosticism which in the same sermon the preacher proceeds to apply to the Trinity and to the divinity of Christ. Not some doctrines are denied, but all doctrines, and what we have left is an agnosticism of the most thoroughgoing kind. The Trinity and the divinity of Christ are indeed verbally affirmed, but like all other doctrines, they are affirmed not as facts, but as formulae for the expression of an experience from which they came. Skepticism could hardly be more complete.

It is that skepticism which is being instilled into the minds of the congregation in the First Church of New York. For there is nothing peculiar in the sermon which has just been quoted; on the contrary, this sermon gives the key to all of Dr. Fosdick's teaching. By placing the stamp of its approval upon such a preacher, the presbytery has made a very definite attack upon the corporate witness of the Presbyterian church.

Another attack has been made by the Modernist "Affirmation" of the one hundred and fifty ministers, for which by an active propaganda many more signatures have now been secured. The Affirmation does indeed employ Christian terminology—and, deceived by this terminology, there are no doubt Christian men among the signers. But the document itself is radically hostile to the Christian faith. It is directed (1) against the creedal character of the Presbyterian church and (2) against the entire factual basis of Christianity.

It is directed against the creedal character of the church because it advocates a kind of interpretation of the creed which makes the creed a dead letter. If a man may "interpret" a perfectly plain confession of faith to mean its exact opposite, what is the use of having any confession at all?

But the Affirmation is also destructive of the entire factual basis of Christianity, for in the fourth section the basic facts of the gospel, notably the bodily resurrection of our Lord, are designated as "theories" to explain something else—theories for which alternatives are said to be also permitted by the Scriptures. Could anything be more absurd? How can the Scriptures teach, for example, that Jesus was born without human father, and at the same time permit an "explanation" which regards him as having a human father—unless indeed the Scriptures are contradictory to themselves? But if the Scriptures are regarded as contradictory to themselves in the account which they give of Jesus, then the trustworthiness of the Bible is given up; and the rejection of the authority of the Bible, really manifest throughout all the Affirmation, becomes here doubly plain. The truth is, however, that it is not merely the Scriptures which are assailed in this Affirmation, but the whole character of our religion founded on historical facts.

The Report of the Presbytery of New York and the Affirmation of the One Hundred and Fifty are not isolated phenomena, but are simply manifestations of the attempt which a great anti-Christian movement[1] is now making to gain control of the Presbyterian church. We speak advisedly of an anti-Christian *movement*, rather than of anti-Christian *men*. What the standing of any individual is before God, what the connection of any individual with Christ, we do not presume for one moment to say. Dr. Fosdick, for example, protests that he loves Christ with all his soul, and we do not in the slightest question the full sincerity of his moving words. The Christ whom he loves is indeed not the Christ of the New Testament, not the Christ who advanced those stupendous claims which Dr. Fosdick rejects. But we do not presume for one moment to say whether that love is or is not connected with saving faith. Certainly we are not without admiration for the ethical fervor which is evidenced by much that Dr. Fosdick says. We do not believe that it will give the sinner peace or lead to the genuine conquest of sin, but we admire it all the same, and we welcome any temporary palliation of evil conditions which may come through such means. But we believe that the fervor of Dr. Fosdick would have fuller scope if, by some means more effective than the gestures of withdrawal which he has made so far, he would put an end to a situation which is radically false. The continuance of such a preacher in a creedal church is, we are constrained to believe, an anomaly which is out of harmony with the ethical qualities of the preacher's life, and counterbalances whatever good, judged by his own standards, he might otherwise accomplish in the world.

At any rate, the public testimony of this preacher, and of the many preachers like him, is diametrically opposed to the gospel of Christ and is

1. See *Christianity and Liberalism* (1923; second edition, 1924), by J. Gresham Machen.

leading men away from the true Savior of their souls; it is producing a confidence in human goodness, in human ability to obey the commands of Christ, which it is the first business of the Christian preacher to break down. For our part, we feel compelled to relinquish all confidence in such goodness and to trust in the crucified Savior alone.

We certainly do not wish to "split" the church; on the contrary, we are working for the unity of the church with all our might. But in order that there should be unity within the church, it is necessary above all that there should be sharp separation of the church from the world. The carrying out of that separation is a prime duty of the hour. Those who try to save men by the ethical principles of a Jesus whom they have reconstructed through rejection of the New Testament witness should form one body; those who glory in nothing save the cross of Christ should form another body. And that latter body is the Christian church. What our Savior demands of us above all else is faithfulness. He has placed us in the world as witnesses, and the supreme duty of his witnesses is that they should testify faithfully to him.

The Presbyterian church, we are convinced, is still predominantly Christian; it would stand for Christ if it knew the real meaning of the hostile propaganda which is now attacking the center of its life. At such a time clearness is demanded of every Christian man; the hour for merely pleasant words is over; love demands the plain speaking of the truth. We are witnesses; and if we are faithful to our sacred trust we must witness truly, whether men hear or whether they forbear.

What shall our decision be? Shall we transfer our allegiance to another gospel? Or shall we, by the help of God's Spirit, be faithful to the Lord and Savior who bought us with his precious blood?

22

THE MISSION OF THE CHURCH

Before we can consider the mission of the church, we must determine what the church is. What are its limits? What forms a part of it and what does not? Where is the true Christian church to be found?

According to the Westminster Confession of Faith of the Presbyterian church, the invisible church is to be distinguished from the visible church. The invisible church consists of the whole number of those who are saved; the visible church consists of those who profess the true religion, together with their children. There is absolutely no warrant in Scripture for supposing that any particular branch of the visible church will necessarily be preserved. Always, it is true, there will be a visible church upon the earth, but any particular church organization may become so corrupt as to be not a true church of Christ, but (as the Confession of Faith puts it) "a synagogue of Satan."

Now the Presbyterian Church in the United States of America has certainly not become a synagogue of Satan. The hostile forces in it are indeed very powerful, and in some sections of it they are dominant, but the majority is still Christian. But the point is that we have absolutely no warrant

"The Mission of the Church" is an address originally delivered on March 1, 1926 before the Presbyterian Ministers' Association of Philadelphia, and appeared in *The Presbyterian* 96 (April 8, 1926) 8–11.

in Scripture for holding that the Christian character of this particular church or of any other particular church will necessarily be preserved. The question whether this church will remain Christian or will become non-Christian (as so many other ecclesiastical bodies throughout the world have done) will probably be determined in the next five or ten years. If the indifferentist party continues (working with the Modernists) to dominate the church, as it did (so far as administrative matters are concerned) by a slight majority at our last General Assembly, and as it does so generally in the boards and agencies, if the great issue continues to be concealed, then the Church will soon become non-Christian; but if, on the other hand, the issue is plainly raised and is decided aright, then the church will continue to be a church of Jesus Christ.

But what needs to be carefully observed is that the church universal is not bound to any one organization. Our Lord established that fact in a great passage in the gospels, which is often misused. A man was casting out demons in the name of Christ. The disciples bade Jesus rebuke him because he followed not with them. But Jesus said: "Forbid him not, . . . he that is not against us is on our part." That utterance is sometimes held to support doctrinal indifferentism—to support the absurd view that a man can be a real disciple of Jesus, no matter what opinions he holds about Jesus. But such a use of the passage is quite preposterous. That man in the gospel held no low view of Jesus, such as is held by the Modernists of today. On the contrary, he held a high view of Jesus, since he believed that Satan was subject to Jesus' name. He certainly had a very lofty creed. There is not the slightest reason to suppose that he differed in doctrine from the rest of the disciples. His fault from the point of view of the disciples was not that he was heretical, but that he was entirely too zealous; his only fault was that he followed not with them, that he did not obey their behests, that he was not—to put the thing in modern language—subservient to their committees. But Jesus accepted him as a disciple, and in so doing he spoke the mightiest word against organizational church union that has ever been spoken. There are those today who look askance upon minorities, who regard with contempt, for example, the Presbyterian church in Canada that is so bravely upholding the cause of liberty and truth in the presence of the United church. There are those today who cherish the notion of one universal church organization, mapping out the work for the whole world through some central committee, assigning a place to every man and allowing no place whatever for the Spirit of God, trying to bring all Christendom under its sway. I am bound to say frankly that for my part I regard it as a depressing and hateful dream. It is the greatest obstacle in the world, I think, to the realization of our Lord's high priestly prayer that "they all may be one." God grant that the dream may not come true! God grant that the Christian church upon this earth may not be brought under one organization! God grant that liberty may be preserved, and that when we contemplate groups of Christians large or small who prefer to do things in their own way, we may remember the words of the Lord Jesus Christ, how he said, "Forbid him not, . . . he that is not against us is on our part."

But where shall a criterion be found to determine which of these many ecclesiastical bodies are truly Christian? The criterion is provided by this same incident in the gospel of Mark, of which we have just been speaking. That man in the gospel was casting out demons, and he was casting them out in the name of Christ. There is found the twofold test. First, the doctrine or the message was right; the work was done in the name of Christ. The "name" means, of course, not merely a word of so many letters, but the stupendous person whom the name represents. In the second place, demons were being cast out; a mighty and beneficent work was being done. That twofold test can be applied today. Many churches (in their corporate capacity) are not Christian because they do not meet the former part of the test. They are not really using the name. They use indeed the word "Jesus," but the word designates for them a poor, weak enthusiast who has little to do with the real Jesus presented in the Word of God. In the second place, to be recognized as a true church of Christ, a church must bring forth works that correspond to the casting out of demons which was possible when miraculous gifts were still in the possession of the church. No organization and no party in any organization can be recognized as Christian when the works that it brings forth are the specious double use of traditional terminology and all manner of chicanery and deceit. By that test again many parties of today are condemned. "By their fruits shall ye know them," said our Lord. A party cannot be recognized as Christian merely because, in a purely external and physical way, it bears the name of Christ; it cannot be recognized as Christian if, in its corporate capacity—we are not speaking about the relation of individuals to Christ—it brings forth Satan's works.

But if the twofold test is met—if, in the first place, the doctrine or the message is right, and if, in the second place, the result is not deceitfulness, but truth—then many a despised company of believers, many a hopeless minority, is to be recognized as a true church of Christ. It is to be so recognized by us, and above all, it is actually so recognized by our Lord. And what warmth of fellowship we enjoy, in these days of stress and strain, with many Christians of many names who are our true brothers in Christ! How hollow is the external unity of committees and boards, and how deep the true unity of the Spirit in the bond of peace!

If, then, the true church is to be found in many places and under many names, for what does the true church stand, and why do we Presbyterians think that it is found in greatest purity in the Reformed or Calvinistic faith?

The church of Christ entered upon the present period in its history in a certain upper room in Jerusalem in the first century of our era. The church had indeed existed before; it had existed under the old dispensation; it had existed in the time of Abraham; it had existed ever since the promise had been given after the fall of man. But under the old dispensation, its life had been derived from a promise of good things to come, and now the fulfillment had arrived. The redemption promised of old had actually been wrought; the Savior had made atonement for the sins of his people, and had completed his redeeming work by his resurrection from the dead.

The little company of his disciples in the upper room were waiting for power from on high, and when the power came they went forth to the conquest of the world.

That first Christian church in Jerusalem had a creed; indeed, upon a creed all its power was based. One part of its creed, of course, is plain; it was "Christ is risen from the dead." A stupendous creed that was in truth; it is just that creed which is really denied by the vast Modernist forces in our Presbyterian church in America today and in the other great churches of the world. But the words "Christ is risen" were not all of the creed of the first Christian church. We have a little extract from the central things of that Jerusalem creed preserved for us in the first epistle to the Corinthians; Paul there tells us what he had "received" from the primitive Jerusalem church. And what was it that he had received? "How that Christ died for our sins according to the Scriptures; and that he was buried, and that he rose the third day according to the scriptures." A wonderful creed in truth! "Christ died for our sins"—there we have the center of Christianity, the blessed doctrine of the atonement. "He has been raised from the dead"—there we have the completion of the redeeming work in the glorious miracle of the resurrection.

That was the good news, the "gospel," the doctrine upon which the church's life was based; that was the message with which it went forth to the conquest of the world.

At first the work was among the chosen people, but soon the leading of the Spirit became plain. The Gentile Cornelius was baptized, and the great apostle to the Gentiles was converted by the Lord himself. The distinctive work of Paul was not the mere geographical extension of the frontiers of the kingdom, but it was the setting forth of the principles of the gospel upon which the worldwide work was based. Those principles indeed were not unknown before—the doctrine of the cross, as we have seen, was at the basis of the life of the Jerusalem church—but to Paul was revealed with special clearness the epoch-making significance of the redeeming work of Christ. Because of that work, certain commands which under the old dispensation had been required of God's people were no longer in force. A new era had begun. Paul recognized that fact; and because he did so, he is sometimes regarded as a "Liberal"—as the precursor of those who in our times reject the authority of the Bible and take the commands of God with a grain of salt. But persons who talk in that way simply show that they have no inkling of what scientific history is. No, the thing is perfectly plain to every historian: Paul was no "Liberal"—not in that low sense of the noble word. He always held with all his heart and mind to the full truthfulness of the Bible, as Jesus of Nazareth had done before; he never separated the "letter" from the "spirit" in the misleading modern way; and he believed that even the ceremonial requirements of the Old Testament law were commands of God. But he held that those ceremonial requirements are represented by God in the Old Testament itself as temporary, so that a man was actually disobeying the Old Testament law if he carried them over in full into the new dispensation. A new era had begun; the time of the promise was over, and the time of the fulfillment had come.

So the church could go forth with a good conscience and with the full favor of God to the conquest of the Gentile world.

That was a great moment in the Antioch church when the missionaries were sent to Cyprus across the narrow seas and then to the conquest of the world. Those missionaries would no doubt have been coldly received by many modern mission boards. Did they not refuse to work with opponents of the cross, both within and without the church? Did not one of them later say: "Though we, or an angel from heaven, preach any other gospel unto you than that which we have preached unto you, let him be accursed"? The idea of sending out a missionary who determined to know nothing save Jesus Christ and him crucified! The thing would be regarded today as quite preposterous. Such men as Paul and Barnabas, I fear, would hardly have been appointed with much enthusiasm by some modern mission boards. But the choosing of missionaries was different in those days. The prophets and teachers were gathered in the church at Antioch, and "the Holy Ghost said, Separate me Barnabas and Saul for the work whereunto I have called them." They received their appointment indeed! And forth they went across the blue waters of the Mediterranean—humble and despised as the world looks upon such things, but with one possession that made them the mightiest of the children of men, with a gospel without which none, high or low, wise or unwise, could be brought into communion with the holy God.

In the years that followed, that gospel had to face attack. What mighty doctrinal conflicts there were in the apostolic age! I sometimes think that those who decry controversy have never read history at all, and certainly have never read the Word of God. The New Testament (gospels as well as epistles) is a controversial book almost from beginning to end; truth in it is always set forth in contrast with error. So it was in the apostolic church; truth was struck forth as a fire from the clash of conflict; the great evangelical epistles, Galatians and Romans, were written in the glorious form in which they actually appear only because of the conflict with the Judaizers, who, like the Modernists of today, though in a much less obviously destructive manner, denied the all-sufficiency of the substitutionary atonement of our Lord. So it will always be, even in uninspired books. Men who decry controversy never in the whole course of the history of the church have produced anything really great; great Christian utterances come only when men's souls are stirred.

God brought the church through those early conflicts. But certainly he did not do so by the instrumentality of theological pacifists, but by the instrumentality of that glorious fighter, the apostle Paul. The Judaistic doctrine of human merit was kept out, at least from the center of the church's life, and also the pagan sublimation of the resurrection into a mere doctrine of immortality—which sublimation is so strikingly like the contention of the thirteen hundred Auburn Affirmationists in our Presbyterian church today.

At last the apostolic age drew to its close. Those who had received the lofty special apostolic commission from Christ were taken away. But two things remained—in the first place, the presence of the Holy Spirit, and in the second place, the Scriptures of the Old and New Testaments that the Holy Spirit used.

In the second century there was another great conflict, and again it was a conflict not without, but within the church. The Gnostics used Christian terminology, like the Modernists of today; but like the Modernists of today they were opposed to Christianity at its root. Despite the insidiousness of the danger, the church was saved. But it was saved only because the leaders were no theological pacifists, but mighty contenders for the faith. Irenæus wrote his great work against heresies, and Tertullian contended against Marcion, and so the gospel was preserved. Those men were not afraid of controversy. God be endlessly praised for that! If they had been opposed to controversy, there would be no Christianity in the world today.

So it has been in all the other great ages through which the church has passed. So it was in the conflicts by which the great ecumenical creeds were produced; so it was in the days when Augustine contended against the Pelagian view of sin; so it was in the heroic days of the Reformation. Always there have been pacifists who have endeavored to conceal the issue and to bring about the false peace of compromise. But always there have been some true men who have resolutely refused.

So it was also when our great Reformed system of doctrine was set forth on the basis of the Scriptures alone. The Reformation had burst the bands of Roman slavery, and had returned to the Magna Charta of liberty in the Word of God. But after the first heroism was over, there had come the days of vacillation and compromise; the Reformation had completed its negative work, but its positive work was yet undone. It had broken with the Roman system, but it had no thorough system of its own. Then came the man of the hour, the man whom God had chosen. In his *Institutes of the Christian Religion*, John Calvin set forth not scattered bits of evangelical truth, but a great system, and a system that was derived from the Bible alone. There is some justification for the dictum which I saw somewhere in that late lamented paper, *The Freeman*, of New York, which differed from most radical papers in that, instead of making radicalism stupid, it made radicalism bright—there is some justification for the dictum of *The Freeman* to the effect that only in the Reformed system has Protestantism overcome the "inferior complex" which elsewhere besets it over against the imposing sys-

THE NATURE AND MISSION OF THE CHURCH

tem of Rome. We need, I think, to learn the lesson. The strongest Christianity, I think, is consistent Christianity; and consistent Christianity is found in the Reformed faith. Strange indeed it is that men should desert that glorious heritage, as in the United Church of Canada, for the hasty creedal formulations to be expected of our intellectually decadent age. I believe in progress in theology. That is the reason why I do not regard theology as a kaleidoscope, but rather prefer to build for the future, in theology as in other branches of science, upon the solid achievements of the past.

At the time of the Reformation, and no doubt at the time of Calvin, there were many voices that counseled compromise. But, thank God, there were also true men who would not listen to the Tempter's voice.

So it is also in our own day. For one hundred and fifty years the church has been in the midst of a conflict greater than all the conflicts that have gone before. Many great branches of the church are completely dominated by the non-Christian forces; our own Presbyterian church in America is in the gravest danger of going on the same path. In 1920, a great attack was made upon the very vitals of our constitution by the Plan of Organic Union, which received a large vote and which, if it had been successful, would have caused the church to cease to be Christian in its corporate capacity at all. In the later years, thirteen hundred ministers of the church have signed the so-called Auburn Affirmation, which attacks the whole factual basis of our religion; and the great Synod of New York is on record officially as approving the licensing of a minister who actually refused to affirm even the virgin birth of our Lord. The boards and agencies have almost no representation from the evangelical party in the church and, to say the least, are failing to sound any ringing evangelical note.

In this time of crisis, when the question is being determined whether our church is to remain Christian or not, there are those who deplore controversy and say that all is well. Among them there are no doubt many who are not really Christian in their preaching at all. These men are not, indeed, conscious of denying the Bible and denying Christ, but the cross really fails to hold the central place in their hearts. But among the ecclesiastical pacifists there are also no doubt many truly Christian men. They belittle controversy because they do not yet see how serious is the danger, or what the controversy is really about. Can they be made to see in time? That is the question of all questions. Upon that question the existence of our church depends. Oh, brethren, you who belittle controversy, you who think that all is well, if you could only be made to see, if the Holy Spirit would only open your eyes! When I contemplate the issue, I feel as though it were a crime for us ever to rise from our knees, except to speak the word that God has given us to speak. God grant, brethren, that the mists may be dispelled from your eyes, and that you may yet witness in this time of crisis, before it is too late, for the Lord Jesus Christ. If you do, then our Presbyterian church will be saved as a true church of Christ, and will go forth again with new power for the salvation of the souls of men.

23

THE CHRISTIAN VIEW
OF MISSIONS

S ome nineteen hundred years ago a remarkable movement emerged from the obscurity of Palestine into the cosmopolitan life of the Roman Empire. That movement was the Christian church. What were its characteristics in those first glorious days?

This question is important for at least two reasons. In the first place, the church in those first days had everything that it so signally lacks today. It had joy, it had power, it had life. Perhaps that life and that power may be regained if we return to what the church was then. In the second place, by considering what the church was then, we can answer the question what can rightly bear the name "Christian" today. If we have a new thing, let us use a new name; but if we claim to be Christian, we must show some conformity to that to which the name "Christian" was first applied.

But what was it to which the name was first applied; what was the Christian movement when it first appeared?

With regard to that question, there may be a certain amount of agreement even between historians who are themselves Christians and historians who are not Christians, even between historians of widely diverse views.

"The Christian View of Missions" originally a radio address delivered on May 7, 1933 on WCAU for the "Church of the Air" program, and appeared in *Revelation* 3 (1933) 203–4, 227. Reprinted in *What Is Christianity?* ed. Ned Bernard Stonehouse (Grand Rapids: Eerdmans, 1951).

Difference of opinion prevails about the question whether Christianity is true, but about the question what Christianity is and what it was in those first days a certain amount of agreement may be attained.

One thing, at least, is clear, on the basis of all our sources of historical information. The earliest Christian church was a missionary church. If Christianity ever settles down to be the religion merely of one nation or of one group of nations, it will have become entirely untrue to the tradition which was established for it at the beginning. There was evidently a tremendous urge among those early Christians to carry their message to the ends of the earth.

What, then, was the mission of that missionary church? What was the Christianity that it propagated in that ancient Roman world?

In the first place, the Christianity that it propagated did *not* present itself as a new religion. On the contrary, it appealed to an ancient revelation, and it claimed to stand in the full continuity of an age-long plan of God. It should never be forgotten—though it often is forgotten—that the Christian church at the very beginning had a Bible. Its Bible was the Old Testament, and it regarded that Bible as the Word of God, just as Bible-believing Christians regard the Scriptures of the Old and New Testaments today.

In so regarding the Old Testament, it was in exact accord with the person whom it presented as the foundation of its life—namely, Jesus Christ. One thing is clear to the historian. Jesus of Nazareth, whether we like it or not, did hold the view of the Old Testament which was generally accepted in the Israel of his day: he did hold the Old Testament to be true throughout; he did hold it to be authoritative and divine. When he said that some of its commands were temporary, and were to be superseded or modified in the new era which his sovereign coming ushered in, he did not at all mean that those commands were not commands of God, absolutely valid in the sphere and in the time in which they were intended by God to prevail. It is a fact of history that Jesus as well as his first disciples held the loftiest view of the divine authority and full truthfulness of the Old Testament Scriptures. From the beginning Christianity was a religion founded upon a book.

That book proclaimed, and the early church proclaimed on the basis of it, in the first place, the one living and true God, Maker of heaven and earth; and that proclamation was the basis of everything else that the church proclaimed. "Ye turned to God," says Paul, in describing his missionary preaching, his preaching to unconverted people at Thessalonica—"ye turned to God from idols to serve the living and true God."

I know that some men have represented that as though it were a mere piece of metaphysics that the church could and can do without. The doctrine of "fiat creation," they tell us, has nothing to do with vital religion; and even in those early days, they tell us, Jesus could be accepted as Savior-God without any settlement of the question regarding his connection with the Creator and Ruler of the world. But men who tell us that are entirely wrong. Certainly Jesus was God, but calling Jesus God has no meaning unless one first tells what one means by "God"; and calling Jesus God while one is indifferent to the existence of a God who is Creator and Ruler of the world runs directly counter to the teaching of Jesus himself. No, both Jesus and his earliest disciples were first of all monotheists; they believed that before the world was God was, that this universe came into being by the fiat of his will, and that he is eternally free as over against the things that he has made. That is what the Bible means by the living and holy God, and it was that living and holy God whom those first Christian missionaries proclaimed.

In the second place, again on the basis of the Old Testament Scriptures, the early church proclaimed the universal sinfulness of mankind—a mankind lost under the guilt and power of sin, and subject to the wrath of God.

Men do not like that doctrine of the wrath of God today. But it is not the historian's business, when he deals with past ages, to find what he likes; it is his business to find what was. And every historian must admit that the doctrine of the wrath of God was at the very foundation of the message of the earliest Christian church. Every historian must also admit, what is more, that that same doctrine was at the very heart of the teaching of Jesus. If you want the really terrible descriptions of the wrath of God and of the divine retribution for sin in the other world, do not turn to the theologians of the church or even to the apostle Paul. But turn to the teaching of Jesus of Nazareth—his teaching not only as it is recorded in the New Testament, but even as it has been reconstructed and reduced by modern negative criticism.

I know that people tell us it is an unworthy thing to appeal to the motive of fear. In missionary endeavor particularly, they tell us, that motive is out of date. But it is strange that those who tell us that should appeal to Jesus as their authority in religion. For if there ever was a religious teacher who appealed to the motive of fear, it was Jesus. "Be not afraid of them that kill the body," he said, "and after that have no more that they can do. But I will forewarn you whom ye shall fear: Fear him, which after he hath killed hath power to cast into Hell; yea, I say unto you, Fear him." These words are no mere excrescence in the teaching of Jesus. No, they are at the very heart of it; they give to the ethical teaching of Jesus its stupendous earnestness. And they are also at the very heart of the missionary message of the earliest Christian church.

One thing is perfectly clear—no missionary work that consists merely in presenting to the people in foreign lands a thing that has proved to be mildly valuable in the experience of the missionary himself, which he thinks may perhaps prove helpful in foreign lands in building up a better life upon this earth, can possibly be regarded as real Christian missions. At the very heart of the real Christian missionary message is the conviction that every individual hearer to whom the missionary goes is in deadly peril, and that unless the message is heeded he is without hope in this world and in the dreadful world that is to come.

Then, on the basis of those two great presuppositions—the awful holiness of God and a mankind lost under the guilt and power of sin—the first Christian missionaries preached Jesus Christ.

But how did they preach him? Did they preach him as a great teacher and example, as a great inspirer of a new religious life? Did they go about the world saying: "We have come under the spell of a great person, Jesus of Nazareth; contact with that person has changed our lives; we proclaim him to you as he lives in our lives; and we beg you to let him change your lives, too"?

Well, that is what modern men might have expected those first Christian missionaries to say, but every historian must admit that as a matter of fact they said nothing of the kind. Every historian must admit that as a matter of fact they proclaimed Jesus not primarily as an example or as an inspirer, but as a Savior from divine wrath and from the awful bondage of sin.

In so proclaiming him, they appealed to their holy book. The case is not as though they appealed to the Old Testament merely for the presuppositions of the gospel and then turned away from it when they preached the gospel itself. No, even in preaching Jesus they turned to God's written Word. They did not preach Jesus as one whose coming was a sort of afterthought of God, one who had no connection with what God had done before. No, they preached him as the fulfillment of a glorious divine promise, as the culmination of a mighty divine plan.

But then they proclaimed him in the great wealth of fresh information handed on by those who had seen and heard him when he was on earth. In particular, they proclaimed his death and his resurrection from the dead. "You are justly subject to God's wrath and curse," they said, "but Christ took that curse upon himself, he died there on the cross in your stead. That just and holy God, Creator and Ruler of the world, is also God of an infinite love; he sent his eternal Son to die for you. That one who died is risen from the dead. He lives, and he is waiting for you to trust him and have life."

At the basis of the Christian message, in other words, was not an exhortation, but a gospel; not a program, but a piece of news.

So much must be admitted by modern historians of all shades of opinion. The early Christian church was radically doctrinal. It proclaimed facts: the facts about God the Father, the facts about mankind lost in sin, the facts about Jesus Christ. That is true not merely of Paul but of the very earliest church in Jerusalem, whose message Paul reproduces for us when he tells us at the beginning of the fifteenth chapter of 1 Corinthians what he had "received."

So much, at least, must be admitted. The early church, even the very earliest church in Jerusalem, did more than proclaim Jesus as an example; it proclaimed him as a Savior. It made him not merely the author, but also the substance, of the gospel. It did more than proclaim what he proclaimed about God; no, it proclaimed him.

But, men tell us, although that is what the early church preached, that is not what Jesus preached, and we can now return from the early church to Jesus himself. The early church proclaimed him as Savior by his atoning death, but he himself, we are told, kept himself out of his gospel and preached a simple and universal gospel of the fatherhood of God and the brotherhood of man—and we ought now, rejecting all doctrinal accretions, to return to that simple gospel which Jesus preached.

But is it not a strange thing that those first disciples of Jesus should so completely have misunderstood their teacher's words and work? And is it not strange that that misunderstanding of the teaching of Jesus should have been so much more powerful in the world than the teaching which it misunderstood? Is it not a strange thing that this supposed gospel of Jesus himself should have been so powerless, and that only when it was perverted into becoming a gospel about Jesus, a gospel which set Jesus forth, it conquered the world? Yes, it is strange; and not only is it strange but it is untrue. Even the most radical criticism is enabling us to see that. All our sources of information—including not only the gospels, but the earliest sources supposed, rightly or wrongly, to underlie the gospels—are dominated by the view that Jesus was no mere proclaimer of a supposed universal fatherhood of God and brotherhood of man, but a divine Redeemer. What is the conclusion? Why, says radical criticism, the conclusion is that we cannot tell what sort of person Jesus was, because all of our sources of information are vitiated by this false Christian notion that he was the Savior of mankind.

A strange conclusion that is, and a conclusion that is contradicted by the self-evidencing quality of the wonderful picture of Jesus which the gospels contain. Our conclusion is different from that of these radical critics. It is that the picture is from the life—that God did walk upon this earth, that the whole Bible that sets forth that divine Christ is true, and that we are in his holy presence today.

I have set forth what Christian missions were in those first glorious days. I have tried to make you understand and sympathize with the joy of those slaves and humble tradesmen in Corinth and in other places who faced the awful wrath of God and then found Jesus to be their Savior from that wrath.

But is that all? Must we be historians merely? Must we look wistfully at the joys of those first glorious days of the church without ever having them for ourselves?

No, my friends, those same joys may be ours, and in exactly the same way.

That is known full well by some of you who are my hearers at this hour. You are listening to my voice that you may receive comfort from one—be he never so humble and never so unworthy—who has resisted the current of the times and has a faith like unto yours. Others of you, I suppose, have listened in out of curiosity—that you may hear for yourselves one of those strange persons, not often heard, whom their opponents call "Fundamentalists." But for whatever reason you have listened, there is one thing that I desire to say to you. I desire to say to you that your hour may come when you expect it least. God may speak to your soul. He may use even my poor words to touch some forgotten chord in your heart and to bring again to your mind the great and precious promises of the holy book. There may even now be one of you who will say: "All my wisdom, all my goodness, all my striving are vain; oh, Lord Jesus, be my Savior now!"

24

THE TRUTH ABOUT THE PRESBYTERIAN CHURCH

I. MODERNISM IN THE JUDICIAL COMMISSION

In 1923 and 1924 the battle between Christianity and Modernism entered upon its last and most acute phase in the Presbyterian Church in the U.S.A. The Christian position was represented by the evangelical pronouncement of the 1923 General Assembly; the Modernist position was represented by the "Auburn Affirmation."

The General Assembly's pronouncement declared that the full truthfulness of Scripture, the virgin birth, the substitutionary atonement, the bodily resurrection, and the miracles of our Lord are essential doctrines of the Word of God and our Standards; the Auburn Affirmation attacked that pronouncement, and declared that not a single one of these great verities is essential even for the ministry.

The issue cannot be evaded by any plea that the Affirmation attacked the General Assembly's pronouncement merely on technical grounds. The Affirmation does, indeed, raise the technical point that the General Assembly had no right to issue such a pronouncement. But it proceeds at once

"The Truth about the Presbyterian Church" originally appeared in *Christianity Today* 2 (November 1931) 5–6; (December 1931) 6–9; (January 1932) 4–6, 12–13.

to something far more fundamental. It attacks the *content* of the pronouncement. It declares that not a single one of the great verities mentioned by the General Assembly is essential; and it declares that all of the five verities are merely "theories" (among other possible theories) which some may and some may not hold to be satisfactory explanations of something else. Thus it excludes all of these verities from the essential message of the church, and in so doing it strikes a blow against the very inmost heart of the Christian religion.

In the battle between the General Assembly's pronouncement and the Auburn Affirmation, between Christianity and Modernism, the Modernist contention has in the main won the victory, and now dominates the machinery of the Presbyterian church.

There are many indications of that fact, but one indication is so unmistakable that it might almost suffice if it stood alone. It is found in the composition of the "Permanent Judicial Commission," which was entirely reconstituted in 1931 with largely increased powers, and is now practically the supreme doctrinal as well as disciplinary authority in the church. In the composition of such a court, we may discover, if anywhere, what the true temper of the church is. Who, then, are members of this all-important court?

The commission consists of fifteen members, chosen by the General Assembly, eight being ministers and seven being elders. Whatever may be said about the elders, it is perfectly easy to tell where the ministers stand in the great issue of the day.

The plain fact is that of the eight ministerial members, four are actually signers of the Auburn Affirmation, and one of the four is the Rev. Robert Hastings Nichols, Ph.D., D.D., of Auburn, secretary of the committee that issued the document. Elders were not invited to sign the Affirmation, so that the signers have been given exactly one-half of the total number of places available to them in the commission. That is, one-half of the ministerial members of a commission which is practically the supreme guardian of doctrine in the Presbyterian church are signers of a public and formal document which, besides being directly polemic against the doctrine of the full truthfulness of Scripture, declares that that doctrine and the virgin birth and three other great verities of the faith are nonessential even for the ministry.

The point is not merely that these four gentlemen have shown by their signing of the Affirmation that they are incompetent persons to sit upon the supreme judicial body of an evangelical Christian church. That point would certainly be well taken. But the real point is far more definite than that. It is that by their signing of the Affirmation these gentlemen have already expressed themselves upon the most important question that has come or is likely to come before the Judicial Commission upon which they sit, and expressed themselves in a way derogatory to the central verities of the Christian faith.

In the presence of that fact, it will at once be seen that all the optimistic talk about the Presbyterian Church in the U.S.A. as being "essentially sound" must surely cease.

But how about the other eleven members of the commission? May there not be found among them such representation of the evangelical position as shall offset the Modernism of the Affirmation which the four members have signed?

Unfortunately, that possibility is, to say the least, very slight. There have been other tests besides the Auburn Affirmation to determine whether a man does or does not stand for the Bible and the Christian faith in the councils of the Presbyterian church.

In 1928, for example, there was presented to the General Assembly a petition of which the ultimate purpose was defense of the doctrine of the virgin birth—defense, that is, of one of the five doctrines attacked as nonessential by the Auburn Affirmation.

The "Virgin Birth Petition" was signed by about seventeen hundred ministers as over against the thirteen hundred who signed the Auburn Affirmation. Not a single one of these seventeen hundred was placed upon the Permanent Judicial Commission, though no less than four of the thirteen hundred signers of the Auburn Affirmation were placed there.

The Virgin Birth Petition was also signed by over four thousand elders. Not a single one of these was given a place on the Commission.

In the same year, moreover, another evangelical memorial was presented to the General Assembly. It was the "Princeton Petition" directed against the reorganization of Princeton Theological Seminary. We shall not stop here to ask whether the signers of the Princeton Petition were or were not justified in thinking that the proposed reorganization of the seminary was inimical to the evangelical cause. As a matter of fact, we think that they were fully justified, and that a very early official pronouncement of the new board of control about its own membership demonstrated the fact beyond peradventure. But whether they were justified or not in the specific request that they made of the General Assembly, it is perfectly evident that they were animated in making that request by an evangelical motive and that they represented the evangelical party in the Presbyterian church.

We do not mean that all the signers of the Princeton Petition represented the evangelical party in any very consistent or vigorous way. The petition was a very mild document, and many of its signers have been anything but thoroughgoing in their championing of the evangelical cause. But though some of the signers of the petition may not have been very consistent or vigorous in their evangelicalism, we do deliberately make bold to say, conversely, that a very great block of the evangelical ministers and elders in the church—perhaps the great majority of them—were among the signers.

Yet not a single one of the twenty-five hundred or three thousand ministers, and apparently only one of the seven thousand or so elders, who signed the Princeton Petition has been given a place on the Permanent Judicial Commission.

Could there possibly be a clearer example of a partisan court? Half of the available ministerial positions have been given to signers of a radical Modernist document that attacks the message of the church at its very root, and not a single ministerial position has been given to the far greater number who signed the mildest possible petitions looking to the defense of God's Word. At most the commission seems to include only one man (an elder) who by signing one of these two petitions has given public indication of zeal for the historic witness of the church.

The ecclesiastical machinery seems to have done its work well. There may, indeed, be gentlemen on the commission, in addition to the one signer of the Princeton Petition, who are opposed to the Auburn Affirmation and in favor of maintaining the church's historic message, but if there are such they seem to have given as yet no very clear public indication of their stand.[1] So far as public utterances could lead the General Assembly to judge, the composition of the commission, as the Assembly constituted it in May 1931, is such as to give assurance not merely that a real believer in the Bible and

1. One of the ministers on the commission, not counted here among the four sign-ers of the Auburn Affirmation, first signed the Affirmation, but then—we cannot now say for what reason—withdrew his name before the Affirmation was printed in its final form.

in the Confession of Faith shall have no sympathetic hearing from a majority of the court, but also that he shall not "disturb the peace of the Church" by receiving even any considerable minority opinion in his favor or in favor of the Bible in which he believes.

It is evident that any consistent Christian man will count it a disgrace to be acquitted on any doctrinal issue by such a court, and an honor to be condemned. But the composition of the court shows that the corporate life of the Presbyterian church is corrupt at the very core, and that until the sin of the church is honestly faced and removed, all the great swelling words about the church's work and all the bustle of its organizational activities can avail but little in the sight of God.

NOTE: In the next number of *Christianity Today*, the present writer hopes to deal with the centralization of power and the attack upon Christian liberty which is involved in measures now before the presbyteries (particularly the dangerous Overture D), and with the secrecy and discouragement of free discussion by means of which the undermining of the church's witness has been carried on.

II. SECRECY IN COUNCILS AND COURTS

Modernism in the Boards and Agencies

Our first article set forth one particular evidence of the triumph of the Modernist contention in the Presbyterian Church in the U.S.A. Half of the ministerial members of the Permanent Judicial Commission, which is practically the highest judicial body in the church, are, we observed, actually signers of a radical Modernist document, the Auburn Affirmation; and evidences of any vigorous evangelicalism in the rest of the commission are, to say the most, exceedingly slight.

Not very dissimilar, we fear, is the situation in the boards and agencies of the church. When one observes, for example, that under the Board of Foreign Missions the secretary of the Candidate Department, to whom is entrusted the delicate and important duty of interviewing candidates for the foreign field and of encouraging or discouraging them in their purpose, is a signer of this Auburn Affirmation—that is, of a document which attacks directly the full truthfulness of Scripture and which removes from the essential message of the church not only that doctrine but also the virgin birth and three other great verities of the faith—when one observes, moreover, that the editor of *The Presbyterian Magazine*, the general secretary and six out of fifteen ministerial members of the Board of National Missions, the secretary of the General Council (who is also secretary for promotion and executive head of the United Promotional Staff), and three out of nine ministerial members of a commission appointed to consider a proposed amendment to the Confession of Faith are signers of the same Auburn Affirmation; when one observes, further, that the General Assembly's Committee on National Missions officially, in its report to the Assembly, commends the Federal Council of Churches of Christ in America as an agency "standing on the rock of Evangelical faith and the Deity of Christ" (*Minutes*, p. 105) and furthermore declares that entrance into home mission work is contingent upon the approval of other super-church interdenominational bodies (ibid., p. 97); when one observes, finally, that representation in these boards and agencies of those who have taken any consistent or prominent or vigorous evangelical stand in the present great issue in the church is, to say the most, very slight—when one attends to these and other facts, one sees clearly that the entire administrative machinery of the Presbyterian church is under such control and devoted to such policy that either one of two things should, in common honesty, immediately be done: either these boards and agencies should be radically reformed, or else independent boards and agencies should be organized to propagate that gospel upon central verities of which the signers of the Auburn Affirmation have cast such despite.

The Effects of Concealment

What has brought the Presbyterian church to such a pass? What has brought a church whose constitution stands toward the Auburn Affirmation in a contradiction that could be recognized, one might think, not merely by theologians or experts but by every man, Christian or otherwise, of ordinary sound common honesty and common sense—what has brought such a church, with such a constitution, into its present anomalous state?

The answer to that question is plain. Secrecy has done the business—secrecy and the discouragement of open and free discussion of the condition of the church.

If the destructive forces had exhibited themselves in their true light, the peace and purity of the church would have been restored long ago, but as it is the work of undermining the church has gone forward in the dark.

At times, indeed, it has seemed, despite all that the ecclesiastical machinery could do, as though light were to be let into the darkness. At the General Assembly of 1925, when the Assembly had handed down a decision in a judicial case declaring that the virgin birth of our Lord is an essential doctrine of our Confession of Faith, certain gentlemen from New York Presbytery are reported, in their indignation, to have threatened withdrawal from the church. But no such step was taken. A "Commission of Fifteen" was appointed, and the matter was hushed up. The hearings before the commission were secret; the Auburn Affirmation was not mentioned in the report, and was alluded to only in the most vague and misleading way; the decision regarding the virgin birth remained a dead letter; the facts about the state of the church were concealed; the cancer that was sapping the church's life was permitted to continue its destructive work in the dark.

The Menace of Secret Courts

It is in judicial cases, of course, where secrecy is most clearly opposed both to general principles of ethics and to the whole spirit of the New Testament. In the time of Henry VIII there was in England a secret court called the "Star Chamber." It was an instrument of tyranny, and against it the great principle of "open court" was finally set up. That principle is at the very foundation of our Anglo-Saxon liberties. It is certainly in profound accord with the Word of God. Yet that principle is being crassly violated at the present moment in the Presbyterian church.

Moreover, the General Assembly of 1931 has sent down to the presbyteries for their examination an entire new Book of Discipline, prepared by the stated clerk, in order that opinions about it may be expressed by the presbyteries before March 1, 1932, or a little later, so that, after the results of such study are embodied in it, it may be sent down finally next May.

That new Book of Discipline expressly provides that "in all cases of judicial process, the judicatory shall sit with closed doors" (*Minutes*, p. 280).

At present, a judicatory *may* sit with closed doors; it may do so at any stage of the case, by a two-thirds vote. That rule makes full provision for exclusion of publicity in certain kinds of cases where publicity might be inimical to public morals or the like; certainly it makes full provision, when taken in connection with the general authority of a judicial body over its own procedure, for the maintenance of good order and for the discouragement of attendance by mere curiosity-seekers.

But the proposed new rule is of an entirely different kind. It allows no discretion whatever. It provides not that judicatories *may* sit behind closed doors, but that they *must* sit behind closed doors, even in cases where the most elementary considerations of fair play demand that open court should be held, and even where the accused person is convinced that by being deprived of an open trial he is being deprived of an inalienable right.

Suppose, for example, that a case should come before the Permanent Judicial Commission, which, as we pointed out last month, is, so far as all indications go, a very one-sided court. Would any advocate of the evangelical contention in the church think he could possibly have a fair hearing if such a court held its sessions in secret? And even if the proceedings were fair, could the world at large ever possibly be convinced that they were fair? Would not the basest suspicions inevitably be aroused? Can anyone imagine a situation more disgraceful to a church that bears the name of Christ?

For my part, I confess that the very notion of "judicial process behind closed doors," of "secret court," is a sinister and disgraceful notion, while the notion of "open court" is at the basis of everything that is fair and aboveboard. That principle is true in the state. It is true with tenfold force in the church of Jesus Christ. The church, we think, should not be less anxious but more anxious to avoid suspicion than is the world at large.

A Proposed Presbyterian Inquisition

I shall not now stop to discuss other features in the proposed new Book of Discipline—for example, the particularly objectionable provision limiting choice of counsel by an accused person. A provision like that tends in the same direction as that in which most proposed changes in the constitution and procedure of the Presbyterian church have tended in recent years. It tends, namely, to destroy the old Presbyterian liberties and put the plain man in the church more and more at the mercy of the gentlemen who control the ecclesiastical machinery.

But whatever other objectionable features there may be in this proposed Book of Discipline, the abolition of open court is the worst of all. The meaning of this feature is perfectly plain. It involves nothing less than the setting up of a secret inquisition in the Presbyterian church.

That step, if it is finally taken, will do two things. In the first place, it will subject the church to the contempt of those who are without—a contempt compared with which all the real or supposed reproach of public ecclesias-

THE NATURE AND MISSION OF THE CHURCH

tical trials is as nothing. Even if these secret courts are fair, their very secrecy will prevent normally minded people in the world at large from ever thinking that they are fair.

But in the second place, as a matter of fact, these secret courts will not be fair. Darkness is a great breeder of sin, and the sin of oppression and unfairness is one to which ecclesiastical courts are notoriously exposed. I do not know altogether why that is so. Perhaps it is because in ecclesiastical courts hatred and oppression are so apt to be concealed by the words of piety and love. In the pursuit of showy and unusual virtues, the simple, homely virtues are so apt to be lost from view. The great ecclesiastic thinks that of course he is above them, but Satan catches him at the unguarded point. At any rate, simple fairness to unpopular men and to the adherents of unpopular causes has, as history teaches, not always been a very marked characteristic of ecclesiastical courts. I am bound to say, for my part, very deliberately, that if this provision of the new Book of Discipline goes into effect, if a secret inquisition is thus set up in the Presbyterian church, I had far rather take my chances in the pursuit of simple justice in even the weaker civil courts, presided over by politically appointed judges who make no profession of religion, than in these secret courts of my own church.

Very sad will be the lot of the plain man, unpopular with the ecclesiastical officials, if he ever falls into the clutches of this secret inquisition. He will be free, indeed, from civil penalties; his body will be safe. But his reputation and his livelihood will be at the mercy of these star-chamber courts that shun the light of day.

Dangerous Overtures and How They Were Sent Down

The present existence of secret courts, with the proposal that all courts be secret, is only one extreme manifestation of a tendency that has made itself felt in many ways in the recent history of our church, and that has come to a head just at the present moment in proposals of a particularly tyrannical kind.

The tendency to which we refer is the tendency to check open discussion and deprive the plain man of his right to be heard in opposition to the ecclesiastical machinery.

That tendency appears, in the first place, in the method by which the General Assembly sends down to the presbyteries overtures involving changes in the constitution of the church.

Five such overtures are now before the presbyteries. They are all harmful measures, and ought to be rejected. One of them, Overture D, prescribes to the individual presbyteries, in considerable detail, how the presbyteries shall exercise their control over vacant churches and shall deal with the all-important matter of vacancy and supply. That overture represents centralization of power in a very dangerous form; it will tend to place congregations more and more exclusively in the hands of pastors who are subservient to the gentlemen in charge of the ecclesiastical machinery; and it will tend more and more to eliminate or push into the background men of independent convictions who love the old gospel and the old liberties of the Presbyterian church.

But our present concern is not so much with the content of these dangerous overtures as with the method by which they were sent down. Technically they were sent down by the General Assembly. But was there any discussion of the merits of them on the floor? Not at all. They came to the General Assembly from the General Council through the Committee on Bills and Overtures, and were handed on to the presbyteries without debate. A similar method has been applied invariably, so far as my observation goes, in recent years. Overtures of the most radical kind are sent down to the presbyteries without the slightest discussion; they come from the General Council and are simply transmitted to the presbyteries as a matter of routine. The plain man on the floor of the Assembly has no opportunity whatever of expressing his views with regard to them or of listening to the views of others.

No Hearing for the Plain Man

It is true, they do finally come before the presbyteries for discussion and action. But in this discussion each presbytery stands alone. There is no way in which the man from New Jersey or Pennsylvania can exchange views with the man from the Pacific Coast; there is no opportunity whatever for general discussion. A man who is opposed to these measures advocated by the General Council can speak against them in his own presbytery, but that is only one presbytery among two hundred and ninety-nine. There is no method for him to make his voice heard before representatives of the whole church.

Yes, there is one method: it is the method of pamphlet distribution. That method has recently been adopted by two members of the General Council, Dr. Cleland B. McAfee and Dr. William E. Brooks (the latter a signer of the Auburn Affirmation) and by one former member, Mr. S. Frank Shattuck. These gentlemen, acting collectively, have received funds to pamphletize the church in favor of the current centralization-overtures as to ordination and as to vacancy and supply. That method is all very well for men of wealth or men who can command wealth. But for others it is either terribly burdensome, as I can testify from personal experience, or else it is completely out of reach.

It must always be remembered that the funds of the church, and not merely private funds like those at the command of Dr. McAfee and his two associates, are often used in the advocacy of these measures. Arguments in favor of them are often printed in the minutes of the Assembly or otherwise distributed. But the plain man who is opposed to them has no way of making his voice heard. His one possible opportunity is taken from him by the absence of discussion on the floor of the General Assembly before the measures are sent down.

The Working of the Ecclesiastical Machinery

The discouragement of discussion at the General Assembly has made itself felt in other ways; indeed, it is one of the chief agencies which has been used for the destruction of Presbyterian liberties and of the evangelical witness of the Presbyterian church. The General Assembly, because of the unfortunate custom of rotation in the choice of commissioners, is composed almost altogether of men unacquainted with the procedure and unacquainted with what the preceding General Assembly has done. Such a situation puts the real power into the hands of the moderator and of the small group of men who are on the platform of the Assembly year after year. This power has sometimes been very ruthlessly used.

If anyone thinks that this language is too strong, let him just turn to the minutes of the General Assembly of 1928 (pp. 79ff.) and read the terms of a resolution in which the Assembly, at the instance of the Committee on Bills and Overtures (Dr. Cleland B. McAfee, chairman), dealt with a petition, couched in very mild and simple terms, which was signed by some ten thousand ministers and elders in the church. According to that resolution of Dr. McAfee, mere ministers and elders, not connected with the all-powerful ecclesiastical machinery, do not know what they are doing, and were not competent even to express confidence in a board of directors which had governed Princeton Seminary for a hundred years and to express very mildly the hope that no change in the government of such an institution might be made. The question here is not whether the signers of the Princeton Petition were right or wrong in their contention. Suppose for the sake of the argument that they were as wrong as wrong can be. Still, it remains true that the whole spirit of that answer to them, with its contempt for the rank and file of the church, was profoundly hostile to Presbyterian tradition and to the most elementary principles of liberty and fair play.

The same spirit was manifested at the General Assembly of the following year, when the gentleman who had brought in that resolution was moderator. At that Assembly, in 1929, the question of Princeton Seminary came up for final settlement. That question, rightly or wrongly, was a matter of deepest concern to many thousands of persons in the church who were convinced that the proposed reorganization would deprive them of the one really important seminary that had resisted the current of the times. Suppose they were wrong in that conviction. As a matter of fact, they were not wrong but right—as, for example, the presence of two signers of the Auburn Affirmation in the new governing board, taken with the board's official commendation of these gentlemen with all the other members to the confidence of the church, has indubitably proved. But suppose for the sake of the argument that they were wrong. Still, it remained true that they had a right to a fair hearing at the General Assembly. Never was there a time when a fair hearing was more obviously in place.

As a matter of fact, no fair hearing was granted. The moderator, against the opposition of three hundred and nine commissioners, pushed through ruthlessly his plan for limitation of debate. That plan resulted, if my recollection is correct, in a grand total of twenty minutes for discussion by ordinary commissioners as distinguished from representatives of various official bodies! And then, when commissioners were pleading for a hearing, the moderator of his own motion, by calling for representatives of the Assembly's committee and of the seminary's financial holding corporation, arranged that two gentlemen on the same side—the moderator's side—should, speaking in succession, close the debate!

Be it observed that the General Assembly was not in the slightest pressed for time. On the contrary, after engaging, as it usually does, in considerable waste of time and of the church's money, it closed, if anything, slightly ahead of schedule. But debate on a question which deeply concerned at least ten thousand ministers and elders in the church was pushed aside to the worst and weariest hours of the afternoon and was practically eliminated altogether so far as the rank and file of commissioners was concerned.

The Need of Moral Reform

I do not think that such tactics are at all unusual in the recent procedure of the Presbyterian church. They have prevailed at least since 1920, when the General Assembly at Philadelphia contemptuously refused to allow even five minutes' debate on a Plan of Organic Union, presented by President J. Ross Stevenson of Princeton Seminary for the Committee on Cooperation and Union—a Plan of Organic Union which relegated our historic Confession of Faith to the realm of the nonessential and sought to unite our church with various other bodies on the basis of a preamble couched in the vague language so dear to popular Modernism. From that time on at least, the attack upon the evangelical witness of the Presbyterian church has gone forward under cover. Free and open discussion has been discouraged; the church's policy has been treated as though it concerned at most only commissioners to the General Assembly or holders of ecclesiastical office; the laity has been kept sedulously in the dark; secret diplomacy has been the rule.

In this discouragement of free discussion, the climax was reached by certain actions of the last General Assembly discouraging "premature" publication of reports. These actions will be discussed in the next number of *Christianity Today*. But enough has been said already, we think, to show that a thoroughgoing moral reform is needed in the Presbyterian church. The church needs to remember that it is not a secret order, whose faults can be concealed either from God or from men; it needs to abandon all secret diplomacy in its negotiations for union with other churches and form only open covenants openly arrived at; it needs to take the laity into its confidence not merely after measures are already formulated but when they are still in process of being formed; it needs to remember that love in the New Testament sense is not merely in word but in deed, and that it is never really present except where simple fairness prevails. In short, it needs to turn resolutely from its present policy and spirit to the wonderful openness and freedom of the New Testament church.

[In the next issue of *Christianity Today*, the present writer hopes to discuss the important matter of publicity for measures proposed for adoption by the church. Is the church's policy a concern only of commissioners or presbyteries or officials, or has the laity still some rights?]

III. The Present Situation

The Proposed Plan of Union

Since the appearance of the last number of *Christianity Today*, a great attack has been launched against the Constitution of the Presbyterian Church in the U.S.A. by the Joint Committee on Organic Union.

We do not at all impugn the motives of the committee. We acknowledge gratefully, moreover, the fact that the proposal is tentative merely, and is submitted to open examination by the Church at large before the General Assembly meets next May. Nevertheless, however laudable may be the motives of the committee, the proposal which it has made does constitute, in fact though not in intention, an attack upon the constitution of the Presbyterian church.

The last attack was made in 1920, by a plan which sought to unite many ecclesiastical bodies on the basis of a preamble couched in the vague language so dear to the popular Modernism of our day. That attack was defeated in the presbyteries. Since then the destructive tendency has continued its undermining work for eleven years. It now comes forward with another public proposal.

The present Plan of Union involves the virtual abandonment of the Westminster Standards and the substitution for them of the creed which the United Presbyterian Church adopted in 1925. In form, indeed, the Westminster Standards are retained together with that United Presbyterian creed. But since the preamble of that creed, which is to be adopted with the rest, states that where that creed differs from the Westminster Standards its declarations are to prevail, what we really have here is the substitution of a new doctrinal standard for our historic Confession of Faith.

That new doctrinal standard is vague and unsatisfactory, as are most creeds produced in this unbelieving age; it contradicts important elements in the Reformed system of doctrine, and is ambiguous, if not definitely destructive, with regard to the authority of the Bible. It contains, indeed, many things that are true. If it had been produced on the way upward to some better presentation of Bible teaching, there is much that might have been said in favor of it. But the important question about any step that is being taken is the question whether it is a step up or a step down. And certainly, from the Christian point of view, this step is a step down. To abandon the Westminster Standards for this vague and unsatisfactory statement is to make vast concessions to unbelief. It is the very opposite of the true creed-making function of the Christian church.

But whatever measure of good there may be in the body of the United Presbyterian creed, the preamble, which is the most important thing in it, is almost wholly evil. It begins, indeed, with apparent adherence to the authority of the Bible as the only infallible rule of faith and practice. But that is apparently contradicted in the very next sentence, which seems to make the "living Church" an authority. No one reading these two sentences consecutively can be quite sure whether the author of the creed holds to the Christian or to the Modernist view as to the seat of authority in religion.

Then the preamble proceeds, in the second paragraph, to indicate that subscription to the Standards means nothing in particular, since "forbearance in love" is to be exercised toward those who are not able fully to subscribe to the Standards but merely do not determinedly oppose them. So a minister does not need to believe in the Standards after all. He can keep silent about the truth that they contain. No, he can even oppose them! Only he must not *determinedly* oppose them. Can anyone imagine a statement more diametrically opposite to the whole letter and spirit of the New Testament, or more utterly abhorrent to a man who is on fire with a zeal to proclaim the gospel of Christ?

What we have in this preamble—at least when its language is taken in the light of the present condition of the church, which it is evidently intended to condone—is Modernism. Only there are different forms of Modernism, and this is Modernism in a particularly confused and shallow form.

We cannot believe that the consistently evangelical part of the United Presbyterian Church would be very sorry to desert this unsatisfactory modern creed and return to the great historic standards of the Reformed faith, which belong to them just as much as they belong to us.

The Policy of Secrecy

Returning now to our presentation of the state of the Presbyterian Church in the U.S.A., we ask our readers to remember what we have said in the first two articles of the series. We have observed that the entire machinery of the church is dominated by a Modernist–indifferentist tendency which is in striking contradiction both to the Bible and to the church's Confession of Faith. Of the ministerial members of the Permanent Judicial Commission, which is practically the supreme court of the church, exactly one-half (four out of eight) are signers of a Modernist document, the Auburn Affirmation, which attacks directly the full truthfulness of Scripture and declares that that doctrine, with four other central verities of the Christian faith, is nonessential even for the ministry; and evidences of any consistent or vigorous evangelicalism in the other members of the commission are, to say the most, very slight. Similar is the condition in the other agencies of the church. Signers of the Auburn Affirmation are prominent in those agencies, and men who have taken any vigorous stand against the point of view of the Affirmation are given scarcely any representation at all. It is not too much to say, therefore, that unless the mission boards are radically reformed, the organization of new boards that can honestly appeal for the support of Bible-believing Christians is one of the crying needs of the hour.

The present anomalous condition of the church has been brought about, we observed further, by a policy of concealment in councils and courts. If the destructive forces had been exhibited in their true light, they might have been checked long ago; but as it is, they have carried on their undermining labors in the dark.

This policy of secrecy is particularly disgraceful in cases of judicial process, where it runs counter to all the fair and honorable traditions of the Anglo-Saxon race, to say nothing of the teachings of the Word of God. In that field, the evil is actually being practiced today; a secret trial has just been completed in the Synod of Pennsylvania. Such procedure is an offense to fair-minded people everywhere, and it is a disgrace to a church bearing the name of Christ. Yet if the proposed new Book of Discipline goes into effect, the evil will be made universal and obligatory, and a secret inquisition will thus be set up in the Presbyterian church. The same outrageous provision is found in the Book of Discipline of the proposed united church.

But the tendency to check open discussion has also proved to be disastrous when applied to the legislative and administrative functions of the church. We traced a few of its workings in the last number of *Christianity Today*. We pointed out how it was operative in the destruction of the old Princeton Seminary—the last important stronghold of a genuine and vigorous evangelicalism among the theological seminaries controlled by the church—and how in general it was made to operate against any fair hearing for the rank and file.

The Anti-Publicity Action

The same tendency—to come to the more immediate subject of the present article—has found special expression in an action of the last General Assembly, meeting in May 1931. At that Assembly, a resolution was passed directing the stated clerk to the effect that he devise means by which "the injudicious or premature publication of matters subject to serious difference of opinion or matters subject to sensational or misleading interpretations may be prevented," and that "Standing Rule No. 29 . . . shall be so interpreted as to carry out the spirit" of this resolution (*Minutes*, pp. 84, 85).

Standing Rule No. 29 provides that "all reports of Special and other Committees shall be delivered to the Stated Clerk on or before April 1, in each year," that they shall be printed by him, that copies shall be sent in bound form to commissioners, and that *"all reports included in the above bound form are thereby released for public comment or quotation"* (italics ours; see *Minutes*, p. 372). It is especially this last provision of the standing rule which, apparently, is to be interpreted in a way to prevent premature publication.

Now in a day when even the Word of God is so frequently "interpreted" to mean its exact opposite, we need not be surprised that a mere standing rule of the General Assembly should meet a like fate. But when that excellent standing rule does meet a like fate, when it is "interpreted" so as to defeat its purpose, the result is that any really free and effective discussion of measures proposed for adoption by the Presbyterian church is either definitely checked or at least committed to the discretion of an administrative officer.

The purpose of that standing rule was that measures proposed to the General Assembly by various committees shall be discussed not merely by commissioners but by the church at large. One medium by which they become known to the church at large is provided by whatever independent church papers there may be. An even more effective and far-reaching medium is provided by the secular daily press. The use of these two media of communication is checked by the present action of the General Assembly.

Just how far it is to be checked, and in what way, is left to the discretion of the stated clerk. We do not know how he will employ the arbitrary power which has been placed in his hands. He may do what I believe was suggested tentatively at the General Assembly—copyright the "Blue Book"—so as to be able to prevent the reports from being copied in any papers except those that are favored by the ecclesiastical machinery. It is almost unthinkable, indeed, that he should venture upon anything quite so outrageous and tyrannical as that. But even if he uses his power in some less tyrannical way, the granting of that power does involve an attack upon the very vitals of Presbyterian liberty.

Autocracy vs. Democracy

What we have in this action of the 1931 Assembly, as over against the standing rule which it nullifies, is a conflict between two widely differing notions of the government of the Presbyterian church.

The notion which underlies the standing rule is a democratic notion. According to that notion, the church—so far as human instrumentalities are concerned—is governed by its entire membership; its presbyters, officers, commissioners to the General Assembly are servants of the people, and the people have a right to know exactly what its servants plan to do. According to the present action of the General Assembly, the real business of the church should be conducted in committee rooms or around board tables, and the people are to have very little real power.

What this action of the General Assembly really means by "premature" publication of reports, or what it will be understood by many persons connected with the ecclesiastical machinery as meaning, is, we fear, publication at such time as to jeopardize the customary process of rushing through the General Assembly the measures favored by the agencies, committees, and boards.

A case in point is provided by the report of the Special Commission on Marriage, Divorce, and Remarriage to the General Assembly of 1931, a report which, we surmise, occasioned the anti-publicity action with which we are now concerned. Publication of that report so aroused the opposition of the church at large that the report was modified before it was presented to the Assembly.

Was the publication "premature"? The answer all depends upon the point of view. It was premature from the point of view of those who *favored* the proposed action; but from the point of view of those who were *opposed* to the action, it was altogether timely—it prevented the Assembly from following its custom of passing committee measures down to the presbyteries without any general discussion.

We do not at all impugn the motives of the stated clerk in welcoming the passage of this anti-publicity resolution, and we hope that he may use wisely the power that has been granted to him. But however wisely or unwisely the authority granted to the stated clerk may be used, the granting of the authority is a very serious sign of the times. The resolution speaks of the "spirit" of the action. Well, it is the "spirit" of the action to which we object. The spirit of the standing rule nullified by this action was a spirit of fairness and openness and liberty; it was the fine old spirit of the Reformed faith. The action nullifying the standing rule will, we fear, with however good intentions on the part of the stated clerk, encourage that spirit of concealment and ecclesiastical expediency and tyranny which is becoming increasingly dominant in the church.

Monopoly in Church Papers

This latter spirit was manifested also in another report that was made to the last General Assembly—the report of the General Council's Committee on Program and Field Activities. That committee presented as part of the "ideal solution" of the problem of publicity for church causes the following:

> (b) To secure the consolidation of weekly church papers so that there should not be more than two in the field, and that such papers should be assisted to become vital and adequate, although not official organs of the work of the entire Church. Such a result to be achieved both by mutual cooperation in the furnishing and publishing of suitable material and also by the furnishing of financial assistance by the General Council and the Boards in the form of paid advertising, the amount and character of such advertising to be determined in the light of the number of subscriptions to such papers, further and active assistance to be afforded by the General Council in the promotion of the circulation and use of such papers. (*Minutes*, p. 224)

What is the meaning of this extraordinary proposal? The answer is only too plain. The proposal means that if this policy is carried out, a monopoly of subsidized church papers is to be established in the Presbyterian church, such papers to publish what the official boards and agencies regard as "suitable material." The consolidation of existing weekly church papers is to be secured so that there shall *"not be more than two in the field"* (italics ours). Thus the "ideal solution" of the problem of publicity, as the committee sees it, is that *all* the church papers are to be controlled by, or complacent toward, the ecclesiastical machinery.

It is true, the subsidized church papers are not, according to the proposal, to be official organs of the entire church; but any thought of real editorial indolence on the part of such subsidized church papers is of course quite out of the question. What we have here is an attempt at monopoly in its most oppressive form.

The time is particularly favorable for such a proposal. There are now only three weekly church papers of general circulation in the Presbyterian Church in the U.S.A. One, *The Presbyterian Advance*, is under the editorship of a signer of the Auburn Affirmation; another, *The Presbyterian Banner*, has for many years been opposed to the ecclesiastical contention of the evangelical part of the church; the third, *The Presbyterian*, was formerly the evangelical organ, but in 1930 removed forcibly the editor, Dr. Samuel G. Craig, and adopted the customary attitude of subservience or complacency toward the present condition of the church.

These are just the sort of papers that will serve the ends of the gentlemen now controlling the ecclesiastical machinery; and if any one of them can be merged with either of the others, the two remaining papers, after being subsidized and made monopolistic, will provide just the kind of "publicity" to prevent any disturbing objection to the prevailing Modernist–indifferentist drift. It is no wonder that the General Council's committee thinks that if such a condition can be secured, *The Presbyterian Magazine* (now under the editorship of a signer of the Auburn Affirmation) can be dispensed with. If papers like *The* (new) *Presbyterian*, *The Banner*, and *The Presbyterian Advance* can be made monopolistic, there will be no danger lest the real condition of the church become known.

The Despised Evangelicals

At first sight, it might look as though the Modernist–indifferentist control of the church were impregnable. It could be shaken only by a true enlightenment of the rank and file, and to prevent that enlightenment an increasing efficiency is being attained by the ecclesiastical machinery. Measures of the most far-reaching importance are being sent down to the presbyteries without debate; in the presbyteries no general, but merely a local, discussion is possible. Objection to the wasting of the church's heritage is discouraged on the absurd ground that it should be made, if at all, only by way of formal judicial process. Judicial process is made worthless as a means of establishing truth not only by the partisanship of the highest Judicial Commission, but more particularly by the secrecy of the church courts. Such secrecy will be made universal and obligatory if the new Book of Discipline goes into effect; men who hold to the unpopular and disturbing evangelical position will be dealt with in a secret inquisition and deprived even of the right of an open trial. The one official journal, *The Presbyterian Magazine,* is edited by a signer of the Modernist Auburn Affirmation; so is one of the three weekly church papers, *The Presbyterian Advance.* The other two weekly papers are either subservient or complacent toward the drift of the church, and it is proposed that the total number of weekly church papers shall be reduced to two, which shall be subsidized and promoted in a monopolistic way. Presentation of ecclesiastical issues by independent papers can be hindered at any time by an arbitrary power given to the stated clerk.

Under such a régime, what chance is there for the despised evangelical part in the church even to obtain a hearing? Be it remembered that the ecclesiastical pressure against it, of which we have been speaking, is reinforced by the vast pressure of the world at large. Adherents of the gospel of Christ— and we mean wholehearted adherents of it, not those who give it lip service, or are willing only to propagate it and not to defend it, or do not believe in controversy, or make their preaching "positive and not negative," or use any of the other miserable phrases by which men seek to conceal from themselves and others the real feebleness of their faith and coldness of their love—wholehearted adherents of the gospel of Christ, we say, are faced today by an overwhelming weight of public opinion. The daily press, though by no means so unfair as the ecclesiastical papers, is for the most part hostile or at least devoid of understanding. It reflects naturally the prevailing popular attitude; it is usually willing to believe the worst of the adherents of an unpopular cause. The secular magazines present for the most part only the opposing view; the schools and colleges have become agencies of propaganda against this unpopular faith. With this vast opposition of the world, the machinery of our church is making common cause. It too uses the current phrases of modern unbelief; it too discourages "controversy"; it too belittles what it regards as divisive contentions; it too, at least in many of its prominent representatives, represents the blessed facts of the gospel as merely "theories," among other possible theories, to explain the vague generalities that are so dear to an unbelieving world.

Under such conditions, faced as they are by the opposition of the world, faced by the opposition more bitter still of an increasingly apostate church, misrepresented, despised, ridiculed, tried in secret courts so that the ridiculousness of the charges against them cannot become generally known, silenced in church assemblies—under such conditions, we say, what help is there for the adherents of a gospel which now as always is diametrically opposed to the thoughts and aspirations and purposes of the generality of mankind?

The answer to that question is perfectly plain. There is no help for believers in the gospel save one, but that help is sure. It is found at the mercy seat of God.

When shall that help be used, my brethren? When shall we cease benumbing ourselves with a baseless optimism; when shall we cease saying that the Presbyterian church is "essentially sound"; when shall we be willing to face the facts before God?

Facing the Facts before God

The facts, alas, are perfectly plain to the man who is not afraid to see. Two mighty forces have been contending for the control of the Presbyterian Church in the U.S.A. One is the religion of supernatural redemption that is presented in the Bible and in the Confession of Faith; the other is the naturalistic or indifferentist Modernism that finds expression in the Auburn Affirmation. Between these two forces, there are many attempts at compromise. We do not presume to look into the hearts of men; we do not presume to say just who in the church is a Christian and who is not; we do not presume to say how far a man can mistakenly serve the cause of unbelief and yet be united to Christ by faith. But whatever may be said about individual *men*, it is perfectly clear that the two *forces* are diametrically opposed; it is perfectly clear that between the Bible and the Auburn Affirmation there can be no peace but only deadly war.

It is perfectly clear, moreover, that in this warfare the anti-evangelical contention has so far won the victory. Of what avail is it to point to general professions of adherence to the faith of the church by this ecclesiastical official or that? The simple fact is that the *policy* of the church organization as a whole is exactly that which so effectively serves the purposes of unbelief in all the churches of the world—discouragement of controversy, tolerance of anti-Christian propaganda, bitter intolerance of any effort to make the true condition of the church known, emphasis on organization at the expense of doctrine, neglect of the deep things of the Word of God. Let us not deceive ourselves, my friends. The Presbyterian Church in the U.S.A. includes, indeed, many true Christian men and women; but in its corporate capacity, through its central organization, it has ceased to witness, in any clear and true sense, to the Lord Jesus Christ.

With this drift away from the faith, there has gone a lamentable moral decline. Life and doctrine, here as always, have been shown to be closely connected. When Christian doctrine is neglected or denied, Christian living sooner or later is abandoned too.

We are not referring to the sins of human weakness to which all Christians are subject. Those sins, alas, are always with us, and with regard to them it must ever be said: "Brethren, if a man be overtaken in a fault, ye which are spiritual, restore such an one in the spirit of meekness; considering thyself, lest thou also be tempted." But we refer to the blatant and settled sins of our ecclesiastical habits—not the sins of this individual or that, but the sins that seem to be inherent in the entire corporate life of the church.

Loving Words or Loving Deeds

At this point, two errors need to be rooted out of our minds and hearts and lives.

The first error is the ancient error which applies a laxer standard of morality to the church than the standard that is applied to the world. Unfairness and oppression and dishonesty are somehow thought to become virtues when they serve ecclesiastical ends; an odor of sanctity in the church is thought to take the place of humble moral considerations which prevail generally between man and man.

That error must be rooted out of the Presbyterian Church in the U.S.A. if it is to be a Christian church in fact as well as in name. Secret courts, depriving a man of his right to an open trial, are disgraceful and outrageous in the world at large; they are even more disgraceful and outrageous in a church that bears the name of Christ. Wrong does not become right merely by being within ecclesiastical walls.

The second error which needs to be rooted out of our minds and hearts is the error that makes loving words a substitute for loving deeds. We hear much about love in the church today, but is it really love? Oh, no, my friends. If a man really loved the church of Jesus Christ, if he really loved with his whole heart the little ones for whom Christ died, he would never repeat the vain swelling words of a foolish optimism; he would never cry, "Peace, peace," when there is no peace; he would never conceal from the church its deadly peril; he would never exalt the smooth working of ecclesiastical machinery above the simple principles of openness and fair play; he would never cherish the wicked and heartless dream of a monopolistic church union; he would never consent to force a single congregation into a church union against its conscience or seek to take its property from it if it declined to conform; he would never deprive any man of his right to an open trial. Instead, he would present the real facts without fear or favor; he would love with a love like that of the apostle Paul, who wrote to the Corinthian Christians a truthful letter that cost him many tears. Above all, in this crisis of the church's life he would come before God in a very agony of prayer—not the prayer that is an evasion of witness-bearing but the prayer that makes even weak men brave. He would pray that those who are leading the church astray may be convicted of their deadly error; he would pray that the great attack just launched in the name of church union against the faith of our church may by God's grace be brought to naught; he would pray that the coldness and indifference of us who hold to the old gospel might be burned away in the flame of the divine love; he would pray that such a thing as secret courts may hardly so much as be named among us; he would pray that the church may renounce the things of darkness and may return to the light and openness and liberty of the gospel of Christ.

Who, in this time of crisis, will engage, very earnestly and very humbly, in such a prayer?

25

IS THERE A FUTURE FOR CALVINISM IN THE PRESBYTERIAN CHURCH?

The future of Calvinism within the Presbyterian Church in the U.S.A. (assuming that that is the particular Presbyterian body which is intended by the editor of *The Banner* in suggesting the title of this article) is certainly, from the point of view of human probabilities, exceedingly dark. The creed of the church remains, indeed, Calvinistic, being the Westminster Confession of Faith; and every candidate for the ministry or eldership is required to subscribe solemnly to that creed. But both creed and creed-subscription are constantly "interpreted" to mean practically nothing at all.

The descent of what was formerly a great church to its present lamentable condition has been for the most part gradual, since here as elsewhere the destructive forces have been content to labor mostly in the dark. At the most, a few landmarks may be distinguished on the downward path.

Such a landmark, for example, was the union in 1906 with the Cumberland Presbyterian Church, which was a church Presbyterian in name but certainly not Calvinistic in doctrine. After the Cumberland union, the undermining efforts of the unionists went on for a time in silence, but in 1920

"Is There a Future for Calvinism in the Presbyterian Church?" originally appeared in *The Banner* 65 (1930) 320, 333.

they came to the surface again in the so-called "Plan of Organic Union," which sought to unite a large number of Protestant bodies on the basis of a preamble couched in the vague language so dear to modern naturalism. The constituting churches were graciously to be allowed to retain each its own creed, but the distinctive features of the individual creeds were to be regarded as nonessential. What was really stamped as essential was the utterly vague statement contained in the preamble. Evidently more than Calvinism was here at stake. The attack in the Cumberland union had been upon the distinctive features of the Reformed faith, but here the attack was rather upon those convictions which even the Roman Catholic and Greek Catholic churches accept in common with us.

This Plan of Organic Union was indeed rejected by the presbyteries in the Presbyterian Church in the U.S.A., but it received a very large vote and thus provided another indication to show how widely the faith of the church had been undermined.

THE AUBURN AFFIRMATION

In 1923, in view of the propaganda of Dr. Harry Emerson Fosdick in the First Presbyterian Church of New York, a propaganda that was hostile to the very roots of the Christian religion, the General Assembly at Indianapolis, after a very close vote, issued a pronouncement in which the virgin birth and four other articles were declared to be essential doctrines of the Word of God and of the Standards of the church.

This pronouncement contained nothing distinctive of the Reformed faith, but merely certain doctrines in which all branches of historic Christendom are for the most part agreed. Certainly it did not err on the side of any undue definiteness or wealth of detail. Yet it was attacked by a document commonly called the "Auburn Affirmation," which was signed by about one thousand three hundred ministers in the Presbyterian church. The Auburn Affirmation declared that not one single one of the five points mentioned in the General Assembly's pronouncement was essential even for the ministry; according to the Affirmation, therefore, a man may be a minister in the Presbyterian church without believing in the virgin birth or in any one of the other four of these basic articles of the Christian faith.

In the ensuing ecclesiastical battle between the General Assembly's pronouncement and the Auburn Affirmation, between the evangelical and the anti-evangelical forces in the church, the anti-evangelical forces have in the main won the victory. They encountered, indeed, some setbacks in their triumphant march. In 1924, for example, Dr. Clarence E. Macartney, representing the evangelical forces, was elected moderator of the General Assembly in a close contest with Dr. Charles R. Erdman, who, despite orthodox declarations made by him and for him, had the support of the Modernist–indifferentist party. But in the ensuing year Dr. Erdman was elected over the candidate of the evangelical party of that year, and the Modernists and indifferentists resumed full control of the machinery of the church. A "Commission of Fifteen" appointed by Dr. Erdman to investigate the trouble in the church really gave the Modernists and indifferentists all that they desired—namely, the glossing over of the real conditions and time for them to tighten their control of the machinery of the church.

That control is at present practically complete. Four out of fifteen ministerial members of the Board of Foreign Missions and seven out of sixteen ministerial members of the Board of National Missions are actually signers of the Modernist "Auburn Affirmation," and those who have taken any clear and effective and prominent evangelical stand in the great ecclesiastical issue of the day are scarcely represented in these boards at all.

DESTRUCTION OF THE OLD PRINCETON SEMINARY

The drift of the church has been seen not only in the ecclesiastical machinery but also in the educational agencies. Only one of the theological seminaries, that at Princeton, was engaging in any really vigorous and effective battle against the destructive forces that were so mightily at work. That seminary indeed, up to the spring of 1929, stood at the very height of its influence; its student body had increased greatly within recent years, and it was honored by all those throughout the world who in the face of the prevailing Modernist tyranny cherished Presbyterian liberty and the glories of the Reformed faith. Evidently, from the Modernist–indifferentist point of view, such an institution constituted a serious menace and had to be destroyed. So destroyed it was in 1929, after a three-year fight. Princeton Theological Seminary now stands under a board of control that is quite out of accord with the doctrinal position that the institution has hitherto maintained.

This destruction of the old Princeton was furthered by representatives of the ecclesiastical machinery who were within the councils of the seminary itself. President J. Ross Stevenson and Dr. Charles R. Erdman, the two advocates of the reorganization who were members of the faculty of the seminary, are both of them members of the Board of Foreign Missions, Dr. Erdman being its president. Dr. Robert E. Speer and Dr. John McDowell, the former being a secretary of the Board of Foreign Missions and the latter of the Board of National Missions, took a particularly vigorous part in the reorganization movement, and Dr. George Alexander and Mr. W. P. Stevenson, members of the Board of Foreign Missions, also were concerned in it, the former being a member of the board of directors of the seminary and the latter a member of the board of trustees. What we have essentially in the change at Princeton is the crushing out of the distinctive features of the seminary by the general administrative machinery of the church. Princeton Seminary has simply been made to conform to the general doctrinal drift.

That doctrinal drift is also in practically complete control of the agencies of public discussion. The official organ of the church, *The Presbyterian Magazine*, is actually under the editorship of a signer of the Modernist "Auburn Affirmation" itself; and among the unofficial organs, the only one, *The Presbyterian*, that has been supporting a clear-cut evangelicalism has just removed its former editor, Dr. S. G. Craig, and has put in his place Dr. W. Courtland Robinson, who was one of those members of the former conservative party in the old Princeton board of directors who joined forces with the "Liberal" party in the board in the fight of last spring, by the adoption of a compromise report which was really no compromise at all but would have given the Liberals practically everything that they desired. Thus the real evangelical party is altogether without any organ of publicity in the Presbyterian church today.

THE PRESENT DUTY OF THE CONSERVATIVES

Under these discouraging circumstances, what should be done by the sound elements in the church? The answer might seem to be that they ought to withdraw from the existing organization and form a real Presbyterian church that should be true to the Reformed faith. From such a course of action—upon which God has put such signal marks of his favor both in Holland and in the Christian Reformed church in America—they have been deterred especially by the conviction, which many of them cherish, that

270

the Presbyterian Church in the U.S.A. is fundamentally sound and that if its rank and file only knew what is going on, it would still stand true to the Word of God.

In support of this conviction, some things undoubtedly may be said. Those who are in control of the ecclesiastical machinery have done everything in their power to prevent light from being shed upon the issues of the day. At the last General Assembly, for example, debate on the Princeton issue was so strictly limited that commissioners on the floor, as distinguished from members of the Assembly's committee and of the seminary boards, were allowed scarcely any time at all. These tactics were particularly successful because of the unfortunate custom of rotation in the choice of commissioners. Of the nine hundred and fifty commissioners, it is safe to say that only an altogether inconsiderable number had listened to the debate of the preceding year. Hence many votes unquestionably were cast in complete ignorance of the issues that were at stake.

It is, indeed, very strange that if the heart of our church is really sound, it does not react vigorously against such unjust and ruthless measures as the suppression of the old Princeton Seminary, and also against the sad vagueness of the pronouncements that come from representatives of the mission boards.[1] But doubtful though we hold the optimistic conviction about the soundness of the church to be, that conviction is at least natural; and since God, alas, has raised up no Abraham Kuyper to lead us in the true path, many of our number are at present uncertain what our immediate ecclesiastical duty is.

WESTMINSTER THEOLOGICAL SEMINARY

One thing, at least, is clear—if there is to be any conservation of the sound element in the Presbyterian church, we must have a truly Reformed, and ringingly polemic, source of ministerial supply. Such a source of ministerial supply has been provided in Westminster Theological Seminary, which has been founded in Philadelphia to continue that Princeton tradition which was so rudely broken at Princeton itself by the action of the last General Assembly.

---

1. As an example of such vagueness, see the recent pronouncement by Dr. Robert E. Speer, entitled "Are Foreign Missions Done For?"

Westminster Seminary will be altogether committed to the Westminster Confession of Faith and to the Presbyterian form of church government, and will remain truly Reformed even if the Presbyterian Church in the U.S.A. altogether abandons the Reformed faith. Thus it will be able to meet whatever eventuality may arise. If the sound elements separate themselves from the existing organization, Westminster Seminary will be ready to serve the truly Reformed church thus formed. If, on the other hand, the existing church organization can still be saved, a large part of that great task will be accomplished, with God's help, by the forces which Westminster Seminary will provide. One thing at least may safely be said—if we do remain in the Presbyterian church, we shall never acquiesce in the program of "peace and work" until the true witness of the Presbyterian church shall have been restored.

But the opportunity for Westminster Seminary is not limited to the Presbyterian Church in the U.S.A. Already it has become evident that it will be worldwide. All over the world there are those who are grieved to their very hearts by the destruction of the old Princeton and are not deceived for a moment by the propaganda which would obscure its true meaning. These persons are looking to Westminster Seminary for a continuation of the service that the old Princeton Seminary was rendering before its destruction by the General Assembly of 1929.

Certainly the work of Westminster Seminary does seem to have had the favor of God during this its first academic year. We have a splendid company of fifty students; and the Christian fellowship that prevails among them, and between them and the faculty, is a joy to the soul.

In the faculty, which consists of eight full-time professors and instructors, there are four young men, who constitute by far the most important influx of new forces for the scholarly defense and propagation of the Reformed faith which we have seen in our Princeton circles for many years. They are Professor Cornelius Van Til (who, after a brilliant career as a student at Princeton Seminary and at Princeton University, where he received his doctor's degree in philosophy, made such a signal success as a teacher at Princeton Seminary last year and is continuing that success in the fullest measure now), the Rev. Paul Woolley, Dr. N. B. Stonehouse, and the Rev. Allan A. MacRae. Three of these men have studied in Europe, and all are admirably equipped. But what is vastly more important than their academic equipment is the true ability which God has given them for their lifework.

They will each have a more and more distinguished place in the scholarly defense of the faith.

As for Professor R. B. Kuiper, it would be quite impossible to express in a few words what his service has meant to our cause. As a teacher of theology, he has the enthusiastic respect and warm affection of the students in a way that really overflows all bounds; and the combination in him of genuine theological learning with ability to move the people in the pulpit and inspire the students in the classroom has made him a veritable tower of strength.

It will at once be seen how profound is our debt to the Christian Reformed church. Without the three men whom you have sent to us—Professor Van Til, Professor Kuiper, and Dr. Stonehouse—it is painful to us to contemplate what our situation would be. You have kept alive in this country the torch of true learning and true devotion to the Reformed faith. Very precious to us have been our relations with your noble church in the days when we were at Princeton. And now you are giving us your help in the hour of our deepest need. We are grateful from the very bottom of our hearts—grateful both to you and to Almighty God.

26

THE NEW
PRESBYTERIAN HYMNAL

The first thing that needs to be said about the new hymnal of the Presbyterian Church in the U.S.A.[1] is that it is really new. It is not a mere revision of the hymnal that has hitherto been in use—the hymnal published in 1895 and revised in 1911 with a supplement of 1917—but a thoroughly new book. Of the 737 hymns in the old book (exclusive of "Ancient Hymns and Canticles"), only 136 have been retained unchanged, with perhaps about twenty more where the changes are slight. Of the 513 hymns in the new book, 214 are entirely new. The changes in the 163 hymns which remain after subtraction of these 214 that are entirely new and of the 136 that are taken unchanged from the old book consist largely, but by no means exclusively, in omissions of whole stanzas.[2]

"The New Presbyterian Hymnal" originally appeared in *Christianity Today* 4 (December 1933) 5–6, 8–9.

1. "The Hymnal," published by authority of The General Assembly of The Presbyterian Church in the United States of America. Philadelphia: Presbyterian Board of Christian Education, 1933. The editors are Clarence Dickinson, M.A., Mus.D., Litt.D., Editor; Calvin Weiss Laufer, M.A., D.D., Assistant Editor.
2. The figures just given are to be regarded as approximate merely. It is quite possible, for example, that some of the hymns here enumerated as entirely new may be partly included in the old book, if, for example, they begin in a slightly different way so that they have been for that reason missed in the search in the

The editors have labored long and earnestly; it is only fair that careful consideration should be given to what those labors have produced. The appearance of this book is an important event in the history of the Presbyterian Church in the U.S.A. and in the history of Protestant Christendom. What is the meaning of that event?

THE GENERAL TENDENCY

A sharp and clear answer to this question was given in *The Chicago Tribune* of May 27, 1933, in a quotation purporting to come from one of the leaders in the Presbyterian Church in the U.S.A. This gentleman was quoted as pointing to the new hymnal as being one of the chief evidences of change now taking place not only in his own church, but also throughout Protestantism generally. "If you want to know the trends of religion, listen to the way religion sings," he was further reported as saying. The quotation continues as follows:

> About 400 old hymns were dropped. The doctrine note in hymns is almost missing. In place of doctrine, brotherhood, international fellowship, and sound service are stressed. In addition to this change the new hymns, instead of stressing outward ecclesiastical conformity, sound the mystical note.
>
> Since the General Assembly last met in Columbus eight years ago great changes have taken place in the Presbyterian Church. Then we faced the crisis in the fundamentalist drive on the church. The thing was fought out on this same platform from which the announcement of DR. JOHN MC-DOWELL'S election as moderator yesterday meant the death of fundamentalism as a party in the church. . . .

We have purposely refrained from mentioning here the name of the gentleman who was reported to have spoken thus, because indirectly we have heard something to the effect that he does not recognize the correctness of the quotation. But however incorrect the quotation may be as a reproduction of what the person quoted actually said, the estimate here given of the

---

index. Moreover, there has been some difficulty in the classification of hymns partly included in the new book among "Opening Responses: Introits," etc.; and there may have been slight errors in counting.

significance of the appearance of the new hymnal is, we are convinced, not so very far from the truth. The "doctrine note in hymns" is indeed "almost missing" in many of the hymns added in the new book; and that means, of course, that the Christian note is almost missing, since the Christian religion is doctrinal to the very heart and core. The Modernist elements in the Presbyterian church will no doubt welcome the new book all the more eagerly when they recognize its true tendency, but what we think important is that the Christian element in the church should continue to use the old hymnal and should not be led into adopting into its worship a book which will sadly impoverish its devotional life.

We do not mean, of course, that there are no truly Christian hymns in the new book, for among the (approximately) 136 hymns that are retained unchanged are to be found many truly evangelical hymns. There are some hymns too deeply entrenched to be dislodged by one generation—even by a generation that desires to get rid of what it calls "doctrine" and that feels little need of the grace of God. Even among the hymns added in this book, moreover, there are some, as we shall see in a moment, that a Christian man can joyfully sing. We do not mean to say that this book is as crassly Modernist as are some of the books now being used in formerly evangelical churches, and particularly we do not mean to say that its editors are consciously or systematically removing the things that conservatives in the church would like to retain. But what we do mean to say is that the book does in rather clear fashion reveal the drift of the times. People do not love now as they once did the things that are at the heart of the Christian faith, and that is the essential reason why this book, reflecting the tendency of the church, is so different from the book that it is endeavoring to replace.

It will be convenient to divide what we shall now say into a treatment (1) of omissions and changes and (2) of additions; but nothing like completeness will be possible. All that we can do is to give examples of what has been done in the new hymnal of the Presbyterian church.

OMISSIONS OF WHOLE HYMNS

Some of the omissions are to be welcomed. Thus we do not see how a believer in the scriptural doctrine of the grace of God can possibly sing the hymn of Charles Wesley (496 in the old book):

A charge to keep I have,
A God to glorify,
A never-dying soul to save,
And fit it for the sky.

Many of the other hymns of Charles Wesley are truly evangelical, and we rejoice in them, but we are glad that that particular hymn has been omitted. So also we are glad that the "Battle Hymn of the Republic" (included as No. 758 in the 1917 wartime supplement in the old book) is absent from the new book. Opinions may differ about the political views out of which that poem was born. Some of us may agree with them; some of us may disagree. But one thing is clear—a fiery war song like that has no place in the worship of a Christian congregation.

Unfortunately, however, such salutary omissions are more than balanced by those which mean genuine loss. Among the whole hymns dear to the Christian heart which are omitted from this book may be noted the following (the numbers being those in the old hymnal revised in 1911 and with the 1917 supplement):

4. Awake, my soul, and with the sun
Thy daily stage of duty run
38. Welcome, delightful morn
54. Safely through another week
God has brought us on our way
86. O God, we praise Thee; and confess
166. Hark! ten thousand harps and voices
188. Shout the glad tidings, exultingly sing
226. Sweet the moments, rich in blessing
Which before the cross I spend
254. O Jesus, Lord most merciful,
Low at Thy cross I lie
281. Come, Holy Ghost, in love
296. God, in the gospel of His Son,
Makes His eternal counsels known
298. The Spirit breathes upon the word,
And brings the truth to sight
306. Lord of our life, and God of our salvation

318. *Jesus, and shall it ever be,*
A mortal man ashamed of Thee?
335. *Not worthy, Lord! to gather up the crumbs*
406. *O'er the gloomy hills of darkness*
421. *Blessed are the sons of God,*
They are bought with Christ's own blood
432. *One there is, above all others,*
Well deserves the name of Friend
439. *Not all the blood of beasts*
On Jewish altars slain,
Could give the guilty conscience peace,
Or wash away the stain.
449. *Father, hear Thy children's call*
452. *No, not despairingly*
Come I to Thee
459. *Weary of earth, and laden with my sin*
465. *My hope is built on nothing less*
Than Jesus' blood and righteousness
471. *I lay my sins on Jesus,*
The spotless Lamb of God
472. *Lord, I believe; Thy power I own*
479. *Oft in danger, oft in woe*
Onward, Christians, onward go
495. *My soul, be on thy guard*
501. *Father, whate'er of earthly bliss*
514. *God is the Refuge of His saints*
571. *From every stormy wind that blows*
643. *There is a land of pure delight,*
Where saints immortal reign
683. *God be with you till we meet again*
708. *Tell me the old, old story*
711. *Awake, my soul, in joyful lays,*
And sing thy great Redeemer's praise
725. *O happy day, that fixed my choice*
On Thee, my Saviour, and my God!
727. *I was a wandering sheep*
729. *I am coming to the cross*

THE NATURE AND MISSION OF THE CHURCH

Corruptions in the Text

Even more revealing, perhaps, than the omission of these and other whole hymns are the omissions and changes in hymns which are in part retained.

At this point a preliminary criticism must apparently be brought against the method used in the new hymnal. The criticism is that changes have been introduced in the text of hymns without any indication whatever that they have been made. Such indications were given in the old hymnal, but in the new one they are lacking. We are well aware of the great difficulty that is involved in the establishment of the true text of hymns—especially in cases where the author himself issued a number of editions—and it is quite possible that we may be mistaken here and there in noting what look to us like corruptions introduced by the editors of the new book. There may be some historical justification in some cases for what they have printed. We lay no claim to competence in this intricate field of study. But the pursuance of an unfortunate method in this matter seems to be clear in the new book.

Thus, in Milton's hymn (64 in the new book), "Let us with a gladsome mind Praise the Lord, for He is kind," the first line in the second stanza reads in the old book and in our edition of Milton, "Let us blaze His Name abroad," whereas in the new book it reads, "Let us *sound* His Name abroad" (italics ours, here and in similar contrasts); and the last stanza in the new book is a repetition of the first with a certain change in the first line which becomes necessary when the stanza is thus used again.

The changes may bring improvement and they may not; personally, we think that they do not. But that is not the point. The point is that John Milton's name is appended in the new hymnal to something that is not his. Milton was a poet of some years ago, whose works are generally thought to possess considerable merit. But we do not think that he ought to be given credit for something—even though it is an improvement—to which he has no right.

Let it not be said that the changes which we have just indicated are slight and that therefore the editors of the new hymnal had a right to make them. In this matter of literary property, we think that only the most complete precision is in place. It was, therefore, altogether what sound scholarship and the best interests of the church demand when the editors of the previous hymnal announced as their policy that "As far as possible, the *hymns* are here printed as their authors wrote them" and that "All deviations from the author's text are indicated in the note beneath the hymn." It is, we think, a very serious backward step when the editors of the present book have departed from these sound literary principles.

Moreover, some of the changes made in the texts of the hymns are by no means so slight as those which we have indicated in connection with that translation of Psalm 136 by John Milton.

Sometimes the wording is changed apparently in the interests of simplicity and uniformity, and very mistaken and pedantic some of these changes seem to us to be. Sometimes they are superficially clarifying, but in instance after instance they will be found really to remove what is really distinctive in the line and reduce it to the level of the commonplace. Thus in the hymn of Isaac Watts, "Begin, my tongue, some heavenly theme," the old book (126) has in the last two lines of the second stanza the following:

> Sing the sweet promise of His grace,
>   And the performing God,

while the new book has (94):

> Sing the sweet promise of His grace,
>   And our redeeming God.

No doubt the new line is superficially easier, but the real point of the stanza is destroyed. The point is the correspondence of God's performance with his promise. That point is beautifully expressed in the last line as it appears in the old book, but in the new book the climax is destroyed by a nondistinctive closing line.

So in the hymn of Charles Wesley, "O for a thousand tongues to sing My dear Redeemer's praise" (147), the new book (199) has "My *great* Redeemer" instead of "My dear Redeemer"; and in the line "His blood can make the foulest clean," it has "the sinful" instead of "the foulest"—to the ruin of what is distinctive in the stanza.

Sometimes the changes, in their removal of what is distinctive, display the tendency, so marked in this book, to turn attention away from the cross of Christ and essential things of the Bible. So in the hymn "Thou didst leave Thy throne And Thy kingly crown When Thou camest to earth for me"— a beautiful hymn, by the way, sadly marred by this objectionable opening, which teaches a wrong, "kenotic" view of the incarnation—the old book

(193) has at the end of the fourth stanza, which deals with Calvary, the words:

> O come to my heart, Lord Jesus,
>   Thy cross is my only plea;

whereas the new book (231) simply inserts the same refrain as that which appears in other verses:

> O come to my heart, Lord Jesus
>   There is room in my heart for Thee!

Again the distinctiveness of the line is destroyed, and this time it is destroyed in a particularly unfortunate way. Many are the places in this new book where mention of the cross of Christ, in its true Christian meaning, is removed.

OMISSIONS OF STANZAS

The tendency toward removal of passages that set forth the death of Christ as a sacrifice to satisfy divine justice and reconcile us to God, and toward removal of passages presenting other basic things of the faith, particularly references to sin and judgment to come, appears with special clearness in the choice of stanzas to be omitted from those hymns of the old book which in part are retained.

Thus, in "Light of light, enlighten me" (37 in the old book, 21 in the new), the stanza is characteristically omitted which prays that the sinner may be led to fly from every error. In the hymn of Heber, "Hosanna to the living Lord!" (55 in the old book, 53 in the new), the climax stanza which deals with the last judgment is omitted. Without that last stanza, the central emphasis of the hymn is changed. Similarly, in John Newton's hymn "Now may He who from the dead Brought the Shepherd of the sheep" (73 in the old book, Response 41 in the new), the last stanza is omitted, which speaks of "that dear Redeemer's praise, Who the covenant sealed with blood."

In "All hail the power of Jesus' Name!" (157 in the old book, 192 in the new), three stanzas are omitted, including (very characteristically) the one which mentions the fall of man and the grace of God:

> *Ye seed of Israel's chosen race,*
> *Ye ransomed of the fall,*
> *Hail Him who saves you by His grace,*
> *And crown Him Lord of all.*

In "O could I speak the matchless worth" (159 in the old book, 203 in the new), in addition to changes in the first and last stanzas, the second stanza is omitted, which speaks of the blood of Jesus as a "ransom from the dreadful guilt":

> *I'd sing the precious blood He spilt,*
> *My ransom from the dreadful guilt*
> *Of sin, and wrath Divine;*
> *I'd sing His glorious righteousness,*
> *In which all-perfect, heavenly dress*
> *My soul shall ever shine.*

That stanza should have been the very last one to be omitted.

In a communion hymn by Horatius Bonar (334 in the old book, 352 in the new), the last stanza, which is the climax and gives point to all the rest, is omitted:

> *Mine is the sin, but Thine the righteousness;*
> *Mine is the guilt, but Thine the cleansing blood;*
> *Here is my robe, my refuge, and my peace,*
> *Thy blood, Thy righteousness, O Lord my God.*

In what clear form we find celebrated in that omitted stanza the imputed righteousness of Christ and the cleansing by his blood—the things that are the very heart and core of the gospel!

In "Who is on the Lord's side?" (369 in the old book, 272 in the new), one of the two stanzas chosen for omission begins thus:

> *Jesus, Thou hast bought us,*
> *Not with gold or gem,*
> *But with Thine own life-blood,*
> *For Thy diadem.*

THE NATURE AND MISSION OF THE CHURCH

That is the only stanza in this fine hymn that deals with the blood of Christ. A hymnal deeply Christian in its tendency would have omitted any other stanza sooner than that.

In the hymn of Frederick W. Fabe, "Was there ever kindest, shepherd" (435 in the old book, 93 in the new), which begins, in the new book, perhaps better, with "There's a wideness in God's mercy," those halves of the old stanzas 2 and 4 are omitted which mention the blood of Christ, so that the hymn as it now appears contains no clear reference to Christ at all!

In "Come, Thou Fount of every blessing" (589 in the old book, 235 in the new), the stanzas beginning "Here I raise my Ebenezer" and "Prone to wander, Lord, I feel it" are omitted. Surely that hymn, at least, might have been spared mutilation.

A particularly clear example of the removal of the gospel which has been brought about by omissions in this book is found in the treatment of the beautiful children's hymn "Around the throne of God in heaven Thousands of children stand" (702 in the old book, 450 in the new). The third stanza of that hymn asks the question about those children whose "sins are all forgiven" (we are here omitting the refrain: "Singing, Glory be to God on high," which occurs after each stanza):

> *What brought them to that world above,*
> *That heaven so bright and so fair,*
> *Where all is peace, and joy, and love;*
> *How came those children there?*

Then the next stanza in the old book gives the answer to that question as follows:

> *Because the Saviour shed His blood*
> *To wash away their sin;*
> *Bathed in that pure and precious flood,*
> *Behold them white and clean.*

That stanza is omitted in the new hymnal, and the answer to the question appears merely in what is said in the last stanza, which now comes immediately after the question:

> On earth they sought the Saviour's grace,
>   On earth they loved His Name;
> So now they see His blessed face,
>   And stand before the Lamb.

Here, in a very characteristic way, the grounding of salvation in the work of Christ is removed, and the true character of saving faith is obscured.

THE ADDED HYMNS

When we come now to the (approximately) 214 hymns which have been added in the new hymnal to those which appeared in the old book, it should be said in commendation that among these hymns are included a series of psalms from the Scottish Psalter of 1650 and from certain other sources, which, if they were not balanced by other things, would constitute a valuable enrichment of the devotional life of the church. We may mention also by way of commendation, for example, the inclusion of a beautiful Christmas hymn by Martin Luther (126), and also—to take a more modern example—the hymn "I am trusting Thee, Lord Jesus, Trusting only Thee" (287), which has come to be very familiar and very dear to many Christian people. There are, moreover, among the added hymns a few that do, in some specific fashion, touch upon the heart of the gospel in the cross of Christ. As examples may be mentioned the hymn of Horatius Bonar, "Glory be to God the Father" (60), which contains the stanza:

> Glory be to Him who loved us.
>   Washed us from each spot and stain.
> Glory be to Him who bought us.
>   Made us kings with Him to reign!
> Glory, glory, glory, glory,
>   To the Lamb that once was slain!

and the hymn by the same author, "Blessing and honor and glory and power" (196), and "Behold the Lamb of God!" (153) by Matthew Bridges, and a good communion hymn (360, by John Morison as in "Scottish Paraphrases"). Others might be mentioned, too, and we do not mean to convey the impression that there is nothing at all that is good in the hymns included in this book.

But these are very distinctly exceptions, and in general it may be said that the added hymns contain little specific reference to the atoning blood of Christ—certainly that they contain little in comparison with the wealth that was found in the hymns, and stanzas of hymns, that have been removed.

What characterizes the new hymns above anything else is their deadly vagueness. Such vagueness cannot, of course, be exhibited in any review; it can be appreciated only when a man reads the new hymns through for himself. This vagueness is altogether attractive to the nondoctrinal Modernism that now dominates the visible church, but to the Christian heart it is almost as depressing as definitely and clearly unscriptural teaching would be. Let it be clearly understood, therefore, that what we shall now say in criticism of individual hymns is only supplementary to the central indictment that they ignore the great central verities of the faith and particularly the heart and core of the Bible which is found in the shed blood of Christ our sacrifice.

How, for example, can a Christian congregation sing the hymn by Ozora Stearns Davis (179), the third stanza of which reads:

> The common hopes that make us men
> Were His in Galilee;
> The tasks He gives are those He gave
> Beside the restless sea.

It is difficult to see what room there is here for the central redeeming purpose that caused our blessed Lord to assume our nature and die in our stead on the cross.

How can a believer in the unique authority of the written Word of God sing the hymn "One holy Church of God appears" (335), by Samuel Longfellow, which in its third stanza says, regarding the "living Church":

> The truth is her prophetic gift,
> The soul her sacred page;
> And feet on mercy's errands swift
> Do make her pilgrimage.

In fairness, however, it ought to be said that the new book contains fewer hymns by this Unitarian writer than the old book did, and that it is to be commended especially for the omission of the hymn "Beneath the shadow of the cross" (542 in the old book), which is far indeed from celebrating the cross of Christ in the Christian sense.

What believer in the new birth, however, and in the sonship which comes to man only through that supernatural act of the Holy Ghost can possibly sing the hymn "In Christ there is no East or West" (341 in the new book), which ends with the words

> All Christly souls are one in Him
>   Throughout the whole wide earth

without any indication whatever that men dead in trespasses and sins can become "Christly" only when they are made alive by God's grace?

The true end of church-union propaganda is rather clearly indicated in the hymn (344) by the New England Quaker writer John Greenleaf Whittier, which begins with the stanza:

> Forgive, O Lord, our severing ways,
>   The rival altars that we raise,
> The wrangling tongues that mar Thy praise,

and in which the hope is expressed that there may be "one Church for all humanity." What kind of church will that one church be? No one who knows Whittier's hymn, I think, can possibly doubt but that it will be the same kind of church as that which was spoken of in my hearing (if I may quote his words roughly as I remember them) by the Unitarian presiding officer at a recent meeting of the American Academy of Political and Social Science in Philadelphia. "Rabbi Fineshriber and I," said he, speaking of the leading "Liberal" rabbi of the city, who was one of the speakers, "are in the same church."

Some of the worst of the new hymns appear under the general heading "The Kingdom of God on Earth" (363–426). Thus, in "O Lord of life, Thy Kingdom is at hand" (370), by Marion Franklin Ham, a Unitarian minister, it appears in the course of the hymn that the kingdom will be here when "man shall rule the world with equity"! Even worse, if anything, from the Christian point of view is the hymn "Once to every man and nation" (373) by another writer of Unitarian background, James Russell Lowell,

THE NATURE AND MISSION OF THE CHURCH

where, in a way that can hardly be regarded as anything other than blasphemous, the poet speaks of "Some great cause, God's new Messiah," and says of himself:

> By the light of burning martyrs,
>   Jesus' bleeding feet I track,
> Toiling up new Calvaries ever
>   With the cross that turns not back.

But it is reserved to a Presbyterian minister, Dr. William P. Merrill, a signer of the Modernist "Auburn Affirmation," to contribute to this book the hymn which perhaps more definitely and clearly than any other indicates the trend of the church. It is the hymn "Not alone for mighty empire" (416), where the closing stanza reads:

> God of justice, save the people
>   From the clash of race and creed,
> From the strife of class and faction:
>   Make our nation free indeed.
> Keep her faith in simple manhood
>   Strong as when her life began,
> Till it find its full fruition
>   In the brotherhood of man.

The inclusion of that stanza in a hymnal of the Presbyterian Church in the U.S.A. certainly raises with particular clearness the issue between Christianity and Modernism. If it is true that "faith in simple manhood" will find "its full fruition in the brotherhood of man," then the Bible is false from beginning to end; all its solemn warnings, all its rebukes to human pride, all its promises of the sovereign grace of God are but idle words, and we have been utterly mistaken in our reliance for salvation simply and solely upon the atoning blood of Christ.

Which shall it be—"faith in simple manhood" or faith in Christ crucified? Shall we regard the cross of Christ merely as an example for us to imitate, a cross upon which we ourselves can die, or shall we regard it as a sacrifice which alone can satisfy divine justice and reconcile us to God? Shall we say, with Dr. Merrill, in another of the added hymns (401):

> *Lift high the cross of Christ!*
> *Tread where His feet have trod,*

or shall we say with the writer of one of the rejected hymns:

> *I lay my sins on Jesus,*
> *The spotless Lamb of God;*
> *He bears them all, and frees us*
> *From the accursed load:*
> *I bring my guilt to Jesus,*
> *To wash my crimson stains*
> *White in His blood most precious,*
> *Till not a spot remains.*

The time has come, in the Presbyterian church and in other churches, when we must choose.

PART SIX

THE PRESBYTERIAN CONTROVERSY

27

STATEMENT TO THE SPECIAL COMMISSION OF 1925

Mr. Chairman: In your letter of November 17th I was requested to express to the Commission of Fifteen my "views as to the best method of forwarding the purposes of its appointment." The purpose of its appointment, according to the constituting resolution of the General Assembly, is "to study the present spiritual condition of our Church and the causes making for unrest, and to report to the next General Assembly, to the end that the purity, peace, unity and progress of the Church may be assured." I shall endeavor to limit what I say strictly to that subject. I shall endeavor to set forth what I regard as the causes of unrest in the church which have affected so unfavorably its spiritual condition.

Those causes I hold to be all reducible to one great underlying cause— namely, the widespread and in many quarters dominant position in the ministry of the church as well as among its lay membership of a type of thought and experience, commonly called Modernism, which is diametrically opposed to the constitution of our church and to the Christian religion. All the disturbances which have agitated the church in our day, all the controversies which have been so much regretted, are necessary consequences of that one cause; and it is as unreasonable to blame those who call atten-

"Statement to the Special Commission of 1925" originally presented to the Special Commission of the General Assembly of the Presbyterian Church U.S.A. to study the causes of unrest in the denomination.

tion to that cause as it would be to regard as disturbers of the peace those who raise an alarm of fire when a building is threatened by the flames. The real cause of the disturbance is not the ringing of fire alarms or the clatter of fire apparatus, but the fire and only that. So the real cause of disturbance in our church today is Modernism and Modernism alone.

The widespread presence of Modernism in the church is evidenced in ways too numerous to mention; no ecclesiastical agency and no individual congregation in our day is altogether free from the effects of this great attack upon the Christian faith. But five indications may perhaps here be singled out for special mention.

The first of these is found in the Plan of Organic Union, which was sent down to the presbyteries by the General Assembly of 1920. That plan found a basis for Christian fellowship among various ecclesiastical bodies in a preamble couched in the vague language of modern naturalism, and clearly relegated to the realm of the nonessential our historic Confession of Faith. I do not mean that all those who favored the plan were fully conscious of its agnostic character, but agnostic it was to the very core, and it never could have received such a large vote both in the General Assembly and in the presbyteries unless the doctrinal—that is, evangelical—consciousness of the church had been very seriously undermined. The plan was indeed defeated, but the menace was very great, and it revealed a most alarming condition in the church. That menace is continued to the present time. One of the principal ways in which anti-evangelical agitation is being carried on in our church today is in the propaganda for agnostic forms of church union, at home and on the mission field, in which the confessional or evangelical character of the Presbyterian church is to be destroyed.

After the Plan of Organic Union was defeated, and thus the unity of the church, for the time, was preserved, the disruptive forces continued vigorously though quietly at work; and it might have seemed as though the Christian character of the church were to be destroyed without even a struggle. But such at least was not to be the case. The issue was raised again by the presence of Dr. Harry Emerson Fosdick as special preacher, over a period of some years, in the pulpit of the First Presbyterian Church of New York. That arrangement is the second outstanding indication which I adduce for the presence of Modernism in our church. Dr. Fosdick is important just because he is by no means original or peculiar in his views. He represents in typical fashion the pragmatist skepticism of our day, which holds that what is really constant in religion is an inner experience that clothes itself from generation to generation in necessarily changing intellectual forms, so that nothing in the sphere of doctrine can ever be permanently true. Evidently such skepticism is opposed in the most radical way to the Confession of Faith of our church and to the Christian religion. Yet the presence of Dr. Fosdick in a Presbyterian pulpit was vigorously defended by a great presbytery, and by many persons throughout the church. There could scarcely have been a clearer indication of the length to which the undermining and disruptive process had gone.

The third indication to which I desire to call your attention is found in the so-called "Auburn Affirmation," which was issued in 1924. That Affirmation represents the basic facts of Christianity, including the virgin birth and bodily resurrection of our Lord, as being merely "theories" in explanation of other things—theories which are by no means the only possible ones, and the acceptance of which is by no means to be required of Presbyterian ministers. Here again we have a very radical denial of the basis of the Christian religion. Yet this Affirmation was signed by no less than twelve hundred and seventy-four ministers of our church. It is possible, indeed, that some of those who signed the document did so carelessly, without full understanding of the true radicalism of the paper. But such carelessness is itself a very grave sign of the times. It is to be feared, moreover, that the Affirmation pamphlet (in its second edition) is correct in holding that many of those ministers who did not sign the document refrained from doing so for other reasons than that they disagreed with what it contained. The Auburn Affirmation is therefore a clear indication of the very widespread presence in the church of a skepticism and doctrinal indifferentism that is opposed to the Christian religion at its roots.

The fourth indication is found in the present attitude of the Presbytery and Synod of New York. Some time ago the Presbytery of New York licensed to preach the gospel Mr. Henry P. Van Dusen and Mr. Cedric A. Lehman, who declined to affirm their belief in the virgin birth of our Lord. Complaint against this action was taken to the Synod of New York, but there was dismissed. A great synod of our church, therefore, was on record as regarding the virgin birth, which is narrated plainly in the Scriptures, as a matter which did not need to be accepted by a candidate for the ministry in our church. A church which acquiesced in any such action as that would simply cease to be a Christian church at all. The General Assembly did not acquiesce, but handed down a clear decision affirming the virgin birth to be essential to the system of doctrine contained in the Scriptures and directing the Presbytery of New York to take appropriate action.

That decision preserved, for the moment, the Christian character of our church; the judicial case was decided in a Christian manner. But the situation revealed by the case is exceedingly grave, and effectually refutes the contention of those who hold that naturalistic or agnostic Modernism has affected only a small number of ministers. Not merely a presbytery but a large synod is here on record as favoring the licensure of candidates who refuse to affirm even the virgin birth of our Lord.

But if the situation revealed by the case is grave, still more disquieting is the way in which the decision in the case has been received. Far from taking "appropriate action" in the case under review in accordance with the decision of the Assembly, the Presbytery of New York has declared that it will not for the present license any candidates for the ministry; and the Synod of New York has deferred action upon other cases which have come up to it by appeal from the presbytery. Thus, when one decision of lower courts has been reversed by the higher court, those lower courts refuse to function at all in other cases. Such an attitude on the part of synod and presbytery, if acquiesced in by the General Assembly, involves the breakdown of the whole judicial system of our church. The constitution of the church lays great stress upon preservation of the doctrinal standards, and provides a definite constitutional procedure for that purpose. That constitutional procedure is here being nullified by a great synod and presbytery of the church.

Most disquieting of all, perhaps, is the reason adduced by the Presbytery and Synod of New York for their actions. The reason adduced is the fact of the appointment of the present Commission of Fifteen. The synod and presbytery desire to wait, in deference to this commission, until the commission has made its report. Why do they desire to do so? Surely it is not in order that the Assembly on the basis of the report of this commission as to the state of the church may reverse a decision which it has rendered when sitting as a court. Perhaps then it is in order that the constitution of the church may be so changed that the Presbytery of New York will not be required, as it now is required, to take appropriate action with regard to its error in the present case and avoid all similar errors in the future. But suppose that that result should be attained. Suppose that the very worst—from the evangelical point of view—should happen. Suppose that on the basis of the report of this commission the General Assembly and the presbyteries, in accordance with the constitutional procedure, should change the formula of creed subscription or substitute a brief modern creed for our great historic Confession of Faith. Such action, if there are any loyal evangelical men in the church at all, would no doubt disrupt the church. The evangelical party would be driven out, and the Modernist party would be left in control. It is hardly likely, we trust, that any such thing will be done; it is hardly likely that the constitution of the church will be changed. But even if that were done, it would not affect the obligation that the present constitution, so long as it remains, should be enforced. The present actions of the Synod and Presbytery of New York are therefore in clear defiance of the constitution. And if the present constitution is not enforced so long as it remains, it is hardly likely that any other constitution will be enforced.

Thus the attitude of the Synod and Presbytery of New York is a very clear indication indeed of the great peril in which the church stands. If the temper of the church at large is such that a great synod can even hope at this time for constitutional changes that will make it possible for a presbytery to license a candidate for the ministry who fails to affirm the virgin birth of our Lord, then the situation is grave indeed.

The last of the five indications to which I desire to call your attention is found in the attitude of the boards and agencies. With regard to this point I shall not pause to cite details. But the great outstanding fact is that the boards and agencies are signally failing to sound any clear evangelical note in the present time of crisis, when the Christian religion all over the world is in the midst of one of the greatest conflicts in its entire history. There are two possible positions that mission boards at home and abroad may take. They may seek to save mankind by Christian influences or Christian principles or Christian civilization; or they may seek to be instruments of God in saving mankind by a new birth of individual men brought about by the Spirit of God using the gospel of the cross of Christ. If the latter position is taken, the former must be abandoned; the first step in evangelization is to destroy the confidence of men in human goodness, in order that recourse may be had simply and solely to the cross of Christ. It is that position which is taken by the Bible and by the constitution of our church. But that position is certainly not being taken in any clear and unequivocal way by the boards and agencies. It often seems to be assumed that if the boards merely refrain from contradicting the gospel, all is well. But that is surely not the case. If the boards and agencies are to fulfill their true function, they must not merely refrain from contradicting the gospel but their members and their representatives must be on fire with the gospel; in the present time of conflict with naturalistic Modernism, they must cease to stand aloof and must support and encourage those men and women all over the world who in the face of opposition and ridicule are taking their stand at the foot of the cross and are looking to the crucified Savior as their only hope for time and for eternity.

The truth is that the boards and agencies, as they are at present, have no really clear right to appeal for funds—certainly no really clear right to appeal for funds for anything save the fulfillment of obligations to workers already in the field. A fundamental requirement of any organization appealing for financial support is that definite information should be given concerning the platform upon which the organization stands and the program which it is endeavoring to carry out. Such information in the case of our boards is now conspicuously absent. The boards therefore have no real right to appeal for funds for any new work. They have no right to appeal to the Modernists—the Modernists who believe that Western creeds cannot be accepted by the Eastern mind and that Christian civilization will save the world—for that is contrary to the constitution under which they are operating. They have no right to appeal to evangelical Christians, for it is perfectly plain that they are not in any unequivocal way proclaiming the gospel of the cross of Christ as the only means of salvation for sinful men. Evidently the present situation is intolerable; it is quite impossible to waver any longer between two mutually exclusive programs; every humble giver has a right to know what is really being done with his gifts; the boards must decide whether they will stand for the gospel or against it. At present they are really failing to stand in any clear fashion for one thing or for the other.

Such is the cause for the unrest in the church. The cause is to be found, as we have seen, despite variety in its manifestations, in one thing and one thing alone—the presence in the church of an agnostic Modernism that is radically opposed to the Christian religion. But what is the total effect of that cause upon the spiritual condition of the church; how is the situation finally to be appraised? Is the situation hopeless, so that disruption must inevitably come; or may the continuity of our church be preserved?

My own attitude to this question is not one of despair. The situation is grave—but it is not, I think, hopeless. The outcome depends upon the choice to which the church in the present crisis is led. If the indifferentist slogan of "peace and work" is successful; if, in defiance of all the lessons of church history as well as of the Bible, controversy is regarded as necessarily evil; if the issue is glossed over; if the church engages in the vain effort of preaching the gospel without settling what the gospel is—then in a very few years the Modernist forces will be in definite control of our church as they are in control of so many other ecclesiastical bodies throughout the world, and the Christian character of our church will be destroyed. In that case there will be disruption—as there has been, for example, in Canada. But if, on the other hand, the issue is resolutely faced, if the judicial decision of the last General Assembly is promptly and definitely enforced, if the boards and agencies are placed gradually by the General Assembly in the hands of men not merely who are evangelical themselves (for that is entirely insufficient) but who know what the great issue of the day is and have decided it aright, if there is a resolute refusal to enter into agnostic forms of church union or to modify the formula of creed subscription or the great historic Confession of Faith, then, without convulsions or any destruction of historic continuity, the unity of the church may yet be preserved; then the Presbyterian ministry will simply cease to be attractive to men like Mr. Van Dusen and Mr. Lehman who cannot accept the virgin birth of our Lord and will become increasingly attractive to men who desire to proclaim the one true gospel of divine grace; then the church can move forward once more with united forces to the conquest of the world for Christ.

I cannot say what the decision will be. God has that in his own keeping. But there are not wanting hopeful signs. All over the world, manifesting themselves in quite independent fashion, there are movements of Christian men who are ready to face the issue and stand for Christ. These movements are despised by the world and too often by ecclesiastical leaders. But I for my part am convinced that they are the work of the Spirit of God. Shall our church discourage them, so that they lose their continuity with the great historic current of ecclesiastical life? Or shall our church itself, in its historic grandeur, shake off its present indecision and become an agency which the Holy Spirit can use? To that result the present commission in my judgment—since you have asked for my counsel—may, under God, render a notable contribution. It may render a notable contribution without departing in the slightest from the scope fixed for it in the constituting resolution, but simply by penetrating beneath all superflicialities and by presenting to the church in unequivocal language the true cause of the present unrest. The church could then, I hope, be trusted to adopt the proper ways and means. It is still predominantly Christian; it would, I think, decide the issue aright if, instead of being deceived, as is now so often the case, by a euphemistic use of conventional language that conceals what is really going on, it knew the facts.

28

STATEMENT TO THE COMMITTEE TO INVESTIGATE PRINCETON

After twenty years of service in Princeton Theological Seminary as instructor and assistant professor, I find myself by the action of the last General Assembly subjected to the extraordinary indignity of having the propriety of my promotion to a full professorship questioned if not as yet actually denied—an indignity almost without precedent in the entire history of our church. The indignity was aggravated by the grounds on which, according to the address of the chairman of the Committee on Theological Seminaries, presenting the majority report, unfavorable action had been advocated before the committee, and in particular by the public appearance against me on the floor of the Assembly of two of my colleagues in the faculty of the seminary, President Stevenson and Professor Erdman.

In presenting the majority recommendation to postpone confirmation

Excerpt from "Statement to the Committee to Investigate Princeton" privately printed in 1926 by the author but not published under the title *Statement by J. Gresham Machen Submitted to the Committee Appointed by the Action of the General Assembly of 1926 to make a sympathetic study of the conditions affecting the welfare of Princeton Seminary, and to co-operate in striving to adjust difference and to report to the next Assembly.*

of my election, the chairman of the committee is credibly reported to have said that there were charges that the professor-elect was "spiritually unqualified to hold the post in question and teach goodwill to students, that he was temperamentally defective, bitter and harsh in his judgment of others and implacable to brethren who did not agree with him." Almost equally derogatory to my good name were the speeches of my colleagues, President Stevenson and Dr. Erdman. President Stevenson not only reported a conversation in which he had said to Dr. Maitland Alexander: "You know this man has serious limitations," but also opposed the confirmation of my election on the ground that I was implicated in certain objectionable actions of the faculty. Finally, Dr. Erdman said: "What is questioned is whether Dr. Machen's temper and methods of defense are such as to qualify him for a chair in which his whole time will be devoted to defending the faith"—thus using language which recalls somewhat a public attack, which, as will be seen in a moment, he himself had made upon me a year and a half before. It is obvious, I think, that by the action itself, as well as by the grounds upon which it was advocated, I have been subjected to serious obloquy.

I cannot, therefore, accept the light estimate which Dr. Erdman placed upon the matter at the conclusion of his speech before the Assembly. "It seems pitiful and painful," said Dr. Erdman, "that we are delaying the Board of Foreign Missions to debate a little question of this kind as to whether we shall decide now or next year in the case of a professional appointment." Perhaps the unparalleled indignity to which one of his colleagues, who has served the seminary with him for twenty years, has been subjected may seem to be a "little matter" to Dr. Erdman, but it does not seem to be a little matter to the one whose good name has thus been attacked. And I am not sure even that it should seem to be altogether a little matter to the Presbyterian church, for not only does it entail derangement for at least an entire year of the work of one our largest seminaries but also it involves principles of rather far-reaching importance.

In view of these considerations, I very respectfully request the committee to receive my present statement, with the appended documents. If, indeed, the position of professor in Princeton Seminary were within the electing power of the Assembly, I should not presume to appear in my own behalf, for then the Assembly could freely choose the man whom it deemed best fitted for the position and other persons would have no right to complain against their being passed by. But as a matter of fact, the Assembly has no such electing power. It cannot elect a professor, but can only veto an election made by the board of directors. Such a veto throws the work of the institution for the time being into confusion and is a very extreme measure. Obviously, recourse should be had to it only for the most imperative of reasons. In the case of an election, the burden of proof rests upon those who favor the entrance of any particular person into an office; in the case of a veto, it rests upon those who oppose the person already elected.

I shall not, of course, make the slightest attempt to establish my own fitness for the chair of apologetics and Christian ethics in Princeton Seminary. According to the board of directors I am a fit person, but whether the board was wise in choosing me I certainly do not presume to say. I am keenly conscious, at any rate, of many faults and failings; no doubt I have made many mistakes. If the professorship of apologetics and Christian ethics demands an incumbent who shall even approximate perfection, then obviously I am not the man for the place. But I do request the privilege of defending myself against certain specific charges which have been brought against me.

In such defense I am seriously embarrassed by never having been confronted with my accusers or furnished with a copy of the precise charges against me. I have heard vague rumors of charges that have been made—and most extraordinary they seem to me to be—but they have been made almost exclusively in my absence. My good name has been gravely injured without any opportunity having been given me to cross-examine or even to answer in any way those who have carried on the attack. I regretted very much, therefore, that the testimony of the persons who appeared against me in the Committee on Theological Seminaries was not given full publicity on the floor of the Assembly and incorporated in the record of its proceedings. Without questioning in the slightest the propriety of the chairman's action or the considerateness that he exercised in his effort to keep my name from being discussed at length before the Assembly, I may yet say that it seemed to me more desirable from my point of view that the charges against me should be made fully known to the church. In that case opportunity might at least have been given to refute the charges if they were false.

As it is, I can deal only with such indications as to the nature of the charges as appeared in the public speeches of the chairman of the Committee on Theological Seminaries and of President Stevenson and Dr. Erdman.

According to the chairman, it had been asserted in the presence of the committee that I am spiritually unqualified to hold the post in question and teach goodwill to students, that I am temperamentally defective, bitter and harsh in my judgment of others and implacable to brethren who do not agree with me. Obviously, this characterization of me—which, if true, casts a serious stain upon my moral character—is of too general a kind to be refuted until information is given as to the specific facts upon which it is based. I am sure, at any rate, that it is not acquiesced in by all the students who have attended my classes during the last twenty years. On the contrary, I have been greatly touched by the many expressions of gratitude and affection from alumni and students of the seminary that have come to me in the trying days since the last meeting of the Assembly. Those expressions have led me to hope, despite the recent attack upon me and despite my own consciousness of faults and failures, that my life has not been altogether in vain.

But obviously I am not qualified to testify with regard to my own personal characteristics. All that I desire here to do is to set forth the facts as regards the one specific matter which has given rise to the chief objections to me and has therefore been the occasion for the appointment of the present committee. I refer to the disagreement between President Stevenson and Dr. Erdman on the one hand, and myself, with the majority of the faculty, on the other. That matter will be treated in its broader aspects in a statement to be presented with supporting evidence by another member of the faculty. Here I shall endeavor to present it principally as it concerns the personal relationship between Dr. Erdman and myself.

In doing so, I shall endeavor to show (1) that there is a serious divergence of principle between Dr. Erdman and myself, and (2) that personal unpleasantness was introduced into the discussion of this divergence not by me but by Dr. Erdman.

The divergence of principle appeared in the clearest possible way so early as 1920, when President Stevenson and Dr. Erdman advocated a "Plan of Organic Union," which, as I have publicly pointed out, relegated our historic Confession of Faith to the realm of the nonessential, and sought a basis for church union in a preamble couched in the vague language of modern naturalism. The adoption of that plan by the presbyteries would have resulted logically in driving out of the Presbyterian church not only myself but also every man of evangelical convictions who detected the real nature of what had been done. It would be difficult, therefore, to imagine a more serious divergence of principle than that which appeared at that time between President Stevenson and Dr. Erdman on the one hand and the majority of the faculty, including me, on the other.

But there was no reason why that divergence of principle should have resulted in unpleasant personalities, and I certainly did nothing to introduce such unpleasant personalities into our relationships at Princeton. I continued to have the highest personal respect for Dr. Erdman, and there seemed to me to be not the slightest reason why he should not continue in the pleasantest personal relations with his colleagues. The fact that he differed from the majority of the faculty about important matters of ecclesiastical policy did not at all prevent me from regarding him as an honored member of our body and as a valued associate.

In 1924, Dr. Erdman was nominated for the moderatorship of the General Assembly. I was opposed to his election and voted for the other nominee, Dr. Clarence Edward Macartney. Apparently this action has been made the basis of attack upon me; for in *The New York Herald Tribune* of June 3, 1926, in the report of President Stevenson's speech at the last Assembly, it is said: "Dr. Stevenson frankly accused Dr. Machen of opposing Dr. Erdman in the moderatorship election last year. . . ." It is perhaps unnecessary to ask whether this newspaper report is at this point verbally accurate; for in any case, my opposition to Dr. Erdman's candidacy for the moderatorship, both in 1925—the year to which Dr. Stevenson here refers—and also in 1924, has certainly been the underlying cause, even where it has not been the express ground, of widespread attack upon me throughout the church.

But was it a crime to oppose Dr. Erdman as a candidate for the moderatorship? If it was, then certainly I stand convicted; but to hold that it was is, I think, to destroy all liberty of conscience in the church. My opposition to Dr. Erdman's candidacy for that particular position was necessarily involved in convictions that are at the basis of my whole life; for me to have made an opposite decision would have been to desert what I was fully convinced was my duty to the church and to God.

In the first place, if I had supported Dr. Erdman in 1924, I should have been obliged to oppose Dr. Macartney; and that I certainly could not do. It is unnecessary to debate the question whether Dr. Macartney was publicly mentioned for the moderatorship before or after the mention of Dr. Erdman. My decided impression was that he was mentioned first. But I am indifferent to the question. What I am clear about, at any rate, is that ever since the General Assembly of 1923, Dr. Macartney was the logical—if I may so say, the inevitable—candidate of the conservative element in the church. Prior to that Assembly, and at the Assembly itself, he had appeared as the spokesman for the overture regarding Dr. Fosdick; and as such, he was the spokesman for the evangelical or conservative party in the church. Could I possibly refuse him my support? I ask you, gentlemen, to put yourselves in my place and view the matter from the point of view of my convictions. For many years I had been convinced that the Presbyterian church was in deadly peril; it was in imminent danger, I believed, of being controlled by that indifference to the central things of the gospel which already had engulfed the larger Protestant churches of the continent of Europe, and unless all indications failed the larger churches of Great Britain. Would the undermining process go on here unchecked, or would our church become aroused to its peril before it was too late?

That question seemed to be answered by Dr. Macartney's courageous act. At last there was a strong, true word in defense of the witness-bearing of the Presbyterian church. Other men *might* have come forward to speak the word that needed to be spoken, but as a matter of fact, for whatever reasons, they had not done so. It was Dr. Macartney who, from my point of view, was the man of the hour.

At the beginning he might have seemed to have little support, and twenty-two out of twenty-three members of the Committee on Bills and Overtures voted against the action that he had favored. But a minority report by one member of that committee out of the twenty-three carried the day, and the movement was begun which finally led to the departure of Dr. Fosdick from his Presbyterian pulpit.

To me it seemed to be the beginning of a new and better day for the church that I loved. I hoped and prayed that the witness of the Presbyterian church might be restored. And the instrument in accomplishing that end seemed to be the man who had so bravely taken the first step—a man of gravity and moderation, scrupulously fair to opponents, singularly free from unworthy personal motives, opposed to extreme or unconstitutional methods, and yet full of a holy zeal for the Word of God. Under such circumstances it seemed to me quite inconceivable that any other person should be the leader of the conservative element in the church. I confess that my whole heart went out to the man who had spoken so brave a word.

I was loyal to him with every fiber of my being, and in being so I was firmly convinced of being loyal to the Lord Jesus Christ.

If that is a fault, I am certainly guilty of it still. I think without any regret of the decision I made in those days when the Spirit of God seemed to me to be moving so mightily in the church.

There was, indeed, one source of sorrow in the midst of my thankfulness and joy. It was found in the fact that our faculty was not a unit in defense of a position that Princeton Seminary had maintained hitherto throughout all its history, and that it was not a unit in support of the movement which had been initiated with such promise and of the man who had already become its leader. Dr. Erdman, in particular, instead of supporting Dr. Macartney, allowed his own name to be put forward as a candidate. In making that decision he did not at all consult me; he did not at all ask for my support or permit me to state to him the reasons why I could not give it. If he had consulted me, it is quite clear what I could have said. In the first place, I could have told him that because of the issue as it had been raised at the previous Assembly, Dr. Macartney was for the moment the logical candidate of the conservative element in the church. Then I could have asked for Dr. Erdman's support, and if he had given it my attitude toward his own candidacy in some future year would have been very different. I could also, however, have asked him whether his attitude toward the Plan of Organic Union and similar movements had remained the same as that to which I had such strong objections in 1920. And in general I could have asked him about the platform upon which he was to be nominated and the ecclesiastical policy which he would pursue if he were elected.

I do not at all mean to say that Dr. Erdman was bound to seek any such conference, but what I do affirm is that such a conference was absolutely necessary if faculty unanimity in such matters was so necessary as apparently it has been thought to be by Dr. Erdman's supporters in the church. The majority of the faculty was opposed to the ecclesiastical policy advocated by Dr. Erdman, and in favor of that advocated by Dr. Macartney; and if collective action was desired, it could be obtained here as always only through the principle of majority rule.

As a matter of fact, I do not think that such collective action is at all necessary. Every member of our faculty should, I think, be free to act in ecclesiastical matters in accordance with his own individual conscience, and such freedom of action is, I think, entirely consonant with mutual respect.

So Dr. Erdman was entirely free to depart from the ecclesiastical position held by the majority of his colleagues, and such departure did not necessarily interfere either with the high regard in which we held him personally or with our appreciation of his services as professor in the seminary.

But if the opposite view is held—if it is maintained that public divergence in the councils of the church among the members of our faculty is undesirable—then it was Dr. Erdman and not I who was at fault, since the majority agreed with me and not with him.

The reason for that attitude of the majority is quite plain. Ever since 1920 Dr. Erdman had consistently favored an ecclesiastical policy to which the majority of his colleagues were conscientiously opposed. The same consistency had appeared in the platform upon which he was nominated for the moderatorship. "We need a moderator," said Dr. Stone in nominating Dr. Erdman at Grand Rapids (see *The Presbyterian Advance* for May 29, 1924), "who stands for presenting a united front rather than the encouragement of controversy." That was said in a great crisis when agnostic Modernism as represented by Dr. Fosdick and his Presbyterian supporters was contending for the control of our church. I disagreed with that platform, and could not support anyone, no matter what his personal relations to me, who was nominated upon it.

Dr. Erdman not only stood upon that platform by accepting the nominating speech by Dr. Stone, but also himself had already enunciated the same principle. In a despatch dated Princeton, N.J., April 29, 1924, in the Philadelphia *Public Ledger* of April 30, it is said that "Dr. Erdman made public a statement in which he put forth the policy he would follow if elected." "In making clear his position, Dr. Erdman said: 'I want the constructive work of the Presbyterian Church to go on without interruption on account of any doctrinal controversy. . . .' " It would be impossible to put in any clearer way than is here done by Dr. Erdman the position of doctrinal indifferentism. And it would be impossible to imagine a position to which I am more conscientiously and more profoundly opposed. How can the constructive work of the Presbyterian church go on without interruption on account of any doctrinal controversy? The thing for which the Presbyterian church exists, I hold, is the propagation of a certain doctrine that we call the gospel of the Lord Jesus Christ. Only in that doctrine is Christ offered to men as their Savior. The church might do many other things—it might tinker with social conditions, it might use all sorts of palliative measures with men who have not been born again—but only by persuading men to accept the blessed "doctrine" or gospel can it save human souls. The church, I hold, is in the world to propagate a message; and if its propagation of the message is not clear, then, whatever else it does, it cannot possibly be said to be engaged in its "constructive work."

Dr. Erdman said indeed: "I believe the question about Dr. Fosdick and those who agree with him should be settled according to the constitutional law of the Church. If these men are not loyal, let the law act."

But what is meant by letting "the law act"? A law never acts of itself; it does not act unless there is someone to enforce it. And what part had Dr. Erdman ever taken in enforcing it? So far as he was concerned, Dr. Fosdick would still be preaching in the First Presbyterian Church of New York. It was Dr. Macartney and not Dr. Erdman who secured the enforcement of the law.

Dr. Erdman makes much of the so-called "Philadelphia Overture" regarding creed subscription on the part of members of the boards. I never favored this overture, and I did not regard it as at all an integral part of the platform on which Dr. Macartney was nominated. But I am convinced that the boards have little representation from the conservative or evangelical party in the church, and I have never observed the slightest effort on the part of Dr. Erdman to correct this evil.

When in the following year at Columbus Dr. Erdman was finally elected to the moderatorship, he stood consistently upon the platform which had previously been laid for him by Dr. Stone, and adhered to the position which he himself had expressly taken.

Thus Dr. Erdman was nominated in 1924 upon a platform to which I am conscientiously opposed, and he has stood consistently upon that platform ever since. In opposition to it, I hold that the Presbyterian church is in deadly peril and that if the peril continues to be ignored, the evangelical witness of the church will soon—as was so nearly the case in 1920—be destroyed. It would be difficult to imagine a more important difference of principle. . . .

Such are my ecclesiastical and theological views. If they disqualify a man for a professorship of apologetics in Princeton Seminary, then of course I am not fit for the position. If professors in our seminaries are to be made to conform to one definite ecclesiastical policy, with which I disagree, I cannot occupy such an office. But if a veto of my election is determined upon,

I only request that it should be based upon the true ground—that if the real objection to me is found in my ecclesiastical views and my consistent carrying out of the implications of them, my character should not continue to be maligned by making alleged "temperamental defects," or harshness or bitterness or the like, the reason for what is done. If zeal for the defense of the faith and for the maintenance of the witness of the Presbyterian church—even a zeal that many think excessive—disqualifies a man for a professorship of apologetics in Princeton Seminary, then I only ask that the fact should be made clearly known.

I venture, however, to hope that you will bring in no such report. I venture to hope that you will either recommend that my election be confirmed next May, or else report that the Assembly had no legal right to postpone action and that therefore my election has already legally been confirmed. I express no opinion upon the correctness of this latter position. But if you do favor it, I venture still to ask that you do not content yourselves with a technical opinion but that you express your judgment regarding the charges that have been brought against me. Whatever the form of your report with regard to the legal aspects of the case, I seek and respectfully request public vindication at your hands.

What I regret most of all is that I have been the occasion, though I think not the underlying cause, of a public attack by President Stevenson upon what is certainly the historic position of Princeton Seminary. Must this institution represent all shades of theological opinion that are found in the Presbyterian church at the present time, or may it continue to represent, in its entirety and in the full historic sense, the Reformed faith as based upon the complete truthfulness of the Bible as the Word of God? That is the really important question at issue. It has been the issue for a number of years, and with regard to it President Stevenson stands opposed to his faculty. If the issue is settled in accordance with the expressed desires of the president, then the distinctive history of Princeton Seminary is at an end. That history has been a long and honorable one. Even by men who are most opposed to our tenets, both at home and abroad, the "Princeton school" (as it is called) has been respected as a scholarly defender of a view that at least deserves to be heard. And never were our opportunity and our prestige greater than just at the present moment. All over the world, and in many communions, men are looking to us as never before for a clear and straightforward presentation of the Reformed faith, and for a defense of the full truthfulness of the Bible against widespread assaults. Is our voice to be silenced? Are we to be made to conform to tendencies that have prevailed in other seminaries of our church? Or is our distinctiveness to be respected, even where it is not shared? Is the Presbyterian church large enough to include one seminary that assumes a position like ours?

Perhaps it may be objected that if we continue to be tolerated, we shall harm the church by an insistence upon the maintenance of a strict view of its doctrinal standards. I think that just from the "Liberal" point of view there ought not to be any such fear. The truth, after all, will prevail. If we are wrong, we shall come to naught. Surely it would be better to tolerate our teaching and to refute it in public discussion than to engage in a method of suppression which clearly would involve a breach of faith.

29

THE ATTACK UPON PRINCETON SEMINARY: A PLEA FOR FAIR PLAY

The action of the General Assembly of the Presbyterian Church in the United States of America, meeting at San Francisco, in adopting the Report of the Special Committee to visit Princeton Theological Seminary, has raised an issue upon which the entire future character of the institution depends. In treating this issue, I shall not deal with the personal attack that has been made upon me. My real sorrow has been due not to the personal indignity that I have suffered by the actions of the last two General Assemblies, but to the fact that I have been the occasion, though certainly not the underlying cause, of the danger which now besets the seminary. That fact gives me, I think, a right to say something in defense of the institution that I so dearly love. There are others far better qualified than I—both by their own ability and by their official position—to defend the institution, and no doubt they will defend it. But since my name has been given such a special, though purely accidental, prominence, I think that I may be permitted to say what my attitude is. In doing so, I am speaking in my own name alone. Since many things have been said about my

"The Attack upon Princeton Seminary: A Plea for Fair Play" privately printed by the author in 1927 under the same title but not published.

views regarding the situation, some of them true and some of them untrue, I think that I have a right to say plainly, for myself, what those views are.

I. For What Does Princeton Seminary Stand?

For over one hundred years Princeton Theological Seminary has stood firmly for the full truthfulness of the Bible as the Word of God and for the vigorous defense and propagation of the Reformed or Calvinistic system of doctrine, which is the system of doctrine that the Bible teaches. This conservative stand of the institution has been due—certainly since 1870, when the present method of electing the professors was introduced—simply and solely to the conservative majority in the board of directors. But now, by action of the last General Assembly, that board is to be dissolved and the control of the institution is to be placed in different hands. What is now a majority in the affairs of the seminary is to become a minority, and the policy of the institution is to be reversed.

Both parties in the present debate are, indeed, professing adherence to "the historic position" of Princeton Seminary. Even the board of trustees—the board which, as distinguished from the board of directors, has had charge of the material, as distinguished from the spiritual, affairs of the institution—has professed such adherence. But since one member of the committee which the trustees have appointed to cooperate in effecting the proposed reorganization is actually a signer of the "Auburn Affirmation," it is evident that the term "historical theological position of Princeton Theological Seminary" must be used by the trustees in a sense widely different from ours. The Auburn Affirmation asserts as plainly as words can express it that even acceptance of the virgin birth and of certain other basic articles of our faith is *not* necessary for the ministry of the Presbyterian church. Does such an Affirmation represent the Princeton position? To anyone who knows the history of Princeton Seminary, the answer will not be difficult.

The truth is that despite all differences of opinion, it is not impossible, whatever one's own personal attitude may be, to determine what the Princeton position is. The question what that position is is quite distinct from the question whether it is right or wrong. And with regard to the former question, as distinguished from the latter, there is a certain unanimity of opinion among outside observers, whether they are friends or foes. Princeton Seminary is known for what it really is, not only by those who have hitherto controlled its destinies, but also by a great host of opponents throughout the world.

What, then, is it for which we at Princeton stand?

I

In the first place, we stand for the complete truthfulness of the Bible as the Word of God. It is often said that the Bible is infallible in the inner, religious sphere, but fallible like other books when it comes to deal with external history. We reject any such distinction. Our religion is no bottomless mysticism, but it is the Christian religion; and the Christian religion is founded squarely upon events, like the death and resurrection of our Lord, that took place in the external world. Unless the Bible can give us knowledge of those basic events, it can be no infallible guide for our souls.

Thus we hold that the Bible is not partly true and partly false, but true throughout. In saying that, we are well aware of the favor that we are sacrificing. There are many who would be inclined to treat with respect what we say about many things—what we say, for example, even in defense of the virgin birth and bodily resurrection of our Lord—but who regard us as having placed ourselves beyond the pale of serious consideration when we hold that the Bible is true from beginning to end. It would be convenient for us to keep in the background what we believe about this point, and thus to retain a larger measure of favor from the modern church. Much could be said, from the point of view of policy, in favor of such an attitude. But it is an attitude which we can never adopt. There is to our mind no profession more despicable than the profession of teaching when one thing is said in the classroom and another thing to the church at large. And so we say plainly—to the ruin, in many quarters, of our reputation, but with the approval of our consciences—that we hold the Bible to be free from the errors that mar other books, to be the blessed, holy, infallible Word of God.

We do not, indeed, *begin* with that conviction in our defense of the Christian religion, and so we can find common ground for discussion with many whose view of the Bible is very different from ours. When, for example, we argue in favor of our belief in a personal God, we do not base our argument at all upon the infallibility of the Bible; what we say in that sphere, therefore, may commend itself to many whose view of the Bible is very unfavorable indeed. Or when we defend our belief in the resurrection of our Lord, again our argument is independent of the question whether the Bible is in-

fallible or not. Even prior to any belief in the infallibility of Scripture, a scientific treatment of the sources of information will, we think, lead the historian to hold that Jesus of Nazareth was raised from the dead on the third
day. There are many Christians who can go with us that far, and yet cannot accept our view of the Bible; and we rejoice in the measure of their
agreement with us. Our view of the Bible is not the beginning, we think,
but it is rather the end, of any orderly defense of the Christian religion. First
the general truth of the Bible in its great outlines as a historical book, and
the supernatural origin of the revelation that it contains, then the full truthfulness of the Bible as the Word of God—that is the order of our apologetic.

Nevertheless, although we do not begin with the doctrine of the infallibility of Scripture, we do come to it in the end; and when we have come to
it, we build upon it our orderly exposition of the Christian faith. As apologists, in other words, we end with the infallibility of Scripture, but as systematic theologians we begin with it. Systematic theology, we think,
logically begins at the point where apologetics has left off. Apologetics establishes the full truthfulness of the Bible, and then systematic theology
proceeds to set forth the teaching that the Bible contains.

II

But what is it that the Bible contains? That question brings us to our second point. We have just said that Princeton Seminary stands for the full
truthfulness of the Bible. In the second place, it stands for the Reformed or
Calvinistic faith as being the system of doctrine that the Bible contains.

The Bible, let it be noted, contains, in our view (which is also the view
expressed in the ordination pledge of ministers and elders in our church),
not merely this doctrine or that, but a *system* of doctrine. A system differs
from a mere agglomeration in the interrelation and mutual necessity of its
parts. And so we cannot agree with those who isolate one part of the system from the other parts as being alone necessary as a basis for Christian
work. Very profoundly, for example, do we differ from those who omit the
doctrines of grace—the Bible teaching about sin, the Bible answer to the
question, "What shall I do to be saved?"—from the things that they regard
essential as a basis for cooperation among various ecclesiastical bodies at
home or on the mission field.

As over against such a reduced Christianity, we at Princeton stand for
the full, glorious gospel of divine grace that God has given us in his Word

and that is summarized in the Confession of Faith of our church. We cannot agree with those who say that although they are members of the Presbyterian church, they "have not the slightest zeal to have the Presbyterian church extended through the length and breadth of the world." As for us, we hold the faith of the Presbyterian church, the great Reformed faith that is set forth in the Westminster Confession, to be true; and holding it to be true, we hold that it is intended for the whole world.

But it would be the greatest mistake to think that the issue with regard to Princeton Seminary stops there; it would be the greatest mistake to suppose that the difference concerns merely the question whether we are to stand for the full heritage of our Reformed faith or are to content ourselves (in the statement of what is essential) with some lesser creed. No, the difference cuts even deeper than that. It concerns not merely the question as to the *content* of the doctrine that we are to set forth, but rather the attitude that is to be assumed with regard to *all* doctrine as such. It concerns not merely the question whether we are to teach this or that, but the question whether what we teach we are to teach with our whole hearts and in clear-cut opposition to the present drift of the times.

The policy of President Stevenson with regard to Princeton Seminary has sometimes been represented as an "inclusive" policy. There is certainly an element of truth in such a representation. Never has Dr. Stevenson given any clear indication, by the policy that he has followed as president of the seminary, that he recognizes the profound line of cleavage that separates the two opposite tendencies within the Presbyterian church, and the necessity that if Princeton Seminary is to be true to its great heritage and true to the moral obligations involved in the distinctive basis upon which it has always appealed for support, it must, in this great contention, definitely and unequivocally take sides. Such recognition, which we seek in vain in President Stevenson, would not necessarily prejudge the question whether both tendencies should be tolerated within the Presbyterian church, but it would certainly mean at least that Princeton has the right and indeed the very solemn obligation of maintaining a *distinctive* position within the larger unity of the church. It is true, then, that Dr. Stevenson's policy is in a very important sense an inclusive policy, and that such an inclusive policy is contrary to the obligations which, on account of its entire history, Princeton Seminary has very solemnly assumed.

But although in one sense the policy with which we disagree is an inclusive policy, in another sense it is not inclusive at all. Formally it is inclusive, but in its deeper meaning and in its practical applications it is very exclusive indeed. No one who has observed with the slightest care the policy of the president can think that if that policy prevails, any man who is consistently conservative or evangelical in the ecclesiastical issue of the present day will have the slightest chance of being elected to a chair in Princeton Seminary. The only men who will be tolerated in the faculty will be men who hold a complacent view of the state of the church, who conceal from themselves and from others the real state of religious opinion in the world, and who consent to conform to the opinions of the party dominant for the moment in the councils of the church. The seminary under the new policy will be inclusive of those who obscure the great issue of the day, but it will be exclusive of those who have determined to warn the church of her danger and to contend earnestly for the faith.

If that policy becomes dominant in Princeton Seminary, then the Princeton position has very definitely been given up. And if the change is wrought by ecclesiastical action, then all the high-sounding words which have recently been uttered about peace and tolerance will be mocked. In that case, there will be liberty in the Presbyterian church for Modernists, but none for conservatives; and those who hold the conservative view will have to go elsewhere for the maintenance of those convictions that are dearer to them than life itself.

III

We have seen that Princeton Seminary stands in the first place for the complete truthfulness of the Scriptures as the Word of God, and in the second place for the Westminster Standards as containing the system of doctrine that the Scriptures teach. In the third place, Princeton Seminary holds that both these things—the full truthfulness of Holy Scripture and the system of doctrine that our Standards set forth—need, and are capable of, intellectual defense.

Hence, we cannot agree with those who think that a theological seminary ought to devote less time to the defense of Christianity and more time to the propagation of it. Certainly it is a grievous sin to propagate what is incapable of defense. The basic question about any message that may be propagated is the question whether it is *true*, and that question has been raised with regard to the Christian message in such insistent fashion in the modern world that the challenge must above all things be squarely and honestly met.

In meeting the challenge, we are fully conscious of the magnitude of our task. We cannot agree at all with those who despise the adversaries in this great debate, who think that the "critics" are to be disposed of with a few general words of adjectival abuse. For our part, we have profound admiration for the great masters of modern criticism; we are fully conscious of their intellectual greatness; we respect them to the full. Who would not admire the imposing reconstructions proposed by a Baur or by a Bousset, or the massive learning of a Schürer, or the brilliancy and versatility of a Harnack, or the incisiveness of radicals like Wrede in Germany or our own American Dr. McGiffert? Certainly we respect such scholars, opponents though they are of all that we hold most dear. Some of them may have respected us in turn; but whether they respect us or not, we shall continue respecting them. They are wrong, we think; all their learning is devoted to the impossible task of reconstructing on naturalistic principles what was really an act of God. But though they are wrong, they are wrong in a grand and imposing way, and they cannot be refuted either by a railing accusation or by a few pious words.

So we try to divest our students of the notion that there is any royal road to sacred learning; we try to divest them of the notion that they can lead the modern church without a knowledge of the original languages of Scripture and without the other tools of research. Above all, we try to give them a sense of the magnitude of the modern debate. We try, indeed, to lead them to faith, but we do not try to lead them by encouraging them to ignore the facts. On the contrary, we believe that Christian faith flourishes not in the darkness but in the light, and that a man's Christian conviction is only strengthened when he has examined both sides. We do, indeed, encourage men to come to Princeton Seminary. For them to do so, we think, is only fair. Historic Christianity deserves, we maintain, at least a hearing before it is finally given up; it is not fair to hear only what can be said against it without obtaining any orderly acquaintance with what it is; and to learn what it is, men should listen not to its opponents but to those who believe it with all their minds and hearts. So we do invite men to Princeton. But after they have studied at Princeton, indeed even while they are studying here, the more they acquaint themselves with what opposing teachers say, the better it seems to us to be. We encourage our graduates, if they can, to listen to the great foreign masters of naturalistic criticism; we desire them to hear all that can be said against the gospel that we believe.

No doubt such a program is full of perils. Might it not be safer for our future ministers to close their ears to all modern voices and remain in ignorance of the objections that the gospel faces in the modern world? We reply that of course it might be *safer*. It is safer to be a good soldier in comfortable barracks than it is on the field of battle. But the great battles are not won in that way.

Thus, we encourage our students to be fearless in their examination of the basis of the faith. Let no one say that such a program is unduly negative—that it involves too much examination of opposing views, and too little positive presentation of the gospel that we believe. Nobly do the graduates of Princeton Seminary refute any such accusation. What is it that the church values in Princeton Seminary? Is it not the positiveness and definiteness of the gospel message that our graduates proclaim; is it not that our former students, amid the vagueness of much modern religious teaching, know so clearly where they stand? No, the teaching of Princeton Seminary is not negative, but positive; all our examination of objections to the gospel is employed only as a means to lead men to a clearer understanding of what the gospel is and to a clearer and more triumphant conviction of its truth.

But the attainment of such conviction leads, for many men, through the pathway of intellectual struggle and perplexity of soul. Some of us have been through such struggle ourselves; some of us have known the blankness of doubt, the deadly discouragement, the perplexity of indecision, the vacillation between "faith diversified by doubt," and "doubt diversified by faith." If such has been our experience, we think with gratitude of the teachers who helped us in our need, and we in turn try with all our might to help those who are in the struggle now. Nothing can be done, we know, by trying to tyrannize over men's minds; all that we can do is to present the facts as we see them, to hold out a sympathizing hand to our younger brethren, and to commit them to God in prayer.

We cannot, indeed, seek to win men by false hopes; we cannot encourage them to think that if they decide to stand for Christ, they will have the favor of the modern world or necessarily of the modern church. On the contrary, if we read the signs of the times aright, both in the church and in the state, there may soon come a period of genuine persecution for the children of God.

If I find Him, if I follow,
What His guerdon here?
Many a sorrow, many a labor,
Many a tear.

Such, we are inclined to think, will be the lot of those who stand against the whole current of the age. It is not an easy thing to oppose a world in arms, nor is it an easy thing to oppose an increasingly hostile church. But when one does so, with full conviction, what a blessed, inward peace!

Such is the peace to which many of our students have attained. Small has been our part in such a result; it has been the work of God. But by the blessing of God's Spirit, through the use of whatever means, there has been emanating from Princeton during the last few years a current of warm Christian life that has refreshed those whom it has touched. It has found a noble expression in the new League of Evangelical Students, but it has found an even nobler expression in the experience of individual men. Conviction has issued here truly into Christian life.

What shall be done with this type of warm and vital Christianity that has been issuing from Princeton? It may come squarely into conflict, at some points, with the present leadership of the church. But because the fervent piety of our recent graduates of Princeton Seminary may be opposed at some points to the ecclesiastical machinery, it does not follow that that ecclesiastical machinery should be allowed to crush it out. Long has been the conflict, during nineteen centuries, between ecclesiastical authority and the free and mysterious operation of the Spirit of God. But under our Presbyterian institutions the tyrannical practices to which ecclesiastical authority has elsewhere resorted are an anomaly and a shame. And so we have some hope that the present tyrannical proposal about Princeton Seminary may yet be rejected and that Princeton may yet be saved. . . .

IV. Two Boards or One Board

The real question at Princeton, as has already been pointed out, is the question whether the conservative majority now in control of the institution is to be ejected and the present minority represented by Dr. Stevenson is to be placed in charge.

The particular means by which this result is to be attained is the establishment, to replace the present boards of directors and trustees, of a single board of control. The question whether we are to have one board or two boards has, indeed, sometimes been represented as though it were a mere administrative question, but in reality it is a question upon which the whole character of the institution depends. Maintain the authority, in spiritual affairs, of the present board of directors, which alone has kept the institution (so far as its theological position is concerned) what it is, and Princeton will continue to maintain its historic stand in the defense and propagation of the faith that is taught in the Word of God; substitute for that authority the authority of a single board of control, and the fine old institution, with all its noble traditions, will be dead.

Conceivably, indeed, there might, under other circumstances, be a single board of control which would maintain the conservative position of Princeton Seminary. That would be, indeed, even under the best of circumstances, extremely difficult; for government by a single board is a very dangerous form of government for a theological institution. Almost certainly it would involve the presence on the board of businessmen who know little or no theology; and in theological matters, ignorance is nearly as likely to throw an institution into the hands of the enemies of the faith as is positive disloyalty to the Word of God. There can be no doubt, therefore, that the form of government which underlies all our Presbyterian polity is essentially sound—one body in charge of spiritual affairs, another body in charge of the investment of funds. That is the polity that underlies the present "Plan" of Princeton Seminary. Any essential departure from it would, even under the most favorable circumstances, be dangerous in the extreme.

But that question is purely academic. Whatever may be the abstract possibilities in the case, there can be no doubt but that under the present circumstances—particularly under the guidance of the overwhelmingly partisan Committee of Eleven which has been appointed by authority of the General Assembly—any single board of control that by any possibility would be nominated would represent a policy diametrically opposed to the policy that has made Princeton Seminary what it is.

What is it, after all, that makes Princeton Seminary a conservative institution? Certainly it is not the general control of the institution by the Presbyterian church, for other theological institutions under the Presbyterian church represent very different points of view. Nor is it the board of trustees, for that board has not been concerned with theological matters, but only with the investment of funds and with the care of the material resources of the institution. Why is it that the present faculty of the seminary is sound in the faith? The fact that the faculty is sound has been mentioned with approval by many persons in connection with the present debate and particularly by the General Assembly's committee. But to what is the soundness of the faculty due? That is the really important question. Most emphatically, it is not due to the board of trustees; for that board has never in the whole history of the institution chosen a single professor. Every professor who has been chosen for the faculty since 1870, when the General Assembly ceased to elect the professors, has been chosen by the board of directors. Thus, if the church approves of the soundness of the present faculty, the credit for such soundness should be given to the board of directors and to the board of directors alone; it is solely to the board of directors and not to the board of trustees that the maintenance of the distinctive evangelical position of Princeton Seminary is due. To turn the spiritual affairs of the institution over to a secular corporation like the board of trustees would be to desert an agency that is tried and true, in these most dangerous times, for one which, to say the least, is quite untried. How would the individual congregations throughout the country like it if their board of trustees, chosen for an entirely different purpose, should suddenly replace the sessions and assume control in spiritual affairs? Yet in the case of an educational institution, the injustice of such a revolution would certainly be greater still.

All that would be true even if the attitude of the board of trustees in theological matters were merely unknown, and not positively known to be hostile to the policy for which the institution has always stood. Even then, an agency that is tried and true would be being deserted for one that is quite untried. Most amazing is the attitude of those who claim to be conservatives and yet are willing to take such a step. In these days when the whole current of the world is contrary to the evangelical position which the seminary holds, and when a most vague and misleading use of traditional terminology so often conceals the true radicalism of men's views—in these perilous days, men who claim to be conservatives are willing to turn over the delicate and difficult task of steering a great institution through the troubled waters to a board which in these matters has, to say the least, never been tried!

But in reality the situation is not even so favorable as that. It is not merely that the board of trustees is not known to be favorable to the historic position of Princeton Seminary; but there are certain positive indications that it is opposed to that position. Its opposition is made clear, to say nothing of less palpable indications, by one fact which cannot possibly be concealed. It is a fact that the board of trustees not only has among its members, but has actually appointed to the committee dealing with the momentous question of the reorganization of the seminary, a signer of the Auburn Affirmation. The Auburn Affirmation may be obscure in many particulars, but at the central point it is plain enough. In language that cannot be mistaken, it declares that acceptance of the virgin birth of our Lord, together with four other basic articles of the Christian faith, is *not* essential even to the ministry in the Presbyterian church. And yet the board of trustees is willing to appoint a signer of such a document to a committee which is to help determine the fate of Princeton Seminary! In view of that fact, the contention of those who say that no doctrinal issue is involved in this Princeton question and that the work of reorganizing the institution is in safe hands—this contention is seen to be quite absurd.

We are not concerned in the slightest, in this connection, with the doctrinal position of individual members of the board of trustees; it is quite possible for men whose own position is of an evangelical kind to be very dangerous guides with regard to the doctrinal policy of an institution—and uncritical optimism about the views of others is fully as dangerous to the maintenance of the things for which an institution like Princeton has always stood as is unsoundness in one's own views. We are not objecting, moreover, to the continuance of the board of trustees in the prerogatives which it now enjoys. Those prerogatives are of a very important kind, and we are as far as possible from desiring to see them interfered with. But those prerogatives do not include, and never have included, the determination of the doctrinal position of the seminary.

The matter is really quite plain. Princeton Seminary is a conservative institution simply and solely because of the conservative majority in its board of directors. That board has had a continuous history of over one hundred years, and since 1870 its members have been elected not by the Assembly, but by the board itself. In the election of its members it is subject, indeed to a veto power of the General Assembly; but the Assembly, very wisely, has refrained from exercising this power, and has allowed the distinctiveness of the institution to be preserved.

What is the result? The result is that Princeton Seminary is still loyal to the full truthfulness of the Bible as the Word of God. In that position it stands, among the older institutions of theological learning in the English-speaking world, practically alone. That may be an unpalatable fact, but a fact it is all the same. The other older institutions, in Great Britain and in America, have one by one drifted away; but Princeton stands firm for the truth of God's Word and for the gospel of redemptive love that the Word proclaims.

For the maintenance of this position, which is so directly contrary to the whole drift of the times, something more than personal orthodoxy has been required. There has also been necessary an unceasing vigilance. Suppose the complacent attitude of Dr. Stevenson with regard to the state of the church had prevailed in the board of directors—who can think that the evangelical position of Princeton Seminary would have been maintained? Suppose the opinion of the minority in the board had been the opinion of the majority—can anyone think that Princeton would be a conservative institution today? Two members of the minority group in the board of directors of Princeton Seminary have recently, in an official letter to the church, actually made the assertion that "our Church stands united in the great truths of the Gospel." It is indeed amazing that such distinguished men—distinguished for their services to our church and to the Christian world—should make an assertion that is so manifestly contrary to the facts; but they certainly have made it, and it represents just the attitude in which the imminent danger to Princeton Seminary lies. If Princeton Seminary comes into the hands of men who, in these days, in the face of the Auburn Affirmation and of plain indications without number, think that "our Church stands united in the great truths of the Gospel," then the long and honorable history of the institution in the propagation of the gospel has indeed come to an end.

As opposed to such dangerous complacency, the vigilance of the majority in our board of directors, its willingness to face the real facts in the world of religious thought, has accomplished the remarkable achievement of maintaining the position of Princeton Seminary in an age of defection and doubt. Despite the drift of the times, our institution still defends the full truthfulness of the Bible as the Word of God, and still propagates, with all its rebuke to human pride, with all its proclamation of God's wondrous love, the gospel of the crucified and risen Lord.

Is such a position to be tolerated in the Presbyterian church? If it is to be tolerated, to say nothing of its being approved, then let the distinctiveness of the institution's life be respected, and let the authority of the board of directors be maintained; if it is not to be tolerated, then let the church put into effect Dr. Thompson's policy of ruthless "frightfulness"; let the board of directors, after its long and faithful service, be wiped forcibly out of existence; let there be a new governing board in which what is now a minority shall become a majority; and thus let the policy of the institution be reversed.

The choice should not be difficult among those in our church who are devoted to the truth of the Bible. Even supposing we have presented the issue with undue sharpness, even supposing there were a *chance* (as in point of fact there is not) that a new, single board of control might maintain the conservative position of the seminary, it would still remain true that a certainty would be deserted for something that is quite untried. The present board of directors not only *might* maintain the conservative position of the seminary, but *has* actually done so; it has done so against opposition of all kinds, and it has done so in the presence of an uncritical complacency that is in such matters far more dangerous than direct attack. Will the evangelical people in the church join the present hue and cry against such a board; will they desert an agency that is tried and true for one that is uncertain at the very best? Or will they insist upon fair play? That is the question that confronts the next General Assembly.

One thing is clear—the really important matter is not the question whether the election of one or the other professor is to be confirmed. But it is the question of the *control* of the institution. If there is a majority of one vote in the new board of control for the policy now represented by the minority, then it does not make the slightest difference how many conservative members, up to that limit, are chosen for that board. In that case, Princeton Seminary, as it has been known and honored for a hundred years, will be dead, and there will be substituted for it a new institution of a radically different kind. And circumstances being what they are, there can be no doubt in the mind of anyone acquainted with the facts where control in the new single board will lie. Princeton Seminary, as a conservative institution, can be saved only by the defeat of the whole ruthless proposal—only by leaving the control of the institution (in spiritual matters) in the hands of the board that has made it what it is.

V. The General Assembly's Committees

It has been shown in what has already been said that the real question concerning Princeton is the question whether the distinctive character of the institution is to be preserved by the continuance of the board of directors that has made it, so far as its theological position is concerned, what it is, or whether, by the formation of a new board of control, a new institution is to be founded that shall be of a radically different kind. That question was raised by the appeal of President Stevenson at the Baltimore Assembly against the policy of the board of directors, and by the consequent appointment of Dr. Thompson's committee.

The ecclesiastical situation was such that Dr. Stevenson's contention was almost certain to be successful. It was almost certain to be successful because the whole machinery of the Assembly was in the hands of one party to the dispute, the party to which Dr. Stevenson belonged.

At the Baltimore Assembly, the retiring moderator was Dr. Charles R. Erdman, who has been the most vigorous advocate of Dr. Stevenson's policy in the councils of the seminary, and the most vigorous opponent of the majority of his colleagues. Dr. Erdman, as moderator, had appointed a strongly partisan "Commission of Fifteen," which had checked the threatened departure of the Modernists who objected to the judicial decision declaring the virgin birth to be an essential doctrine of the church, and which in its first report had engaged in a somewhat veiled but really very bitter attack upon the conservative party in the church. Dr. Thompson, the new moderator, who appointed the Princeton investigating committee, was one of Dr. Erdman's appointees on the Commission of Fifteen, and had himself, by a report to the Indianapolis Assembly in 1923, shown his thoroughgoing opposition to the things for which Princeton stands in the field of theological education. The committee that Dr. Thompson appointed was of a thoroughly partisan kind. One of its members was Dr. Luccock, who had previously been appointed to the chairmanship of the Standing Committee on Theological Seminaries by Dr. Thompson, and who in that position had already led the attack upon Princeton in a very vigorous way. There was no offset to this appointment; no representative of those members of the Standing Committee on Theological Seminaries who opposed Dr. Luccock's report was given a place on Dr. Thompson's committee. In general, it would be difficult to imagine a more perfect example of a partisan committee.

From such a committee no impartial report could reasonably have been expected. And yet one could scarcely have anticipated quite such unfairness as that which characterizes the report that was actually produced—the misrepresentation of various kinds, the omission of vitally relevant evidence, the unjudicial tone throughout. It is safe to say that seldom has a more unfair document been submitted to a body such as the General Assembly of our church.

Such a document never could have been submitted with any reasonable certainty of its being adopted if time had been allowed for the commissioners to peruse it with any care and for the persons whom it attacked to prepare their defense. Quite essential, therefore, to any certain adoption of the report was the delay in the publication of it until over a month after the time prescribed by the rules of the General Assembly. And so, in this unfair manner, the destruction of our largest seminary, which has had a continuous history under its board of directors for a hundred years, was railroaded through the Assembly almost without any consideration at all.

Final adoption of a plan for the new control of the institution is, indeed, postponed until May 1928; and the Committee of Five has been enlarged to become a Committee of Eleven. But there is no likelihood that the enlarged committee will be much more impartial than the old.

Indeed, it might conceivably be questioned whether the appointment of an impartial committee was not precluded by the very form of the instructions which the committee received from the Assembly. As a matter of fact, at any rate, the Committee of Eleven is overwhelmingly partisan. Little sympathy will be found among the great majority of its members for the position that the seminary has maintained.

Thus, the entire ecclesiastical machinery by which Princeton Seminary is to be destroyed next May has been under the control of one of the two parties to the dispute. It is hardly to be expected that such procedure will bring any sort of conviction to those who are of a different way of thinking. And surely such a policy of "frightfulness" is rather a singular method of promoting peace.

The whole action would be stopped if the rank and file of the church were given the slightest real voice in the questions in dispute. In particular, if the laymen whose well-justified fear with regard to the church's maintenance of the necessity of belief in the virgin birth of our Lord was quieted by the repetition of the Apostles' Creed last May had had the slightest inkling of what is really going on, we may be sure that our strongest center of evangelical Christianity would not be so ruthlessly crushed out.

But the present method of procedure is such that the laity is given little voice. If the commissioners to the Assembly next year were men who had sat in the Assembly this year, the matter could be given genuine consideration. But unfortunately the great majority of commissioners in 1928—probably almost all of the lay commissioners—will be men who were not at the previous Assembly. They will be, for the most part, men totally ignorant of the Princeton situation, and they will naturally not understand that the men in charge of the whole ecclesiastical machinery are in reality active partisans in the dispute. And so, without any real consideration at all, and with the best intentions in the world on the part of the lay members of the Assembly and on the part of many ministers, a very great injustice may be consummated. In view of the inexperience and lack of information of the bulk of the commissioners, the ecclesiastical machinery may again be supreme. The only hope is that the sound Christian heart of the church, despite all the obstacles, may become genuinely interested at last in this supremely important matter, and that thus there may be fair play.

It is to the rank and file of the church that we must make our appeal. We do so not altogether without hope. From the human point of view, indeed, everything is against us. The men representing the fine old institution which is now being done to death are for the most part entirely without skill in the arts of ecclesiastical politics, while their opponents are in full control of the machinery of the church. We cannot hope to win this battle by any reliance upon human influences or by any concealment of the real issue. Our only hope for victory is by a frank appeal from the present ecclesiastical authorities to the rank and file of the church. We have a just cause, and the inner heart of our church, we hope, is still sound. If the facts could only be made known, we think that justice would be done.

VI. The Future of Evangelical Christianity

In discussing "the future of evangelical Christianity," we do not mean the ultimate future. The ultimate future, according to the great and precious promises of God, is sure; if evangelical Christianity is true, it cannot ultimately fail.

But the future of which we are speaking is the immediate future. The gospel will triumph in the end, but meanwhile we are living in a time of conflict when we need to ask what it is God's will that we should do.

In that time of conflict, an epoch will unquestionably be marked by the reorganization of Princeton Seminary, if such reorganization is finally authorized by our General Assembly next May. What we shall have here is not merely the destruction of a single institution, but an event typical of a mighty movement of the times. The end of Princeton Seminary will, in some sort, mark the end of an epoch in the history of the modern church and the beginning of a new era in which new evangelical agencies must be formed.

What we shall have in the destruction of Princeton is nothing less than the severing of almost the last link, in the English-speaking world at least, between present-day evangelicalism and the traditions of a glorious past. Formerly, evangelical Christianity was rooted in a fine, scholarly tradition; the great universities, in Great Britain, in Protestant Europe, and in America, were in some instances the direct products of the Reformation, or at any rate were thoroughly devoted to the propagation of the Protestant faith. But now the universities have all, or nearly all, deserted the faith which they formerly held. There are here and there evangelical Christians in the faculties of the great universities of Europe and America, but such men are, to say the least, few and far between. For the most part, the universities are hostile or indifferent to the evangelical faith.

What is true of the universities in general is also true of the theological faculties. Not one of the older theological colleges in Great Britain, so far as I know, holds really, in any consistent way, to the evangelical position; and in America almost the same condition prevails. But in America, unlike Great Britain, one notable exception—not to prejudice the question whether there are others—is to be found. It is to be found in Princeton Theological Seminary. At Princeton, the oldest seminary of our Presbyterian church still maintains the unpopular evangelical cause.

In that position Princeton has come to stand, among the older institutions of theological learning, almost alone; and its uniqueness has won for it a certain measure of respect. Robertson Nicoll, the distinguished editor of the British Weekly, intimated in a letter to James Denney written in 1894 that "the only *respectable* defenders of verbal inspiration" (as *he* called it) were the Princeton school of Warfield and William Henry Green.[1] In that intimation

1. Robertson Nicoll, *Life and Letters*, by T. H. Darlow (1925), 341.

he was no doubt indulging in rhetorical exaggeration; no doubt there were really other defenders of plenary inspiration (as we call it) who were well worthy of respect. And yet the utterance was at least near enough to the truth to deserve being well taken to heart. Since the time of Robertson Nicoll's letter, the distinctiveness of Princeton has become even more marked. It may be questioned in some quarters whether we are still "respectable" in our defense of the full truthfulness of the Bible, but it will be widely admitted that if we are not respectable in such a position, no one else is.

This solitary position of Princeton will, of course, seem to many men to be due simply to the fact that we are supporters of a hopelessly discredited cause and adherents of a creed outworn; in the march of progress, it will be said, we have been left hopelessly behind. But of course there is another possible way of looking at the matter. Instead of holding that we have been left behind in the march of progress, one might also conceivably hold that in a time of general intellectual as well as moral decadence, we are striving to hold aloft the banner of truth until the dawn of a better day.

Which of these views is correct is of course a question far too great to be dealt with here. But this much at least can be said—the solitary position of Princeton in the modern world, though it has brought opposition, has also brought opportunity. As other avenues of evangelical learning have one by one been closed, earnest seekers after truth have turned to Princeton in their need. And so we have had in recent years a magnificent body of students from all over the world—from New Zealand, from South Africa, from Protestant districts on the continent of Europe, from Scotland, from the North of Ireland, from the Far East. Our students have come, moreover, not merely from many lands, but from many ecclesiastical bodies. The great Methodist church has sent us many splendid men; the Protestant Episcopal church, the Lutherans, the Baptists, have all been notably represented; members of the various Reformed bodies throughout the world have looked to us for training in the faith that they hold in common with us. And of course our greatest privilege of all has been to serve a large body of students from our own American Presbyterian church. Never has the prestige of our ancient institution been quite so wide as it is today. It is almost pathetic to observe the eagerness with which Princeton is looked to by men all over the world who in the face of the prevailing Modernist tyranny love the Bible as the Word of God and cherish the full gospel of the Lord Jesus Christ.

Such an institution it is that is being attacked by the ecclesiastical leaders in our church. If the present committee of the General Assembly works its will, there will be no really evangelical seminary at Princeton after next May. Let no one deceive himself into thinking that the transition will stop halfway; let no one think that although Princeton relinquishes the entirety of the Reformed faith, it will stop in the mediating position represented by some of the advocates of the present proposed change. No, the lesson of experience in these matters is only too plain. Such movements do not stop halfway. The institutions that have drifted away from the Christian faith have begun not with definite Modernism, but with just such doctrinal indifferentism, just such ignoring of the real seriousness of the issue, as that which appears in those who are attacking the present control of Princeton Seminary today. We do not need, therefore, to discuss the personal views of the men who are engaged in the attack; for although they may not be Modernists themselves, the inevitable result of their policy will be to make Princeton a Modernist institution in a very few years.

The transition may, indeed, be disguised. It is possible that some members of the present evangelical faculty may prefer to continue in their professorships even after the control of the institution has passed into hostile hands, and possibly there may be an avoidance for some years of any election of honest and outspoken Modernists to fill vacant chairs. But no one who has the slightest inkling of what is going on can possibly doubt but that the really decisive step will have been taken if the authority of the board of directors is destroyed next May.

It may seem at first sight strange that in a church professing to be evangelical, a seminary which is just now at the height of its success—attracting a very large body of students from all over the world, holding the respect even of some who disagree most strongly with its position, looked to with almost pathetic eagerness by evangelical people in many communions and in many lands—it may seem strange that such an institution should be the one that is singled out for attack. But the truth is that Princeton is being attacked not in spite of its success, but because of it. The warm and vital type of Christianity that has emanated from Princeton—the type of Christianity that not only proclaims the gospel when it is popular to proclaim it, but proclaims the gospel in the face of a hostile world, the type of Christianity that resolutely refuses to make common cause, either at home or on the mission field, with the Modernism that is the deadliest enemy of the cross of Christ, the type of Christianity that responds with full abandon of the heart and life to the Savior's redeeming love, that is willing to bear all things for Christ's sake, that has a passion for the salvation of souls, that holds the Bible to be not partly true and partly false, but all true, the blessed, holy Word of God—this warm and vital type of Christianity, as it has found expression, for example, in the League of Evangelical Students, is disconcerting to the ecclesiastical leaders; and so Princeton Seminary, from which it emanates, must be destroyed. Such has often been the fate of those who have felt compelled to warn the church. The ecclesiastical machinery rolls smoothly on, and the church proceeds to destroy that wherein its real safety rests.

Ecclesiastical action can never, indeed, destroy vital Christianity from human hearts. No one who has come into close contact, for example, with these young men who have formed the League of Evangelical Students can suppose that such consecration can ever be vanquished or discouraged by hostile actions of the organized church. Vital Christianity never will be crushed out of the world by action of church legislatures or courts. The gospel of Christ is still enshrined, even in these sad, cold days, in the hearts of men.

But though vital Christianity cannot be destroyed by ecclesiastical action, it may be driven out of the Presbyterian church; and in driving it out a very important step will be taken by the General Assembly if it adopts the reorganization plan for Princeton Seminary next May.

If that step is taken, no good can be accomplished by concealment of the loss. On the contrary, it will be the duty of evangelical Christians to consider carefully and prayerfully what ought to be done. One thing, of course, is clear—there will be imperative need of a truly evangelical seminary to take the place of the institution that will have been lost. The greatest weakness of evangelical effort in many parts of the Christian world today is the absence of any sound source of ministerial supply; Christian people are trying vainly to keep the waters sweet when the fountain is corrupt. It will be a sad day if Presbyterianism in America falls into such a condition as that. If Princeton is lost, there must certainly be a new institution that shall not conceal the really great issue of the day, but that shall contend earnestly for the faith.

But even if such an evangelical institution is founded, a vast deal will certainly have been lost. Who can measure the value of an institution like Princeton? Even its material equipment could hardly be replaced, even by unlimited resources. Its library is a magnificent instrument of research that has been built up by the loving care of generations of evangelical scholars.

Without such an instrument it is almost impossible to engage, in any intelligent way, in the defense and exposition of the faith. And such a library could hardly be replaced at all today, even by the expenditure of many millions of dollars. But even more valuable than such material equipment is the high tradition of Princeton, a possession that can never possibly be measured in any external way. No, it is no light thing when such an institution as Princeton passes into hostile hands.

We think, therefore, that before such a loss is acquiesced in, every effort ought to be made between now and next May to see whether the loss may not be avoided and Princeton may not yet be saved. Princeton could be saved still, if the evangelical people in our church had any understanding of what is going on. Indeed, even among those who disagree with our position regarding the great religious issue of the day, there are some, we think, who will hardly be willing to stoop to methods so unfair as those which were employed by Dr. Thompson's committee last year. And if there are any persons in our church in whom evangelical convictions are really clear and strong, they will engage earnestly in prayer that the continuity of Princeton Seminary may be preserved and that thus we may have at least one institution in the Presbyterian church that shall proclaim clearly and without compromise the gospel of our Lord Jesus Christ as it is found in God's Word. Even among the present ecclesiastical leaders, the men whom we have been obliged by conscientious reasons to oppose, there may be some who, when they really come to consider the matter, may shrink back from the ruthless measure that has been proposed. At first sight, it may seem so easy to crush the troublesome conservatives by destroying their Princeton base of supply. But possibly the leaders may come to see, on sober second thought, that even from their point of view the end is being attained at too great a cost, that in running roughshod over the principles of liberty in the church they are really harming their own cause, that theological pacifism will hardly prosper in the long run if it is stained with crime. Thus we have hope of every man; and we shall rejoice with all our heart if the present leaders of the church show that although they are against us in many matters, they prefer at least to fight with weapons that are fair.

But our chief appeal is to the rank and file of our church. We have a just cause, and the heart of the church, we hope, is still true. If the whole body of the church could only be acquainted with the facts, we think that Princeton might be saved next May.

30

STATEMENT TO THE PRESBYTERY OF NEW BRUNSWICK

WHY I CANNOT OBEY THE ORDER OF THE GENERAL ASSEMBLY.

A. Obedience to the order in the way demanded by the General Assembly would involve support of a propaganda that is contrary to the gospel of Christ.

1. The order plainly implies that in withdrawing from the Independent Board for Presbyterian Foreign Missions I shall support the present program of the Board of Foreign Missions in the Presbyterian Church in the U.S.A.

    a. The Action of the General Assembly expressly declares that support of the specific missionary program of the church is as much

Excerpt from "Statement to the Presbytery of New Brunswick" privately printed in 1935 by the author under the title, "Statement to the Special Committee of the Presbytery of New Brunswick in the Presbyterian Church in the U.S.A. which was Appointed by the Presbytery . . . to Confer Further with Dr. Machen with Respect to His Relationship with the Independent Board for Presbyterian Foreign Missions."

a duty of every member of the church as is participation in the Lord's Supper. The Action says (*Minutes*, p. 110):

> A church member or an individual church that will not give to promote the officially authorized missionary program of the Presbyterian Church is in exactly the same position with reference to the Constitution of the Church as a church member or an individual church that would refuse to take part in the celebration of the Lord's Supper or any other of the prescribed ordinances of the denomination as set forth in Chapter VII of the Form of Government.

That plainly implies that failure on my part to contribute to the present program of the official Board of Foreign Missions of the Presbyterian Church in the U.S.A. is an offense that makes me liable to discipline.

    b. The whole attack of the General Assembly upon the Independent Board for Presbyterian Foreign Missions is based upon the charge that the Independent Board for Presbyterian Foreign Missions is interfering with that support of the Board of Foreign Missions of the Presbyterian Church in the U.S.A. which the General Assembly holds to be obligatory upon every member of the church.

2. The present program of the Board of Foreign Missions of the Presbyterian Church in the U.S.A. includes support of and encouragement to propaganda that is contrary to the gospel of Christ.

    a. Evidence in support of this assertion was adduced in my argument entitled "Modernism and the Board of Foreign Missions of the Presbyterian Church in the U.S.A." The charges against the policy of the Board of Foreign Missions of the Presbyterian Church in the U.S.A. that were made in the argument have never been refuted.

    b. Actions of the General Assembly and of the Board of Foreign Missions of the Presbyterian Church in the U.S.A. which have been taken after the issuance of my argument have not all served to invalidate the charges made in that argument, but have rather served to substantiate them.

(1) The Board of Foreign Missions took action on March 20, 1933 (see *Report of Board of Foreign Missions, 1933*, p. 16), declaring that it was not in agreement with the view as to the aim of missions set forth in the first five chapters of the (Modernist) book *Re-Thinking Missions*. But:

(a) This expression of disagreement with the book was not only belated but also altogether general in character and did not at all serve to undo the harm which had been done by the Board in calling attention hopefully beforehand to the laymen's inquiry out of which the book *Re-Thinking Missions* came.

(b) The 1933 General Assembly's Standing Committee on Foreign Missions, whose report endorsing the policy of the board has been regarded by the board itself and by its supporters as being the primary document in refutation of the charges brought against the board, actually had among the majority in its membership approving its report a member of the Appraisal Commission that issued the book *Re-Thinking Missions*. Thus, the report which has been regarded as the chief document in vindication of the Board of Foreign Missions of the Presbyterian Church in the U.S.A. was perfectly agreeable to one of the persons issuing a book—the book *Re-Thinking Missions*—which is an attack upon the very heart of the Christian religion. Christian people who know the facts will say that that report, far from being a real vindication of the Board of Foreign Missions, is really a terrible indictment not only of that board but also of the two General Assemblies (1933 and 1934) that have adopted this part of the 1933 report of the 1933 Standing Committee.

(c) Certain members of the Board of Foreign Missions of the Presbyterian Church in the U.S.A. have been actively engaged in promoting the movement begun by the laymen's inquiry that authorized the issuance of the book *Re-Thinking Missions*. These promoters of a Modernist movement have been endorsed by the General Assembly, since the General Assembly elected them to the board, and by the board itself, since the board insists upon its essential internal unity and essential soundness.

(2) Mrs. Pearl S. Buck has resigned from her position as a missionary under the Board of Foreign Missions of the Presbyterian Church in the U.S.A. But the board accepted her resignation with "deep regret" and expressed "its earnest prayer that her unusual abilities may continue to be richly used in behalf of the people of China." Thus, the board is still involved in the propaganda of this writer, who has shocked Christian people throughout this country and the world by her published utterances regarding our Lord Jesus Christ.

(3) The Rev. Lindsay S. B. Hadley, a signer of the Modernist document commonly called the "Auburn Affirmation," is no longer candidate secretary of the Board of Foreign Missions of the Presbyterian Church in the U.S.A. But particular pains have been taken by the spokesmen of the board to make clear that the board still regards Mr. Hadley as an admirable person to occupy the position of candidate secretary and that his resignation was not due to any dissatisfaction of the board with him. The board is therefore still clearly on record as tolerating in a particularly responsible post a man who has signed this formal document which attacks the inerrancy of Holy Scripture and relegates to the realm of nonessential "theories" the virgin birth of our Lord and four other great verities of the Christian faith.

B. Obedience to the order of the General Assembly would involve the substitution of a human authority for the authority of the Word of God.

The passage already quoted from the Assembly's action not only requires support of the present policy of the Board of Foreign Missions of the Presbyterian Church in the U.S.A. and of the other boards of that church but also requires support of *any future* program of those boards that may be established by any subsequent General Assembly.

1. This is clearly indicated in that passage of the action of the General Assembly which was cited above. There it is plainly stated that a member of the Presbyterian Church in the U.S.A. who will not support "the officially authorized missionary program of the Presbyterian Church is in exactly the same position with reference to the Constitution of the Church as a church member or an individual church that would refuse to take part in the celebration of the Lord's Supper or any other of the prescribed ordinances of the denomination as set forth in Chapter VII of the Form of Government." Thus, if I obey the command of the General Assembly, I shall clearly be understood to adhere to the principle that is here set forth—namely, that a minister or member of the Presbyterian Church in the U.S.A. must support whatever missionary program successive General Assemblies may set up regardless of the question whether such program is or is not in accordance with the Holy Scriptures as they are understood by the individual minister or member.

2. That obedience on my part will generally be taken to mean just this is also made clear by the fact that the principle of implicit obedience to boards and agencies is being widely advocated in the church.

    a. That principle was practically adopted by the Presbytery of New Brunswick when it placed in its manual, at its meeting on September 26, 1933, a provision that "all candidates seeking licensure or ordination shall be examined as to their willingness to support the regularly authorized Boards and Agencies of the Presbyterian Church in the U.S.A., particularly the Board of Foreign Missions."

    b. It is also advocated by the complainants against the licensure of certain persons in the Presbytery of Chester. The complainants urge against the action of this presbytery in licensing those candidates that the candidates would not give a blanket promise to support the agencies and boards. (The Presbytery of Chester itself, however, has now ordained these candidates and therefore plainly holds that under Presbyterian law a candidate for licensure or ordination need not take a pledge to support the boards and agencies.)

c. The same principle is involved in the complaint against the action of the Presbytery of Philadelphia in receiving me from the Presbytery of New Brunswick. The complainants desired to question me about my attitude regarding the agencies and boards. Back of these questions was evidently the principle that support of the boards is required by a man's pledge as minister in the Presbyterian Church in the U.S.A.

d. The same principle is involved in the action of the Presbytery of Baltimore in refusing to license Mr. Calvin K. Cummings.

e. The same principle is definitely stated by the stated clerk of the General Assembly, in a letter to the stated clerk of the Presbytery of Baltimore, the following passage of which was read in the Presbytery of Baltimore of its spring meeting, 1934:

> If and when any students from Westminster Seminary come before your Presbytery, they should be informed that the Presbytery will neither license nor ordain them until they have given a written pledge that they will support the official agencies of the Church as a part of their pledge of loyalty to the government and discipline of the Church.

f. The same principle has been advocated widely in the church in other ways.

Enough has surely been said to show that this command of the General Assembly raises the issue: Is support of the official boards and agencies (no matter how their policies may change in accordance with the shifting votes in successive General Assemblies) an obligation of all ministers and members in the Presbyterian Church in the U.S.A.? I cannot evade the issue. If I obey the order of the General Assembly, I shall plainly be taken as answering this question in the affirmative; I shall plainly be taken as holding that support of the official boards and agencies is an obligation of all ministers and members in the Presbyterian Church in the U.S.A.; and that will plainly mean that I shall have substituted a human authority for the authority of the Word of God.

C. Obedience to the order of the General Assembly would mean acquiescence in the principle that support of the benevolences of the church is not a matter of freewill giving but the payment of a tax enforced by penalties.

This is shown clearly by the passage in the action of the General Assembly which has been cited above. It is true, the action of the General Assembly in another place does give lip service to freedom. It says (*Minutes*, p. 113):

> On the contrary, it [the General Assembly] has always maintained that the right to control the property of the members of the Church, to assess the amount of their contributions, or to prescribe how they shall dispose of their money, is utterly foreign to the spirit of Presbyterianism. Every contribution on the part of an individual member of the Church must be purely voluntary. In fact, the Presbyterian Church itself is a voluntary association. All of its members voluntarily associate themselves with the Church, and maintain their affiliation with it no longer than they voluntarily choose to do so. All that they do for its support, therefore, is a voluntary donation, and there is no power which can compel them to contribute to any ecclesiastical object to which they are not willing to give.

But then this liberty is at once withdrawn in the first sentence of the following paragraph (*Minutes*, p. 113):

> In maintaining, however, this personal freedom of individual members, in their contributions to the Church, the General Assembly has never recognized any inconsistency in asserting with equal force, that there is a definite and sacred obligation on the part of every member of the Presbyterian Church to contribute to those objects designated by the authorized judicatory of the denomination.

The liberty is also withdrawn in the passage which we cited above—namely, the passage to the effect that support of the missionary program of the boards is just as obligatory upon a member of the Presbyterian Church in the U.S.A. as is attendance upon the Lord's Supper.

What the General Assembly therefore says in effect (if we may use colloquial language) is: "Support of the boards is voluntary—don't you dare to say that it is not voluntary—but all the same, if you do not come right across with it, we shall see that it will be the worse for you."

Indeed, it is not quite clear but that all that the General Assembly means by the voluntariness of support of the boards is that *entrance* into the Presbyterian Church in the U.S.A. or into the ministry in that church is voluntary. "You may enter the Presbyterian Church in the U.S.A. or not as you please," says the General Assembly in effect; "but if you do enter, you must leave your Christian liberty behind. If you once enter, you are our slaves. Henceforth support of whatever missionary program successive General Assemblies may set up is obligatory upon you, whether you think the program is right or wrong. If you think that the missionary program of any General Assembly is so wrong that you cannot conscientiously support it, then the only thing for you to do is to leave the church."

D. All three of the aforementioned implications of obedience to the order of the General Assembly are contrary to the Bible.

1. The Bible not only requires a Christian man to preach the gospel of Christ, but forbids him to preach any other gospel. "Though we, or an angel from heaven, preach any other gospel unto you than that which we have preached unto you, let him be accursed" (Gal. 1:8). That is only one text among many. Indeed, it is only a summary expression of what runs through the Bible from beginning to end—the utter exclusiveness and imperiousness of the gospel of Christ.

    As a minister of the Lord Jesus Christ, I am in the presence of a world lost in sin. Men are going down into the darkness of eternal separation from God. There is one gospel and one only that can save them. If by my words or by my gifts I lead them to have the false hope that any other gospel can save them, I am guilty of an awful sin of bloodguiltiness. So if I lead men to think that the vague or antibiblical teaching being furthered by the

Board of Foreign Missions of the Presbyterian Church in the U.S.A. in many ways can save a soul from death, I am an unfaithful watchman. To me in that case there applies in full measure the warning of Ezekiel: "But if the watchman see the sword come, and blow not the trumpet, and the people be not warned; if the sword come, and take away any person from among them, he is taken away in his iniquity; but his blood will I require at the watchman's hand" (Ezek. 33:6).

That warning applies not only to a watchman who has what the world regards as an important post or large influence. It applies to every servant of God without exception. Every steward of the mysteries of God must be faithful in the place in which God has put him, no matter how small the world may hold that place to be. So I must be faithful in the place where God has put me, to the very best of my ability and in reliance upon God's grace.

2. The Bible forbids a man to substitute any human authority for the Word of God.

"Ye were bought with a price," says the Bible; "be not ye the servants of men" (1 Cor. 7:23). That verse only summarizes the whole teaching of the Bible with regard to the seat of authority. The conflict between the Bible and the General Assembly is here particularly plain. I cannot hesitate about the side that I shall take in that conflict.

In demanding that I shall shift my message to suit the shifting votes of an Assembly that is elected anew every year, the General Assembly is attacking Christian liberty; but what should never be forgotten is that to attack Christian liberty is to attack the Lordship of Jesus Christ.

I desire to say very plainly to the Presbytery of New Brunswick that as a minister I have placed myself under the orders of Jesus Christ as his will is made known to me through the Scriptures. That is at the heart and core of Protestantism. It is also at the heart and core of the teaching of the Word of God. I cannot give it up.

If I read the Bible aright, a man who obtains his message from the pronouncements of presbyteries or General Assemblies instead of from the Bible is not truly a minister of Jesus Christ. He may wear the garb of a minister, but he is not a minister in the sight of God.

By the issuance of this command, the General Assembly has attacked the authority of the Bible in very much the same way as the way in which it is attacked by the Roman Catholic church. The Roman Catholic church does not deny the authority of the Bible. Indeed, it defends the truth of the Bible, and noble service is being rendered in that defense, in our times, by Roman Catholic scholars. But we are opposed to the Roman Catholic position for one great central reason—because it holds that there is a living human authority that has a right to give an authoritative interpretation of the Bible. We are opposed to it because it holds that the seat of authority in religion is not just the Bible but the Bible interpreted authoritatively by the church. That, we hold, is a deadly error indeed: it puts fallible men in a place of authority that belongs only to the Word of God.

The same thing exactly was done by the 1934 General Assembly of the Presbyterian Church in the U.S.A. That Assembly abandoned the Reformation and returned essentially to the Roman Catholic position. It held that it is the duty of every officer and minister and member in the Presbyterian Church in the U.S.A. to support whatever missionary program may be set up by casual majorities in the General Assembly. It held, in particular, that a minister in the Presbyterian Church in the U.S.A. may not examine the missionary program to determine whether it is in accord with the Word of God, giving his support if it is in accord with the Word of God and withholding it if it is contrary to the Word of God. No, it held that a minister must take his Bible from his pulpit desk and put the last minutes of the General Assembly in its place—or rather, that he must keep the Bible there but put the minutes of the General Assembly on top of it, limiting his interpretation of the Bible to what the last General Assembly says the Bible means.

That command was contrary to the heart and core of Protestantism. But it was contrary to something more than Protestantism; it was contrary to the Word of the living God.

I desire to say very plainly to the Presbytery of New Brunswick that I cannot obey such a command. If I obeyed it, in order to obtain ecclesiastical favor, then the ministry would have become for me only a profession, and rather a contemptible profession too. I cannot thus deny my Savior and Lord. I must obey God rather than men.

3. The Bible forbids a man to regard support of the benevolences of the church as a tax enforced by penalties, but requires him to look upon them as freewill offerings.

In 2 Corinthians 9:7 we read: "Every man according as he purposeth in his heart, so let him give; not grudgingly, or of necessity: for God loveth a cheerful giver." This verse only puts in particularly clear and beautiful form something that really runs through all the teaching of the Bible regarding the new dispensation in which we are now living.

It would be easy, of course, to show that the General Assembly, in making support of boards and agencies of the church a tax rather than a matter of free will, has really defeated its own object; it has offended against the canons even of worldly wisdom. This money-or-your-life method of obtaining support for the boards really degrades the boards and dries up the real springs from which their support comes. Thinking people in the long run are not going to have much confidence in benevolent agencies, holding trust funds, that depend upon pressure or upon threats. They will have confidence, on the contrary, only in agencies that are always ready to give a full account of their stewardship and seek only gifts that come freely from the hearts of the givers.

But it is not such considerations which lead me to take my stand upon this question. Here as elsewhere I take my stand upon the teaching of the Word of God. I cannot give a penny to any mission agency if such a gift means acquiescence in the principle that support of the boards and agencies of the church is something required of me by membership in the church and enforceable by the disciplinary agencies of the church. I must take my stand on the teaching of the Word of God which declares that there shall be no compulsion in this matter.

4. The action of the General Assembly, involving as it does, and as I have shown above, the substitution of a human authority for the Word of God, is contrary to the express provisions of the Constitution of the Presbyterian Church in the U.S.A. and to the entire tenor of that constitution from beginning to end.

It has been shown above that the action of the General Assembly requires ministers and members in the Presbyterian Church in the U.S.A. not merely to support the present program of the boards and agencies of the church but to support any future program which any future General Assembly may establish.

The action plainly holds that support of the boards and agencies is an obligation which is necessarily involved in membership in the Presbyterian Church in the U.S.A. A man, the action holds, is perfectly free to enter the Presbyterian Church in the U.S.A. or not; but when he has once entered that church, it is his duty to support the boards and agencies as long as he remains a member.

The policy of the boards and agencies may change completely from year to year, since the boards are elected by successive General Assemblies. Therefore, the program of the boards may be one program this year and an opposite program next year. "Never mind," says the action of the General Assembly in effect; "a man must support any program which the General Assembly establishes no matter how much that program may differ from the program which it established the previous year."

The meaning of this principle, thus plainly held by the action of the General Assembly, may be seen if we examine the provision which now stands, as I have shown above, in the manual of the Presbytery of New Brunswick. The Presbytery of New Brunswick now requires that everyone who enters into the presbytery by licensure, ordination, or transfer shall be examined as to his willingness to support the boards and agencies of the church. I was present at the presbytery when this provision was put into effect. A young man appeared, in order to be received from another presbytery. He was asked to come up to the front. Then he was asked the question whether he would support the boards. That question was asked him in practically the same way as that in which the constitutional questions are asked, as they are set forth in the Form of Government.

The young man answered without any reservation that he would support the boards and agencies.

That could mean only one thing. It plainly meant that that young man was obtaining his ecclesiastical status, whether it was being licensed, being ordained, or being received from some other presbytery, by a blanket promise to shift his missionary program in accordance with the shifting votes in the General Assembly.

Now the placing of that provision in the manual of the Presbytery of New Brunswick was simply the logical consequence of the principle which was later set forth in the action of the 1934 General Assembly.

It is perfectly clear that both actions were unconstitutional.

a. The General Assembly's action and the addition to the manual of the Presbytery of New Brunswick both mean the addition of a question to the constitutional questions required by the Form of Government of the Presbyterian Church in the U.S.A. Those questions do not include any questions as to whether a man will support the boards and agencies of the church. A question to that effect can lawfully be added to the constitutional questions not by any presbytery and not by the General Assembly but only by the constitution-amending agency of the church—namely, the General Assembly plus a majority of the presbyteries (indeed, perhaps, even the General Assembly plus two-thirds of the presbyteries, since, as will be shown in a moment, this change would really be contrary to the Confession of Faith as well as contrary to the Form of Government).

The Form of Government of the Presbyterian Church in the U.S.A. contains certain provisions as to the examination of candidates. Those provisions are in two places.

They are found, in the first place, in the constitutional questions (Form of Government, Chapter XIV, Section viii and Chapter XV, Section xii). The constitutional questions contain certain pledges as to future conduct of the candidates in case they are received. The other place is in the section on the examination of candidates (Form of Government, Chapter XIV, Sections iv–vi).

Neither of these parts of the constitution permits the examination of a candidate as to his future support of particular programs.

In the constitutional questions, any such pledge is conspicuous by its absence, though there are very important pledges there of an entirely different character.

In the section on examinations, there is no provision whatever for examination of the candidate as to his future conduct in any particular. The candidate, according to that section, is to be examined on his knowledge and on his piety, but there is no provision there for any pledges to be exacted of him at all.

It is entirely contrary to the constitution, therefore, to put in this additional pledge as something to be required of candidates.

b. This Action of the General Assembly, the meaning of which is, as I have said, made perfectly plain by the application of the principle involved in it in the addition to the manual of the Presbytery of New Brunswick, is contrary to the Confession of Faith, which contains the following paragraph (Chapter XX, Section ii):

> II. God alone is lord of the conscience, and hath left it free from the doctrines and commandments of men which are in any thing contrary to his Word, or beside it, in matters of faith or worship. So that to believe such doctrines, or to obey such commandments out of conscience, is to betray true liberty of conscience; and the requiring of an implicit faith, and an absolute and blind obedience, is to destroy liberty of conscience, and reason also.

If anything in this world could be held to involve "the requiring of an implicit faith, and an absolute and blind obedience," it is the action of the General Assembly and the addition to the manual of the Presbytery of New Brunswick, of which we were speaking just now.

c. The action of the General Assembly, with the addition to the manual of the Presbytery of New Brunswick, is contrary also to the following paragraph of the Confession of Faith (Chapter XXXI, Section iii):

> III. All synods or councils since the apostles' times, whether general or particular, may err, and many have erred; therefore, they are not to be made the rule of faith or practice, but to be used as a help in both.

It is true that the immediately preceding section in the Confession of Faith is as follows (Chapter XXXI, Section ii):

> II. It belongeth to synods and councils, ministerially, to determine the controversies of faith, and cases of conscience; to set down rules and directions for the better ordering of the public worship of God, and government of his Church; to receive complaints in cases of mal-administration, and authoritatively to determine the same: which decrees and determinations, if consonant to the Word of God, are to be received with reverence and submission, not only for their agreement with the Word, but also for the power whereby they are made, as being an ordinance of God, appointed thereunto in his Word.

But in the use which has been made argumentatively of this section, great mischief has been wrought by failure to notice the momentous words "if consonant to the Word of God." The decrees and determinations of synods and councils are not to be received unless they are consonant to the Word of God. To ignore those words is to do away with Protestantism, and return, essentially, to the Roman Catholic position. If those words are ignored, one has to ignore the rest of our Protestant and particularly Presbyterian view of the government of the church.

d. This action of the General Assembly, again as its meaning is made clear by the addition to the manual of the Presbytery of New Brunswick, is shown to be contrary to the whole tenor of the Constitution of the Presbyterian Church in the U.S.A., because persons who submit to it are binding themselves either to conduct which is contrary to common honesty or else to conduct which is an evasion of the plain responsibilities of a member or a minister in the Presbyterian Church in the U.S.A.

Suppose a minister obtains his ordination by promising to support the boards and agencies, as he is required to do by the plain intent of that addition to the manual of the Presbytery of New Brunswick and by the plain intent of the action of the 1934 General Assembly. Suppose he later becomes convinced that the boards and agencies are unfaithful to their trust. Let us even take an extreme case. Let us suppose that he has become convinced that those in charge of the boards and agencies are guilty of actual embezzlement. That case is, of course, entirely hypothetical, but an extreme case does illustrate plainly the principle that is involved. Let us insist upon putting that extreme case. Here is a minister who has promised that he will, as long as he remains a minister in the Presbyterian Church in the U.S.A., support the boards and agencies as they are established by successive General Assemblies. Yet he has become convinced that those boards and agencies are positively dishonest, even with the kind of dishonesty that is contrary to the criminal laws of the land.

What course of action is open to such a minister? He is convinced that the boards and agencies are dishonest. The General Assembly is convinced that they are honest. What shall he do in such a situation?

In accordance with this action of the General Assembly, and in accordance with the plain intent of the addition to the manual of the Presbytery of New Brunswick, only two courses of action are open to a minister who is in such a quandary.

In the first place, he may continue to support boards and agencies which he holds to be dishonest. That course of action would plainly involve him in dishonesty. An honest man cannot possibly recommend to people that they should give to agencies which he holds to be dishonest.

In the second place, a minister who is in such a quandary may withdraw from the Presbyterian Church in the U.S.A. That plainly means evasion of the solemn responsibility which he has as a minister. I really wonder whether those who advocate this action of the General Assembly have ever thought this thing through. Do they really mean to tell us that just because a majority in the General Assembly has made a mistake one year and has placed in charge of the missionary funds of the church men who are dishonest, therefore a minister should withdraw from the church and allow that dishonesty to go on? I say that such conduct is an evasion of a solemn responsibility. No, it is the duty of a minister in such a situation to remain in the church and to seek by every means in his power to bring about a change in that policy of the General Assembly which he regards as involving dishonesty. Meanwhile (and this should be particularly observed), he cannot for any consideration whatever give a penny to what he regards, rightly or wrongly, to be a dishonest agency; and still less can he recommend to any other persons the support of such an agency.

I am perfectly well aware of the fact that this is a case which does not exist. It is not, indeed, an inconceivable case. Sin is rampant in the world, and it is perfectly conceivable that trust agencies like the boards and agencies of the Presbyterian Church in the U.S.A. should become dishonest even in that outrageous fashion—particularly if they are put beyond effective criticism, as this action of the General Assembly tends to put them. But I want to make perfectly clear, of course, that I am not charging the boards and agencies with any such thing. I am just using that extreme case to show the logical result of this action of the General Assembly and the logical result of the principle underlying that addition to the Manual of the Presbytery of New Brunswick. A man must think of what the outcome of principles is before he subscribes to them.

The same situation, essentially, faces a minister who believes that the boards and agencies, while not guilty of embezzlement, are unfaithful, no matter how good their motives may be, to their great trust of proclaiming the one true gospel. That is my position now. I believe that the Board of Foreign Missions of the Presbyterian Church in the U.S.A. is unfaithful. Thus, I cannot possibly support it or urge others to support it. That would plainly be contrary to common honesty. Neither can I withdraw from the ministry of the Presbyterian Church in the U.S.A. That would be evasion of what I regard as a very great and solemn trust. It would be a violation of my ordination pledge to maintain the purity and peace of the church, whatever "persecution or opposition may arise" unto me on that account.

But what I particularly desire to make plain is that this action of the General Assembly is unconstitutional no matter what the present condition of the Board of Foreign Missions or of any other board may be. I could never promise to support any human agency as a condition of my being ordained. I could not promise to support the Independent Board for Presbyterian Foreign Missions, which I believe now to be sound in the faith. I could not promise to support even the very best and soundest of human agencies as a condition of my being ordained. It is at the very heart and core of my ordination pledge, in accordance with the law of the Presbyterian church, that I should repeatedly examine any agency that appeals to me for support in the light of the Word of God, and support it only if it is in accord with that blessed Word. Moreover, in determining whether it is in accord with that Word, I must be governed by my conscience, as God may give me light, and not by the pronouncements of any human councils or courts.

If that is contrary to Presbyterian law, then I should certainly be removed from the Presbyterian Church in the U.S.A. But all the glorious history of the Reformed faith should teach a man, if the Word of God does not teach him, that it is not contrary to Presbyterian law but is at the very heart of Presbyterian law.

5. This action of the General Assembly is contrary to the Constitution of the Presbyterian Church in the U.S.A. in that it makes support of the boards and agencies of the church to be, in effect, a tax enforced by penalties and not a matter of freewill giving.

I have shown above that this is exactly the import of the action of the General Assembly, despite lip service in that action to the principle of freewill giving.

Surely it does not require many words to exhibit the contradiction between such an import on the one hand and the Constitution of the Presbyterian Church in the U.S.A. on the other. A man need only turn to the chapter in the Directory for Worship on "The Worship of God by Offerings" (Chapter VI in the Directory for Worship) to see that any notion that the support of any particular board or agency is to be required of members or ministers in the Presbyterian Church in the U.S.A. or to be supported by disciplinary measures is conspicuous by its absence. Moreover, it is specifically provided that "the specific designation by the giver of any offering to any cause or causes shall always be respected and the will of the donor carefully carried out." The chapter does say that "It is the duty of every minister to cultivate the grace of liberal giving in his congregation, that every member thereof may offer according to his ability whether it be much or little"; but nothing whatever is said about the enforcement of such giving by discipline, and certainly nothing is said about a duty of supporting any one particular program. Certainly there is no hint of justification for the assertion in the General Assembly's action that "a church member or an individual church that will not give to promote the officially authorized missionary program of the Presbyterian Church is in exactly the same position with reference to the Constitution of the Church as a church member or an individual church that would refuse to take part in the celebration of the Lord's Supper or any other of the prescribed ordinances of the denomination as set forth in Chapter VII of the Form of Government." Attendance upon the Lord's Supper is required of every Christian by the *Word of God*. Support of any particular human agency is most emphatically not required in the Word of God. It is really a very dreadful thing when a fallible human agency sets up its particular program for any one year as being on a par with a holy ordinance instituted by Christ and given by him to the church. I really do not see how human presumption could go much further than that presumption of which the last General Assembly has made itself guilty.

That dreadful sentence, which has seemed to some devout men in the church to be almost blasphemous, is certainly abhorrent not only to the express provisions of the Constitution of the Presbyterian Church in the U.S.A. but to the whole tenor of that constitution from beginning to end.

6. The action of the General Assembly errs in holding that the Independent Board for Presbyterian Foreign Missions is an organization within the Presbyterian Church in the U.S.A.

If the Independent Board for Presbyterian Foreign Missions were within the Presbyterian Church in the U.S.A., it could be held to be subject to that provision of the Form of Government which provides (Chapter XXIII, Section ii):

> II. Where special organizations of the character above indicated exist in a particular church, they shall be under the immediate direction, control and oversight of the session of said church; where they cover the territory included within a presbytery or synod, they shall be responsible to the judicatory having jurisdiction; and where they cover territory greater than a synod, they shall be responsible to the General Assembly.

This paragraph, in accordance with the very heading of the chapter, which is "Of the Organizations of the Church: Their Rights and Duties," and also in accordance with the plain implications of the chapter, refers to organizations of the Presbyterian Church in the U.S.A. and in the Presbyterian Church in the U.S.A. It refers to such organizations as women's societies or the like which owe their existence to their claim to belong to the Presbyterian Church in the U.S.A.

The plain fact is that the Independent Board for Presbyterian Foreign Missions makes no such claim. Indeed, such a claim is distinctly contrary to its charter. It has no more connection with the Presbyterian Church in the U.S.A. than has the China Inland Mission or a host of other organizations.

As for the fact that it has the word "Presbyterian" in its name, we must remember that that name is borne by a great number of churches that are entirely independent of one another and also by a great number of organizations that are not connected with any church. The Presbyterian Church in the U.S.A. happens to be the largest of the Presbyterian bodies in this country, but any claim on its part to have an exclusive right to the name "Presbyterian" would be nothing short of outrageous.

As for the charge that the Independent Board for Presbyterian

Foreign Missions is discharging "ecclesiastical functions," that charge is so utterly baseless that we can fairly hold that no words are necessary in refutation of it.

7. The action of the General Assembly is contrary to the Constitution of the Presbyterian Church in the U.S.A. because it requires support of an agency, the Board of Foreign Missions of the Presbyterian Church in the U.S.A., which at present is unfaithful to the Word of God.

It is not necessary to labor this point. *If* the Board of Foreign Missions of the Presbyterian Church in the U.S.A. is unfaithful to what is set forth in the Word of God, then I doubt whether anyone would be quite bold enough to argue that the Constitution of the Presbyterian Church in the U.S.A. can possibly require support of such a board.

But what I want to make perfectly plain is that all the rest of my argument in the present statement is entirely valid even if I am wrong in holding that the Board of Foreign Missions is at present unfaithful. The point is that if I am conscientiously convinced that it is unfaithful, then, whether I am right or wrong in that, the constitution of the church forbids my being coerced in the manner that is involved in the action of the General Assembly.

CONCLUSION

It has been shown in the foregoing statement that the action of the 1934 General Assembly ordering certain persons to sever their connection with the Independent Board for Presbyterian Foreign Missions and ordering certain presbyteries to take disciplinary steps in case these persons should not obey that part of the order addressed to them is contrary to the Constitution of the Presbyterian Church in the U.S.A.

What should be done about the matter?

The answer to that question is very simple. Since the action of the General Assembly was unconstitutional, it should be ignored both by the individuals concerned and by the presbyteries.

PART SEVEN

CHURCH
AND SOCIETY

31

CHRISTIANITY AND LIBERTY

When I was honored by an invitation to contribute an article to *The Forum*, it could only be because the editor is broadminded enough to accord a hearing to a humble representative of a very unpopular cause. To be an adherent today of that redemptive religion that has always hitherto been known as Christianity, and to be at all in earnest about the logical consequences of that conviction, is to stand sharply at variance not only with the world at large but also with the forces that dominate most of the larger Protestant churches. These churches, many of them, instead of engaging in the sweet and gentle ministrations to the human soul in which they formerly engaged, have made themselves political lobbies or agencies of the police. Church organizations, already proud of their bigness, have sought to unite themselves in the gigantic monopoly of one Protestant body. Amid the rattle of all this machinery, amid the bustle of all this efficiency, there is little sympathy for the man who asks what it is at bottom that the church is in the world to do. The churches often profess belief, indeed, in the Bible and in the ancient creeds; but for an individual in the churches to believe in the Bible and in the creeds and to be at all earnest about the logical consequence of such belief—this is regarded as an unpardonable ecclesiastical crime.

"Christianity and Liberty" originally appeared in a shorter form in *Forum and Century* 85 (1931) 162–66. Reprinted in *What Is Christianity?* ed. Ned Bernard Stonehouse (Grand Rapids: Eerdmans, 1951).

Whatever may be thought of such an unpopular step as that, it can hardly be any unworthy motives of self-interest that lead a man to take it. It is not easy to stand against the whole current of an age, and the sacrifice which is involved in doing so is far from being light. Why then do we adherents of the religion of the Bible insist on being so peculiar; why do we resist in such perverse fashion the pronouncements of the "modern mind"?

Perhaps, for one thing, it is because we do not think so highly as some persons do of the modern mind—of the modern mind and of the modern world that that modern mind has produced.

It is not the incidental defects of the modern mind of which I am thinking just now. Those incidental defects are surely plain enough even to the most enthusiastic modernity.

I suppose my experience is similar to the experience of a good many men. When I was a student in Europe in 1905–06, the argument from modern authority seemed to me to be a very powerful argument against the super-naturalistic Christianity in which I had been brought up. I was living in an environment where that Christianity had long been abandoned, where it was no longer regarded even as being worthy of debate. It was a very stimulating environment indeed, dominated by men whom I enthusiastically admired then and whom I still admire. And the world in general might have seemed to a superficial observer to be getting along very well without Christ. It was a fine, comfortable world—that godless and Christless European world prior to 1914. And as for anything like another European war, that seemed to be about as well within the bounds of possibility as that medieval knights should don their armor and set their lances again in rest. The international bankers obviously would prevent anything so absurd. But we discovered our mistake. Our comfortable utilitarian world proved to be not so comfortable after all.

In some directions, indeed, there was advance even in warfare over conditions that had prevailed before. Antiseptic surgery no doubt had accomplished much. But in other directions there was a marked decline. The notion of the nation in arms, that redoubtable product of the French Revolution, was carried out to something approaching its logical result. Even more logical and even more damnable, no doubt, will be its results in the next war.

Modern scientific utilitarianism, in other words, did not produce the millennium prior to 1914; and there is not the slightest evidence that it has produced the millennium since that time or that it ever will produce the millennium in the ages to come.

In further incidental indictment of the age in which we are living, I might point to the brutal injustices and enormities of the peace that followed upon a war which was supposed to be waged for justice and liberty. And I might point also to the appalling spiritual decline which has come over the world within the last fifty years. High poetry, for the most part, is silent; art is either imitative or bizarre. There is advance in material things, but in the higher ranges of the human mind an amazing sterility has fallen on the world. Very extraordinary is the complacency of such an age; indeed, that complacency is perhaps the most appalling indication of decadence that could possibly be conceived.

But serious as are such incidental defects of the age in which we are living, it is not those incidental defects of which I am thinking just now. After all, there has been advance in some directions to balance the retrogression in others. Humanitarian effort has no doubt accomplished much; war has been declared against the mosquito and the germ, and someday we may be living in a world without disease. I doubt it, for my part; but at any rate the possibility cannot altogether be denied.

What, then, if it is not found in incidentals—even so stupendous an incidental as the world war—is the real indictment against the modern world? The answer seems clear enough to some of us. The real indictment against the modern world is that by the modern world human liberty is being destroyed.

At that point, no doubt, many readers will only with difficulty repress a smile. The word "liberty" today has a decidedly archaic sound. It suggests G. A. Rnety, flag-waving, the boys of '76, and the like. Twentieth-century intellectuals, it is thought, have long ago outgrown all such childishness as that. So the modern historians are writing "liberty" in quotation marks, when they are obliged to use the ridiculous word: no principle, they are telling us, for example, was involved in the American Revolution; economic causes alone produced that struggle; and Patrick Henry was indulging in cheap melodrama when he said: "Give me liberty or give me death." Certainly, at any rate, whatever our estimate of history, liberty is out of date in modern life. Standardization and efficiency have very largely taken its place.

Even nature is being made to conform to standard. In the region that I have visited in Maine off and on for the past thirty years, I have seen the wild exuberance of woods and streams gradually giving place to the dreary regularities of a national park. It seems almost as though some sweet, delicate living creature were being ruthlessly destroyed.

But that is only a symbol of what is also going on today in the higher sphere of human life: the same ruthless standardization of human souls. That is particularly true in the all-important field of education. If, it is said, we allow all sorts of queer private schools and parochial schools to confuse the mind of youth, what will become of the welfare of the state? How can we have a unified nation without a standardized school?

I know that this process of standardization has recently been checked in America here and there. The Supreme Court of the United States declared unconstitutional the Oregon school law that simply sought to wipe all private schools and Christian schools out of existence in that state, and it also declared unconstitutional the Nebraska language law (similar to laws in other states) that made literary education even in private schools a crime. The abominable Lusk laws in the State of New York, one of which placed private teachers under state supervision and control, were repealed. The bill establishing a federal department of education, despite the powerful interests working in behalf of it, has not yet become a law. The misnamed "child-labor amendment" to the Constitution of the United States, which would have placed the youth of the country under centralized bureaucratic control, has not yet received the requisite ratification from the states. But I fear that these setbacks to the attack on liberty, unless the underlying temper of the people changes, are but temporary, and that the process of standardization and centralization will go ruthlessly on.

In some spheres, no doubt, standardization is a good thing. It is a good thing, for example, in the making of a Ford car. But it does not follow that it should be applied to human beings, for a human being is a person and a Ford car is a machine.

The typical modern experts deny this distinction, and that is our fundamental quarrel with the "modern mind." I know that there are those who tell us that this tendency to which we object is merely incidental to a change in the physical conditions of life. The liberty of the individual, they tell us, has always had to be limited somehow in the interests of the community and of the race; and the limitation, as life becomes more complex, merely has to appear in somewhat more intricate form. We may be passing through a period just now when the pendulum between individualism and collectivism has swung too much to the latter extreme, but it will swing back, and all will be well.

I should like to think that this view of the situation is correct, but I am unable to think so. The trouble is not that the modern world has been unsuccessful in an effort to preserve liberty, but that it is not seeking to preserve liberty at all. Mussolini is thought to be a benefactor of the race because, although liberty of speech is destroyed in Italy, the streets of Italian cities are clean. The Soviet tyrants in Russia are said not to be efficient, but it never seems to occur to modern critics that they would be far more dangerous tyrants if they were. Mankind, in other words, has become willing to buy material benefits at any price. I do not know how the bargain will turn out in detail. But in the bargain something at any rate will have been lost. We may have gained the whole world, but we are in danger of losing our own soul.

What sort of world is it to which we are tending today? What is really the modern ideal? I suppose it is a world in which the human machine has arrived at the highest stage of efficiency. Disease, I suppose, may be abolished; and as for death, although we shall not have abolished it, we shall at least have abolished its terrors. Vague, childish longings, pre-scientific speculations as to a hereafter, will all be gone; and we shall have learned, as reasonable and scientific men, to stand without a pang at the grave of those whom in a less-scientific age we should have been childish enough to love.

What is to be thought of such a mechanistic world? I will tell you what we think of it: we think it is a world in which all zest, all glory, all that makes life worth living will have been destroyed. It will no doubt have its advantages. In it, no doubt, the span of our life may be extended far beyond the previously allotted period of threescore years and ten. Experts appointed by the state will always be by our side to examine our physical and mental condition and keep us alive upon the earth. But what will be the use? Who would want to live longer in a world where life is so little worth living?

From such a slavery, which is already stalking through the earth in the materialistic paternalism of the modern state, from such a world of unrelieved drabness, we seek escape in the high adventure of the Christian religion. Men call us, indeed, devotees of a book. They are right. We are devotees of a book. But the book to which we are devoted is the Magna Charta of human liberty—the book which alone can make men free.

At that point I am particularly desirous of not being misunderstood. I do not mean for one moment that a man ever became a real Christian merely through a desire to attain civil or political freedom or even the very highest of worldly ends. Valuable are the by-products of Christianity, and one of them is the civil liberty of the race. But if a man carries on this undertaking for the sake of the by-products, the undertaking and the by-products are both sure to be lost. Jesus said indeed: "Seek ye first the Kingdom of God and His righteousness, and all these things shall be added unto you"; but if a man seeks the kingdom of God and his righteousness in order that all these things may be added unto him, he will miss the kingdom of God and those other things as well.

But what I do mean is that the defects of the modern world, though they will never make a man a Christian in themselves, may yet lead him to a consideration of far profounder needs. He may begin by seeking escape from mechanism and go on to seek escape from sin. In the Christian religion, we find a liberty that is far deeper than the civil and religious liberty of which we have spoken. It is a liberty that enters into the depths of the soul.

In the Bible, we find, in the first place, God. Back of the stupendous mechanism of the world there stands, as the Master of it and not as its slave, no machine but a living person. He is enveloped, indeed, in awful mystery; a dreadful curtain veils his being from the gaze of men. But unlike the world, he is free, and he has chosen in his freedom to lift the veil and grant us just a look beyond. In that look we have freedom from the mechanism of the world. God is free, and where he is, there is liberty and life.

In the Bible, in the second place, we find man; we regain that birthright of freedom which had been taken from us by the modern mind. It is a dreadful birthright indeed. For with freedom goes responsibility, and with responsibility, for us, there goes the awful guilt of sin. That conscience awakens which makes cowards of us all. Gone for us Christians is the complacency of the modern mind; gone is the lax, comforting notion that crime is only a disease; gone is the notion that strips the ermine from the judge and makes him but the agent of a utilitarian society; gone is the blindness that refuses to face the moral facts. The Christian world, unlike the modern world, is a world of nameless terrors; the Christian views man as standing over a bottomless abyss. Such a view will find little sympathy from the experts of the present day; they will doubtless apply to it their usual method of dealing with a thing that they do not understand—they will give it a long name and let it go. But is their judgment really to be trusted? There are some of us who think not. There are some of us who think that the moral judgments of us sinners, even when they are the judgments of experts, are not always to be trusted, and that the real pathway of advance for humanity lies through a rediscovery of the law of God.

In the third place, in the Bible we find redemption. Into this vast universe, into this world of sin, there came in God's good time a divine Redeemer. No mere teacher is he to us, no mere example, no mere leader into a larger life, no mere symbol or embodiment of an all-pervading divinity. No; we stand to him, if we are really his, in a relationship far dearer, far closer than all that. For us he gave his precious life upon the cross to make all well between us sinners and the righteous God, by whose love he came.

At that point, I despair of finding words to tell the readers fully what I mean. Perhaps we may tell you what we think, but it is harder to tell you what we feel. You may dismiss it all as "theory of the atonement," and fall back upon the customary commonplaces about a principle of self-sacrifice exemplified in the cross of Christ or the culmination there of a universal law or a revelation of the love of God or the hallowing of suffering or the similarity between Christ's death and the death of soldiers who gave themselves for others in the world war. And then, by God's grace, there may come, when you least expect it, a flash of light into your soul, and all will be as clear as day. Then you will say with Paul, as you contemplate the Savior upon the cross: "He loved me and gave Himself for me." Thus will the ancient burden fall from our back; then do we become true moderns at last. "Old things are passed away; behold, they are become new." Then and then only will you have true freedom. It will be a freedom from mechanism, but the freedom from mechanism will be rooted in a freedom from sin.

At this point I think I know what some of the readers may say. Do we not agree, they may say, with much that has been said? Do we not reject behaviorist psychology; do we not believe in the freedom of the soul; do we not believe in God? But need such beliefs be connected with such very doubtful conclusions in the sphere of external history; may we not believe in the eternal worth of the human soul, and enter into communion with God, without insisting upon the external miracles of the Bible? May we not have a true Christian experience without believing in the empty tomb?

This attitude lies at the basis of what may be called, by a very unsatisfactory and question-begging term, "Liberalism" in the church. It is a very imposing phenomenon. I hope I do not approach it without sympathy. I have listened to many of its representatives during the last twenty-five years with high admiration—ever since I sat in Herrmann's classroom at Marburg and obtained some impression of the fervor and glow of that remarkable man. I can quite understand how men desire to escape if they can the debate in the field of science; I quite understand how they seek to avoid disputing about what happens or has happened in the external world and fall back upon an internal world of the soul into which scientific debate cannot enter. It seems to be such a promising solution of our apologetic difficulties just to say that science and religion belong in two entirely different spheres and can never by any chance come into conflict. It seems to be so easy for religion to purchase peace by abandoning to science the whole sphere of facts in order to retain for itself merely a sphere of feelings and ideals.

But in reality these tactics are quite disastrous. You effect thus a strategic retreat; you retreat into a Hindenburg line, an inner line of defense whence you think that science can never dislodge you. You get down into your pragmatist dugout and listen comfortably to the muffled sound of the warfare being carried on above by those who are old-fashioned enough to be interested in truth; you think that whatever creedal changes, whatever intellectual battle there may be, you at least are safe. You have your Christian experience, and let science and biblical criticism do what they will!

But do not comfort yourself. The enemy in this warfare is good at mopping up captured trenches; he has in his mechanistic psychologists a very efficient mopping-up squad. He will soon drive you out of your refuge; he will destroy whatever decency and liberty you thought you had retained; and you will discover, too late, that the battle is now lost, and that your only real hope lay not in retreating into some anti-intellectualistic dugout but in fighting bravely to prevent the initial capture of the trench.

No, the battle between naturalism and supernaturalism, between mechanism and liberty, has to be fought out sooner or later; and I do not believe that there is any advantage in letting the enemy choose the ground upon which it shall be fought. The strongest defense of the Christian religion is the outer defense; a reduced and inconsistent Christianity is weak; our real safety lies in the exultant supernaturalism of God's Word.

And is the case for that supernaturalism really so weak? There are many things that lead us to think that it is not; but if you want to learn of one of them, just read the four gospels for yourselves. Do not study them this time,

362   CHURCH AND SOCIETY

important though it is to study them at other times. Just read them; just let the stupendous figure of Jesus stand before your eyes. Has not that figure the marks of truth? Could that figure ever have been produced in impersonal fashion to satisfy the needs of the primitive church? No, the figure of Jesus in the gospels possesses an individuality that is irreducible, a shining, startling vividness against which criticism will ultimately fail. Yet criticism has had its beneficent results; it has shown with increasing clearness that the picture of Jesus in the New Testament is essentially one. Gone is the day when men thought that a few miracles could be removed from the gospels to leave a "Liberal Jesus," a mere preacher of the "fatherhood of God and the brotherhood of man."

Recent New Testament criticism has tended strongly against any such easy solution of the problem as that. Increasingly the great alternative is becoming clearer: give Jesus up, and confess that his portrait is forever hidden in the mists of legend; or else accept him as a supernatural person, as he is presented by all the four gospels and by Paul.

We have chosen the latter alternative for ourselves, and we believe that only in that alternative are true progress and true liberty to be attained for mankind.

32

THE RESPONSIBILITY OF THE CHURCH IN OUR NEW AGE

The question of the church's responsibility in the new age involves two other questions: (1) What is the new age? (2) What is the church?

The former question is being answered in a number of different ways; differences of opinion prevail, in particular, with regard to the exact degree of newness to which the new age may justifiably lay claim. There are those who think that the new age is so very new that nothing that approved itself to past ages can conceivably be valid now. There are others, however, who think that human nature remains essentially the same and that two and two still make four. With this latter point of view I am on the whole inclined to agree. In particular, I hold that facts have a most unprogressive habit of staying put, and that if a thing really happened in the first century of our era, the acquisition of new knowledge and the improvement of scientific method can never make it into a thing that did not happen.

"The Responsibility of the Church in Our New Age" originally appeared in *Annals of the American Academy of Political and Social Science* 165 (1933) 38–47. Reprinted in *What Is Christianity?* ed. Ned Bernard Stonehouse (Grand Rapids: Eerdmans, 1951).

Such convictions do not blind me to the fact that we have witnessed astonishing changes in our day. Indeed, the changes have become so rapid as to cause many people to lose not only their breath but also, I fear, their head. They have led many people to think not only that nothing that is old ought by any possibility to remain in the new age, but also that whatever the new age favors is always really new.

Both these conclusions are erroneous. There are old things which ought to remain in the new age; and many of the things, both good and bad, which the new age regards as new are really as old as the hills.

In the former category are to be put, for example, the literary and artistic achievements of past generations. Those are things which the new age ought to retain, at least until the new age can produce something to put in their place, and that it has so far signally failed to do. I am well aware that when I say to the new age that Homer is still worth reading, or that the Cathedral of Amiens is superior to any of the achievements of the *art nouveau*, I am making assertions which it would be difficult for me to prove. There is no disputing about tastes. Yet, after all, until the artistic impulse is eradicated more thoroughly from human life than has so far been done even by the best efforts of the metallic civilization of our day, we cannot get rid of the categories of good and bad or high and low in the field of art. But when we pay attention to those categories, it becomes evident at once that we are living today in a drab and decadent age, and that a really new impulse will probably come, as it has come so many times before, only through a rediscovery of the glories of the past.

Something very similar needs to be said in the realm of political and social science. There, too, something is being lost—something very precious, though very intangible and very difficult of defense before those who have not the love of it in their hearts. I refer to civil and religious liberty, for which our fathers were willing to sacrifice so much.

The word "liberty" has a very archaic sound today; it is often put in quotation marks by those who are obliged to use the ridiculous word at all. Yet despised though liberty is, there are still those who love it; and unless their love of it can be eradicated from their unprogressive souls, they will never be able to agree, in their estimate of the modern age, with those who do not love it.

To those lovers of civil and religious liberty I confess that I belong; in fact, civil and religious liberty seems to me to be more valuable than any other earthly thing—than any other thing short of the truer and profounder liberty which only God can give.

What estimate of the present age can possibly be complete that does not take account of what is so marked a feature of it—namely, the loss of those civil liberties for which men formerly were willing to sacrifice all that they possessed? In some countries, such as Russia and Italy, the attack upon liberty has been blatant and extreme, but exactly the same forces which appear there in more consistent form appear also in practically all the countries of the earth. Everywhere we have the substitution of economic considerations for great principles in the conduct of the state; everywhere a centralized state, working as the state necessarily must work, by the use of force, is taking possession of the most intimate fields of individual and family life.

These tendencies have proceeded more rapidly in America than in most other countries of the world; for if they have not progressed so far here as elsewhere, that is only because in America they had a greater handicap to overcome. Thirty years ago we hated bureaucracy and pitied those countries in Europe that were under bureaucratic control; today we are rapidly becoming one of the most bureaucratic countries of the world. Setbacks to this movement, such as the defeat, for the present at least, of the misnamed "child-labor amendment," the repeal of the Lusk laws in New York placing private teachers under state supervision and control, the invalidation of the Nebraska language law making literary education even in private schools a crime, the prevention so far of the establishment of a federal department of education—these setbacks to the attack on liberty are, I am afraid, but temporary unless the present temper of the people changes.

The international situation, moreover, is hardly such as to give encouragement to lovers of liberty, especially in view of the recent proposal of Premier Herriot that a policy of conscription, inimical as it is to liberty as well as to peace, shall be made general and permanent. Everywhere in the world we have centralization of power, the ticketing and cataloguing of the individual by irresponsible and doctrinaire bureaus; and worst of all, in many places we have monopolistic control of education by the state.

But is all that new? In principle it is not. Something very much like it was advocated in Plato's *Republic* over two thousand years ago. The battle between collectivism and liberty is an age-long battle, and even the materialistic paternalism of the modern state is by no means altogether new. The technique of tyranny has, indeed, been enormously improved; a state-controlled compulsory education has proved far more effective in crushing out liberty than the older and cruder weapons of fire and sword, and modern experts have proved to be more efficient than the dilettante tyrants of the past. But such differences are differences of degree and not of kind, and essentially the battle for freedom is the same as it always has been.

If that battle is lost, if collectivism finally triumphs, if we come to live in a world where recreation as well as labor is prescribed for us by experts appointed by the state, if the sweetness and the sorrows of family relationships are alike eliminated and liberty becomes a thing of the past, we ought to place the blame for this sad denouement—for this sad result of all the pathetic strivings of the human race—exactly where it belongs. And it does not belong to the external conditions of modern life. I know that there are those who say that it does belong there; I know that there are those who tell us that individualism is impossible in an industrial age. But I do not believe them for one moment. Unquestionably, industrialism, with the accompanying achievements of modern science in both the physical and the social realm, does constitute a great temptation to destroy freedom; but temptation is not compulsion, and of real compulsion there is none.

No, my friends, there is no real reason for mankind to surrender to the machine. If liberty is crushed out, if standardization has its perfect work, if the worst of all tyrannies, the tyranny of the expert, becomes universal, if the finer aspirations of humanity give way to drab efficiency, do not blame the external conditions in the world today. If human life becomes mechanized, do not blame the machine. Put the blame exactly where it belongs—upon the soul of man.

Is it not in general within that realm of the soul of man that evils of society have their origin today? We have developed a vast and rather wonderful machinery—the machinery of our modern life. For some reason, it has recently ceased to function. The experts are busily cranking the engine, as I used to do with my Ford car in the heroic days when a Ford was still a Ford. They are wondering why the engine does not start. They are giving learned explanations of its failure to do so; they are adducing the most intricate principles of dynamics. It is all very instructive, no doubt. But the real explanation is much simpler. It is simply that the driver of the car has forgotten to turn on the switch. The real trouble with the engine of modern society is that it is not producing a spark. The real trouble lies in that unseen realm which is found within the soul of man.

That realm cannot be neglected even in a time of immediate physical distress like the present. I do not know in detail how this physical distress is to be relieved. I would to God that I did. But one thing I do know: it will never be relieved if, in our eagerness to relieve it, we neglect the unseen things. It is not practical to be merely practical men; man cannot successfully be treated as a machine; even the physical welfare of humanity cannot be attained if we make that the supreme object of our pursuit; even in a day when so many material problems are pressing for our attention, we cannot neglect the evils of the soul.

But if that is so, if the real trouble with the world lies in the soul of man, we may perhaps turn for help to an agency which is generally thought to have the soul of man as its special province. I mean the Christian church. That brings us to our second question: What is the church?

About nineteen hundred years ago, there came forth from Palestine a remarkable movement. At first it was obscure, but within a generation it was firmly planted in the great cities of the Roman Empire, and within three centuries it had conquered the Empire itself. It has since then gone forth to the ends of the earth. That movement is called the Christian church.

What was it like in the all-important initial period, when the impulse which gave rise to it was fresh and pure? With regard to the answer to that question, there may be a certain amount of agreement among all serious historians, whether they are themselves Christians or not. Certain characteristics of the Christian church at the beginning stand out clear in the eyes both of friends and of foes.

It may clearly be observed, for example, that the Christian church at the beginning was radically doctrinal. Doctrine was not the mere expression of Christian life, as it is in the pragmatist skepticism of the present day, but— just the other way around—the doctrine, logically though not temporally, came first and the life afterward. The life was founded upon the message, and not the message upon the life.

That becomes clear everywhere in the primary documents. It appears, for example, in the first epistle to the Thessalonians, which is admitted by all serious historians, Christian and non-Christian, to have been really written by a man of the first Christian generation—the man whose name it bears. The apostle Paul there gives us a summary of his missionary preaching in Thessalonica—that missionary preaching which in Thessalonica and in Philippi and elsewhere did, it must be admitted, turn the world upside down. What was the missionary preaching like? Well, it contained a whole system of theology. "Ye turned to God," says Paul, "from idols to serve the living and true God, and to wait for His Son from heaven, whom He raised from the dead, even Jesus, which delivereth us from the wrath to come." Christian doctrine, according to Paul, was not something that came after salvation, as an expression of Christian experience, but it was something necessary to salvation. The Christian life, according to Paul, was founded upon a message.

The same thing appears when we turn from Paul to the very first church in Jerusalem. That too was radically doctrinal. In the first epistle to the Corinthians—again one of the universally accepted epistles—Paul gives us a summary of what he had received from the primitive Jerusalem church. What was it that he had received; what was it that the primitive Jerusalem church delivered over unto him? Was it a mere exhortation; was it the mere presentation of a program of life; did the first Christians in Jerusalem say merely: "Jesus has lived a noble life of self-sacrifice; we have been inspired by him to live that life, and we call upon you our hearers to share it with us"? Not at all. Here is what those first Christians said: "Christ died for our sins according to the Scriptures; he was buried; he has been raised on the third day according to the Scriptures." That is not an exhortation, but a rehearsal of facts; it is couched not in the imperative but in the indicative mood; it is not a program, but a doctrine.

I know that modern men have appealed sometimes at this point from the primitive Christian church to Jesus himself. The primitive church, it is admitted, was doctrinal; but Jesus of Nazareth, it is said, proclaimed a simple gospel of divine fatherhood and human brotherhood, and believed in the essential goodness of man. Such an appeal from the primitive church to Jesus used to be expressed in the cry of the so-called "Liberal" church, "Back to Christ!" But that cry is somewhat antiquated today. It has become increasingly clear to the historians that the only Jesus whom we find attested for us in our sources of information is the supernatural Redeemer presented in the four gospels as well as in the epistles of Paul. If there was back of this supernatural figure a real, nondoctrinal, purely human prophet of Nazareth, his portrait must probably lie forever hidden from us. Such, indeed, is exactly the skeptical conclusion which is being reached by some of those who stand in the van of what is called progress in New Testament criticism today.

There are others, however—and to them the present writer belongs—

who think that the supernatural Jesus presented in all of our sources of information was the real Jesus who walked and talked in Palestine, and that it is not necessary for us to have recourse to the truly extraordinary hypothesis that the intimate friends of Jesus, who were the leaders of the primitive church, completely misunderstood their Master's person and work.

Be that as it may, there is, at any rate, not a trace of any nondoctrinal preaching that possessed one bit of power in those early days of the Christian church. It is perfectly clear that that strangely powerful movement which emerged from the obscurity of Palestine in the first century of our era was doctrinal from the very beginning and to the very core. It was totally unlike the ethical preaching of the Stoic and Cynic philosophers. Unlike those philosophers, it had a very clear-cut message—and at the center of that message was the doctrine that set forth the person and work of Jesus Christ.

That brings us to our second point. The primitive church, we have just seen, was radically doctrinal. In the second place, it was radically intolerant. In being radically intolerant, as in being radically doctrinal, it placed itself squarely in opposition to the spirit of that age. That was an age of synchronism and tolerance in religion; it was an age of what J. S. Phillimore has called "the courtly polygamies of the soul." But with that tolerance, with those courtly polygamies of the soul, the primitive Christian church would have nothing to do. It demanded a completely exclusive devotion. A man could not be a worshiper of the God of the Christians and at the same time be a worshiper of other gods; he could not accept the salvation offered by Christ and at the same time admit that for other people there might be some other way of salvation; he could not agree to refrain from proselytizing among men of other faiths, but came forward, no matter what it might cost, with a universal appeal. That is what I mean by saying that the primitive Christian church was radically intolerant.

In the third place, the primitive church was radically ethical. Religion in those days, save among the Jews, was by no means closely connected with goodness. But with such a nonethical religion the primitive Christian church would have nothing whatever to do. God, according to the primitive Christians, is holy; and in his presence no unclean thing can stand. Jesus Christ presented a life of perfect goodness upon earth, and only they can belong to him who hunger and thirst after righteousness. Christians were, indeed, by no means perfect—they stood before God only in the merit of Christ their Savior, not in their own merit—but they had been saved for holiness, and even in this life that holiness must begin to appear. A salvation which permitted a man to continue in sin was, according to the primitive church, no matter what profession of faith it might make, nothing but a sham.

These characteristics of primitive Christianity have never been completely lost in the long history of the Christian church. They have, however, always had to be defended against foes within as well as without the church. The conflicts began in apostolic days; and there is in the New Testament not a bit of comfort for the feeble notion that controversy in the church is to be avoided, that a man can make his preaching positive without making it negative, that he can ever proclaim truth without attacking error. Another conflict arose in the second century, against Gnosticism, and still another when Augustine defended against Pelagius the Christian view of sin.

At the close of the Middle Ages, it looked as though at last the battle were lost—as though at last the church had become merged with the world. When Luther went to Rome, a blatant paganism was there in control. But the Bible was rediscovered; the ninety-five theses were nailed up; Calvin's *Institutes* was written; there was a counter-reformation in the church of Rome; and the essential character of the Christian church was preserved. The Reformation, like primitive Christianity, was radically doctrinal, radically intolerant, and radically ethical. It preserved these characteristics in the face of opposition. It would not go a step with Erasmus, for example, in his indifferentism and his tolerance; it was founded squarely on the Bible, and it proclaimed, as providing the only way of salvation, the message that the Bible contains.

At the present time, the Christian church stands in the midst of another conflict. Like the previous conflicts, it is a conflict not between two forms of the Christian religion but between the Christian religion on the one hand and an alien religion on the other. Yet—again like the previous conflicts—it is carried on within the church. The non-Christian forces have made use of Christian terminology and have sought to dominate the organization of the church.

This modern attack upon the Christian religion has assumed many different forms, but everywhere it is essentially the same. Sometimes it is frankly naturalistic, denying the historicity of the basic miracles, such as the resurrection of Jesus Christ. At other times it assails the necessity rather than the truth of the Christian message—but, strictly speaking, to assail the necessity of the message is to assail its truth, since the universal necessity of the message is at the center of the message itself. Often the attack uses the shibboleths of a complete pragmatist skepticism. Christianity, it declares, is a life and not a doctrine; and doctrine is the expression, in the thought-forms of each generation, of Christian experience. One doctrine may express Christian experience in this generation; a contradictory doctrine may express it equally well in a generation to come. That means, of course, not merely that this or that truth is being attacked, but that truth itself is being attacked. The very possibility of our attaining to truth, as distinguished from mere usefulness, is denied.

This pragmatist skepticism, this optimistic religion of a self-sufficient humanity, has been substituted today, to a very considerable extent, in most of the Protestant communions, for the redemptive religion hitherto known as Christianity—that redemptive religion with its doctrines of the awful transcendence of God, the hopelessness of a mankind lost in sin, and the mysterious grace of God in the mighty redemptive acts of the coming and death and resurrection of Jesus Christ. Many of the rank and file of the churches, many of the individual congregations, are genuinely Christian; but the central organizations of the churches have in many cases gradually discontinued their propagation of the Christian religion and have become agencies for the propagation of a vague type of religion, to which Christianity from its very beginning was diametrically opposed.

So, in speaking about the responsibility of the church in the new age, I want it to be distinctly understood that I am not speaking about the responsibility of the existing Protestant church organizations (unless they can be reformed), but about the responsibility of a true Christian church. The present ecclesiastical organizations may have their uses in the world. There may be a need for such societies of general welfare as some of them have become; there may be a need for the political activities in which they are increasingly engaged—but such functions are certainly not at all the distinctive function of a real Christian church.

Even in the sphere of such worldly functions, I am inclined to think that there are agencies more worthy of your attention then these Protestant church organizations, or than, for example, such an organization as the Federal Council of the Churches of Christ in America. The trouble is that the gentlemen in control of these organizations are, though with the best and most honorable intentions in the world, in a hopelessly false position. The churches are for the most part creedal; it is on the basis of their creeds that they have in the past appealed, and that to some extent they still appeal, for support; yet the central organizations of the churches have quietly pushed the creeds into the background and have devoted themselves to other activities and a different propaganda. Perhaps in doing so they have accomplished good here and there in a worldly sort of way. But in general, the false position in which they stand has militated against their highest usefulness. Equivocation, the double use of traditional terminology, subscription to solemn creedal statements in a sense different from the sense originally intended in those statements—these things give a man a poor platform upon which to stand, no matter what it is that he proposes, upon that platform, to do.

But if the existing Protestant church organizations, with some notable exceptions, must be radically reformed before they can be regarded as truly Christian, what, as distinguished from these organizations, is the function of a true Christian church?

In the first place, a true Christian church, now as always, will be radically doctrinal. It will never use the shibboleths of a pragmatist skepticism. It will never say that doctrine is the expression of experience; it will never confuse the useful with the true, but will place truth at the basis of all its striving and all its life. Into the welter of changing human opinion, into the modern despair with regard to any knowledge of the meaning of life, it will come with a clear and imperious message. That message it will find in the Bible, which it will hold to contain not a record of man's religious experience but a record of a revelation from God.

In the second place, a true Christian church will be radically intolerant. At that point, however, a word of explanation is in place. The intolerance of the church, in the sense in which I am speaking of it, does not involve any interference with liberty; on the contrary, it means the preservation of liberty. One of the most important elements in civil and religious liberty is the right of voluntary association—the right of citizens to band themselves together for any lawful purpose whatever, whether that purpose does or does not commend itself to the generality of their fellow men. Now, a church is a voluntary association. No one is compelled to be a member of it; no one is compelled to be one of its accredited representatives. It is, therefore, no interference with liberty for a church to insist that those who do choose to be its accredited representatives shall not use the vantage ground of such a position to attack that for which the church exists.

It would, indeed, be an interference with liberty for a church, through the ballot box, or otherwise, to use the power of the state to compel men to assent to the church's creed or conform to the church's program. To that kind of intolerance I am opposed with all my might and main. I am also opposed to church union for somewhat similar reasons, as well as for other reasons still more important. I am opposed to the depressing dream of one monopolistic church organization, placing the whole Protestant world under one set of committees and boards. If that dream were ever realized, it would be an intolerable tyranny. Certainly it would mean the death of any true Christian unity. I trust that the efforts of the church-unionists may be defeated, like the efforts of the opponents of liberty in other fields.

But when I say that a true Christian church is radically intolerant, I mean simply that the church must maintain the high exclusiveness and universality of its message. It presents the gospel of Jesus Christ not merely as one way of salvation, but as the only way. It cannot make common cause with other faiths. It cannot agree not to proselytize. Its appeal is universal, and admits of no exceptions. All are lost in sin; none may be saved except by the way set forth in the gospel. Therein lies the offense of the Christian religion, but therein lies also its glory and its power. A Christianity tolerant of other religions is just no Christianity at all.

In the third place, a true Christian church will be radically ethical. It will not be ethical in the sense that it will cherish any hope in an appeal to the human will; it will not be ethical in the sense that it will regard itself as perfect, even when its members have been redeemed by the grace of God. But it will be ethical in the sense that it will cherish the hope of true goodness in the other world, and that even here and now it will exhibit the beginnings of a new life which is the gift of God.

That new life will express itself in love. Love will overflow, without questions, without calculation, to all men whether they are Christians or not; but it will be far too intense a passion ever to be satisfied with a mere philanthropy. It will offer men simple benefits; it will never pass coldly by on the other side when a man is in bodily need. But it will never be content to satisfy men's bodily needs; it will never seek to make men content with creature comforts or with the coldness of a vague natural religion. Rather, it will seek to bring all men everywhere, without exception, high and low, rich and poor, learned and ignorant, compatriot and alien, into the full warmth and joy of the household of faith.

There are certain things which you cannot expect from such a true Christian church. In the first place, you cannot expect from it any cooperation with non-Christian religion or with a non-Christian program of ethical culture. There are those who tell us that the Bible ought to be put into the public schools, and that the public schools should seek to build character by showing the children that honesty is the best policy and that good Americans do not lie or steal. With such programs a true Christian church will have nothing to do. The Bible, it will hold, is made to say the direct opposite of what it means if any hope is held out to mankind from its ethical portions apart from its great redemptive center and core; and character building on the basis of human experience may be character destruction; it is the very antithesis of that view of sin which is at the foundation of all Christian convictions and all Christian life.

There is no such thing, a true Christian church will insist, as a universally valid fund of religious principles upon which particular religions, including the Christian religion, may build; "religion" in that vague sense is not only inadequate but false, and a morality based upon human experience instead of upon the law of God is no true morality. Against such programs of religious education and character building, a true Christian church will seek from the state liberty for all parents everywhere to bring up their children in accordance with the dictates of their conscience, will bring up its own children in accordance with the Word of God, and will try to persuade all other parents, becoming Christians, to bring up their children in that same Christian way.

In the second place, you cannot expect from a true Christian church any official pronouncements upon the political or social questions of the day, and you cannot expect cooperation with the state in anything involving the use of force. Important are the functions of the police, and members of the church, either individually or in such special associations as they may choose to form, should aid the police in every lawful way in the exercise of those functions. But the function of the church in its corporate capacity is of an entirely different kind. Its weapons against evil are spiritual, not carnal; and by becoming a political lobby, through the advocacy of political measures whether good or bad, the church is turning aside from its proper mission, which is to bring to bear upon human hearts the solemn and imperious, yet also sweet and gracious, appeal of the gospel of Christ.

Such things you cannot expect from a true Christian church. But there are other things which you may expect. If you are dissatisfied with a relative goodness, which is no goodness at all; if you are conscious of your sin and if you hunger and thirst after righteousness; if you are dissatisfied with the world and are seeking the living God, then turn to the church of Jesus Christ. That church is not always easy to distinguish today. It does not always present itself to you in powerful organizations; it is often hidden away here and there, in individual congregations resisting the central ecclesiastical mechanism; it is found in groups, large or small, of those who have been redeemed from sin and are citizens of a heavenly kingdom. But wherever it is found, you must turn to that true church of Jesus Christ for a message from God. The message will not be enforced by human authority or by the pomp of numbers. Yet some of you may hear it. If you do hear it and heed it, you will possess riches greater than the riches of all the world.

Do you think that if you heed the message you will be less successful students of political and social science; do you think that by becoming citizens of another world you will become less fitted to solve this world's problems; do you think that acceptance of the Christian message will hinder political or social advance? No, my friends. I will present to you a strange paradox but an assured truth—this world's problems can never be solved by those who make this world the object of their desires. This world cannot ultimately be bettered if you think that this world is all. To move the world, you must have a place to stand.

This, then, is the answer that I give to the question before us. The responsibility of the church in the new age is the same as its responsibility in every age. It is to testify that this world is lost in sin; that the span of human life—no, all the length of human history—is an infinitesimal island in the awful depths of eternity; that there is a mysterious, holy, living God, Creator of all, Upholder of all, infinitely beyond all; that he has revealed himself to us in his Word and offered us communion with himself through Jesus Christ the Lord; that there is no other salvation, for individuals or for nations, save this, but that this salvation is full and free, and that whoever possesses it has for himself and for all others to whom he may be the instrument of bringing it a treasure compared with which all the kingdoms of the earth—no, all the wonders of the starry heavens—are as the dust of the street.

An unpopular message it is—an impractical message, we are told. But it is the message of the Christian church. Neglect it, and you will have destruction; heed it, and you will have life.

33

THE CHURCH IN THE WAR

I n many cases the church has done nobly in the war. There have no doubt been many chaplains, many Y. M. C. A. secretaries, and many soldiers in the ranks who have proclaimed the gospel of Christ faithfully and humbly and effectively to dying men. Any discouraging estimate of the situation is subject to many noble exceptions. But in general, in view of the manifest estrangement between the church and large bodies of men, there is at least some plausibility for the common opinion that the church has failed.

Fortunately, if the church has failed, it is at least perfectly clear why she has failed. She has failed because men have been unwilling to receive, and the church has been unwilling to preach, the gospel of Christ crucified. Men have trusted for their own salvation and for the hope of the world in the merit of their own self-sacrifice rather than in the one act of sacrifice which was accomplished some nineteen hundred years ago by Jesus Christ. That does not mean that men are opposed to Jesus. On the contrary, they are perfectly ready to admit him into the noble company of those who have sacrificed themselves in a righteous cause. But such condescension is as far removed as possible from the Christian attitude. People used to say, "There was no other good enough to pay the price of sin." They say so no longer.

"The Church in the War," a chapel address at Princeton Seminary on May 6, 1919 and originally appeared in the *Presbyterian* 89 (May 29, 1919) 10–11. Reprinted in *What Is Christianity?* ed. Ned Bernard Stonehouse (Grand Rapids: Eerdmans, 1951).

On the contrary, any man, if only he goes bravely over the top, is now regarded as plenty good enough to pay the price of sin.

Obviously, this modern attitude is possible only because men have lost sight of the majesty of Jesus' person. It is because they regard him as a being altogether like themselves that they can compare their sacrifice with his. It never seems to dawn upon them that this was no sinful man, but the Lord of glory who died on Calvary. If it did dawn upon them, they would gladly confess, as men used to confess, that one drop of the precious blood of Jesus is worth more, as a ground for the hope of the world, than all the rivers of blood which have flowed upon the battlefields of France.

But how may this Christian conception of the majesty of Jesus' person be regained?

Some people think it may be regained simply by more knowledge. If people would only read the gospels more, we are told, they would come to know Jesus, and, knowing him, they would revere him. But knowledge, important though it is, is not sufficient. Many men knew Jesus in the days of his flesh—intelligent men, too—who never became his disciples. Who then were those who did come to reverence him? The answer is plain. During the earthly lifetime of Jesus and all through the centuries, the men who really understood the majesty of Jesus' person were the men who were convicted of their sin. Peter was one of those who said, "Depart from me, for I am a sinful man, O Lord." The dying thief was another; he knows more about Jesus today than many a modern preacher who has the name of Jesus forever on his lips. Paul was another—a brave, clean man he was, too, as the world looks on it, even before he found forgiveness in Christ. The real reason why men no longer understand the majesty of Jesus' person is that they do not contrast his holiness with their own sinfulness; they are without the conviction of sin.

The leading characteristic of the present age is a profound satisfaction with human goodness. The popular war -literature, for example, is redolent of such satisfaction. Get beneath the rough exterior of men, we are told, and you find sufficient self-sacrifice in order to found upon that self-sacrifice the hope of the world.

What has produced such a spirit of self-satisfaction?

In the first place, the war has provided us with a convenient scapegoat. In wartime, men have been interested in the sins of others; they have been called upon to fight in hot indignation against injustice and oppression on the part of the Germans. Such indignation has been necessary. But it has not been without its moral dangers. In attending to the sins of others, men have sometimes lost sight of their own sins.

In the second place, the sense of sin has sometimes been blunted by the consciousness of a great achievement. Certainly the achievement is very great; the men who march in triumph up Fifth Avenue deserve not less but more honor than they are receiving from their fellow citizens. But honor from men can be received with perfect satisfaction only where it is joined, as it is joined in the case of many a Christian soldier, with utter humility in the presence of God.

But the roots of modern self-satisfaction lie far deeper than the war. During the past century a profound spiritual change has been produced in the whole thought and life of the world—no less a change than the substitution of paganism for Christianity as the dominant principle of life. We are not here using "paganism" as a term of reproach; ancient Greece was pagan, but it was glorious. What we mean by "paganism" is a view of life which finds its ideal simply in a healthy and harmonious and joyous development of existing human faculties. Such an ideal is the exact opposite of Christianity, which is the religion of the broken heart.

We would not be misunderstood. In saying that Christianity is the religion of the broken heart, we do not mean that Christianity ends in the broken heart; we do not mean that the characteristic Christian attitude is a continual beating of the breast and a continual crying of "Woe is me." On the contrary, the Christian should not be always "laying again the foundation of repentance from dead works"; sin is dealt with once for all, and then a new and joyous life follows. There is thus in Christianity a higher humanism. The trouble with the humanism of ancient Greece, as with the humanism of modern times, lay not in the superstructure, which was glorious, but in the foundation, which was rotten. Sin was never really dealt with and removed; there was always something to cover up. In the higher Christian humanism there is nothing to cover up; the guilt has been removed once for all by God, and the Christian may now proceed without fear to develop every faculty which God has given him.

But if Christianity does not end with the broken heart, it does begin with it. The way to Christ lies through the conviction of sin.

Unfortunately, the fact is not always recognized. Modern preachers are inclined to suggest some easier way. They are saying to men in effect this:

"You men are very good and very self-sacrificing, and we take pleasure in revealing your goodness to you. Now, since you are so good, you will probably be interested in Christianity, especially in the life of Jesus, which we believe is good enough even for you." Such preaching is very attractive—much more attractive than the preaching of the cross. But it is quite useless. It is useless to try to call the righteous to repentance.

But it is hard for men to give up their pride. How shall we find the courage to require it of them? How shall we preachers find courage to say, for example, to the returning soldiers, rightly conscious as they are of a magnificent achievement: "You are sinners like all other men, and like all other men you need a Savior." It looks to the world like a colossal piece of impertinence. Certainly we cannot find the courage in any superior goodness of our own. But we can find the courage in the goodness and in the greatness of Christ.

Certainly the gospel does put a tremendous strain upon Jesus of Nazareth. The gospel means that instead of seeking the hope of the world in the added deeds of goodness of the millions of the human race throughout the centuries, we seek it in one act of one Man of long ago. Such a message has always seemed foolish to the wise men of this world. But there is no real reason to be ashamed of it. We may feel quite safe in relinquishing every prop of human goodness in order to trust ourselves simply and solely to Christ. The achievements of men are very imposing. But not in comparison with the Lord of glory.

> When I survey the wondrous cross
> On which the Prince of glory died,
> My richest gain I count but loss,
> And pour contempt on all my pride.

34

VOICES IN THE CHURCH

A Debate about the Child-Labor Amendment

It is rather unfortunate that Professor Vandenbosch, in his criticism of my lecture, was able to use not the lecture itself but only the report of it in *The Banner*. That report is, indeed, excellent; but after all, even the best of reports or summaries is a dangerous guide when one is accusing a speaker of being ignorant of that which the summary report does not contain. Thus, if my lecture itself had been read, I do not think that I could have been accused of not knowing that the so-called child-labor amendment does not *require* federal regulation and prohibition of labor of all persons under eighteen years of age but merely *empowers* the federal government to regulate and prohibit if it sees fit. But I feel somewhat surprised that Professor Vandenbosch should think that anybody at all could be quite so ignorant as he thinks me at this point to be.

Of course, the so-called child-labor amendment does not require the exercise by Congress of the stupendous powers which it grants. That is clear. But how can any student of recent history possibly doubt that if those powers are granted, they will be exercised in very full measure? We have witnessed in the last few years the rapid growth of the vast federal bureaucracy.

"Voices in the Church" originally appeared in *The Banner* 70 (January 4, 1935) 5–7.

That is not a surmise but a simple fact. Whatever may be said of Congress, it cannot be said to have been backward in the use of powers granted to it. One thing is perfectly clear—if we do not want Congress to exercise certain powers, then we must not grant it the right to exercise those powers. The lesson of history is really too plain. We cannot possibly unlearn it.

Indeed, this whole notion that Congress may be trusted is contrary to the basic notion of the Constitution of the United States. The Constitution is essentially a system of checks and balances. It carefully guards each of the departments of the federal government from encroachments by the others; it carefully guards the states from encroachments by the federal government; and it carefully guards individual rights from encroachments by any government. Jealous distrust by governmental powers is at the heart and core of our institutions.

Those institutions were not an arbitrary invention of the framers of the Constitution, but were the culmination of a long and glorious history. Professor Vandenbosch seems to regard the defense of those institutions as being "reaction." I am compelled to disagree with him. I am compelled to call it progress, and I am compelled to regard the growing tendency in our day to disregard basic human rights in the interests of an all-powerful state as being at bottom nothing in the world but a reversion to savagery.

If someone accuses me at that point of being an alarmist, I would just bid such a one to open his eyes and look out upon the countries of the world today. Russia stands under the most crushing tyranny that history has ever seen. Italy and Germany are now under a régime which, despite all superficial differences, is essentially the same as the system that prevails in Russia. And then—at such a time, when all over the world these elemental forces of evil are mightily at work, these forces that have given us Stalin and Mussolini and Hitler—at such a time Professor Vandenbosch is telling us that Congress can be trusted. I am bound to say that a man would have to be blind not to see that the forces which in this country have given us our present vast bureaucracy, a bureaucracy to which yet vaster additions will be made if this so-called child-labor amendment is ratified, are exactly the same forces as those which have led to the destruction of all liberty in Russia and Italy and Germany.

Professor Vandenbosch designates as "sheer nonsense" the view that the proposed amendment confers upon Congress powers which no state in the union has ever possessed. I may just point out in passing that if this is sheer nonsense, it is sheer nonsense that is shared (for example) by a former Attorney General of the United States and by a great number of the ablest men in America. I have in my hands, for example, a formal "protest" which was issued by the American Constitutional League at the time when the child-labor amendment was first presented to the states. That protest is signed not only by George W. Wickersham, whom I have just mentioned, but by (for example) such men as Dr. Arthur T. Hadley, President Emeritus of Yale University, and by other distinguished persons in the most varied walks of life. In paragraph 2 of that protest it is said, in very plain language, that "the amendment will give to Congress a power which no state legislature now possesses." Thomas F. Cadwalader, Esq., a member of the Maryland bar, wrote in *The Woman Patriot* of March 1, 1925, as follows:

> The purpose of the Constitution was "to secure the blessings of liberty to ourselves, and our posterity." In pursuance of this purpose the Fifth Amendment provides that no person "shall be deprived of life, liberty or property without due process of law." The proposed Twentieth Amendment will in effect change this to read: "No person, except those under eighteen, shall be deprived of life, liberty or property without due process of law, and the judgment of parents as to the welfare of their children under eighteen shall not be construed to constitute a part of their liberty."

Professor Vandenbosch insists that the states now have the power to regulate child labor. So they have. But it is not merely that power which the proposed amendment gives to Congress. The proposed amendment gives to Congress the power to "limit, regulate and *prohibit* the labor of persons under eighteen years of age." No state now has the power to prohibit the labor of a youth of seventeen years of age. It seems rather strange that anyone who is severe upon his opponents as Professor Vandenbosch is severe upon me should not base his arguments upon a simple reading of the clause that is under discussion.

Apparently Professor Vandenbosch is concerned lest I, in the ignorance and guilelessness which he seems to attribute to ministers as a class, should be the dupe of "highly financed propaganda organizations out to discredit social and economic reforms." In reply, I desire to say that I am a member of a "propaganda" organization myself, having been for a number of years a member of the Executive Committee of the Sentinels of the Republic, but that I challenge anyone to show either that it is highly financed or that its purpose is anything other than a disinterestedly patriotic purpose. As for the other organizations to which Professor Vandenbosch alludes, I am bound to say that I am not impressed in the slightest with such vague and unfounded charges. It is very sad indeed when inculcation, not of some abstruse political doctrines, but of the most elementary principles of civil and religious liberty, should be regarded as being explainable only by some ulterior motive. Professor Vandenbosch may not be aware of it, but there are some real patriots left in this country—some men and women who are not ready to relinquish without a struggle those liberties which our fathers won at such cost and which are now being so generally trampled ruthlessly underfoot.

But then the argument from silence is used against me. I have not, in my address, it seems to be argued, said anything about the prevention of war; therefore, I am unqualified to speak on any other subject! In reply, let me say that I do not claim to be an expert on all subjects. It is just barely possible that there may be one or two subjects about which my knowledge may be slightly short of superhuman and about which my judgment may be slightly short of being completely definitive! Yet I do not quite see how ignorance or uncertainty about these subjects prevents me from giving expression to my opinions on other subjects if I think—still without any claim to any unusual wisdom or knowledge on my own part—that on those other subjects I have anything at all to say.

As a matter of fact, however, I have certain convictions even on this subject of war. First, I am opposed to war with all my heart and soul and mind. That should surely be a matter of course. Second, I am opposed to "pacifism," as that term is ordinarily understood. It involves logically the abandonment of all protection of helpless people from violence, and tends to produce the very evil that it is intended to check. Third, I am opposed to a government monopoly in the manufacture of arms. It would mean the reduction of our own citizenry to the position of serfs, and would also mean the unchecked tyranny of the strong over the weak in nonindustrial countries of the world. Fourth, I am opposed to conscription. It is supposed to prevent wars by bringing home the sacrifices of war to every citizen. As a matter of fact, it has exactly the opposite effect. The whole notion of the "nation in arms" has been one of the most disastrous notions that has ever entered the mind of man. So I think that all efforts of the American Legion and of others to make America quick on the trigger by setting up a scheme of conscription of wealth and manpower which shall operate automatically with a declaration of war ought to be opposed. The whole notion of putting into the hands of one man, the President, a button by the pressure of which he can beat down all opposition and confiscate the property and the lives of the citizens is dangerous in the extreme. It would be a mighty breeder of wars. The good motives of many of those who advocate it should not blind us to its disastrous effects.

But we may profitably return now from this digression to the point under discussion. I hope it may be remembered that the digression was due to Professor Vandenbosch, not to me.

I am opposed to the so-called child-labor amendment to the Constitution of the United States. Even if that amendment merely gave to the federal government powers which the states now possess—instead of conferring a vast power now possessed by no state—it would still be a most destructive and reactionary proposal. It would mean not really an amendment to the Constitution, but practically the destruction of the Constitution, since it would take the control of the 45,000,000 persons in the United States who are in the formative period of their lives away from the states and would place them under whatever bureaus the federal government would choose to set up. If that is done, the whole American idea in government is abandoned.

Some people seem to be perfectly willing to make this stupendous change. The American idea in government means nothing to them. To me it means a great deal; to me it seems to be profoundly rooted in fundamental principles of civil and religious liberty. I am not ready to see it abandoned without a struggle.

Does that mean that I favor the exploitation of children in industry? It means nothing of the kind. It only means that I am opposed to the turning over of children and youth to the tender mercies of centralized and despotic bureaus. If there ever was any kind of legislation that ought to be kept under state control and ought not to be handed over to a central federal authority, it is this matter of the regulation of the lives of children and youths. The contrary arguments, whatever their force, all sink into insignificance compared with the tragic evil of centralization and bureaucracy in this field.

Regulation of the labor of children, even by the states, is a much more delicate and difficult matter than is sometimes supposed. I do not think it can be accomplished through the thoughtless and emotional reiteration of a few stock phrases. In particular, I think we ought never to forget that while harmful child labor is a great evil, child idleness is perhaps almost a greater evil still.

I think there is a real danger lest we fall victim to that evil sometimes when we are trying to prevent the other. Just now this country is passing through a period of depression. Jobs are scarce; the right to work is being restricted in various ways. At such a time, what is more natural than that youths should be prevented from working in order that more work may be left to be divided among older persons?

But when that is done, one thing seems often to be forgotten. It is the moral welfare of the youths who are affected. Here is a youth of seventeen years of age, let us say. There is an aged mother and young brothers and sisters. Shall that youth be prevented from turning in to help out? Or here, let us say, is a farmer's son or a son of a man in some other kind of business. The son is seventeen years of age. His father is in difficulties. Shall the son be prevented from helping the father out in leisure time? If youths in such circumstances are prevented from acting on an impulse that every decent and generous youth ought to have, I hate to think of the kind of men that they are apt to turn out later on to be.

I am saying that not because I am trying now to discuss the details of child-labor legislation, but just to show that this matter is far too delicate to be turned over to remote and irresponsible bureaus. It is evidently a matter that should be kept under state, as distinguished from federal, control; and I wonder whether those who favor federal child-labor legislation have ever really contemplated the necessity that will then be found of duplicating state enforcement agencies with federal agencies all along the line. In general, one has the feeling that many of those who are becoming aroused against real or alleged child labor have never asked themselves with any very great seriousness whether the remedy that is being proposed is not even worse than the disease. Comparatively few of those who have fallen in with the agitation for the so-called child-labor amendment have ever even begun to think the thing through.

That is not the case, however, with the persons who are really the initiators of this whole movement. They have certainly thought the thing through; they have thought it clear through to the end, and the end is the destruction of our civilization and the establishment of collectivistic society.

It seems not to be denied that the person principally concerned with the drafting of this amendment was Mrs. Florence Kelley. Professor Vandenbosch objects to my reference to her radical activities. But when he backs up his objection merely by such general considerations as that "to many industrialists any person who is at all sympathetic with the laboring classes is a Marxist," that really will not do at all; the evidence with regard to Mrs. Kelley is really too definite and too plain to be brushed aside in any such fashion. I may be just as much an innocent dupe of "highly financed propaganda organizations" as Professor Vandenbosch thinks I am; but the fact remains that Mrs. Kelley did translate at least one book of Friedrich Engels, the associate of Marx; the fact remains that after she had been associated with Engels in Europe, she became the recipient of correspondence with him that shows him to have regarded her as an advocate of his program in America (see the *Congressional Record*, as below); the fact remains that she is designated, and no doubt rightly designated, by Lillian D. Wald in an article appearing in the March 1934 number of The *Atlantic Monthly* as "one of the first members of the Socialist Party in this country"; the fact remains that none of her subsequent activities seems to indicate any real recession from the essentials of her early position. If Professor Vandenbosch really desires to defend Mrs. Kelley, the thing that he needs to do is not to bring general strictures against the gullibility of ministers as a class, including the present writer, but to examine the mass of evidence regarding her which is contained in the *Congressional Record*, 69th Congress, First Session (Remarks of the Hon. Thomas F. Bayard on the Maternity and Infancy Act, transmitting the material presented by *The Woman Patriot*). Facts are not to be put out of the way by a few general criticisms of those who call attention to them.

In Mrs. Kelley's books intended for general American consumption, the true import of her propaganda may not always appear. Yet what shall be thought of passages like the following (from her book *Modern Industry in Relation to the Family, Health, Education, Morality*, 1914):

We suffer the disadvantage of living in a period when the morality of our great-grandparents is outgrown, and that of our grandchildren is not yet established. (p. 116)

The fundamental moral teaching that prevailed on this continent when the Republic was founded had its roots in the experience of an agricultural people—its precepts and maxims were in harmony with and adequate to the clear demands of responsibility and decency within the rural family"—and then Mrs. Kelley goes on to say that this "morality of agricultural individualism" "affords no adequate guidance in the intricate relations of our rapidly changing life. (p. 117)

Between that obsolete morality which remains embodied in our laws, and our human needs in modern daily life, the contradiction has become intolerable. (p. 117ff.)

Now I want to be fair to Mrs. Kelley. She is not in this book saying quite what one might suppose her to be saying when these quotations are taken out of their context. She is not here saying anything specifically about new ideas regarding marriage, for example; she is talking rather about industrial relations as they affect the family. She does even, in this book, intimate that the old commandment, "Thou shalt not kill," still is valid, and that it merely has new and wider implications in our modern life. All that is true. And yet the fact remains that "morality" is here treated as the product of human experience, and that the old morality of the agricultural family is regarded as out of date. Can Professor Vandenbosch blame us if we pause to ask where such principles lead? Whatever others may think about these quotations from Mrs. Kelley, I will tell the readers of *The Banner* plainly what I think about them. I think they are destructive of the very basis of human life. I confess frankly that I am very old-fashioned about this matter. I am old-fashioned enough to believe in the moral law. I believe that the "morality of our great-grandparents" was not rooted in the experience of "an agricultural people" or in any other human experience, but that it was and is rooted in the law of God.

What does Professor Vandenbosch think about this question? Does he agree with me? Does he, unlike Mrs. Kelley (in accordance with the plain implication of her words), believe in obligatory morality? If so, why does he play with fire? Why does one offend Christ's little ones by excusing a woman who regarded the morality of our great-grandparents as out of date and who gave every indication that she regarded all morality as being merely the product of human experience?

Perhaps it may be asked what relevance all this has for the question of the so-called child-labor amendment. Suppose it really is the case that some advocates of that amendment are seeking unworthy ends. Is it not also the case that some opponents of the amendment are seeking equally unworthy ends? Must not the proposed measure be judged on its own merits, irrespective of the purposes of those who are advocating or opposing it?

In reply, two things need to be said. In the first place, we are perfectly ready to judge the proposed amendment on its own merits, and when it is so judged we are convinced that it is condemned. In the second place, we think that there is a great difference between advocacy of a measure and the actual framing of it. We are not merely saying that this proposed amendment has been advocated by socialists, but that it was actually framed by a socialist, and that that socialist and some at least of her associates in framing it regarded it as an important step toward the destruction of our existing order of society.

Suppose this so-called child-labor amendment is ratified. What sort of persons will be in charge of the federal bureaus which will be established under the vast powers which the amendment will grant? A man has to be rather blind not to see that the same kind of persons will be in charge of those bureaus as the persons who were allowed the determinative influence in framing the amendment in the first place and as the persons who were placed, for example, in charge of the federal "Children's Bureau" when it was formed some years ago. If anyone doubts that, just let him read the evidence which is presented in the part of the *Congressional Record* cited above regarding the propaganda activities of the "Children's Bureau" (propaganda activities under the camouflage of fact-finding and of philanthropy). And if those activities were carried on even under the limitations of the present Constitution, what will be done when the federal bureaus are given the stupendous and tyrannical powers contemplated in the present proposed amendment, and when practical socialism in the United States has made the vast strides that it has undoubtedly made since 1912?

If you want your children and the most intimate affairs of your family life to be turned over to the tender mercies of persons whose views are like those of Mrs. Florence Kelley and like the persons who were put in charge of the Children's Bureau, then favor this so-called child-labor amendment; if, on the contrary, you want to preserve the decency of your home, then oppose this amendment with all your might and main. If your state has not already ratified it, try to prevent that disastrous step from being taken; if it has already ratified it, then seek to get that ratification withdrawn, as some constitutional lawyers think to be quite lawful.

If, however, I am right—as I certainly am—in holding that this proposed amendment would be a great stride towards socialism, perhaps it may be asked what is wrong with socialism from the Christian point of view. I shall try in closing just to say a word about that, and what I shall say will apply very largely, I think, to socialism of the "pink" as well as the "red" variety.

A flood of light is shed upon this question by the antipathy which modern socialists feel for "philanthropy," as when Mrs. Kelley, for example, speaks of "the new ideal of the democracy of the future: the ideal of service performed not as philanthropy, not as charity, not alone in the care of childhood and old age, but in a transformed industry, a universal service of men and women of tomorrow." That is a central point where the ethics of communism and socialism and collectivism in all its forms is obviously opposed to the ethics of the Lord Jesus Christ. Our Lord Jesus Christ says: "And whosoever shall give to drink unto one of these little ones a cup of cold water only in the name of a disciple, verily I say unto you, he shall in no wise lose his reward."

The communists and their more or less consistent allies are seeking to produce a condition of society where it shall no longer be necessary or desirable that anybody shall give a cup of cold water to anybody. It is a degrading thing, they hold, for one human being to be beholden to another; love and compassion and the tender care of the individual for another are becoming out of date.

Such a régime is commended to us because of its "security." Well, I do not think that it will really be secure at all. Tyranny often begins by being superficially beneficent; but it always ends by being both superficially and radically cruel. But one thing is perfectly clear—if that collectivistic régime does give security, the security which it will give is like the security now possessed in Russia, the security of fed beasts of burden in a stable. If this collectivistic régime does guarantee physical life—as in point of fact it does not—the life which it guarantees is certainly not worth living.

We can place this great issue before us if we just ask the question what ought to be said to a youth starting out in life—a youth, let us say, who has a position in some industrial establishment. What is the Christian thing to tell him? Is it Christian to tell him that "industrialists" are a band of robbers and that no Christian man can possibly "make good" in business? That seems to be just now the fashionable thing to tell him. Or shall we tell him to save a portion of his salary and to invest it wisely; shall we tell him to try to get out of the rut, to try, by qualities of industry and of initiative, so to commend himself to his employers that he may ultimately be taken into the firm and attain a position of great influence in the world?

I have no hesitation whatever about holding that this latter thing is what we ought to say. I am opposed to the subjection of all citizens to the hopeless treadmill of service in government offices, where initiative is regarded as a crime. I am opposed to that depreciation of love and charity and kindness between man and man which is the keynote of socialism or communism in its various forms. I am opposed to this notion that "making good" in business or getting out of the rut in any walk of life is a thing to be ashamed of. I hold that the entire tendency toward bureaucratic centralization, which appears in such an extreme form in the so-called child-labor amendment, means the abandonment of civilization and a return to barbarism.

Is that attitude of mind, which is the attitude of all real lovers of free institutions, a Christian attitude? I believe with all my heart and soul that it is. People talk glibly about taking the "profit motive" out of industry. I am dead opposed to people who talk in that way. I think the profit motive ought to be kept right in industry. Only—and this is the important thing—I think that that profit motive ought to be consecrated, as ought also every other human ambition, to the service of God. I hold, indeed, that it is a highly un-Christian thing to desire success in business for its own sake; but I hold that it is a truly Christian thing to desire it for the good that it enables a man to do. I hold that it is very wicked to desire success in order to enter into a round of selfish pleasures; but I hold also that it is very noble to desire it in order that one may serve one's fellow men and labor for the glory of God.

What, at bottom, is the difference between the ethics of socialism and the ethics of Christianity? In some ways the two look very much alike. Both are seeking to relieve creature distress; and both require men of wealth, at least under certain circumstances, to give up their wealth and become poor. But the socialist seeks to accomplish that by force, and the Christian seeks to accomplish it by love. There lies the profound difference. The socialist says to the man who possesses this world's goods: "We intend to compel you to distribute your wealth as we see fit: we should regard ourselves as degraded if we received it from you as a gift, but we intend to take it from you by force." The Christian, on the other hand, says to the man of wealth, or rather to the man who has any amount, large or small, of this world's goods: "The Lord loveth a cheerful giver; will you not have compassion upon those less fortunate than yourself; and will you not take any possible sting of degradation from the receivers of such a gift by letting your gift be prompted truly by love?" I think there is a deep-seated conflict between these two views of life; I do not think that that conflict between them can permanently be concealed.

35

STATEMENT ON THE
EIGHTEENTH AMENDMENT

Prior to the action of the Assembly of 1926, refusing immediate confirmation of my election to the chair of apologetics and Christian ethics, there was widespread comment on my vote against a motion in the Presbytery of New Brunswick placing the presbytery on record with regard to the Eighteenth Amendment and the Volstead Act. The matter was not mentioned on the floor of the Assembly, but there is, I think, not the slightest doubt that because of its influence upon many commissioners it contributed very largely to the refusal of the Assembly to ratify my election. At this point also, as with regard to certain other charges against me, it would have seemed to me fairer that a policy of full publicity should have been adopted. The ground upon which I stood was quite unassailable, in accordance with the constitution of the church, and whatever the result, it would have been better for the issue to be openly faced.

The resolution endorsing the Eighteenth Amendment or the Volstead Act was introduced in the Presbytery of New Brunswick at the very end of the meeting on April 13, 1926. The attendance, which had been large during the early part of the session, had dwindled until only a very few persons were present—my estimate would be ten or twelve, exclusive of the offi-

"Statement on the Eighteenth Amendment" was prepared in 1926 to explain the author's vote in the Presbytery of New Brunswick on a motion supporting the Eighteenth Amendment to the United States Constitution.

cers, though I believe someone else estimates the number at about five. Under these conditions, the resolution was put to a *viva voce* vote. I voted "No"; but I did not speak to the motion or in any way ask that my vote should be recorded. The moderator, the Rev. Peter K. Emmons, then turned to me personally and said, "Do you want your vote recorded?" I cannot remember the wording of my reply, but certainly I indicated that I did *not* want my vote recorded. I had no intention of concealing my vote; but neither had I any intention of obtruding it and thus introducing a new issue when other issues are engaging my full attention and should, I think, engage the full attention of the church.

It is a misrepresentation to say that by this vote I expressed any opinion on the merits of the Eighteenth Amendment or the Volstead Act—and still less on the general question of Prohibition. On the contrary, my vote was directed against a policy which places the church in its corporate capacity, as distinguished from the activities of its members, on record with regard to such political questions. And I also thought it improper for so small a group of men as were then in attendance to attempt to express the attitude of a court of the church with regard to such an important question. Hence, I voted "No" in a *viva voce* vote. But I did only that.

Such are the facts about my vote. I desire now to say one or two things about my attitude regarding the issues involved.

In the first place, no one has a greater horror of the evils of drunkenness than I or a greater detestation of any corrupt traffic which has sought to make profit out of this terrible sin. It is clearly the duty of the church to combat this evil.

With regard to the exact form, however, in which the power of civil government is to be used in this battle, there may be difference of opinion. Zeal for temperance, for example, would hardly justify an order that all drunkards should be summarily butchered. The end in that case would not justify the means. Some men hold that the Eighteenth Amendment and the Volstead Act are not a wise method of dealing with the problem of intemperance, and that indeed those measures, in the effort to accomplish moral good, are really causing moral harm. I am not expressing any opinion on this question now, and did not do so by my vote in the Presbytery of New Brunswick. But I do maintain that those who hold the view that I have just mentioned have a perfect right to their opinion, so far as the law of our church is concerned, and should not be coerced in any way by ecclesiastical authority. The church has a right to exercise discipline where authority for condemnation of an act can be found in Scripture, but it has no such right in other cases. And certainly Scripture authority cannot be found in the particular matter of the Eighteenth Amendment and the Volstead Act.

Moreover, the church, I hold, ought to refrain from entering, in its corporate capacity, into the political field. Chapter XXXI, Article iv, of the Confession of Faith reads as follows:

> Synods and councils are to handle or conclude nothing, but that which is ecclesiastical; and are not to intermeddle with civil affairs which concern the commonwealth, unless by way of humble petition in cases extraordinary; or by way of advice for satisfaction of conscience, if they be thereunto required by the civil magistrate.

This section, I think, establishes a very great principle which was violated by the Presbytery of New Brunswick. Hence I voted in the negative. In doing so I did not express any opinion on the question whether the action of the presbytery was contrary to the law of the church, though I think that it was (see *Digest*, Vol. I, 1922, pp. 56–64); but merely voted "No" in a *viva voce* vote on a motion which seemed to me unwise.

In making of itself, moreover, in so many instances primarily an agency of law enforcement, and thus engaging in the duties of the police, the church, I am constrained to think, is in danger of losing sight of its proper function, which is that of bringing to bear upon human souls the sweet and gracious influences of the gospel. Important indeed are the functions of the police, and members of the church, in their capacity as citizens, should aid by every proper means within their power in securing the discharge of those functions. But the duty of the church in its corporate capacity is of quite a different nature.

PART EIGHT

CHRISTIANITY AND CULTURE

36

CHRISTIANITY AND CULTURE

O ne of the greatest of the problems that have agitated the church is the problem of the relation between knowledge and piety, between culture and Christianity. This problem has appeared first of all in the presence of two tendencies in the church—the scientific or academic tendency, and what may be called the practical tendency. Some men have devoted themselves chiefly to the task of forming right conception as to Christianity and its foundations. To them no fact, however trivial, has appeared worthy of neglect; by them truth has been cherished for its own sake, without immediate reference to practical consequences. Some, on the other hand, have emphasized the essential simplicity of the gospel. The world is lying in misery, we ourselves are sinners, men are perishing in sin every day. The gospel is the sole means of escape; let us preach it to the world while yet we may. So desperate is the need that we have no time to engage in vain babblings or old wives' fables. While we are discussing the exact location of the churches of Galatia, men are perishing under the curse of the law; while we are settling the date of Jesus' birth, the world is doing without its Christmas message.

The representatives of both of these tendencies regard themselves as

"Christianity and Culture" is an address delivered at the opening of the fall semester at Princeton Seminary on September 20, 1912 and originally appeared in the *Princeton Theological Review* 11 (1913) 1–15. Reprinted in *What Is Christianity?* ed. Ned Bernard Stonehouse (Grand Rapids: Eerdmans, 1951).

Christians, but too often there is little brotherly feeling between them. The Christian of academic tastes accuses his brother of undue emotionalism, of shallow argumentation, of cheap methods of work. On the other hand, your practical man is ever loud in his denunciation of academic indifference to the dire needs of humanity. The scholar is represented either as a dangerous disseminator of doubt, or else as a man whose faith is a faith without works. A man who investigates human sin and the grace of God by the aid solely of dusty volumes, carefully secluded in a warm and comfortable study, without a thought of the men who are perishing in misery every day!

But if the problem appears thus in the presence of different tendencies in the church, it becomes yet far more insistent within the consciousness of the individual. If we are thoughtful, we must see that the desire to know and the desire to be saved are widely different. The scholar must apparently assume the attitude of an impartial observer—an attitude which seems absolutely impossible to the pious Christian laying hold upon Jesus as the only Savior from the load of sin. If these two activities—on the one hand the acquisition of knowledge, and on the other the exercise and inculcation of simple faith—are both to be given a place in our lives, the question of their proper relationship cannot be ignored.

The problem is made for us the more difficult of solution because we are unprepared for it. Our whole system of school and college education is so constituted as to keep religion and culture as far apart as possible and ignore the question of the relationship between them. On five or six days in the week, we were engaged in the acquisition of knowledge. From this activity the study of religion was banished. We studied natural science without considering its bearing or lack of bearing upon natural theology or upon revelation. We studied Greek without opening the New Testament. We studied history with careful avoidance of that greatest of historical movements which was ushered in by the preaching of Jesus. In philosophy, the vital importance of the study for religion could not entirely be concealed, but it was kept as far as possible in the background. On Sundays, on the other hand, we had religious instruction that called for little exercise of the intellect. Careful preparation for Sunday-school lessons as for lessons in mathematics or Latin was unknown. Religion seemed to be something that had to do only with the emotions and the will, leaving the intellect to secular studies. What wonder that after such training we came to regard reli-

CHRISTIANITY AND CULTURE

gion and culture as belonging to two entirely separate compartments of the soul, and their union as involving the destruction of both?

Upon entering the seminary, we are suddenly introduced to an entirely different procedure. Religion is suddenly removed from its seclusion; the same methods of study are applied to it as were formerly reserved for natural science and for history. We study the Bible no longer solely with the desire of moral and spiritual improvement, but also in order to know. Perhaps the first impression is one of infinite loss. The scientific spirit seems to be replacing simple faith, the mere apprehension of dead facts to be replacing the practice of principles. The difficulty is perhaps not so much that we are brought face to face with new doubts as to the truth of Christianity. Rather, it is the conflict of method, of spirit that troubles us. The scientific spirit seems to be incompatible with the old spirit of simple faith. In short, almost entirely unprepared, we are brought face to face with the problem of the relationship between knowledge and piety or, otherwise expressed, between culture and Christianity.

This problem may be settled in one of three ways. In the first place, Christianity may be subordinated to culture. That solution really, though to some extent unconsciously, is being favored by a very large and influential portion of the church today. For the elimination of the supernatural in Christianity—so tremendously common today—really makes Christianity merely natural. Christianity becomes a human product, a mere part of human culture. But as such it is something entirely different from the old Christianity that was based upon a direct revelation from God. Deprived thus of its note of authority, the gospel is no gospel any longer; it is a check for untold millions—but without the signature at the bottom. So in subordinating Christianity to culture we have really destroyed Christianity, and what continues to bear the old name is a counterfeit.

The second solution goes to the opposite extreme. In its effort to give religion a clear field, it seeks to destroy culture. This solution is better than the first. Instead of indulging in a shallow optimism or deification of humanity, it recognizes the profound evil of the world, and does not shrink from the most heroic remedy. The world is so evil that it cannot possibly produce the means for its own salvation. Salvation must be the gift of an entirely new life, coming directly from God. Therefore, it is argued, the culture of this world must be a matter at least of indifference to the Christian. Now in its extreme form this solution hardly requires refutation. If Christianity is really found to contradict that reason which is our only means of apprehending truth, then of course we must either modify or abandon Christianity. We cannot therefore be entirely independent of the achievements of the intellect. Furthermore, we cannot without inconsistency employ the printing press, the railroad, the telegraph in the propagation of our gospel, and at the same time denounce as evil those activities of the human mind that produced these things. And in the production of these things not merely practical inventive genius had a part, but also, back of that, the investigations of pure science animated simply by the desire to know. In its extreme form, therefore, involving the abandonment of all intellectual activity, this second solution would be adopted by none of us. But very many pious men in the church today are adopting this solution in essence and in spirit. They admit that the Christian must have a part in human culture. But they regard such activity as a necessary evil—a dangerous and unworthy task necessary to be gone through with under a stern sense of duty in order that thereby the higher ends of the gospel may be attained. Such men can never engage in the arts and sciences with anything like enthusiasm—such enthusiasm they would regard as disloyalty to the gospel. Such a position is really both illogical and unbiblical. God has given us certain powers of mind, and has implanted within us the ineradicable conviction that these powers were intended to be exercised. The Bible, too, contains poetry that exhibits no lack of enthusiasm, no lack of a keen appreciation of beauty. With this second solution of the problem we cannot rest content. Despite all we can do, the desire to know and the love of beauty cannot be entirely stifled, and we cannot permanently regard these desires as evil.

Are then Christianity and culture in a conflict that is to be settled only by the destruction of one or the other of the contending forces? A third solution, fortunately, is possible—namely, consecration. Instead of destroying the arts and sciences or being indifferent to them, let us cultivate them with all the enthusiasm of the veriest humanist, but at the same time consecrate them to the service of our God. Instead of stifling the pleasures afforded by the acquisition of knowledge or by the appreciation of what is beautiful, let us accept these pleasures as the gifts of a heavenly Father. Instead of obliterating the distinction between the kingdom and the world, or on the other hand withdrawing from the world into a sort of modernized intellectual monasticism, let us go forth joyfully, enthusiastically to make the world subject to God.

Certain obvious advantages are connected with such a solution of the problem. In the first place, a logical advantage. A man can believe only what he holds to be true. We are Christians because we hold Christianity to be true. But other men hold Christianity to be false. Who is right? That question can be settled only by an examination and comparison of the reasons adduced on both sides. It is true, one of the grounds for our belief is an inward experience that we cannot share—the great experience begun by conviction of sin and conversion and continued by communion with God—an experience which other men do not possess, and upon which, therefore, we cannot directly base an argument. But if our position is correct, we ought at least to be able to show the other man that *his* reasons *may* be inconclusive. And that involves careful study of both sides of the question. Furthermore, the field of Christianity is the world. The Christian cannot be satisfied so long as any human activity is either opposed to Christianity or out of all connection with Christianity. Christianity must pervade not merely all nations, but also all of human thought. The Christian, therefore, cannot be indifferent to any branch of earnest human endeavor. It must all be brought into *some* relation to the gospel. It must be studied either in order to be demonstrated as false, or else in order to be made useful in advancing the kingdom of God. The kingdom must be advanced not merely extensively, but also intensively. The church must seek to conquer not merely every man for Christ, but also the whole of man. We are accustomed to encourage ourselves in our discouragements by the thought of the time when every knee shall bow and every tongue confess that Jesus is Lord. No less inspiring is the other aspect of that same great consummation. That will also be a time when doubts have disappeared, when every contradiction has been removed, when all of science converges to one great conviction, when all of art is devoted to one great end, when all of human thinking is permeated by the refining, ennobling influence of Jesus, when every thought has been brought into subjection to the obedience of Christ.

If to some of our practical men these advantages of our solution of the problem seem to be intangible, we can point to the merely numerical advantage of intellectual and artistic activity within the church. We are all agreed that at least one great function of the church is the conversion of individual men. The missionary movement is the great religious movement of our day. Now it is perfectly true that men must be brought to Christ one by one. There are no labor-saving devices in evangelism. It is all handwork.

And yet it would be a great mistake to suppose that all men are equally well prepared to receive the gospel. It is true that the decisive thing is the regenerative power of God. That can overcome all lack of preparation, and the absence of that makes even the best preparation useless. But as a matter of fact, God usually exerts that power in connection with certain prior conditions of the human mind, and it should be ours to create, so far as we can, with the help of God, those favorable conditions for the reception of the gospel. False ideas are the greatest obstacles to the reception of the gospel. We may preach with all the fervor of a reformer and yet succeed only in winning a straggler here and there, if we permit the whole collective thought of the nation or of the world to be controlled by ideas which, by the resistless force of logic, prevent Christianity from being regarded as anything more than a harmless delusion. Under such circumstances, what God desires us to do is to destroy the obstacle at its root. Many would have the seminaries combat error by attacking it as it is taught by its popular exponents. Instead of that, they confuse their students with a lot of German names unknown outside the walls of the universities. That method of procedure is based simply upon a profound belief in the pervasiveness of ideas. What is today matter of academic speculation begins tomorrow to move armies and pull down empires. In that second stage, it has gone too far to be combated; the time to stop it was when it was still a matter of impassionate debate. So as Christians we should try to mold the thought of the world in such a way as to make the acceptance of Christianity something more than a logical absurdity. Thoughtful men are wondering why the students of our great Eastern universities no longer enter the ministry or display any very vital interest in Christianity. Various totally inadequate explanations are proposed, such as the increasing attractiveness of other professions—an absurd explanation, by the way, since other professions are becoming so overcrowded that a man can barely make a living in them. The real difficulty amounts to this—that the thought of the day, as it makes itself most strongly felt in the universities, but from them spreads inevitably to the masses of the people, is profoundly opposed to Christianity, or at least—what is nearly as bad—it is out of all connection with Christianity. The church is unable either to combat it or to assimilate it, because the church simply does not understand it. Under such circumstances, what more pressing duty than for those who have received the mighty experience of regeneration, who, therefore, do not, like the world, neglect that whole series of vitally relevant facts which is embraced in Christian experience—what more pressing duty than for these men to make themselves masters of the thought of the world in order to make it an instrument of truth instead of error? The church has no right to be so absorbed in helping the individual that she forgets the world.

There are two objections to our solution of the problem. If you bring culture and Christianity thus into close union—in the first place, will not Christianity destroy culture? Must not art and science be independent in order to flourish? We answer that it all depends upon the nature of their dependence. Subjection to any external authority or even to any human authority would be fatal to art and science. But subjection to God is entirely different. Dedication of human powers to God is found, as a matter of fact, not to destroy but to heighten them. God gave those powers. He understands them well enough not bunglingly to destroy his own gifts. In the second place, will not culture destroy Christianity? Is it not far easier to be an earnest Christian if you confine your attention to the Bible and do not risk being led astray by the thought of the world? We answer that of course it is *easier*. Shut yourself up in an intellectual monastery, do not disturb yourself with the thoughts of unregenerate men, and of course you will find it *easier* to be a Christian, just as it is easier to be a good soldier in comfortable winter quarters than it is on the field of battle. You save your own soul—but the Lord's enemies remain in possession of the field.

But by whom is this task of transforming the unwieldy, resisting mass of human thought until it becomes subservient to the gospel—by whom is this task to be accomplished? To some extent, no doubt, by professors in theological seminaries and universities. But the ordinary minister of the gospel cannot shirk his responsibility. It is a great mistake to suppose that investigation can successfully be carried on by a few specialists whose work is of interest to nobody but themselves. Many men of many minds are needed. What we need first of all, especially in our American churches, is a more general interest in the problems of theological science. Without that, the specialist is without the stimulating atmosphere which nerves him to do his work.

But no matter what his station in life, the scholar must be a regenerated man—he must yield to no one in the intensity and depth of his religious experience. We are well supplied in the world with excellent scholars who are without that qualification. They are doing useful work in detail, in biblical philology, in exegesis, in biblical theology, and in other branches of study. But they are not accomplishing the great task, they are not assimilating modern thought to Christianity, because they are without that experience of God's power in the soul which is of the essence of Christianity. They have only one side for the comparison. Modern thought they know, but Christianity is really foreign to them. It is just that great inward experience which it is the function of the true Christian scholar to bring into some sort of connection with the thought of the world.

During the last thirty years there has been a tremendous defection from the Christian church. It is evidenced even by things that lie on the surface—for example, by the decline in church attendance and in Sabbath observance and in the number of candidates for the ministry. Special explanations, it is true, are sometimes given for these discouraging tendencies. But why should we deceive ourselves, why comfort ourselves by palliative explanations? Let us face the facts. The falling off in church attendance, the neglect of Sabbath observance—these things are simply surface indications of a decline in the power of Christianity. Christianity is exerting a far less powerful direct influence in the civilized world today than it was exerting thirty years ago.

What is the cause of this tremendous defection? For my part, I have little hesitation in saying that it lies chiefly in the intellectual sphere. Men do not accept Christianity because they can no longer be convinced that Christianity is true. It may be useful, but is it true? Other explanations, of course, are given. The modern defection from the church is explained by the practical materialism of the age. Men are so much engrossed in making money that they have no time for spiritual things. That explanation has a certain range of validity. But its range is limited. It applies perhaps to the boomtowns of the West, where men are intoxicated by sudden possibilities of boundless wealth. But the defection from Christianity is far broader than that. It is felt in the settled countries of Europe even more strongly than in America. It is felt among the poor just as strongly as among the rich. Finally, it is felt most strongly of all in the universities, and that is only one indication more that the true cause of the defection is intellectual. To a very large extent, the students of our great Eastern universities—and still more the universities of Europe—are not Christians. And they are not Christians often just because they are students. The thought of the day, as it makes itself most strongly felt in the universities, is profoundly opposed to Christianity, or at least it is out of connection with Christianity. The chief obstacle to the Christian religion today lies in the sphere of the intellect.

That assertion must be guarded against two misconceptions. In the first place, I do not mean that most men reject Christianity consciously on account of intellectual difficulties. On the contrary, rejection of Christianity is due in the vast majority of cases simply to indifference. Only a few men have given the subject real attention. The vast majority of those who reject the gospel do so simply because they know nothing about it. But whence comes this indifference? It is due to the intellectual atmosphere in which men are living. The modern world is dominated by ideas which ignore the gospel. But it is out of all connection with it. It not only prevents the acceptance of Christianity. It prevents Christianity even from getting a hearing.

In the second place, I do not mean that the removal of intellectual objections will make a man a Christian. No conversion was ever wrought simply by argument. A change of heart is also necessary. And that can be wrought only by the immediate exercise of the power of God. But because intellectual labor is insufficient, it does not follow, as is so often assumed, that it is unnecessary. God may, it is true, overcome all intellectual obstacles by an immediate exercise of his regenerative power. Sometimes he does. But he does so very seldom. Usually he exerts his power in connection with certain conditions of the human mind. Usually he does not bring into the kingdom, entirely without preparation, those whose mind and fancy are completely dominated by ideas which make the acceptance of the gospel logically impossible.

Modern culture is a tremendous force. It affects all classes of society. It affects the ignorant as well as the learned. What is to be done about it? In the first place, the church may simply withdraw from the conflict. She may simply allow the mighty stream of modern thought to flow by unheeded and do her work merely in the back-eddies of the current. There are still some men in the world who have been unaffected by modern culture. They may still be won for Christ without intellectual labor. And they must be won. It is useful, it is necessary work. If the church is satisfied with that alone, let her give up the scientific education of her ministry. Let her assume the truth of her message and learn simply how it may be applied in detail to modern industrial and social conditions. Let her give up the laborious study of Greek and Hebrew. Let her abandon the scientific study of history to the men of the world. In a day of increased scientific interest, let the church go on becoming less scientific. In a day of increased specialization, of renewed interest in philology and in history, of more rigorous scientific method, let the church go on abandoning her Bible to her enemies. They will study it scientifically, rest assured, if the church does not. Let her substitute sociology altogether for Hebrew, practical expertness for the proof of her gospel. Let her shorten the preparation of her ministry; let her permit it to be interrupted yet more and more by premature practical activity. By doing so she will win a straggler here and there. But her winnings will be but temporary. The great current of modern culture will sooner or later engulf her puny eddy. God will save her somehow—out of the depths. But the labor of centuries will have been swept away. God grant that the church may not resign herself to that. God grant that she may face her problem squarely and bravely. That problem is not easy. It involves the very basis of her faith. Christianity is the proclamation of a historical fact—that Jesus Christ rose from the dead. Modern thought has no place for that proclamation. It prevents men even from listening to the message. Yet the culture of today cannot simply be rejected as a whole. It is not like the pagan culture of the first century. It is not wholly non-Christian. Much of it has been derived directly from the Bible. There are significant movements in it, going to waste, which might well be used for the defense of the gospel. The situation is complex. Easy wholesale measures are not in place. Discrimination, investigation is necessary. Some of modern thought must be refuted. The rest must be made subservient. But nothing in it can be ignored. He that is not with us is against us. Modern culture is a mighty force. It is either subservient to the gospel or else it is the deadliest enemy of the gospel. For making it subservient, religious emotion is not enough; intellectual labor is also necessary. And that labor is being neglected. The church has turned to easier tasks. And now she is reaping the fruits of her indolence. Now she must battle for her life.

The situation is desperate. It might discourage us. But not if we are truly Christians. Not if we are living in vital communion with the risen Lord. If we are really convinced of the truth of our message, then we can proclaim it before a world of enemies, then the very difficulty of our task, the very scarcity of our allies becomes an inspiration, then we can even rejoice that God did not place us in an easy age, but in a time of doubt and perplexity and battle. Then, too, we shall not be afraid to call forth other soldiers into the conflict. Instead of making our theological seminaries merely centers of

CHRISTIANITY AND CULTURE

religious emotion, we shall make them battlegrounds of the faith, where, helped a little by the experience of Christian teachers, men are taught to fight their own battle, where they come to appreciate the real strength of the adversary and in the hard school of intellectual struggle learn to substitute for the unthinking faith of childhood the profound convictions of full-grown men. Let us not fear in this loss of spiritual power. The church is perishing today through the lack of thinking, not through an excess of it. She is winning victories in the sphere of material betterment. Such victories are glorious. God save us from the heartless crime of disparaging them. They are relieving the misery of men. But if they stand alone, I fear they are but temporary. The things which are seen are temporal; the things which are not seen are eternal. What will become of philanthropy if God is lost? Beneath the surface of life lies a world of spirit. Philosophers have attempted to explore it. Christianity has revealed its wonders to the simple soul. There lie the springs of the church's power. But that spiritual realm cannot be entered without controversy. And now the church is shrinking from the conflict. Driven from the spiritual realm by the current of modern thought, she is consoling herself with things about which there is no dispute. If she favors better housing for the poor, she need fear no contradiction. She will need all her courage, she will have enemies enough, God knows. But they will not fight her with argument. The twentieth century, in theory, is agreed on social betterment. But sin, and death, and salvation, and life, and God— about these things there is debate. You can avoid the debate if you choose. You need only drift with the current. Preach every Sunday during your seminary course, devote the fag ends of your time to study and to thought, study about as you studied in college—and these questions will probably never trouble you. The great questions may easily be avoided. Many preachers are avoiding them. And many preachers are preaching to the air. The church is waiting for men of another type. Men to fight her battles and solve her problems. The hope of finding them is the one great inspiration of a seminary's life. They need not all be men of conspicuous attainments. But they must all be men of thought. They must fight hard against spiritual and intellectual indolence. Their thinking may be confined to narrow limits. But it must be their own. To them theology must be something more than a task. It must be a matter of inquiry. It must lead not to successful memorizing, but to genuine convictions.

The church is puzzled by the world's indifference. She is trying to overcome it by adapting her message to the fashions of the day. But if, instead, before the conflict, she would descend into the secret place of meditation, if by the clear light of the gospel she would seek an answer not merely to the questions of the hour but, first of all, to the eternal problems of the spiritual world, then perhaps, by God's grace, through his good Spirit, in his good time, she might issue forth once more with power, and an age of doubt might be followed by the dawn of an era of faith.

37

RELATIONS BETWEEN JEWS AND CHRISTIANS

The present gathering, as I understand it, is intended to promote a better relationship between Jews and Christians in America and particularly New York. I have been asked to consider the problem from the point of view of orthodox Christianity, and I regard it as a very high privilege, and also as a very great pleasure, to accede as best I can to the request.

In doing so I might choose either one of two possible methods of approach. In the first place, I might put my best foot forward; I might present first the positive side—I might tell you what I think can actually be done toward the solution of the problem. That method would seem at first sight to be desirable. But as a matter of fact it would be fraught with considerable danger. The concessions which it might seem to involve would almost certainly be misinterpreted and exaggerated, and when in the latter part of my remarks those misinterpretations would be corrected my hearers might have the feeling that they had been unfairly treated, that pleasant words had been used to cloak a really fundamental divergence of opinion.

The danger of misunderstanding always presents itself in discussions like

"Relations between Jews and Christians" is an address originally delivered on October 29, 1924 in New York City before a meeting of The Fellowship of Reconciliation. Reprinted in *What Is Christianity?* ed. Ned Bernard Stonehouse (Grand Rapids: Eerdmans, 1951).

411

that in which we are engaged tonight; the *suaviter in modo* sometimes obscures the *fortiter in re*. If you will pardon a personal example, I may say that last year I was invited to engage in a discussion at the Rutgers Presbyterian Church of this city with a leader of the Modernist point of view in the Protestant Episcopal church. A correspondent in one of our Presbyterian church papers drew rather far-reaching conclusions from the meeting. He was delighted with it, he said in effect; these two gentlemen did not call each other names; and thus it became evident that conservatives and Modernists in the church could stand on common ground after all. Now is that not absurd? The meeting between this man and myself was, I trust, a courteous one; but its courtesy did not at all obscure the fact that in my opinion he is a vigorous opponent of the Christian religion and that there is in the religious sphere absolutely no common ground between us. We are fellow citizens, and I trust that when we discuss serious questions we can be courteous to each other, but "brethren" in the religious sense we certainly are not.

The fact is that in discussing matters about which there are differences of opinion, it is really more courteous to be frank—more courteous with that deeper courtesy which is based upon the Golden Rule. For my part, I am bound to say that the kind of discussion which is irritating to me is the discussion which begins by begging the question and then pretends to be in the interests of peace. I should be guilty of such a method if I should say to a Roman Catholic, for example, that we can come together with him because forms and ceremonies like the mass and membership in a certain definite organization are, of course, matters of secondary importance—if I should say to him that he can go on being a good Catholic and I can go on being a good Protestant and yet we can unite on a common Christian basis. If I should talk in that way, I should show myself guilty of the crassest narrowness of mind, for I should be showing that I had never taken the slightest trouble to understand the Roman Catholic point of view. If I had taken that trouble, I should have come to see plainly that what I should be doing is not to seek common ground between the Roman Catholic and myself but simply to ask the Roman Catholic to become a Protestant and give up everything that he holds most dear.

It is a similar begging of the question when the Modernist preachers represent themselves as speaking in the interests of peace. "Let us," they say in effect, "recognize the right both of conservatives and of Liberals in the church; let us not allow doctrinal differences to separate us, for doctrine,

CHRISTIANITY AND CULTURE

after all, is simply the necessarily changing expression of Christian experience, and various doctrines will find their unity if they can only be translated back into the experience from which they came." The man who speaks in that way is, it seems to me, guilty of a really astonishing narrowness of mind. For he has simply begged the whole question, and has shown that he has never given himself any trouble to understand the other man's point of view. Of course, if doctrine is merely the necessarily changing expression of experience, then the whole debate is ended; but it is ended not by a compromise but a complete victory for the Modernist and a complete relinquishment by us of everything that we hold most dear.

The very center and core of our faith is the conviction that instead of doctrine springing from life, life springs from doctrine; that doctrine is not the necessarily changing expression of experience—that seems to us to be simply the most abysmal skepticism—but, on the contrary, the setting forth of those facts upon which experience is based—facts which are facts now, which are facts not only for us but for whatever demons there may be in hell, and which will remain facts beyond the end of time. It is not necessarily narrow-minded to combat that view of ours. It is, I think, wrong; but it is not necessarily narrow-minded. But what is narrow-minded is to combat that view and then represent oneself as speaking, not in defense of one's own opposing view, but in the interest of peace. For that simply shows that one has not given oneself the trouble to understand one's opponent's point of view.

So to my mind the most inauspicious beginning for any discussion is found when the speaker utters the familiar words: "I think, brethren, that we are all agreed about this . . ."—and then proceeds to trample ruthlessly upon the things that are dearest to my heart. Far more kindly is it if the speaker says at the start that he sees a miserable narrow-minded conservative in the audience whose views he intends to ridicule and refute. After such a speaker gets through, perhaps I may be allowed to say that I regard him as just as narrow-minded as he regards me, and then having both spoken our full mind we may part, certainly not as brothers (it is ridiculous to degrade that word) but at least as friends.

Accordingly, I am going to put what may seem to be my *worst* foot forward, and speak first of those things about which agreement with a part of you at least cannot possibly be attained. It is better to speak of those things first in order that the conditions of the problem may be known at the start.

In the first place, then, let me say that Christianity as we hold it begins with the most thoroughgoing pessimism that could possibly be imagined. I was almost amused a short time ago in reading in the *Atlantic Monthly* an article by Dr. Gordon of the Old South Church in Boston which held that, although many things formerly connected with Christianity have been given up, we are still Christians because we hold an optimistic view of the future of the human race. As a matter of fact, not optimism but the deepest pessimism is the starting point of Christianity. It is paganism which finds hope in the development of the resources of man, whereas Christianity is the religion of the broken heart. Paganism finds popular expression in sermons like a recent one of Dr. Fosdick, the burden of which was that a central article of our creed should be the clause "I believe in man." In one sense, indeed, Christians "believe in man." They believe in the reality of man's soul, as over against the materialistic psychology of our day. But that belief in the reality of the soul leads of itself not to hope but to the greater despair; it is a terrible belief; it means that the soul of man is capable of falling into depths which otherwise could not be conceived. A stick or stone cannot be "lost" in the Christian sense, but the soul of man, just because it exists, can be lost and is lost indeed. How terrible a thing is the true Christian belief in the soul of man! How totally different at any rate from the pagan optimism which masquerades under the name of Christianity today! "I believe in man"—that is paganism. "Strait is the gate and narrow the way that leadeth unto life, and few there be that find it"; "There is none righteous, no, not one"; "All sinned and came short of the glory of God"—that is Christianity.

There are some phenomena of the present day which seem to support this Christian doctrine of sin and guilt. There was a time a few years ago when to the superficial observer all might have seemed to be going well. But now our complacency has been destroyed and we are facing elemental depths. I am not referring merely to the war or to the orgy of vindictive cruelty which has followed upon the alleged "peace" of Versailles. But I am referring rather to the appalling intellectual as well as moral decadence which was going on before the war began and which is enormously hastened today. When one contemplates the decadence of our age, the lamentable growth of ignorance, the breakdown of education, the absence of great men, the silence of true poetry, one ceases to be much impressed with the corresponding advance in the material realm. We have improved the means of

CHRISTIANITY AND CULTURE

communication, but in doing so we have ceased to have anything to say. We have the radio, but what is broadcast through it is rather pitiable stuff. Strange indeed is the complacency of such an age.

But the true grounds for holding the Christian doctrine of sin are far deeper than all that—they lie in the terrible law revealed in the Bible and most terribly of all in Jesus, and they lie in the confirmation of that law in the depths of our own souls. A man who has never been under the conviction of sin—not the sins of other people but his own sin—can never even begin to understand what the Christian man feels. At the very basis of Christianity is the cry "Woe is me" and woe to a lost and sinful world.

But that is not the end of Christianity but its beginning. For the darkness has been lightened by a radiance of divine light. It has been lightened by the coming of our Lord. Nineteen hundred years ago, the Christian holds, a strong Savior came from the outside into this sinful world and led mankind out from Egyptian bondage into a land of freedom and hope. It was done not by a discovery but by an act; not by an influence brought to bear upon man, but by a change in the relationship between man and God. We were under God's just wrath and curse; the Lord Jesus took upon himself the curse and set us free. But how pitiful are my words! I despair of letting you see how we Christians *feel*, how we hang with all our hearts upon just the thing that other men despise, how we abhor any subjectivizing of the work of Christ, how we depend above all just upon the fact that Christ has done not merely something *in* us but something *for* us when he died for us upon the cross and made all well between us and the holy God. What a mystery it is—and how simple to the man who believes!

It is that sheer objectivity of our salvation, that sheer factual basis of our religion, which the Modernist preachers cannot understand, and because they cannot understand wound us yet more and more by every reference that they make to the cross of Christ. Christianity, we hold, is rooted not in something that was discovered, but in something that *happened* when the Lord Jesus died for our sins and rose again for our justification.

The narration of that happening constitutes the "gospel," the good news, which puts a new face on life. Without it the world is dark, and particularly dark is the awful God whom Jesus bade men to fear. But when the gospel comes into a man's heart, then for him, despite the blackness of his former despair, there is naught but light—light and yet more glorious light. Can you not put yourselves for a moment into our place? Can you not understand how inexpressibly grieved and hurt we are when a preacher not out-side but within our church pours out the vials of his scorn upon this thing to which we cling with all the energy of our souls?

But however the sheer factual basis of our religion may be misunderstood now, it was not misunderstood in the first days. At the center of early Chris-tianity were the words "Christ died for our sins according to the Scriptures, he was buried, he rose again the third day according to the Scriptures." That was the gospel, "the good news." And when it was heard, and was accepted and received in faith, then there was life. Without it, all was lost in the blackness of sin; with it, when it was received by faith and used by the re-generating power of the Spirit, all was shouting and joy for time and for eternity.

Such was Christianity then and such is Christianity, we hold, now. But then as now it was offensive to the world. The offense was found not at all in the fact that a new Savior was offered to the attention of men. Then as now the world was looking for new saviors and welcomed them when they came. But the offense came because this Savior was offered as the one and only Savior. Without him every single man, no matter what his relative goodness, and no matter what his achievements and what his pride, was represented as lost forever under the wrath of God. With him alone, the early Christians held, there was life. The offense of Christianity was found in the universality and exclusiveness of its appeal. Without that exclusive-ness, the Christians would have been honored by the Roman world; be-cause of it, and because of it alone, they suffered and died.

Similar is the case today. The offense of Christianity is still found in the universality and exclusiveness of its appeal. Christians would be welcomed, no doubt, as the benefactors of the race if they would only acquiesce in the proposal of "Nathan der Weise"—if they would only allow Judaism, Mo-hammedanism, and Christianity to live peacefully side by side, each con-tributing its necessary quota to the welfare of humanity. But be perfectly clear about one thing—Christianity, if it ever accedes to such a program, has ceased to be Christian at all.

Here no doubt, you will say, is the chief obstacle which orthodox Chris-tianity (or as we would say, all Christianity that is really Christian) opposes to the purposes aimed at by your group. And we do not think that the ob-stacle can be dodged. The plain fact is that we Christians regard all of you who are not Christians as lost under the guilt of sin. And since we regard you thus, what do you expect us to do? Do you expect us to promise that we will avoid proselytizing? Do you not see that such a promise would involve, from our point of view, the most awful bloodguiltiness of which a man could ever possibly be guilty? Do you not see that holding the view that we hold—a view that is at the very root of the Christian religion—we cannot possibly avoid proselytizing, but must say, "Woe is me, no matter in whose presence I am, if I preach not the gospel"? Do you not see that, holding the view which we hold, we should, if we ceased to proselytize among you, be not kind and considerate but guilty of the most heartless neglect that could possibly be conceived?

No, it is perfectly clear, I think, that "Nathan der Weise" cannot help us at all tonight. Our religion makes an absolutely universal appeal, and it refuses to stop short at the bounds of the people that we regard as the chosen people of God, from whom all our joy and all our salvation came. We look for real unity only when you as well as we have been saved by the one Savior of all.

But meanwhile, what can be done? Can we respect each other even without such a consummation which you indeed expect never to come? Can we help each other in certain of the affairs of life? I think that we can.

First, we can help each other in the promotion of tolerance. But what do we mean by tolerance, and what do we mean by intolerance? We mean almost exactly the reverse of what often seems to be meant by these terms today. Thus, it is often held that the Presbyterian church is guilty of intolerance if it excludes a heretical minister. To me, on the other hand, the real intolerance seems to be found in those who would deny the right of the church to exclude him. Let us look at the thing in its simplest terms. Here is a group of people who believe that the greatest thing in the world is to proclaim a way of salvation, a system of "doctrine," if you will, that is summarized in the Westminster Confession. For mutual help they come together in a body called the Presbyterian church. The real question is whether they are to be allowed to do so. No doubt the purpose of their organization, which is set forth as plain as day in their constitution, seems to be very foolish to many. It seems so very foolish that they can hardly grant such a foolish organization the right to exist. So to prevent its existence they regard themselves as justified in doing what they would never do in any other sphere of life: they regard themselves as justified in making the necessary subscription with a mental reservation which completely reverses its meaning, in order that the character of the organization may then, when they have entered into it, be changed. Is that tolerance? Surely not. Surely it is, on the contrary, intolerance of the crassest kind. It is intolerance because it is based upon the denial of that right of voluntary association which is at the very basis of liberty. A creedal church seems foolish to the Modernist preachers, but if they are really tolerant they will recognize its right in a free country to exist and to maintain its existence by insisting that its accredited representatives shall not combat its fundamental purpose from within. We who insist upon honesty in creed-subscription are really insisting not merely upon honesty but also upon the central principles of freedom.

But such right of voluntary association—voluntary association even for purposes which to other persons seem foolish and absurd—is possible only where there is tolerance on the part of the state. There is a fundamental distinction between an involuntary organization like the state, an organization to which a man must belong whether he will or no, and a purely voluntary organization like the church. It is absolutely no interference with liberty for the church to insist upon one type of teaching on the part of its accredited representatives who are speaking not merely with their own authority but with the authority of the church. For if a man does not agree with that type of teaching, he can seek another platform in which he can really speak his full mind. How absurd it is, then, to say that the Presbyterian church, for example, is trying to "silence" certain men! Surely it is doing nothing of the kind. Surely it is merely seeking to avoid the dishonesty of allowing a creedal church to carry on a propaganda which is the very opposite of that for which the church exists. I suppose I have an old-fashioned view of the moral law, but I am bound to say that I do not think that plain honesty of speech ought to stop at the church door.

But entirely different is an involuntary association like the state. For the state to force any one type of teaching upon its citizens, or upon the children of its citizens, is the crassest tyranny. Within the state there should be tolerance, or liberty is at an end.

Tolerance, moreover, means not merely tolerance for that with which we are agreed but also tolerance for that to which we are most thoroughly opposed. A few years ago there was passed in New York the abominable Lusk Law requiring private teachers in any subjects whatever to obtain a state license. It was aimed, I believe, at the socialists, and primarily at the Rand School in New York City. Now certainly I have no sympathy with so-

CHRISTIANITY AND CULTURE

cialism. Because of its hostility to freedom, it seems to me to be just about the darkest thought that has ever entered the mind of man. But certainly such opposition to socialism did not temper in the slightest degree my opposition to that preposterous law. Tolerance, to me, does not mean merely tolerance for what I hold to be good, but also tolerance for what I hold to be abominably bad.

The attack upon tolerance in America is appearing most clearly in the sphere of education. The Oregon school law, it is true, with its provision that children should be taken by brute force from their parents and delivered over to the tender mercies of whatever superintendent of education happens to be in power in the district where they reside, will probably be declared unconstitutional by the Supreme Court. And the Nebraska language law, which made literary education a crime, was thrown out by the same tribunal. But the same ends may well be accomplished by indirect means, and if the Sterling–Reed Bill is passed by Congress, we shall have sooner or later that uniformity of education under the control of the state which is the worst calamity into which any nation can fall.

Against such tyranny, I do cherish some hope that Jews and Christians, Roman Catholics and Protestants, if they are lovers of liberty, may present a united front. I am for my part an inveterate propagandist; but the same right of propaganda which I desire for myself I want to see also in the possession of others. What absurdities are uttered in the name of a pseudo-Americanism today! People object to the Roman Catholics, for example, because they engage in "propaganda." But why should they not engage in propaganda? And how should we have any respect for them if, holding the view which they do hold—that outside of the Roman church there is no salvation—they did not engage in propaganda first, last, and all the time? Clearly they have a right to do so, and clearly we have a right to do the same.

But in insisting upon the right of unlimited proselytizing, we hope that we shall not throw all discretion to the winds. Certainly in trying to convert other people we do not mean that we are ourselves setting up to be better than they. On the contrary, we are doing exactly the opposite. It is just because we are so conscious of our own unworthiness that we are unable to satisfy ourselves with the skeptical view that Christianity is a life and not a doctrine. It is just because we are not able to stand upon the basis of our lives before God—or, to use a figure proper to the present moment, upon our "record"—that we cling to the gospel of Christ and try to bring to others the joy that that has brought to us.

Does that mean, then, that we must eternally bite and devour one another, that acrimonious debate must never for a moment be allowed to cease? We do not think that it does. But how can it help doing so? We Christians think that you—as we should be ourselves—are lost and hopeless without Christ. How then shall we live with you in peace and avoid making ourselves insufferable by constant arguments and appeals?

There is a common solution of the problem which we think ought to be taken to heart. It is the solution provided by family life. In countless families, there is a Christian parent who with untold agony of soul has seen the barrier of religious difference set up between himself or herself and a beloved child. Salvation, it is believed with all the heart, comes only through Christ, and the child, it is believed, unless it has really trusted in Christ, is lost. These, I tell you, are the real tragedies of life. And how trifling, in comparison, is the experience of bereavement of the like! But what do these sorrowing parents do? Do they make themselves uselessly a nuisance to their child? In countless cases they do not; in countless such cases there is hardly a mention of the subject of religion; in countless cases there is nothing but prayer, and an agony of soul bravely covered by helpfulness and cheer.

There is the solution of the problem presented by the inveterately proselytizing tendency of Christianity. It is a solution which, I admit, in the larger sphere about which we are talking tonight, is only very, very imperfectly tried. But if it were tried, it would work. The problem is very difficult. But love would find a way.

38

THE CHRISTIAN AND HUMAN RELATIONSHIPS

"For I long to see you, that I may impart unto you some spiritual gift, to the end ye may be established; That is, that I may be comforted together with you by the mutual faith both of you and me."   *(Rom. 1:11–12)*

Into the communion of the early church were called not many wise according to the flesh, not many mighty, not many noble; yet it is a great mistake to suppose on that account that the early church was characterized by anything like vulgarity. In almost every country, and at almost every time, there are among the uneducated classes individuals who, by a native fineness of perception and delicacy of feeling, fully atone for the lack of the acquired refinements of culture and education. Especially was this the case with the class of the poor in the land of Israel at the time of Christ, to which many of the early disciples of Jesus belonged. True, into those humble circles had not penetrated to any great extent the philosophy or learning of Greece, yet those peasants were possessed of an exquisite delicacy of thought and feeling which, through its poetical expression in the hymns of

"The Christian and Human Relationships" was originally delivered to students at Princeton Seminary sometime in 1915. Reprinted in *What Is Christianity?* ed. Ned Bernard Stonehouse (Grand Rapids: Eerdmans, 1951).

421

the first chapter of Luke, has been the wonder of the civilized world. Similar is the conclusion from the New Testament writings in general. It is true that the language is for the most part not the approved language of literature, even of a degenerate stage of the Greek tongue, but is rather the language of daily life; yet after all, language is primarily valuable merely as the expression of thought, and behind the plainness of the mere outward dress, we can clearly discern not merely a greatness of spiritual truth but also an exquisite fineness of mold in the form in which that truth is conceived and presented. We are not really following out the practice of the New Testament if we imagine that any form of expression will do, if only real spiritual truth lies back of it. A study of the New Testament should make us rather more cautious in taking up new religious phrases than are many of our modern religious teachers. To receive spiritual truth, faith alone is sufficient, but to give that truth adequate expression, to mold a religious phraseology, one must also have good taste. With that gift, as well as with other still greater ones, the New Testament writers were richly endowed.

Take Paul, for example. It is rather remarkable that the man who so powerfully emphasized the absolute transcendence of the Christian life, so that he could say that there can be neither bond nor free, no male and female, for ye are all one man in Christ Jesus—it is rather remarkable that this same Paul, who more than any other emphasizes the absolute independence of the Christian of earthly conditions, should yet show himself to be such an accurate student of human relationships. Paul does not address a king in the same way that he addresses one who is his equal in station—though he regards him as just as much a sinner in the sight of God. He does not, according to Acts, address the philosophers of Athens in the same way as the Jews of Pisidian Antioch. He does not write to Christians whom he had never seen in quite the same tone as his own spiritual children. There is the same gospel for all; all human distinctions are subordinate and secondary; and yet these human distinctions are carefully to be observed. Paul was a man of tremendous spiritual power, but he was also a man of admirable tact.

As an example of this, take the verses which I have just read. Paul says, "For I long to see you, that I may impart unto you some spiritual gift, to the end ye may be established." With that an ordinary man might well have been content. Paul was in a position to impart spiritual good to others; he felt himself to be the recipient of revelation from God. Yet he seems to detect a possible objection, for he half-corrects himself: "that is, that I may be

422   CHRISTIANITY AND CULTURE

comforted together with you by the mutual faith both of you and me." A coarser nature would have seen no reason to make the correction, but Paul had that ability to put himself in the other man's place which is the essence of true courtesy. He wished to remove all possibility that his hearers might feel hurt in supposing that Paul meant to regard them as men who could receive only and had no power to give. He gives his readers full credit for all that could by any possibility be theirs; it is a charming bit of fine discernment and delicate courtesy.

But like all true courtesy, it is based not on hypocrisy but on truth. It results simply from the clear discernment and generous recognition of conditions that really exist. When Paul says that he hopes to receive spiritual benefit from his association with them, he shows that he was really capable of friendship with other men; and wonderfully does his whole life bear this out. So we have two sides to the life of Paul: a supreme devotion to Christ and the things of the other world in which all outward conditions are held to be comparatively valueless; and a delicate tact in the various relationships of this life, in union with a wonderful intensity in affections for other men. How are the two things to be reconciled? We have here brought before us the great question of the position of Christianity with regard to human relationships.

In the history of the church, three answers to the question have been given.

In the first place (our order is not the order of time), there is the worldly tendency in the church. Christians find themselves living in a world where their social needs seem, after all, to be pretty well satisfied. Their time is so much taken up with their human friends that their Savior is thrust into a secondary place. Usually, this process has been unconscious merely—men have gradually without knowing it drifted away from their first enthusiasm. But today we see this worldly tendency openly defended by professing Christians. Men say, Yes, Christianity is good, but it must be kept in its proper place; it must not be allowed to interfere with those natural relations between man and man which have been ordained by God himself. Religion occupies merely one part of our nature; it should not be neglected just as the physical and the intellectual sides of our nature should not be neglected; but (this is really implied, at least) it should not be allowed to encroach on those other spheres. Who has not heard Y. M. C. A. speeches that amount to little more than that? And then, it is said, of course, we should send missionaries to foreign lands, but we should caution them to be very careful not to create trouble. If they find that the preaching and the acceptance of the gospel begins to go too much below the surface, so as to break up ancient customs or families, or worst of all to affect the healthy development of commerce—then by all means let them desist. Religion is thus degraded to a mere part of our life or to a mere means to an end.

It scarcely requires argument to show that this conception of the position of Christianity with regard to human relations is sharply opposed to the teaching of him who said, If any man cometh after me and hateth not his own father, and mother, and wife, and children, and brethren, and sisters, yea and his own life also, he cannot be my disciple; of him who represented the beginning of the Christian life, not as the development of any one side of our nature, but as a new birth, as a new beginning for the entire life.

Not less harmful in its effects, though possessing more of fundamental Christian truth, is the second answer to our question—namely, the answer of ascetics of various degrees of strictness. Since the relation to Christ is the supreme relation in which we stand, therefore we should seek to give it free room by lopping off all other affections. We should seek to avoid not only love of self, but also love for our friends. The latter stands higher than the former, but even it must make way for the supreme devotion to Christ. Natural affections, not only under special conditions but of necessity in themselves, are regarded as entangling alliances with the world. Now in the Presbyterian church we do not seem to be much troubled with asceticism; the error seems at first sight to lie all in the opposite extreme. Yet I am not sure but that some ministers do not in principle err in this way also. I do not refer to exaggerated opposition to certain forms of pleasure, but to a negative attitude toward human relationships. I know some preachers who are very good men, and very devoted to Christ, who seem somehow to let their Christianity make them cold and dead to all the movings of friendship. They do not outwardly lead the lives of hermits; on the contrary, their greatest joy is to be serving Christ by preaching his Word. Yet somehow there is an impenetrable barrier between them and other men. You always have the feeling that whenever they speak to you it is out of a stern sense of duty, in order that they may do you some good. They have no spontaneous affection for individual men—all men are to them alike, for all alike simply form a field for preaching. The consequence is their sermons always

CHRISTIANITY AND CULTURE

sound as though they were coming out of a phonograph. In order to prevent your words from being sounding brass or tinkling cymbal, two kinds of love are necessary—love to God and love to your hearers. It will not do to let your hearers say, Yes, the preacher loves Christ devotedly, but he cares not one cent for me.

It is pretty evident, as a matter of homiletics and pastoral theology, then, that there is something wrong with this second answer to our question. Nor does our New Testament desert us here; for we have, for instance, the example of Paul. Paul saw as clearly as anyone the truth which the ascetics emphasize—he is very clear with regard to the absolute independence of the Christian life of all earthly relationships, and the absolute supremacy of the place which Christ holds as over against all earthly affections—and yet, somehow, he avoids admirably the error which seems to lie so near. For so far is he from living a calm sort of life away from the world, in a kind of cold isolation, that it is hard to find in all history any man of intenser affection than he. The affection which he feels for his spiritual children is not something that he has to force upon himself as a Christian duty, but springs spontaneously right out of the depths of a warm heart. Nor is his affection confined to Christians alone. Read, for example, the touching expression of his patriotism in Romans 9: "For I could wish that myself were accursed from Christ for my brethren, my kinsmen according to the flesh." Paul was no stranger to natural affection—his becoming a Christian did not make him any the less a man.

In opposing the ascetic answer to our question, we can claim not only the testimony of experience, but the example of an apostle and the authority of Scripture. We have, therefore, concluded (1) that natural affections are not to be allowed to choke our affection for Christ and (2) that neither are they to be rooted out. This brings us to the third and correct solution of the problem. Human relationships are not to be broken off, but they are to be consecrated. They are to be regarded as one of the means which God has given us for serving him. They therefore should not only not be neglected, but should be furthered in every possible way. Far from seeking to isolate ourselves from our friends, we should seek, by every means in our power, to strengthen the bonds which unite us with them, for thus shall we be better enabled to serve Christ.

The difficulty of reconciling human relations with absolute devotion to Christ disappears the minute we see that the two things lie in different spheres. Of course, if our devotion to Christ is not different in kind from our feelings for our friends, then in a certain sense it comes into competition with them, but in that case, it is not really a religious feeling. It may be a very ennobling sentiment, but it is not truly religious. When we become Christians, the true statement of the case is not that we substitute for our human affections the love of Christ, but rather that we set Christ up in a place in our lives which has really been vacant, whether we were aware of it or not—the place which can be filled only by God. If we tear out of our heart our natural affections, we are not, except under certain conditions, making room for Christ, but we are simply making ourselves less efficient servants of his. Love for Christ and love for our fellow men are different in kind and need not under healthy conditions come into competition. It is possible for one to be developed to the highest extent without affecting the other.

True, it is not always easy to carry on this work of consecration—it requires the help and guidance of the Spirit of God. Very often it seems simpler and easier and safer to break off absolutely all connection with the world; and sometimes God uses a great sorrow in order, by depriving the Christian of human solace, to cast him back more completely upon Christ. But for us to withdraw ourselves from the world is usually to usurp the disciplinary function which is the prerogative of God alone. It is a lesser sin of the same kind as suicide.

Undoubtedly the hardest kind of worldly relation to consecrate to the service of Christ is a relation with one who is not a Christian. Suppose I have a friend who is an out-and-out opponent of the Christian faith who yet is very dear to me and from whom I have received a great deal of moral aid. Does it not seem as though the help which I receive from such a man and the joy I have in his friendship must of necessity weaken the feeling of absolute devotion to Christ? It seems so until you bethink yourself who Christ is. Christ is God, and God has created the world and all the men in it. It was he who endowed my friend with those noble qualities which have been such a help to me on the pathway of life; what I owe to my friend I owe also to my God, and to him I can give thanks.

And if we Christians should break off relations with our non-Christian friends, or if we should put between us and them a hidden wall—what hope would there be that the world would ever be brought to Christ? If we have Christ's cause at heart, we ought to rejoice that the bonds that bind us to other men are ever so strong and enter ever so deeply into the depths of the heart. For it is through the instrumentality of these real bonds of friendship that God will draw them into his fold. Without such friendship, any persuasion that we may attempt will usually be mere empty words.

But far easier is the course of affairs when our friends are Christians, and far more important. Christian fellowship is not only an aid to Christian service; it is a necessity for Christian life. It is not only a necessity for the weak, for even the great Paul, the strongest of Christians, felt the need to strengthen his faith by communion with his weaker brethren. There is none so strong that he does not need help from his fellows; there is none so weak that he may not help the strongest. No wonder that the church is a divine institution; it satisfies a universal need.

If any one of us has ever known what it is to be helped on upon the path of life by an older and stronger Christian, if he knows by experience that calm pardon of the worst sin, that unselfish sympathy, that desire to help, by which the true disciple reveals the great Master—if any one of us has had that experience, he will never be inclined to undervalue the church. For the activities of the church are manifold: she performs her office not merely by public services but by all kinds of intercourse between Christians, and for the formation of these we have special opportunities at the seminary.

Now I know perfectly well that friendships cannot be made to order—it is far too subtle a thing for that; it has its roots too deep down in the human soul. All that we can do is to remove obstacles that may stand in its way.

The first of such obstacles—and one that stands in the way not only of intimate friendship but also of all Christian intercourse—is intolerance. I am not speaking so much of intolerance for different views on questions of theology—though where there is a real religious devotion to Christ, the Son of God and the Savior of the world, tolerance is certainly a virtue— but rather of intolerance for different ways of giving expression to the common Christian faith. One man can give day and hour of his conversion, and loves to have the name of Jesus always on his lips; to another, Christian experience seems a deep and holy mystery, which must not be breathed except to sympathetic ears. One can conceive of no Christian activity other than that of preaching the gospel, and regards as part of the wisdom of this world which is foolishness with God the researches of the Christian scholar; another is filled with a deep longing for knowledge as to the way things actually happened in the time of Christ and the apostles, and is inclined to look rather askance upon the more emotional temperament of the evangelists. To one, Christianity seems a thing that is diametrically opposed to the arts; another loves to give his faith poetical expression, to bring it into some kind of connection with literature. This diversity will be a stumbling block until we remember Paul's words about diversity of gifts but the same Spirit. We must learn to thank God that he did not make all men alike—especially that he did not make all men like us. Let us do our own work, in the special sphere and in the special way for which our gifts may fit us; but let us not disparage the work of that other man of entirely different habits of thought. Christ came to save not only the ignorant man but the scholar; not only the scholar but the ignorant man. Let us thank God that he raises up various instruments to accomplish his infinitely various work.

The second obstacle to Christian friendship is that old enemy selfishness. It takes some time to help the other man, as well as perform our own work; and we are often so much engrossed in our own affairs that we are unwilling to go out of our way. We have our eyes so steadily fixed upon some great work of our own that we are to do in the future that we do not step aside to help in work for which we shall get no credit.

But I really believe the greatest obstacle in the way of our receiving the greatest benefit from our association with our brother Christians is not selfishness but pride. Selfishness makes us unwilling to give aid; pride makes us unwilling to receive it. We all love to think of ourselves as standing firm on our own feet, without leaning upon anyone but Christ. Let us remember the words of Paul—"That is, that I may be comforted together with you by the mutual faith both of you and me."

39

MOUNTAINS AND
WHY WE LOVE THEM

What right have I to speak about mountain climbing? The answer is very simple. I have none whatever. I have, indeed, been in the Alps four times. The first time I got up Monte Rosa, the second highest of the Alps, and one or two others of the easier Zermatt peaks. On my second visit I had some glorious days in the Grossglockner group and on a few summits in the Zillerthal Alps and also made my first visit to that beautiful liberty-loving land of South Tirol, where, as a result of a war fought to "make the world safe for democracy," Mussolini is now engaged in the systematic destruction of a language and civilization that has set its mark upon the very face of the landscape for many centuries. On my third visit, in 1913, I did my most ambitious climbing, all in the Eastern Alps, getting up the Kleine Zinne by the north face, certain of the sporty Cortina courses, and also the Campanile di Val Montanaia, which is not considered altogether easy. In 1932 I was on three of the first-class Zermatt peaks.

Why, then, have I no right to talk about mountain climbing? For the simple reason that I did all of these climbs with good guides, safeguarded by

"Mountains and Why We Love Them" is a paper originally delivered on November 27, 1933 before a body of Philadelphia clergy and published in *Christianity Today* 5 (August 1934) 66–69. Reprinted in *What Is Christianity?* ed. Ned Bernard Stonehouse (Grand Rapids: Eerdmans, 1951).

perfectly good Alpine ropes. An Alpine guide is said to be able to get a sack of meal up the Matterhorn about as well as he can get some tourists up; and then those tourists go home and boast what great mountaineers they are. Well, I differed from the proverbial sack of meal in two particulars: (1) I am a little superior to the sack of meal in climbing ability; (2) the sack of meal is unaware of the fact that it is not a mountaineer, and I am fully aware of the fact that I am not. The man who leads on the rope is the man who has to be a real mountaineer, and I never did that. I am less than the least of the thousands of real climbers who go to the Alps every summer and climb without guides.

But although I am not a mountaineer, I do love the mountains and I have loved them ever since I can remember anything at all. It is about the love of the mountains, rather than about the mountains, that I am venturing to read this little paper today.

Can the love of the mountains be conveyed to those who have it not? I am not sure. Perhaps if a man is not born with that love, it is almost as hopeless to try to bring it to him as it would be to explain what color is to a blind man or to try to make President Roosevelt understand the Constitution of the United States. But on the whole I do believe that the love of the mountains can at least be cultivated, and if I can do anything whatever toward getting you to cultivate it, the purpose of this little paper will be amply attained.

One thing is clear—if you are to learn to love the mountains, you must go up them by your own power. There is more thrill in the smallest hill in Fairmount Park if you walk up it than there is in the grandest mountain on earth if you go up it in an automobile. There is one curious thing about means of locomotion—the slower and simpler and the closer to nature they are, the more real thrill they give. I have got far more enjoyment out of my two feet than I did out of my bicycle; and I got more enjoyment out of my bicycle than I ever have got out of my motor car; and as for airplanes—well, all I can say is that I wouldn't lower myself by going up in one of the stupid, noisy things! The only way to have the slightest inkling of what a mountain is is to walk or climb up it.

Now I want you to feel something of what I feel when I am with the mountains that I love. To that end I am not going to ask you to go with me to any out-of-the-way place, but I am just going to take you to one of the most familiar tourist's objectives, one of the places to which one goes on every ordinary European tour—namely, to Zermatt—and in Zermatt I am not going to take you on any really difficult climbs but merely up one or two of the peaks by the ordinary routes which modern mountaineers despise. I want you to look at Zermatt for a few minutes not with the eyes of a tourist, and not with the eyes of a devotee of mountaineering in its ultra-modern aspects, but with the eyes of a man who, whatever his limitations, does truly love the mountains.

In Zermatt, after I arrived on July 15, 1932, I secured Alois Graven as my guide; and on a number of the more ambitious expeditions I had also Gottfried Perren, who also is a guide of the first class. What Ty Cobb was on a baseball diamond and Bill Tilden is on the courts, that such men are on a steep snow or ice slope, or negotiating a difficult rock, *Ueberhang*. It is a joy, as I have done in Switzerland and in the Eastern Alps, to see really good climbers at work.

At this point I just want to say a word for Swiss and Austrian guides. Justice is not done to them, in my judgment, in many of the books on climbing. You see, it is not they who write the books. They rank as professionals, and the tourists who hire them as "gentlemen"; but in many cases I am inclined to think that the truer gentleman is the guide. I am quite sure that that was the case when I went with Alois Graven.

In addition to climbing practice on the wrong side of the cocky little Riffelhorn and on the ridge of the Untergabelhorn—which climbing practice prevented me from buttoning my back collar button without agony for a week—and in addition to an interesting glacier expedition around the back side of the Breithorn and up Pollux (13,430 feet) and Caster (13,850) and down by the Fellikjoch through the ice fall of the Zwillingsgletscher, on which expedition I made my first acquaintance with really bad weather in the high Alps and the curious optical illusions which it causes—it was perfectly amazing to see the way in which near the summit of Caster the leading guide would feel with his ice-axe for the edge of the ridge in what I could have sworn to be a perfectly innocent expanse of easy snowfield right there in plain view before our feet, and it was also perfectly amazing to see the way in which little pieces of ice on the glacier were rolled by way of experimentation down what looked like perfectly innocent slopes, to see whether they would simply disappear in crevasses which I could have sworn not to be there (if they disappeared, we didn't because we took the hint and chose some other way through the labyrinth)—after these various preliminary expeditions and despite the agony of a deep sore on my right foot in view of which the Swiss doctor whom I consulted told me that as a physician he would tell me to quit but that as a man he knew I would not do so and that therefore he would patch me up as well as possible, and despite the even greater agony of a strained stomach muscle which I got when I extricated myself and was extricated one day from a miniature crevasse and which made me, the following night in the Theodul hut, feel as helpless as a turtle laid on its back, so that getting out of my bunk became a difficult mountaineering feat—after these preliminary expeditions and despite these and other agonies due to a man's giving a fifty-year-old body twenty-year-old treatment, I got up three first-class Zermatt peaks: the Zinalrothorn, the Matterhorn, and the Dent Blanche. Of these three, I have not time—or rather, you have not time (for I for my part should just love to go on talking about the mountains for hours, and Niagara would have nothing on me for running on)—I say, of these *you* have not time for me to tell about more than one. It is very hard for me to choose among the three. The Zinalrothorn, I think, is the most varied and interesting as a climb; the Dent Blanche has always had the reputation of being the most difficult of all the Zermatt peaks, and it is a glorious mountain indeed, a mountain that does not intrude its splendors upon the mob but keeps them for those who will penetrate into the vastnesses or will mount to the heights whence true nobility appears in its real proportions. I should love to tell you of that crowning day of my month at Zermatt, when after leaving the Schönbühl Hut at about 2:30 A.M. (after a disappointment the previous night when my guides had assisted in a rescue expedition that took one injured climber and the body of one who was killed in an accident on the Zmutt Ridge of the Matterhorn, opposite the hut where we were staying, down to Zermatt so that we all arrived there about 2 A.M., about the time when it had been planned that we should leave the hut for our climb) we made our way by lantern light up into the strange upper recesses of the Schönbühl Glacier, then by the dawning light of day across the glacier, across the bottom of a couloir safe in the morning but not a place where one lingers when the warmth of afternoon has affected the hanging glacier two thousand feet above, then to the top of the Wandfluh, the great south ridge, at first broad and easy but contracting above to its serrated knife-edge form, then around the "great gendarme" and around or over the others of the rock towers on the ridge, until at last that glorious and unbelievable moment came when the last few

CHRISTIANITY AND CULTURE

feet of the sharp snow ridge could be seen with nothing above but a vacancy of blue, and when I became conscious of the fact that I was actually standing on the summit of the Dent Blanche.

But the Matterhorn is a symbol as well as a mountain, and so I am going to spend the few minutes that remain in telling you about that.

There is a curious thing when you first see the Matterhorn on a fresh arrival at Zermatt. You think your memory has preserved for you an adequate picture of what it is like. But you see that you were wrong. The reality is far more unbelievable than any memory of it can be. A man who sees the Matterhorn standing at that amazing angle above the Zermatt street can believe that such a thing exists only when he keeps his eyes actually fastened upon it.

When I arrived on July 15, 1932, the great mountain had not yet been ascended that summer. The masses of fresh snow were too great; the weather had not been right. That is one way in which this mountain retains its dignity even in the evil days upon which it has fallen when duffers such as I can stand upon its summit. In storm, it can be almost as perilous as ever even to those who follow the despised easiest route.

It was that despised easiest route, of course, which I followed—though my guide led me to have hopes of doing the Zmutt ridge before I got through. On Monday, August 1st, we went up to the "Belvedere," the tiny little hotel (if you can call it such) that stands right next to the old Matterhorn Hut at 10,700 feet. We went up there intending to ascend the Matterhorn the next day. But alas for human hopes. Nobody ascended the Matterhorn the next day, nor the day after that, nor that whole week. On Wednesday we with several other parties went a little way, but high wind and cold and snow soon drove us back. The Matterhorn may be sadly tamed, but you cannot play with it when the weather is not right. That applies to experts as well as to novices like me. I waited at the Belvedere all that week until Friday. It is not the most comfortable of summer resorts, and I really think that the stay that I made in it was one of the longest that any guest had ever made. Its little cubbyholes of rooms are admirable as Frigidaires, but as living quarters they are "not so hot." People came and people went; very polyglot was the conversation; but I remained. I told them that I was the hermit or the *Einsiedler* of the Belvedere. At last, however, even I gave it up. On Friday I returned to Zermatt, in plenty of time for the Saturday night bath!

The next Monday we toiled again up that five thousand feet to the

Belvedere, and this time all went well. On Tuesday, August 9th, I stood on what I suppose is, next to Mt. Everest, the most famous mountain in the world.

From the Belvedere to the summit is about four thousand feet. The Matterhorn differs from every other great Alpine peak that I know anything about in that when you ascend it by the usual route you do not once set foot on a glacier. You climb near the northeast ridge—for the most part not on the actual ridge itself but on the east face near the ridge. In some places in the lower part there is some danger from falling stones, especially if other parties are climbing above. There is scarcely anything that the blasé modern mountaineer calls rock climbing of even respectable difficulty, but it is practically all rock climbing or clambering of a sort, and it seems quite interesting enough to the novice. The most precipitous part is above what is called "the shoulder," and it was from near this part that the four members of Whymper's party fell 4,000 feet to their death when they were descending after the first ascent in 1865. There are now fixed ropes at places in this part. You grasp the hanging rope with one hand and find the holds in the rock with the other. It took me five hours and forty minutes to make the ascent from the Belvedere. It would certainly have been no great achievement for an athlete; but I am not an athlete and never was one, and I was then fifty-one years of age and have an elevator in the building where I live. The rarefied air affected me more than it used to do in my earlier years, and the mountain is about 14,700 feet high. I shall never forget those last few breathless steps when I realized that only a few feet of easy snow separated me from the summit of the Matterhorn. When I stood there at last—the place where more than any other place on earth I had hoped all my life that I might stand—I was afraid I was going to break down and weep for joy.

The summit looks the part. It is not indeed a peak, as you would think it was from looking at the pictures which are taken from Zermatt, but a ridge—a ridge with the so-called Italian summit at one end and the so-called Swiss summit three feet higher at the other. Yes, it is a ridge. But what a ridge! On the south you look directly over the stupendous precipice of the south face to the green fields of Valtournanche. On the north you look down an immensely steep snow slope—with a vacancy beyond that is even more impressive than an actual view over the great north precipice would be. As for the distant prospect, I shall not try to describe it, for the simple reason that it is indescribable. Southward you look out over the mysterious infinity of the Italian plain with the snows of Monte Viso one hundred miles away. To the west, the great snow dome of Mont Blanc stands over a jumble of snow peaks, and it looks the monarch that it is. To the north the near peaks of the Weisshorn and the Dent Blanche, and on the horizon beyond the Rhone Valley a marvelous glittering galaxy of the Jungfrau and the Finsteraarhorn and the other mountains of the Bernese Oberland. To the east, between the Strahlhorn and Monte Rosa, the snows of the Weisshorn are like a great sheet let down from heaven, exceedingly white and glistering, so as no fuller on earth can white them; and beyond, fold on fold, soft in the dim distance, the ranges of the Eastern Alps.

Then there is something else about that view from the Matterhorn. I felt it partly at least as I stood there, and I wonder whether you can feel it with me. It is this. You are standing there not in any ordinary country, but in the very midst of Europe, looking out from its very center. Germany just beyond where you can see to the northeast, Italy to the south, France beyond those snows of Mont Blanc. There, in that glorious round spread out before you, that land of Europe, humanity has put forth its best. There it has struggled; there it has fallen; there it has looked upward to God. The history of the race seems to pass before you in an instant of time concentrated in that fairest of all the lands of earth. You think of the great men whose memories you love, the men who have struggled there in those countries below you, who have struggled for light and freedom, struggled for beauty, struggled above all for God's Word. And then you think of the present and its decadence and its slavery, and you desire to weep. It is a pathetic thing to contemplate the history of mankind.

I know that there are people who tell us contemptuously that always there are croakers who look always to the past, croakers who think that the good old times are the best. But I for my part refuse to acquiesce in this relativism which refuses to take stock of the times in which we are living. It does seem to me that there can never be any true advance, and above all there can never be any true prayer, unless a man does pause occasionally, as on some mountain vantage ground, to try, at least, to evaluate the age in which he is living. And when I do that, I cannot for the life of me see how any man with even the slightest knowledge of history can help recognizing the fact that we are living in a time of sad decadence—a decadence only thinly disguised by the material achievements of our age, which already are beginning to pall on us like a new toy. When Mussolini makes war deliberately and openly upon democracy and freedom, and is much admired for doing so even in countries like ours; when an ignorant ruffian is dictator of Germany, until recently the most highly educated country in the world— when we contemplate these things, I do not see how we can possibly help seeing that something is radically wrong. Just read the latest utterances of our own General Johnson, his cheap and vulgar abuse of a recent appointee of our President, the cheap tirades in which he develops his view that economics are bunk—and then compare that kind of thing with the state papers of Jefferson or a Washington—and you will inevitably come to the conclusion that we are living in a time when decadence has set in on a gigantic scale.

What will be the end of that European civilization, of which I had a survey from my mountain vantage ground—of the European civilization and its daughter in America? What does the future hold in store? Will Luther prove to have lived in vain? Will all the dreams of liberty issue into some vast industrial machine? Will even nature be reduced to standard, as in our country the sweetness of the woods and hills is being destroyed, as I have seen them destroyed in Maine, by the uniformities and artificialities and officialdom of our national parks? Will the so-called child-labor amendment and other similar measures be adopted, to the destruction of all the decencies and privacies of the home? Will some dreadful second law of thermodynamics apply in the spiritual as in the material realm? Will all things in church and state be reduced to one dead level, coming at last to an equilibrium in which all liberty and all high aspirations will be gone? Will that be the end of all humanity's hopes? I can see no escape from that conclusion in the signs of the times: too inexorable seems to me to be the march of events. No, I can see only one alternative. The alternative is that there is a God—a God who in his own good time will bring forward great men again to do his will, great men to resist the tyranny of experts and lead humanity out again into the realms of light and freedom, great men, above all, who will be the messengers of his grace. There is, far above any earthly mountain peak of vision, a God high and lifted up who, though he is infinitely exalted, yet cares for his children among men.

What have I from my visits to the mountains, not only from those in the Alps, but also, for example, from that delightful twenty-four-mile walk which I took one day last summer in the White Mountains over the whole Twin mountain range? The answer is that I have memories. Memory, in some respects, is a very terrible thing. Who has not experienced how, after we have forgotten some recent hurt in the hours of sleep, the memory of it comes back to us on our awaking as though it were some dreadful physical blow. Happy is the man who can in such moments repeat the words of the psalmist and who in doing so regards them not merely as the words of the psalmist but as the Word of God. But memory is also given us for our comfort; and so in hours of darkness and discouragement I love to think of that sharp summit ridge of the Matterhorn piercing the blue or the majesty and the beauty of that world spread out at my feet when I stood on the summit of the Dent Blanche.

40

THE BENEFITS OF WALKING

Having the great joy of three weeks of climbing in the Canadian Rockies, I am writing this little article to see whether I cannot help even those readers who cannot climb and cannot go to the Canadian Rockies to get some of the benefits which I am getting here.

Climbing mountains is good, in the first place for the body, and in the second place for the soul.

It is good for the body because of the wholesome buffeting of the body which it brings. To get such buffeting, the "tired American businessman" is wont, I believe, to place himself under the despotic control of some ex-prizefighter until he comes out of the ex-prizefighter's (very expensive) establishment feeling fit. There are, I suppose, cruel and unusual punchings of the bag and pulling of the chest weights most severe. I shudder when I think of it. Such drudgery will people submit to in order to harden their bodies and make them a little better able to undertake the duties of life. I admire people who thus recognize the fact that a soft body will not do hard work.

But there are even better ways of hardening the body, and one of these is to learn to climb. Let that tired businessman get a good Swiss guide, like the one that I have here; let him be initiated into the mysteries of rock

"The Benefits of Walking" originally appeared in the *Presbyterian Guardian* 2 (1936) 190. Reprinted in *What Is Christianity?* ed. Ned Bernard Stonehouse (Grand Rapids: Eerdmans, 1951).

climbing, and he will find that his softness of body will soon disappear. What a thoroughgoing twisting and pulling and bumping the body gets, at every conceivable angle and in every conceivable way, on a rock climb even of moderate difficulty! It is glorious exercise indeed.

Now I know that it is only a few people who can climb. Climbing without expert guides, unless one is oneself a real expert, is highly dangerous; and there are now, I believe, only four mountaineering guides in all of Canada. Since the Canadian Pacific Railway speaks of western Canada as "fifty Switzerlands in one," that makes just about one guide for every dozen Switzerlands—hardly enough to go around!

But the point that I am making is that many of the same benefits as those that are obtained in climbing may be obtained also without climbing and without the expense of guides. They may be secured through that cheapest and simplest of all forms of exercise—the exercise of walking.

I can testify to that from personal experience, for I have been a walker all my life. I do not, indeed, underestimate those comparatively rare occasions when I have been able to climb. They would hardly have justified the expense involved in them if they had brought to me merely the pleasure of the moment, but as a matter of fact when the climbs have been over, the benefit of them has just begun. During a period of nineteen years, when I did no climbing at all, how I used to live over again in memory those glorious days in the Eastern Alps in 1913! How eagerly did I read countless descriptions, in books and Alpine journals, of precipitous mountains of South Tirol! Then in 1932 and 1935 came the crowning joy of standing on the great Zermatt peaks. When I get discouraged I love to think of that unbelievable half hour when, after having climbed the Matterhorn by the Zmutt Ridge, we sat on the Italian summit, with our feet over Italy and our backs to a little wall of summit snow, and let our eyes drink in the marvelous beauty of the scene. What a wonderful help it is in all discouragements, what a blessed gift of God, to be able to bring before the mind's eye such a vision as that.

But do you know, my friends, a man can have very much that same joy in much simpler ways.

The more I see of the high mountains, the more I love the simple beauty of the woods and hills, and the more I love to walk.

What a very simple amusement walking is! You do not need any elaborate equipment; you just "up and do it" any time you like.

But perhaps you say that as a matter of fact you do *not* like it. All right, I say; but will you not learn to like it?

There are many things that man does not like at first, and yet that he comes to like. A man says, for example, that he cannot see anything at all in golf. It seems to him a very silly game. But then a friend persuades him one day to go out and have a try. He has "beginner's luck." He manages just once to hit the ball instead of the earth. To his amazement he watches that ball go. How amazingly far that little pellet will sail when you happen to hit it right! Well, the man understands the fascination at last. He plays golf and talks golf all the rest of his life. He is a hopeless victim of the well-known "hoof and mouth disease."

So when you say you do not love to walk, I do wish I could just get you to try. I do wish I could persuade you to use the old Ford this summer just to get to the edge of the woods. If you did choose that kind of a holiday, it would not cost you much, shoe-leather being much cheaper than gasoline and rubber tires. And the wholesome exercise you would get, and the close contact with the beauties of nature, would be a wonderful thing "as well for the body as the soul."

PART NINE

REVIEWS

41

REVIEW OF SPEER'S
SOME LIVING ISSUES

T he author of *Some Living Issues* has been for many years one of the most distinguished missionary leaders in the world. As a secretary of the Board of Foreign Missions of the Presbyterian Church in the U.S.A., he has wielded an influence that extends far beyond the bounds of any one church or any one country, but rather is in the truest sense worldwide.

This worldwide influence has been due not merely to administrative experience and to a wide acquaintance with the mission fields, but also, and primarily, to spiritual gifts of a high order. Dr. Robert E. Speer is a truly eloquent man. Though quiet and restrained in the manner of his public address, he yet exerts an extraordinary power over his hearers. What sympathetic hearer does not fall under his spell? For nearly forty years Dr. Speer has been a real leader of men.

It cannot be an event without importance when such a leader, at a time of uncertainty and transition in the church, publishes a book which sets forth in something like comprehensive form his position with regard to the issues of the day. Such a book is the one now under review. The book is not, indeed, intended to be comprehensive; it is in part made up of addresses de-

"Review of Robert E. Speer's *Some Living Issues*" originally appeared as "Dr. Machen Surveys Dr. Speer's New Book," *Christianity Today* 1 (October 1930) 9–11, 15.

livered at various times, and it deals with somewhat disconnected subjects. Yet when it is taken as a whole, it does serve to indicate fairly well the general trend of the teaching of its distinguished author.

With that general trend we find ourselves, if we may speak plainly and briefly, in disagreement. There are, indeed, many things in the book with which we heartily agree. We do not mean the general declaration on page 136 that the author "accepts the whole of Christianity as set forth in the New Testament," and that he accepts the doctrine of the Westminster Confession as to the Bible. Such general declarations are constantly being interpreted in so many diverse ways at the present time that in themselves they mean almost nothing. But, as will appear in what we shall say presently, there are many points at which our agreement becomes far more specific.

Nevertheless, when the book is taken as a whole, our general attitude toward it is one not of agreement but of disagreement. The disagreement is due to the fact that Dr. Robert E. Speer shows himself in this book to be, as indeed he has with increasing clearness become, a representative of that tendency in the church which seeks to mediate and obscure an issue about which we think that a man must definitely take sides.

That issue is the issue between Christianity as set forth in the Bible and in the great creeds of the church and a nondoctrinal or indifferentist Modernism that is represented in the Presbyterian Church in the U.S.A. by the "Auburn Affirmation" and that is really more or less dominant in most of the large Protestant churches of the world.

With regard to that issue, three positions are possible and are actually being taken today. In the first place, one may stand unreservedly for the old faith and unreservedly against the indifferentist tendency in the modern church; in the second place, one may stand unreservedly for Modernism and against the old faith; and in the third place, one may ignore the seriousness of the issue and seek, without bringing it to a head, to preserve the undisturbed control of the present organization in the church. It is this last attitude that is represented by the book now under review. Dr. Robert E. Speer certainly presents himself not as a Modernist but as an adherent of the historic Christian faith; yet he takes no clear stand in the great issue of the day, but rather adopts an attitude of reassurance and palliation, according high praise and apparently far-reaching agreement to men of very destructive views.

It is this palliative or reassuring attitude which, we are almost inclined to think, constitutes the most serious menace to the life of the church today; it is in some ways doing more harm than clear-sighted Modernism can do. The representatives of it are often much further from the faith than they themselves know, and they are leading others much further away than they have been led themselves. Obviously, such a tendency in the church deserves very careful attention from thoughtful men.

But when it is considered, fairness demands that it should be considered not in its poorest, but in its best, representatives. That is our justification for occupying so much space with the present review. Dr. Robert E. Speer is perhaps the most distinguished and eloquent popular representative of what is commonly called the "middle-of-the-road" or pacifist position with regard to the great religious issue of the day. As such, he is certainly worthy of a careful hearing by those who differ from him in the church.

The first chapter of the book deals with "The Place of Christ in the World Today." That chapter begins well. Dr. Speer refers with evident condemnation to the common view that Jesus had a religion which was "the religion of Jesus" and not "a religion about Jesus that made Him its object and elevated Him to the place of God to be regarded and worshipped as God," a religion about Jesus which "was the doing of His disciples in later years." Surely, we may be inclined to say, a book that states the issue so well on its first page and evidently rejects the prevailing nonredemptive view of Christianity will be a book that evangelical Christians can heartily commend.

But we are not left very long in this state of favorable anticipation. On the very next page, we find Dr. Speer actually appealing to the late A. von Harnack of Berlin in support of "the historic judgment of the Church" regarding Jesus' "character and significance." Now we share to the full Dr. Speer's admiration of Harnack's intellectual ability. We will not, indeed, call him, as Dr. Speer does, not only the ablest but the "most authoritative" of the critics; for we do not think that any critic is "authoritative," the plain man having an inalienable right to make up his own mind regarding the credentials of the New Testament books. But certainly Harnack was an exceedingly able scholar. Who would not admire such prodigious learning, such limpid clearness of expression, such earnestness in the search for truth? Yet, after all, Harnack, with all his extraordinary gifts, was a representative of just that view of Christianity as "the religion of Jesus," just that view that regards as later accretions the whole redemptive content of Christianity, which Dr. Speer has apparently rejected. What possible comfort can the evangelical Christian obtain from being told that Harnack regarded the gospels as being essentially true? The plain fact is that Harnack removed from the pages of history those things in the gospels that are dear to the Christian's heart—namely, their whole supernatural and redemptive content. Yet we are told by Dr. Speer that the Christian need not fear New Testament criticism because Harnack, "the ablest and most authoritative of all the critics," has assured us that New Testament criticism has resulted in a confirmation of the plain man's reading of some, at least, of the New Testament books!

Does Dr. Speer mean that we are to accept Harnack's historical criticism, or at least regard as essential no more of the biblical account of Jesus than Harnack retains? Does he mean that the plain man is well enough off if he contents himself with that reading of the New Testament which Harnack thinks modern criticism confirms? Or is the reference to Harnack due only to unawareness of what Harnack's real position is? We should like to think that the latter is the case. It seems, indeed, almost incredible that such unawareness of Harnack's position should exist in the mind of any modern educated man who has ever dealt with these questions at all, especially in the mind of one who pronounces Harnack's book on "The Expansion of Christianity in the First Three Centuries" to be "one of the greatest missionary books ever written" (p. 96); but on the other hand, the other explanation of Dr. Speer's attitude toward Harnack seems to be excluded by the fact that Dr. Speer does believe in the virgin birth and no doubt in the true, bodily resurrection of Jesus, which, with all the other miracles of the New Testament, Harnack rejects. A middle position, we surmise, is correct—Dr. Speer no doubt affirms many things that Harnack denies, but we hardly think he could speak of Harnack as he does unless he had gone much further with Harnack, and much further away from clear-cut evangelicalism than a careless reader of his book might suppose. One thing at least is plain—there can be no real compromise between the naturalism of Harnack and the supernaturalism of the Bible and of the Christian faith. Was the real Jesus the Jesus reconstructed by Harnack, or was he the stupendous Redeemer whom the Bible presents? That question ought never to be trifled with, but must be resolutely and clearly faced.

In the facing of the question, the reader obtains no help in the rest of Dr. Speer's first chapter. A considerable amount of space is occupied by testimony from non-Christians in support of the thesis that "Christ is more looked up to today throughout the whole world as the supreme moral authority and the ultimate and absolute ethical ideal than ever before in human history." We confess that sadness comes over us as we read these testimonies. If the true Jesus, with his stupendous claims, had always been presented in mission lands, would there ever have been this polite recognition of him as a moral leader by those who have not been born again and are not willing to desert all other saviors and endure the offense of his name? Dr. Speer does recognize, indeed, the inadequacy of these testimonies in themselves. Jesus Christ, he observes, claimed to be more than the moral Lord of life; he claimed also to be "the unique Son of God." But even with regard to this claim, he continues, important acknowledgments have been obtained from adherents of non-Christian faiths. Here again, however, we are filled with little but sadness as we read. The testimonies cited here do not really go beyond those cited under the other head, and it seems very sad that a great missionary leader should regard such testimonies as these as in any sense testimonies to the Christian view of Christ. But, says Dr. Speer in the same chapter, modern ideas of development and personality have "helped many minds toward faith in the Incarnation." Then follows a long quotation from Dr. George A. Gordon, of the Old South Church in Boston, in the course of which it is said that "the true relation of mankind to the Lord Jesus is not grasped until He is regarded as the Incarnation of the Eternal Humanity in which the race is constituted." We can only say that if it is easier for the modern world to accept an incarnation like that, it is no doubt correspondingly harder to accept the incarnation spoken of in the fourteenth verse of the first chapter of John. Here, as always, a minimizing apologetic ends logically in the loss of everything distinctive of the Christian faith.

Finally, in the same chapter, Dr. Speer points out that "the Church's claim for Christ has involved not only His moral authority and His Deity, but also His Saviourhood." Is Christ "any nearer His rightful place in these regards in the life and thought of the world"? Here again Dr. Speer appeals to the testimony of non-Christian men—particularly to one who "was, at the time of his death in 1923, the leading Indian in eastern India." This leading Indian said: "I am a Hindu, but I believe in Christ as the highest fulfilment of Hinduism." And more in that vein. Dr. Speer can see in such testimonies "the evidence of Christ's steady advance toward His sovereignty as moral ideal, as Son of God, as Saviour of mankind." We, however, can see little in them but evidence that the visible church has mitigated the true offense of Christ's words and has lowered his lofty claims. The true and stupendous Lord and Savior presented in God's Word could hardly thus be treated with complacent admiration by those who will not bear his name. God keep us in the church from seeking testimonies such as these! The world will never be saved by "the mind of Christ" becoming in this manner supreme; it will only be saved when men and women lost in sin are begotten again by God's Spirit and have their sin washed away in the blood of the Lamb. If missionaries always proclaimed that message in all its poignancy and offense, no doubt fewer distinguished Hindus would testify to the value of Christ's moral ideals. But, on the other hand, more precious souls would be saved.

The second chapter deals with "The Grounds for Belief in the Deity of Christ." The essential and conclusive ground, Dr. Speer says, is to be found not in the inimitable uniqueness of Christ's moral character, not in his "unique character and message as a teacher," not in the miracle of his "spiritual consciousness, His sense of perfect harmony with God," not in his "central place in history," not in the miracles of his ministry, but rather in his resurrection from the dead. So thought Paul, says Dr. Speer, and so we ought to think. "So today the Resurrection ought to be conceived by us as the demonstration of our Lord's deity, and the power and principle of the Resurrection as the central essence of Christianity."

Here, as so often in connection with the book, agreement is mingled with disagreement as we read. Certainly we agree with the author's attribution of importance to the resurrection of Christ. We do not, indeed, think that the resurrection of itself would be sufficient to establish the deity of our Lord. Lazarus was raised from the dead; yet he was not God. But when taken in connection with the whole New Testament account of Jesus, above all when taken in connection with Jesus' own stupendous claims, the resurrection does set the seal upon the testimony. We confess, further, that we do not know what Dr. Speer means by "the power and principle of the Resurrection" as being "the central essence of Christianity." To us, the really essential thing to say about the resurrection of Christ seems to be not that it was a principle or possessed a principle, but that it was a fact. By it our Lord completed the redeeming work that he had come into the world to do. At any rate, however, we do not think that we attribute less importance to it than does Dr. Speer.

The third chapter, entitled "The Son of God Is the Son of Man," deals largely with the significance of the title "Son of Man" as it appears in our

Savior's words. Here the author, as is unfortunately very common, has missed the origin and significance of the term with which the chapter deals. The true key to the term is almost certainly to be found in the stupendous vision of the seventh chapter of Daniel, where "one like unto a son of man" appears in the presence of the Ancient of Days. The title "Son of Man" in the gospels is not a designation of our Lord's humanity as distinguished from his deity, still less a designation of any real or supposed character of his as a summation or recapitulation of humanity as a whole, but rather is expressive of his supernatural office as heavenly Messiah. Dr. Speer regrets the avoidance of the title in the usage of the church. Yet he himself admits that in the New Testament the title occurs almost exclusively in the words of Jesus himself. Apparently the only exception is found in Acts 7:55ff., where the ultimate origin of the title is particularly plain. The dying martyr, Stephen, like Daniel, saw the heavenly Messiah in the presence of God. We must say plainly that in our judgment the church would do well to imitate the reserve of the New Testament writers in the use of this title in referring to Christ. Certainly the use of the title would be very unfortunate if it led to any confusion between the humanity and the deity of our Lord. Dr. Speer, in this chapter which deals with "the Son of Man," actually quotes from Myers's "St. Paul," which he calls "one of the most nobly Christian of all the poems of the centuries," a passage ending with the line:

Jesus, divinest when Thou most art man!

That line, from the Christian point of view, is little short of blasphemous. Never should we forget that our Lord is "God and man, in two *distinct* natures, and one person, forever." A supremely important truth is involved in that word "distinct." It was well worth the theological conflict that led to its inclusion in the creeds of the church.

In connection with the fourth chapter, which deals with "The Virgin Birth," our agreement with Dr. Speer is probably as great as it is at any other point in the book. The author accepts the virgin birth of Christ and so do we, and in that agreement we greatly rejoice. But then, in the next chapter, entitled "Why Was Christ Crucified?" our disagreement becomes particularly acute, and it is a disagreement not only of the head but also of the heart. Dr. Speer, like so many other modern men, seems to linger at the threshold of the great truth of the atonement without ever really entering in. He says many fine and true things about the cross of Christ, but neither here nor in any other of his recent books, so far as we have been able to observe, does he give any clear expression to that which seems to us to lie at the inmost heart of Christianity—the true substitutionary death of our Lord as a sacrifice to satisfy divine justice and reconcile us to God. He comes near to the great doctrine; he quotes on page 79 a passage of Scripture which implies it, but he himself somehow always stops short at the really decisive point. After quoting the words, "Unto him that loveth us and loosed us from our sins by his blood," and a verse from an old gospel hymn, he says:

> We do not know how. We only know that nineteen hundred years ago a tragedy had to be wrought to cure the tragedy of the sin of mankind.

And then he trails off, in the customary way, about "the illustration of God's absolute and utter faithfulness and His willingness to pay the price, even with His own life, for the failure of man." Thus the true and blessed doctrine of the cross is passed by.

Here our disagreement, we must say frankly, concerns the very heart of the Christian faith and life. Dr. Speer says with regard to salvation by the cross of Christ: "We do not know how." We say, on the contrary: "Praise be to God, we *do* know how." There are many things that we do not know. But one thing, thank God, we do know; we do know that the Lord Jesus took upon himself the just penalty of our sins and bore it in our stead upon the cross. We do not know it by any wisdom of our own. Indeed, all the wisdom of all the philosophers, all the insight of all the poets, all the experience of all the ages were quite powerless to discover it. But it can be well known to every simple reader of God's holy book. This mystery at least God has forever hidden from the wise and prudent; but, thank God, he has revealed it unto babes.

In the sixth chapter, which deals with "The Resurrection—The Centre of Christianity," we agree with much that is said. Certainly we agree as to the supreme importance of the resurrection in the Christian faith. But we cannot see why the resurrection should be used, as Dr. Speer uses it, to belittle the cross. Dr. Speer says with regard to Paul: "In some of his Epistles he says nothing of the Cross, but in almost every one he makes much of the Resurrection." To our mind, that is a very unfortunate assertion. The fact seems to be that the death of Christ, in one way or another, is mentioned

450

in every one of the Pauline epistles except 2 Thessalonians and Philemon, while the resurrection is not mentioned in 2 Thessalonians or in Philemon or in Titus. But how utterly useless is such a calculation! It is perfectly clear, when Paul's teaching is taken as a whole, that both the cross and the resurrection were quite fundamental to everything that he said, being presupposed even where they are not mentioned. Why should the one be pitted against the other?

We cannot pass the other chapters of the book in any sort of detailed review. They contain many things with which we heartily agree, many things, too, which are eloquently and finely said. Thus, on page 118, Dr. Speer points out well and forcibly the unfairness of the charge of narrowness which is so often brought against evangelical Christianity:

> Men will speak tolerantly of liberalistic Christianity or of institutional or sacerdotal or prelatical or Papal religion, or of the use of religion as a force to control the ignorant, but evangelical Christianity, with its clear doctrinal convictions and its warm religious experience, is narrow.
>
> Now let us at once recognize that there is an element of truth in this view. Truth is narrow and exclusive. All truth is so. The search for it, whether in science or religion, involves the rejection of every false and untenable hypothesis.

That is well said indeed. Our central criticism of Dr. Speer is that he does not apply it in his own teaching and in his own attitude in the church. Certainly he does not apply it in the present book. Particularly does he fail to apply it in what he says, on pages 141ff., with regard to "the limits of tolerance." What becomes of the Christian message if "the possession of Christian spirit ["spirit" being spelled with a small letter] is the essential and sufficient credential" (p. 142)? Dr. Speer seems to forget, here and at other places, that which he himself recognizes (see, for example, page 227), that the world cannot be saved by the loveliness of Christians or by any human goodness, but only by the gospel of the Lord Jesus Christ. Certainly the New Testament passages cited in such profusion on page 144 do not at all warrant the inclusiveness for which Dr. Speer seems to plead.

Finally, we come to the last chapter, on "Returning to Jesus." The title is somewhat ominous. It recalls the famous shibboleth of modern Liberalism, "Back to Christ," by which the followers of Harnack and of others of his way of thinking sought to justify their rejection of the way of salvation as it is set forth, in particular, in the epistles of Paul. Here, indeed, as at other places in the book, Dr. Speer detects the lurking danger; he shrinks back from the apparent implications of his words. He says (p. 258):

> There is a second sense in which the conception of returning to Jerusalem to find Jesus is inadequate and untrue. It is inadequate and untrue if it is a proposal to go back of John's Gospel and Paul's Epistles and to eliminate the miracle and mystery from the Synoptic Gospels and to reduce Jesus to the naturalistic figure of a good man who taught nobly but was self-deceived, and around whom delusion soon grew up which transformed the simple, human teacher of Galilee into a supernatural Saviour and a dying God.

And again (p. 260):

> The Jesus we return to Jerusalem to find is the full Jesus of the New Testament, of Matthew and Mark and Luke, of John and Peter and Paul.

These are salutary words. But the trouble is that they have little influence upon the main current of the book. Only a few pages after the words that we have just quoted, we find the author saying (pp. 263ff.):

> Jesus only is the fundamental and adequate theology. What was enough for Peter and James and John, when Jesus was transfigured before them, is enough for us.

What becomes, then, of the cross; what becomes of Pentecost? What becomes of that which Christ did for us once for all, as distinguished from that which he was and is? It is all pushed, as nonessential, aside. We can return without essential loss, according to Dr. Speer, to the experience of Peter and James and John, in the days before Jesus had yet died for men's sins.[1]

The truth is that in this book we have two distinct strains. We have, in the first place, elements of evangelical conviction; and we have, in the sec-

---

1. We cannot think that this objection is removed by the fact that Dr. Speer himself, almost in the same breath with the passage just quoted, mentions the cross and the empty tomb among the things that designate the Christ who is sufficient for us.

ond place, a type of religious faith and life in which those elements have no logical place. This latter type has exerted a large influence upon Dr. Speer's book. The author does manfully strive, indeed, to hold on to elements of the former type. We do not for a moment mean to imply that the evangelical utterances in the book are put there by the author merely in order to quiet the fears of evangelicals in the church. Rather is Dr. Speer, in those utterances, really striving to be conservative; he is really striving to avoid the radicalism that is so prevalent in the religious world today. But the trouble is that logic is a great dynamic, and that things contradictory to each other cannot permanently exist side by side. Whether or not Dr. Speer ever draws the full logical conclusions from the erroneous elements in his thinking, many of those who are influenced by him will probably draw those conclusions only too well. Indeed, we find even Dr. Speer himself, almost at the very end of his book, quoting with the utmost enthusiasm vague and verbose utterances of the Lausanne and Jerusalem Conferences. That is surely a sad ending for a book that contains so many things that are true. It is as though the verbiage of church-unionism had at last swept away as in a mighty flood the elements of the historic faith that Dr. Speer had tried so manfully to maintain.

Dr. Speer pleads, in his last chapter, for simplicity. But we venture to think that in doing so he is confusing very different things. He is confusing simplicity with vagueness, and the two are really quite distinct. Dr. Speer's teaching is often vague, but is it really simple? We venture to think that it is not. We venture to think that in its combination of tendencies really opposite, in its attempt to be evangelical and yet make common cause with profoundly anti-evangelical tendencies in the church, it is a highly subtle, painfully labored thing that the plain man can never really grasp. Many great theologians, on the other hand—perhaps all really great Christian theologians—possess a true simplicity which comes straight from God's Word. And that true simplicity can be the possession of every humble Christian as well. "How can I learn about God and my relation to him?" says the truly simpleminded man. "I can learn it in God's holy book. What does that book tell me about the present state of my soul? It tells me that I am a transgressor of God's law and under its wrath and curse. Is there, then, for me no hope? Oh, yes, the book tells me that God sent his own Son to be my Savior. What, then, did he do to wash away my sin? He took my place and died in my stead upon the cross. But how can I, who am dead in trespasses and sins, ever lay hold upon the benefit of Christ's death? The Holy Spirit can make me alive by the new birth. How, then, when I am born again, am I justified before God? Not by good works, not by love, but by faith alone. What, then, must I do henceforth, with my new life in Christ, and with the guilt of my sins washed away? I must use the weapons that God has given me in the battle of this world; I must read his holy Word, I must partake of the sacraments that Christ instituted, I must pray in Christ's name. How then shall I show that I am truly Christ's? By living a life of love and by telling others the blessed story of God's grace."

Such is the simplicity that is found in the Confession of Faith of the Presbyterian church; such is the simplicity that is found in God's Word. Those who hold to that simplicity are at present undergoing hardship and reviling in the church. But it is worth all that it costs. Those who possess it would not exchange it for all the favor of all the churches or for all the kingdoms of all the world.

42

REVIEW OF FOSDICK'S *MODERN USE OF THE BIBLE*

he "modern use of the Bible,"[1] as Dr. Fosdick sets it forth, consists first in a somewhat naïve application of the evolutionary point of view, and second in a separation between "abiding experiences" and the temporary "mental categories" in which those experiences were expressed. These two closely related aspects of the book may be considered briefly in turn.

In the first place, then, our author applies to the Bible the evolutionary point of view; the Bible, he insists, must not be treated as though it lay all on the same plane, but on the contrary "the new approach to the Bible saves us from the necessity of apologizing for immature stages in the development of the Biblical revelation" (p. 27).

"Review of Harry Emerson Fosdick's *The Modern Use of the Bible*" originally appeared in *The Princeton Theological Review* 23 (1925) 672–75. Reprinted in *What Is Christianity?* ed. Ned Bernard Stonehouse (Grand Rapids: Eerdmans, 1951).

1. *The Modern Use of the Bible*, by Harry Emerson Fosdick, D.D., Morris K. Jessup Professor of Practical Theology, Union Theological Seminary (New York: The Macmillan Company, 1924), 291.

From the purely scientific point of view this [the arrangement of the documents of the Bible in their approximately chronological order] is an absorbing interesting matter, but even more from the standpoint of practical results its importance is difficult to exaggerate. It means that we can trace the great ideas of Scripture in their development from their simple and elementary forms, when they first appear in the earliest writings, until they come to their full maturity in the latest books. Indeed, the general soundness of the critical results is tested by this fact that as one moves up from the earlier writings toward the later he can observe the development of any idea he chooses to select, such as God, man, duty, sin, worship. . . No longer can we think of the Book as on a level, no longer read its maturer messages back into its earlier sources. We know now that every idea in the Bible started from primitive and childlike origins and, with however many setbacks and delays, grew in scope and height toward the culmination in Christ's Gospel. We know now that the Bible is the record of an amazing spiritual development. (pp. 7ff)

We have called this evolutionary view of the Bible "naïve" for several reasons. In the first place it does not do justice to the possibility of retrogression as well as advance—a possibility which certainly exists if history is looked at from the naturalistic point of view. It is true that Dr. Fosdick speaks of the roadway that leads any religious and ethical idea of the Bible "to its climax in the teaching of Jesus" as a roadway that is "often uneven" (p. 8); it is true that he speaks of "setbacks and delays" that occurred in the development. But despite these admissions, it seems fairly clear that the fact of progress is a dogma with Dr. Fosdick. Yet we are inclined to doubt whether that dogma is in such complete accord with the findings of modern science as our author seems to suppose.

In the second place, Dr. Fosdick does not seem to see that the chronological arrangement of the biblical sources upon which the evolutionary reconstruction depends is itself based upon that elimination of supernatural revelation which it in turn is made to support. As it stands, of course, the biblical history does not fall into the evolutionary scheme, but involves supernatural interpositions of God in miracle and in revelation; and if, after the sources are first arranged at will in the order that will show a regular development from crude beginnings to a higher spiritual religion, the rearranged Bible shows that beautifully regular development which is the goal of the rearrangement, the result can scarcely be called significant. The truth is that the critical reconstruction itself presupposes the naturalistic principle which it is made to demonstrate. The whole argument moves in a vicious circle.

But we have not yet commented on the most astonishing thing about Dr. Fosdick's presentation of the modern use of the Bible. The most astonishing thing is that in exalting the historical method of approach, our author displays so little acquaintance with that to which he himself appeals. It would be difficult to discover a book which exhibits less understanding than this book does for the historical point of view.

It is not merely misinformation in detail to which we refer. Such misinformation is indeed at times surprising. It is somewhat surprising, for example, to find a modern man, professor in Union Theological Seminary, writing about textual criticism as though it were "a powerful help in correcting obscure and perverted renderings," and as though it enabled us to select "the more ancient or more sensible renderings" (pp. 39ff.). What has textual criticism, which concerns (as Dr. Fosdick himself says) the task of getting back as nearly as possible to "the original autograph copies of the Scriptures," to do with the selection of the more ancient or more sensible "renderings"— that is, translations? The reader is almost tempted to doubt whether our author has any clear understanding of what textual criticism is.

But what is far more important than all such confusions in detail is the rejection of historical method at the central point—that is, in the presentation of the teaching of Jesus and of the apostles. Our author is very severe upon the ancient allegorizers who read their own ideas into the biblical writings, but what he does not seem to see is that he has made himself guilty, in a far more extreme form, of the fault which he blames in them. It would be difficult to discover a more complete abandonment of grammatico-historical exegesis, in fact though not in theory, than that which is to be found in the present book.

The prerequisite of grammatico-historical exegesis is a sharp separation between the question what the modern reader could have wished the biblical writers to say and the question what the writers actually did say. This method has been practiced, we believe, best of all by those scholars who have themselves been willing to learn from the Bible, who have been willing to mold their own views of God and the world and salvation upon the views which the biblical writers present. But it has also been practiced with considerable success by many modern scholars who have not at all accepted for themselves the teachings of the biblical writers and yet have honestly endeavored to present those teachings as they are without admixture of their own modern predilections. In Dr. Fosdick's case, however, such historical method is abandoned, and the teachings of Jesus and of the apostles are presented not as the sources—even the critically reconstructed sources—show them to have been, but as the modern author would have liked to have them be.

We do not mean that our author is entirely unaware of the fact that the apostles and even Jesus taught things that he himself cannot believe to be true; he does, for example, face in passing the possibility that Jesus shared the apocalyptic ideas of his people, which "the modern man" of course rejects. He does, moreover, deal incidentally with the question of the Messianic consciousness. But at this point he finds refuge in an extreme skepticism about the gospels which few even of modern naturalistic historians have been willing to share; he is doubtful whether Jesus ever presented himself as the Messiah—a view which makes the origin of the church an insoluble enigma. At other points he takes refuge in a total ignoring of the problems. One could read Dr. Fosdick's presentation of the teaching of Jesus and not have the slightest inkling of the central place which Jesus gave, for example, to that theistic view of God which Dr. Fosdick so vigorously rejects, and to the awe-inspiring doctrine of heaven and hell which runs all through the words of Jesus and is at the very foundation of the terrible earnestness of his ethical demands. These central characteristics of Jesus' teaching are for Dr. Fosdick as though they did not exist; he does not even face the problem which they present to the "modern man." Very different is the attitude of real (however radical) scholarship like that of Dr. McGiffert, who in his *God of the Early Christians*,[2] despite a false limitation of the sources, has presented, though of course not explicitly, as devastating a refutation of Dr. Fosdick's anti-historical account of Jesus as any refutation which we might undertake.

Our author's abandonment of historical method appears at many points; it appears, for example, as has already been observed, in his ignoring of Jesus' theism and of his teaching about future rewards and punishments. But it appears most crassly of all, perhaps, in his complete failure to recognize the

2. Cf. *Princeton Theological Review* 23 (October 1924), 544ff.

REVIEWS

factual or dispensational basis of all the New Testament teaching. The plain fact of history, a fact which must be recognized by all impartial historians, is that Jesus was conscious of standing at the threshold of a new era which was to be begun by a catastrophic event, and that the apostles were conscious of looking back upon that event and of having had its meaning revealed to them by God. In Dr. Fosdick's book this central feature of the New Testament is consistently or almost consistently ignored. The result appears in exegetical monstrosities like the following:

> In the second place, having thus appealed to the Old Testament against the clever and sophistical interpretations that had been fathered [?] on it, he [Jesus] distinguished in the Old Testament between significant and negligible elements. He rated ceremonial law low and ethical law high. The Mosaic laws of clean and unclean foods were plainly written in the Book, but Jesus abolished them from the category of the ethical. . . .
>
> In the third place, having appealed from the oral law to the written law, and within the written law having appealed from ceremonial elements to ethical principles, he went on to recognize that some ethical principles in the written law had been outgrown. . . . His whole Sermon on the Mount, starting with its assurance that the old law is to be fulfilled and not destroyed, is a definite endeavor to see that it is fulfilled, carried to completion, with its outgrown elements superseded and its abiding ideals crowned and consummated.
>
> What the Master did, in a word, was to plunge deep beneath the sophisticated exegesis of his time, the timid literalisms, which bound men by a text instead of liberating them by a truth, and in the abiding experiences and principles of the Old Testament find a revelation of God that was fruitful and true.
>
> Let it be clearly noted that this attitude of Jesus involved the recognition of the fact that the Scriptures did contain outgrown elements.
>
> Let us then frankly take our stand with the Master on this basic matter! Of course there are outgrown elements in Scripture. How could it be otherwise in a changing world? (p. 91ff.)

A similar method of treatment is applied even to Paul:

> In this [that is, in "translating the formula back into the life out of which it came"] they [modern liberals] are like Paul. Brought up a Jew, indoctrinated

in the strictest sect of Hebrew orthodoxy, he discovered that much of the religious framework in which he had trusted was for him untenable. He gave up his old interpretation of the Scripture, dropped circumcision, clean and unclean foods, and the burden of ceremonial requirement. He gave up his old view of worship and left the temple behind. A more radical transition in mental framework and practical religious expression it would be hard to find. Paul, however, did not give up religion. He went deeper into it. His casting off of old forms sprang from the positive expansion of his religious experience. Cramped and prisoned in Judaism, he sought more room for his enlarging life. He became a liberal, from the standpoint of his older thinking, not because he was less religious, but because he was more religious. He struck out for air to breathe and he found it in the central regenerative experiences which lie at the heart of the Gospel. And when he was through he was sure that he understood the depths of the Old Testament as he had never understood them before. That is the very genius of liberalism. Its first step is to go through old formulas into the experiences out of which all religious formulas must come. In Phillips Brooks's figure, it beats the crust back into the batter. (pp. 186ff.)

Such is Dr. Fosdick's presentation of Jesus and of Paul. Both Jesus and Paul appear, according to our author, to have been pragmatists of the most approved modern kind. But of course such a presentation has nothing in the world to do with history; it increases our knowledge of the agnostic Modernism of the present day, but as an account of those who lived in the first century it is nothing short of absurd.

To the historian, as distinguished from the propagandist, it should be abundantly plain that when Jesus opposed his stupendous "I say unto you" to the requirements of the Old Testament, he was not appealing to a general right of man as man to take the commands of God with a grain of salt—to penetrate (if we may borrow from the very common misuse of 2 Corinthians 3:6) behind the "letter" to the "spirit"; but he was appealing to his own exalted right, as Messiah, to legislate for the new age which his coming was to usher in. Certainly he was not holding that the requirements of the Old Testament had been "outgrown" (what a really astonishing departure from historical method is involved in our author's repeated use, as expository of Jesus, of that word!), but he was announcing the beginning of an entirely new dispensation which was to be opened by an act of his which was also an act of God the Father.

So also it is a historical blunder of the crassest kind to represent Paul as though he were a "liberal" who rejected the ceremonial parts of the Old Testament law because of "the positive expansion of his religious experience." On the contrary, the teaching of Paul is based not upon a lax, but the strictest possible understanding of the law. And, to speak precisely, he did not "give up" the ceremonial law at all; circumcision, just as truly as love and mercy, he believed, was a command of God. But it was a command intended for the old dispensation, and by the death and resurrection of Christ a new dispensation had been ushered in. The freedom of Paul was supported not by an appeal from positive commands to inner experiences, but by an exhibition of the epoch-making significance of the cross of Christ. It was not an anticipation of modern Liberalism but the diametrical opposite of it.

The whole of the New Testament centers in an event, the redeeming work of Christ in his death and resurrection. To that event Jesus himself in the days of his flesh pointed forward; to it the apostles looked back. But both in Jesus and in the apostles the "gospel" did not consist in the setting forth of what always had been true, but in the proclamation, whether in advance or in retrospect, of something that happened. When that central feature of the New Testament is ignored, true historical exegesis is impossible. And ignored it is in Dr. Fosdick's book from beginning to end. The author of this book displays little acquaintance with scientific historical study of the New Testament.

Before we turn from the first aspect of the book, it may be well to point out that the Christian, as well as the naturalistic historian, has a conception of progress in revelation, though a very different conception. The Christian thinks of the progress as being due to the unfolding of a gracious plan of redemption on the part of the transcendent God. That conception is certainly not wanting in grandeur. And it has the advantage, as compared with the naturalistic conception, of being true.

The other principal aspect of "the modern use of the Bible," as Dr. Fosdick sets it forth, is the separation between "abiding experiences" and the "mental categories" in which those experiences were expressed. "All doctrines," he says, "spring from life," and peace can be attained in the midst of controversy if the doctrines will only be translated back into the life from which they came; the theologies of various ages (including the "mental categories" contained in the New Testament) are merely codes in which experience is expressed, and if these codes become obsolete, all that we have to do is to decode the underlying experience and start fresh. It is true that according to Dr. Fosdick even modern Liberalism cannot do without theology; it must seek to clothe the religious experience which it shares with Jesus and other men of Bible times in the forms of thought that are suited to the modern age. But in doing so it incurs the disadvantage of establishing a new orthodoxy, which in some future generation will have to give place to a new Liberalism (p. 190), and so on (we suppose) *ad infinitum*.

Dr. Fosdick places this theologizing which he thinks modern Liberals must undertake in parallel with the creed-making labors of the historic church. But of course the difference is profound. It is not merely that the results of the activity are different in the two cases, but that the whole nature of the activity is different. The greatest difference between the doctrine which our author thinks that modern Liberalism must produce and the great creeds of the church is not that the historic creeds differ from the new doctrine in this detail or that, and it is not even that they differ from the new doctrine in *all* details. But the real difference is that the authors or compilers of the historic creeds meant their creeds to be true, whereas the authors of these proposed Modernist compendia of belief do not believe their own assertions to be true but only believe them to be useful, as symbolic expressions of a really ineffable experience. But if theologizing is no more than that, we venture to think it is the most useless waste of time in which an able-bodied man could possibly engage. Very different were the great creeds of the church, which were efforts to set forth what was not merely useful but also true.

There is no doubt that we have at this point the very center and core of Dr. Fosdick's teaching. The assertion that "all doctrines spring from life" recurs like a refrain in the present work, and the changes are rung upon it in many different connections. But it involves, of course, the most radical skepticism that could possibly be conceived. It means simply that, abandoning objective truth in the religious sphere, our author falls back upon pure positivism. Prior to all questions about God and creation and the future world, our lives can be changed, he holds, by the mere contemplation of the moral life of Jesus; we can enter into the experience which Jesus had. Then, Dr. Fosdick holds further, that experience into which Jesus leads us finds symbolic expression in doctrines like the divinity of Christ. Men used to apply the word "divinity" to a transcendent God, Maker and Ruler of the world.

In such a God the Modernists no longer believe. But the word "God" or the word "divinity" is useful to express our veneration for the highest thing that we know, and the highest thing that Modernists know is the purely human Jesus of modern critical reconstruction.

At no point, then, does Dr. Fosdick's hostility to the Christian religion appear more clearly than in his assertion of the divinity of Christ. "Let us," he urges his readers, "say it abruptly: *it is not so much the humanity of Jesus that makes him imitable as it is his divinity*"(p. 270). There we have Modernism in a nutshell—the misleading use of Christian terminology, the blatancy of human pride, the breakdown of the distinction between God and man, the degradation of Jesus, and the obliteration of the very idea of God.

In view of the underlying pragmatist skepticism of our author, it hardly seems worthwhile to examine his teaching in detail. Since he does not believe in the objective truth of his own teaching, but regards it only as the temporary intellectual form in which an experience is expressed, we might be pardoned if we failed to be interested in it. He might affirm every jot and tittle of the Westminster Confession, for example; yet, since he would be affirming it merely as useful and not as true, he would be separated by a tremendous gulf from the Reformed faith. As a matter of fact, however, the system of belief which Dr. Fosdick does set forth (as the temporary intellectual form in which his experience is expressed) is somewhat as follows.

God, according to Dr. Fosdick, is to be thought of as the "ideal-realizing Capacity in the universe or the creative Spirit at the heart of it" (p. 161), and he quotes with approval words of John Herman Randall that set forth the ancient pagan *anima mundi* view of God: "The universe as we see it is God's body; then God is the soul of the universe, just as you are the soul of your body" (p. 266). The transcendence of God, which is at the root of all the ethical glories of the Christian religion, is by this preacher vigorously denied; Dr. Fosdick's whole teaching, in marked contrast to that of Jesus— even the reduced Jesus to whom he appeals—is passionately antitheistic. He has "a live cosmos," but has given up the living God.

Equally opposed to Christianity is his view of man, the root of which is found in his rejection of any real consciousness of sin. "I believe in man," Dr. Fosdick thinks, according to a recent sermon and according to the plain implications of this book, ought to be a fundamental article in our creed. Here we have the thoroughgoing paganism—the thoroughgoing confidence in human resources—which runs all through this preacher's teaching.

But if Dr. Fosdick is opposed to the Christian view of both these presuppositions of the gospel, he is also opposed to the Christian view of the book in which the gospel is set forth:

> Men have always gone to any sacred Scriptures they possessed primarily that they might find out how to live. That the Bible is "the infallible rule of faith and practise" is one of the most familiar statements which the church has ever framed, but in the historical development of our religion in the Old Testament the second item of that statement came first. The primary use of Scripture was to guide conduct, not to control belief. . . . When, therefore, among the Hebrews we see the canon of sacred Scripture growing, when Josiah swore the people to a solemn league and covenant—the first example of a formal Hebrew Bible that we know—or when Ezra pledged the nation's loyalty to the keeping of the Levitical law, the Bible which thus was coming into being was primarily a book of divine requirements. It told the people what they ought to do. . . . (pp. 235ff.)

Now, it is true that according to Dr. Fosdick Jesus broke with this legalism of the Old Testament. But he did so, the author holds, not at all because he restored truth to the primary place as over against conduct, but because he substituted "a form of conduct, a quality of spirit" for detailed rules (p. 240). Thus, according to our author, the New Testament as well as the Old Testament is valuable primarily as setting forth a way of life and not as recording facts.

But the Christian view is the exact opposite: the Bible, according to the Christian, first sets forth truth—both eternal truth regarding God and also redemptive facts of history—and upon that truth grounds its ethical demands. That is the case with the Old Testament as well as with the New Testament. Dr. Fosdick is quite wrong in thinking that the Old Testament law is, like the ethics of skeptical Modernism, left hanging in the air; on the contrary, it is grounded throughout in the nature of God. Law in the Old Testament is always rooted in doctrine: the Ten Commandments are preceded by the words, "I am the Lord thy God, which have brought thee out of the land of Egypt, out of the house of bondage" (Ex. 20:2); and the law of love in Deuteronomy is based upon the great Sh'ma, "Hear, O Israel: The Lord our God is one Lord" (Deut. 6:4). Similar is the case with regard to the New Testament. The "practical" parts of the epistles are always based upon the great doctrinal passages that precede them, and the ethical demands of Jesus are always based upon his presentation of the facts not only about God but about his own person and about heaven and hell.

Thus, the *Shorter Catechism* is true to the Bible from beginning to end in the order which it observes in the answer to the question, "What do the Scriptures principally teach?" "The Scriptures principally teach," it says quite correctly, "*what man is to believe concerning God* and what duty God requires of man." The reversal of the order, or rather the virtual elimination of the former part of the answer, by Dr. Fosdick exhibits the great gulf which exists between his teaching on the one side and the Christian religion on the other. Christianity, in accordance with the whole Bible but unlike Dr. Fosdick, founds morality upon truth, and life upon doctrine.

Of course, in speaking of Dr. Fosdick's view of the Bible it would be easy to point out the vast sections of Scripture which he holds to be directly untrue. He does not indeed make the matter always perfectly clear to the unsophisticated reader, and his failure to do so is from the ethical point of view one of the most disappointing features of the book. If this writer stated in plain language, which the lay reader could understand, his critical views about the New Testament, for example, the favor which he now enjoys among many misinformed but devout persons in the church would at once be lost. But such frankness is not his; he prefers to undermine the faith of the church by an entirely different method—more immediately effective, perhaps, but ethically far inferior.

But if Dr. Fosdick is opposed to the presuppositions of the Christian message and the Christian view of the book in which the message is set forth, he is also opposed to the Christian view of the person whose redeeming work forms the substance of the message. Jesus, according to Dr. Fosdick, is simply the fairest flower of humanity, divine in the sense in which all men are divine, the culmination of a process, not the entrance of a creative interposition of God. "That differential quality in Jesus," he says, "is the most impressive spiritual fact that this earth has seen. It is the best we know. It is the fairest production that the race has to show for its millenniums of travail" (p. 260). What an abysmal distance there is between this view of Christ as "the fairest production that the race has to show" and the Christian view of the eternal Son of God who entered freely into the world for our redemption!

Certainly the difference is not diminished but only exhibited in the clearer light when in the passage that has just been quoted the author speaks of the "differential quality in Jesus" as being "a revelation of creative reality." For here we have in striking form the degradation of the word "creative" which runs all through the book and which is involved in the passionate antitheism which is a central characteristic of the Modernism of the present day.

The plain fact, of course, is that Dr. Fosdick eliminates from the pages of history all the miracles in the New Testament account of Jesus from the virgin birth to the empty tomb, as well as all the miracles in the Bible as a whole. He does speak, it is true, of miracles of Jesus that he accepts; but these "miracles," it turns out, are miracles which we also can experience. The miracles that show Jesus to have been unique are of course gone; what we have here is the elimination of the whole supernatural content of the Word of God. And how indeed can it be otherwise? There can be no supernatural interposition of a transcendent God if no transcendent God exists—if "God," like ourselves, is bound to the course of this world!

Corresponding to this degraded *view* of Jesus is the author's *attitude* toward Jesus. There is not the slightest evidence in this book that Dr. Fosdick has ever exercised faith in Jesus or indeed has the slightest notion of what faith in Jesus means. Jesus is to him a leader whom he loves, but never really a Savior whom he trusts. "Say 'Jesus' to a medieval Christian [rather, we should put it, to *any* Christian] and he instinctively would think of a king sitting on his throne or coming in the clouds of heaven. Say 'Jesus' to a man of to-day and he instinctively thinks of that gracious and courageous Nazarene who lived and worked and taught in ancient Palestine" (p. 220). Here we have the contrast between the Christian attitude to Christ and Dr. Fosdick's attitude: the Christian thinks of the Christ now living in glory, Dr. Fosdick thinks of the Christ who instituted a type of religious life long ago; Dr. Fosdick calls Christ "the Master," the Christian calls Him "the Lord." The difference is profound, and it is a difference of the heart and of the inner life fully as much as of the head. Dr. Fosdick speaks of a personal Savior "with whom to fall in love" (p. 231); the Christian thinks of Christ as one who first loved us. Dr. Fosdick *loves* the reconstructed Jesus of modern naturalism; the Christian *trusts* as well as loves the Jesus to whom is given all power in heaven and on earth.

In view of what has already been said, it is quite needless to point out our author's scorn for the gospel itself—the account of the redeeming work of

Christ in his death and resurrection. *"The historic Jesus,"* he says, *"has given the world its most appealing and effective exhibition of vicarious sacrifice"* (p. 229). Here the cross of Christ is treated as a mere member of a series of acts of self-sacrifice, and so it is treated in the book throughout. But to the Christian, such words about the tenderest and holiest thing in the Christian religion seem so blasphemous that even in quotation he can hardly bear to take them on his lips.

In reply to such an estimate of Dr. Fosdick as that which has here been made, the exponents of naturalistic Modernism in the creedal churches, who themselves are just as much opposed to Christianity as this author is, are accustomed to point to individual utterances in the book, torn from their context—individual utterances in which Christian terminology is used. But that use of Christian terminology only serves to set in sharper light the divergence between this preacher and the whole tendency of Christianity; for it involves a certain carelessness about plain straightforwardness of speech, which would be thoroughly abhorrent to anyone who appreciated the Christian point of view. The truth is that the similarity between Dr. Fosdick and the Christian religion is largely verbal; both in thought and in feeling (so far as the latter can be revealed by words) the divergence, despite undoubted influences of Christianity upon Dr. Fosdick in certain spheres, is profound.

In closing, a word of explanation may be due as to the reason why we have treated this book at such great length. It is because the author is representative of a very large body of persons in the modern world. He himself has asserted that theological views similar to his are held by hundreds of ministers in the Presbyterian church, and certainly similar conditions prevail in most other ecclesiastical bodies. The author of this book represents in fairly typical, and certainly in very popular, fashion the attack upon Christianity which is being carried on with such vigor at the present time.

It cannot be said that this fact reflects credit upon the intellectual standard of the day; on the contrary, it is only one among many instances of the intellectual decadence which has set in with such force. It is just the faults of Dr. Fosdick, as much as his undoubted gifts, which make him popular. The disinclination of this writer to clear definitions, the use of Christian terminology to veil a totally alien meaning, the lack of that breadth of mind which leads a man to enter at least into some sort of comprehension of the thing against which he is directing his attack—these faults, distressing as they may be to thoughtful persons, make the book typical of the present age, and hence contribute no doubt very largely to the popularity which the author enjoys.

But this is not the first period of decadence through which the world has passed, as it is not the first period of desperate conflict in the church. God still rules, and in the midst of the darkness there will come in his good time the shining of a clearer light. There will come a great revival of the Christian religion; and with it there will come, we believe, a revival of true learning: the new reformation for which we long and pray may well be accompanied by a new renaissance.

43

REVIEW OF MCGIFFERT'S
GOD OF THE
EARLY CHRISTIANS

A marked characteristic of the present time is the intellectual decadence which has affected most departments of human endeavor
except those that are concerned with purely material things.
This decadence has been felt in no department more clearly than in the
sphere of the Christian religion. And the reason is not far to seek—it is
found in the pragmatist philosophy of the day, which divorces right living
from right thinking and supposes that religion may be the same no matter
what may be the intellectual conceptions with which it is connected. Such
exclusion of the intellect from the highest sphere of human life has very
naturally degraded the intellect, and the result is a lamentable intellectual
decline. No doubt the men who laid the foundations of the modern anti-
intellectualistic philosophy and anti-intellectualistic religion were men of
great intellectual power, and for a time the logical results of their endeavors were obscured. But today the inevitable result is becoming more and
more clear. The intellect has been browbeaten so long in the field of theory that one cannot be surprised if it is now ceasing to function in the field

"Review of Arthur Cushman McGiffert's *The God of the Early Christians*" originally
appeared in the *Princeton Theological Review* 22 (1924) 544–88.

of practice. Schleiermacher and Ritschl, with all their intellectual gifts, have, it may fairly be maintained, contributed largely to produce that indolent impressionism which, at least in the New Testament field, has now largely taken the place of the patient researches that were being carried on a generation or two ago.

But in this development from anti-intellectual theory to anti-intellectual practice, the distinguished president of Union Theological Seminary is to be connected clearly not with the latter, but with the former phase. In the sphere of theory, Dr. McGiffert is clearly to be included among the enemies of the intellect; few men have separated more sharply than he between theology and religion, and few have more ruthlessly drawn the skeptical conclusions from that separation. But even in dethroning the intellect, Dr. McGiffert, like the older Ritschlians, has displayed marked intellectual power; unlike most contemporary writers on biblical themes, he belongs spiritually to a better day when scholarship was at least thought to involve painstaking intellectual work.

And so in this volume of Nathaniel William Taylor Lectures, delivered before the Divinity School of Yale University in 1922, the author has produced a learned and brilliant, though at the same time provocative and (we are constrained to think) erroneous, book. Underlying the book, it is true—and more fundamentally, we suppose, than the author himself realizes—is the anti-intellectualistic philosophy of our day, with its separation into watertight compartments of theology and philosophy on the one hand and religion and ethics on the other. But this philosophy, though it does, we think, influence and even determine the conclusions, does not lead to the shallow sentimentality and meaningless repetition of cant phrases which characterize the great mass of religious books at the present time. On the contrary, Dr. McGiffert has examined the problem of Christian origins for himself, with ruthless disregard of what is usual in the ecclesiastical circles to which he belongs. And far from falling into sentimentality, he has, we are almost tempted to say, erred on the other side—he has, despite his own exaltation of experience at the expense of theology, displayed not too great, but too little, sympathy with religious feeling, at least where religious feeling is connected with convictions which he does not himself share. Such a book, with its learning and its originality, whatever may be its faults, repays careful examination far more than many a five-foot shelf of the ostensibly startling and progressive but really thoroughly conventional religious books which are so popular just now.

470

Jesus, according to Dr. McGiffert, did not teach a new view of God, but simply continued the teaching which was common among his people and in his day. In particular it is a great mistake, according to Dr. McGiffert, to suppose that Jesus emphasized in any revolutionary manner the love or the fatherhood of God—indeed, he says, in the synoptic gospels (which are here treated as the sole authentic sources of information), the love and the forgiveness of God are very seldom directly in view, and the fatherhood of God was perhaps even more prominent in the teaching of Jesus' contemporaries than in his own. Indeed, our author insists, if any element in Jesus' teaching about God is distinctive, it is the awful severity of God rather than the love of God; Jesus had much to say about punishment as well as bliss in the future world, and differed from his contemporaries in breaking down their easy complacency and bringing them face to face with the dread decision between death and life. "Strait is the gate," according to Jesus, "and narrow is the way, which leadeth unto life, and few there be that find it." But even in this element in his teaching, Dr. McGiffert maintains, Jesus clearly was following in the line of an Old Testament prophet such as Amos; and in general, in the whole outline of his teaching about God—his thoroughgoing theism, with its insistence upon the sovereignty of God with which none can argue or bargain, and his doctrine of creation—he was simply a child of his people and was not the originator of distinctively Christian ideas.

It will not be possible here to examine these contentions in detail; they are based, we think, upon a false limitation of the sources, and even within those sources that are used they are at a number of points clearly one-sided. But if they are one-sided, they constitute at least a salutary protest against a modern presentation that is more one-sided still. In a few ruthless strokes Dr. McGiffert has here demolished the entire sentimental picture of the "Liberal Jesus." It is only necessary to compare, for example, Professor Ellwood's absurd but exceedingly popular and altogether typical assertion that "Jesus concerned Himself but little with the question of existence after death"[1] with our author's insistence upon Jesus' utterances about heaven and hell and upon the central place which they had in his teaching in order to detect the difference between popular Modernism,[2] with its thoughtless

1. Ellwood, *The Reconstruction of Religion* (1922), 141.
2. We are using this word in a broad sense, in which it would include Harnack, for example, as well as Loisy.

repetition of current phrases and its complete refusal to separate the question what we should have said from the question what Jesus actually said, on the one hand, and real scholarship, no matter how radical, on the other. The truth is that our author has indicated with admirable clearness, despite the one-sidedness of his presentation in detail, how false is the appeal of the dominant optimistic and positivist Modernism to the real Jesus of Nazareth. To put the matter briefly, Modernism (including Dr. McGiffert himself) thinks of religion exclusively "in terms of salvation," whereas the real Jesus of Nazareth thought of it also in terms of judgment; Modernism relegates the doctrines of creation and the divine sovereignty to the realm of metaphysics, whereas the teaching of the real Jesus was theistic through and through.

Thus, according to our author, Jesus was and always remained a Jew, and his doctrine of God was Jewish and not Christian. In what sense, then, was he the founder of the Christian religion? The obvious answer might seem to be, from the point of view of our author, that he was not the founder of the Christian religion at all, and that Christianity originated after his time and had little to do with him. But we desire earnestly to be fair; indeed, at this point we want, if possible, to be fairer to Dr. McGiffert than he is to himself. He does not himself make the matter very clear—certainly he does not lay very much stress upon it—but still he does find something in Jesus that was distinctive as over against His contemporaries. That something was not his teaching, but it was his life; in Jesus the gospel of the kingdom was "irradiated by the intimacy and beauty of Jesus' own relation to God and by the quality of his life of service and sacrifice" (p. 193). No doubt, Dr. McGiffert holds that without that *life* of Jesus, the whole subsequent development, the whole formation and development of Christianity, would have been impossible.[3] Accordingly, our author is not so very far away from the current Modernism after all—he probably agrees with the Modernist preachers in holding that Jesus was the founder of Christianity because he was the first to live the Christian life. But at any rate, he does emphasize with a salutary clearness the falsity of the customary Modernist appeal to the *teaching* of Jesus. The impression is constantly being produced by the popular exponents of Modernism that although they have given up the authority of the Bible, they do hold to the "authority of Christ." That im-

3. See, for example, p. 21.

pression would be removed by a perusal of Dr. McGiffert's book. Our author has shown with all requisite clearness that the God of Modernism is quite different from the God of Jesus of Nazareth. The admission, we think, ought to be taken with very great seriousness. It will not indeed bring the Modernists back into conformity with the Word of God; for when, learning from Dr. McGiffert, they have to choose between their own view of God and the view which Jesus held, they will no doubt hold to their own view and let the teaching of Jesus go. But at least the alternative will have been placed clearly before the rank and file of the church, and that will be immense gain. Dr. McGiffert has shown very boldly and very clearly, in the brief but weighty first section of his book, that the God of Nazareth was quite different from the God proclaimed by the antitheistic Modernism of the twentieth century, including Dr. McGiffert himself.

So much for Jesus' view of God; it was, according to our author, simply the view commonly held by the Jewish teachers of Jesus' day. But an important step in advance, it is held, was taken by the apostle Paul. Paul did indeed retain his allegiance to the God of the Jews and of Jesus, but he added to that God a second object of worship—namely, Jesus himself. At this point it is interesting to observe the insistence of Dr. McGiffert upon the Pauline doctrine of the deity of Christ; indeed, the reference of the word "God" (Theos) to Jesus in Romans 9:5, which was singled out by Jülicher for special criticism in his review of a book by the writer of the present article,[4] here receives the weighty support of one who certainly cannot be accused of orthodox prejudices. But at any rate, whether or not Paul applies the word "God" to Jesus, he constantly applies to him the word "Lord" (Kyrios), and refers to him Old Testament passages where in the Septuagint that word is used to translate the "Jahwe" of the Hebrew text. What is more important still, Paul recognizes Christ throughout as an object of worship and even addresses prayers to him. With this second object of worship whom Paul added to God the Father, and with the closely related idea of the Holy Spirit, the distinctive mystical piety of the apostle, according to our author, was connected. At this point, Dr. McGiffert believes, is to be found the influence, important though indirect, of the non-Jewish and non-Christian religion of Paul's day; Paul "illustrates in his own thinking the twofold strain

4. See *The Origin of Paul's Religion* (1921), 198, and Jülicher in *Christliche Welt*, 36 (1922), col. 625.

which has run through nearly all Christian thought since his day, for Christianity was the child both of Judaism and of the orientalized Hellenism of the Roman world" (p. 34). "The God of Paul was the God of the Jews, expanded to include the divine Saviour Jesus Christ the Lord, by mystical union with whom believers are transformed from flesh into spirit and are thus saved" (pp. 193ff.).

This exposition of Paul is correct, of course, in emphasizing Paul's full belief in the deity of Christ, and also in representing Paulinism as in the fullest sense a religion of redemption. But it is wrong, we believe, in several respects: it is wrong positively, in finding the origin of Paul's redemptive religion in the orientalized Hellenism or the Hellenized oriental mysticism of Paul's day; and it is wrong negatively because of its ignoring of important elements in Pauline thought and Pauline experience. It ignores in the first place the entire forensic aspect of Paul's doctrine of salvation—the aspect which is concerned with justification or with the question how a sinful man becomes "right with God"—and it ignores in the second place the factual or historical basis which the apostle himself clearly attributed to his religious life. Paul's religion was not founded, as the reader of Dr. McGiffert's book might suppose, merely upon what Christ was, but it was founded also, and primarily, upon what Christ had done; Paulinism is based not merely upon things that always were true but something that happened—namely, the redemptive work of Christ in his death and resurrection.

We understand, of course, that Dr. McGiffert is discussing, not soteriology, but theology in the narrower sense; he is discussing not Paul's doctrine of the way of salvation, but Paul's doctrine of God. Yet even in such a discussion, the strictly factual basis of Paul's religion should not have been ignored. Attention to it might have led to a clearer recognition of the identity between the God of the old dispensation, with his promises of redemption to come, and the God of the new dispensation holding closer fellowship with his people because of the redemption already accomplished through the death and resurrection of Christ; and it might have led also to a recognition of the difference between the mystery religions, with their dimly conceived savior-gods, whose experiences, even if they were really regarded as taking place at all otherwise than in the constantly repeated cult, lay at best in the remote past, and the religion of Paul, with its clear account of a redeeming act that had taken place before the gaze of the multitude outside the walls of Jerusalem only a few years before. Paulinism was founded upon a plain account of something that had happened, upon a piece of good news, a "gospel." Ignore that fact and you are without the key which unlocks the meaning of all the rest.

But it is time to return to the exposition of Dr. McGiffert's book. Two steps in the reconstruction have so far been noticed. There was, according to our author, first the thoroughly Jewish monotheism of Jesus; and there was in the second place, added to this Jewish monotheism, the Pauline notion of Jesus as a Savior-God. These two elements in Paul's thought were, according to Dr. McGiffert, brought together in a sort of rough, provisional way by the Pauline designation of Jesus as "Son of God." This designation, or rather the Pauline use of it, shows, Dr. McGiffert thinks, that Paul had come to conceive of God in quite an un-Jewish way as a sort of substance in which two persons (God the Father and Jesus the Son) could share, and that this conception involves the conception of the divine immanence and the momentous notion, common to Paul and to the mystery religions, that salvation consists in a sharing, on the part of men, of the nature of God. All of this, our author thinks, is non-Jewish, and the union of it with Paul's Jewish monotheism, which conceives of God in a strictly personal way, means merely that two elements, really disparate, were allowed to rest side by side in the mind of Paul. Paul began, it is supposed, with Jewish monotheism, like that of Jesus, but added to it, as an entirely new and disparate element in his thinking, the Christ-mysticism which made of Jesus a Savior-God.

Yet, according to Dr. McGiffert, disparate as the two elements really were, they were both present in Paulinism and in the thought of some men, like the author of the fourth gospel, who were his followers. But—and here we come to the boldest and most distinctive contention in this remarkable book—there were many persons who accepted one of the two elements in Paulinism and did not accept the other, who accepted Jesus as a savior-god, but did not accept the monotheism which Jesus and Paul derived from their Jewish inheritance. These persons, it is supposed, were not at all exceptional, and did not creep into the church at any late date, but on the contrary formed the rank and file of primitive Gentile Christianity. There were no doubt, it is admitted, some Gentile Christians who, coming into the church through the gateway of the synagogue, believed in the one God, Maker and Ruler of the world, before they came to believe in Jesus. But the great majority, it is thought, were of the way of thinking which has just been indicated: the great majority accepted Jesus as *their* savior-god, but were not at all concerned to deny the existence of other gods, and in particular were not at all interested in the connection of Jesus with the Maker and Ruler of the universe or indeed with the question whether there is any Maker and Ruler of the universe at all. At an early date, Dr. McGiffert says, "there came into the Christian church from the Gentile world many who found in Jesus Christ their saviour, and to whom the God of the Jews—the God worshipped by both Jesus and Paul—meant nothing" (pp. 193ff.). A somewhat extended quotation may be necessary to set forth this central thesis of the book (pp. 46ff.):

> The saviour gods of the current mystery religions were not supreme gods—creators and rulers of the world—nor were they thought of by their votaries as the only gods. Initiation into this or that cult did not mean the denial of other deities, but only the special consecration of oneself to the service of a particular deity. This may well have been the situation of many early Christians. Their personal piety centred in the Lord Jesus Christ. In communion with him and in devotion to him they found their religious life. But they may not have felt it necessary to deny the existence of other deities or to accept the one God of Israel as their God.
>
> There was no antecedent reason, indeed, why the Gentile Christians should accept the God of the Jews whom Jesus worshipped, any more than the Jewish ceremonial law which he observed and the Jewish practices in which he was brought up. The fact that Jesus himself and his personal disciples were Jews no more required the Gentile Christians to be Jews in their customs and beliefs than the fact that Adonis was a Syrian deity, Attis a Phrygian, and Isis and Serapis Egyptian deities required their adherents to become Syrians or Phrygians or Egyptians, and to accept the religious tenets of those peoples. Whether Judaism or any part of it was to be regarded as permanently essential to Christianity was a matter to be determined, and by no means went without saying. The early Jewish disciples thought the whole of it essential and regarded the new faith as only a form of Judaism. Paul broke with Judaism and made of Christianity a new religion, but he did not break with the Jewish God. On the contrary, he recognized him as the God of Christians as well as Jews.
>
> But by what right did he reject a part of the old system and retain another part? Evidently there was room for a difference of opinion. Paul's authority was not great enough to compel the general adoption of his doctrine of re-

demption, nor were other Christians under the necessity of accepting the Jewish God simply because he did. We can hardly avoid the conclusion that if belief in the God of the Jews was finally universal among Christians it was because it commended itself as sound rather than because it was from the beginning an essential part of the new faith. As already said, most of the early Gentile converts were not seeking monotheism, but salvation through Christ. This being so, it is gratuitous to assume that they must have accepted monotheism when they accepted Christianity. On the contrary, they may well have taken Christ as their Lord and Saviour, without taking His God and Father as their God.[5]

Thus, according to Dr. McGiffert, primitive Gentile Christianity thought of religion "in terms of salvation" but not in terms of metaphysics; it was Christian without being theistic; it accepted Jesus but did not accept Jesus' God.

It would be difficult to imagine a more revolutionary thesis; and if such a thesis were proposed by one of the merely impressionistic historians of the day, who either dispense themselves from any examination of the sources or else, completely abandoning scientific historical method, make the sources subservient to the practical needs of the modern church, then the thesis could perhaps safely be passed by. But when it is proposed by one of the most distinguished American scholars, who in his *Apostolic Age* has produced perhaps the ablest American exposition of the older "Liberal" view of primitive Christianity—a view widely different from the one which the author now sets forth—and who by the solid learning of his commentary on Eusebius has placed all students of Christian literature very deeply in his debt—when so revolutionary a thesis is proposed by such a scholar, it certainly ought to be examined with some care.

But before the examination, it is important to fix in our minds, just as clearly as possible, exactly what it is that Dr. McGiffert is undertaking to prove. If he were maintaining merely that individual Gentiles, not understanding the apostolic proclamation of the one God, found their way into the church without having really freed themselves of their polytheistic point of view, then we should not perhaps venture upon a summary denial. Cer-

5. *The God of the Early Christians*, by Arthur Cushman McGiffert. New York: Charles Scribner's Sons, 1924.

tain Athenians supposed that when Paul spoke of "Jesus and the resurrection," he was a setter forth of "strange gods"; they did not understand or perhaps mockingly pretended to misunderstand the monotheism which underlay everything that the apostle said. These Athenians were indeed certainly not received into the primitive Christian community; they are spoken of, rather, as typical representatives of those who scornfully rejected the new faith. But it is conceivable, though perhaps improbable, that individual Gentiles made their way into the apostolic churches without inwardly relinquishing their polytheistic point of view and without becoming deeply interested in the apostolic teaching about the one living and true God. In the subapostolic age, moreover, there were those who perhaps called themselves Christian and who accepted some at least of the Christian claims for Christ and yet were very far from accepting the central elements in New Testament Christianity. It is conceivable, though by no means certain, that such heresies as those of Cerinthus and Carpocrates, for example, had their precursors even in the earlier part of the apostolic age. And it is conceivable, though again by no means probable, that among such isolated phenomena is to be put a nontheistic[6] Gentile Christianity such as that which Dr. McGiffert describes.

But even if such an admission should be made, it would not at all touch the matter now under discussion. What Dr. McGiffert is undertaking to establish is not merely the existence, in individual converts in the apostolic and subapostolic age, of a nontheistic Christianity, but the existence of such a Christianity as embracing the great mass of early Gentile Christians, as having a recognized place in the church instead of being rigidly excluded as were the adherents of Carpocrates and Cerinthus and the later Gnostics, and indeed as forming the basis for the whole subsequent development of the Christian religion. That, and nothing less than that, is the astonishing thesis which our author endeavors to establish. Indeed, so fundamental does he regard this nontheistic Christianity in the subsequent history of the church that at times he seems almost to ignore the possibility of any other influence, and in particular the possibility of any considerable direct influ-

6. It is hoped that the reader will pardon the use of this hybrid word. "Atheistic" would obviously not do at all. And even "antitheistic" would perhaps be too strong, since Dr. McGiffert does not maintain that these Christians expressly denied theism but only that they were not interested in it.

REVIEWS

ence of the New Testament. Were the primitive Gentile Christians so predominantly worshipers of Jesus without being worshipers of the God of Israel, were they so predominantly Christians without being monotheists, that this nontheistic Gentile Christianity could form the basis of the whole subsequent development of the church? That is the question which is raised by Dr. McGiffert's book.

In proposing so provocative a thesis, it is unfortunate that the author has not allowed himself more space than is afforded by a short volume of lectures. Dr. McGiffert is proposing nothing less than a rather radical reconstruction of early Christian history, yet he has flung his suggestion out into the world with only very sketchy argumentative support. One could wish that like Baur or Bousset he had made public at once the materials upon which his reconstruction is based. Nevertheless, he has at least clearly indicated the main arguments by which his thesis is to be supported, and we do not think that the addition of details could essentially change our estimate. We shall therefore endeavor briefly to set forth and criticize the arguments by which the existence of a nontheistic Gentile Christianity as a dominant factor in the life of the primitive church is here thought to be established.

In the first place, the author deals with the antecedent probabilities of the case. Before adducing positive evidence as to the existence of a nontheistic Gentile Christianity, he seeks to show that the existence of such a Christianity is only what might have been expected, especially on the basis of the epistles of Paul. The early converts from the Gentile world, except those who had already been attracted by the synagogue, were, Dr. McGiffert insists, in a very different situation from that which prevailed among the Jewish Christians; the "Christians of Jewish birth or training worshipped the God of the Jews from the beginning, and only afterward worshipped Christ and recognized him as divine, as many of them never did.[7] But converts drawn directly from the Gentile world were in a different situation. They did not begin with the God of the Jews, but with the Lord Jesus Christ. Not the former, but the latter, brought them into the Christian circle" (p. 44).

---

7. There is really not the slightest evidence that the words "as many of them never did" are correct for the early period. Even in arguing with his bitterest Jewish Christian opponents, Paul gives no evidence of any difference of opinion between himself and them with regard to the person of Christ.

It cannot be said, however, that this consideration supports Dr. McGiffert's thesis. Indeed, it is not even clear that the situation of the Gentile Christians is here correctly stated; it is by no means clear that the Gentile Christians "began" with the Lord Jesus Christ and not with the God of the Jews. In the precious summary of missionary preaching to Gentiles which Paul gives in 1 Thessalonians 1:9–10, the apostle indicates the contrary; in that summary, the proclamation of "the living and true God" comes before the proclamation of Jesus. "For they themselves," Paul says, "show of us what manner of entering in we had unto you, and how ye turned to God from idols to serve the living and true God; and to wait for his Son from heaven, whom he raised from the dead, even Jesus, which delivereth us from the wrath to come." But even if it should be granted that the primitive Gentile Christians began with Jesus rather than with God, it would still not follow that acceptance of Jesus was ever possible without acceptance of God. For in all our sources of primitive information, the Lordship of Jesus and his Saviorhood are represented as being indissolubly connected with the relation that he sustained to God the Father. There is not the slightest evidence for the opinion that the title "Son of God" was a mere invention of Paul to show a relation between Jesus the Savior-God and the God of the Jews whom Paul continued to worship. On the contrary, Jesus is presented in every aspect, including his aspect as Savior, which Dr. McGiffert makes the sole aspect in which he appeared to the Gentile Christians, as standing in relation to God. Indeed, the very idea of salvation involves the idea of the one God. What did the primitive Gentile Christians understand by "salvation"? Did they not understand by it—whatever else it might mean—did they not understand by it salvation from the final condemnation *of God?* Will Dr. McGiffert venture to remove—and just in the case of the simple-minded rank and file—this eschatological reference? He insists indeed that the primitive Gentile Christians thought of religion in terms of salvation, not of judgment. But does not the very idea of salvation involve, as its correlative, the idea of judgment; and does not the idea of judgment involve the idea of God as judge?

Moreover, if the result of salvation or the very nature of it thus involves the idea of God, so does also the act by which salvation was consummated; in speaking of the resurrection of Christ, Paul speaks, in the Thessalonian passage just quoted and elsewhere in the epistles, of the one who raised him from the dead. So it is also with regard to all other aspects of salvation. In attributing to those supposedly simpleminded Gentile Christians of the first century the sublimated mysticism of the twentieth century, which is not interested in the thought of a life after death or in the relation of man to the inscrutable and terrible power that the ancients called fate, Dr. McGiffert is, we are constrained to believe, guilty of a very serious anachronism. Indeed, even in connection with the Holy Spirit, where the affinity with a mere mysticism might naturally be expected to appear, if it appears anywhere, Paul speaks of the sending of the Spirit or the supplying of the Spirit *by God*. So monotheism is connected even with what might be regarded as the most mystical aspect of salvation. The truth is that so far as the primitive sources permit us to judge, Christ was valued as Savior just because of his relation to the one supreme God; it is, so far as we can see, quite typical of primitive Christianity when Paul couples "God our Father and the Lord Jesus Christ" together regularly at the beginnings of his epistles. There is not the slightest evidence that in the apostolic age Jesus was ever preached in such a way that the acceptance of him as Savior and Lord was possible without the acceptance of God his Father.

Against this conclusion Dr. McGiffert employs one of the most extraordinary arguments in the whole book. In certain passages, he says, Paul speaks of the gospel as having "to do only with Christ, not God"—for example, in 1 Corinthians 15:1ff. But could there be any greater conceivable misuse of the passage? Paul was led to give this excerpt from his fundamental missionary teaching because of an error that was concerned specifically with the resurrection and with nothing else; it is absurd to expect him, in such a connection, to reproduce other elements in his teaching, which, no matter how fundamental, would here have been entirely irrelevant. Again Dr. McGiffert refers to Philippians 1:15–21, where the rival teachers are tolerantly spoken of because they are preaching Christ, and where nothing is said about God. But would Paul ever have spoken with tolerance of a preaching which ignored God the Father? The question needs only to be put in order to be answered. The truth is that preaching "Christ" for Paul necessarily involved preaching the one God the Father; the idea of "Christ" had as its absolutely necessary correlative the idea of God; the former could never be thought of without the latter. Finally, Dr. McGiffert asks that with the tolerance of Philippians 1:15–21 there should be contrasted the stern words of Galatians 1:7–8: "There are some that trouble you and would pervert the gospel of Christ. But though we or an angel from heaven preach another gospel than that we have preached unto you, let him be anathema." The point seems to be that Paul was intolerant, whereas in Galatia "Christ" or the way of salvation was not correctly set forth, but could be very tolerant about errors concerning other things, including the doctrine of God. But could there be any more complete abandonment of grammatico-historical interpretation? The reason why Paul does not in Galatians pronounce an anathema upon those who fail to proclaim God the Father is simply because he is there arguing against Jews, whose doctrine of God the Father was presumably all that could be desired; very naturally he refers to the matter that was in dispute and not to other matters, important though they might be, which were utterly irrelevant at that particular time. If the opponents in Galatia had failed to proclaim the one true God set forth in the Old Testament and in the teaching of Jesus, then we can be sure that Paul's anathema would have lacked nothing in sternness. But as a matter of fact, a proclamation of Christ which was not also a proclamation of God the Father was so absolutely inconceivable in the early church that anathemas against it were never needed. Where Paul does refer, as in the case of the Thessalonians, to his missionary preaching among Gentiles, he places the proclamation of "the living and true God" at the very beginning.

But Dr. McGiffert has not quite finished with Galatians 1:7–8. "Of this gospel preached to the Galatians," he continues, "Paul says: 'Neither did I receive it from man, nor was I taught it, but by revelation of Jesus Christ,' showing that it was something different from Judaism and Jewish monotheism." Here appears, in a peculiarly poignant way, the failure of our author to recognize the dispensational or factual and historical character of Paul's teaching. It is perfectly true that the doctrine of God did not, strictly speaking, form a part of Paul's "gospel"; for "gospel" meant to Paul, as the very word implies, a piece of good news, an account of something that had happened. The doctrine of God sets forth what God was and always had been and in itself, far from being a gospel or a piece of good news, can lead us sinners only to despair; whereas the "gospel" sets forth something that God did at a definite point of time near Jerusalem when he saved sinful mankind through the death and resurrection of the Lord Jesus Christ. But although the gospel itself does not contain the doctrine of God, it presupposes it and is absolutely meaningless without it. In isolating the gospel from its presuppositions, Dr. McGiffert, in accordance with the dominant tendency of today, has made of the gospel something totally different from that which

Paul understood it to be. If the gospel of Paul is said to be "something different from Judaism and Jewish monotheism," that is perhaps true, provided that "Jewish monotheism" (in what is really a thoroughly unhistorical way) is abstracted from the element of promise with which it was always connected. But if the assertion is true, it is also valueless. "Jewish monotheism" sets forth what God is; the gospel of Paul sets forth something that he has done—but what he has done is entirely unintelligible without a knowledge of what he is.

The same consideration—namely, insistence upon the factual or historical nature of Paul's gospel—serves to refute the next argument which Dr. McGiffert brings forth. "Paul's teaching about the law in his Epistle to the Galatians—that they were not justified by works of law but by faith in Jesus Christ, and that they who were justified by law were severed from Christ— and his declaration that circumcision is nothing nor uncircumcision, but a new creation, might easily lead his converts to think the whole Jewish system including Jewish monotheism itself of small importance" (p. 50). "There was no antecedent reason . . . why the Gentile Christians should accept the God of the Jews whom Jesus worshiped, any more than the Jewish ceremonial law which he observed and the Jewish practices in which he was brought up" (p. 47). This argument ignores the difference between a command, which deals with what *ought to be*, and a doctrine of God, which deals with what *is*. A command may be absolutely authoritative and yet temporary, whereas a doctrine of God, if it is abandoned, can be abandoned only because it never was true at all. If a boy's father, to use a homely example, tells him to chop up the wood on the woodpile, that does not mean that he is to continue chopping wood to the end of time; he is not at all disobeying or setting aside his father's command if he quits chopping wood when the job is done. So it is exactly with the ceremonial requirements of the Old Testament law; they were, according to Paul, commands of God, but they were commands which God intended from the beginning to be in force only until the coming of Christ. When their purpose was fulfilled, it was not obedience but disobedience to insist upon the observance of them. But to reject the "Jewish" doctrine of the one living and holy God would not be to declare a command to be temporary, but it would be to declare an assertion of fact to be false. The two things are entirely incommensurate. If God commanded Jewish fasts and feasts and the separation of Israel from other nations, it was quite conceivable that he should declare that the purpose of those commands was fulfilled with the completion of Christ's redeeming work. And if he did so, that did not involve at all any confession that those previous commands had been, under the old dispensation, anything but holy and just and good. But to say that the God of Israel was not really the Maker and Ruler of the world—indeed, to say that there was no supreme Maker and Ruler of the world at all—that would be an entirely different matter. Dr. McGiffert says: "Paul broke with Judaism and made of Christianity a new religion, but he did not break with the Jewish God. . . . But by what right [the Gentile disciples are represented as possibly saying to themselves] did he reject a part of the old system and retain another part?" The answer to this question of Dr. McGiffert's is that Paul did not reject any part of the old system at all. He did not reject the ceremonial law, but believed that it was authoritative throughout. But he believed that though absolutely authoritative, it was intended by God to be temporary.

So the whole notion that Paul was picking and choosing in Judaism, and that in retaining the Old Testament idea of God while rejecting the ceremonial law he was stopping arbitrarily in a halfway emancipation, is based upon an ignoring of the dispensational or historical basis of Paulinism. Paul preached his gospel of Gentile freedom not because he took the Old Testament law with a grain of salt, but on the contrary because he took it strictly—so strictly that he could not be satisfied with halfway measures, but was led on to a clear recognition of the epoch-making significance of the cross of Christ. He emancipated his converts from the ceremonial law not because he accepted part of what the Old Testament teaches and rejected the rest, but on the contrary just because he accepted all of it; his doctrine of redemption is based not upon a lax or eclectic, but upon a strict and comprehensive, view of the law of God.

No doubt it may be said in reply that, although Paul himself was not really rejecting the authority of any part of the Old Testament, yet simple-minded Gentile converts might have thought that he was doing so, and so might have thought that they were only going a little further in the path in which Paul had led if, in addition to the rejection of the ceremonial law, they rejected or at least ignored the Old Testament teaching about God. But the reply is hardly satisfactory. Despite the epistle of Barnabas, with its different teaching (which was due to the anti-Jewish polemic of the second century), the Pauline doctrine of the temporary character of the ceremonial law may probably have made its way generally in the early church. The point was so very simple that even simpleminded, untheological Gentile Christians could understand it. And were any human beings ever quite so simpleminded and quite so untheological as Dr. McGiffert's Gentile Christians are thought to have been?

But even if the Pauline teaching about the one God, Maker and Ruler of the world, was perfectly clear, would the authority of Paul and of the other Jewish Christian apostles and teachers be sufficient to compel the Gentile converts to accept this "Jewish God"? Dr. McGiffert thinks that it would not. "Paul's authority," he says (p. 48), "was not great enough to compel the general adoption of his doctrine of redemption, nor were other Christians under the necessity of accepting the Jewish God simply because he did." This reference to the Pauline doctrine of redemption is ingenious but hardly convincing. The point here made seems to be that many post-Pauline writers—for example, the apostolic fathers and the later writers of the old Catholic church—display a woeful lack of understanding for the Pauline doctrine of redemption. Might not others in the church, then, have displayed a similar lack of acceptance of the Pauline doctrine of God? In answer, it must be admitted that there is in early Christian literature outside of the New Testament evidence of a failure to understand or at least to state at all fully or clearly the Pauline doctrine of justification by faith. That is why the achievement of Augustine and of the Reformation, in bringing to light things that are indeed at the very center of the Bible but that the church had failed fully to understand and use, must be rated very high; and that is also why the true "progressives" are not those who now busy themselves with the "simplification" of creeds but those who value the rich theological heritage which on the basis of Scripture the Holy Spirit has given to the church. Nevertheless, the failure of the sub-apostolic church to make full use of the Pauline doctrine of redemption is not at all comparable to that ignoring of Pauline monotheism which Dr. McGiffert attributes to the primitive Gentile disciples. The Pauline doctrine of redemption was not denied, nor even altogether ignored, but was merely not made use of in its full richness and depth; whereas this supposed ignoring of Pauline monotheism would mean the missing of that feature of Paul's preaching which according to 1 Thessalonians came at the very beginning, which was perhaps most strikingly distinctive as over against the beliefs from which the Gentiles were won, and which appeared in the simplest possible way in everything that Paul said. What did those Gentile Christians, according to

Dr. McGiffert, make of the terms "God" and "the Father" which appear every few lines in the Pauline epistles and which were undoubtedly equally frequent, if not more frequent, in his oral missionary teaching? Did they suppose that those terms meant nothing at all, so that they could be safely passed by? The supposition, we think, is nothing short of absurd.

But Dr. McGiffert has raised the question of authority, and it is an important question which cannot be ignored. What, according to our author, were the authorities or the influences which led the early Gentile converts to ignore monotheism, and what were the authorities or influences on the other side which, in order that they might thus ignore monotheism, they were obliged to overcome?

On the former side, as an influence hostile to monotheism, Dr. McGiffert places the religions from which the converts had come. "While monotheism and polytheism," he says, "were both represented in the religious world of the period, the former was usually the affair of the philosopher, and it is improbable that the mass of the early Gentile converts, who were certainly not drawn from the philosophic schools, had any initial interest in monotheism or any understanding of it" (p. 41). "Had the Gentile Christians lived in a monotheistic world, they might have been expected to subordinate Christ to God as Christians of Jewish antecedents did. As it was, they needed no supreme God above and beyond Christ, and to suppose such a God central in their thought is to misinterpret their interest and attitude. Jewish Christianity was monotheistic and Gentile Christianity became monotheistic under influences to be referred to later, but there is no reason to suppose that the latter was monotheistic from the start. The Jews had won their monotheism only gradually and by many struggles;[8] to imagine that Jewish Christians could impose it without more ado upon converts to the new faith from the polytheistic civilization of the day is to overestimate their influence" (pp. 45ff.). "The saviour gods of the current mystery religions were not supreme gods—creators and rulers of the world—nor were they thought of by their votaries as the only gods. Initiation into this or that cult did not mean the denial of other deities; but only the special consecration of oneself to the service of a particular deity. This may well have been the situation of many early Christians. Their personal piety cen-

8. This is obviously not the place to discuss the view of the Old Testament which Dr. McGiffert here assumes.

tred in the Lord Jesus Christ. In communion with him and in devotion to him they found their religious life. But they may not have felt it necessary to deny the existence of other deities or to accept the one God of Israel as their God" (pp. 46ff.).

It will not here be possible to examine in detail the questions of fact involved in this argument—particularly the question whether the Gentile converts in any considerable numbers had been adherents of the mystery religions. That question, we think, must be answered, for the early period, with an emphatic negative.[9] But the fundamental weakness of the argument is independent of all such questions, no matter how important the questions may be in themselves. The clearest defect of the argument is that it ignores one of the most outstanding features of early Christianity—namely, its uncompromising exclusiveness. That was the characteristic which impressed itself most plainly even upon outsiders; that was the characteristic which gave the new religion all its offensiveness, but also all its power. If the early Christians had been what Dr. Giffert represents them as being, if they had simply accepted Christ as *their* Savior without being concerned to deny the existence of other saviors, then there would have been no persecutions, but also there would have been no conquest of the world. The most obvious single feature of this religion was just the thing that Dr. McGiffert denies; the strange thing about these hated Christians, the thing which aroused the opposition of the world, was not that they accepted a new Savior, but that they held him to be the *only* Savior and the only Lord. But to what was this exclusiveness of the early church due? The answer is perfectly plain—it was due to the lofty, universalistic, uncompromising monotheism which runs all through the Old Testament and which appears in supreme glory in the teaching of Jesus himself. Is Dr. McGiffert correct in representing the universalistic and exclusive monotheism of the Christian church as being the cold invention of theological schemers who say that without it the church could not extend its dominion over the whole world? Surely not. Rather, it was the thing for which plain men and women were willing, with a glad smile on their faces, to suffer and die.

Our author is making a great mistake in assuming that because monotheism has no place in *his* religious life, it had no place in the religious life of

9. See *The Origin of Paul's Religion* (1921), p. 273, and the passage there cited from Oepke, *Die Missionspredigt des Apostels Paulus* (1920), 26.

the early church. And just the prevalent polytheism of that age, upon which this argument lays stress, placed in the very forefront of the disciples' mind and heart their belief in the one God the Father Almighty and the one Lord Jesus Christ.

Thus, the previous polytheism of the Gentile disciples, far from making them indifferent to the apostolic teaching about God, had if anything exactly the opposite effect. Adherence to an exclusive monotheism was one of the things that acceptance of the new faith, in a polytheistic environment, most clearly meant. Nothing is to be said, therefore, in favor of the antitheistic influence which Dr. McGiffert finds in the previous beliefs of the early Gentile converts.

But what were the authorities on the other side?

In the first place, there was the authority of the apostle Paul. Dr. McGiffert tries to minimize its importance, but surely without success. It is true, the authority of Paul was called in question in the early days, in accordance with the information contained in the epistles. But by whom was it called in question? It was called in question not by Gentiles who refused to accept the Jewish Christian teaching about God, but, quite the contrary, by Jews who appealed to the Jerusalem apostles and to the Old Testament. In their case Paul's authority was undermined not by a rejection of apostolic authority but by an appeal to one apostle against another. As a matter of fact, the appeal was unsuccessful; Paul was in agreement even about the way of salvation with the original apostles, and the old Catholic church was quite correct in appealing not to Peter alone or to Paul alone but to Peter and Paul together. But whatever may have been the differences of opinion in the early days about the way of salvation and the place of the Jewish law, there was at any rate full agreement among all the apostles about the God of Israel. Where Paul's authority was undermined, it was undermined not because of an objection to Judaism on the part of Gentile converts, but on the contrary because of an excessive readiness of Gentile converts to accept even the most burdensome parts of the Jewish ceremonial law. The receptiveness of the Galatian converts to the Judaizers would be very strange if Dr. McGiffert's picture of the polytheistic and anti-Jewish tendencies of the Gentile Christians were at all correct. At any rate, in the matter of monotheism all the early teachers of the church, to say nothing of all the apostles, were fully agreed. If the Gentile disciples had not accepted this element of the apostolic preaching it is difficult to see how they could have accepted anything at all.

In the second place, there was on the same side the authority and influence of the Old Testament. This influence, again, Dr. McGiffert underestimates in a very extraordinary way. He does not, of course, deny altogether the use of the Old Testament. "I do not," he says, "mean, of course, to suggest that all the primitive Gentile Christians took Christ as their Lord and Saviour without taking his God and Father as their God. On the contrary, I have no doubt that many of them accepted the Jewish God and the Jewish Bible when they accepted Jesus Christ" (p. 49). But surely this admission, in its inadequacy, only sets in sharper light the gross underestimate of the influence of the Old Testament in the early church which runs all through the book. To say that "many" of the Gentile converts accepted the "Jewish Bible" completely fails to do justice to the place which the "Jewish Bible" holds in all our accounts of the primitive Gentile mission. Is it not clear that one of the chief instruments in the missionary work of the church was just the appeal to this ancient and authoritative book? The world of that day was seeking for ancient authority; no religion which represented itself as really new could have any chance of success. Even those Gnostics of the second century who rejected the Old Testament could not do without a Bible, but appealed to New Testament books or to sacred books of their own. Dr. McGiffert has therefore clearly failed to give due attention to the attitude of the converts, just as he has also failed to appreciate the attitude of the missionaries, when he represents the Old Testament as a piece of baggage which might easily be dropped by the way. There is evidence, moreover, that just that feature of Old Testament teaching which our author supposes to have been ignored was the feature which appealed especially to the Gentile world of that day, for the progress of the pre-Christian Jewish mission shows clearly that the pagan world was susceptible to monotheistic influences. It is true, that mission would never in itself have succeeded in conquering the world, but the reason for its failure was not unattractiveness in monotheism but the national exclusiveness of the Mosaic Law. Judaism could only have removed this limitation by rejecting the Old Testament, or at least by taking it "with a grain of salt." But to have done so would have destroyed all the power which the Jewish mission possessed. The Christian mission, on the other hand, because of its presentation of the epoch-making, dispensational significance of the coming of Christ offered all that Judaism had offered and yet offered it with a good conscience and with full retention of the authoritative book which had been the chief strength of the previous missionary effort. Without the Old Testament, Gentile Christianity would have been at best only one religion among many; an absolutely essential element in its world-conquering power was just the thing that Dr. McGiffert rejects.

A third authority in favor of monotheism in the early Gentile church was the authority of Jesus. This authority Dr. McGiffert not merely minimizes, but almost ignores. The only reference to it seems to be as follows:

> There was no antecedent reason, indeed, why the Gentile Christians should accept the God of the Jews whom Jesus worshipped, any more than the Jewish ceremonial law which he observed and the Jewish practices in which he was brought up. The fact that Jesus himself and his personal disciples were Jews no more required the Gentile Christians to be Jews in their customs and beliefs than the fact that Adonis was a Syrian deity, Attis a Phrygian, and Isis and Serapis Egyptian deities required their adherents to become Syrians or Phrygians or Egyptians, and to accept the religious tenets of those peoples. (p. 47)

But surely this reference to the gods of various pagan cults only places in the sharper light the weakness of Dr. McGiffert's contention. Where is anything said in antiquity about the *teaching* of Adonis or Attis or Isis? Where is there any even pretended record of their words? It is no wonder that the worshipers of Adonis did not have to be Syrians and the worshipers of Attis did not have to be Phrygians, for nothing whatever about the personality of those deities was recorded. They were pale mythical figures, whose experiences, even if they were conceived as taking place at any definite time at all—rather than being merely repeated again and again in the cult—lay in the dim and distant past. But Jesus, the "Savior-God" of the Christians, was a historical personage who had lived and died but a short time before. And he was a historical personage whose words were recorded and treasured. Even Dr. McGiffert will not deny that fact, for he himself makes use of the tradition contained in the synoptic gospels as providing precious information about the real Jesus. But here, in defending his main thesis, he treats the tradition of the words of Jesus as though it did not exist; and his parallel between Jesus and the pagan cult-gods shows as clearly as anything possibly could do how far he is from doing justice to the real facts of primitive Christianity. The worshipers of Adonis were not bound by the teaching of their god, for no teaching of Adonis was handed down. But the worshipers of Jesus were worshipers of a historical character, whose words, as we know and as even Dr. McGiffert admits, were carefully treasured among his followers. At this point our author has almost outdone the radicalism of Wrede. Wrede supposed (quite erroneously) that the apostle Paul cared little about the words which Jesus uttered when he was on earth, but even Wrede would hardly have denied that the tradition of Jesus' words was carefully preserved in the primitive Gentile church taken as a whole. But if the tradition of Jesus' words was treasured at all, then his teaching about God the Father could certainly not be ignored. It was quite impossible for disciples of Jesus to accept anything that Jesus said, and not accept this. But to suppose that the mass of Gentile Christians in the early period accepted nothing that Jesus said, not even this central part of his teaching, and treated him merely as the worshipers of Adonis treated the mythical figure that was supposed to be connected with their cult—this is to exceed by far all bounds of historical possibility. If the mass of early Gentile Christianity had been what Dr. McGiffert supposes it to have been, then the memory of Jesus' words and deeds would probably have been lost and Christianity would probably long ago have taken its place among the half-forgotten cults of a decadent age. A primitive Gentile Christianity that cared nothing for Jesus' teaching about God is a historical monstrosity, which Dr. McGiffert's whole reconstruction indeed demands, but which a little reflection shows to be nothing short of absurd.

Historic Christianity as a whole has certainly retained the influence of Jesus' life; and Dr. McGiffert would probably maintain, with the current Modernism, that Jesus was the founder of Christianity just because of the ethical and religious life that he lived. But does he not see that, in supposing the primitive Gentile church—which, as we shall observe, he makes the basis of the whole subsequent development of Christianity—to have been ignorant of the teaching of Jesus about God, which lay at the center of Jesus' own religious life, he has placed an insurmountable barrier between the life of Jesus and the Christianity of which Jesus is thought to have been the founder? Dr. McGiffert's primitive Gentile Christians could have had no contact with Jesus' religious life, for if they had had contact with Jesus' religious life, they could not possibly have ignored the thing that lay at the very heart of it. But if they had no contact with Jesus' religious life, then, since they formed the basis of the whole subsequent development, the religious life of Jesus could have exerted no central influence upon the historic Christian church. That is absurd, but it is an absurdity which follows with relentless certainty from Dr. McGiffert's thesis. Shall the thesis be abandoned, or shall the Christian church be regarded as having only a nominal and no essential connection with the real Jesus of Nazareth? The answer, we think, can hardly be uncertain.

Thus our author has failed to render his extraordinary thesis antecedently probable; he has entirely failed to put out of the world the overpowering weight of *prima facie* evidence that is against it. His nontheistic Gentile Christianity did not exist, for the simple reason that, in view of the whole character of the primitive Christian mission and in view of the authorities upon which that mission was based, it never *could* have existed. It is with much more brevity, therefore, that we can deal now with the positive arguments for the actuality, as distinguished from the antecedent possibility, of this reconstructed Gentile Christianity.

These arguments may apparently be placed under six heads (pp. 52–87).

(1) In the first place (pp. 52–64), Dr. McGiffert says, it is "beyond dispute that Christ was widely recognized as divine among the early Christians." That fact may certainly be admitted—indeed, we do not understand why Dr. McGiffert does not say that Christ was *always* instead of only *widely* recognized as divine. But how does the recognition of the divinity of Christ prove that there ever was a time when God the Father was not also recognized? Paul, for example, as Dr. McGiffert himself insists, recognized Christ as divine; yet he also recognized the God of Jesus and of the Old Testament. The only answer which our author can give is that in certain writers it cannot always be determined whether Christ or God the Father is being spoken of, whereas in Paul there is no such confusion. But surely this answer is quite inadequate. In Paul the same terms are sometimes used in referring to God the Father as those which are used in referring to Christ; and if confusion is avoided usually in his epistles, surely that may be merely a matter of linguistic clearness as over against other writers, or at most a mere difference of the degree to which a certain phenomenon appears. Dr. McGiffert, under the same head, points to the frequency with which in certain quarters prayers were offered to Christ; but as he himself admits, Paul also offers prayers to Christ, and the difference is again a difference not of principle, but of degree. The entire argument, therefore, clearly breaks down. Recognition of the divinity of Christ certainly does not indicate any denial

492

or ignoring of God the Father; for Paul recognizes the divinity of Christ, yet his theism cannot be called in question.

Of course, that simply raises the central question how it was that a strict monotheist like Paul could place the worship of a Jew, one of his contemporaries, alongside of the worship of Jehovah. With that question, in the present book, Dr. McGiffert does not attempt to deal. It is answered, of course, if the New Testament account of Jesus is true. But it has never been satisfactorily answered by any naturalistic reconstruction. Certainly no progress toward the answering of it has been made by Dr. McGiffert's addition to it of the other question how a primitive nontheistic belief in the divinity of Christ came to have added to it in the later history of the church the belief in the one God the Father, Maker of heaven and earth. If our author could only maintain that there was (1) a Jewish Christian monotheism without the divinity of Christ and (2) a Gentile Christian belief in the divinity of Christ without monotheism, then he might explain the later belief of the church by the conjunction of these two elements. But unfortunately, this way is closed to him by the testimony of Paul. The whole problem therefore remains in all its troublesomeness; belief in the divinity of Christ and worship of him arose, unfortunately for all naturalistic reconstructions, not on Gentile Christian ground but among the monotheistic Jews.

(2) In the second place (pp. 64–67), Dr. McGiffert points to Marcion, the heresiarch of the second century, who "read Christianity solely in terms of salvation, and rejected the creating God, the God of the Jews." "The presence in the church of the second century of Marcion and his followers, as well as of their fellow heretics, the Gnostics, who also rejected the God of the Jews on grounds to be referred to later, goes to show that conversion to Christianity did not necessarily carry with it the acceptance of the God of the Jews. Had it done so, their attitude would have been difficult, not to say impossible. At any rate, if Jewish monotheism was an essential element in Christianity, and to be a Christian meant to believe in the Jewish God, they could not have regarded themselves in good faith as Christians."

This argument involves the customary use of the second-century heresies as witnesses to a primitive Christianity which is supposed to have been left behind, and so have come to be despised, by the main body of the church. But the argument is extremely precarious. A living religion, such as the Christian religion was in the second century, is constantly assailed from within and from without by totally alien types of faith and life. So it was in the ancient period, and so it is also today. That Marcion and the Gnostics called themselves Christians is no more a proof that they really were Christians than the fact that the disciples of Mrs. Eddy call themselves "Christian" Scientists is a proof that their acutely pagan teaching has any real affinity for the religion whose name they choose to bear. It is certainly very precarious, to say the least, to find any foothold for the dualism of Marcion or of the Gnostics in the piety of the apostolic age. Moreover, in the specific case of Marcion, it must be remembered that he did not venture to identify Jesus with the supreme "good God," as over against the "just God" of the Jews, but regarded Jesus as having been sent by that good God. Thus, he does not even plausibly attest the type of belief which our author attributes to primitive Gentile Christianity, but rather is a witness (if such witnesses were really needed) to the necessary connection in Christian thinking between Jesus and a Father who sent him into the world.

(3) In the third place (pp. 67–75), Dr. McGiffert finds a polemic against, and so a testimony to the existence of, his primitive nontheistic Gentile Christianity in Polycarp, Ignatius, the first epistle of John, and even in the epistles of Paul—particularly in the epistle to the Ephesians. The first epistle of John, for example, is regarded by our author as being directed not, as has always been supposed, against those who made too little of Christ but against those who made too little of God. But this polemic—certainly the reference of it to nontheistic Gentile converts within the church—is found only by the most unnatural reading of the epistle, and particularly by reading into the text what is not there. For example, Dr. McGiffert quotes in support of his thesis 1 John 4:2–3: "Every spirit that confesseth that Jesus Christ is come in the flesh (and so was connected historically with the Jewish people) is of God; and every spirit that confesseth not Jesus is not of God." Here the only words which support Dr. McGiffert's thesis instead of actually telling against it are the words in parentheses, which Dr. McGiffert himself supplies. And so it is throughout the whole argument. Particularly unwarranted is the use of the epistle to the Ephesians as a polemic against those in the church who did not accept the God of the Jews. And any references of Paul to the evils of idolatry are surely explained quite adequately by the fact that Christianity was engaged in an active propaganda against the polytheism outside of the church. In general, the Pauline epistles and all the other books to which Dr. McGiffert refers create the clear impression that monotheism did not need to be defended among Chris-

tians, but could always be assumed. This impression is dealt with by our author in a very extraordinary way. "It may be objected," he says, "that if there
were Gentile Christians who did not accept the God of the Jews, Paul would
not have contented himself with references of so casual a sort, but would
have denounced and condemned them in unsparing terms, as he did the Judaizers. It should be noticed, however, that such Christians as I have been
speaking of accepted Jesus Christ as their saviour and were thus one with
Paul in the chief matter." Here the last words simply beg the question. Were
Christians who accepted Jesus Christ and ignored God the Father one with
Paul [in Paul's view] "in the chief matter"? Indeed, would Christians who
"accepted Jesus Christ" in this manner have been regarded by the apostle
as having accepted the real Jesus Christ at all?

(4) In the fourth place (pp. 76–78), "in support of the assumption that
there were Christians in the primitive church whose God was Jesus Christ
and Jesus Christ alone, attention may be called," Dr. McGiffert says, "to the
continued use of the original formula of baptism in his name" [that is, baptism in the name of Christ alone instead of in the name of Father, Son, and
Holy Ghost]. "Of course," Dr. McGiffert continues, "the use of the simple
formula among the early Jewish disciples meant that they and their fellow
countrymen already believed in God, and hence did not need to be baptized into his name. But in the Gentile world the situation was altogether
different." Here our author weakens his own case by supposing that the formula which mentioned Christ alone was earlier than the triune formula of
Matthew 28:19. For if that simple formula was earlier, then the continuance of it even in the Gentile world could be easily explained by faithfulness to tradition. But in any case, the whole argument altogether fails to
bear the weight that Dr. McGiffert rests upon it. No matter how firm and
vital was the belief of the Gentile church in God the Father, the brief designation of baptism simply as baptism in the name of Christ would be thoroughly natural. And Marcion's rejection of the triune formula must probably
be regarded as simply connected with his system and (for the reasons mentioned above) as being quite without significance for the facts of primitive
Gentile Christianity.

(5) In the fifth place (pp. 78–80), Dr. McGiffert points to the wide prevalence in the second century of "Modalism, the belief, namely, that Christ
is himself the supreme God, the Father of the world and of men." But surely
this denial of the personal distinction between Father and Son is adequately

to be explained simply as one of the unsuccessful attempts to set forth the mysterious teaching of the New Testament. The Modalist solution of the problem presented by the relation of God the Father and God the Son is rightly designated by Tertullian (quoted on p. 78) as belonging to "the simple"; but this (false) simplicity is to be explained—quite naturally, in view of human weakness—as an attempt of second-century Christians to interpret the New Testament, rather than as any survival of a primitive nontheistic Christianity.

(6) The last argument (pp. 80–87) is drawn from the "extraordinary lack of vivid and fervent piety" and indeed of devotional writings of any kind in "most of our early Christian literature, aside from the New Testament." But what is the bearing of that interesting fact—interesting if true—upon Dr. McGiffert's thesis? The bearing of it is certainly not obvious. "If such piety toward Christ" (as that which is discovered in Ignatius), Dr. McGiffert says, "found frequent expression in the literature of the early church, it would be easy to explain the situation on the ground that Christ was the real God of the early Christians and the Father God only a theological abstraction. But except in the writings of Ignatius piety toward Christ finds no larger and more vivid expression than piety toward God." The admission is certainly significant, and would seem to deprive the observation of all possible significance for the main thesis of the book. But Dr. McGiffert is not ready to surrender so easily. "In these circumstances," he says, "I can only suggest that the lack may have been due to the divided object of worship. The singleness of devotion felt by the Jews toward Jehovah may have been difficult for a Christian whose real God was Jesus Christ, but who was compelled to subordinate him to another God, a theological or philosophical figure—as will appear in the next lecture—not at all calculated to arouse deep personal devotion." Could there possibly be a weaker argument? If the real God of the Gentile Christians was Jesus and only Jesus, why did the fact that they were compelled to connect him with God the Father prevent them from giving joyous expression to their devotion to him any more than the voluntary connection of Jesus with God the Father on the part of Paul and the other New Testament writers prevented them from giving joyous expression to *their* devotion to both of these divine persons?

Thus, the positive arguments for Dr. McGiffert's thesis break down as completely as do his attempts to establish an antecedent probability in its favor. Enough has been said, we are bold enough to think, not merely to show that the thesis is not proven, but to show positively that it is proven to be false. There never was a prevalent Gentile Christianity in the early church that read Christianity only in terms of salvation and was not interested in the God whom Jesus taught his disciples to worship and love.

But if so, then the rest of the book can be treated very briefly. It is indeed full of interesting observations, but despite the hope expressed at the conclusion of the lecture which has just been reviewed, the attentive reader can hardly say that it provides any "added reason" for positing the existence of "a Christianity whose God was Jesus Christ alone."

"In the previous lecture" (that is, the one which has just been discussed), Dr. McGiffert says in summing up the subject of the latter part of his book, "I showed that the God of the primitive Gentile Christians, or at any rate, of many of them [but he has really claimed far more than that], was Jesus Christ; that they began with him and only afterward associated him with the God of the Jews and worshipped two divine beings, Son and Father. In the present lecture I wish to trace this development and explain the addition of God the Father to the original object of worship, the Lord Jesus Christ. Many writers have described the process by which Christ came to be associated with the God of the Jews, and to be thought of as the second person of the Trinity, subordinate only to God the Father, and I shall not repeat the story here. I am interested, rather, in the other problem and shall confine myself to that. So far as I am aware, it has hitherto escaped notice. How, then, did it come about that Christians who originally worshipped Jesus Christ alone were led to worship also the God of the Jews and even to subordinate Christ to him as a son to a father?"

It is no wonder that this second problem has "hitherto escaped notice." It has escaped notice for the simple reason that its existence depends upon the existence of the primitive nontheistic Gentile Christianity which until the appearance of the present book was unknown. And since that condition has just been shown not to be satisfied, it is only with a qualified, though (because of Dr. McGiffert's mastery of details) still with a keen, interest that we turn to the solution of the problem which his hypothesis has raised.

How did Dr. McGiffert's Gentile Christianity whose only God was Jesus come to give place to the monotheism of the historic Christian church? The answer which our author gives may be put almost in a word. The transition was due not to religion, but to theology; it was due to the necessity of exhibiting a worldwide scope for the Christian religion. The simple Gentile Christians, it is supposed, were perfectly willing to accept Jesus as their Savior without asking whether he stood in any relation to the whole world. In this respect, as in many other respects, they were the precursors of those who in the modern church accept certain beliefs for themselves without being interested in the question whether those beliefs are accepted by others, and are perfectly willing to make common cause with men whose beliefs are diametrically opposite to their own. But this simple, nontheological, nontheistic religion, it is supposed, would have been only one religion among many, and the theologians and apologists were unwilling to be satisfied with any such position as that. They therefore had to show the connection of Jesus the God of the early Christians with a God who would require the devotion of all the dwellers on earth; in short, they had to show the connection of Jesus with the one supreme God, Maker and Ruler of the world. There were unsuccessful attempts, it is supposed further, at attaining this result, notably Gnosticism; but after such errors had been overcome, the result was the addition of the Jewish God to the Savior-God Jesus and the connection between the two as Father and Son. "The Christianity that emerged from the [Gnostic] conflict was not a mere gospel of salvation, but a theology and cosmology, a doctrine of God and a philosophy of the universe" (p. 107). But this connection of Jesus with God the Father "did not mean the displacement of the Saviour Jesus Christ . . . but the extension of his functions to include creation, providence, and judgment" (p. 194). "The association of the two was as close and the identification of the two as complete as philosophy would allow" (p. 195).

One thing that strikes the careful reader forcibly as he examines this hypothesis is the evident disregard by the author of the law of scientific parsimony: ingenious and far-fetched explanations are here sought for things of which a simple explanation lies ready to hand. Why is there all this labor to explain how God the Father came to be added to Jesus Christ as an object of worship in the Christian church? Does he not appear as an object of worship, side by side with Christ, at the very beginning of the development, in all the New Testament and particularly in the epistles of Paul? Does not Christ also appear in the New Testament as associated with the Father in creation and in judgment? Why then may not the appearance of exactly these same views in the later church be due to the simple influence of the New Testament (to say nothing of the teaching of Jesus himself) instead of to this elaborate theological and apologetic scheming of men who wanted by such means to extend the power of the church over the whole world? The question is unanswerable to the man who stations himself on the basis of the plain historical facts. But it is easily answerable on the basis of Dr. McGiffert's theory. The reason why, if Dr. McGiffert's theory is correct, the simple influence of the apostolic teaching and of the teaching of Jesus cannot at this point be made determinative is that if it is made determinative the entire hypothesis of a primitive nontheistic Gentile Christianity falls to the ground. Such a Christianity could have come to exist in the first place only if there was in the early days the most abysmal neglect of the teaching of Jesus and of the Jewish Christian apostles. But if there was such a neglect of the New Testament and of the teaching underlying it, then and then only does the final victory of the New Testament idea of God become a problem— a problem which must be solved in the extraordinary ingenious and intricate way which Dr. McGiffert proposes.

The truth is that the primitive nontheistic Gentile Christianity of Dr. McGiffert is without beginning of days or end of life. It had no root in what preceded, and it left no real trace in what followed. All the labor of the latter part of the book—instructive and interesting though it is in detail— could have been spared if the problem had not been artificially created by the insertion into history of a phenomenon which is not attested in the sources, and which throws the whole development of the church into a confusion from which even Dr. McGiffert's learning and skill have not succeeded in extricating.

But another observation is more important still. The really important thing about this elaborate reconstruction of the history of the church is not the historical improbability of it in detail, but the presupposition upon which it is based. We do not indeed demand that a historian should be without presuppositions. But the important question is whether the presuppositions are true or false. And in the case of Dr. McGiffert, we think that they are false. The entire book is really based upon the pragmatist assumption that religion can be separated from theology and that a man can obtain the values of the religious life apart from the particular intellectual conception which he forms of his God. This assumption leads in the first place to an artificial treatment of history, which altogether fails to do justice to the real complexity of human life; and it leads, in the second place, and in particular, to the reconstruction, contrary to all the evidence, of a primitive Gentile Christianity which shall exhibit just the type of nontheological religion which the modern pragmatist desires.

Dr. McGiffert is not able, it is true, to carry out his separation between theology and religion in a thoroughly consistent way. At one moment, for example, he tells us that "the Gnostic controversy . . . was a theological controversy pure and simple," and that "the Gnostics, as well as their opponents, believed in Christ and in salvation through him" (p. 107), and at another moment he implies that Gnosticism outraged traditional Christian piety (p. 108). And even Dr. McGiffert's nontheological Gentile Christians have at times attributed to them interests which never ought to have been theirs. Thus it is said that to have made Christ less and lower than God would have doomed the doctrine "with the great mass of pious Christians" (p. 99), and that the Gnostic degradation of Jesus to a mere place in a series of emanations "seemed particularly offensive to common Christian sentiment as tending to degrade the Lord Jesus Christ and remove him from his place of pre-eminence" (p. 103). No doubt these observations are in themselves perfectly true. But the trouble is that they do not at all agree with the main thesis of the book. What did those simpleminded Gentile converts care about the preeminence of Christ, just so he was allowed to still be their Savior? Our author has here attributed to the supposedly nontheological converts just that "theological" interest which it is the chief point of his book to keep separate from them.

Nevertheless, despite such inconsistencies, the anti-intellectualistic philosophy of our author does color and determine his conclusions throughout. Philosophy and theology and religion are in this book kept rigidly separate; and where they are supposed to have combined in the production of any historical phenomenon, the proportion contributed by each of the ingredients is determined almost with the accuracy of a chemical analysis. Thus the book ends with this characteristic utterance: "Religion speaks in the historic doctrine of the deity of Christ; philosophy speaks in the Logos Christology which means the distinction of the Son from the Father, and that, too, even though both are declared to be equally divine" (p. 195). In Dr. McGiffert's treatment of history, the pragmatist philosophy of the present day is fully as determinative as was the Hegelian philosophy in the Tübingen reconstruction of Baur and Zeller. And even far more plainly than in that former case the result is failure. The sources fail utterly to lend themselves to the attempted reconstruction; history refuses to be forced into the pragmatist mold; and all religious life—certainly all Christian life—is found to be based upon a doctrine of God.

The incorrectness of Dr. McGiffert's assumptions appears at many points. Particularly faulty is the separation of "salvation" from theism—a separation which appears again and again in the book. "That there were philosophical thinkers," he says, "who were attracted by the monotheism of the Jews and became Christians because of it is undoubtedly true, but they were vastly in the minority and the Roman world was not won to Christianity by any such theological interest. On the contrary, faith in Christ and in his salvation converted the masses then, as it has converted multitudes in every age since" (pp. 44–45). "Christianity ceased," he says again with evident disapprobation, "to be a mere religion of salvation—a mere saving cult—and Christ ceased to be a mere saviour. He was the creator, ruler, and judge of all the earth. This is really a very remarkable fact, not adequately accounted for in my opinion by the influence of Jewish tradition. I see no satisfactory explanation of it except the one I have suggested, the [theological and apologetic] desire to associate Christ with God in all the divine activities, and thus to make the connection between the two as close as possible" (p. 191).

This distinction ignores the simple fact that there can be no salvation without something from which a man is saved. If Christ saves the Christians, *from what* does he save them? Dr. McGiffert never seems to raise that question. But the answer to it is abundantly plain, and it destroys the entire reconstruction which this book so brilliantly attempts. Is it not abundantly plain that Christ saves Christians from sin, and from the consequences which it brings at the judgment-seat of God? And is it not plain also that this was just the thing that appealed most strongly to simple people of the first century, as it appeals most strongly to many persons today? The truth is, it is quite impossible to think of Christ as Savior without thinking of the thing from which he saves; the justice of God is everywhere the presupposition of the Saviorhood of Christ. No doubt modern men, especially in the circles where Dr. McGiffert moves, have lost the sense of sin and guilt and the fear of God's awful judgment-seat. But with this loss there goes the general abandonment even of the word "salvation," to say nothing of the idea. Without the sense of sin and the fear of hell, there may be the desire for improvement, "uplift," betterment. But desire for "salvation," properly speaking, there cannot be. Modernism does not really "read Christianity in terms of salvation," but reads salvation out of Christianity. It gives even the word "salvation" up. For salvation involves the awful wrath of a righteous God; in other words, it involves just the thing which the antitheistic Modernism of Dr. McGiffert and others is most eager to reject. Very different was the situation in the early days of the Christian church. Modern men have lost the sense of guilt and the fear of hell, but the early Gentile Christians had not. They accepted Christ as Savior only because he could rescue them from the abyss and bring them into right relation to the Ruler and Judge of all the earth. The Saviorhood of Christ involved, then as always, the majesty and justice of God.

Even more radically at fault is another distinction which is at the very root of Dr. McGiffert's thinking throughout—the distinction "between a god of moral and a god of physical power" (p. 154). This distinction underlies the "ethical theism" presented in *The Rise of Modern Religious Ideas*—an "ethical theism" which is really the most radical possible denial of everything that the word "theism" can properly be held to mean. In accordance with the distinction, Dr. McGiffert holds that it is or should be a matter of indifference to Christians how the world came into being; the doctrine of creation belongs, he thinks, to a region of metaphysics with which religion need have nothing to do. Similar is really the case with respect to the doctrine of providence; the whole thought of the power as distinguished from the goodness of God is, our author evidently thinks, quite separable from religion. We can, he thinks, revere God's goodness without fearing his power or relying upon his protection from physical ills. And that really means that we can cease thinking of God as personal at all.

Such skepticism may be true or may be false—with that great question we shall not now undertake to deal—but indifferent to religion it certainly is not. Give up the thought of a Maker and Ruler of the world; say, as Dr. McGiffert really means, that "the Great Companion is dead," and you may still maintain something like religious fervor among a few philosophic souls. But the suffering mass of humanity, at any rate, will be left lost and hopeless in a strange and hostile world. And to represent these things as matters of religious indifference is to close one's eyes to the deepest things of the human heart. Is the doctrine of creation really a matter of no religious moment; may the religious man really revere God without asking the question how the world came into being and who it is that upholds it on its way? Is the modern scientist wrong who, pursuing his researches into nature's laws, comes at length to a curtain that is never lifted and stands in humble awe before a mystery that rebukes all pride? Was Isaiah wrong when he turned his eyes to the starry heavens and said: "Lift up your eyes on high, and behold who hath created these things, that bringeth out their host by number: he calleth them all by names by the greatness of his might, for that he is strong in power; not one faileth"? Was Jesus wrong when he bade his disciples trust in him who clothed the lilies of the field and said: "Fear not, little flock; for it is your Father's good pleasure to give you the kingdom"?

To these questions, philosophy may return this answer or that, but the answer of the Christian heart at any rate is clear. "Away with all pale abstractions," it cries, "away with all dualism, away with Marcion and his modern followers, away with those who speak of the goodness of God but deprive him of his power. As for us Christians, we say still, as we contemplate that field gleaming in the sun and those dark forests touched with autumn brilliance and that blue vault of heaven above—we say still, despite all, that it is God's world, which he created by the fiat of his will, and that through Christ's grace we are safe forever in the arms of our heavenly Father."

But what do we have left when, according to Dr. McGiffert, our heavenly Father is gone? The answer that he gives is plain: "We have goodness left," we are told in effect; "we do not know what brings out the stars in their courses, we do not know how the world came to exist, we do not know what will be our fate when we pass through the dark portals of death. But we can find a higher, disinterested worship—far higher, it would seem, than that of Jesus—in the reverence for goodness divested of the vulgar trappings of power."

It sounds noble at first. But consider it for a moment and its glory turns into ashes and leaves us in despair. What is meant by a goodness that has no physical power? Is not "goodness" in itself the merest abstraction? Is it not altogether without meaning except as belonging to a person? And does not the very notion of a person involve the power to act? Goodness altogether divorced from power is therefore no goodness at all. And if it were goodness, it would still mean nothing to us—included as we are in this physical universe which is capable apparently of destroying us in its relentless march. The truth is that overmuch abstraction has here destroyed even that which is intended to be conserved. Make God good only and not powerful, and both God and goodness have really been destroyed. The moral law will soon succumb unless it is grounded in the nature of a personal God.

Feeling, even if not fully understanding, this objection, feeling that goodness is a mere empty abstraction unless it inheres in good persons, many modern men have tried to give their reverence for goodness some sort of subsistence by symbolizing this "ethical" (and most clearly antitheistic) "theism" in the person of the man Jesus of Nazareth. They read Christianity only in terms of salvation and take the man Jesus as their only God. But who is this Jesus whom they make the embodiment of the goodness that they revere? He is certainly not the Jesus of the New Testament, for that Jesus insisted upon everything that these modern men reject. But he is not even the Jesus of modern reconstruction; for even that Jesus, as Dr. McGiffert has shown with devastating clearness, maintained the theism which these modern men are rejecting with such contempt. The truth is that it is impossible for such men to hold to Jesus even as the supreme man, even as the supreme embodiment of that abstract goodness which Modernism is endeavoring to revere. For the real Jesus placed at the very center, not merely of his thinking but of his life, the heavenly Father, Maker and Ruler of the world.

Is then the antitheistic Modernism of our day, reading Christianity solely in terms of salvation and taking the man Jesus as its only God, to relinquish all thought of continuity with the early glories of the Christian church? Dr. McGiffert here comes with a suggestion of hope. He abandons indeed the former answers to the question; he destroys without pity the complacency of those who have supposed that the early history of Christianity on naturalistic principles is all perfectly settled and plain; he throws the historical problem again into a state of flux. Hence we welcome his brilliant and thought-provoking book. Such books, we believe, by their very radicalism, by their endeavor after ever new hypotheses, by the exhibition which they afford of the failure of all naturalistic reconstructions—especially their own—may ultimately lead to an abandonment of the whole weary effort, and a return to the simple grounding of Christian history upon a supernatural act of God.

But meanwhile Dr. McGiffert comes to the Modernist church with a word of cheer. The continuity with primitive Christianity, he says in effect, does not need to be given up even by an antitheistic, nontheological Christianity which at first sight seems very nonprimitive indeed.

It would be a great mistake, we think, to ignore this practical reference of the book. It is no doubt largely unconscious; Dr. McGiffert writes no doubt with the most earnest effort after scientific objectivity. But as we have said, no historian can be altogether without presuppositions, and the presupposition of the present author is that an antitheistic Christianity is the most natural thing in the world. And so, as many notable historians have done, he finds what he expects to find. Baur, on the basis of his Hegelian philosophy, with its "thesis, antithesis, and synthesis," expected to find a conflict in the apostolic age with a gradual compromise and settlement. And so he found that phenomenon surely enough—in defiance of the sources, but in agreement with his philosophy. Similarly, Dr. McGiffert, on the basis of his pragmatist skepticism, expects to find somewhere in the early church a type of religious life similar to his own.

Why is it that despite our author's own admission of the precariousness of many of his arguments, he yet "cannot resist the conclusion that there was such a primitive Christianity" as that which he has just described (p. 87)? The answer is plain. It is because Dr. McGiffert is seeking a precursor in early Christianity for the nontheistic Modernism which he himself holds. Others have found precursors for it in the New Testament—even in Paul. But Dr. McGiffert is far too good a scholar to be satisfied with any such solution as that. Still others have found it in Jesus, and so have raised the cry, "Back to Christ." But Dr. McGiffert has read the gospels for himself, and knows full well how false is that appeal of the popular Modernist preachers to the words of the one whom they call "Master." Rejecting these obviously false appeals, our author is obliged to find what he seeks in the nonliterary, inarticulate, and indeed unattested piety of the early Gentile Christians. "There," he says in effect to his fellow Modernists, "is *our* religion at last; there is to be found the spiritual ancestry of a religion that reads Christianity exclusively in terms of salvation and will have nothing to do with 'fiat creation' or the divine justice or heaven or hell or the living and holy God." And so for the cry, "Back to Christ"—upon which Dr. McGiffert has put, we trust, a final quietus—there is now apparently to be substituted the cry, "Back to the nontheistic Gentile Christians who read Christianity only in terms of salvation and were not interested in theology or in God." But if that really is to be the cry, the outlook is very sad. It is a sad thing if the continuity of Christianity can be saved only by an appeal to the nontheistic Gentile Christians. For those nontheistic Gentile Christians never really existed at all.

The truth is that the antitheistic religion of the present day—popularized by preachers like Dr. Fosdick and undergirded by scholars such as the author of the brilliant book which we have just attempted to review—the truth is that this antitheistic Modernism, which, at least in one of its characteristic forms, takes the man Jesus of naturalistic reconstruction as its only God, will have to stand at last upon its own feet. With the historic Christian church, at any rate, it plainly has little to do. For the Christian church can never relinquish the heavenly Father whom Jesus taught his disciples to love.

44

REVIEW OF MULLINS'S
CHRISTIANITY
AT THE CROSS ROADS

T he distinguished president of the Southern Baptist Theological Seminary has made a distinct and very important place for himself in the modern religious world. He has come to be spokesman not merely for the Southern Baptist church or for the Baptist churches in America, but also, to a considerable extent, for the Baptist churches throughout the world. And there are many in other communions also who look to him as to their spiritual guide. Nevertheless, spokesman though he is for a large section of the evangelical Christian church, he has yet preserved a full measure of individuality both in thought and expression; and in addition to other graces of style, a delightful humor, manifested especially in spoken discourse, is fruitful also in his published work, though if it is there exercised directly at all, it is exercised so gently as not to mar in the slightest the real gravity and sincerity of the discussion.

It is not surprising to find that *Christianity at the Cross Roads*, the latest work of so distinguished an author is an important contribution to religious

"Review of E. Y. Mullins *Christianity at the Cross Roads*" originally appeared as "The Relation of Religion to Science and Philosophy," *Princeton Theological Review* 24 (1926) 38–66.

literature and that it is a very delightful book to read. Dr. Mullins has placed the Christian public distinctly in his debt.

With a very large part of what the author says we are in heartiest agreement. He sees clearly that the religious issue of the present day is not between two varieties of evangelical Christianity, but between Christianity on the one hand and something that is radically opposed to Christianity on the other. He insists, also, upon a genuine theism, as over against that pantheizing way of thinking which is so prevalent at the present time. "What is the difference," he asks, "between a God locked out of the world, and a God locked in?"[1] The God of Dr. Mullins is a transcendent, as well as an immanent, God; he is no mere additional name for the totality of the universe, but the Creator and Ruler of all.

Such a genuine theism, our author sees further, involves the possibility of miracles; Dr. Mullins rejects resolutely that "compromise" between Christianity and the new "religion of biology" which is found in a religion based upon a "non-Christian theism":

> One of the most unfortunate phases of the present situation is that there are leaders of thought, calling themselves Christian, who are merely theists. The danger lies in putting the Christian label on a non-Christian or half-Christian world-view. This so-called Christian or half-Christian world-view classes Jesus with Plato, Buddha, Socrates and other great teachers. His knowledge of God was due to his human instinct, not to a unique relation as divine Son to an eternal Father. His supernatural works and resurrection from the dead are disallowed as contrary to natural law. The future life is accepted, but no appeal is made in its defense to the resurrection of Christ. (p. 121)

Dr. Mullins correctly sees that this non-Christian theism is in actual practice unstable. At this point he agrees with what seems to us to be perhaps the root idea of Bishop Gore's recent trilogy—the idea, namely, that although theoretically no doubt theism may be held without an acceptance of the miracles of the New Testament and without an acceptance of the supernatural revelation which the Bible records, yet practically it always tends under such conditions to fall back into some lower view: those who reject

1. E. Y. Mullins, *Christianity at the Cross Roads* (New York: George H. Doran Company, 1924), 105.

the miracles may try to be theists, but their theism often turns out to be merely a "higher pantheism." Dr. Mullins puts the thing very well in a passage which is the continuation of the one that we have just quoted:

> This form of so-called Christian [really non-Christian] theism is always under the influence of the law of physical continuity. It feels constantly the backward pull of Naturalism. It begins well but comes to a bad end. It sets out to recognize human personality with its meaning, and ends by denying the resurrection of the body and leaving a half instead of a whole man. It sets out with the idea of the personality of God and pares down the conception almost beyond recognition in particular applications. (pp. 121ff.)

But this non-Christian theism (which tends to become no theism at all) not only is unstable, but also fails utterly to satisfy man's religious needs:

> If the idea of a personal God is to be of any value for men, God must be a Being who can do things. An idle God who does nothing is of no avail. And a God who can do no more than nature does is of no avail. In that event we are locked up hopelessly in the chain of continuity along with God. (p. 127)

Thus our author pleads not only for theism, but for a consistent theism; and a consistent theism involves the acceptance of the biblical miracles, their attestation being what it is. Dr. Mullins presents cogently the attestation of the miracles—and what is more, he does not explain them away; he does not speak of them as being manifestations of some "higher law," but allows them apparently to remain as immediate acts of God to be distinguished sharply from his works of providence. It is true, he does say in arguing against a certain type of modern biologist:

> Now a consistent logic would see in this supernatural revelation through Christ, the next stage in the upward course of the universe. A well-poised judgment, a judicial frame of mind, would see the new stage as the necessary outcome of the old. (p. 150)

If these sentences are intended to represent the author's own view, they are disappointing, and certainly they are out of accord with the rest of the book. Dr. Mullins does not elsewhere represent the supernatural revelation through

Christ as the necessary result of a previous upward course of the universe; but he would represent it, if we understand him aright, as involving a redemption from sin, and a redemption from sin that was absolutely mysterious and undeserved. We hope that the author at this point is intending merely to construct an argumentum ad hominem against the naturalistic biologists, and not to present his own view.

Another point of our agreement with Dr. Mullins is found in his clear recognition of the grounding of Christianity in historical facts. He does, it is true, at times separate fact from doctrine in a way that we regard as subject at least to misunderstanding:

> I shall not deal primarily with theological doctrines. I am chiefly concerned here with the Christian facts. (p. 24)

And again:

> By the Christian religion, I mean that religion of which Jesus Christ is the center and of which the New Testament is the record. I do not mean any doctrinal system which has arisen since the New Testament was written. So far as this argument is concerned the Nicene and Chalcedonian decisions as to the Person of Christ and the Godhead, might be blotted out of existence. So also might other schemes of doctrine, the Calvinistic, Arminian and so on. The main question concerns the realities set forth in the record of the life and work of Jesus Christ. All the vital and essential elements of the doctrinal systems would come back if we should make a new start from the facts. And while I have the profoundest appreciation of the need and value of correct doctrines, nevertheless the argument of this book is concerned primarily with facts rather than formal systems of doctrine. (p. 43)

And again:

> The purpose here has been to make clear the issue now before the religious world. Fundamentally it is an issue as to the facts of Christian history, and the facts of Christian experience. A doctrine of incarnation, of sin and atonement, of the deity of Christ, of regeneration and justification and so on through the great circle, is implicit in all that has been said. But the strength of the Christian position is the stability of the foundations in the New Tes-

tament records, the deeds of Christ in history, and the experience of redemption through his power. Doctrines are inevitable as arising out of these facts. Indeed a statement of many of the facts is virtually the statement of the doctrines. But for the purposes in view in the present discussion, formal doctrinal discussion has not been necessary. (pp. 272ff.)

In these passages there is in our judgment an element that is good, and there is also an element that is misleading.

The element that is misleading is found, as has already been intimated, in the undue separation between fact and doctrine. Dr. Mullins sometimes gives the impression that what we have in the New Testament are the bare facts, while the doctrinal interpretation of the facts is left to later generations. It is hardly to be supposed that such is actually his meaning, but certainly he does give that impression. At any rate, the impression is quite incorrect. It is certainly not true to say that the New Testament presents merely the facts and leaves it to later generations to set forth the meaning of the facts. On the contrary, the New Testament sets forth the meaning of the facts as well as the facts themselves, and it sets forth the meaning of the facts as a result of supernatural revelation. From the beginning, the apostles said not merely, "Christ died"—that would have been a bare fact— but they said, "Christ died for our sins," and that was a doctrine. And so we do not think at all that the Nicene and Chalcedonian creeds are merely inferences from the facts that are set forth in the Bible. On the contrary, they are systematizations of the doctrinal instruction that was given by the inspired writers themselves. Also, we are not for a moment satisfied with regarding the Calvinistic system (which happens to be the system that we hold) as a mere inference from biblical facts. On the contrary, it is a systematization of what the Bible says in the sphere not merely of bare facts but of doctrine. And we do not think that devout Arminians would be satisfied with regarding *their* system as merely an inference from the facts. They regard it as a systematization of what the Bible teaches. The only question is whether the Bible teaches Arminianism or Calvinism. We think that it teaches Calvinism; the Methodists think that it teaches Arminianism; but in either case the system arose not by a mere independent process of reflection upon the data provided by biblical facts, but by an effort to gather up the doctrinal instruction that is actually contained in the biblical books.

In the last passage that we have quoted it is said: "Fundamentally it is an issue as to the facts of Christian history, and the facts of Christian experience." We have just been discussing this passage so far as it concerns the relation which doctrine sustains to the facts of history. But it also seems to concern the relation which doctrine sustains to "the facts of Christian experience." Dr. Mullins says: "But the strength of the Christian position is the stability of the foundations in the New Testament records, the deeds of Christ in history, and the experience of redemption through his power." And then he continues: "Doctrines are inevitable as arising out of these facts." Here again we think that the words are at least misleading. Does the author mean that we have (1) the bare historical facts, (2) the experience of redemption through Christ's power (that is, "the facts of Christian experience"), and then (3) "the doctrines"? Does he mean that doctrine is logically subsequent to the facts of Christian experience? We can hardly think that that is his meaning, in view of the whole tenor of his book. But in this passage, and perhaps in some other places, he might seem to an unwary reader to be creating that impression.

At any rate, the impression would certainly be unfortunate. It is quite incorrect to say that not only the historical facts about Christ but also the facts of Christian experience come first and then the doctrinal interpretation of these facts comes afterwards. On the contrary, it is of the very essence of Christianity that doctrine comes (logically though not temporally) before Christian experience. The presentation of the bare fact that "Christ died" never was an instrument in saving a single soul; what saves souls—and what has saved souls from the very beginning of the church's life—is the blessed *doctrine* that "Christ died *for our sins*." Doctrine, in other words, is not a mere inference from the gospel, but it is itself the gospel.

We do not think that Dr. Mullins has made that quite clear, and certain paragraphs of his, if taken by themselves, might seem to contradict it. Such is the element that we think to be misleading in his exposition of the relation between facts and doctrine. But in that exposition there is also an element that we hold to be good, and we turn gladly to the pleasanter duty of pointing out what that element is.

The thing that our author is driving at in his insistence upon the factual, as distinguished from doctrinal, character of his present discussion is that the Modernism of the present day differs from evangelical Christianity not merely in its interpretation of the facts but also in its attitude to the facts themselves. The impression is constantly produced, at least upon the lay mind, that the Modernist theologians accept the facts about Christ and merely present a new interpretation of the facts. Dr. Mullins's book brings a most forcible and salutary correction of any such impression. The real issue is not so much whether the meaning which the New Testament and the creeds of the church assign to the great redeeming events is correct, but whether the events really took place. Was Christ born of a virgin? Did he work miracles? Did his body emerge from the tomb by the power of God? Modernism says "No"; Christianity says "Yes." It is not merely a question of "interpretation," but it is primarily a question of fact; it is not a question what the meaning of the New Testament is but whether what the New Testament says is true or false. Dr. Mullins deserves the thanks of the church for having made the issue so clear.

Accordingly, we rejoice in the testimony to the facts of the New Testament record (and also really to the redemptive significance of the facts) which is contained in this notable book. At the same time we should not be giving to the book the consideration that it deserves if we did not point out the measure of our disagreement with it. Such a book deserves more than perfunctory praise; it deserves really careful consideration. And careful consideration, here as frequently, involves a certain amount of disagreement.

It ought to be observed, however, that the disagreement, though it is not altogether without importance, is distinctly a disagreement between friends. In the time of crisis that now appears in the church, we have often been obliged to argue with men who (despite friendly personal relations) are, in the sphere of principle, not our friends, but opponents of everything that we hold most dear. It is therefore rather refreshing to engage, for once, in argument with a true friend. Such argument, it may be hoped, may lead, if not at once to agreement, at least to better mutual understanding and ultimately to a better common service of the evangelical cause.

The central point with regard to which we disagree with Dr. Mullins is found in his sharp separation between the spheres of science and philosophy and religion:

> What are the rights involved in the modern controversy about religion? There are at least three great rights to be considered: the rights of science, the rights of philosophy, and the rights of religion. No one will dispute the general state-

ment that the right of each of these is freedom to pursue its own task in its own way. Confusion and conflict arise when these tasks and the corresponding rights are forgotten. . . .

Physical science deals with nature. It observes facts and phenomena. It traces sequences and causes. It explains events in nature by antecedents. It assumes continuity in all events. It rigidly limits itself to explanation in one particular way. In a word, science works with the principle of causality.

Philosophy, on the other hand, seeks to find satisfaction for the reason. It assumes the facts and data supplied by science and experience. Its chief aim is to find a single principle which will explain the universe. . . . Philosophy works with the principle of rationality.

Religion differs from science and philosophy in that its chief quest is for God and salvation from sin. Religion is a personal relation. It seeks adjustment with the infinite life. . . . Religion works with the principle of personality. (pp. 30–32)

It is true, Dr. Mullins does admit that science, philosophy, and religion "are harmonious and should coöperate" and that they are alike in that they "all seek to know the truth." He also admits that there are points of contact and overlapping between them. "Religion," he says, "is not irrational, science is not concerned to deny personality, and philosophy must take account of both." "There is," he continues, "necessarily a higher unity in which some day these three will meet when their tasks are done" (p. 32).

Meanwhile, however, the three are each of them, according to our author, autonomous; and when one of them "has attempted to invade the sphere of the other, trouble has arisen" (p. 32). "Christians make a mistake when they invade the scientific sphere and seek to impose alien principles and criteria and to make demands based on unwarranted assumptions" (p. 33). On the other hand, "it is also true that science and philosophy commit an equally grievous sin when they attempt to invade the religious realm" (p. 33).

This principle of the sharp separation between science and philosophy and religion leads, we think, logically into an abyss of skepticism. Of course, we do not for a moment mean to imply that Dr. Mullins carries it out to any such dire conclusion. On the contrary, he contradicts it almost at every turn; indeed, the very center of his book, with its insistence upon the factual basis of Christianity, is really a protest against his own separation between religion and science, and his exultant theism is really a protest against his own separation between religion and philosophy. Yet the false principle—deserted though it is at many points by a salutary inconsistency in which we heartily rejoice—is present, and again and again it turns up to mar the clearness of the author's defense of the Christian faith. It is not merely a momentary phenomenon in Dr. Mullins's thinking, but has entered rather deeply into his entire attitude in the crisis of the present day. Consideration of it is necessary in any careful view of the present book.

Let us see, in the first place, how the supposed separation between science and religion works out. Of course, as it is ordinarily interpreted, it at once destroys the entire doctrinal or factual basis of the Christian religion. The conflict between science and religion, it is often said, may be very easily settled: religion may hold to a realm of ideals, but science must be given the entire realm of facts. It is perfectly evident that our author does not acquiesce in any such settlement of the conflict as that; for he insists that certain facts, such as the appearance of Jesus upon the earth and his resurrection from the dead, are absolutely necessary to the Christian religion. But what is to be made of a passage like the following:

So-called conflicts between science and the Bible are all imaginary. The Bible is the inspired literature of religion. Science is the uninspired literature of nature. These two literatures move on different levels. They can never collide any more than an eagle flying high in the air can collide with a lion walking on the earth. (p. 26)

Or this:

So also with science and religion. They are distinct in the forms of reality with which they deal: matter and spirit. They are distinct in their aims—classified knowledge of nature, and redemption. They are distinct in the principles of causation which they wield: continuity and freedom. They are distinct in their methods of verification: objective experimentation and spiritual experience. But underneath all these diversities there is a common unifying bond: the desire for truth. For science truth is formulated knowledge of the world. For religion it is the clearly expressed meaning of the immediate experience of God. As there is no way to merge the differences in the unity, so there is no way to cancel the unity by the differences. (p. 56)

Such assertions, we are compelled to believe, lead logically to skepticism. But fortunately they are not true. We agree, to be sure, that the "so-called conflicts between science and the Bible are all imaginary"; but we think that these conflicts are all imaginary not because the Bible does not teach things with which science has a right to deal, but because what the Bible says about those things is true. There are, indeed, many departments of science with which the Bible does not deal, but in the departments into which it does enter it does, we think, represent the facts as they are.

Our meaning may become plain if we take as an example the resurrection of Christ. That event, if it really took place, was an event in the external world: a certain tomb near Jerusalem first contained the body of Jesus and then became empty. Is the question whether it became empty, and is the related question whether natural causes can be found for its becoming empty, to be regarded as a matter for scientific investigation or not? Do these questions belong to science? And if they do belong to science, do they also belong to religion?

This last question, according to the letter of what Dr. Mullins says, would have to be answered in the negative. Religion, according to our author, deals with "spirit" as distinguished from "matter" (p. 56). But the question of the resurrection of our Lord, in accordance with the commonsense definition of "resurrection" which Dr. Mullins certainly holds, does concern "matter"; it concerns the emergence or nonemergence of the body from the tomb. Therefore, because of the sharp separation between the spheres of science and of religion, it cannot be a religious question at all.

Such is the logical conclusion to be drawn from the utterances to which we object. Yet the conclusion is emphatically rejected by Dr. Mullins himself: almost the root idea of his book is that the Christian religion is based upon external happenings like the resurrection of Jesus from the tomb.

We are therefore forced apparently upon the other horn of the dilemma: since the question of the resurrection of Christ is certainly a religious question, and since religion and science are quite distinct in their subject matter, it cannot be a scientific question; there can be no scientific certitude, whatever religious certitude there may be, with regard to the miracle of the resurrection.

Now just exactly this position is held by a very large body of persons in the modern world; indeed, it is on the basis of this position that the modern attack upon the factual basis of Christianity to a very considerable extent has come. All that can be established by science—that is, scientific history—it is said, is simply the belief of the disciples in the resurrection, and the question of what caused that belief is a question not for scientific history but for "faith." The practical result of such a position is, of course, skepticism; for very naturally, when "faith" is thus deprived of its proper basis in knowledge, it fails to establish anything whatever, and the miracle is given up.

What is Dr. Mullins's attitude toward such assertions? Logically he ought to agree with them, for they seem to follow quite logically from his sharp separation between science and religion. But as a matter of fact, we are glad to say that he does nothing of the kind. In an interesting passage he seems to express his sharp dissent from those students of the New Testament who "repudiate the right of the critical scholar to indulge in dogmatic negations [and, we may add, affirmations] about the supernatural elements in the New Testament":

> As I see it, the view of these critics as to the relation of historical science to supernatural facts, is incorrect. If it is meant that we do not fully understand supernatural causes I raise no objection. We do not fully understand any causes, natural or supernatural. In so far as a man's attitude will influence his interpretation of the historical data, I raise no question. We all bring a subjective element to bear upon facts. But to affirm that a supernatural event, like the resurrection of Jesus, lies outside the realm of historical research, is to rob history of its most vital factor. . . . Thus we come to the absurd conclusion that the Christian movement in history, the most momentous of all movements, arose out of something which lies outside the range of historical research. (pp. 181ff)

These are golden words. It is true, we cannot give unqualified approval to what immediately follows them, where supernatural events like the resurrection of Christ are brought into analogy with the new factors which the evolutionary hypothesis is obliged to recognize. Such an analogy may be held to obscure the sharp distinction between miracles and those works of God which, however "new" and however surprising to us they may be, are part of the natural order. But the words that we have just quoted are themselves, we think, thoroughly sound, and they constitute a complete refutation of the sharp separation between religion and science to which we object.

It should be noticed in particular that the author refers to historical research as "historical science." Such a use of the word "science" is, we think, quite correct; science can establish, and if it is truly scientific will actually establish, the resurrection of our Lord. Yet the resurrection of our Lord is vitally important for religion. The Bible then, in recording the resurrection, most emphatically does teach science, and the separation between science and religion breaks down.

We are in harmony, therefore, with Dr. Mullins himself (in other elements of his thinking) if we disagree with him rather sharply when he says: "The greatest recent gain in thought about religion and science is the increasing recognition of the distinctiveness of their spheres" (p. 59). For our part, we hold that the notion of the distinctiveness of the spheres of science and religion, far from being a great recent gain, is one of the chief forms that have been assumed by modern unbelief, and that its increasing prevalence is one of the most disastrous features of our time. It is highly significant that this notion of the separation between religion and science is held by a certain distinguished biologist whose rejection of the supernatural our author is refuting with much learning and skill. Dr. Mullins himself quotes the passage: "Strictly speaking, science and religion deal with different subjects. The purpose of science is knowledge, of religion faith and conduct." "The organ of science primarily is intellect, of religion the emotions and will; the goal of science is mechanism, of religion spirit" (p. 86). To do our author justice, he does not himself formulate the separation between science and religion in the way in which it is formulated by this advocate of naturalism.[2] But with the separation itself he himself, in some places in his book, formally at least, agrees; and in doing so he has adopted one of the chief shibboleths of modern skepticism. The biologist of whom we have just spoken has a right to represent "the increasing recognition of the distinctiveness" of the spheres of religion and science as "the greatest recent gain in thought about religion and science"; certainly it *is* the greatest recent gain in thought from his point of view—but when a Christian theologian regards it so, he is introducing a skeptical lever into the foundation of his Christian belief, which if allowed to remain will cause the entire building to fall.

The inconsistency which we have just found in Dr. Mullins's book may

2. Indeed, on p. 108, he seems to be polemic against it. "The fact is," he says, "that religion includes cognition or knowledge as well as emotion."

be due partly to his employment of the word "science" now in a broader and now in a narrower sense. At one time, as we have already observed, he uses it in a sense broad enough to include historical research; but at another time apparently it designates merely such sciences as physics and biology, or at any rate only those methods of research that operate merely with the doctrine of "physical causation." But for our part, we are unable to regard even physics and biology as being without rights in the sphere of religion; and at any rate, we deprecate the narrowing of the use of the word "science." That word ought to be used in a sense broad enough to include, for example, theology. Theology, we think, is just as scientific as chemistry, and if we fail to recognize its scientific character, we are in danger of delivering ourselves over to that anti-intellectualism which is now attacking the Christian religion at its roots—and which is also, by the way, leading rapidly in the modern world into a very lamentable intellectual decline. Dr. Mullins shares our conviction that Christianity is based upon truth, and it is in the interests of that conviction that we ask him to give up the separation between religion and science.

But if the separation of science from religion is unwarranted, so also, it may be remarked in passing, is the separation of science from philosophy. Dr. Mullins seems, in one place at least,[3] to be supposing that there is such a thing as a "modern scientific criticism" of the New Testament which is independent of philosophical presuppositions, and the results of which can safely be accepted by men of differing shades of philosophical and religious opinion—a modern scientific criticism which has established, for example, the "two-document theory" as to the synoptic gospels. As a matter of fact, we do not think that such a neutral, purely scientific criticism exists. The study of the New Testament, even in the sphere of literary criticism, and certainly in the sphere of historical criticism, cannot get along without presuppositions. And the presuppositions of much of the criticism which our author apparently accepts as purely "scientific" are often really naturalistic—proceed, that is, upon the basis of a philosophy which Dr. Mullins himself rejects. Everywhere we are led to the same conclusion—the relations between science and religion and between science and philosophy are very much closer than our author seems to suppose; the independence of science

3. Mullins, *Christianity at the Cross Roads*, 196.

is by no means so complete as he is inclined to represent it as being. That conclusion is certainly not dishonoring to science. On the contrary, we object to the independence of science only because we insist that the sphere in which science moves is so very broad. That sphere is broad enough to include even the knowledge of God that he has given us in nature and in his Word. There is a breadth and sweep about true science of which many scientists have no conception; true science takes account not merely of some, but of all of the facts. And if it takes account of all of the facts, it will not neglect what God has told us about himself.

We are not at all sure but that Dr. Mullins would himself agree with us here, but there are passages in his book which seem to make the thing obscure; there are passages in his book where he seems to present what we are constrained to regard as an incorrect view of the separation of science both from philosophy and from religion.

Equally unfortunate, we think, and equally inconsistent with the real aim of the book are certain things that are said about philosophy. At times philosophy, like science, is given an unwarranted independence, and, as is also the case with science, in being given independence is at the same time narrowed and degraded.

"Philosophy," Dr. Mullins says, "works with the principle of rationality; religion with personality" (p. 164). But what can be made out of such a disjunction? How can religion possibly work with the principle of personality without also working with the principle of rationality, which personality certainly involves? And how can philosophy possibly work with the principle of rationality without also working with the principle of personality if, as Dr. Mullins believes, it is objectively true that a personal God is the author of all being?

But it is necessary to look a little more closely at this principle of "rationality." And when we look a little more closely, it seems to lead to a skeptical conclusion so far as philosophy is concerned. Any one of a number of contradictory philosophies is apparently regarded as good (*qua* philosophy) equally with any other, provided only it hangs together:

> The philosopher is free to select his world-view on any level of reality from matter up to man and personality. It is perfectly legitimate, from the standpoint of reason, for a man to attempt to prove that matter is the fundamental reality, and that all else is reducible thereto. It is, of course, quite as

legitimate to begin with man and spirit and personality and freedom, and explain all things from this point of view—or indeed from any intermediate point between matter and man. I am not here speaking of the cogency of the logic of the respective views, but only of the intellectual rights involved. The rights of reason cannot be gainsaid. (pp. 160ff)

One sentence in this passage is, we confess, to us quite obscure. "I am not here speaking," Dr. Mullins says, "of the cogency of the logic of the respective views, but only of the intellectual rights involved." We confess that we do not see how any philosophy can possess "intellectual rights" if its logic is not cogent. But in general, despite what inconsistencies there may be in detail, the impression seems to be produced by chapter 8 of the book that philosophies must necessarily differ and that in the field of philosophy no one system can be established against the others, that any one of a number of contradictory systems can be regarded equally with the others as a "sound metaphysic":

The chief point here is that the great number of metaphysical systems indicates the variety in the perfectly legitimate forms of rationality. Philosophy, planting its feet firmly on scientific fact, or some fact of experience, moves out to the frontiers. By speculative thought it seeks to solve the ultimate problems. As a result of this effort *there are now in existence a dozen or more world-views*.

We recur now to our question: which of these many world-views answers to the requirements of a "sound metaphysic"? Each philosopher undoubtedly would claim that his own system does so; and if we are sound in our definition of philosophy, every one of them would be right. Each begins with a valid assumption or type-phenomenon. Each pursues legitimate method in constructing his system. Each world-view is unified and coherent, and attempts to explain all phases of being. No one of these contradictory systems can be read out of court on the ground that it is not "a sound metaphysic." It follows, therefore, that the phrase is meaningless when employed to discredit the evangelical Christian faith. That faith gives rise to its own metaphysic which bears perfectly valid credentials in the intellectual and philosophical realm. It is one of a dozen or more systems, all of which, of course, are not equally true, but which are equally "sound" as metaphysical efforts to explain the world. (pp. 162ff.)

Here again we confess to a certain amount of bewilderment: we do not see how two systems can be equally "sound" and not equally "true." But the main tenor of the passage, as of the whole chapter, is, we fear, fairly plain; it involves a discrediting of philosophy as a merely academic exercise to which religion can be more or less indifferent:

> And this brings us to the crucial point. Religion cannot wait upon philosophy, because philosophy cannot supply a stable basis for religion. Every great religious verity is constantly called in question in philosophic thought. An adequate view of the soul is set forth strongly supported by rational arguments. But at once it is attacked and apparently destroyed by some other system. A clear demonstration of a personal God is set forth. But at once on some other assumption it is questioned and the clouds of uncertainty gather about the idea. We prove by philosophic reasoning the immortality of the soul. Before our ink dries on the page we hear the cynical reply of some "modern" man who asks: "Who are you to imagine that your survival after death is of any importance to the universe?" And not only so, he proceeds to construct a philosophic or speculative disproof of immortality which seems to many to be based upon a metaphysic just as "sound" as any other.
>
> I am not implying in all this any question as to the rights of philosophy. Let men strive for as many insights as they will. Let the systems evolve into as many varieties as may be. Let the antagonisms and contradictions become as sharp and decisive as temperament and assumption and speculative acumen may necessitate. In it all something is going on distinct from religion. The process is one which religion cannot employ save in a secondary way. This is not because religion is against reason but because it broadens reason into something richer and more conformable to human need than is the case with philosophy. (pp. 172ff.)

It will be observed that Dr. Mullins admits that philosophy has its "rights." But if those rights are only what they are here said to be, then they are but sorry "rights" after all, and philosophy is degraded from its high estate.

In order to see whether this account of the relation between philosophy and religion is true or false, it may be well, as in the case of the relation between science and religion, to take an example. In the former case we took as our example the question of the resurrection of Christ. That question, we saw, is a matter for scientific consideration, and yet is of vital importance to religion; by it, therefore, the separation between science and religion is disproved. In the present case we choose as our example the question of the existence of a personal God.

The question of the existence of a personal God belongs, Dr. Mullins will admit, to religion. There are, indeed, many persons in the modern world who would make no such admission; religion, these persons hold, is an ineffable experience which is not indissolubly connected with any particular intellectual conception of the nature of God. But with such persons Dr. Mullins certainly does not agree: he is neither a pragmatist nor a mystic; the Christian religion, he certainly holds, could never conceivably exist without a conviction on the part of its adherents that there is a personal God, Maker and Ruler of the world.

How, then, should the existence of such a God be established? The old answer to that question was that it should be established by the so-called "theistic proofs," in which an inference is drawn from the existence and from the character of the world to a personal Creator and Ruler. With these proofs must no doubt be included the "moral argument" which infers from the presence of the moral law in the conscience of man the existence of a great Lawgiver.

Now evidently the consideration of these proofs belongs to philosophy; if this does not belong to it, nothing does. Philosophy, if it is philosophy at all, must at least consider (whatever answer it may give) the question whether the universe is to be explained ultimately by the existence of a personal God.

If then the theistic proofs belong to philosophy, the question becomes important what place Dr. Mullins assigns to these proofs. If he regards them as basically important to religion, then after all he has restored philosophy to what we regard as its rightful place. What then is his attitude to the philosophic proofs of the existence and personality of God?

It is not altogether easy to answer this question. Dr. Mullins quotes from Julian Huxley as follows:

> There remains to search in the external world to find if possible a foundation of fact for the belief drawn from the inner world of mind, to test the conceptions of a supreme being or supereminent power against ever more and more touchstones of reality, until the most skeptical shall acknowledge that the final construction represents, with whatever degree of completeness, yet

not a mere fragment reduced to fill a void, however inevitable, to satisfy a longing, however natural, but the summary, the essence of a body of verifiable fact, having an existence independent of the wishes or ideals of mankind. (pp. 78ff.)

This passage seems to set forth the desire which men have felt for the theistic proofs—that is, for objectively valid arguments for the existence of God. Dr. Mullins's comment is as follows:

From the point of view of the author this is a finely expressed and comprehensive statement of the aim in view. The objection to it is that for religious purposes it is inadequate. To search in "the external world," for a foundation of fact for the "belief drawn from the inner world of mind," is just the ancient process of theologians to find a new proof of the existence of God. The "modern mind" has long ago pronounced such "proofs" unconvincing. And it must be said that the outcome is merely a philosophy of the universe, not a religion. The further result that "the most skeptical shall acknowledge" the truth of the outcome, is to convert religious certainty into a form of logic which deals not with religious forces, but with external facts of nature. Even intellectual stability is not attained in that way. The proof is conclusive, of course. But the "most skeptical" are very stubborn. (p. 79)

Here our author says that the "modern mind" is hostile to the theistic proofs. But what is his own attitude? We cannot help feeling that at this point he regards the "modern mind" with considerable sympathy. To be sure, he does say that "the proof is conclusive, of course." But in the context this is apparently to be regarded as almost ironical, and on the whole very little importance is here attributed to those proofs of the existence of God which operate with the "external facts of nature."

How then, according to our author, is the existence and personality of God to be established? We are afraid that the answer is: "Through Christ." The evangelical Christian faith "gives rise," Dr. Mullins says, "to its own metaphysic" (p. 162):

Christianity is primarily not a philosophy of the universe. It is a religion. It is not founded upon metaphysics. Like all things known to us, there is an implied philosophy. There is a certain view of God and nature and man and the world in the background of our faith. But Christianity is a historical religion, and a religion of experience. It is grounded in facts. Its credentials are well-established facts and clearly defined experiences. God has revealed himself to man in and through Jesus Christ. The Christian world-view rests upon these facts. (p. 163)

So also, after his depreciation of philosophy, in the course of which he points out the fact that the moment the existence of a personal God is established by one system of philosophy it is questioned by another, he says that "God has revealed himself to man through Christ" (p. 173), that as a result of our "experience of God in Christ" Christianity has fulfilled the ideal of religion and has forever set religion free, that hence "it stands on its own foundations, brings its own credentials, performs its own function" (pp. 173ff.).

It is difficult to avoid the impression that our author is here making the establishment of theism dependent upon the revelation of God that has come through Christ:

The plea that the eternal and universal truths of reason and religion are not dependent upon history cannot be made good. Christianity completes religion as an ideal, as an experience and as a program. To go behind Christ and his gospel by referring them to speculative philosophy, is to go backward and not forward. (p. 174)

And in one place Albrecht Ritschl is commended (despite an accompanying recognition of his errors) because "he retained the New Testament truth that we know God only through Christ" (p. 269).

Now for our part we hold it to be not a "New Testament truth" but a very serious error to say that "we know God only through Christ." At least we hold it to be a very serious error in the sense in which it is apparently meant by Dr. Mullins. There is indeed a sense in which it is true: the eleventh chapter of Matthew does seem to teach either that all knowledge of God which men have comes through the second person of the Trinity, the eternal Logos, or else that a really full, intimate knowledge of God—a knowledge worthy of the name—comes only through Christ. But to say that there is no valid establishment of the existence of a personal God apart from the historic manifestation of Jesus is to do despite, for one thing, to what the

Bible (especially Jesus himself) says about the revelation of God in nature. The Bible holds that "the heavens declare the glory of God: and the firmament showeth his handywork." There is, as Paul says, a knowledge of God which ought to be obtained through the things that he has made.

It is true, this knowledge of God has been obscured. Of modern men as of the men of the first century it can be said that "their foolish heart was darkened." And that fact explains those contradictions of philosophy with which Dr. Mullins is so much impressed. But the fault does not lie in philosophy but only in philosophers; the evidence for the existence of a personal God was spread out before us all the time, but we failed to discern it because of the intellectual effects of sin.

Now these effects of sin are removed by Christ. But that does not mean that he causes us to relinquish the theistic proofs which were open to us even in our unredeemed state, or that he causes us to despise that measure of understanding of those proofs which, through common grace, was attained even by unregenerate men. What it does mean is that we are enabled through the redemption offered by Christ to see clearly where formerly our eyes were darkened. The experience of regeneration does not absolve us from being philosophers, but it makes us better philosophers. And so far as the intellectual defense of Christianity is concerned, the fact should never be obscured that theism is the logical prius of faith in Christ. "Believe in God," said Jesus; "believe also in me." To reverse that order is to throw the entire organism of apologetics out of joint. The old order of apologetics is correct: first, there is a God; second, it is likely that he should reveal himself; third, he has actually revealed himself in Christ. It is a very serious fault when the last of these points is put first.

Certainly we do not mean to deny that in actual experience it is through Christ that men are brought to believe in a personal God. It would be absurd to send men, in our effort to establish theism, to this teacher and that, and lead them to neglect the greatest teacher of all. And the greatest teacher of theism that has ever lived upon the earth is Jesus of Nazareth. In his teaching, a theistic view of the world appears in its true reasonableness, and thus carries important credentials with it. But what we do affirm is that when the logical as distinguished from the temporal order is being established, theism does precede the acceptance of Jesus as Redeemer and Lord. The gospel sets forth the way in which God saved man; that gospel cannot be understood unless its presuppositions are accepted; those presuppositions are the Christian view of God and the Christian view of man; and the Christian view of God is based upon theism.

Thus, we disagree with our author in his low estimate of philosophy. "Is Christianity," he asks, "dependent upon 'a sound metaphysic' in the ordinary popular meaning of that phrase?" "The reply," he answers, "is a decided negative" (pp. 163ff). Our reply, on the contrary, is a decided affirmative. We should hate to think that "the rational process in metaphysics is often in open antagonism to religion" (p. 164). If we thought that, we should be in great danger of skepticism. On the contrary, we hold for our part that wherever a process in metaphysics is in antagonism to Christianity, it is not rational but irrational. Christianity does depend, we hold, upon a sound metaphysic. Only that dependence fills us with no misgivings. For a sound metaphysic is not impossible of attainment; it may be attained wherever philosophers see clear. And philosophers come to see clear when their minds are illumined by the Holy Spirit of God.

We have spoken of Dr. Mullins's doctrine of the autonomy of science and of philosophy. It remains to speak of his doctrine of the autonomy of religion. But here we can perhaps speak more briefly, since most of what we should like to say is implied in what we have already set forth.

The autonomy of science and of philosophy is correlative, according to our author, to an autonomy of religion:

Religion also is autonomous. It has its own methods, its own criteria of truth, its own approach to the great Reality, and its own conditions for attaining certainty. (p. 33)

Fifth, religious certainty is religiously conditioned. . . . The Christian act of faith is a self-committal to God as revealed in Jesus Christ. Instantly it brings the soul into contact with spiritual Reality. (pp. 46ff)

Sixth, we are led by the preceding to the next principle: religious rationality is religiously achieved. (p. 49)

It is clear from the preceding that disputants are working at cross-purposes when this truth as to religious rationality is not recognized on both sides. Use reason in the narrow Aristotelian sense and your conclusion about God and religion is insecure. It can be attacked on other logical grounds. But bring reason over into the larger context of the religious life itself and it attains stability. (p. 51)

I note, as an eighth principle, that religious life and experience must be religiously evaluated. All kinds of confusions and controversies have arisen in recent times by failure to keep this truth in mind. How shall a critic approach religion? With what principles of explanation, with what tests of truth, with what norms and criteria of thought shall the various religions of the world be judged? There can be but one answer to these questions. Religion must be judged as religion. (p. 53)

But the more accurate and thorough and self-consistent is the physicist, chemist, biologist, or psychologist, the less justification he finds for bringing religion to the test of the non-religious sciences. . . . We must conceive it, define it, analyze it, expound it and defend it, not as physics, chemistry, biology, psychology or anything else, but as religion. (p. 54)

It is a false issue when men deal with religion as if it were physics or chemistry or biology, or psychology, or sociology. There is no necessary conflict between any of these and religion. But when men crave religion and a solution of its problems, then religious criteria must be employed. (p. 62)

It follows from this that we are on a false trail when we strive to make the Christian religion conform to science or philosophy, or anything else. (p. 230)

But it [the Christian faith] does not depend upon scientific research for its justification or vindication. (pp. 257ff.)

If these passages stood alone, they might seem to place our author in the full current of present-day anti-intellectualism. What is this "religious rationality" which is so distinct from other rationality, and which seems to absolve the Christian from subjecting his religion to the criteria of science and of philosophy? At first sight it might seem to be another name for that ineffable experience which the mystics make to be the sum total of religion. But such is plainly not the case. Dr. Mullins is no mystic: he grounds Christianity in a genuine theism and in historic facts. In one passage at least he is definitely polemic against a view which "simply sets aside the history and transfers the problem of Christianity to the inner realm of our moral and spiritual intuitions" (p. 179). It is true that in that very passage the transferring of the problem of Christianity "to the inner realm of our moral and spiritual intuitions" is repudiated not in the interests of a general objectivity of religious knowledge (which is what we should like to see done) but in the interests of what we regard as somewhat anti-philosophical polemic against the validity of moral intuitions when they are not supported by the New Testament history. Still, it remains true that Dr. Mullins is not a mystic but a theist, and not a pragmatist but a believer in the objective validity of Christian theology. So much is established by the whole tenor of his book.

Nevertheless, we hold the whole notion of a special "religious rationality" to be open to the gravest objections. What these objections are need not be set forth here in detail, for the simple reason that Dr. Mullins himself has really provided the best possible presentation of the objections in the whole course of his interesting book. Sometimes he provides even formal contradictions to those elements in the book to which we are now objecting. "It [the Christian faith] does not depend primarily upon what men usually call a sound metaphysic, although it rests upon unassailable philosophical foundations" (p. 257). The second part of this sentence, however contradictory it may be to the former part, does seem to restore philosophy to its rightful place. And what is more important than such individual passages is the whole tenor of the book. Is religion entirely autonomous? Must it be tested only by itself? Dr. Mullins's own defense of the New Testament facts, on the basis of scientific historical criticism, is the best refutation of any such view.

Nevertheless, the epistemological error (we are constrained to regard it) in certain passages in the book is not altogether unimportant; for however the consequences may be avoided (through a salutary inconsistency) by Dr. Mullins himself, those consequences are likely not to be altogether avoided by others. It is dangerous to adopt the shibboleths of modern anti-intellectualism in the course of an intellectual defence of the Christian faith.

Is there, then, no element of truth in this notion that religion possesses its own credentials and should be judged as religion and not as something else? There is, we think, such an element of truth.

In the first place, it is of course true that religion is far more than science and philosophy. A man might conceivably hold a perfectly correct view of

God and of Christ, he might attain a complete intellectual acceptance of the facts that are at the basis of our religion, and at the same time not be a religious, or a Christian, man. Religion is not merely intellectual.

But although religion is not merely intellectual, it *is* intellectual. Dr. Mullins himself says that it "includes cognition or knowledge as well as emotion" (p. 108).

In the second place, we admit freely that in human nature as it is at present constituted, a full intellectual conviction of the truth of Christianity is not attained without the experience of the new birth; no man was ever brought to Christian conviction merely by argument.

But because argument is insufficient, it does not follow that it is unnecessary. It is often an instrument that the sovereign Spirit of God is pleased to use. What the new birth does is not to absolve men from being scientific in their defense of the Christian faith, but rather to enable them to be truly scientific because a veil has been taken from their eyes.

In the third place, in application of what has just been said, we admit that there are certain convictions, so closely connected with the heart of religion that they can be called specifically religious, without which a conviction of the truth of Christianity cannot be attained. Such, for example, is the conviction of sin. Convictions such as that cannot be attained by ordinary methods of research, but come more obviously (though not more really) than is the case with other convictions through the illumination of the Spirit of God.

But attainment even of these convictions is not really to be separated from philosophy or from science. A man cannot be truly scientific if he neglects relevant facts; he cannot be truly scientific if he neglects the fact of sin.

Thus, we do hold that as defenders of Christianity we must meet non-Christian scientists and non-Christian philosophers on their own ground. But we meet them on their own ground armed with certain weapons which they do not possess—armed with certain facts to a knowledge of which they have not attained. That knowledge has been attained by us not by our own merit or by our own diligence in research but by the gracious illumination of the Holy Spirit.

Such knowledge of new facts which Christians alone have does not absolve us from a consideration of other facts which are known to non-Christian men. On the contrary, the truth can be attained only by a consideration of *all* of the facts. We ought, therefore, not to despise either science or philosophy; we ought not to hold that the arguments even of non-Christian men are without importance for the defense of the Christian religion. We ought to try to lead scientists and philosophers to become Christians not by asking them to regard science and philosophy as without bearing upon religion, but on the contrary by asking them to become more scientific and more philosophic through attention to all, instead of to some, of the facts.

We are pleading, in other words, for a truly comprehensive apologetic— an apologetic which does not neglect the theistic proofs or the historical evidence of the New Testament account of Jesus, but which also does not neglect the facts of the inner life of man. The force of such an apologetic is, we think, cumulative; such an apologetic is strong in its details, but it is even stronger because the details are embraced in a harmonious whole.

Dr. Mullins would hardly disagree with us here; there are indeed some specific utterances in his book which show that he does not disagree. But in the separation which in other places he sets up between science and philosophy and religion, he has introduced, we think, an inconsistent element that mars the symmetry and the stability of the apologetic edifice. That inconsistent element does not destroy our admiration for the many splendid features of this defense of the Christian faith. Most splendid of all, we think, is the fact that this author is ready to be polemic in defense of his faith. Dr. Mullins for his part detects the great issue of the day, and has decided it aright. We rejoice in the noble testimony of this Christian leader in our perplexing times.

But just because of our admiration for Dr. Mullins we have plucked up courage to set forth the points at which we feel constrained to differ from him. In the case of a writer less able and less truly Christian than he, the thing would have been hardly worthwhile. But in this book the good is so very good that we feel the more constrained to separate it from that which we are forced to regard as misleading if not bad. And we are not altogether without hope that consistency in Dr. Mullins's thinking may ultimately be attained—attained by an elimination of that to which we object in the interests of that which we sincerely and profoundly admire.

At any rate, we for our part cannot with safety go one step upon this anti-intellectual path. It may be safe for others; Dr. Mullins, for example, will never follow it to the end. But it would never be safe for us. We are not indeed without appreciation of its attractiveness. The apologetic battle in which Christianity is engaged is so sore that it is not surprising if men desire to avoid it. When scientists are attacking Christianity in the name of science and philosophers are attacking it in the name of philosophy, it seems to be such an easy escape from the battle to say that religion has its own credentials which it alone can judge; it seems so easy to withdraw thus into a place that shall be free from all possible attack. Such is the epistemological Bypath Meadow which is found in the separation of religion from science. It is pleasant to weary eyes and soothing to weary feet, and it seems to lie close along the way. But ultimately it leads to the castle of Giant Despair. We, therefore, are obliged to keep, by God's help, to the high, rough, intellectualistic road of a sound epistemology. That road leads past many a difficulty and through many a conflict. But there are some cooling arbors beside the way, for the refreshment of weary pilgrims. And at the end there is the City of God.

45

KARL BARTH AND "THE THEOLOGY OF CRISIS"

Karl Barth, the leader of the movement about which I am venturing to say a few words today, is a man of about forty-two years of age, having been born in 1886 in German Switzerland. After study at a number of the German universities, he entered into the pastorate in his native country. For a number of years he engaged in what seems to have been a kind of socialistic endeavor; but then, becoming convinced that such effort was merely an affair of this earth and did not touch the real issues of life, he launched forth into the remarkable course of teaching and writing that has so profoundly influenced the youth of Germany and that bids fair to make itself felt throughout the world.

Closely related in the character of their teaching with the leader of the movement are Iduard Thurneysen, Friedrich Gogarten, and Emil Brunner. The two first names of these, with Barth himself, are frequent contributors to the journal *Zwischen den Zeiten*, which is the organ of the school.

There are differences between these individual teachers; Brunner, in particular, does not, I am told, have the complete endorsement of the other

"Karl Barth and 'The Theology of Crisis' " was originally presented on April 23, 1928 before a meeting of Philadelphia clergy and published in the *Westminster Theological Journal* 53 (1991) 197–207.

leaders of the movement. But these differences will not here be taken into account. All that I can hope to do is to present a very rough composite picture, using now one and now another of the four writers that I have named and even now and then some less prominent or less regular adherents of the same general point of view. I am fully conscious of my incompetence for such a task. The Barthian teaching is by no means altogether a simple thing, and it is quite possible that my present understanding of it might have to be radically modified if my knowledge of it were more complete; I can only give you my present impression for what it is worth.

The teaching of Karl Barth and his associates is commonly called "the theology of crisis." The "crisis" or "decision" that is meant in this title is the one that is forced upon a man when he is placed before the dreadful antinomy between time and eternity, the world and God. That antinomy is at the root of the Barthian teaching. At the very foundation of everything that Barth says is the conviction of the awful transcendence of God, the awful separateness between the created world in which man lives and the boundless mystery of the Creator. Away then, say these writers, with all efforts to find God in the world itself! Away with the mysticism of Schleiermacher, discovering God in one particular area of the human soul, in the feeling of absolute dependence; away with the intellectualism of Hegel, setting up an antinomy that is not final, a thesis and antithesis transcended in a higher synthesis still within the world, a dialectical process that is itself thought to be God; away with the moralism of Ritschl, finding God in the human goodness of Jesus, looking upon Jesus as the highest embodiment of human goodness and regarding that human goodness as revealing in itself the nature of God! These three great movements, say Barth and his associates (especially Brunner), are just so many efforts of man to transcend the gulf that separates him from God; they are just so many efforts to drag God down into the sphere of this world. Quite different from all such imaginings of man's heart is the living and true God. From such a God, man is never so remote as when he thinks that he has found him; religion as well as civilization comes under the same great condemnation; it is finite, not the infinite, time not eternity; it is of man, not of God. God is not another name for the totality of this world, and he is not to be found in any experience of man. He is, with respect to this world, the "completely Other," *der schlechthin Andere*, the one who is incommmensurate with anything that can possibly enter into the life of man.

Such is the stupendous dualism between the world and God that is at the root of the thinking of Karl Barth. But this dualism seems not to be ontological; it is not based upon any denial of the Creatorship of God. On the contrary, the dualism between the world and God is conceived of as being due to sin. There we have one of the most profoundly Christian elements in the thinking of these writers. The world, they hold, has been estranged from God by the awful fact of sin. God is Creator; but the creature has been estranged from him by this awful gulf. Sin is no merely individual thing— it has a cosmic significance; it determines the whole situation in which the world stands with respect to God.

As the world is now constituted, there is no possibility for the world to bridge the gulf that separates it from God. All efforts of man to bridge that gulf are only so many manifestations of sin; the very essence of sin is found in the overweening pride that leads men to think that they can by searching find out God.

It looks, then, as though the darkness were complete—God enveloped in impenetrable mystery, man separated from God by a chasm that can never be bridged. But then the darkness is relieved by a divine and glorious light. Man can never bridge that chasm, but God has bridged it. It is impossible and inconceivable that time can have contact with eternity, that man can have communion with God; but the impossible has actually been accomplished, the inconceivable has actually been done. Barth is never tired of ringing the changes upon this paradox. The impossible has become a fact.

It has become a fact by the act of God and God alone. That act of God is not to be thought of under the mere category of cause; it is not to be thought of as merely the sowing of a new seed in humanity, which has flowered into the glories of historic Christendom. Such merely biological analogies will not do. God has not dealt with us in any such impersonal fashion. He has come to us not in the gift of a new impulse but in a true communication addressed to responsible beings; he has come to us not in a feeling or in an experience, but in his *Word*. That Word of God is not something that grows out of the life of man; psychology can never reveal it; it has come *senkrecht von oben*, directly from above. It is not an idea, but "revelation."

By this revelation from God the helplessness, the sinfulness, the awful guilt of man are made clear; in fact, a man never truly knows the guilt of sin until the message of salvation is already knocking at the door of his soul. The fate of the sinner is to be contented in his sin, to hope by his relative goodness to attain unto God. But then comes God's Word. It is a message of wrath. We are far removed here from the Ritschlian notion that God is only love, and that salvation consists in destroying in our minds the delusion of God's anger. Little difficulty have Barth and his associates in showing that the wrath of God is at the very center of the Bible and of all true Christian teaching. That wrath is concealed from the men of the world, but when God's Word comes to a man, then wrath is revealed.

Thus the Word of God, according to Barth and his associates, brings in a complete negation of all the achievements of man, a complete negation of human wisdom, human feeling, human goodness, human religion. So long as a man defends these things, he is still in rebellion against God. But when his last defenses are broken down, when he knows that he is guilty and lost, when he utters over against all civilization, all religion, all feeling, all willing, all thinking an utterly despairing "No," when he acquiesces in the terrible judgment of God, then indeed the Word of God has come nigh to him.

And that Word is not only a word of condemnation: it is also a word of grace. The wonder has been accomplished. God has bridged the impassible chasm; we could never go to him, but he has come to us.

He has come to us, say these writers, in the person of Jesus Christ. It is inconceivable, indeed, that God should come in the flesh. It would not be inconceivable if God were what he is thought to be in the immanence philosophy of modern times; on such a view, the incarnation becomes merely the highest illustration of a permanent truth that God and man are one. Very different is the view of Brunner and of Karl Barth. To them the incarnation is the wonder of wonders. How can the infinite thus condescend to the finite; how can eternity thus enter into time? How can God become man?

These questions, according to Barth and his associates, are unanswerable; the incarnation can never be comprehended or conceived. Never can we support by any argument this inconceivable, this stupendous Word of God. What then can we do? We can only receive it by faith.

And faith itself is no work of man; it is the work of God. God alone can speak this word, and God alone can hear. God can hear in the person of his Holy Spirit, who returns the answer of faith in the human heart to the word which has been spoken by God.

So we have, in the *Dogmatik,* the latest book of Karl Barth, a doctrine of the Trinity. It is hardly the doctrine that has been held by the historic church. But I do not think that it is merely a modal Trinity; certainly it is not a Trinity that is found only in the operations of God within this world. Rather, God has revealed to the eye of faith something of the eternal mystery of his being.

So God's Word, according to Barth and Brunner, has come to man. When it comes, it puts man at the place of decision. Here we have the "crisis" that gives "the theology of crisis" its name. Time or eternity; the world or God; rebellion or obedience? Faith is the answer to that stupendous challenge, which God brings to man.

But when the answer of faith is given, it is no merely static condition in which the redeemed man stands. We live in this world by faith, not yet by sight. We have not yet entered into eternity; we are living still "between the aeons," *zwischen den Zeiten*, between eternity and time. And so our theology must be expressed in questions, in antinomies, in paradoxes. There we have the strange "dialectic" of Karl Barth. Do not ask me to explain it. I cannot explain it, for I should find it difficult to explain what I do not understand.

But that dialectic does not seem to mean, at any rate, that the church, according to Barth, has no positive message. On the contrary, she has a message, which she derives solely from the Scriptures of the Old and New Testaments, not (God forbid) the Scriptures as a record of human experience, but the Scriptures as containing the Word of God. By the Scriptures all preaching must be tested—the church teaching on the basis of the Scriptures, and the Scriptures bringing a revelation from God. There we have the links that unite us with God. There is no immediacy here, no mysticism, but God speaks to us through his Word, and as the substance of his Word the Logos, Jesus Christ, the only mediator between God and man.

This teaching of Barth and his associates, which we have just tried to outline, sounds—much of it, at least—like a simple return to evangelical Christianity. What is there new in most of what we have just said? The living and holy God, man lost in sin, God's grace in the gift of Jesus Christ his Son, faith as itself the gift of God—it sounds like John Bunyan and John Calvin and the Shorter Catechism and the Reformed faith. And indeed Barth does regard himself as a follower of Calvin and a follower of the apostle Paul. It is no wonder that malicious tongues have uttered against the Barthian school a charge, the most insulting that could possibly be uttered against a modern German—the charge that their teaching is nothing but "orthodoxy" after all.

That charge of orthodoxy is denied by these writers in the most indignant way. What is the substance of their defense? How do they differ from what we on our part have been accustomed to think of as the teaching of the historic church?

They differ, I think (if we may ignore details and come at once to the center of things)—they differ in their epistemology, and they differ in their attitude toward the plain historical information that the Bible contains.

On the former point I speak with much hesitation, for I am not at all certain that I understand what the Barthian position is. There is certainly a large measure of agreement, regarding the knowledge that is at the basis of Christianity, between us who are not ashamed of being "orthodox," who are not ashamed of trying, however unworthily, to practice that "straight thinking" which orthodoxy, in accordance with the etymology of the word, involves—there is a large measure of agreement between us on the one hand and these denouncers of orthodoxy on the other.

Barth and Brunner, for one thing, have restored theology to something like the place of real dignity which we think it can rightfully claim. They have made short work of the notion that what is primary is a religious experience that clothes itself indifferently in various thought-forms to suit the intellectual needs of different generations. It is true, Barth regards the function of theology as being critical merely; he regards theology as not dealing directly with God but as protecting the human proclamation of the Word of God from the introduction of matters extraneous or hostile to the Word itself. Nevertheless, the actual operation of Barthian teaching is to restore theology to something more like its rightful place: the Word of God is prior to Christian experience, not identical with it or subsequent with it, and theology deals not with Christian experience but with the proclamation of the Word.

This attitude toward theology, or rather this attitude toward the divine revelation with which ultimately theology is concerned, has as its corollary an attitude toward differences of opinion in the doctrinal sphere which is very different from the prevailing attitude today. There could be no more salutary reading for the modern church than the work of Brunner on "Mysticism and the Word" (*Die Mystik und das Wort*), in the course of which he shows how inevitably the boundless tolerance and syncretism of the modern religious world grows out of the mysticism of Schleiermacher which finds God in an experience of the human soul, and how totally contrary such tolerance and syncretism are to the very roots of the Christian faith. I wish also that the leaders of our church would peruse the noble essay of Karl Barth, which he submitted in an English form, I think, to the Cardiff Conference of the Alliance of Churches Holding the Reformed System, on the question whether the formation of a common creed for the Reformed churches is at present possible or desirable—an essay in which he contrasts this modern business of forming a creed for mere purposes of convenience, merely with the notion that it is convenient for various ecclesiastical bodies to come together and that convention requires that a common church should have a common creed—in which he contrasts this whole business with the true creeds of the church which were born in agony and conflict, when the church felt compelled to set forth God's truth in the face of the error that was rampant in the world. Certainly most persons who talk so lightly about creedal statement today have not the slightest inkling of what a creed really is, and it would be well for them if they would listen to Karl Barth.

But despite all that, despite the fact that this new teaching in practice involves a mighty reaction against the anti-intellectualism of the modern church, I cannot be quite sure that the knowledge of God which it sets forth is, in theory at least, real knowledge at all. The Word of God can be received, Barth says, only by faith; it cannot possibly be supported by argument; apologetics must be altogether eschewed; argue in defense of the truth of God's Word, and you show that the Word has not really come to you; the Word of God will brook no human advocate; faith is distinct from all reasoning; God speaks, and that is all. A great truth certainly underlies such an attitude. It is certainly true that argument alone never made a man a Christian; there must be a mysterious act of the Spirit of God; God's message must be brought home to a man by God himself; "ye must be born again." But because argument is insufficient, it does not follow that it is unnecessary; and as a matter of fact it is God's will that his Word should be so presented to men that acceptance of it shall be a profoundly reasonable thing. What the Holy Spirit does is not to render unnecessary the gift of reason, but to free reason from the effects of sin and enable a man again to see clearly. We could never indeed reason out the truth of the things that God has told us in his Word, but to accept it as God's Word is not contrary to reason but on the contrary is possible only when reason, by the act of God's Spirit, ceases to be blinded by sin.

I have an uneasy feeling, therefore, with regard to the Barthian epistemology. Does Barth mean that the doctrine of the Trinity, for example, and the doctrine that sets forth the redeeming work of Christ are not true until they are accepted in faith, and that they are true only to the man who thus accepts them? Does he do away with the objectivity of truth; does he fall back at last into that subjectivity against which his whole teaching starts out to be a mighty protest? I am not sure that such is his meaning. But there is a side of his teaching that might seem to bring us near to such an epistemological abyss. What, moreover, do the Barthians mean by "creation," for example, and by "sin"? One cannot escape the impression that similarity of terminology in these writers, as over against historic Christianity, makes a very profound difference of view.

My objection becomes acute when we come to the second point that I mentioned, when we come to the attitude of Barth and his associates toward the historical information that the Bible contains.

We have seen that the writers of the Barthian school regard Jesus of Nazareth as the incarnate Son of God. Brunner in particular in his notable book "The Mediator" (*Der Mittler*) is concerned to set forth the sheer, the absolute, uniqueness of Jesus. Not only, Brunner says, is there as a matter of fact only one mediator between God and man, but in the very nature of the case there could be only one, and that one is Jesus Christ. Surely, we might say, holding such a view of Jesus as that, the Barthian writers must join issue sharply with the historical criticism of the present day. But that is not at all the case. Indeed, Rudolf Bultmann, who represents the very extreme of skepticism in the historical sphere, who holds that our sources of historical information are so uncertain as to prevent us from any certain knowledge of what sort of person Jesus was—Rudolf Bultmann is a contributor to the journal *Zwischen den Zeiten* and is apparently accepted by Barth as an orthodox member of the school! Thus, the Barthian writers try to make Christian faith quite independent of the findings of scientific history with regard to the life of Christ.

That effort might be understood in various ways. It might be held, for example, that although scientific history can never establish the facts about Jesus, particularly the fact of the empty tomb, yet faith can do so. If that understanding were correct, then the negative criticism of Bultmann, to which he subjects the NT documents, would merely be a *tour de force* to show how, when history proceeds on naturalistic principles, and with aloofness of the historian from this subject matter, it can never establish the facts upon which Christianity is based. Thus, scientific history would be discredited simply in order to leave a clear field for faith. We should then still have the facts that are set forth in the NT, but these facts established by a more immediate method than the historical evidence in the ordinary sense can afford. But I fear that no such thing as that is meant. Certainly it is not meant by Bultmann, and probably is not meant by Barth. I fear that the real meaning is that we can hear the Word of God in the NT, as addressed to our own soul, no matter what the facts about Jesus of Nazareth were. Thus, a consistent Barthian might even not be disturbed if scientific history should prove that Jesus of Nazareth had committed, for example, positively immoral acts; Jesus, on Barthian principles, might still bring to us the Word of God, the great central message of justification by faith, no matter what sort of person he was according to the flesh. I cannot think that all the writers of the school would push consistency so far; Brunner, for example, would, if I understand aright, repudiate such a view. But if so, then Christian faith cannot be indifferent to the findings of historical criticism after all. Certainly if it *is* indifferent, it cannot be true to the NT. The NT does, indeed, present a message of God to the individual soul. But that message contains the homely testimony of men and women who saw certain things in the external world; it contains, for example, the testimony of women who went early to the sepulchre and repeated what they there had seen and heard. We cannot possibly evade the question whether that testimony is true or false.

The truth is that the radicalism of Barth and Brunner errs by not being radical enough. These men have broken with the whole development of theology since Schleiermacher and with the entire immanence philosophy upon which it is based. That is a notable and courageous act. It may prove to have introduced a new era in the history of the church. But they must carry their radicalism a step further if what they have done is to be permanent; they must break not only with the immanence philosophy of the past century, but also with the application of that immanence philosophy to the historical problem that the NT presents. And why not? I do not wonder at it, if the Barthians are impressed by the mighty edifice of modern negative criticism in the NT field. I do not wonder, if they desire to avoid attacking such a fortress. But attack it I think they must if they are really to proclaim the Word of God to a lost and dying world. And why should they fear? Modern skepticism is, indeed, imposing, as it is applied to the NT field. But it may fall away like a house of cards if once its presuppositions are attacked. And its presuppositions are attacked, and attacked in the very citadel, by the assault of Barth and Brunner upon the evolutionary philosophy of Schleiermacher and his successors. What we need is a more consistent Barthian than Barth; we need a man who will approach the NT documents with presuppositions that are true instead of false, with presuppositions that will enable him to accept at its face value the testimony of salvation that the NT contains.

But as it is, the attitude of Barth and his associates toward historical criticism constitutes a deadly weakness of the school. These writers are bringing to us the Word of God, but they are trying to enable us to accept it on entirely too easy terms. Much more radical still must be our break with the philosophy that would prevent us from finding in the midst of human history, in the coming and in the resurrection of Jesus Christ, a creative act of God.

I have also another word of criticism that is intimately connected with the one that I have just ventured to express. It concerns the attitude of Barth and his associates toward the detailed account of the words and deeds of Jesus that the gospels contain. With much in that attitude I have the warmest sympathy. I agree fully with Barth and Brunner in holding that what is primary in the NT account of Jesus is not his teaching or his example but his redeeming work. I agree fully with the emphasis that they place upon the cross and resurrection of Christ (though what they mean by the resurrection I do not quite know) as distinguished from his words and deeds in Galilee. I rejoice with all my heart in their rejection of the modern notion that a mere contemplation of the character of the man Jesus will wipe away the guilt of sin or bring a man into communion with God; I rejoice in their final rejection of "the Liberal Jesus." That Jesus never existed upon this earth, and if he did exist, he could not bring salvation to the souls of men. It is profoundly true, as these writers hold, that a man who merely studies the life of Christ as a record of a man who lived long ago is without real understanding even for the simplest things which according to the synoptic record Jesus said and did. Such knowledge is superficial indeed; it involves knowing Jesus only according to the flesh. A man who knows Jesus only so knows him really not at all. Only in the light of the cross can the Sermon on the Mount be truly understood. The true Jesus everywhere, even in his simplest acts, is the divine Logos who came into this world for the redemption of men.

But while all that is true, it does not follow that the Christian can be indifferent to the details of what Jesus said and did. In their effort to make the Christian message independent of historical criticism, one has the disturbing feeling that Barth and his associates are depriving the church of one of its most precious possessions—the concrete picture of Jesus of Nazareth as he walked and talked upon this earth. These writers insist indeed upon the reality of the incarnation; it is important to them that Jesus lived in this world. But what sort of person he was when he was here—that question at times seems, in the logic of their view, to be of no concern. They speak of the *offense* of Jesus' human life; it was, they say, such as to conceal from the unredeemed the fact that Jesus was truly the Word of God. But is that altogether true to NT teaching? Does not the NT speak also of the glory of the incarnate Word that was manifested here upon earth? "The Word was made flesh, and dwelt among us, (and we beheld His glory, the glory as of the only-begotten of the Father,) full of grace and truth." There have been many efforts to cut Christianity loose from the concrete picture of Jesus of Nazareth that is contained in Matthew, Mark, Luke, and John. Is the Barthian movement only another such effort? I am not quite sure that it really is. I am not inclined hastily to apply the term "Gnosticism" to a teaching that in some respects seems to me to be a recovery of precious truth. But unquestionably there is a danger here. In their effort to avoid a clash with naturalistic criticism, these teachers must not be allowed to deprive us of the Jesus whom we love, the Jesus of the gospels, the Jesus who spoke words such as never man spoke, the Jesus who went about doing good.

Only let us not take that Jesus merely as one who lived long ago; let us not be deaf to the dreadful immediacy of his claim upon us; let us not hide ourselves from him by a sentimental contemplation of events of the first century; let us rather say here and now, as in a dread crisis from which we cannot escape, as though this moment were our last, as being indeed between time and eternity, between God and the abyss—let us say to Jesus here and now: "My Lord, I have heard thy voice to me." That much at least we can learn from Karl Barth.

PART TEN

AUTOBIOGRAPHICAL

46

CHRISTIANITY IN CONFLICT

An account of personal experiences may be interesting for one of two reasons: (1) because the writer is in some way remarkable; (2) because, not being at all remarkable, he may be able to set forth in a concrete way the experience of a considerable body of men. It is for the latter reason, if at all, that the present little sketch may justify its place in the volume of which it is to form a part. I have been asked to contribute to the volume, I suppose, in order that I may show by the example of my own very imperfect, but for that reason all the more typical, experience how it is that a considerable number of persons have been led to resist the current of the age and to hold with mind and heart to that religion of supernatural redemption which has always hitherto been known as Christianity.

In the pursuance of this task, however, I shall not seek to distinguish those elements in my experience which are peculiar from those which I share with others, but shall simply set forth certain observations of mine in the concrete, in the hope that here and there they may by way of example shed some light upon something less unimportant than they are in themselves. It seems to me, even with that explanation, to be rather a presumptuous undertaking—but the responsibility is the editor's, not mine.

"Christianity in Conflict" was originally published in *Contemporary American Theology*, vol. 1, ed. Vergilius Ferm (New York: Round Table Press, 1932), 245–74.

If the question is asked how it has come about that contrary to the majority of the men of our day I am a believer in the truth of the Bible and an adherent of the redemptive religion which the Bible presents, the answer will be found, to a far greater extent than in any other one place, in the home in Baltimore in which, in company with my brothers, Arthur W. Machen Jr. and Thomas Machen, I was brought up. My father, who died in 1915 at the age of eighty-eight, and my mother, who died in 1931 at the age of eighty-two, were both Christians; from them I learned what Christianity is and how it differs from certain modern substitutes. I also learned that Christian conviction can go hand in hand with a broad outlook upon life and with the pursuit of learning.

My father was a lawyer, whose practice had been one of the best in the State of Maryland. But the success which he attained at the bar did not serve in the slightest to make him narrow in his interests. All his life he was a tremendous reader, and reading to him was never a task. I suppose it never occurred to him to read merely from a sense of duty; he read because he loved to read. He would probably have been greatly amused if anyone had called him a "scholar"; yet his knowledge of Latin and Greek and English and French literature (to say nothing of Italian, which he took up for the fun of it when he was well over eighty and was thus in a period of life which in other men might be regarded as old age) would put our professional scholars to shame.

With his knowledge of literature there went a keen appreciation of beauty in other fields—an appreciation which both my brothers have inherited. One of my father's most marked characteristics was his desire to have contact with the very best. The second-best always left him dissatisfied; and so the editions of the English classics, for example, that found place in his library were always carefully chosen. (As I think of them, I am filled with renewed dismay by that provision of the Vestal Copyright Bill, nearly made a law in the last Congress, which would erect a Chinese wall of exclusion around our country and prevent our citizens from having contact with many things that are finest and most beautiful in the art of the printing and binding of books.)

My father's special "hobby" was the study and collection of early editions—particularly fifteenth-century editions of the Greek and Latin classics. Some fine old books were handed down to him from his father's home in Virginia, but others he acquired in the latter part of his long life. His modest means did not suffice, of course, for wholesale acquisitions, but he did try to pick up here and there really good examples of the work of the famous early printers. He was little interested in imperfect copies; everything that he secured was certain to be the very best. I can hardly think of his love of old books as a "hobby"; it was so utterly spontaneous and devoid of self-consciousness. He loved the beautiful form of the old books, as he loved their contents; and the acquisition of every book on his shelves was a true expression of that love.

He was a profoundly Christian man, who had read widely and meditated earnestly upon the really great things of our holy faith. His Christian experience was not of the emotional or pietistical type, but was a quiet stream whose waters ran deep. He did not adopt that "Touch not, taste not, handle not" attitude toward the good things or the wonders of God's world which too often today causes earnest Christian people to consecrate to God only an impoverished man, but in his case true learning and true piety went hand in hand. Every Sunday morning and Sunday night, and on Wednesday night, he was in his place in church, and a similar faithfulness characterized all his service as an elder in the Presbyterian church. At that time the Protestant churches had not yet become political lobbies, and Presbyterian elders were chosen not because they were "outstanding men [or women] in the community," but because they were men of God. I love to think of that old Presbyterian session in the Franklin Street Presbyterian Church of Baltimore. It is a refreshing memory in these days of ruthless and heartless machinery in the church. God grant that the memory may some day become actuality again and that the old Christian virtues may be revived!

Even stronger was the influence of my mother. Like my father, she was an exceedingly wide reader; her book on *The Bible in Browning* is only one gleaning from a very rich field. Her most marked intellectual characteristic, perhaps, was the catholicity of her tastes. She loved poetry with a deep and discriminating love, but she loved with equal ardor the wonders and beauties of nature. Long before the days of "Outlines of Science" and "Outlines" of everything else, she was a student of botany and also a student of the stars in their courses. I shall never forget the eager delight with which she used to stand with me, when I was very young, upon a ridge in the White Mountains and watch the long shadows creep upward upon the opposite heights. She loved nature in its more majestic aspects, and she also loved the infinite sweetness of the woods and fields. I suppose it is from her that I learned to escape sometimes from the heartless machinery of the world, and the equally heartless machinery, alas, of a church organization nominally dedicated to Christ, and refresh my soul with the friendliness of the hills. But beneath my mother's love of nature and beneath her love of poetry that was inextricably intertwined with that other love, there lay her profound reverence for the author of all beauty and all truth. To her God was all and in all, and her access to God she found only through the new and living way that the Scriptures point out. I do not see how anyone could know my mother well without being forever sure that whatever else there may be in Christianity, the real heart of Christianity is found in the atoning death of Christ.

I am glad that in my very early youth I visited my grandfather's home in Macon, Georgia, where my mother was brought up. Its fragrance and its spaciousness and simplicity were typical of a bygone age, with the passing of which I am convinced that something precious has departed from human life. In both my father and my mother, and their associates whom I saw from time to time, I caught a glimpse of a courtlier, richer life and a broader culture than that which dominates the metallic age in which we are living now. It is a vision that I can never forget. I cannot, indeed, hope to emulate the breadth of education attained by both my parents and successfully emulated especially by my older brother; my own efforts seem utterly puny when compared with such true and spontaneous learning as that. But at least I am glad I have had the vision. It has taught me at least that there are things in heaven and earth never dreamed of in our mechanistic world. Someday there may be a true revival of learning, to take the place of the narrowness of our age; and with that revival of learning there may come, as in the sixteenth century, a rediscovery of the gospel of Christ.

In Baltimore I attended a good private school. It was purely secular, and in it I learned nothing about the Bible or the great things of our Christian faith. But I did not need to learn about those things in any school, for I learned them from my mother at home. That was the best school of all; and in it, without any merit of my own, I will venture to say that I had acquired a better knowledge of the contents of the Bible at twelve years of age than is possessed by many theological students of the present day. The Shorter Catechism was not omitted. I repeated it perfectly, questions and answers, at a very tender age; and the divine revelation of which it is so glorious a summary was stored up in my mind and heart.

When a man has once come into sympathetic contact with that noble tradition of the Reformed faith, he will never readily be satisfied with a mere "Fundamentalism" that seeks in some hasty modern statement a greatest common measure between men of different creeds. Rather will he strive always to stand in the great central current of the church's life that has come down to us through Augustine and Calvin to the Standards of the Reformed faith.

My mother did more for me than impart a knowledge of the Bible and of the faith of our church. She also helped me in my doubts. Having passed through intellectual struggle herself, having faced bravely from her youth the objections to the truth of the Christian religion, she was able to help those who had doubts. And of doubts I certainly had no lack. In this connection, I cannot forbear to speak also of my older brother, Arthur W. Machen Jr., and of my cousin, LeRoy Gresham, both of whom I greatly admired. A man is in sad case if he must fight the battle of faith and unbelief entirely alone. In most instances, God uses the help and example of older and wiser men and women to bring him safely through.

When I was seventeen years of age, I entered the Johns Hopkins University as an undergraduate student, and in 1901 I received my bachelor of arts degree. At that time, the initial impulse of the Johns Hopkins, which had made such a profound impression upon the entire intellectual life of our country, had not yet run its course. Daniel Coit Gilman, the first president, was still in office; and of the famous original faculty, Remsen, Rowland, and Gildersleeve still occupied their chairs. Even an undergraduate could appreciate to some extent the stimulus of such an environment; and in my case the stimulus was enormously increased when, in the autumn of 1901, I entered as a graduate student into the Greek seminar (or, as it was better called, the Greek seminary) of Gildersleeve himself.

Gildersleeve may perhaps be regarded as the most notable classical scholar that America has yet produced. In him was found a rare combination of accurate philological learning with something akin, at least, to literary genius. I shall never forget the hours that I spent with the little company of students that gathered around the table in his seminary room. There were no undergraduates in that company and no candidates for the master of arts degree. They were all men who intended to make the teaching of language their life work and who had altogether transcended the schoolboy or undergraduate point of view. Never was there an environment where earnest study was had in more honor than in that group of students of Latin and Greek under Gildersleeve and C. W. E. Miller and Kirby Smith. In such a company Gildersleeve would let himself go. With a magisterial disregard of anything like system, he started with Greek syntax and then allowed his thought to range over the literature of the world. His successor, C. W. E. Miller, has preserved much of the work of the great teacher in the splendidly edited volume *Selections from the Brief Mention of Basil Lanneau Gildersleeve;* but particularly fortunate were we who actually sat in the seats of the learners in that classroom.

I shall always be glad that I obtained contact with the rigidly scientific method and with the contempt for mere claptrap which characterized the Johns Hopkins University in its best days. But as my first year of graduate study drew to its close, the thought did occur to me (more or less vaguely, perhaps, at the time) that that method might be applied with even greater advantage to a subject matter different from that which engaged our attention there. The year 1901–02 was the Plato year in the cycle that governed the choice of studies in Gildersleeve's seminary, and in addition to our wider reading we were each assigned brief passages from Plato's dialogues for detailed discussion. It was a useful exercise. But I could not help reflecting that there are certain other ancient Greek books whose detailed interpretation is of profound interest not merely to scholars or philosophers but to the rank and file of mankind. Could I aspire to devote my life to that far more important field?

I was still undecided when the academic year came to an end, and during part of the summer continued my Greek studies at the University of Chicago. I took only one course. It was a course in Pindar under Paul Shorey, and it brought plenty of hard work as well as contact with another true man of letters in a philological chair. A student who can count both Gildersleeve and Shorey among his teachers—even for brief periods of time—is fortunate indeed.

But when the summer was over, I turned at last to the field upon which I had for some time been casting longing eyes. How much more worthwhile it is, if one is to apply modern scientific methods of research to ancient books, to apply them to those books whose every word is of an importance to humanity with which the importance even of Homer and Plato can never for one moment be compared!

So I entered Princeton Theological Seminary in the autumn of 1902. In doing so, I was encouraged particularly by Francis L. Patton, who was just coming to the presidency of the seminary. He had been a guest repeatedly at my father's home in Baltimore. I admired him then greatly, and I came afterwards to love him with all my heart. With infinite patience he brought me through my doubts and helped me in my difficulties. Never did a doubter and a struggler have a better friend than I had in this wonderfully eloquent and brilliant man.

From the start, when I went to Princeton, I was impressed by William P. Armstrong, the head of the New Testament department, who later became my most intimate friend. I had been in contact at the Johns Hopkins University, with modern scientific method applied to the study of ancient books. That same method was applied by Armstrong to the New Testament. No student in his classroom who knew anything whatever of modern methods of philological and historical research could help seeing that he was a modern university man of the very highest type. It seemed significant to me then, as it seems today, that, applying such modern methods of criticism to the New Testament, he could arrive at a result confirmatory, and not destructive, of the trustworthiness of the New Testament books.

One of Armstrong's strongest points is that he combines detailed knowledge of critical and historical questions with an understanding of great underlying principles. His wide reading in philosophy enables him to show the connection between schools of New Testament criticism and various schools of modern philosophy, but above all, he is able to exhibit the connection between the supernaturalistic view of the New Testament and the theistic view of God and the world upon which the Christian religion depends. I think that this union between detailed scholarship and an understanding of great principles was characteristic of the old Princeton Seminary.[1] Princeton differed from other seats of conservative scholarship in that more clearly than was done elsewhere it found the center of the curriculum in the department of systematic theology. For my part, I have always regarded the study of the New Testament, to which I have given my life, as ancillary to that other department. New Testament study has its own

1. Dr. Armstrong has remained, indeed, at the new Princeton Seminary after the recent reorganization, but he certainly belongs spiritually to the old, and it is extremely unlikely that scholars of his type will be added to the faculty of the institution henceforth.

methods, indeed; but ultimately its aim should be to aid in the establishment of that system of doctrine that the Scriptures contain.

At Princeton the chair of systematic theology was occupied by a man who effected a personal, as well as a logical, union between that department and the departments devoted to biblical research. B. B. Warfield had won his reputation as a New Testament scholar. In the field of textual criticism he had been among the first to recognize the epoch-making importance of the labors of Westcott and Hort, and he had supplemented those labors by independent research. In New Testament exegesis his contributions were highly valued in Great Britain as well as in America. Then, with his coming to Princeton, he turned to the field of systematic theology, bringing to that field the broad exegetical and critical foundation without which the systematic theologian is hampered at every turn. Warfield became one of the greatest authorities in the history of doctrine, and it may certainly be said, in general, that he had a truly encyclopedic mind.

When I was a student at Princeton I admired Warfield, as we all did, but I was far from understanding fully his greatness both as a scholar and as a thinker. I was still playing with the notion that a minimizing apologetic may serve the needs of the church, and that we may perhaps fall back upon a biblical Christianity which relinquishes the real or supposed rigidities of the Reformed system. Subsequent investigation and meditation have shown me, as over against such youthful folly, that Warfield was entirely right; I have come to see with greater and greater clearness that consistent Christianity is the easiest Christianity to defend, and that consistent Christianity—the only thoroughly biblical Christianity—is found in the Reformed faith.

In general, I need only to think of my own immaturity when I was a student at Princeton in order to be convinced that theological students are far from being so well qualified in the field of theological encyclopedia as they sometimes think they are. An educational institution, I am convinced, should present its curriculum with a certain clear-cut, though sympathetic, decisiveness. If it is governed by its students or its alumni or the donors of its funds, it might just as well close its doors.

There is not space for me to speak of the rest of the old Princeton Seminary faculty. From every one of them I obtained something distinctive and something of real value. I also profited very greatly by the courses in the history of modern philosophy which I pursued at Princeton University under

A. T. Ormond. How Ralph Barton Perry can speak of Ormond as "ponderous, high-minded, and unintelligible"[2] is a complete mystery to me, unless the explanation is found in the fact that this writer refers to his studies at Princeton as belonging to his "prenatal" experience in philosophy. As a matter of fact, anything more utterly limpid and more broadly illuminating than Ormond's lectures it would be difficult to conceive.

On my graduation from Princeton Seminary in the spring of 1905, I went to Germany, having also spent the previous summer there. In Germany I obtained practically no contact with conservative scholarship, but listened almost exclusively to those who represented the dominant naturalistic point of view.

During the winter semester of 1905–06, I was a student at Marburg. Since I was intending to be a teacher of the New Testament, I confined myself for the most part to New Testament courses. But I did hear the lectures on systematic theology by W. Herrmann, and I have always rejoiced greatly that I had that privilege. In one's contact with any great movement, it has always seemed to me important to attend to its best, and not merely to its worst, representatives; and Herrmann certainly represented Ritschlianism at its best. He was a man, moreover, who could never fully be understood or appreciated through his books alone. Only personal contact could reveal the contagious earnestness, the deep religious feeling, of the man. I felt, as I sat in that classroom, that it was the center of worldwide influence, a place from which a great current went forth, for good or ill, into the whole life of mankind.

That current has now run its course. Certainly the power of Ritschlianism is diminishing. Its popular phrases, used often by men who know little of their origin, are still heard in the pulpits of America; but in those circles whence come the real springs of influence, the Ritschlian solution of our religious difficulties has already had its day. I was not insensible of the attractiveness of that solution when I sat in Herrmann's classroom, and I am not insensible of it now. How happy we might seem to be if we could only avoid the debate about the existence of a personal God—if we could only relegate all that to a sphere of metaphysics with which the Christian man need have nothing to do! What a world of trouble it would save us if we could only make ourselves independent of the findings of detailed histori-

2. Ralph Barton Perry, in *Contemporary American Philosophy*, vol. 2 (1930), 187.

cal research and find in the gospel picture of the moral life of Jesus all that we need to give us the value of God! But in reality this solution has proved to be utterly fallacious. It is fallacious for at least two reasons.

In the first place, the religious experience that it seeks to conserve is not really independent of apologetic debate. The picture of "the Liberal Jesus," which called forth Herrmann's unbounded reverence—the picture which Harnack presented in *What Is Christianity?* and which was set forth in many other learned and popular books—has by no means escaped criticism. Radicals have denied its historicity; "consistent eschatologists" have pointed out in the sources elements which contradict it at its root. The picture is faulty, moreover, in itself. The Ritschlians thought that the moral life of Jesus—*their* Jesus, reconstructed by their particular type of naturalistic criticism of the gospels—was capable of calling forth mankind's unbounded reverence, was capable of having for all mankind the value of God. But, alas, that is far from being the case. The "Liberal" or Ritschlian Jesus has in his Messianic consciousness a moral contradiction at the very center of his being; such a Jesus is very far indeed from being a perfect moral ideal, to say nothing of being worthy to assume the place in human affection and reverence that used to be assumed by the Creator of heaven and earth.

A second reason why the Ritschlian solution of our apologetic difficulties has failed is that the type of religious experience which it endeavors to conserve is hardly true Christian experience at all. W. Herrmann was a deeply religious man; no one who came into contact with him can doubt that. But was the religion of which he was so noble an adherent really the Christian religion? That may well be doubted. If Herrmann was a Christian, he was a Christian not because of but despite those things that were most distinctive of his teaching. At the heart of Christianity is a view of sin whose profundities were a sealed book to Herrmann and to all of his school. A man under true conviction of sin will never be satisfied with the Ritschlian Jesus, but will seek his way into the presence of that Jesus who redeemed us by his precious blood and is ever living to make intercession for us at the throne of God.

In the New Testament field, I heard at Marburg lectures by no less than four men. Easily foremost in my estimation at that time was A. Jülicher, then at the very height of his powers. I shall never forget my first hour in his classroom. Even comparatively trivial things stand out in my mind as I think of the thrill of that hour. I remember, for example, that in speaking of commentaries on Galatians he said of Lightfoot's commentary that it was "a masterpiece of learned work" (*ein Meisterstück gelehrter Arbeit*). What a homelike feeling it gave me to hear our revered Lightfoot praised by a leader in such an opposite school of thought!

In general, I have found from that day to this that the really able men do not by any means share the contemptuous attitude toward conservative scholars which seems to be regarded as a mark of learning in certain circles in America. That may serve to give comfort to us believers in the truth of the Bible. On the other hand, I have never been able to give myself the comfort which some devout believers seem to derive from a contemptuous attitude toward the men on the other side of the great debate; I have never been able to dismiss the "higher critics" *en masse* with a few words of summary condemnation. Much deeper, it seems to me, lies the real refutation of this mighty attack upon the truth of our religion, and we are not really doing our cause service by underestimating the power of the adversaries in the debate.

When I was at Marburg, J. Weiss seemed to me to be somewhat overshadowed by Jülicher. He was a very delightful man, who showed his kindness by inviting me to his house and by befriending me in every way. Also he was a clear and popular lecturer. But I thought of him rather as a popularizer than as a profound scholar. I have since then come to see that this impression was totally incorrect. His *Urchristentum* and above all his amazingly rich and learned commentary on 1 Corinthians have made me repent of my youthful injustice to one of the ablest of modern New Testament scholars.

Rudolf Knopf, who later went to the Protestant faculty at Vienna, lectured when I was at Marburg on "New Testament Introduction." It was a clear and methodical course of lectures, in which the entire field of special introduction was covered. As I compared it with the treatment of the same subject by Armstrong at Princeton, I observed to my delight that the old Princeton had placed the real questions before me in a thoroughly fair and comprehensive way. The conclusions arrived at in the two cases were very different, but at least my Princeton teacher had not concealed from me either the position of the opponents or the evidence upon which their contentions were based. Many criticisms have been brought against the old Princeton Seminary, but whoever brings against it the charge that it substituted passionate dogmatism for fair and scholarly treatment of the opposing views can be set down as either violently prejudiced or completely ignorant about that of which he is venturing to speak.

At Marburg, I listened also to lectures on the gospel of John by Walter Bauer, then a young *Privat-dozent,* now the distinguished successor of Schüerer and Harnack in the editorship of the *Theologische Literaturzeitung.* The course, which came at eight o'clock on the dark winter mornings, was attended by four students—two Germans, one Englishman, and myself. On a number of occasions the two Germans were absent; and once, I remember, the Englishman was absent too, so that the lecture was delivered (with all the academic formality characteristic of a German lecture room) for my sole benefit. On another occasion, I confess that the regularity of my attendance was impaired. That was on the morning after a hastily organized *Nachtbummel* which took me with a crowd of my German fellow students on an expedition through the surrounding country that lasted from midnight until seven o'clock.

One thing that surprised me in Germany was the amount of intellectual labor that can be accomplished by a German student with a minimum of sleep. The secret, no doubt, is that German students have learned to work at the *Gymnasium* before the joyous university semesters are begun. Our American students for the most part have never learned to work, and what little acquaintance with intellectual application the students of twenty-five years ago may have attained is today being destroyed partly by a ruthless standardization, which is standardization down and not standardization up, and partly by the untrammeled operation of our great American pedagogic discovery that it is possible to think with a completely empty mind. Solid subjects have almost been removed from American schools, and a really distressing intellectual decadence is the not unnatural result.

At Göttingen, during the summer semester of 1906, I heard Schürer, Bousset, Heitmüller, and (in another department) Kattenbusch. Schürer had the reputation in some quarters of being tiresome, but I did not find him so at all. The careful, methodical character of his mind was well expressed in his lectures, and one came away from them impressed with the kind of mental process necessary for massive learning such as that which is displayed in "The History of the Jewish People." Heitmüller had promise of brilliant achievement, but for some reason his published contributions afterwards were less extensive than might at that time have been expected. His death was untimely, like the death of J. Weiss, Knopf, and Bousset. Bousset's lectures were brilliant, as might have been expected from an examination of his published work. I can see him now as he chopped off some sharp, incisive utterance, and looked around with his great round eyes while the effect would sink into the mind of the class. His official position was only that of an *extraordinarius*, but already he was one of the really commanding figures in the theological world.

My admiration for Bousset's learning and brilliancy were later increased by his book, *Kyrios Christos*, which appeared in 1913. Not since the time of F. C. Baur, it seems to me, has there appeared such an original, comprehensive, and grandly conceived rewriting of early Christian history. The construction is mistaken—of that I am firmly convinced and tried to give some expression to my conviction in *The Origin of Paul's Religion*—but it is mistaken in a grand and incisive way. It is such books which at least present, even though they do not solve, the really central problems.

A comparison of Bousset on the one hand with Norden and Reitzenstein on the other will show the difference between mere theologians in Germany and the occupants of philological chairs. The difference is not found in any agreement on the part of the theologians with the Bible or the Christian faith, nor is it found in any inferiority of their scholarship. But it is found in the fact that whereas the philologians seem to regard it as the mark of a true scholar to be obscure, the theologians are not ashamed to be clear. Certainly nothing could exceed the clarity of Bousset's *Kyrios Christos*. It is an immensely learned book, but the facts that it adduces are marshaled like a well-disciplined army; the reader is never in any doubt as to what every fact, whether mistakenly or not, is intended to prove.

The type of thing that Bousset represented and that Jülicher represents is to a certain extent out of date in Germany at the present time. Owing partly to the Barthian depreciation of historical studies in the biblical field, and partly, I am obliged to think, to the bankruptcy of the naturalistic reconstruction of the beginnings of Christianity, New Testament studies occupy by no means the place in the intellectual life of the country that they occupied twenty-five years ago. But the pendulum will swing back. The interest of the human race in those amazing historical documents that form the New Testament will never permanently be lost.

The way in which I was received in Germany by both students and professors aroused in me a gratitude which, it is needless to say, the war has done nothing to destroy. I had in many respects a happy time when I was there in 1905–06. In other respects, it was a time of struggle and of agony of soul. I was living in an environment where the Christian religion as I knew and loved it had long been abandoned. No Christian man could live in such an environment without facing questions of a very serious kind.

It was not Germany, however, that first brought doubts into my soul, for I had been facing them for years before my German student days. Obviously, it is impossible to hold on with the heart to something that one has rejected with the head, and all the usefulness of Christianity can never lead us to be Christians unless the Christian religion is true. But is it true or is it not? That is a serious question indeed.

I may perhaps be subserving the purpose of this series of sketches if at this point I mention certain considerations that were useful to me as I passed through the long and bitter experience that the raising of this question brought into my life.

One consideration was presented in particularly clear-cut fashion by an illustration which Francis L. Patton used to employ in one of his lectures or sermons, which I heard in my college days. I do not think it ever found a place in any of his published work, and I cannot remember the details of it with anything approaching accuracy. But he likened the man who faces the problem of living to a man who stands on the waterfront looking over the ships that might take him across the sea. *He is obliged to go*, and the only question is in which ship his voyage shall be made. Two ships lie at the dock. One of them, he is told, is new and well found, has a careful captain, and is rated A-1 at Lloyd's. He is favorably impressed, but being a cautious man turns by way of comparison to the other. That, he is told, is old and rotten, has a drunken captain, and is ready to be condemned. Will he then choose the former ship? "No," he says, "despite the evidence for the goodness of that ship, I cannot be *certain* of its goodness, and so I must choose the second ship after all!"

Such, said Patton in effect, is *our* conduct if we refuse to act on reasonable probability in this matter of religion. We have no choice about undertaking this business of living—and of dying. We cannot choose but to make the voyage. The only question is in which ship we shall go. One ship presents itself with evidences of safety far superior to those of all others. It is the ship of Christianity, the way of living and dying founded upon the supernatural revelation that the Bible contains. Shall we desert that ship for one far less approved, simply because the evidence in its favor does not amount to apodictic certitude? Or, acting on the best evidence that we can obtain, shall we make the great venture of faith and launch forth into the deep at Christ's command?

Bishop Blougram, too, was a great help to me as Patton used to quote him in the pulpit and in the home; and that comfort was to be had no matter what sort of character Browning meant Bishop Blougram to be. The question is not merely whether we can rest in our faith, but whether we can rest in the doubt that is the necessary alternative of faith. We pass sometimes through periods of very low spiritual vitality. The wonderful gospel which formerly seemed to be so glorious comes to seem almost like an idle tale. Hosts of objections arise in our minds; the whole unseen world recedes in the dim distance, and we think for the moment that we have relinquished the Christian hope. But then let us just face this situation: let us just imagine that we had really given up all these things that formerly seemed to us so dear. Ah, when we do that, life seems to us to be a hopeless blank. It is all very well to toy with the thought of a Christless world, but when we once imagine ourselves living in it we see that really, in our heart of hearts and mind of minds, we have not given up our Savior after all.

Another thing used to be said to me by my mother in those dark hours when the lamp burned dim, when I thought that faith was gone and shipwreck had been made of my soul. "Christ," she used to say, "keeps firmer hold on us than we keep on him."

That means, at least, when translated into worldly terms, that we ought to distrust our moods. Many a man has fallen into despair because, losing the heavenly vision for the moment, passing through the dull lowlands of life, he takes such experience as though it were permanent, and deserts a well-grounded conviction which was the real foundation of his life. Faith is often diversified by doubt, but a man should not desert the conviction of his better moments because the dark moments come.

But my mother's word meant something far deeper than all that. It meant rather that salvation by faith does not mean that we are saved because we keep ourselves at every moment in an ideally perfect attitude of confidence in Christ. No, we are saved because, having once been united to Christ by faith, we are his forever. Calvinism is a very comforting doctrine indeed. Without its comfort, I think I should have perished long ago in the castle of Giant Despair.

When I returned from Germany in 1906, I entered, as instructor in the

New Testament department, into the teaching staff of Princeton Theological Seminary. Except for an interval in France and Belgium from January 1918 to March 1919, I was at Princeton (first as instructor and then as assistant professor of New Testament literature and exegesis) from 1906 until the reorganization of the seminary in 1929.

During the first part of this period, life in the faculty of the seminary was of a most delightful kind. Francis L. Patton was president, and in him the finest traditions of the institution were preserved. Warfield was professor of systematic theology (or "professor of didactic and polemic theology," as the chair was then more sonorously and vigorously called). And what a wonderful man he was! His learning was prodigious. No adequate notion of its breadth can be obtained even from his voluminous collected works. Consult him on the most out-of-the-way subjects, and you would find him with the "literature" of each subject at his tongue's end and able to give you just the guidance of which you had need. Now and then, in wonderfully generous fashion, he would go out of his way to give a word of encouragement to a younger man. The old Princeton was an environment in which a man felt encouraged to do his very best.

My best was none too good, but it was done at least with my whole heart. At the beginning of my senior year as a student, I remember a piece of advice which was given me by Kerr Duncan Macmillan, then instructor in Semitic philology, who later left the seminary and entered, as president of Wells College, into an entirely different field. I mentioned to him the question that was being debated in my mind as to whether during my senior year I should find time for general reading or compete for the New Testament fellowship. He advised me to do the latter. I could do general reading, he told me, at any time in my life, but the opportunity to do that piece of detailed research would come then and then only. Excellent advice it was. Many a student might be saved from a desultory life if he could receive and act upon advice like that. I acted upon it, to the very best of my ability, by writing a thesis on "The New Testament Account of the Birth of Jesus," and I have always been grateful to the one from whom the advice came.

My schedule as a teacher at Princeton was rather a heavy one, and I do not regret the fact. There were some advanced courses to keep me alive, and I also had the job of teaching elementary Greek. This latter was never mere drudgery to me, as it is to some men. I have notions about it different from those that often prevail, and after fifteen years' experience I embodied them in my little textbook, *New Testament Greek for Beginners*. A teacher of language, it seems to me, or the writer of an elementary textbook, should never yield to the temptation of displaying his philological learning—I myself was greatly helped in my resistance to this temptation by having so little philological learning to display—but should ruthlessly sacrifice everything else to the impartation of a reading knowledge of the language. Philological discussion is very interesting and very important, but it should come later. It is not learning, but often mere pedantry, to discuss the detailed history of a language that one cannot read. The more general observance of that principle might have delayed, even if it could not have prevented, the sad disfavor into which the classics have fallen in our day.

In 1921, I had the honor of delivering the James Sprunt Lectures at Union Theological Seminary in Virginia. The resulting book, *The Origin of Paul's Religion*, 1921, in which the lectures appeared in greatly enlarged form, deals really with the problem of the origin of the Christian religion. It cannot be doubted that what is commonly known as "historic Christianity"—the Christianity of the main body of the church—is found in essentials in the epistles of Paul, whose genuineness is not denied by serious historians, whether they are Christians or not. Paul thought that his religion was based upon Jesus of Nazareth, one of his contemporaries, who had recently died a shameful death. If Paul was wrong in that, how did the religion of Paul actually arise? I attempted to pass in review the various generically different hypotheses which in modern times have been advanced to answer that question, and in doing so I endeavored to exhibit the inadequacy of all naturalistic hypotheses and present reasons to show, instead, that Paul's view of the origin of his religion is correct. In particular, I tried to show (1) that the "Liberal" or Ritschlian historians were right over against Wrede and other radicals in insisting that Paul possessed and cherished a knowledge of the real Jesus, but (2) that the radicals were right over against the "Liberals" in insisting that the Jesus whom Paul's religion presupposes is no mere teacher of righteousness but a supernatural Redeemer come into the world for the salvation of men. The true synthesis, I argued, is found only when that supernatural Redeemer, presupposed in the epistles of Paul and presented in detail in the gospels, is held to be the real Jesus who walked upon this earth.

In my little book *Christianity and Liberalism*, 1923, I tried to show that the issue in the church of the present day is not between two varieties of the same religion but, at bottom, between two essentially different types of thought and life. There is much interlocking of the branches, but the two tendencies, Modernism and supernaturalism, or (otherwise designated) non-doctrinal religion and historic Christianity, spring from different roots. In particular, I tried to show that Christianity is not a "life" as distinguished from a doctrine, and not a life that has doctrine as its changing symbolic expression, but that—exactly the other way around—it is a life founded on a doctrine.

In *What Is Faith?*, 1925, I tried to combat the anti-intellectualism of the Modernist church—the false separation which is set up between faith and knowledge—and to present the New Testament teaching as to what faith is. That endeavor involved necessarily some treatment of the object of faith, so that the little book contains a brief and summary treatment of considerable portions of Christian doctrine.

In *The Virgin Birth of Christ*, 1930, a book which contains in enlarged form the Thomas Smyth Lectures which I had the honor of delivering at Columbia Theological Seminary, I have tried to present the subject indicated by the title in a somewhat comprehensive way. Whether it is a good book is a question which I shall not presume to answer, but no one can deny that it is a big one!

At present I am engaged in a series of expository studies for the monthly journal, *Christianity Today*, which is the organ of the evangelical party in the Presbyterian Church in the U.S.A., and is devoted to the propagation and defense of the Reformed faith throughout the world. I can scarcely imagine a greater privilege than to serve in such an enterprise. The journal is in many respects unique among church papers. It is not at all technical, and is intended for laymen as well as for ministers. But it seeks to avoid the superficiality of the average church paper and addresses itself, under the able editorship of Samuel G. Craig, assisted by J. McAllister Griffiths, to thinking men and women who believe that knowledge and piety should go hand in hand.

The period of twenty-seven years during which, with two short intervals, I was connected, first as student and then as teacher, with Princeton Theological Seminary witnessed the conflict between the old Princeton and the newer forces now dominant in the Presbyterian church, and finally it witnessed the triumph of the latter in the reorganization of the seminary in 1929.

The old Princeton Seminary may have been good or it may have been bad—opinions differed about that—but at least it was distinctive, and at least it was a power in the affairs of men. It was known throughout the world as the chief stronghold of a really learned and really thoroughgoing "Calvinism" in the English-speaking peoples. Even its opponents, if they were scholars, spoke of it with respect.

The old Princeton Seminary first resisted, then succumbed to, the drift of the times. It did not succumb of its own free will, for the majority of its governing board as well as the majority of its faculty desired to maintain the old policy, but that board was removed by the General Assembly of the Presbyterian church in 1929 and another board was placed in control. Thus, the future conformity of Princeton Seminary to the general drift of the times was ensured.

This view of the matter has been strenuously opposed by many of those responsible for the change, but how any other view can possibly be taken by any real observer it has always been beyond my power to comprehend.

When the reorganization of Princeton Seminary took place, some men felt that so fine a scholarly tradition as that of the old Princeton ought not to be allowed to perish from the earth. Obviously, it could not successfully be continued at Princeton, under the new and unsympathetic board, but elsewhere it might be carried on.

It is being carried on at the new Westminster Theological Seminary in Philadelphia, which was founded in 1929, largely through the initiative of self-sacrificing laymen, "to carry on and perpetuate the policies and traditions of Princeton Theological Seminary, as it existed prior to the reorganization thereof in 1929, in respect to scholarship and militant defense of the Reformed Faith."

The new seminary is vigorously opposed to the intellectual decadence which is so widely manifested in our day. It sets its face like a flint, for example, against the indolent notion that scholarly preparation for the ministry can be carried on without a knowledge of the original languages of the Bible. It is opposed to shortcuts and easy lines of least resistance. It is in favor of earnest work, and its students as well as its faculty share that attitude. In particular, it believes that the Christian religion flourishes not in the darkness but in the light.

My whole heart is in this institution and in the cause that it represents. I believe that that cause involves not reaction, but true progress, and I rejoice in my comradeship with the hopeful group of men who constitute its faculty. Particularly do I rejoice in my comradeship with the students. Technically I stand to them in the relation of teacher to scholar, but in reality I often receive from them more than I can give. They have taught me by their brave devotion to principle, by their willingness to sacrifice all for the sake of Christ, that the old gospel is an ever new and living thing. The true hope of the church rests in such men as these. Meanwhile, as I meet with them in prayer and labor, I feel anew what a blessing Christian fellowship is in the midst of a hostile world.

We who are reckoned as "conservatives" in theology are seriously misrepresented if we are regarded as men who are holding desperately to something that is old merely because it is old and are inhospitable to new truths. On the contrary, we welcome new discoveries with all our heart; and we are looking, in the church, not merely for a continuation of conditions that now exist but for a burst of new power. My hope of that new power is greatly quickened by contact with the students of Westminster Seminary. There, it seems to me, we have an atmosphere that is truly electric. It would not be surprising if some of these men might become the instruments, by God's grace, of lifting preaching out of the sad rut into which it has fallen, and of making it powerful again for the salvation of men.

There are certain root convictions which I hold in common with Westminster Seminary and with the journal *Christianity Today*—in common with these representatives of the ancient yet living tradition of the old Princeton. I hold (1) that the Christian religion, as it is set forth on the basis of Holy Scripture in the Standards of the Reformed faith, is true, and (2) that the Christian religion as so set forth requires and is capable of scholarly defense.

The former of these two convictions makes me dislike the term "Fundamentalism." If, indeed, I am asked whether I am a Fundamentalist or a Modernist, I do not say, "Neither." I do not quibble. In that disjunction, as the inquirer means it, I have very definitely taken sides. But I do not apply the term "Fundamentalist" to myself. I stand, indeed, in the very warmest Christian fellowship with those who do designate themselves by that term. But for my part, I cannot see why the Christian religion, which has had a rather long and honorable history, should suddenly become an "-ism" and be called by a strange new name.

The second of the two convictions just formulated—that the Christian religion requires and is capable of scholarly defense—does not mean that a man ever was made a Christian merely by argument. There must also be the mysterious work of the Spirit of God in the new birth. But because argument is insufficient, it does not follow that it is unnecessary. From the very beginning, true Christianity has always been presented as a thoroughly reasonable thing. Men sometimes tell us, indeed, that we ought not to be everlastingly *defending* Christianity, but rather ought simply to go forth to *propagate* Christianity. But when men talk thus about propagating Christianity without defending it, the thing that they are propagating is pretty sure not to be Christianity at all. Real Christianity is no mere form of mysticism, but is founded squarely upon a body of truth.

The presentation of that body of truth necessarily involves controversy with opposing views. People sometimes tell us that they are tired of controversy in the church. "Let us cease this tiresome controversy," they say, "and ask God, instead, for a great revival." Well, one thing is clear about revivals—a revival that does not stir up controversy is sure to be a sham revival, not a real one. That has been clear ever since our Lord said that he had come not to bring peace upon the earth but a sword. A man who is really on fire with a message never thinks of decrying controversy but speaks the truth that God has given him to speak without thought of the favor of men.

In all controversy, however, the great principle of liberty should be preserved. I am old-fashioned in my belief that the Bible is true, but I am equally old-fashioned in my love of freedom. I am opposed to the attack on freedom in whatever form it may come. I am opposed to the Soviets, and I am opposed to Mussolini. For the same reason also, I am opposed to the rapidly growing bureaucracy in this country. I am opposed to a federal department of education; I am opposed to monopolistic public schools; I am opposed to a standardization that treats human beings as though they were Ford cars.

For the same reason, to say nothing of far deeper reasons, I am opposed to a church union, which is the deadliest enemy of Christian unity. I am opposed with all my mind and heart to the depressing dream of a monopolistic Protestant church organization placing the whole Protestant world under one set of tyrannical committees and boards. I am opposed to the growing discouragement of free discussion in my own church and other churches. I am opposed to secret church courts of judicial commissions. In all ecclesiastical affairs I believe in open covenants openly arrived at. I am opposed with all my might to actions like the action of the last Presbyterian General Assembly tending to discourage publicity regarding measures proposed for adoption by the church.

Just because I believe in liberty, I believe in the right of purely voluntary association. I believe in the right of a voluntary association like the Presbyterian church. If a man does not believe that the Bible is true, and in his interpretation of the Bible is not an adherent of the Reformed faith, I am opposed to exerting any compulsion on him to become a Presbyterian minister. If he adopts some position other than that of the Presbyterian church, let him have full liberty to become a minister in some other body. But if he does choose to become a Presbyterian minister, I hold that he should be able honestly, and without mental reservation, to subscribe to the ordination pledge setting forth that for which the Presbyterian church exists. Without such honesty there can be no possibility of Christian fellowship anywhere for those who do with their whole heart hold to what that pledge sets forth. And true Christian fellowship, not forced organizational union of those who disagree in the whole direction of their thought and life, is the real need of the hour.

I take a grave view of the present state of the church; I think that those who cry, " 'Peace, peace,' when there is no peace," constitute the greatest menace to the people of God. I am in little agreement with those who say, for example, that the Presbyterian church, to which I belong, is "fundamentally sound." For my part, I have two convictions regarding the Presbyterian church. I hold (1) that it is not fundamentally sound but fundamentally unsound; and I hold (2) that the Holy Spirit is able to make it sound. And I think we ought, very humbly, to ask him to do that. Nothing kills true prayer like a shallow optimism. Those who form the consistently Christian remnant in the Presbyterian church and in other churches, instead of taking refuge in a cowardly anti-intellectualism, instead of decrying controversy, ought to be on their knees asking God to bring the visible church back from her wanderings to her true Lord.

We can, if we are Christians, still be confident and joyous in these sad days. This is not the first time of unbelief in the history of the church. There have been other times equally or almost equally dark, yet God has brought his people through. Even in our day, there are far more than seven thousand who have not bowed the knee to the gods of the hour. But our real confidence rests not in the signs of the times, but in the great and precious promises of God. Contrast the glories of God's Word with the weak and beggarly elements of this mechanistic age, contrast the liberty of the sons of God with the ever-increasing slavery into which mankind is falling in our time, and I think we shall come to see with a new clearness, despite the opposition of the world, that we have no reason to be ashamed of the gospel of Christ.

FOR FURTHER READING

F or readers whose appetite has been whetted by this book for more of J. Gresham Machen's biblical, theological, and cultural writings, the good news is that most of his books remain in print.[1] Machen was arguably the greatest conservative American New Testament scholar of the first half of the twentieth century. His skills are amply evident in two important books, *The Origin of Paul's Religion* (1921; Wipf & Stock, 2002); and *The Virgin Birth of Christ* (1930; James Clark Co., 2000). He also wrote a grammar for teaching New Testament Greek to seminary students, *New Testament Greek for Beginners* (1922; Prentice Hall, 1998). Machen's most popular books were his double-barreled critique of liberal Protestantism, first in the classic *Christianity and Liberalism* (1923; Eerdmans, 1956); followed by *What Is Faith?* (1925; Banner of Truth Trust, 1996). Toward the end of his life, Machen gave a series of radio talks on basic Christian doctrine that have been published in two volumes, *The Christian Faith in the Modern World* (1936; currently not in print); and *The Christian View of Man* (1937; Banner of Truth Trust, 1984). Ned B. Stonehouse, Machen's junior colleague in New Testament at Westminster Seminary, also edited a collection of Machen's sermons, published as *God Transcendent* (1949; Banner of Truth Trust, 1984). Stonehouse was also responsible for gathering many of the essays reprinted in this anthology in *What Is Christianity? and Other Addresses* (Eerdmans, 1951).

Books about Machen have not been plentiful, but neither has he been a

---

1. A virtually complete bibliography of Machen's published writings compiled by James T. Dennison Jr. and Grace Mullen is available in Charles G. Dennison and Richard C. Gamble, eds., *Pressing toward the Mark: Essays Commemorating Fifty Years of the Orthodox Presbyterian Church* (Committee for the Historian of the OPC, 1986), 461–85.

neglected figure. The standard biography is Ned B. Stonehouse, *J. Gresham Machen: A Biographical Memoir* (Eerdmans, 1954). D. G. Hart, *Defending the Faith: J. Gresham Machen and the Crisis of Conservative Protestantism in Modern America* (1994; P&R Publishing, 2003) is an intellectual biography that situates Machen in a crucial period in American cultural history. Terry A. Chrishope, *Toward a Sure Faith: J. Gresham Machen and the Dilemma of Biblical Criticism, 1881–1915* (Christian Focus, 2001) is a close examination of Machen's interaction with the biblical scholarship of his day. Shorter studies of Machen are available in the following: George M. Marsden, *Understanding Fundamentalism and Evangelicalism* (Eerdmans, 1991); C. Allyn Russell, *Voices of Fundamentalism: Seven Biographical Studies* (Westminster Press, 1976); Henry W. Coray, *J. Gresham Machen* (Kregel, 1981); and Paul Woolley, *The Significance of J. Gresham Machen Today* (P&R Publishing, 1977).

A variety of contexts are important to consider when reading Machen. The most obvious, though perhaps not the best, is the so-called fundamentalist controversy of the 1920s and 1930s in which Machen played the role of highbrow-fundamentalist. The best accounts of the controversy remain Ernest R. Sandeen, *The Roots of Fundamentalism: British and American Millenarianism, 1800–1930* (University of Chicago Press, 1970) and George M. Marsden, *Fundamentalism and American Culture: The Shaping of Twentieth-Century Evangelicalism* (Oxford University Press, 1980). An impressive contribution to the history of Protestant Liberalism, which includes attention to its conservative critics, is William R. Hutchison, *The Modernist Impulse in American Protestantism* (1976; Duke University Press, 1992). Valuable intellectual biographies of important Protestant leaders during the fundamentalist controversy are Grant Wacker, *Augustus H. Strong and the Dilemma of Historical Consciousness* (Mercer University Press, 1985); William Vance Trollinger Jr., *God's Empire: William Bell Riley and Midwestern Fundamentalism* (University of Wisconsin Press, 1990); and Barry Hankins, *God's Rascal: J. Frank Norris and the Beginnings of Southern Fundamentalism* (University of Kentucky Press, 1996).

Because the doctrines of creation (versus evolution) and Christ's second coming (i.e., dispensational premillennialism) were such important sources for fundamentalist conviction, the following studies are especially helpful for understanding the controversy that divided American Protestantism: Timothy P. Weber, *Living in the Shadow of the Second Coming: American Pre-*

millennialism, 1875–1925 (Oxford University Press, 1979); Paul Boyer, *When Time Shall Be No More: Prophecy Belief in Modern American Culture* (Harvard University Press, 1992); Ronald L. Numbers, *The Creationists: The Evolution of Scientific Creationism* (Alfred A. Knopf, 1992); and Edward J. Larson, *Summer for the Gods: The Scopes Trial and America's Continuing Debate over Science and Religion* (Harvard University Press, 1998).

The reason why the fundamentalist controversy may not be the most useful study for understanding Machen better is that much of the literature on that episode in American church history overlooks important differences among America's largest Protestant denominations. Machen himself preferred to be called a Calvinist rather than a fundamentalist. For that reason, the history of American Presbyterianism is a more important context for appropriating Machen. One piece of American Presbyterian history particularly relevant to Machen's theological development is that of Princeton Seminary. The following are reliable guides to the seminary's theological tradition: David C. Calhoun's two-volume history, *Faith and Learning, 1812–1868*, vol. 1 of *Princeton Theological Seminary* (Banner of Truth Trust, 1994), and *The Majestic Testimony, 1869–1929*, vol. 2 of *Princeton Theological Seminary* (Banner of Truth Trust, 1996); Mark A. Noll, ed., *The Princeton Theology, 1812–1921: Scripture, Science, and Theological Method from Archibald Alexander to Benjamin Warfield* (1983; Baker Book House, 2001); W. Andrew Hoeffecker, *Piety and the Princeton Theologians: Archibald Alexander, Charles Hodge, and Benjamin Warfield* (P&R Publishing, 1981); Lefferts A. Loetscher, *Facing the Enlightenment and Pietism: Archibald Alexander and the Founding of Princeton Theological Seminary* (Greenwood Press, 1983); Hugh Thomson Kerr, *Sons of the Prophets; Leaders in Protestantism from Princeton Seminary* (Princeton University Press, 1963); and John C. Vander Stelt, *Philosophy and Scripture: A Study in Old Princeton and Westminster Theology* (Mack Publishing, 1978).

The literature on twentieth-century American Presbyterianism tilts in favor of the mainline denomination, but it has included valuable material on Machen and the issues he addressed in the church. Lefferts A. Loetscher, *The Broadening Church: A Study of Theological Issues in the Presbyterian Church since 1869* (University of Pennsylvania Press, 1954); Bradley J. Longfield, *The Presbyterian Controversy: Fundamentalists, Modernists, and Moderates* (Oxford University Press, 1991); and William J. Weston, *Presbyterian Pluralism: Competition in a Protestant House* (University of Tennessee Press,

1997) are particularly useful. On the conservative side, Edwin H. Rian, *The Presbyterian Controversy* (1940; Committee for the Historian of the OPC, 1992) and Gary North, *Crossed Fingers: How Liberals Captured the Presbyterian Church* (Institute for Christian Economics, 1996) offer a different perspective.

For more general treatments of twentieth-century American Presbyterianism, a series edited by Milton J Coalter, John M. Mulder, and Louis B. Weeks is especially interesting even if geared toward the mainline denomination. Its titles include the following: *The Confessional Mosaic: Presbyterians and Twentieth-Century Theology* (Westminster/John Knox, 1990); *The Diversity of Discipleship: Presbyterians and Twentieth-Century Christian Witness* (Westminster/John Knox, 1991); *The Mainstream Protestant "Decline": The Presbyterian Pattern* (Westminster/John Knox, 1990); *The Organizational Revolution: Presbyterians and American Denominationalism* (Westminster/John Knox, 1992); *The Pluralistic Vision: Presbyterians and Mainstream Protestant Education and Leadership* (Westminster/John Knox, 1992); *The Presbyterian Predicament: Six Perspectives* (Westminster/John Knox, 1990); and *The Re-Forming Tradition: Presbyterians and Mainstream Protestantism* (Westminster/John Knox, 1992). For treatments of Machen's role in the founding of the Orthodox Presbyterian Church, readers should consult Charles G. Dennison and Richard C. Gamble, eds., *Pressing toward the Mark: Essays Commemorating Fifty Years of the Orthodox Presbyterian Church* (Committee for the Historian of the OPC, 1986); and D. G. Hart and John R. Muether, *Fighting the Good Fight: A Brief History of the Orthodox Presbyterian Church* (Committee on Christian Education and Committee for the Historian of the OPC, 1995).

One last set of works covers the place of theology in American culture in the late nineteenth and twentieth centuries. These books provide a backdrop to important changes that saw the decline of religion in American intellectual life and provided the context for labors and arguments of Protestant scholars such as Machen. They include Robert M. Crunden, *Ministers of Reform: The Progressives? Achievement in American Civilization, 1889–1920* (Basic Books, 1982); D. G. Hart, *The University Gets Religion: Religious Studies and American Higher Education* (Johns Hopkins University Press, 1999); Bruce Kuklick, *Churchmen and Philosophers: From Jonathan Edwards to John Dewey* (Yale University Press, 1985); T. J. Jackson Lears, *No Place of Grace: Antimodernism and the Transformation of American Culture,*

1880–1920 (New York: Pantheon, 1981); George M. Marsden, *The Soul of the American University: From Protestant Establishment to Established Nonbelief* (Oxford University Press, 1994); Henry F. May, *The End of American Innocence: The First Years of Our Time, 1912–1917* (Alfred A. Knopf, 1959); Mark A. Noll, *Between Faith and Criticism: Evangelicals, Scholarship, and the Bible in America* (Harper & Row, 1986); and James Turner, *Without God, Without Creed: The Origins of Unbelief in America* (Johns Hopkins University Press, 1985).

INDEX

Adonis, 490–91
airplanes, 430
alcohol, 12
Alexander, George, 270
Alexander, Maitland, 300
allegorizers, 68, 181, 457
Alliance of Churches Holding the Reformed System, 539
Allis, Oswald T., 192
Alps, 429–34, 436, 439
American liberty, 161–67
American Revolution, 357
Americanization, 173
anthropomorphism, 70
anti-intellectualism, 117, 135, 138, 144, 469–70, 519, 528, 531, 564
apologetics, 145–46, 313, 531–32, 554
apostasy, 264
Apostles' Creed, 58
applied Christianity, 121
argument, 144–45, 150, 409, 421
Arminianism, 510–11
Armstrong, William P., 553, 557
art, 357, 365, 428
ascetics, 67, 424–25
assurance, 200–201
atonement, 31, 41, 233, 241, 285, 361, 449–50
Attis, 490
Auburn Affirmation, 221, 225–26, 235, 264, 268–69, 293, 444
    and Board of Foreign Missions, 335
    and boards and agencies of the church, 247–48, 258
    and church papers, 263

and hymnody, 287
and Permanent Judicial Commission, 196, 243–47, 258
and *Presbyterian Magazine*, 270
and Princeton Seminary, 193, 311, 321
on the resurrection, 233
Augustine, 191, 234, 371, 485, 551
Augustinian Christianity, 4, 7
authority, 335–38, 340–41, 343, 486–90
automobile, 430

Baltimore, 2, 548, 550
Banner, The, 267, 381
baptism, 495
Baptist churches, 507
Barth, Karl, 181–82, 533–45, 559
"Battle Hymn of the Republic," 277
Bauer, Walter, 558
Baur, F. C., 316, 479, 500, 505, 559
Bayard, Thomas F., 387
beauty, 402, 548
begging the question, 412–13
benevolences of the church, as a tax, 338–39, 342, 349–50
Bible
    as absolutely unique, 212
    and Auburn Affirmation, 264
    authority of, 23, 72, 341
    as controversial book, 198
    Fosdick on, 455–68
    as foundation of the church, 108
    as history, 56, 97
    inerrancy of, 6
    infallibility of, 6, 56, 312–13

inspiration of, 327–28
on Jesus, 99–108
as Magna Charta of human liberty,
    359–60
original languages of, 316
in public schools, 12, 169–70, 375
richness of, 155–60
specialists in, 155, 193, 211
teaching on Jesus, 23, 25, 28–32, 33
at Westminster Seminary, 188–89
Bible in Browning, The, 549
Bible League of Great Britain, 23, 33,
    45, 135, 143, 153
Biblical theology, 190–91
Bill of Rights, 163
biologists, 509–10, 518
Blougram, Bishop, 561
Board of Foreign Missions, 247, 270,
    332–35, 348–49, 352, 443
Board of National Missions, 248, 270
body, buffeting of, 438–39
Bonar, Horatius, 282, 284
Book of Discipline (PCUSA), 249,
    250–51, 258, 263
Bousset, Wilhelm, 316, 479, 558–59
Bridges, Matthew, 284
Briggs, Charles, 9
Brooks, William E., 253
brotherhood of man, 241–42, 275, 369
Brunner, Emil, 181, 182, 533, 534, 536,
    537, 538, 540, 541
Buck, Pearl S., 335
Bultmann, Rudolf, 177, 180, 540–41
bureaucracy, 10, 113, 162, 164, 366, 385,
    391
Burkitt, F. C., 63

Cadwalader, Thomas F., 383
Calvin, John, 7, 15, 191, 234–35, 371,
    537, 551
Calvinism, 5, 11, 15–16, 191, 267, 311,
    313–14, 510–12, 561, 565
centralization, 12–13, 162, 252, 366,
    385, 391
ceremonial law, 459
Chalcedonian creed, 510–11
character, 113, 164, 168–69

charity, 390–91
Chicago Tribune, 275
child-labor amendment, 163–65, 358,
    366, 381–89, 391, 436
Christ-mysticism, 475
Christian America, 13
Christian civilization, 295
Christian liberty, 13, 208, 230, 338–39,
    340
Christian life, 94, 160, 200, 427
"Christian" (name), 237
Christian Reformed Church, 270, 273
Christian scholarship, 7–9, 405–6
    and the church, 153–60
    and defense of the faith, 143–52
    and preaching, 137–42
Christian school, 161, 167, 171–73
Christianity
    as consistent, 554
    and culture, 11–14, 212, 399–410
    decline in power of, 406
    defense of, 315–17, 566–67
    as doctrinal, 114
    exclusiveness and universality of mes-
        sage, 374, 416–17
    as higher humanism, 379
    as historic religion, 92–93
    as human product, 401
    intellectual objections to, 406–7
    and liberty, 359–63
    as life founded upon doctrine, 93–95,
        118, 217, 368, 564
    as means to end or end in itself, 108
    origin of, 77, 178, 563
    propagating of, 567
    as religion of broken heart, 379, 414
    as social and individual, 111–12
    See also historic Christianity
Christianity and Liberalism, 3, 563–64
Christianity Today, 564, 566
Christology, 65, 140
church, 207
    and cooperation with non-Christian
        religion, 375
    corporate witness of, 219–21, 227
    creedal character of, 225–26
    as democratic, 221, 260

function of, 373–76, 395
mission of, 10, 13–14, 228, 238
origin of, 104–5, 106
and politics, 375, 394–95
as radically doctrinal, 373
as radically intolerant, 373
and separation from world, 227
unity of, 227
as voluntary association, 113,
 338–39, 373, 418, 568
worldly tendency in, 423–24
church attendance, 406
church history, 152, 192
church papers, 261–62
church union, 266, 292, 355, 567
civil liberty, 12, 13, 161, 360, 365–66
civilization, 391
Codex Sinaiticus, 62, 175
Codex Vaticanus, 62, 175
collectivism, 112, 167, 258–59, 366–67,
 390
colleges and universities, 196
Columbia Theological Seminary, 564
comfort, 200–201, 203
Commission of Fifteen. See Special
 Commission of 1925
Committee of Eleven. See Special Committee to Visit Princeton Theological Seminary
Committee on Theological Seminaries
 (PCUSA), 299, 301, 324
common grace, 526
common sense, 92–93, 189, 190
communication, 415
Communists, 12, 390
comparative religion, 70, 71, 181
compromise, 234–35
compulsion, 114
Congress, 381–83
conscription, 366, 384–85
consecration, 402, 425–26
conservatives, 4
Constitution of the United States, 162,
 163, 164, 382, 385
controversy, 34–35, 39, 125, 146–49,
 198, 233–35, 263, 265, 297, 306,
 371, 409, 567

conversion, 27, 139–40
courtesy, 412, 423
covenant, 27
Craig, Samuel G., 262, 270, 564
creation, 25–26, 49, 155–56, 471–72,
 502
 Barth on, 540
creationism, 4, 5, 6
creeds, 132, 225–26, 231, 256, 373, 462,
 539
 as useful, 462–63
cross of Christ, 30–32, 36, 140, 281, 295,
 361, 380, 415, 542–43
cultural homogeneity, 12, 13
culture, 13–14, 212, 399–410
Cumberland Presbyterian Church,
 267–68
Cummings, Calvin K., 337
Cynic philosophers, 370

darkness, 251, 255, 535
Davis, Ozora Stearns, 285
de Boor fragment, 176
debate, 254
decadence, 115, 162, 357, 414, 468, 469
deceit, 230
defense of the faith, 143–52. See also
 apologetics
Deissmann, Adolf, 175
democracy, 162
Democrats, 12–13
demons cast out, 230–31
Denney, James, 327
Dent Blanche, 432–33, 437
depression, 162, 386
despair, 561
dialectic, 537
Dibelius, Martin, 177
Directory for Worship (PCUSA), 350
discernment, 423
disciples, 76–77, 105, 378
discipleship, cost of, 198, 202
disease, 357, 359
dishonesty, 347–48
disinterestedness, 158
dispensationalism, 4, 5, 6
divinity, 462–63

doctrine, 9–10, 93–95, 118, 200,
217–19, 230, 231, 368–70, 417,
462, 465
attitude toward, 314
as changing expression of experience,
117, 372, 413
and Christian living, 265
as comes before experience, 512
and drift in PCUSA, 270
in early church, 241
and fact, 510–12
as the gospel, 140, 512
in hymnody, 275–76
Modernists on, 219, 224–25
in PCUSA, 306–7
springs from life, 462
doubt, 317, 551, 560–61
Downs, Francis Shunk, 121
Drews, Arthur, 50
drunkenness, 394
dualism, in Barth, 535

early church, 240, 421–22, 496
on Jesus, 55
missions of, 237–42
as radically doctrinal, 241, 368–70
as radically ethical, 370
as radically intolerant, 370
ecclesiastical machinery, 125, 246, 250,
251–52, 253–55, 257–58, 260,
262–63, 325, 326, 330, 355, 550
ecumenism, 9–10, 230
edification, 154
education, 112–13, 136–37, 162,
165–66, 358, 414, 419
experts in, 168
federal department of, 165, 358, 567
modern, 210–11
uniformity in, 166–67, 173
Edwards, Jonathan, 15
efficiency, 12, 92, 210, 357, 359, 367
Eighteenth Amendment, 393–95
Ellwood, Charles A., 471
Emmons, Peter K., 394
emotions, 400
Empire State Building, 203–5
empty tomb, 80, 82, 85–86

Engels, Friedrich, 387
equal opportunity, 167
equivocation, 373
Erasmus, 371
Erdman, Charles R., 269, 270, 299–300,
301–5, 324
error, 151
ethical preaching, 370
ethical theism, 502–4
etymology, 127
Europe, 356, 435–36
European war. See World War I
evangelical Christianity, 327, 451
at Princeton, 326–31
in Speer, 452–53
evangelism, 138–41, 403
and apologetics, 145
and polemics, 148
evil, 98
evolutionary view of Bible, 455–56
exegesis, 190
expedience, 261
experience, 26–27, 31, 34, 36, 94, 372,
470, 538
and evangelism, 141
Fosdick on, 218–19, 224, 461–62
and the gospel, 131–32
and history, 107–8
of Paul, 41
and resurrection, 87

Fabe, Frederick W., 283
facts, 95, 110, 114, 117, 128, 510–12,
528–29
fair play, 254, 255, 261, 266, 323
faith, 122, 287, 400, 517
Barth on, 536–37, 539
intellectual element of, 138–40
in Jesus Christ, 38
false ideas, 404
family, 164, 172, 388, 420
fatherhood of God, 241–42, 369, 471
fear, 239–40
Federal Council of Churches of Christ in
America, 9, 248, 372
federal department of education, 165,
358, 567

fellowship, 135, 427–28
Fellowship of Reconciliation, 411
fiat creation, 155–56, 223, 239
First Presbyterian Church of New York, 218, 220, 222, 225, 292, 307
Form of Government of the PCUSA, 344
Formgeschichte, 177
Fosdick, Harry Emerson, 218, 221–26, 268, 292–93, 304, 306, 307, 414, 455–68, 506
France, 435
Franklin Street Presbyterian Church (Baltimore), 549
Free Church of Scotland, 91
Frenssen, Gustav, 54
friendship, 423, 424, 426–28
Fundamentalism, 5–7, 14, 109–15, 116, 149–50, 551, 566

Galilee, 78, 79–80, 83
General Assembly, 332, 338, 339
General Assembly of 1923, 243–44, 324
General Assembly of 1925, 249
General Assembly of 1926, 324, 393
General Assembly of 1928, 253
General Assembly of 1929, 254
General Assembly of 1931, 249, 259–60
General Assembly of 1933, 334
General Assembly of 1934, 341, 344–47, 352
General Council (PCUSA), 248, 252
Gentile Christianity, 475–505
Gentiles, 232
Germany, 161, 382, 435–36
    injustice and oppression, 378–79
    Machen's study in, 555–61
Gildersleeve, Basil, 551–52
Gilman, Daniel Coit, 551
Gnostics, Gnosticism, 73, 234, 371, 478, 493–94, 500, 543
God
    doctrine of, 118, 482
    holiness of, 118, 240
    justice of, 501–2
    as love, 32, 98, 536
    as personal, 25–26, 156–57, 523–26

sovereignty of, 471–72
    transcendence of, 27, 118, 182, 360, 463, 508, 534
    wrath of, 119, 239, 502, 536
God Transcendent, 1
Gogarten, Friedrich, 181, 533
Golden Rule, 64, 149, 412
golf, 440
goodness, 156, 369, 376, 503–4
Gordon, George A., 414, 447
Gore, Charles, 508
gospel, 30, 92, 119, 121, 123–32, 232, 241, 339, 395, 399, 415–16, 461
    in boards and agencies of PCUSA, 295–96
    and doctrine of God, 482
    Fosdick on, 466–67
    glory of, 200–201
    as history, 98
    modern threats against, 195–200
    and Paul, 475
    presuppositions, 526
gospels, 29–30, 46–48, 50–56, 101
Gothic architecture, 203
Göttingen, 558
grace, 32, 536, 537
grammatico-historical exegesis, 181–82, 457
Graven, Alois, 431
Great Britain, 327, 554
Greek, 189, 551–52, 562–63
Greek mythology, 69–70
Greek New Testament, 210–13
Green, William Henry, 327
Gregory, Casper René, 174
Gresham, LeRoy, 551
Griffiths, J. McAllister, 564
guilt, 98, 239, 240, 360, 414

Hadley, Arthur T., 383
Hadley, Lindsay S. B., 335
hallucinations, of appearances of risen Christ, 77, 79, 86
Ham, Marion Franklin, 286
Harnack, A. von, 46, 59, 68, 71, 177–78, 316, 445–46, 451, 471n.2, 556, 558

Heber, Reginald, 281
Hebrew, 189
Hegel, G. W. F., 534
Hegelian philosophy, 500, 505
Heitmüller, W., 558
Henry, Patrick, 357
heresy, 147
Herrmann, W., 362, 555–56
higher critics, 557
Hinduism, 447
historians, 83–85, 237–42
  on liberty, 357
  on the resurrection, 76–80
historic Christianity, 116–22, 316, 563
historic Jesus, 102–3, 179–80
historical criticism, 182, 446, 519, 529,
  542, 543
history, 30–31, 92–93, 95, 97, 105, 106,
  109–10, 435, 459, 517–18, 528
  and experience, 107–8
  Fosdick on, 457–61
"history-of-religion" school, 181
Hitler, Adolf, 382
Hodge, Caspar Wistar, 14
holiness, 370–71
Holland, 270
Holtzmann, H. J., 38, 100
Holy Spirit, 87, 96, 148, 234, 236, 473,
  481, 527
home, 436
Homer, 210, 365
homiletics, 192
honesty, 189, 418, 568
Hoover, President, 165
hope, 204
Hort, F. J. A., 174–75, 554
human authority, 335–38, 340–41, 343
human goodness, 110, 369, 378–80
human nature
  optimism about, 119
  pessimistic view of, 110
human relationships, 421–28
humanism, 379
humanities, 210–11
humility, 379
Hutchison, William R., 15
Huxley, Julian, 523

hymnody, 274–88
hypocrisy, 423

Ignatius, 58, 494
ignorance, 140, 319, 414
  in the church, 24–25
  of the gospel, 124–25
immanence philosophy, 541
implicit faith, 345
imputed righteousness of Christ, 282
incarnation, 73, 447, 543
Independent Board for Presbyterian Foreign Missions, 4, 11, 332, 349,
  351–52
independent church papers, 259
indifferentists, indifferentism, 72,
  124–25, 147, 229, 264, 266, 269,
  293, 297, 306, 329, 371, 444–45
individualism, 358
individuals, 111
industrialism, 367, 385, 390, 436
injustice, 378
inquisition, in the Presbyterian Church,
  250, 258
intellect, 400, 402
interpolation hypothesis (virgin birth),
  60–62, 70, 71
interpretation, 86, 128, 189, 511, 513
intolerance, 265, 373–74, 417–19, 427
invisible church, 228
Isaac, 68
Isis, 490
Italy, 359, 366, 382

James (brother of Jesus), 59
Jehovah, 37
Jerusalem, 78, 80
Jesus
  allegiance to, 207, 208
  authority of, 490–91
  Barth on, 540–41, 542–43
  burial of, 81–82, 85
  coming in glory, 131
  death of, 30–32, 33, 40, 43, 93, 95,
    128, 231
  death and resurrection of, 98–99,
    114, 129, 241

deity of, 37–38, 239, 448, 473
divinity of, 219, 462–63
as example of faith, 55, 99, 120–21, 240–41, 465
Fosdick on, 225, 458–59, 465–66
goodness and greatness of, 380
humanity of, 38
in hymnody, 281–85
as insane, 53–54, 103, 106
according to liberalism, 48, 50–56, 102–3, 105–7, 179–83, 222–23, 369, 504
Lordship of, 37, 340, 480
majesty of person, 378
as Master, 37
Messianic self-consciousness of, 53, 54, 103, 106, 458, 556
miracles of, 178
not a Christian, 120–21
as object of faith, 38, 55, 121, 178, 473
personal influence of, 34
as purely human, 52, 54–55
redemptive work of, 30, 131, 159–60, 415–16, 474
resurrection of, 40, 43, 66, 72–73, 74, 77–87, 95, 105, 107, 110, 128, 231, 446, 448, 480, 516–17, 542
as Savior, 55, 99, 120–21, 240–42
as second Adam, 65
as Son of God, 447
as supernatural person, 40, 48, 50, 73, 101, 102, 120, 183, 563
teaching of, 99, 129–30
teaching on God, 239–40, 471–73
Jews, 411, 419
John, 47, 48
    epistles of, 494
Johns Hopkins University, 2, 551–52, 553
Joint Commission on Organic Union, 256
Jones, E. Stanley, 28
Joseph of Arimathea, 86
joy, 208
Judaism, 39, 43, 179, 416
judgment, 98, 472, 480, 501–2

Jülicher, A., 473, 556, 557, 559
justification, 474, 485
Justin Martyr, 58

Kalthoff, A., 50
Kattenbusch, F., 558
Kelley, Florence, 386–88, 389
kenotic view of the incarnation, 280
kingdom of God, 130–31, 360, 403, 539
Knopf, Rudolf, 557, 558
knowledge, 136, 137, 142, 151, 378, 399–401
knowledge of God, 118, 526
Koiné Greek, 175–76
Kuiper, R. B., 273
Kuyper, Abraham, 13, 15, 271
kyrios, 37

laity, 189, 255, 325–26
language, accuracy in, 223
Latin, 210
law of God, 26, 56, 158, 169, 361, 375, 388, 459, 464
League of Evangelical Students, 195, 197, 199, 318, 330
learning, revival of, 136–37
Lehman, Cedric A., 293, 297
"Liberal Jesus," 84, 102–3, 182, 471, 542, 556
liberalism, 4, 10, 361
    Fosdick on, 462
    in New Testament studies, 179–83
    on Paul, 40–42
    See also Modernism
liberty, 112, 113, 200, 357–63, 365–67, 382, 418–19, 436, 567–68
    and intolerance in the church, 373–74
    of conscience, 91, 303
    of speech, 112
    See also Christian liberty; civil liberty; religious freedom
life, springs from doctrine, 413
Lightfoot, J. B., 557
Lippmann, Walter, 158
literary criticism, 46, 48, 176–78, 182, 519

literary education, 112
literature, 428
logic, 521
Loisy, A. F., 471n.2
Longfellow, Samuel, 285
Lord's Supper, 333, 336, 339, 350
love, 149, 255, 266, 374, 391, 424
Lowell, James Russell, 286
Lowrey, Mr., 165
Luccock, Dr., 324
Luke, 46, 177–78
    on virgin birth, 58–62, 64
Lusk Laws, 112, 163, 358, 366, 418–19
Luther, Martin, 140, 192, 284, 371

McAfee, Cleland B., 253
Macartney, Clarence E., 269, 303–4, 307
McDowell, John, 270, 275
McGiffert, Arthur Cushman, 316, 458,
    469–506
Machen, Arthur W. (father), 548–49
Machen, Arthur W., Jr. (brother), 548,
    551
Machen, J. Gresham
    alleged temperamental defects of,
        300–302, 308
    promotion to chair in apologetics and
        Christian ethics, 299–301, 307
    as Southerner, 12
Machen, Mary Gresham (mother),
    549–51, 561
Machen, Thomas (brother), 548
machines, 167, 200, 204–5, 358, 367,
    436
MacLean, John Allan, Jr., 123–25, 132
Macmillan, Kerr Duncan, 562
Macon, Georgia, 550
MacRae, Allan A., 272
McReynolds, Justice, 163
Maine, 357–58, 436
man, 118–19, 360
Marburg, 555–58
Marcion, 234, 493–94, 495, 503
Mark, 47, 48, 230
    on the resurrection, 85
    silence on virgin birth, 65–66
Mary (mother of Jesus), 66

material benefits, 359
materialism, 406
mathematics, 172
matter, 515–16
Matterhorn, 430, 432, 433–35, 437, 439
Matthew, on virgin birth, 58, 62–64
mechanistic world, 359–62, 550, 569
medieval cathedrals, 203–4
memory, 436–37
Mencken, H. L., 15
Merrill, William P., 287
Merx, Adalbert, 68
Messiah, 54, 449
metaphysics, 156, 527
Methodists, 511
Meyer, Eduard, 59, 177–78
Micaiah, 207
Middle Ages, 189–90, 371
Miller, C. W. E., 552
Milton, John, 114, 279–80
ministers, 205, 207, 211
miracles, 48–50, 51–52, 77, 87, 120, 218,
    466, 509
missionaries, 232–33, 239
missions, 240, 242
Modalism, 495–96
moderator of General Assembly, power
    of, 253, 254
Modernism, 109, 110, 124–25, 264, 269,
    444–45
    as anti-intellectual, 114, 144, 219,
        564
    as antitheistic, 504–6
    on doctrine, 219
    God of, 473
    in hymnody, 285, 287
    on Jesus, 219, 229
    as non-redemptive religion, 36
    preachers, 7
    in United Presbyterian Church, 257
    and unrest in PCUSA, 291–92, 296
    use of Christian terminology, 234
    on virgin birth, 69
    See also liberalism
"Modernism and the Board of Foreign
    Missions" (Machen), 333–35
modernity, 192

Mohammedanism, 416
monasticism, intellectual, 402, 405
monotheism, 39, 70, 475–78, 481,
    482–83, 486–88, 493, 497
Moody, D. L., 55, 145
moral argument, 523
morality, 169, 375, 387–88, 465
"More Abundant Life, The" (Fosdick),
    223–24
Morison, John, 284
Mormons, 12
Moulton, J. H., 176
mountains, 26, 429–37, 438
Mudge, Lewis, 208
Mullins, E. Y., 507–32
Mussolini, 161, 359, 382, 429, 435, 567
mystery religions, 487
mysticism, 92, 111, 219, 275, 312, 475,
    481, 534, 539

narrow-mindedness, 412–13
"Nathan der Weise," 416–17
National Education Association, 165
national parks, 358, 436
National Union of Christian Schools,
    161
natural affections, 424–26
natural religion, 26
natural science, 168
naturalism, 42, 72, 101, 105, 222, 362,
    401, 446, 466, 467, 509, 518
    in Plan of Organic Union, 292, 302
nature, 26, 430, 549–50
Nebraska language law, 112, 163, 358,
    366, 419
"Neutral text," 175
neutrality, 171
new age, 364–65, 372, 376
new birth, 27, 286, 530, 567
New Testament, 174–83, 212, 559
    as controversial book, 125, 198, 233
    conversions in, 139–40
    on Jesus, 50, 71
    mythical theory of, 67, 218
    on resurrection, 78
    study of, 553
    on virgin birth, 58–74

New Testament Greek for Beginners, 563
New York City, 203
Newton, John, 281
Nicene creed, 510–11
Nichols, Robert Hastings, 244
Nicoll, Robertson, 327–28
Niebuhr, H. Richard, 13
non-Christian theism, 508–9
non-Christians, friendships with,
    426–27
nontheistic Christianity, 477–505
Norden, E., 559

obedience
    to boards and agencies, 336
    to General Assembly, 332, 339
offerings, 342, 349–50
old Princeton, 3–4, 15, 258, 269, 271,
    272, 553–54, 557, 562, 564–65
Old Testament, 25, 26, 159, 238, 239,
    459–61, 489–90
    ceremonial law in, 483–84
    Fosdick on, 464
    prophets of, 67, 471
    on resurrection of Jesus, 83
open courts, 249–50, 265
oppression, 378
optimism
    in human race, 119, 414
    in PCUSA, 245, 568
    in state of the times, 197
order of nature, 120
ordination pledge, 345, 349
Oregon school law, 112, 113, 162–63,
    358, 419
Origin of Paul's Religion, The, 3, 559, 563
original languages, 565
Ormond, A. T., 555
Orthodox Presbyterian Church, 4, 11,
    12
orthodoxy, and Karl Barth, 538
Owen, John, 15

pacifism, 235, 384, 445
paganism, 110, 379, 414
    and the resurrection, 84–85
    and the virgin birth, 60, 62, 68–70, 71

pamphlet distribution, 252–53
pantheism, 26, 118, 182, 509
papyri, 175
paradox, 537
past, 435
pastoral epistles, 176
Patton, Francis L., 61, 553, 560–61,
    562
Paul
    and Christology, 65
    on doctrine, 369
    epistles of, 29–30, 35, 39, 43, 45–46,
        99–101, 153–54, 176, 178, 452,
        494, 563
    Fosdick on, 459–61
    as founder of Christianity, 41, 179
    on the gospel, 127
    as a liberal, 232, 461
    McGiffert on, 473–85, 488, 492–93
    religion of, 35–43, 178
    on the resurrection, 80–85, 450–51
    on salvation, 473–74
    as scholar, 140
    silence on virgin birth, 64–65
    as student of human relationships,
        422–23
Paulus, H., 52
peace, 318, 412–13, 568
Pelagius, 371
Pentecost, 148
Permanent Judicial Commission, 196,
    244–47, 250, 258
Perren, Gottfried, 431
Perry, Ralph Barton, 555
persecution, 317
personality, 520
Philadelphia Overture, 307
philanthropy, 390
Philippian jailer, 139
Phillimore, J. S., 370
Philo of Alexandria, 68
philological learning, 563
philosophy, 156, 500, 513–14, 519,
    520–27, 529, 530–32, 554–55
piety, 399–401
    of early church, 496
    of Princeton Seminary, 318, 329–30

Plan of Organic Union (1920), 235, 255,
    256, 268, 292, 302, 305
Plato, 210, 366, 552
pneumatic exegesis, 181
poetry, 114, 200, 205, 357, 402, 414,
    428, 549–50
polemics, 147–48. See also controversy
Polycarp, 494
polytheism, 477, 486–88
popularity, 150
poverty, 114, 115
power, and goodness, 502–4
practical studies, 211
practical theology, 192
pragmatism, 117, 218, 219, 223, 460,
    463, 469, 500–501
prayer, 147, 266
prayer in public schools, 12
preaching, 92, 125, 137, 141, 148,
    153–55, 192, 205, 211, 380, 427
premillennialism, 109
Presbyterian Advance, The, 262, 263
Presbyterian Banner, The, 262
Presbyterian Church in Canada, 229
Presbyterian Church in the U.S.A, 3, 8,
    9, 10–11, 196, 206, 217, 227, 228,
    235–36
    boards and agencies of, 247–48, 258,
        295–97, 336, 343–51
    Constitution of, 208, 225, 251–52,
        256, 345, 346–47, 349–50
    corruption in, 247
    as fundamentally unsound, 568
    future of, 267, 272
    moral decline of, 265
    optimism about, 245
Presbyterian law, 219, 349
Presbyterian liberties, 250, 252, 254,
    261
Presbyterian Magazine, The, 248, 262,
    263, 270
Presbyterian, The, 262, 270
presbyteries, 252, 263
Presbytery of Baltimore (PCUSA), 207,
    337
Presbytery of Chester (PCUSA),
    336–37

Presbytery of New Brunswick (PCUSA), 4, 206, 208, 332, 336–37, 340–42, 343–48, 393–95
Presbytery of New York (PCUSA), 221–26, 249, 293–95
Presbytery of Philadelphia (PCUSA), 206, 337
presuppositions, 131, 499, 505, 519, 526
pride, 30, 204, 287, 380, 428
Princeton Petition, 245–46, 254
Princeton Theological Seminary, 2, 3, 6, 8–9, 10–11, 155, 193–94, 269–70, 305, 307–8, 562
    historic position of, 311
    during Machen's student days, 552–55
    piety of, 318, 329–30
    reorganization of, 245, 254, 310–11, 319–21, 564–65
    stood for truth of gospel, 322
    world-wide prestige of, 328–29
Princeton University, 554–55
probability, 107, 560
progress, 109–15, 363
    Fosdick on, 456
    in revelation, 461
    in theology, 235, 485
Prohibition, 394
promises of God, 201
propaganda, 383, 389, 419
property, 266
proselytizing, 417, 419–20
prosperity, 162
Protestantism, 340–41
providence, 502, 509
psalms, 284
psychology, 361
psychology of religion, 142
public schools, 12, 113, 162–63, 165, 167–71, 375, 567
publicity, 259–62

"quest of the historical Jesus," 179–80

race, 28
Rademacher, A., 176
radio, 415

Rand School (New York City), 418
Randall, John Herman, 463
rationality, 520
rationalizing method, 51–52
Re-Thinking Missions, 4, 334–35
reading, 548
redemption, 36, 44, 129, 361
redemptive religion, 36, 178, 264, 372
Reformation, 115, 189–90, 234–35, 327, 341, 371, 485
Reformed faith, 5, 91, 191, 192, 257, 272, 273, 308, 313–14, 551
    at Princeton Seminary, 329
    as consistent Christianity, 235
regeneration, 526
Reitzenstein, R., 559
relativism, 435
release time, in public schools, 171
religion, 170, 193
    autonomy of, 527–29
    as intellectual, 530
    and science, 400–401, 513–20, 530
    and theology, 41, 178
religious education, 137, 142
religious freedom, 161, 365–66
Renaissance, 136
Republicans, 12
resurrection, 82, 448, 450–51
revelation, 118, 535, 538
revival, 199
    born in controversy, 125, 148
    of Christianity, 115
Ritschl, A., 40–41, 470, 525, 534
Ritschlians, 178–79, 555, 556, 563
Robertson, A. T., 176
Robinson, W. Courtland, 270
rock climbing, 438–39
Roman Catholic Church, 12, 113, 341, 345, 412, 419
Russia, 161, 359, 366, 382, 390

Sabbath observance, 406
salvation, 122, 158–60, 480
    objectivity of, 415
    as separated from theism, 501–2
Samaritan woman, 139

Schleiermacher, Friedrich, 182, 470,
534, 539, 541, 542
scholarship, 405, 553
Schürer, Emil, 316, 558
science, 49, 95, 109, 114, 120, 362, 367,
530–32
and religion, 400–401, 513–20, 530
scientific criticism, 519
Scottish Psalter (1650), 284
second causes, 120
secret church courts, 248–51, 255,
257–58, 261, 263, 264, 265, 567
secular press, 259, 263
self-satisfaction, 378–80
selfishness, 428
Sentinels of the Republic, 164, 383
Sermon on the Mount, 53, 56, 459, 543
servants of Jesus Christ, 208
servants of men, 208
"Shall the Fundamentalists Win?" (Fosdick), 221–22
Shattuck, S. Frank, 253
Shorey, Paul, 552
"simple faith," 138–40
simplicity, 453–54
sin, 26–27, 36, 98, 121, 140, 169, 239,
240, 348, 360, 371, 378–80, 414,
415, 556
Barth on, 535, 537, 540
Bible on, 157–58
Fosdick on, 463
conviction of, 110, 530
in corporate life of church, 265
Sinaitic Syriac, 62–63, 175
skepticism, 94, 117, 124, 130, 137, 145,
177, 182, 183, 225, 292–93, 372,
413, 463, 505, 514, 516, 527
slavery, 200
Smith, Alfred E., 163
Smith, Kirby, 552
Smith, W. B., 50
Smyth Lectures (Columbia Seminary),
564
social gospel, 13
socialism, 112, 387, 390–91, 418–19
Soden, Hermann von, 174
Son of God, 53, 72, 119, 475, 480

Son of Man, 53, 448–49
soul of man, 367–68, 414
Southern Baptist Theological Seminary,
507
Soviets, 359, 567
Spanish-American War, 81
Special Commission of 1925, 249, 269,
291–98, 324
Special Commission on Marriage, Divorce, and Remarriage, 260
Special Committee to Visit Princeton
Theological Seminary, 310, 319,
325
specialization, 193
Speer, Robert E., 270, 443–53
spiritual decline, 357
Sprunt Lectures (Union Seminary), 563
Spurgeon, Charles, 145
Stalin, J., 382
standardization, 167, 357–58, 367, 558,
567
star-chamber courts, 249, 251
state, 418
stated clerk, power of, 259–60, 261
Sterling-Reed Bill, 419
Stevenson, J. Ross, 255, 270, 299–300,
301–3, 308, 314, 318, 322, 324
Stevenson, W. P., 270
stewards, of mysteries of God, 205
Stoics, 370
Stone, Dr., 306, 307
Stonehouse, Ned B., 1–2, 12, 272, 273
Strauss, David Friedrich, 51–52, 218
subjectivism, 132, 540
subscription, 257, 373, 568
suffering, 98
Sunday school, 154
supernatural, supernaturalism, 50–51,
72, 119–20, 179, 212, 264, 362,
401, 446
false, 51
in life of Jesus, 48, 102
synchronism, 171, 370
syncretism, 538
Synod of New York (PCUSA), 235,
293–95
Synod of Pennsylvania (PCUSA), 258

synoptic gospels, 177, 471, 519
system of doctrine, 313–14, 554
systematic theology, 191–92, 313, 554

tact, 422
taste, 365
temperance, 394
Ten Commandments, 464
Tertullian, 234, 496
textual criticism, 62–63, 174–76, 457,
    554
Thayer, J. H., 176
theism, 98, 118, 501–2, 508, 525
theistic proofs, 523–26, 531
theological education, 8–9, 211
theological pacifists, 233–35
theological seminaries, 196
theology
    as science, 118, 519
    separated from religion, 470, 497–500
    in Sermon on the Mount, 53
theology of crisis, 181, 534, 537
theology proper, 140
theosophy, 61
third day, 82–85
this age, 199–200, 203–5, 357
Thompson, Dr., 323, 324, 331
Thurneysen, Iduard, 181, 533
Tischendorf, C. von, 174
tolerance, 314, 370, 371, 417–19, 427,
    451
Torrey, C. C., 59
tradition, 177
transformation of culture, 13–14
Tregelles, S. P., 174
Trinity, 37, 495, 537, 540
truth, 118, 151, 172, 218, 219, 231, 309,
    372, 423, 451, 465, 519, 540
two-document theory, 176, 519
tyranny, 114, 162, 261, 366, 367, 374,
    382, 384, 390, 418
    of the expert, 162, 367

unbelief, 124, 150, 203–4, 568
Union Seminary Review, 123, 174
Union Theological Seminary in Vir-
    ginia, 563

Union Theological Seminary (N.Y.), 7,
    457, 470
Unitarians, 126, 285, 286
United Church of Canada, 235
United Presbyterian Church, 256, 257
universal church, 229
University of Chicago, 7, 552
utilitarianism, 111, 115, 356

vagueness
    in modern religious teaching, 317
    in new hymns, 285
    in Plan of Organic Union, 255,
        256–57, 302
    vs. simplicity, 453
Van Dusen, Henry P., 293, 297
Van Loon, H. W., 114
Van Til, Cornelius, 272, 273
Vandenbosch, Professor, 381–88
Versailles, 414
Vestal Copyright Bill, 548
virgin birth, 6, 57–74
    in Auburn Affirmation, 335
    Fosdick on, 221–22, 466
    as Jewish concept, 67–68, 70, 71
    pagan influences, 60, 62, 68–70, 71
    in Presbytery of New York, 235, 249,
        293–95, 297
    Speer on, 446, 449
Virgin Birth of Christ, The, 3, 564
Virgin Birth Petition, 245
visible church, 228
vocation, 14
Volstead Act, 393–95
voluntary association, 113, 338–39, 373,
    418, 568

Wald, Lillian D., 387
walking, 438–40
war, 377, 384–85, 414
Warfield, B. B., 6, 327, 554, 562
Watts, Isaac, 280
wealth, 390–91
Weiss, J., 557, 558
Wells, H. G., 114
Wesley, Charles, 276–77, 280
Westcott, B. F., 174–75, 554

"Western text," 175
Westminster Confession of Faith, 191,
    194, 228, 256–57, 267, 272,
    293, 297, 314, 395, 417, 444,
    454, 463
Westminster Shorter Catechism, 6,
    157, 465, 550
Westminster Theological Seminary, 3,
    8–9, 11, 151, 155, 187–94, 202,
    206, 271–73, 565–66
  and the PCUSA, 208, 337
What is Christianity?, 1, 2, 4, 12
What is Faith?, 3, 564
White Mountains, 436
Whittier, John Greenleaf, 286
Wickersham, George W., 383
Wilke-Grimm, 176
Winona Lake Bible Conference, 57, 75

witness-bearing, 96, 217–20, 227
Woolley, Paul, 272
Word of God, 207
  authority, 335–38, 340–41, 343, 346
  Barth on, 537, 539, 542
  riches of, 205
word of man, 207
world, 202, 376
World War I, 2, 356–57
Wrede, William, 41–42, 179, 316, 491,
    563

Yale Divinity School, 470
YMCA, 2

Zahn, Theodore, 183
Zeller, E., 500
Zermatt peaks, 429, 431, 432, 434